ILLINOIS CENTRAL COLLEGE
PR4023.H6
STACKS
Matthew Arnold, a life /

A12900 723509

P9-DMH-981

71803

PR 4023 .H6

Honan, Park.

Matthew Arnold, a life /

Illinois Central College
Learning Resources Center

MATTHEW ARNOLD

A LIFE

MATTHEW ARNOLD

A LIFE

Park Honan

I. C. C. LIBRARY

McGRAW-HILL BOOK COMPANY

New York St. Louis San Francisco Mexico Toronto Hamburg

71803

Copyright © 1981 by Park Honan
All rights reserved. Printed in the United States of America.
No part of this publication may be reproduced, stored in a
retrieval system, or transmitted, in any form or by any means,
electronic, mechanical, photocopying, recording, or otherwise,
without the prior written permission of the publisher.

1 2 3 4 5 6 7 8 9 DODO 8 7 6 5 4 3 2 1

LIBRARY OF CONGRESS CATALOGING IN PUBLICATION DATA

Honan, Park.
Matthew Arnold, a life.
Includes bibliographical references and index.
1. Arnold, Matthew, 1822–1888—Biography.
2. Poets, English—19th century—Biography.
3. Critics—England—Biography. I. Title.
PR4023.H6   821'.8 [B]   80–26131
ISBN 0–07–029697–9

Book design by Nancy Dale

For Jeannette, Corinna, Tasha, and Matthew

who lived in Fox How with me and
climbed the Gemmi Pass

PREFACE

IN the English Midlands where I live, people often think it strange Matthew Arnold became a poet—since he was the eldest son of "the greatest Headmaster who ever lived," the intense, commanding Dr. Arnold of Rugby School. Despite an imposing father, Matthew became a vitally brilliant elegiac poet and even a poet of poets. (Allen Tate was to prefer Matthew Arnold to Browning or Tennyson and Arnold's lyric "The Forsaken Merman" inspired Sylvia Plath.)

Yet an artistic and vain young man who rebels against the earnest good sense of an unpoetic father may not surprise us. Today, the "family rebel" is a familiar concept and Matthew as a lazy dilettante will be familiar. But what *is* surprising is that in his poetry and critical prose, he introduced a new, subtle, comparative attitude to central problems in Western society and culture, and helped to form the modern consciousness. An understanding of him is really more useful to us than an understanding of any other Englishman of the last century. Critics, creative artists, and our wisest leaders have turned and will continue to turn to Arnold for social perspective, and for that critical attitude which is the best help in our national and our international difficulties. His career is a study in sensitivity, courage, and endurance. After he became a School Inspector and married, he began to investigate the towns and cities of England and the Continent and to apply what he learned. His *Essays in Criticism* is a work of literary criticism enriched by a strong, close sense of the failings of a modern industrial society; his later *Culture and Anarchy* is an enduringly important work of social criticism enriched by a keen feeling for ideas. He turned from literary, to educational, and then to religious topics in his essays and books—with a sense of the complex interrelatedness of the forces that make modern life what it is. He was the first to delve deeply into the feelings of city dwellers, and to show what we have lost, and where we are, after the ending of medieval certainties. His essays furthermore display what "criticism" is, or can be, and illuminate its open exploratory nature. He is a very great critic: *every* English and American critic of distinction since his time has felt his impact.

He was hardly an optimist and in this sense was different from Voltaire, with whom he is compared. Arnold's tragic vision of ignorant armies that clash by night never left him. But there *is* hopefulness in his ideas. Arnold's "culture," for example, refers to a psychological condition of an openness-of-mind which involves a growing, a becoming, a process whereby the individual moves towards realizing his mental, emotional, and creative potential, or his humanity. And he saw much of common humanity in his traveling life as a School Inspector. Arnold spoke to more schoolchildren, teachers, and petty officials than any other man of letters. As the first social critic to make full use of the new railway network of the 1840s, he was able to compare and contrast, day in and day out, towns and cities in different parts of England and Europe. It is this breadth of experience that informs his literary criticism and makes it so influential and important to us today.

From the start, he had to contend with an unusual father, who as Headmaster of Rugby School expected intellectual and even physical wonders of his children. Standing in his drawing room, Dr. Arnold might lean backwards, grip his small daughter's hands, and let her walk horizontally up his body until her feet touched his shoulders and her laughing head rose near the ceiling. But Dr. Arnold could as easily raise big, crimson welts on a child's bottom with a thin oak cane. He was literal-minded, earnest and cheerful, sometimes emotive and violent. A motionless boy was, for the moment, beyond criticism. But when the boy *did* anything, that boy might be fiercely judged. His wife Mary Arnold lacked his severity but had a sharp, quick intuitiveness about people that supplemented her husband's literal-mindedness.

If Matthew as the eldest son was normally lazy, full of himself, slow to do anything required, and idle at his books, how did he survive at Dr. Arnold's energetic hard-working Rugby? How did he find an inner life of his own, in his family, and develop into a remarkable poet and thinker? His story is an illuminating and important one. I was a student when I first read Lionel Trilling's intelligent study, *Matthew Arnold* (1939), which was written as a "biography of a mind." Trilling's book challenged and delighted me but failed to take me close to Matthew Arnold's life. Trilling had a secondary interest in biography and based his discussion of Arnold's life on the heavily censored texts in George Russell's edition in 1895 of the *Letters of Matthew Arnold*. Russell complained after editing the letters that Matthew Arnold's widow had crossed out of the texts "every admiring reference to herself" and Arnold's sister Fan had deleted "every trace of humour." (Much was kept out of Russell's edition on other principles besides these.) The Arnold of the *Letters* was a "curious obscuration" lacking his "most characteristic traits," as Russell admitted. The holograph letters were seldom mutilated; they were preserved; but the only book-length Arnold biographies before the present one—a brief life by E. K. Chambers and a psychological study in French by Louis Bonnerot—are based on Russell's "obscuration."

Convinced that much of the published work on Arnold is of good quality, and that a large amount of unpublished material lay in the hands of his descendants or in archives, I decided in 1970 to write a definitive biography—or as Painter said he attempted for Proust, a book close, full, and scholarly, accurate in every detail—for the Arnold specialist and general reader alike. I respect the distinction between life and art, but have tried to show how Arnold amplified and defined himself in his work, and have offered a guide to further reading in the References. I have tried to find every known fact relating to Arnold; and over ten years have worked with very many unpublished letters, journals, and diaries. Three-quarters of the biographical data in this book, I may say, has not appeared in a previous study of Arnold. My aim, always, has been to come as close to Matthew Arnold as the evidence will permit—and not to violate the truth that an unpredictable future lay ahead of him as he lived. That is, though alluding to "future" matters, I have tried to give an authentic sense of Arnold's own historical present and what Augusto Centeno called "livingness" —or the sense of real life.

Ten years spent in research and writing would not have been enough time without unceasing help from Arnold's and Clough's living descendants. Mrs. Mary Moorman let me borrow diaries, visited me at Fox How and walked with me over Arnold's grounds, offering encouragement and aid from the start. Professor Arnold Whitridge let me borrow unreleased Arnold letters, answered many questions, and—as Mrs. Moorman did—permitted me to quote from unpublished Arnold documents. Miss Katharine Duff, Clough's great-niece, encouraged my researches and criticism while lending manuscripts by Anne Jemima Clough. Miss Duff let me quote anything I wished, and I say with emphasis that no one ever inhibited my work. I found in Anne's diaries and in the easy and natural letters between Anne and Arthur Clough, and Jane and Matthew Arnold, no evidence of "incestuous" relationship; but brother-and-sister friendships within the "Clougho-Matthean set" were close, affectionate, and important —and I have not neglected them in the narrative. I thank Mr. Tom S. Arnold and Mrs. H. C. Arnold-Forster for replies to requests, and Mr.

A. H. B. Coleridge for letting me quote from Hartley Coleridge's unpublished letters.

Professor Kathleen Tillotson helped materially and intellectually during all ten years of the project—and not least by letting me consult the late Geoffrey Tillotson's unpublished notes, which have affected my attitude towards several problems. Professor Ruth apRoberts read every chapter of the work, commented in detail, modified my critical views, and enlightened me on Arnold, his religion, and the Rothschilds.

Many others commented on my notions, gave stimulus and encouragement, or helped with very detailed problems. I thank a number of "Professors" who (with those mentioned above) give to that academic title a humane, erudite connotation Arnold hoped it might have: Edward Alexander, Eugene August, R. M. Bennett, James Bertram, James H. Broderick, William E. Buckler, Thomas D. Clareson, Philip Collins, A. Dwight Culler, Carl Dawson, Ian Gregor, Edward Guiliano, Michael Hancher, Geoffrey Hartman, Fred Kaplan, Jacob Korg, Cecil Lang, Allan B. Lefcowitz, James C. Livingston, Patrick S. McCarthy, C. R. Moyer, W. S. Peterson, David A. Roos, S. P. SenGupta, and John F. Stasny. My remark on professors applies just as strongly to those listed, for convenience, below.

I remember listening to T. S. Eliot, and then hearing Norman Maclean and Larry Ragan compare our visiting "Poetry Professor" with Arnold (when I was a student). Twice, during work on this book I. A. Richards spoke to me about Arnold: "Well, Mr. Honan," he merrily began, "and are you showing that he was a *prophet*? For you know, he was!"

I also remember the late Professors Kenneth Allott, James D. Boulger, and Basil Willey for listening to my notions and for much vigorous discussion of Arnold, the Coleridges, and the Brontës. For comments on draft chapters, notes, or articles, I thank Professors Miriam Allott, David J. DeLaura, Robert Langbaum, and David Lodge—several of whom sent copies of their own Arnold work, all of whom debated Arnold with me. I have used Professor R. H. Super's edition of Matthew Arnold's prose, and benefited from Robert Super's letters on sources. The editor of Arnold's important, difficult Yale MS. desk-notes, Professor S. O. A. Ullmann—who finds his way even in the most obscure, unlikely European sources dating over four or five centuries—shared his research into the "Pride is Madness" allusions, advised me on Arnold's handwriting and letter dating, and discussed many points. I thank Mr. Paul Turner (who long ago did his best to teach me Greek) for advice on Epictetus and help with Arnold's Latin; Professors A. E. Douglas and R. F. Willetts for advice on the classics;

and Professor Roy Pascal and Drs. Richard Littlejohns and James Simpson for help with Arnold and Germany. My knowledge of Winchester College was improved by its Archivist, and by Gerald Studdert-Kennedy and James and Julia Birley. At Harrow, I was aided by Miss Kathleen Pennefather, J. S. Golland, and Mrs. Rosemary Hudson. At Rugby School, I thank its Archivist Mrs. Jennifer Macrory, Robin Alden, and also the scruffy, thoughtful Sixth-Form boys who replied to my lecture on their greatest Headmaster.

For help with sources relating to the Oxford years, and other matters, I am grateful to J. P. Curgenven for a valuable talk, to Bernard Richards of Brasenose College for many notes, and to Mrs. Elsie Duncan-Jones. At the Arnolds' Fox How, where I lived for two weeks, Mrs. F. Harrison and her daughter answered many questions, and at Ambleside the Rev. J. P. S. Morton, Mr. B. L. Thompson, and the late H. O. Roberts illuminated Arnold's Westmorland.

For improving my understanding or for aid in locating sources, I am glad to acknowledge Lady Mander; Fr. Ian Ker and the late Fr. Stephen Dessain of the Birmingham Oratory; Gordon Phillips the Archivist of *The Times,* and the following scholars or specialists: Dr. Nadean Bishop, Eve Herring the sculptor, Dr. Arthur Kincaid, Mr. Paul Merchant, Dr. Marcia Pointon, and Mrs. Joan K. R. Stubbs. At Austin, Texas, I was aided by Mrs. Iris Tilman Hill, Peter Fox Johnston, and Chris Tawwater.

The Rev. John Leonard Miller, who sent two books Arnold owned, in effect took me closer to Keble and the High Church party. Dr. Robert Woof of Newcastle sent me a valuable résumé of genealogicial data on Claudes and Reclams. For comments on the evidence relating to Arnold's health, I thank Keith Norcross, F.R.C.S., Dr. W. H. P. Cant, and Professors Peter Eckstein and W. A. Littler. I recall the help in matters of Arnold's letters given me during days and nights at Virginia by Arthur Kyle Davis, Jr., as well as the aid of Edmund Berkeley, Jr., at the Alderman Library of the University of Virginia, and the generous assistance of E. V. Quinn at Balliol. My gratitude to many other librarians must be mentioned in a token way, with a word of thanks to the staff of the University of Birmingham Library, and to Marjorie G. Wynne and her colleagues at Yale. My own colleagues Professor J. T. Boulton and Drs. Brian Harding, Ian Small, and Dorothy Thompson generously helped with their specialized knowledge. Three of my postgraduate students, Miss Christina Hill, Rev. David Lockwood, and the late Deryck Cumming, made suggestions about sources.

David Hopkinson the historian, and formerly one of H. M. Inspectors of Schools, advised me on Arnold's brothers and the Council Office. Gordon Ray and Edward A. Bloom, as it will not surprise their friends to hear, were wise and encouraging. But no one mentioned here is responsible for my mistakes; debate over Arnold with my friends has been vigorous. The debate continued along with much practical exercise (for biographers need to get out of their rooms) in my family: my children will recall duplicating Mrs. Arnold's seven hours' walk from Fox How to Fairfield's ridge and back, the Gemmi climb, the walk to Toulx, fishing in Arnold's streams, invading the Hôtel Bellevue at Thun, and similar incidents. I thank my mother, my brother William H. Honan, and for help with French sources and much other aid, my wife, Jeannette.

For printing my Arnold notes, articles, or Fox How diary and letting me use material from these pieces, I thank the editors of *Victorian Poetry, Victorian Newsletter,* and *The Arnoldian.* I express gratitude to the British Academy and to the Leverhulme Trust Fund for research grants, to the John Simon Guggenheim Foundation for a fellowship, and to Birmingham's Faculty of Arts Research Fund. I also thank Mrs. Anne Buckley and Miss Mary Parker for their typing.

For editorial help, I am especially grateful to Sally Mapstone, Gladys Carr, and Gail E. Greene.

Finally, for permission to quote from unpublished Arnold letters or other unpublished material, I am glad to mention the Alexander Turnbull Library at Wellington, New Zealand; the Alderman Library at the University of Virginia, Balliol College and the Bodleian Library at Oxford, Boston Public Library, the Brotherton Collection at Brotherton Library in the University of Leeds, Dr. Williams's Library in London, Harvard College Library, Houghton Library at Harvard, the New York University Library, the Humanities Research Center at the University of Texas in Austin, the Pierpont Morgan Library in New York City, Trinity College at Cambridge, Wellesley College Library in Massachusetts, the Beinecke Rare Book and Manuscript Library at Yale, and the Wordsworth Library at Grasmere.

January 1970–April 1980
Birmingham, England

CONTENTS

PART ONE

What youth, Goddess, what guest
Of Gods or mortals?
                                 —*"The Strayed Reveller"*

1

CHILDHOOD
1822–1836

Now it came to pass that when they wer'e [sic] come to about the middle of the wood that LOVE saw a monstrous cave, and all that he could see of it was blood and . . . two great giants their names were Hurt and Cruel. battle cried L O V E.
　　　　　　　—Matthew Arnold, age 7, to "dear papa"

IN their immense sentimental autobiographies and nostalgic memoirs, the later Victorians rediscovered childhood. They tended to forget that children of the poor had been condemned to death in unheated factories and subterranean mines; they looked back wistfully and eagerly to the comforts and securities of the middle-class English home. To some extent, they were justified. Living in what Shaw called "the dark night of the nineteenth century," adults frequently had the impression that the dark thickened as years passed. In earlier years of the century, the middle-class family had been a well-regulated monarchy—and fathers often had been benevolent despots.

Mothers tried to understand their difficult, unruly children. Certainly the wife of the Headmaster of Rugby studied her eldest son with great care. A dark-haired and physically clumsy boy, with bright eyes and a very good memory, "dear Matt" had a penchant for violence. He loved guns and blasted at blackbirds and at one point, he actually set himself on fire! He pretended one summer—apparently for a whole night—to be a corpse at the bottom of Lake Windermere. And with his fists, he gave his delicate younger brother Tom bloody noses.

Yet in 1836, Matthew Arnold was less "obstinate"[1] than he had been. Reprimanded, exiled from home, and specially drilled, he had made laudable progress in Latin and Greek. And in one additional respect he had begun to emulate Rugby School pupils, for he was scribbling poetry.

3

And yon murmuring fountain is never dry
And all is joy in the sparkling eye
of the maidens dancing merrily.

In her careful hand, Mrs. Arnold jotted his entire poem, "The First Sight of Italy," in one of her household notebooks. Of course, Matthew had never *seen* Italy! Lost, now and again,

In the depths of the sea
Where the Whale and the Dolphin are rolling in glee,[2]

he couldn't manage to deflect her attention from his persistent failings, and Mrs. Arnold clearly thought about those failings repeatedly: "vanity & love of ease—and admiration of rank & fashion."[3]

In 1836 she set Matthew and his sister Jane the task of composing brief autobiographies for her newest notebook. Encouraging self-awareness in her children, Mrs. Arnold discerned a moral benefit in this exercise. At fourteen, Jane composed a modest, pretty piece of recollection, and directly after it, dropping an inkblot or two, Matthew scrawled in the boldly sloping hand of a thirteen-year-old historian: "Tradition says that I was born at Laleham on the 24th of December in 1822 . . . I have not however any string of facts in my head, but only abstruse ones."[4]

But strings of *particular* facts ran throughout Mrs. Arnold's letters to her unmarried Penrose sisters, and also through columns of abundant memoranda . . . in pocket-diaries, handsome leather-bound journals, and modest small black-covered books preserved to this day by her descendants. She may not have needed so many *aides-mémoire,* but she recognized that her husband was one of the most distinguished of men, and nine children would need to be reminded of that salient fact. There were the three "Elder Ones," born at Laleham:

Jane Martha Arnold, or "K," born August 1, 1821
Matthew Arnold, or "Crabby" the poet, born December 24, 1822
Tom Arnold, or "Prawn," born November 30, 1823

And then three "Little Ones," also of Laleham:

Mary Arnold, or "Bacco," born March 29, 1825
Edward Penrose Arnold, or "Didu," born October 28, 1826
William Delafield Arnold, or "Widu," born April 7, 1828

Then came the ones born after she had left Laleham in the south, for the flat midlands at Rugby School where her husband, Dr. Thomas Arnold, was Headmaster:

Susanna Elizabeth Lydia, or "Susy," born in 1830
Frances Bunsen Trevenen Whately, or "Bonze" or "Fan," born in 1833
Walter Thomas, or "Quid," born in 1835

What could she remember of the childhood of Matthew, or "Crabby" the poet?

A few months before his marriage, in partnership with his sister's husband who was ten years older than he, Mr. Thomas Arnold had established at Laleham in the Thames Valley a modest school, consisting of two houses, to prepare boys for university. The Rev. John Buckland and his wife (the former Frances Arnold) lived at one end of the village with thirty smaller pupils. With a handful of bigger, somewhat grimier, and less tractable boys (who at first thought little enough of him as a disciplinarian and rioted under his nose), Thomas lived in a mansion he rented from an East India captain in the middle of town, not far from a bend in the swift and narrow Thames. In 1820, he married Mary Penrose, a lady from Fledborough Parsonage in Nottinghamshire.

The following summer, Mrs. Mary Arnold nearly died of a "violent inflammatory fever" after giving birth on August 1 to her first child, Jane Martha. She recovered slowly. Then—at almost the worst possible moment in 1822, during her second pregnancy—she tumbled from a pony near the schoolhouse gate: "My confinement was so soon expected that I was considerably alarmed, but thank God! no mischief followed."[5] A Penrose sister arrived, and Matthew Arnold the poet was safely born on December 24 near a beautiful reach of the Thames during a school holiday. He was named after his paternal uncle, the Reverend Matthew Arnold, who had been an army chaplain and then a classical professor in a military college before he drowned in the Irish Sea.[6]

The Reverends John Keble and John Tucker were the new infant's godfathers. After the baptism Mr. Tucker left his duties at Anglican madhouses (giving religious instruction)[7] to carry the Bible with missionary zeal to the Far East. But Mr. Keble, who shook Mrs. Arnold's hand with "cheerful earnestness" and gave Matthew an inscribed Bible before he could read, frequently returned to Laleham.[8] Thomas Arnold admired Keble's "hymns" in *The Christian Year,* only reversing himself with exasperation when this old friend became a Romeward-tending "High Church" reactionary in the 1830s. ("I should be very glad indeed to hear that anybody was going to put Keble's *Christian Year* into good English," Thomas duly remarked with startling effect to his niece Laura Ward, after he became Headmaster of Rugby. "There is such a feebleness and want of power about the language.")[9]

But despite her husband's feelings, Mrs. Mary Arnold never blotted a vivid Keble lyric from her journal. "If ever your lives are passing away in careless peace," she told her children, "I would entreat you to think of the injunction contained in these lines. God grant that your mother herself may bear it in mind—

> *Think not of rest; though dreams be sweet*
> *Start up & ply your heavenward feet.*
> *Is not God's oath upon your head*
> *Ne'er to sink back in slothful bed,*
> *Never again your loins untie,*
> *Nor let your torches waste and die . . . ?*[10]

Not surprisingly, an intimate friend (Mrs. Fletcher) felt that she demanded too much of herself and, later on, of her sons Matthew and Tom, but the friend rejoiced in her great "frankness, vivacity, and quickness of observation."[11] Other people wondered. Was the vivacity charming and romantic, or, perhaps, superficial and vexing? Charlotte Brontë thought after a tense interview that Mrs. Arnold lacked the highest intellectual qualities—but Aubrey de Vere was enchanted to find the mother of nine Arnolds "a dark, eager, enthusiastic, vivid, interesting, and apparently strong-minded woman."[12]

In an early portrait by Howell, Mrs. Arnold appears to be on the point of starvation, with a thin bending torso and enormous eyes. Her aquiline nose and meager visage in the portrait are set off by the neat frivolity of Louis Philippe curls—which she often combed straight, preferring an upswept coiffure and a Spanish comb to hold her hair. Of Celtic ancestry, born in Cornwall in August 1791, she was in her thirties, and extremely fragile. She had cause to be gloomy about her prospects. Each confinement seemed to bring to her bedside the Angel of Death, along with Mr. Tothill's quinine and laudanum, and the terrible day was preceded by prayerful admonitions and farewells. "I rejoice to think," she wrote of Howell's painting, "that you my darlings might recognise something motherly in those eyes resting upon you—even if the eyes themselves . . . have closed for ever!"[13]

Even the punctuation in her journals is dramatic. Somewhat bored on the northern plains at Fledborough, to which she had migrated at the age of ten, she had acted in family theatricals and teased a quantity of older sisters and a younger brother Trevenen Penrose (when he was home on holidays) until Trevenen's best friend married her and took her to Laleham. Here she adjusted with efficiency to pupils, thieves, a suicidal housemaid named Harriet, and even to her husband Thomas —whose appetite for lovemaking was as keen as his letters announced; after becoming Dr. Arnold of Rugby he could fly into a rage over a clergyman who wanted to take sexual allusions out of the classics. Thomas's energy for love and work she viewed with the wonder she felt for spectacular European mountains, or the boiling green-and-black sea. "When you see the Jura," she told her children, "think of me." Unlike many frail people, she loved tumult and turmoil. She felt it natural to share family life with pupil-boarders, visitors, and Thomas's relatives in the village—and to live in a beehive. The breakfast room, main parlor, and schoolroom on the ground floor of her house were seldom empty; upstairs were freshly painted simple bedrooms for eight or ten teenage pupils, the bedroom she shared with Thomas, the sleeping nursery and play nursery and maidservants' quarters. She could see the spacious garden from upstairs rooms, and hear murmurs from the room where Thomas gave lessons in history, the Bible, and other subjects for five or six hours a day. But Laleham was sleepy enough to make her recite to her family reports from London of hangings, murders, and revolutions. She yearned to visit foreign locales, to see thrilling sights and vistas—and longed to have her own children become active Christian reformers.

England after the Napoleonic wars seemed to Mrs. Arnold heartless and a little stupid, smugly content with new factories and industries, neglectful of the plight of the poor and the glory of Europe. She could agree with her husband that exchanges with German and French thinkers might be needed for the nation's well-being, and modestly understood why Thomas made twelve journeys to the Continent to feed his *mind*. England was vigorously industrializing; factories sprang up; commercialism and materialism richly prevailed in the 1820s. Yet the nation was riddled with inequalities which only faith, enthusiasm, and unrelenting boldness might correct. She loved the social idealism of her middle-class husband, and lived with joy in dramatic action and beauty and with a generous, wide-eyed interest in the world, despite her physical weariness. She composed verses,

> *In an Exeter coach, all shut up in the dark*
> *Without pen or pencil to aid me,*

and even lighter poetry when nearly exhausted on her sofa, sixteen miles from the attractions of London:

> *When lately I went up to town*
> *I thought again before come down*
> *That I like other country wights*
> *Must go & see some London sights—*
> *But feeling rather dull & flat*
> *But weak & languid, & all that*
> *I could not like the well & gay*
> *See all the humours of a play,*

. . . . . .
But I could go & see Corfu [an illuminated panorama]—
. . . . . .
The groups of figures scattered round,
The hills which all the distance bound,
Albania's mountains crowned with snow
The purple tint on all below
The gallant ships that come and go—
What wonder that so fair a sight
Had power to charm a Lalehamite![14]

At least in 1823, Matthew pleased this eager and intelligent woman by doing everything he ought to do. He conquered the drawing-room carpet by not toppling over on it, and then leapt to a celestial object. "My dear Matt," his mother wrote with prescience, "will you not laugh when you find it on record that you first took notice of the moon on the 14th of September?"[15]

But Matthew was so active and loud, he pleased his father a little less. He was to come deeply under the influence of his father's ideas; yet in these days he observed nothing more striking than Thomas Arnold's firm, shaven chin and good looks.

The father, for his part, peered at his son—but some vexing imbecilities in the Laleham schoolroom caused Thomas, at twenty-eight, to take a qualified delight in infancy. He was irritated by his own puzzling mental insurrections and by the sudden extension of family responsibilities.

As his wife's ancestors had been learned and unworldly, Thomas Arnold's tended to be ordinary and practical. The Cornish Penroses had produced a string of intelligent and respectable divines; but the Arnolds apparently had produced neither robber-barons, warriors, philosophers, educators, nor reformers. The genealogical evidence indicates that they had bartered, farmed, and fished for centuries. A good many of them had sold their hake and their squid at Lowestoft —where Thomas Arnold himself discovered a great-grandfather, and "so many Matthew Arnolds as to prove quite clearly that it was a family name."[16] In the eighteenth century, William Arnold sired a child with an unfortunate lady of the London streets, while working as a postal clerk. He confessed to, and married, a former sweetheart and then raised seven lawful children, while pursuing smugglers and collecting customs fees at the Isle of Wight—where Thomas Arnold was born in June 1795.

Sisters and aunts conspired to keep "DEAR, DEAR, DEAR little Tom" in a bath of affection and moral encouragement for five years. Dr. Goddard of Winchester praised Thomas for hard work as a schoolboy; but, in fact, Thomas rioted. He invented a clever booby trap and played

enough illicit games to convince himself that Goddard's praise was "a
Bounce, and a wopping one too . . . !"[17] At Oxford, he debated with
Corpus Christi College Tories, and wrote a typically affecting song:

> *May his health in a Bumper go round, Sir.*
>
> *Though now as our Tutor he perhaps may not suit, Sir,*
>   *Though he cram us with old Aristotle,*
> *The deeds we must praise of his juvenile Days,*
>   *For he gain'd us the Rights of the Bottle!*[18]

But he kept his Greek concordances and dictionaries on his desk, in a
fine "Order of Battle" at Oxford, and became a first-classman and then
an Oriel College Fellow. In those days the Senior Common Room of
the Oriel College intellectuals or "Noetics" smelled of coffee, if not of
logic. John Davison and Richard Whately sharpened their wits on the
old, evangelical assumptions about biblical prophecy and miracles. In
the best classical manner, Thomas threw javelins in a meadow with
Whately—who was to teach Thomas's sons, little Matthew and Tom
Arnold, how to carve Australian boomerangs and rise to become
Archbishop of Dublin at the age of forty-four in 1831. Indoors, Thomas
filled ledgers with historical notes and Anglican Church problems.
Could he become a clergyman if he doubted the literal interpretation
of the Bible, and quarreled with the Thirty-nine Articles?

"The management of my own mind is a thing so difficult, and brings
me into contact with so much that is so strangely mysterious," he
complained to John Tucker in 1819, "that I stand at times . . . in a
chaos."[19] As a young deacon and schoolmaster at Laleham, Thomas
hated teaching Sunday school! Searching theology with a quick
practical eye, he faulted the Doctrine of the Trinity.

> *There is a fire whose flame unquenched glows,*
> *Thoughts inly brood that never know repose,*

he jotted in his wife's journal in 1822, and again the next month:

> *Where thorny Questions vex our Mind*
> *And Doubts which can no answers find—*
> *Shall we our Christian faith forego . . . ?*[20]

Actually, the volcano in his mind seethed and glowed with intellectual
zeal. Wisely, he *trusted* the guidance of a good Diety; but he doubted
the historical and social awareness of most English clergymen, and
the usefulness of a "corrupt" ecclesiastical establishment.[21] At Laleham, he simplified his aims and principles with the practical instinct
of a man who dislikes subtleties and paradoxes. He would "sink into
nothing the difference between Christian and Christian," as he later
told his friend Mr. Empson, "and insist strongly on the difference

between Christian and non-Christian"²²—until the rudimentary
moral principles of the gospels were recognized by the sects and every
civic institution became Christianized. Clearly, the state and the
Church ought to be one and the same. In the moral battlefield of the
world, *reform* was the Christian's flag.

Meanwhile, his hold on adolescents was rather loose. A whole crowd
left the schoolhouse for an unauthorized, moonlit ride on the Thames,
and, according to Mary's journal, refused to apologize. Having been
struck on the head by an orbiting washbasin at Winchester, Thomas
had a pretty good notion of the "ordinary meannesses, coarsenesses,
and littlenesses" of pupils and the "nakedness of boy-nature."²³ He
resolved not to be aloof from his students. Craving exercise, he turned
part of his ample garden into a "Campus Martius"—complete with a
trench for leaping, a peg-pole for climbing, and a tall sturdy gallows for
chinning and target practice. He speared and fenced and "skir-
mished" in between tutorials, and merrily plunged after the pupil-
boarders into the river. By oil and candlelight, he fed historical articles
to a London encyclopedia, and put Edward Gibbon in his place by
starting to write a history of Rome. But for all his concern for his
students, he failed to understand very small children. His own
Matthew and Jane were puzzling. At six months of age, Matthew
seemed "backward and rather bad-tempered" because he wouldn't lie
still;²⁴ and at the age of one year, little Jane reminded Thomas Arnold
of the sin of Adam and Eve's Fall, by refusing to curtsy.

But he recovered charity in the mild summer of 1824 when five
Arnolds traveled to the Penrose home, in the north, at Fledborough on
the Trent. Mrs. Arnold sat outside on the coach. Adding her own
father, and leaving Matthew and his brother Tom at Fledborough
Parsonage, the party made a journey into the pretty Lake District.
Thomas once had met William Wordsworth—but his wife had never
encountered the poet. In the Lake District, they received invitations to
take tea first at Rydal Mount, and then with the Southeys at Keswick.
Mrs. Arnold expected to find "a trifling sentimental wild-looking
person" in the leading poet, and was very relieved to find a polite
countryman with a homely nose: "I was agreeably surprised in Mr.
Wordsworth," she declared later. "I found him mild and gentlemanly,
with considerable dignity in his appearance and manner—but it
seems to me to want that variety and animation . . . which afterwards
struck me so much in Southey." Happily, even more animated than
Southey were his "active quick-looking girls." Almost as an anticli-
max, Mrs. Arnold tested her nerves by climbing a mountain on
horseback: Thomas walked, but "three sorry hacks" took the others up
Skiddaw Mountain and down. Mrs. Arnold noted, "My father's

stumbling Rosinante was actually unsafe—and Jane's very unceremoniously took her into the [River] Greta on our return."[25]

Refreshed and mainly undamaged, the Arnolds returned to Fledborough Parsonage. Instructing his infants in oarsmanship, the father now took them out on the Trent in the *Frolic,* "letting them row," as Mrs. Arnold delightedly recorded, "or fancy they did so."[26] Within a day or two of this time, she noticed that something was wrong with Matthew's leg.

As a boy of almost two, Matthew splashed water in a grand style; and, indeed, his kicking in a crib and slamming of an oar suggest his gusto. Matthew spent a lifetime persuading people that he was jolly and urbane—while surprising his friends with his sense of impotent tears, and of the sad inevitability of things. His later childhood visits to Fledborough were remembered, in his maturity, when he saw again "the grey church. . . . the immense meadow, and the sparkling Trent"[27]—images that suggest his own poetic tribute to family life, the lyrical "Forsaken Merman," in which a pagan of the sparkling ocean chants so accusingly:

> *Call her once before you go—*
> *Call once yet!*
> *In a voice that she will know:*
> . . . . . .
> *Children's voices should be dear*
> *(Call once more) to a mother's ear;*
> *Children's voices, wild with pain—*
> . . . . . .
> *One last look at*
> *. . . the little grey church on the windy shore,*
> *Then come down!*
> . . . . . .
> *Singing: 'There dwells a loved one,*
> *But cruel is she!*
> *She left lonely for ever*
> *The kings of the sea.'*[28]

The gray church, sparkling water, and the theme of children in pain, even a sense that it gives of a mother's unintentional cruelty, need not connect "Forsaken Merman" with the beginning of Matthew's time "in irons." But within ten days of leaving the River Trent, the Arnolds consulted Mr. Tothill, back at home, and then a London specialist —with the result that a frightening iron apparatus arrived at Laleham to be fitted to his limbs. His father was not deeply worried: "We have had some anxiety about Matt," Thomas Arnold wrote to a friend this autumn, "from the Effects of a bad habit of crawling before he could walk, and which has greatly bent one of his Legs, so that he has been obliged to wear Irons, and must continue to do so for some time."[29]

At two or three, most children become excitedly aware of themselves in relation to other people; but Matthew found that thick leg-straps and leg-braces of the heaviest iron made him peculiar and decidedly ugly. He found it difficult to move about and reacted very audibly. "I also remember," he writes at thirteen, "wearing irons and being obstinate and being taken up to London about my crooked legs."[30] Mrs. Arnold understood her little boy's obstinacy and tears. Pediatricians who have examined her comments believe that rickets had increased bowing of the tibia in her young child; the weight of cast-iron braces soon bent his one good leg.[31] She took him up to town to plead with an orthopedic specialist—but Dr. Carpus was invisible on one occasion, and quite adamant on another. Beside herself with worry, she thought of defying Dr. Carpus's explicit orders—and wavered. Arthur Stanley[32] was to observe "her watchful care, always anxious, even to nervousness, at the least indication of illness," and she was very alert. The braces were removed in the evening, when with the dreadful fetters standing by in the large sleeping nursery the boy learned to "repeat" Keble's lyrics in exchange for his mother's ardent attention: "I used to go round your little beds at night to kiss and bless you," she told her children later, "and be careful of every little trouble of body or mind!"[33]

Matthew enjoyed a lion's share of her attention—even before he delayed a holiday by opening his head on the claw foot of the dining-room table. But the psychological effect of his mother's attention had limits: for what Mrs. Arnold hardly concealed was her joy at each "fearful tottering step"[34] taken by her *normal* infants. She hungered to witness tangible signs of progress, to see their big and little victories. To move about in a tiny pelisse and straw hat, however unsteadily, as she explained in the household journal, was "going alone—which always seems to me a great advance in the dignity of a boy's or girl's condition." "You trot about in the gaiety of your little heart," she notes of her child Susy. Little Tom, while his brother stayed near the pink acacia, won great praise for toddling all the way home from Chertsey.[35] Matthew's strenuous exertion in maturity, his lethally effective critical manner, and his deep, fierce pride are connected to early and repeated sensations of being outstripped.

At Laleham Thomas Arnold had set up school in administrative partnership with the Rev. John Buckland, who ran classes nearby. The two men now ended their agreement. Thomas, at last, was solely in command of his *own* school. The new operational freedom made him more relaxed, demonstrative, and loving as a father. He seemed a dynamo of energy, a geyser of affectionate exuberance, a roving scientific laboratory of inquisitive zeal. On holidays, he roamed out of the Thames valley, with the Ordnance map on his knees—and returned with plants and fossils, and whole wads of his loving wife's pocketed letters. He swept Matthew up, irons and all, for hugs and pickaback rides—once carrying him bumpily up to the top of Peterborough Cathedral—and showered the boy with little bricks and soldiers. Lady Franklin wondered if he knew how to laugh. "My father," Tom Arnold recalled as an elderly Catholic in *Passages in a Wandering Life*, "was not witty, nor—though he could appreciate humour—was he humourous; but the comic and grotesque side of life attracted him strongly. He gave to each of us children some nickname more or less absurd, and joked with us, while his eyes twinkled, on the droll suggestions and comparisons which the names suggested."³⁶ Jane almost defeated drollery as "K"; and Matthew at three was rechristened "Crab" or "Crabby," for he scuttled slowly when he scuttled at all. With further twinkling merriment, Thomas turned his namesake into "Prawn," the next three children into "Bacco," "Widu," and "Didu," an old Greek philosopher into "Tottle," and three roads in the Lake District into "Radical Reform," "Bit-by-Bit Reform," and "Old Corruption." Collectively and ingloriously, the Arnold children were "the dogs" or "the fry."

From the Campus Martius, Laleham schoolhouse appeared as a reddish bulk with a luminous and airy aspect. Large windows gaped from the ground-floor and upper-floor levels, and five dormers between solid chimneys looked out on a dirt road. Not all of the greenery had been consecrated to the exercise gallows. Mrs. Arnold recalled for her children the "shade and liberty—where your . . . steps first tottered . . . till becoming stronger and stronger you ran through the walks with your Hoops or Whips—or gathered violets in the spring time, both blue and white in the ash plantation."³⁷ Even as an ordinary boy from the waist up, and something odder from the thighs down, Matthew couldn't avoid gigantic tea parties under the cedar of Lebanon. Sometimes thirteen infants ("including . . . the Whateleys & Bucklands") made as much noise as a cow, in a nearby field, whose mooing quite upset and frightened Jane. Near the lilacs and syringa grew two enormous trees, "which I used to make the boundaries of your wanderings when I allowed you to run about alone," and "under which your Aunt Susanna's crib used to be placed."³⁸ A lady with an incurable spinal complaint, Miss Susanna Arnold exuded great hilarity and common sense, and thoughtfully left her godson (Matthew) her watch and her Shakespeare and £100 in her will.

Freed from leg-braces when he was four, Crabby walked slowly, but his limbs were straight. He took more interest in his family, and a cautiously superior interest in his father's pupils.

> One of the first things I remember [Matthew recalled at thirteen] is my asking one of Papa's pupils . . . one morning to get me a bough, and he greatly vexed me by making a bow. We used also to be in the parlour after breakfast, putting together our dissected maps. I also remember when one of the pupils gave a book of beasts to Papa, and the going out to see a particular pig killed, & seeing a great hole dug till they came to water . . . & seeing Aunt Lydia copy the house from the lawn. Also cutting the thistles with Willy Buckland & Jane & Tom, in the garden.[39]

Sometimes Papa's clever pupils would put Jane and himself "into a little carriage we had . . . and harness Spot to it and make him drag us round the garden."[40] Otherwise, Crabby was at the still point of the turning world, and indeed his mother agonized over "his clumsy manner of walking . . . & inactive habits" in his sixth year: for fourteen months he had refused even to gain weight, and had maddeningly registered "43" pounds on the Marriott scales! Matthew *looked* normal. But had the "incumbering irons" saved him from deformity —or in some way ruined him for life? "I cannot help thinking that they would have been equally safe and efficacious if *much* lighter."[41]

With Jane, he received from his Papa his first Latin lesson, in the niceties of *amo, amas, amat* according to the "Hamiltonian system," on February 14, 1828,[42] but Thomas Arnold had much else besides Latin on his mind at this time. Always enthusiastic, he was about to reform the very bricks of a noble old public school; already he had predicted that Time's footsteps would separate him from Laleham's "low Church tower" and garden groves forever—

> *And for some far ignobler Tide*
> *I may thy stream, sweet Thames resign.*[43]

As it happened, the schoolmaster woke up one morning to learn from a letter, that a "thousand" testimonials for other candidates had been passed over in favor of his own papers, and that he had been elected Headmaster of Rugby School—to take up duties beginning in August 1828. With little to do, now, except to remind Rugby School's trustees that he was *not* a violent radical—several "noblemen and gentlemen" in Warwickshire oddly nursed doubts on that score—and then to revolutionize Rugby School from top to bottom, Thomas scarcely contained himself. While Laleham village buzzed with fervent expectation,[44] he wrote cheerily, "Forwards, forwards, forwards, —should be one's motto."

Sadly, in this year or the next, Crabby received parental spankings.

Why was grammar "pain and grief"[45] to him? Perhaps Papa was impatient; and surely Miss Rutland, as a governess, made a poor substitute for Mrs. Arnold. Her "coming to live with us," as Jane recalled, was "an arrangement which neither Matt, Tom or myself liked . . . but we got used to it."[46] Tutored by Miss Rutland, and more occasionally by his father, Matthew defied the law that an Arnold should *progress*, mainly because he had appealed very deeply to his mother by flouting it. Barred at first from competitive play with other children, he had wrung the hearts of parents and visitors alike by dragging his silver legs; he had gained sympathy by doing almost nothing in a house where everyone else did everything. After the leg-braces, the oddity of his comportment set a pattern. Soon he would be unusual among mortals; he would try very smoothly and coolly to amaze and astonish people without repelling them, and instead of being uniquely ugly, would try to become *beautiful*.

Yet at what price? Unreasonably, he was a vexing little David who defied a conscientious Goliath: "I should *not* be anxious to make a Child's Conscience very enlightened," wrote his father, trying to be firm, "but I should strive . . . to make him obey what it did tell him." Matthew hardly knew that he had a conscience, but he disliked lessons, and he disliked Miss Rutland. Sometimes Thomas was vehement, and spoke with a passion that lightly scorched his children as it would later scorch a few Rugbeians. "If, my little boys," the father announced, placing one hand on Crabby's dark brown head and another on Tom's, "I were to find that you had grown hard . . . & did not love your Papa and Mamma—how unhappy it would make me." Then as light in the drawing room struck two pairs of anxiously upturned eyes, Thomas Arnold pronounced: "I had rather my little boys should die." Mary observed this scene: "Little Tom's eyes filled with tears," she wrote, "& he seemed to think it impossible he should cease to love us."[47] Matthew failed to sob or even to choke—but he would soon pay bitterly for being stubborn at lessons.

In July, a rainstorm broke through a scholar's roof. "We were awoke by the plaistering of the ceiling falling into our Bedroom . . . to sleep in this storm was impossible," Mary Arnold admitted. "The water began to pour down violently into both nurseries."[48] Clearly it was time to leave Laleham. In August, Thomas took inventories with normal zeal and accounted for everything except the family dog. Filled with small, dismayed, red-eyed Arnolds—Jane's face was swollen with crying, because her tummy didn't travel very well and she couldn't bear to leave Grandmamma—Layton's coach rolled inexorably and horrendously towards the Colnbrook crossroads and then stopped. A breathless workman materialized, with a black-and-white hound in tow! "Spot sprang up with glee," Mrs. Arnold gratefully recalled, "& we pursued our way to Oxford."[49] Next day—August 6, 1828—they rolled over the Dunchurch Road and saw in the distance between elm trees the battlements of one of England's great public schools.

On tableland rising from the Avon's south bank in Warwickshire, Rugby School had the look of a massive fortified church. It was strange to find it at the edge of a sunny market town. Over the main gateway rose a windowed tower from which archers might have shot down at passersby; merlons and crenels ran along the top of a gray central building which seemed of brick and Portland stone—with a glinting, leaded roof. The headmaster's house had a turreted high military entrance. Beyond a neat quadrangle, a simple chapel, and the Upper Bench and Lower Bench rooms in the gray library tower there spread eight acres of green playing fields. These were nearly surrounded by rows of enormous English elms. One came to a muddy pond and then to a delightfully tree-shaded mound known as the "Island," which was thought to be a Roman lookout point. The flat meadows beyond were so infested and broken up by hedgerows and clumps of trees, however, that the far view proved disappointing: "no hills—no plains—not a single wood," wrote Thomas as if the map were insubordinate, "no rock, no river . . . scarcely any flowers . . . nothing but one endless monotony of inclosed fields and hedgerow trees." Unlike Shakespeare he had no love for Warwickshire.

But by the time his family settled into the headmaster's house and noisy, well-dressed Rugby students returned from their holidays, he was delighted to be in command of Rugby. His power was "perfectly absolute," as he wrote, so "I have no excuse if I do not try to make the school something like my beau ideal."[50] Enrollment had slumped under old Dr. Wooll, the last Headmaster; and Thomas meant to revive the school by giving power and responsibility to older boys, and intelligent Christian zeal to lessons. While lifting the morale of teachers or masters, he would himself become an exemplary teacher in history and religion—and he had other plans.

He took his children on fine days to bathe at "Roly Poly" in the Avon. In a nearby wood, he led the boys in a hunt for anemones and coltsfoot, and in flat lanes pointed out honeysuckles and "hedgeroses." Under a machicolated turret, he roused "the dogs" every morning and listened to their biblical recitations Sunday evening. Meanwhile, Rugby pupils flowed in and out of the family downstairs drawing room like tidal water in an estuary; and if Rugby boys, of all ages, were omnipresent, so was Papa. Very evident were the Faustian syllabuses he prepared for "K," Crab, and Prawn. There were history and geography, scripture and arithmetic, Italian, French, and German, and the classical verbs for dessert. (Yielding to Miss Robertson, poor Miss Rutland felt that there might be an easier way to make a living. In fact none of the Arnolds' overworked governesses lasted for very long.) Matthew recited the catechism well enough to earn a copy of Sellon's *Abridgment of Holy Scriptures;* and with Jane he mused over a famous, gory head of John the Baptist in a Bible *Bilderbuch.* Also, he read animal stories and looked at pictures in Thomas Bewick's *British Birds and Quadrupeds*—which Papa had received from a grateful pupil—and he quickly went through little histories of France and England written by one Aunt Penrose, known as "Mrs. Markham." No mortal child could shut his ears while Thomas told the stories in Herodotus, moreover, or could fail to love "Men riding on Dolphins, Ants eating Men, and the Sun blown out of Heaven by a high Wind."[51]

But Matthew stumbled as badly in the large syllabuses as he stumbled in the garden. "I must . . . get a drill sergeant and a dancing master," vowed his mother, who administered tea and sympathy to dozens of Rugbeians. "His awkwardness strikes me more than ever."[52] Looking for ways to impress his mother, Matthew learned to recite a purple patch from Edmund Burke about "Hyder Ali's ferocious desolation of the Carnatic."[53] He *had* to do something gloriously wonderful soon for he was being neglected in these exhilarating days. His father Thomas took a divinity degree and became "Dr." Arnold—a change Mary deemed "almost ludicrous."[54] Working hard, Thomas or Dr. Arnold (as we shall call him with respect) wrote essays and annotated Thucydides, taught the Sixth Form with exactitude from an undignified kitchen chair, and addressed God and the whole school very sensibly in the great hall.

Dr. Arnold's enthusiasm was fired by events that were sweeping the Continent as well as by his own ambitions. In France the reactionary King Charles X suppressed his legislature and gagged the press: his minister Polignac had gone too far and proved himself a fool. In July 1830, Charles X was overthrown and replaced by a constitutional monarchy so that for sixteen years England and France were to move closer in an *entente cordiale.* Next the Belgians revolted against union with the Dutch and within a month revolts occurred in Saxony, Hesse, and Brunswick, where rulers fell and popular constitutions were granted. If democracy was dawning in Europe, loud cries for Parliamentary reform were heard at home. The election of 1830 resulted in a Whig, or Liberal, government pledged to reform and headed by Lord Grey, with capable Lord Palmerston in the Foreign Office and "Little Johnny" Russell in the wings. This election thrilled Mrs. Arnold and lifted Dr. Arnold's spirits with the force of a trumpet call. National feeling for reform after 1830 encouraged bold experiments at Rugby School, and Dr. Arnold achieved publicity and fed the national spirit for reform. In November 1830, Lord John Russell, a shy and forgetful man 5 feet 4¾ inches tall, was only Paymaster-General (a post not even in the Cabinet until 1831). During the next twenty-five years "Little Johnny" achieved more than any British statesman had ever done—he was to shepherd through the House of Commons a Reform Bill which in 1832 added 300,000 middle-class voters to the polls and consolidated a mood for slow reform. As Prime Minister from 1846 to 1852 and again briefly in the 1860s, he was the shrewdest leader in the first half of the Victorian age—or before Disraeli and Gladstone alternated as Tory and Liberal Prime Ministers between 1868 and 1886. What was *not* so apparent in 1830 was that inequities of the Industrial Revolution, the staggering complexity of the economy, the terrible plight of the cities would be too much even for Russell. In 1830 as cholera came to London, millions of citizens lived with hunger, fear, and a degrading Poor Law, with dreadfully poor schooling, in ignorance and insecure jobs, their bodies affected by conditions of work and life in ramshackle, infested, overcrowded, ugly, filthy, and stinking English cities.

While Charles X toppled in Paris on the distant Continent, children roamed over an enormous green close with its admonitory border of English elms in the lazy, hot July days of 1830. Mrs. Arnold read the newspapers aloud; and in "the cool shade of the purple beech" Matthew took turns, with Jane, reciting from Bunyan's *Pilgrim's Progress*.

Matthew noticed that his father loved this book, with its martyrdom of Pilgrim Faithful and battle between Christian and a scaly, wicked devil and was inspired to set to work with a pencil. He soon handed Papa a new classic called "Pimgrim's Progress, in 4 vol., 8th Edition, Vol 1st," by one "Matthew Arnold, LATE Fellow of CHRISTCHURCH COLLEGE OXFORD." Written in pencil by a seven-year-old, the tiny manuscript is eloquent, even if Late Fellow's punctuation is a little unsteady:

> then said the, pilgrim [Matthew wrote in a clear hand for "dear papa"] my name is Love . . . Now it came to pass that when they wer'e come to about the middle of the wood that LOVE saw a monstrous cave, and all that he could see of it was blood and brains . . . [and] two great giants their names were Hurt and Cruel.

Any father concerned with spiritual victories would have to admire a fine denouement:

battle cried LOVE. then Hurt tried to knock Love, down with his club but as HURT was just going to do it he got a cut in his right hand [,] which being given by the sword of the Spirit it made Hurt fall faint to the ground [.] so cruel came up And knocked Love down straight upon the ground. but Love manffuly getting up again hit Cruel such A knock on his forehead that it quite killed him.[55]

But this work—a few scraps of paper with an absurd title—didn't please Papa. Matthew did worse than ever at lessons, to the despair of his current governess. Unable to get ahead in Latin and Greek, at the fringes of a Christian public school, Matthew was sent off by his own mother to learn grammar at Uncle Buckland's school, back at Laleham.

With all good intentions toward her son, Mrs. Arnold, by sending him to Buckland's, ensured that he would suffer exquisitely. What made Buckland's "a really bad and injurious school in my time," Matthew told her in 1863, was the "confinement." "We never left that detestable little gravel playground except on Sundays."[56] And what made things worse for Matthew was his mother's absence; there were miles between Buckland's school at Laleham and her loving, palpable presence at Rugby. He felt lost, betrayed: "Jane is the only one I connect with Laleham," he later declared with feeling. His *sister's* loyalty he couldn't question; partly because she had left her dolls to join him in the garden "diggings" when he had been in leg-braces, and partly because she always admired him, his sister Jane was to him "what no one else could be"—and what no one else would "ever be again."[57] Mrs. Arnold's love had been a little less dependable.
"My dear Crabby," Dr. Arnold wrote after Matthew had scuffed the gravel for a few months at Laleham School, "I am afraid that you are become a Tory . . . since you have got *Malé* [unsatisfactory] twice in one week. . . . I am very sorry for it, be it what it will,—for it makes me sadly afraid that my Boy Matt is an idle Boy, who thinks that God sent him into the world to play and eat and drink . . . —I do not like writing to my Crabby when I am obliged to find fault with him . . . but I must write to him . . . God bless you, my dearest Crabby, and believe me to be your very loving *Pappy,* as you used to call me."[58] Actually, the Rev. Mr. Buckland knew that even insufferable boys liked to "eat & drink," and hence banished insufferable boys who did badly at lessons to a lonely and inferior dinner regularly on Fridays. "Whenever I hear of your dining in on a Friday," Mrs. Arnold wrote to her son in the second year of exile, "I will directly give you the pleasure of a letter with news. . . . You have therefore only to write and tell me you have

given proof of a week's diligence & our letter shall be written."[59]

Fighting fire with fire, Matthew became careless about writing home.

"My dearest Crabby," Rugby's Headmaster wrote with a stern allusion to *Gulliver's Travels,* "you want a Flapper sadly to put you in Mind of Things, and I had better ask Uncle Buckland to become a Flapper." And then—in Dr. Arnold's merriest manner—"O Crabby the great, who make your Letters long to wait, that we get them about a week too late."[60]

Matthew spent two years at Buckland's strict school, between January 1831 and December 1832. There were compensations for the horrid playground and the puritanical, bitter smell of the room. Trembling, devoted Arnold ladies lived nearby in the village, and his schoolmates included his cousins. On *one* day a week, he was free. On Sundays, he had the heaths and pines of Surrey, a barge path and a gravelly road to follow, and a clear, swift river to fill his eyes—swifter than anything in Virgil—and, later, he was to return impulsively to Chertsey Lock and watch again "the wide sheet of the gray Thames gleaming through the general dusk." Also, Uncle John Buckland's manner was "honest"; he was a rosy, broad-shouldered man who set boys to memorizing seven *Eclogues* of Virgil as a "prize task." Really learning grammar, Matthew at last saw "the beauty of poetry"[61] while sweating through the Latin of Virgil's fourth *Eclogue.* "Crab certainly does construe Virgil very well . . . when made to think about it," Dr. Arnold noted.[62] Wisely, back at Rugby, he felt that his son would have to be treated with gentle flattery, with the careful distinction an eldest son deserves: "The Fry do some Delectus every Day with me, . . . get on quite fast:—I do not mean," he wrote to Matthew, "that they are at all equal to such a grand Crab as you are, who can construe Virgil, and quote Ovid."[63]

On holidays, Crabby came home to amaze his brothers with the latest, worldliest schoolboy slang. He seemed very grand to Tom, who had begun to "hesitate" and would later manage to call Matthew the "Emperor"—probably after reading an essay of Emerson's in 1844*—while still hesitating. Matthew, too, stuttered a little—and then inexplicably stopped stuttering. "Your godson is now turned of 10 years old," Dr. Arnold wrote to the Rev. John Tucker, "and I think of keeping him at home to familiarize him with home feelings."[64] Matthew was delighted to hear this news, since he adored home feelings. To keep Matthew and Tom stuffed full of Latin and Greek, Mr.

---

*"The poet is not any permissive potentate, but is emperor in his own right," Emerson wrote in "The Poet."

Herbert Hill was now summoned to Rugby. A cousin of Southey, Hill married one of the poet laureate's own daughters. Tom thought Herbert Hill "rather severe" and Dr. Arnold lost patience because the new tutor was ignorant of mathematics and was too timid to master "the six books of Euclid"[65]—but Hill sheltered in the literary classics and found a reward in longevity. Even as late as 1891, "the old gentleman had a place in some endowed school in Warwickshire, which yielded him an income of £900," says Judge Fishback, who met Hill in his eighties and found him polished and softened "to a temper that was alert, intelligent and courteous."[66]

Mr. Hill tutored the two brothers until they left for Winchester in 1836. Anxious to prevent another enforced exile, Matthew demonstrated a satisfactory command of everything—and began to show off. "My dear Uncle Trevenen," he writes knowingly in the month he turned eleven.

> I can quite well remember when I used to construe Herodotus with you. . . . When I first went to Mr. Hill's, I used to construe only Homer and Xenophon, but I have lately been put into Aeschylus and am construing the Persae, where the Chorus and the Messenger are calling out O T O T O T O I.

Southey's cousin was not only teaching him classical tragedies, but helping him to be a perfect Arnold:

> I spear with Mr. Hill [Matthew testifies] or play battledore or shuttlecock. . . . I can drive my hoop quite round the school-field. . . . I like drawing armed men as well as ever, but I wish very much to draw cavaliers, . . . therefore as Mr. Hill is going to Oxford with us he says he will get a trooper which he had at college and show it to me. I have got a wooden sword.[67]

Still, no matter how well he did at lessons, there were boys in the Rugby library tower to outshine him: they won prizes and achieved miracles. (His parents treated school as an extension of the family.) As an outcast at the Bucklands', Matthew had enjoyed a special status, for even as an inglorious Crab, with "Claws, reposing in the Shade of a large Sea Weed,"[68] he had appealed to his mother by worrying her almost to distraction. Now, pride wilted in the furnace of the paternal will. Feeling extraordinary, while looking quite ordinary, Matthew sought out delectable private worlds in which he could freely luxuriate—proving himself clever and wise or sadly beautiful and forlorn. Roaming in Aeschylus, he was oddly slow and languid, and apologized to Mr. Hill for "a peculiar dullness in learning orally."[69] What the Arnold children often lacked was neither love nor understanding, but the experience of anonymity in order to discover themselves and explore their own feelings—and Matthew was ferociously interested in himself. With glee, he got Jane's and Tom's help in digging in the garden a great fort about three yards square, "surrounded by a ditch and ramparts of earth." Four smaller, awed children constructed a nearby bomb shelter—and "missiles, in the shape of clay balls, were easily manufactured," as Tom recalls of the warfare.[70] Matthew's structure was parent-free; but one of the littlest of the enemy was captured and immured in it, and Mrs. Arnold prohibited the forts thereafter, for she was very watchful.

More than watchful, she was intuitive. Mrs. Arnold saw into a boy's head. Matthew's fondness for poetry and increasing interest in theatricals were not lost upon her. Quietly, she could even sympathize with his tendency to dramatize aches and pains, and with his glittering natural preeminence among the children, for she was herself susceptible to everything poignant and grand. (Her husband, for example, hated Maria Edgeworth's novels; neither the Irish setting in *Castle Rackrent,* drawing-room comedy in *Belinda,* nor scenes of low life in *The Absentee* could please him. But Mary read the thrilling Miss Edgeworth—as later, though Dr. Arnold found nothing very good or inspiring in Dickens, Mary Arnold got him to recite the *Pickwick Papers.*) Her husband's faith in the poet of Rydal Mount she suddenly had discovered was quite justified: before seeing Wordsworth in the summer of 1831, however, the whole Arnold family had taken a tour in the north. On their journey, they visited the famous Speedwell Mine. Uneasy, that day, at the thought of a descent into Hell, "Bacco" or Little Mary stayed with "the old woman who guarded the mouth of the cavern"; but the rest of the family plunged underground and Matthew described the "long dark subterranean passage" so vividly that his mother was impressed.[71] From there, they went on up to Scotland, where Matthew broke out in a nettle-rash, and then into the Lake District where the older boys extended their hands to the bemused Robert Southey. "So, now you've both seen a live poet!" remarked that gentleman with scandalous, memorable condescension.[72] But a much greater poet, at Rydal Mount, spoke so pointedly and helpfully about house-rents that they found themselves "at the corner of the lane that leads up to Wordsworth's house"[73] at Christmas, in Brathay Hall at the head of Lake Windermere the following summer, and in Fox Ghyll under Loughrigg Fell, at the end of 1832. In the summer of 1833, they rented in the radiant green bowl of Grasmere Valley, Allan Bank, in which Wordsworth had once lived. By this time, the Headmaster of Rugby School and the author of the Immortality Ode were grumbling together not only about the recent Reform Bill—which either saved England from revolution or perhaps entirely ruined the country—but about the relative merits of blue and reddish slate, and round and square chimney-quoins. A holiday home for the Arnolds was under construction at Fox How—a very pretty site jammed between the River Rotha and the boulders and tarns of Loughrigg and not far from the bluestone houses of Ambleside. Mrs. Arnold contemplated the region while drinking tea in a skeletal, spacious drawing room "with planks over the rafters."[74]

Once again in the heaven he had first visited as an Oriel Fellow in 1819, Dr. Arnold contemplated a region that put Arcadia to shame, that had been prowled over by Roman legionaries and lately been invested with wonderful, magical, if supererogatory qualities by native poets. Skirmishing on the green fells with his children, with cousins and in-laws and Sixth Formers; with the literary Captain Hamilton who had written *Cyril Thornton;* and with a taciturn sixty-three-year-old Wordsworth who stepped heavily and wore a green eyeshade, Dr. Arnold felt guilty and suspicious of his happiness. "Mere mountain and lake hunting," he firmly impressed his children, were "time lost."[75] The lovely stone house of Fox How, which stands today, drew from him the guiltiest of his testaments of adoration.

In July Dr. Thomas Arnold briskly led a detachment of rather light infantry—"K," Crab, Prawn, and the author of *Cyril Thornton*—from Wythburn all the way over to Keswick. Matthew, who was then ten-and-a-half, never forgot this walk. He wrote later in "Resignation:"

> *High on a bank our leader stands*
> *Reviews and ranks his motley bands[.]*

Captain Hamilton must have pulled himself together. A dashing, romantic figure who had thought of dueling with a book reviewer and had ended in a tavern, Hamilton could of course recognize a born commander. Dr. Arnold displayed common sense and understanding by stopping en route at the Nag's Head Inn, at Wythburn, where Keats had stayed overnight; Matthew had either walked or ridden in his mother's carriage up to this point.

Near a sedentary innkeeper, Papa now

> *Makes clear our goal to every eye—*
> *The valley's western boundary.*

And off they go, observing and drinking in

> *Mild hollows, and clear heathy swells,*
> *The cheerful silence of the fells.*
> *. . . . . .*
> *Through the deep noontide heats we fare;*
> *The red-grouse, springing at our sound,*
> *Skims, now and then, the shining ground.*

Oddly, in the poetic version of this grand trudge over open countryside in "Resignation," two adults and three children are elongated in a "wavering, many-coloured line" reminiscent of the army of humanity in "Rugby Chapel." Mountains loom in the distance, challenging even the eye:

> *In front, behold outspread*
> *Those upper regions we must tread!*

Jane wavered so much that she had to lie down. Having proved that his legs were indubitably stuck on straight, Matthew was parched, pricked, scratched, boiled, and exhausted by the time he collapsed into his mother's carriage for the ride to Cockermouth, and then, through significant gathering darkness, to the coast of Whitehaven—where "I remember well"—

> *We bathed our hands with speechless glee,*
> *That night, in the wide-glimmering sea.*[76]

He remembered, too, the stunning silence of Papa during the walk. Matthew associated the grandeur of the Lake District, as later of the Alps, with the aspiration and purity of his father.

Occupied in July 1834, Fox How became the worldly paradise for members of the family until they died. Matthew's youngest sister, Fan, lived there through the First World War—and on the patio told a visitor, Theodore Roosevelt, how to run the United States. Fox How connected generations and epochs, immortal bards and mortal politicians. The view of Wansfell from one drawing-room window elicited a sonnet by Wordsworth. The whole setting taxed poor Charlotte Brontë's accuracy and even her descriptive powers ("beautiful as imagination could dream"[77]) and kept Matthew and Tom out of doors in all weather. Tom remembered the twice-yearly excursion up from Rugby in the most reverent detail, "the boxes belonging to the olive-green carriage," the landaulet and sword-case and imperial duly packed, the three-day trip to Westmorland on bad macadam and worse pavé, the gray and chestnut horses and the dusty postboys, the geological and botanical talk of his father, as everyone's teeth rattled, and the triumphal arrival at "Bacco's Brook"—with Fairfield streaked by snow or entirely white in the distance. A boy needed only to fall out of bed to find himself going up Loughrigg, to half-concealed tarns and "little streams," each in the winter "forcing its way down its own obstructed gully through a succession of . . . ice grottoes."[78] At thirteen and fourteen, Matthew was less moved by sublimity than by dace and brown trout; and less concerned to hear the "strangled sound" of a black torrent than to patronize the Elterwater Gunpowder

Company. Fox How holidays freed him from unremitting parental vigilance, sharpened his senses, and put him amid beauty unparalleled in England. His landscape poetry and sanity of mind—alike —owe much to Loughrigg and Fairfield.

Of late, Dr. Arnold had been imitating the English poets. Having discovered the River of Life in Coleridge's "Kubla Kahn," if not in Wordsworth's Duddon Sonnets, he soon flung it gurgling and bursting with exclamations through fourteen stanzas. After her husband poeticized over the Lake District, Mrs. Arnold naturally followed:

> *Here the grey rock, precipitous—*
> *There the bank's grassy bound*
> *With the deep Tarn within—'tis ever thus*
> *Through the year's varied round.*[79]

Matthew could do no less. But he first struck home by writing a poem, in Latin, to celebrate the second birthday of little Fan Arnold in October 1835. "Mr. Hill gave him the subject," Mrs. Arnold told her brother, "and [Matthew] brought it up without the least idea of its being better than his ordinary productions."[80] Encouraged, he continued to bring up unassigned poems. Welding an episode to a song from *Childe Harold,* Matthew wrote lyrics about Mary Queen of Scots that look—unsurprisingly—like bad early Byron. In 1836, he also produced "The First Sight of Italy," which combined Scott's chivalry with Byron's bright frothy seawater and nostalgia. "Alas!" Matthew wrote three months after his thirteenth birthday, "when thou"

> *hears't the voice of the light guitar*
> *That tells of the Knight of the Chivalrous Lance,*
> *The gay in peace, the bold in war,*
> *. . . . . .*
> *Then beat thy brow*
> *For Rome is low*
> *And woe to them who have made her so! . . .*
>
> *Italy, Italy*
> *The mountains echo thy name!*
> *In the depths of the sea*
> *Where the Whale and the Dolphin are rolling in glee*
> *Is stor'd thy never ending Fame.*[81]

Hundreds of English boys worth their salt had found that Scott and Byron were the only poets worth imitating. Though confused, "The First Sight" botanized on the grave of the Roman Empire with great lyric energy, incidentally wringing the last drop of pathos out of the subject of Dr. Arnold's then-progressing *History.* Hearing her brother Matt recite the poem at her private audition, Jane thrilled to the roots of her hair.

In the summer of 1836, the Arnold family thought eagerly of Winchester. Some of the family went down to Southampton Water, by way of Windsor Park—"about which I dare say Willy has got a poem in his book of Poetry," Matthew grandly declared in a letter, "beginning with, 'Thy forests, Windsor, and thy green retreats,' which Mr. Pope wrote when he was only 13 years old."[82] From Farnham, they drove to Winchester College, where the boys saw the long cathedral and met their future headmaster. "Dr. Moberley's House is not near such a nice one as the School House at Rugby," Matthew observed.[83] Later they proceeded to the fine myrtles and excellent seaview of Eaglehurst, then inhabited by Dr. Arnold's sister Lydia. Shortly before sailing on the *Amazon* for the Isle of Wight, Mrs. Arnold called in vain for her truant son. "It was suggested that he might have gone down to the shore"—as was the case—for as the carriage began to roll, Matthew ran up and poked through the window a very pretty lyric:

> *Naiads were wont of old to dwell*
> *Beneath the boundless ocean's swell,*
> · · · · · ·
> *What naiad, then, what nymph presides*
> *To shelter thee from wind and tides . . . ?*[84]

Clearly, his poetic imagination lived a life of its own. In other respects, Matthew seemed less shimmering and tuneful. Lazy and indifferent to facts he didn't want to know, deeply envying people who hadn't a care in the world, jealous and envious of the docile and obedient Tom, he lived in the grandest juvenile defiance of the fact that he was an Arnold. But he had scarcely encountered the conflicts within himself, or the world's conflicts. Rugbeians felt the bewildering, stunning impact of a Headmaster's obsessive concern with a roaring and jangling modern industrial society. What chance would a boy's Muse have? Through the preliminary crucible of Winchester and the much fiercer one of Rugby School, and out through Oxford into that maelstrom, Matthew was destined to go. "Everything is against one . . . ,"[85] he told Arthur Hugh Clough later, when he knew that he was fighting the only battle that mattered.

Whatever her virtues, Mrs. Arnold kept her eyes open. Fretting about her son, she recorded his enjoyments. There was the high, broken barricade that he built one winter on the dark, barren mountain behind Fox How. "You will be . . . amused to hear of the pleasure which you took in your *Fort* in Loughrigg," she wrote for the benefit of her two eldest boys, "& how valiantly you brought down trees to help you, & how Mr. Wordsworth came and found you in your Strong hold."[86]

2

TO WINCHESTER AND THEN TO
DR. ARNOLD'S SCHOOL
1836–1841

susy owes me twopence for ducking
my head when i bathed.

The first of July it is a grand day
When all of us do have, our pay
Leaving out none from Jane to Fan
even great matt though he's not a man.
—*Two of the Arnold children, in 1839*

THE French Revolution—which ushered in brilliant scientific, intellectual and cultural achievements in the West, and in due course gave nightmares to some of the Victorian middle class—seldom upset Dr. Thomas Arnold, the new Headmaster of Rugby School. On the whole, he detested the crude violence of the Reign of Terror. However, he understood with clear satisfaction and approval that the French had dealt a shattering blow to wealth and social privilege before they wavered with Napoleon.

With British moderation, he brought the spirit of 1789 to Rugby while keeping himself so busy that he was often exhausted or despondent. He spoke of retreating to Tasmania, even of going to a revolutionary land. "You remember how Papa talked of New Hampshire," Matthew reminded his sister Jane, "and said he would emigrate there if he emigrated to the States at all."[1] But in less wearily despondent moods, Dr. Arnold was combative, cheerful, athletic, and alert. He could dictate "to twenty secretaries"[2] at those times. Not at his intellectual best in chapel, he delivered sensible, ethical Sunday sermons, dashed off in the hour or two before the service, in a brisk, gravelly, unemotional voice. On weekdays, he filled gloomy and tradition-ridden halls with the noise of a modern newspaper office and sometimes with the bizarre atmosphere of a revivalist's camp. He introduced "praeposters" or Sixth Formers of sixteen and seventeen into the school government, converting them into guardians of morality and protectors of the weak at the risk of making them prigs. He met with his staff-members and raised their dignity by improving salaries. Turning the clock back to the Renaissance he placed history with the classics at the center of his new curriculum. He raised the status of French, German, and mathematics—while doing little about the sciences, even if his wife coated dead butterflies in the Rugby Museum with protective layers of varnish. Grumblingly, he recognized the fine arts. Paintings of anything except battles and Swiss and Italian mountains bored him; statues of almost everything except dogs and horses made him fairly indignant;[3] and he passed along his tonal deafness to his sons. But he stimulated clever boys who, in effect, were living proof of his intellectual brilliance in class. In 1833, the slim and girlish Arthur Penrhyn Stanley, who had entered Rugby in a frilly shirt with a pink watch-ribbon, won an Open Balliol Scholarship; William Charles Lake matched that feat in 1834; and Charles John Vaughan went on to Cambridge, to win every academic prize in sight. Dr. Arnold was rapidly becoming a "hero-schoolmaster"[4] and a vigorous, brilliant fighter in important social and religious causes.

His reputation made even Matthew, so delightfully wrapped up in himself, aware of his father's exalted position. "The loftiness and fine address of Papa's spirit and life"[5] would be his normal impression of his parent. In 1836, setting out for a year of study at Winchester before he should begin as a pupil at Rugby, he felt princely enough.

A day or two after unpacking in Dr. Moberly's horrible Commoners dormitory, he sent back a sedative for his parents' nerves in the form of a poem. Winchester may have seemed a much rougher place than he had thought it to be the year before, and he knew that his parents were worried. "Lines Written on First Leaving Home for a Public School" barely alludes to a drafty "School" hall ninety feet long, in which boys cowered on narrow oak benches and masters bawled competitively at either end of the hall, but the poem suggests that Matthew will welcome letters from a midlands drawing room,

> To cheer the drooping heart of man,
> The sound of home will cheer the mind when naught beside it can,

although he implies that he can get along without Mrs. Arnold by remembering to pray.

No doubt, every battle is preceded by small warnings. There is in "Lines" a clairvoyant hint that deep disturbances may occur in Matthew's interior. Can he please Papa by being very dutiful and Mamma by being very affecting? Perhaps he can climb "life's toilsome hill" while finding comfort "where'er . . . fancy strays," but there may be troubling conflicts ahead:

> *Though all human aid forsake us [Matthew concludes]*
> *. . . . . .*
> *Though conflicting passions shake us,*
> *Do Thou, O Lord, be present still.*[6]

We have to see him in the Winchester year mainly through Tom's sketchy recollections and his mother's at first happy and then anguished comments, but it seems Matthew didn't catch cold while walking "two regulation hours" on St. Catherine's Hill. Armed with a letter from Herbert Hill, he presented himself to a Wykehamist Fellow named Lawrence, who took him to a book-box filled with plum pudding. Lawrence "furtively regaled" both Arnold brothers. One day Dr. Moberly stopped Matthew, who was then a Commoner in the *Quinta Classis Senior Pars.** Would he care to become a Heathcote Scholar by taking a test "chiefly in the 39 Articles of the Church?"

Thinking that that might be desirable, he wrote home to Papa for some help.

> My dearest Matt, [Dr. Arnold replied in a very long letter on November 4, 1836.] I am afraid that this long sheet will not give you much entertainment, & my dearest Tom must forgive me for writing what will to him, I fear be neither entertaining, nor very useful. . . . You ought not now to study the Articles, because they were not meant to teach Christianity, but to state the line which the Church of England meant to hold upon disputed questions. Scarcely any thing therefore comes forward in the Articles, which has not been disputed. . . . Now if you look into the Catechism which *was meant to teach Christianity* you will find all this very different. . . .[7]

Accepting this advice, he remained a Winchester Commoner. Having met a boy named Manley Hawker who was amusing, and having also made a friend of a prestigious boy named Herman Prior, whom he would try to see in London, he got back to Rugby at Christmastime in fine fettle.

Most of the family were then up at Fox How with a governess who lacked spirits and energy "for a situation demanding both";[8] but Matthew found an exceptional, older boy in the Arnolds' drawing room. At eighteen, Arthur Hugh Clough had just worn himself to a pallor in order to win a Balliol College Scholarship. Tom and Matthew knew him already as a goalkeeper who wore "neither jersey nor

---

*In 1836 there were six classes at Winchester—the Sixth, Fifth Senior, Fifth Middle, Fifth Junior, Fourth Senior, and Fourth Middle. Boys in Matthew's class would have been aged between fourteen and sixteen. Tom was in the class below, the *Quinta Classis Media Pars*. As Commoners, the Arnold brothers were ordinary fee-paying students.

cap"—and from the sidelines on the close they had seen his black hair, white dome, and perspiring shirt charging against loud hordes in "desperate struggles."[9] They knew that Clough was called "Tom Yankee" because his parents had taken him from Liverpool over to Charleston, South Carolina, for a few years, and that he had left his mother behind in America—and he had edited the *Rugby Magazine,* won prizes and the Derby Run, and visited France. Matthew at fourteen was too full of himself to appreciate the older boy's brilliance, but he made a friend of him this holiday. Here was a scholar who did everything more or less wonderfully—while printing rather a good deal of verse. Clough, after a bad cold, had written accomplished lines about the Arnold family for the *Rugby Magazine,*

I watched them from the window, thy children at their play,
And I thought of all my own dear friends, who were far, oh! far away,[10]

and he had confessed in secret to a confidant, "I love Arnold, and Mrs. Arnold, and the children very much."[11]

Clough spent ten days at Fox How in January 1837 before leaving to write a Latin essay in "real earnest." Matthew himself, who reached Fox How with Tom in time for Christmas Day, showed how cooperative he could be by playing the part of the Beast in "The Beauty and Beast." His mother thought the children's play very admirable. Jane acted Lady Beauty in a "straightforward" way—and "Matt [wore] my cloak for his furry garment, and a Boa to complete his equipment as a tail."[12]

In February he got back to Dr. Moberly's with no inkling of impending trouble. Early in the spring with Tom, he emerged from the Commoners dormitory and cut across open rolling downs on a frosty morning towards nearby Hursley. The boys had an invitation from the Reverend John Keble. Matthew's godfather did everything for them that an enemy of liberalism could do, it seems, to be civil. Stuffed with pastry, the brothers were taken into a gloomy church that had small, dim clerestories and carved angels soaring up under the rafters. Matthew left Hursley rectory with an amusing memory of a "Flibberti-gibbet, fanatical, twinkling" man,[13] a rational memory, perhaps, of wincing John Keble, a view which corresponded to Papa's view of that friend as a High Church fanatic, although his feelings often clashed with his own rational views and that of his father's. He would cite Keble's *Christian Year* in school essays and later find in that book—which he certainly associated, in part, with his mother—a very rare "ethereal light."[14]

"My brother always talked freely," recalls Tom Arnold, whose speech defect often kept him silent. At a spring breakfast with the

Winchester Headmaster, Matthew blurted out with remarkable freedom that his class assignments were "light and easy."

"Indeed," replied Dr. George Moberly, laughing. "We shall see to
that."

Matthew had been bored by the slow-paced reading of Virgil's
Aeneid, Horace's *Satires,* and Sophocles' *Electra* in a ninety-foot room.
His downfall was quite as sudden as Electra's. A big boy "attacked"
him after breakfast. Later he was pulled out like a medieval witch and,
for the crime of "making light to the head-master of the difficulty of
schoolwork," pelted with "pontos" (made from bread rolls) amid hoots
and jeers at a public ceremony.[15]

He tried to redeem himself in the eyes of the Winchester Senior
Fifth by reciting the Doge's scurrilous harangue from Byron's *Marino
Faliero* for elocution at Easter, and did it so well he was asked to repeat
the performance at Commoner Speaking. But he didn't write home
about his elocution victory, for the simple reason that he had caught
on fire.

"My dearest Prawn," Dr. Arnold had written at this time, "You are so
correct in your Accounts generally, that I shall beg of Dr. Moberly to
let you have your £1.3.0, and Matt his 7 [shillings]. . . . I do not
understand whether Easter Speaking is over,—as we have heard
nothing of Matt's speech." And Mrs. Arnold adds in a postscript,
written just after hearing that her eldest son had ignited himself: "Tell
us whether dearest Matt is likely to have the full use of his fingers
again."[16]

Though he admired Cato's suicidal courage and later wrote of
Empedocles' leap into a fiery crater, it is possible Matthew didn't
intend to burn himself at Winchester in 1837. He seems to have been
playing with a firearm. The phosphorus wound to his hand was
fortuitous. The accident was somewhat strange, and he waited a little
before running for help. He received much attention. Wrapped in a
bandage that saved him from some bullying, he returned after medical
treatment and psalms at Aunt Buckland's to Winchester. He also
survived the year—though the school was savage, and he was
dangerously unpopular for having told Moberly that class assignments
were light.

Furthermore, his pain distressed his mother deeply. With her
feeling for tragedy and her vivid imagination, his mother could well
visualize Matthew's suffering. "Even now it is painful to think of that
first sight," Mrs. Arnold wrote months after Matthew's accident,
"when all alone you had to bear the suffering of so severe a
burn—actually seeing the light about your hand from the fire

unextinguished by the lotion."[17] It was his mother who made Matthew a master of pathos. Minor themes in her journals of the 1830s, such as time's evanescence, the poignancy of the past, and the inconsequence of the world's routine hubbub, swell into major ones in his own poetry. Mrs. Arnold was satirical about Rugby speeches that have to be "speechified" and the "lack of wit about us,"[18] and she was becoming a decided enemy of the hands of the clock. Even before Baron Bunsen announced with Prussian candor that Dr. Arnold would soon die, that he would drop, that he could not and *would not* last at the pace he set for himself, Mary Arnold had certain fears. "I wish I could make the picture of time present complete by Inventories," she writes, filling up more than a page with poignant trivia, elegiac lists, and cinematic glimpses of the present:

> There on the sopha table beside me reposes *Bacco* the Doll . . . with her outstretched hands. . . . Then there is the Album for entrances into the school—& a sheet of his Thucydides open at the place where he left his notes last night—& a paper of Lozenges, & Boys Exercises—& a Demosthenes—& a Chapel Hymn Book & Boyles Court Guide & Bakewells Geology, & Quentin Durward . . . your precious Bible my Matt: which your Godfather Mr. Keble gave you—with Stories of animals . . . one of my Geneva Baskets, Files of Bills . . . in this very room—where with you our darlings sometimes about us—down to the playful little Susy herself;—sometimes alone . . . we have passed hours & days & years.[19]

Back from Winchester, Matthew had an amazing year ahead of him. In August his father led him up Fairfield Mountain and from the summit pointed to humps and alligator-backs hanging under a clear blue sky—the Old Man, Great Gable, Helvellyn, the Pillar, and the jagged Langdale Pikes. The next day Dr. and Mrs. Arnold and three children set out for London. "That enormous city," Dr. Arnold commented, "sublime with the Sublimity of . . . Mountains, is yet a Place that I should be most sorry to call my Home."[20]

Matthew's gaiety and effervescence this summer suggest that he knew he was the apple of his mother's eye, and he may have foreseen that whatever the horrors of being Headmaster's son at Rugby might be, he'd be living in a comfortable apartment. "Flogged Marshall," Dr. Arnold penned in a neat hand. "Flogged Curie. . . . Flogged Hains for Cotton's report."[21] The days ahead could be painful, but the worst danger might be Rugby Fifth and Sixth Formers jealous of a boy with a fine memory. Matthew protected himself from the masculine world of the public school and from the desiccating effects of Papa's intensity by consciously appealing to Mrs. Arnold, by dazzling and surprising her; he even unconsciously preserved, through his mother, connections to the world of his early childhood and a strong line to a source of his imagination. While his father was busy getting passports in Poland Street, Matthew, now fourteen, walked into an oculist's shop and bought a monocle. Alarmed, his parents drove him to a Blackfriars dentist, who knew as much about eyes as teeth. "[Mr. Ware] told me not to wear a glass," Matthew noted ruefully, "and said plenty more which I need not repeat." Only *one* of his eyes was myopic and the dentist strongly believed a glass would further damage the eye. But the glass became a part of the theatrical shell he was building for himself—and it corrected myopia and impressed Mamma. Matthew had his way, and wore a monocle. He needed to impress his younger brothers too: he dedicated a travel journal to Edward, since poor "Didu" had been left repining at Fox How and would miss this wonderful trip. "You will find it useful to your . . . Natural Piggish Propensities," he told Didu, "in its' being in some small measure a 'journale Gastronomique,'" but on the way to the Channel there wasn't much gastronomy to record. Sitting atop the family carriage Matthew was "frizzeled" by the dew "in a style no Tonseur could have surpassed" and later he was sick on the jolting *Water-Witch;* but as the Channel boat neared the shore, he sat bolt upright and saw "quantities of white bathing machines." Then he was going down a pier amidst a "confusing"[22] assortment of dresses and hearing a language spoken in a way that nobody ever spoke it at school, and he was going straight into the heart of France.

In ten days he recorded things from his father's viewpoint, while discovering his own viewpoint. He drank *Bourgogne* out of a tumbler and made an inventory of the dress of a French postilion, and noted the incredible luxurious elegance of hotels. "We have more to learn from France than from any other nation," he told his mother later, "mainly because she is so unlike ourselves."[23] The sheer pleasantness of France was noteworthy. And the romantic passion, despair, and lyricism he would find in this vibrating land were similar to forces existing in what he would call his own "buried life."

A visit to Chartres Cathedral in August exhausted his best adjective: the stonework over its portals was "most beautiful," he felt, but "beautiful as this was, the carving along the Quire inside . . . seemed to me more beautiful still."[24] Then he was at the hub of the earth's civic grandeur. "We are at Paris," he told his journal hastily, "a capital . . . in fashion elegance public buildings &c inferior to none."[25] An aesthetic progress continued to the Louvre where he saw Rembrandts and Rubenses and Vandykes and found the statuary rather less good, but "much admired the Aegyptian Porphyry Vases." He ate a refreshing ice and saw a live giraffe. "I am hot tired sleepy, and what not?" he wrote in his journal and the "what not?" is eloquent. Everything he noted in two days at Paris, including the live giraffe, belonged to an exquisitely refined world, and the aesthetic world would figure in Matthew's reaction to an important experience ahead. "No 10 days' tour," he informed Didu in the *Journale gastronomique*, "ever gave me more gratification."[26]

Matthew Arnold began with caution as a pupil at his father's Rugby School, having enrolled on June 26. Boys in "The Twenty" or Upper Fifth Form at Rugby first noted him in their ranks late in August 1837.

Matthew talked in a "very reserved manner," as a classmate thought, and showed "a singular constraint towards his father." Arthur Hugh Clough, living near Rugby School House for a few weeks before starting as a Balliol undergraduate, told a friend in a journal letter that seemed unlikely to end: "Mat. Arnold is in the School and the Upper [Fifth]. His compos [ition] Tutor is Lee, his Mathematical, Price—a balance of favour, I suppose."[27] Matthew slept in the adult portion of School House, but joined his fellow students by day. He told Clough later, "the mathematics were ever foolishness to me."[28] but he admired Bonamy Price—a voluble tutor who mixed liberal German divinity with quadratic equations, rode in the lanes with a smartly dressed wife (a Macaulay), and at last got the Drummond Chair of Political Economy at Oxford. In the presence of Dr. Arnold, Matthew failed to be at all brilliant. "Examined the Twenty," his father wrote on March 20, 1838. "Matt floored [unable to answer]."[29] He recited "nonsense-verse" of a seditious character, but he did astonishingly well for James Prince Lee—a Composition tutor so eager that he was known in the family drawing room as Michael, "short," Dr. Arnold announced, "for 'Michael Scott's Devil,' the said Devil who was so restless . . . he could only be settled by being told to weave Ropes of Sea Sand."[30] At the end of the year, Lee became Headmaster of King Edward VI School in Birmingham, and later a dignified bishop, who received the well-to-do at the front door of his palace and clergymen at the back.

Responding to Mr. Lee's assigned theme, "Juvat Ire Jugis" (It Is Pleasant to Walk in the Mountains), Matthew invented in 1837 a point-of-view character—apparently a compound of Byron's Manfred and Matthew Arnold on Fairfield Mountain—who exults over the wonders of nature though finding nature less wonderful than he finds himself:

> *Mystica quaerendi, tu, rerum arcana cupido!*
> *Spesque fatigatae carissima mentis imago,*
> *Tu potes in campos rupes mutare minaces*

Obscuram et noctem vestire in luce diei:
Jam, jam, summa patent scopulosa cacumina montis
Invitantque pedes juga celsa—[31]

(Thou, Passion for search into mysteries, the secrets of things!
And Hope, dearest image of a tired mind,
Thou canst turn threatening rocks into plains
And clothe dark night in the light of day:
Now, now, the high craggy peaks of the mountain are open to view,
And the lofty mountain-ridges invite the feet.)

Another school theme, carefully preserved in an elegant notebook, is reminiscent of his mother's feeling about time's evanescence. Matthew shows that the present is illusory:

Inter diversa hominum negotia, discedenti simul ac incipienti vitae. . . .

(Since among the various activities of various people, life departs as soon as it begins. . . .)

Fatalities are conjured up to prove that grief may give pleasure, and as authorities on human memory, Keble, Pope, Byron, Southey, and Juvenal are all cited. Of course much that we can remember in our maturity, at fourteen, is amusing:

. . . sed curas doloresque pueriles, tunc graves, nunc contra irridendas, meminisse fere jucundum est.[32]

(. . . but it is usually enjoyable too to remember childish agonies and pains, serious at the time, now on the contrary to be laughed at.)

Promoted at fifteen into Rugby's Sixth Form, where he would be guardian of morality, Matthew did well enough to emerge "very high" in a June exam. He collected writing prizes and "spoke well" in front of a constellation of Old Boys on Speech Day. Later Arthur Stanley "and others"[33] perhaps monopolized Mrs. Arnold's attention—as they often did. Jealous of three Old Rugbeians who were too close to his mother's heart, Matthew would have something to say about Stanley's vulgarity, Lake's childishness, and Vaughan's ignorance.

At Fox How, in the summer of 1838, he showed much independence by avoiding normal entertainments and coming back from fishing too late for prayers. He refused to set foot in old Mr. Roughsedge's boat the *Nautilus,* even though Mrs. Arnold and Tom often sailed in the lumbering schooner. The frequent winner at the Windermere regattas was often the *Dolphin,* a sleek cutter owned by a rich "sugar-boiler"[34] of Liverpool named James Brancker.

Dr. Arnold referred to James Brancker's deific "cut," engineered to prevent the River Rotha from flooding. Frightening away the trout, the sugar-boiler had caused almost a mile of stream to flow over a new course—and Matthew in hiking far afield must have passed his bizarre mansion at Clappersgate with strong feelings. A mile from home he passed Rothay Bank, a villa designed with continental restraint and then inhabited by Brancker's friends, the Claudes, who included a German-born widow, her son Louis, and four daughters. Matthew would write familiarly to Louis Claude and conceive a "romantic passion" for the young author Mary Sophia Claude—one of Louis's sisters—and he may have seen the Claudes this summer in Brancker's *Dolphin*.

According to his mother, Matthew was befriending strangers in a region noted for oddities. He could easily have met three famous oddities. There was William Bowe or "Billy Boo," who trolled Derwentwater to the accompaniment of music, according to the angler Braithwaite, for he blew "a tune on his bugle" in moonlight to please the fish.

> *Banner by turns and bugle woo:*
> Ye shy recluses, follow too!

Joe Winn wore an eighteenth-century blue frockcoat and ran up hillsides at the approach of anglers of whom he was "jealous,"[35] or threw rocks into their pools; and young Hebson fished and tied flies with a whirling hand (the only one he had). In the middle of August when Jane was *châtelaine* of Fox How during their parents' absence, Matthew pushed out on Windermere with two strange companions. He didn't return for evening prayers but "that had happened before," so Jane didn't worry until midnight. Recalling that the wind had blown up that afternoon, she sent Tom and the servants out into the dark—but no one awake in the village had seen her brother's boat. Pacing in a copse after midnight, she imagined hideous things *hadn't* happened to her brother though "firmly believing . . . all the time that they had," and at dawn she ran to the lake and scampered up misty lookout hills.

She couldn't see anything! She ran to the lake and asked a boatman if the *Black Dwarf* could possibly upset and got a reply: "It had been blowing *fresh*." Matthew must be dead!

Then she ran ashen-faced into town and collapsed on "the Warden of the Post," who set out on the lake and returned at noontime with news that made him seem "beautiful." Matthew now appeared, twenty-two hours after his disappearance, without his boat; somebody was rowing him in a smaller craft. With a burgeoning talent for the plausible, he explained that he and his crew were "knocked up" with rowing and quite simply put in "at the Ferry"[36] where they spent most of the night. But why hadn't he used six or seven hours to walk home? "We are not much encouraged," Mrs. Arnold told her sisters, "to leave them fatherless and motherless again."

Her leniency suggests that Mrs. Arnold believed her children to be deprived of attention: indeed Fox How was often full of guests; at Rugby, the family in effect included three hundred souls. Jane complained—in a manner that aggravated Mrs. Arnold's guilt—"Papa becomes less when his company has to be divided among so many," and Matthew took advantage of his mother's obvious leniency by demanding a "double barrelled gun."[37] Having bought him the weapon, she laid down optimistic rules about "hedge-popping," but he blasted behind the hollies at Spring Cottage in the Lake District whenever he liked (his myopia being among the birds' main defenses) and back at school courted Sir Grey Skipwith, a Liberal trustee who fathered eighteen children and kept an arsenal at Newbold Hall. Hunting became a "mania," as Mrs. Arnold felt. Her son was insatiable however badly he shot—and "I believe it is a vain hope that the want of success will sicken him of it."[38] Underlying the "mania" were boyish spirits and a lasting aggressiveness, owing much to frustrations in early childhood as well as to a lasting need to astonish and baffle his mother without quite horrifying her. She notes on Matthew's sixteenth birthday, "The present holidays will show us whether there is really any more manliness of character or thoughtfulness than there has been."[39]

How delicious, aristocratic, and wicked to carry a gun under a noble army of mountains! Irreverent when others were somber, Matthew looked somber when his brothers and sisters were lighthearted.

> *She died* [he wrote]—*unwept, perchance unknown*
> *She laid her calmly down to die.*
> *By mountain cliff she stood alone. . . .*[40]

His poem about Miss Pardoe's *City of the Sultan* is the most polished and nearly the most lugubrious entry in the first issue of the *Fox How Magazine,* which the children launched in 1838.

All of them except Jane contributed to its second issue, which Dr. Arnold read aloud on New Year's Day, and for which Matthew had written some good Popeian couplets on the departure of God at the siege of Jerusalem.

> *Calm is the Touch, and noiseless the Decay*
> *That sweeps the Relics of the Past away—*

But frequent still before the entranced Eye
Visions of Long Ago come fleeting by:
· · · · · ·
All is silent now. On Salem's Hill,
God's voice, that talked of old with man, is still.[41]

Matthew accepted applause with magisterial ease because he had versified one of his father's difficult themes—the withdrawal and mystery of God. Dr. Arnold was reserved and troubled when speaking to adults at Rydal Chapel (Crabb Robinson found one of his sermons "cold . . . as the morning itself") and in his own poems he exhibited an unusual sense of man's *aloneness:* "Our senses cannot pierce the Skies, our Mind/Some nearer Object evermore enchains," Dr. Arnold had written for the household journal. ". . . The Sky is closed."[42] This holiday he was very badly shaken by a recent drunken display of Rugby pupils and such "vileness and folly which . . . would soon," as he told William Lake, "if it went on, end either my life at Rugby or my life altogether."

Go my Friends & dig my grave
· · · · · ·
There would I myself lie down
There no pain no Care are known,[43]

he had indited in translation of a German hymn two days before reciting his children's pieces.

Matthew's own poetry, on occasion, caught and reflected darker, half-hidden moods of his father. Normally his father's mood was refreshingly tolerant. Aware of Matthew's loyalty, the father lightly dismissed juvenile faults in a sprightly monologue for the *Fox How Magazine* called "CRAB," written from his son's viewpoint:

Now welcome to the Rotha, where I stand & fish all day,
And where I shoot the Birds, when they do not get away
And I like the Railway well, for we sit there at our ease,
And no fat intruding Gentleman does your Sides to thummy
    squeeze.[44]

"Matt & K. went over to the Mount," Dr. Arnold wrote in December, 1838.[45] Jane Arnold was attached to Wordsworth's invalid sister Dorothy, who since her derangement had become pathetically bald. An obese woman in her sixties with beautiful eyes, she huddled over soapsuds near a fire that threatened her heavy shawls, spoke to her nailbrush, and now and then used "bad language" and cried and shrieked. But she smiled when William pushed her wheelchair out of doors, and "her countenance," says Mrs. Wordsworth, "is often the image of a child-like innocence and simplicity . . . except when she is angry."[46] Mrs. Wordsworth, with her quiet voice and intelligent squint, kept alive at Rydal Mount the cult of natural beauty, and Jane at sixteen and seventeen cooperated by making apt comments on local scenery. Matthew's remarks were equally apt. He had encountered William Wordsworth in a fort on Loughrigg, walked with his own father and the poet, picnicked with the poet's family and chatted with the thin, tubercular daughter, Dora, and—no doubt with unfeigned attention—had listened to recitals of new works in the Fox How drawing room. To be sure, Wordsworth had begun to find moral principles in such unimportant things as copyright legislation; but for Benjamin Haydon he had tolled out his poems like the funeral bell of St. Paul's and the music of Handel "mingled." Matthew must have seen that inside the crotchety, lumbering eminence was a more remarkable being:

> Hardly his voice at his best
> Gives us a sense of the awe,
> The vastness, the grandeur, the gloom
> Of the unlit gulph of himself,[47]

he would write when Wordsworth died in 1850. Mrs. Arnold approved the grandeur and praised the success with which Wordsworth had "conquered . . . public opinion" and "ascended among our highest and best." In these years, Matthew found Wordsworth deeply impressive and found Mrs. Arnold's approval of him important, too. Despite reservations, he would rank him as highly as his mother did—and find in the lyrics and ballads models of spareness, lucidity, and directness, and indeed "draw out" the great man successfully on Coleridge and Italian poetry as the great man sat on Mrs. Arnold's stool at the fire.[48]

Immortal presences were palpable in or near Fox How. Wordsworth had known Keats; and Southey, Shelley. Crabb Robinson must have out-talked Lamb as well as Blake; he had listened to Schelling's lectures and had taken coffee with Goethe—whose *Faust* libeled divinity, in Dr. Arnold's opinion. S. T. Coleridge's son Hartley, sent down in an alcoholic cloud from Oriel College, had tried lately to teach little boys at Parson Dawes' school in Ambleside, while writing love letters to little girls. Rotund and gray, he caught children in the lanes with outstretched arms on the way to the local pothouse, adored the Arnolds because "they were suckled on Latin and weaned on Greek"—and once, thirsting and embarrassed, he confronted Mrs. Arnold's water jug. "May I," Mr. Coleridge exploded, "ask for a glass of *beer*?"[49] (Mrs. Arnold obliged.) Matthew pitied "poor Hartley" who had taken "perfidious refuge" in teaching. The ruined state of romanticism's survivors added a touch of pathos to Matthew's dreams, even as he read the romantic poets for "bursts of sentiment"[50]—which he admired most of all in narratives.

Noisy schoolboys flooded up to Fox How. Matthew made such a fuss about traveling with his family that when they came up from Rugby by train, he rode up in a coach with George Bradley. As conventional then as he proved to be in Westminster's Deanery, Bradley thought Matthew amiably "jocund." The two boys found a party of twenty-four ahead of them at Fox How—including Herbert Hill and the under-sized Walronds of Rugby. When the morning of rain yielded to a foggy afternoon Matthew struck out for the fields, leaving Tom hollowing out a boat, Edward making geographical cards, Willy learning Greek, and "Bradley reading"[51] in a deafening drawing room: the future Dean left before Christmas with few glimpses of his jocund friend.

When George Hughes appeared on New Year's Day, Matthew became very sociable. An older brother of Tom Hughes who wrote *Tom Brown's Schooldays,* he was a warmhearted, reticent, handsome, and ill-starred rebel. As football captain he kept order genially with his fists and bullying quite disappeared from School House. But Dr. Arnold expelled George for not naming miscreants who had broken some pottery and then in a gesture of goodwill invited him up north. George would be reinstated, but he had lost a University scholarship, and obscure failings continued to defeat him until his early death.

After looking in vain for a skating pond on Loughrigg, "I and Matt Arnold," George wrote home to his parents, "went down to a swampy sort of lake to shoot snipes."[52] Rain struck and the boys were drenched through when they got back from Elterwater. Having wrung out, they hired horses next day and set out through dark fields past Rydal Lake and "beautiful little" Thurlmere to the "most beautiful view" overlooking Keswick. "At odd moments," George wrote, in further apparent imitation of Wordsworth, "we caught a glimpse of Helvellyn free from clouds."[53]

Matthew flitted around Rugby as the airiest guardian of morality and protector of the feeble. He was late to class more often, in one half-year, than thirty other boys in his small class, and he plunged dismally in Greek.[54] Mrs. Arnold threatened not to let him go to college unless he showed "a more decided sense of duty in . . . school work." She saw him writing Latin verses after ten at night, by her table, but also scrambling to get work done, or half done, moments before "2nd lesson."[55]

Deeply impressed by his father's sermons in Rugby chapel, he later thought only one other divine was like "Papa in . . . force and earnestness. . . . Every word tells." The later man (Temple) threw "more emotion and even passion into preaching than Papa did," but lacked depth and solidity.[56] Perhaps anyone with a theatrical sense could recognize that Dr. Arnold's black-gowned form and rasping, frank voice in chapel were splendid. If he didn't hear the call of a light-infantry bugle (as Tom Brown did), Matthew did get a sense of the importance of authority in chapel, and of moral value as the highest test of worth. His admiration for the tenacity of Wellington, Napoleon, and Ulysses S. Grant, and his feeling for the Church as a "national society for the promotion of what is commonly called goodness"[57] owe to Dr. Arnold—whose sermons ruined Matthew for humdrum pulpit oratory and impaired his ability to stomach theologians, good, bad, or indifferent, later on.

Matthew learned to survive as a natural aristocrat at more or less democratic Rugby without arousing fatal envy. He avoided "Hare and Hounds" (though that cross-country run was required of Lee's pupils) and played just enough rugby football not to seem a prig. Tom Hughes may have portrayed him in *Tom Brown's Schooldays* as the School House boy who holds the ball in a great match for a kick: "Call Crab Jones. . . . Here he comes he comes, . . . the coollest fish in Rugby: if he were tumbled into the moon this minute, he would just pick himself up without taking his hands out of his pockets."[58] In Franklin Lushington's Greek poem about a rugby match, of 1839, "Matthew and Thomas, the two sons of Arnold" (Ματθαῖος Θώμας τ', 'Αρνόλδου υἱέε δοιώ.)[59] make an appearance as players. Befriending everybody and nobody, he mixed at the edges of most activities. "[Matt] is not likely to form intimate friendships," reports Dr. Arnold. "He does not like being alone. . . . He flitters about from flower to flower, but is not apt to fix."[60]

But he could defy public opinion partly to please his mother. When the Dowager Queen Adelaide watched a football match played for her Matthew chatted with her; but a few days after she left he noted his mother in distress because the boys toasted "Queen Adelaide"—to the neglect of England's young Queen. Still, Matthew waited to set that matter straight. On December 7, 1839, the Arnolds gave a supper to "all our School House Boys in their hall—& Matt & Tom were invited." No sooner was the Dowager's health drunk, than Matthew rose at an iron-bound table and said "they should not show their loyalty" if they didn't drink to Victoria of England, "which was done accordingly," notes Mrs. Arnold. Yet he greatly displeased his mother when Sixth Formers and masters danced with sober hilarity one night on the close, at the "Annual Festival of the Tea-Totallers." "Matt," says Mrs. Arnold, "did not approve."[61] How could he? Lately, at headmaster's soirées, he had been quaffing champagne with the nobility!

After Queen Adelaide's visit to the school in October 1839, and with

Dr. Arnold's rising notoriety, the fashionable and titled made a point of calling at Rugby. The champagne here was perhaps not good, but better than might be thought. And the Doctor's sons were charming! Four or five lords and ladies chatted and dined on special weekends —and Matthew, looking like a penguin, walked into a candlelit dinner on more than one evening with a beaming, elderly noblewoman on his arm.

He deeply identified with the exceptional and the great and socially superior; his friendship with Wordsworth, and at seventeen his eager mixing with "titled ladies" at headmaster's dinners, inflated his sense of importance and ensured that his future would be difficult. To satisfy his noble view of *himself,* he would have to become a dazzling success—or life would be a nightmare. He lived complacently, now, in a safe, glittering, rich evening world, infinitely far removed from that of schoolboys, and within view of sapphires, diamonds, and lovely eyes.[62] "So many titled ladies," remarks Mrs. Arnold in 1840. "Lady Lydia [Lambert] is by the fire, having just written out a song for Matt . . . while Matt and Laura [Ward, Matthew's beautiful marriageable niece] are playing at chess."[63]

Taking time out to read a schoolbook, Matthew opened his French textbook, by Mignet, to find electrifying sentiments:

"Soldiers," said Napoleon, "I am satisfied with you. You have adorned your eagles with immortal glory. . . . Those who escaped your steel have been drowned in the lakes."[64]

Mignet's *Histoire de la Révolution Française* (1824) penetrated his vanity by appealing to it and left him impressed; no other school used so modern a text. The twin objects of the French Revolution, Matthew read in Mignet's *Histoire,* had been a free constitution and "a more perfect state of civilization." Far from being diabolic, Napoleonic armies "carried with them the ideas and customs of the more advanced civilization of France."[65] and by agitating nations really helped to sophisticate them. Adapting the idea, Matthew would tell Clough that Gothic hordes in turning over the soil of Europe had been an animating cause of Elizabethan literature.[66] He also digested, at least in part, *Histoire de la Révolution d'Angleterre, en 1640,* for Sixth-Form French, along with Guizot's choleric view of the British as practical and sound in action, but lost and ignorant in the realm of ideas.

At a London soirée in the spring of 1840, Dr. Arnold met the scourge of British intellect, François Guizot, who had organized public

instruction throughout France, and chatted amiably with Lord Lansdowne, then trying to do something about the chaos of public
instruction in England.[67]

In one way or another, the Headmaster animated a large number of
vivid figures in the history classes Matthew attended. Dr. Arnold
taught history in the paneled library tower Socratically, drawing
analogies between epochs in the manner of his astute earlier friend
Barthold Niebuhr (a proponent of "historicism"), who elucidated
ancient trade through a personal knowledge of the Danish and North
German peasantry. Ranging beyond Niebuhr, Dr. Arnold brought the
ghost of the Italian historian Vico to class to illustrate that history is
cyclical. For Dr. Arnold the world moved through "modern" ages in a
spiraling temporal glide. England had come round to late Greece and
imperial Rome in sharing a modernity in which morality and feeling
are endangered by restless skepticism, doctrinal conflict, and the
dissatisfied intellect. Men of wisdom and faith retained steadfastness
and inwardness by turning to older civilizations for subtle paradigms
of the present. One must read widely to understand the "national
spirit"—or Goethe's evolving, efficacious *Zeitgeist*—that year by year
alters the quality and fixes the exact character of a society. "[Papa's]
mind was constantly working, and open," Matthew later wrote with
qualified approval. "Still, while he held a thing, he held it very hard,
and without the sense of . . . two sides to the question."[68] Sometimes
Matthew failed to see any side of the question—as when he couldn't
illustrate "from Scott's novels" (which his sisters were reading to
pieces) Aristotle's view of old age—and one time it seems, when he
was ordered to stand in disgrace in front of the class, he "amused the
whole form by making faces derisive of his father."[69] Sailing in the
teacher's time machine, he now and then met a few moral signposts,
and perceived topics inadmissable of debate. But whether or not he
wiggled his ears in history class, Matthew absorbed ideas, as well as
many glowing examples of broad-mindedness and cosmopolitanism,
and these were Dr. Arnold's greatest gifts to his son.

"Alaric at Rome" illustrates what history meant to a romantic
seventeen-year-old. Eyeing a Sixth-Form prize in 1840, Matthew
surely had in mind his mother's astonishment and Wordsworth's
approval. When the previous poetry prizewinner had been invited up
north, Mrs. Arnold had exhibited Franklin Lushington's poem, and a
little later Franklin Lushington himself, to the poet of Rydal Mount,
who reacted to the former with delight and to the latter with a grunt of
disgust. That to Mr. Wordsworth Franklin Lushington "should be so
ugly" understandably offended Mrs. Arnold: the boy was "no beauty,
but I should not have expected his plainness to make quite so much

impression."[70] At any rate, in writing "Alaric" Matthew distilled Gibbon's *Decline and Fall* through the familiar alembic of Byron's *Childe Harold* for exquisite effects. The poem turns historic Rome into a chaos, a grave, a poor widow "with sad prophetic eye," and even into a time capsule reminiscent of Rugby's history class,

> *Where all we see, or do, or hear, or say*
> *Seems strangely echoed back by tones of yesterday:*
>
> ······
>
> *And memory's gushing tide swells deep and full,*
> *And makes [Rome's] very ruin fresh and beautiful.*[71]

Rome has witnessed the picturesque tragedy of history. Alaric has conquered Rome, but he will die within the year. Rome is a city of valiant defenders, but they all happen to be dead and gone. Perhaps only the poet with his lofty and intelligent grasp of the whole sweep of history, can intuit

> *So stern a lesson as necessity.*

Is the poet superior to the historian? In "Resignation" and other works of Arnold's early manhood, he is at least more philosophic than other mortals. Though dismissive of historical detail, the poet in "Alaric at Rome" surmises that the doomed Goth on a misty Capitoline hill may have thought any number of things, or of nothing much at all:

> *Perchance his wandering heart was far away,*
> *Lost in dim memories of his early home,*
> *And his young dreams of conquest; how to-day*
> *Beheld him master of Imperial Rome.*[72]

After a city's collapse and its victor's foretold demise, four or five stanzas conclude with Rugbeian homelies that justly "dash our holiest raptures." While pointing up wasted energies and thoughtless words, Alaric's story shows that "wildest visions" beautifully relieve the "dull and low"[73] world—only to prove in themselves disappointing and ephemeral. Indeed, the poem exists for the sake of its romantic scenery and beautifully elegiac visions.

Matthew recited it defiantly with a "roll and vigour" on Rugby Speech Day and some of his feeling for it lasted a lifetime. "Yes!" he wrote at sixty-five to Edmund Gosse, this was his prize-poem—"and I think it better than my Oxford one, 'Cromwell'; only you will see that I had been very much reading *Childe Harold*."[74] Mrs. Arnold didn't record Wordsworth's praise of it, if the immortal of Rydal ever lifted his eyeshades to read it. She almost forgot to tell her sisters it had won a prize—though she was quick to tell them everything else. "How have I omitted to say that dear Matt has gained the English verse?"[75] But she was overjoyed when Matthew got an award for an historical essay, and found herself on "tenterhooks" over June Exhibition prizes and pleased enough when he was beaten by Lushington, Bradley, and a mere nonentity to come in *fourth*: "—then comes Matt! . . . of course Matt does not take the fragment [of the Exibition award] which comes to him—but how encouraging for both him . . . —& us."[76]

Matthew found that the manner in which he had always held pride of place in her heart was becoming less effective; his talent for appearing debonair counted for little when she worried about whether he was sober enough for life. Unwilling to "thwart" him, Mrs. Arnold felt, with misgivings, that he might go to Oxford, which he "especially" desired. Dr. Arnold looked about for a summer tutor, and found one in Lake, to prepare him for the Balliol Scholarship contest.[77] But his mother's unwillingness to be deeply or quickly enthralled by "Alaric" must have qualified—or robbed—his sense of triumph. Her fretful attitude about his lack of steadiness became a major factor in his life.

In the summer of 1840, after a few weeks' respite, Matthew kept a rendezvous at Chester with his lean tutor. Then twenty-three, William Lake was to reveal to Balliol College men enough slyness and pedantry on alternate days, it seems, to be nicknamed "Serpent" and "Puddle," but he knew books. After rattling through Welsh valleys, Matthew found himself with his tutor and a boy with an Irish brogue named Carden, at Beddgelert, where for a fortnight they had nothing to do but read "with constant Rain the whole Time." As he told his aunts, "I got heartily tired of it."[78] Then they went to Abergele, where he fled from Lake's stupid soul into the rain. The Balliol Serpent hissed or recoiled with damp sarcasm. "Lake . . . is a perfect child," Matthew later assured "K"; "—if all does not go as he wishes it, he can neither keep his temper, nor conceal that he has lost it."[79] The tutor committed angry feelings to paper when the reading party was over, and Dr. Arnold, who wrote with exaggeration when furious and with yieldingness when not, bent to conciliate a very gallant tutor. "I agree with all you say," the Headmaster replied to William Lake in August 1840. "Matt does not know what it is to work because he so little knows what it is to think. I am hopeful," the father continues of Matthew, who was now almost eighteen and going to Oxford, "and he is so loving to me that it ought to make me not only hopeful, but very patient and long-suffering. . . . Alas! that we should have to talk of prospect only, and of no performance as yet which deserves the name of 'earnest reading.' "[80] On the whole, this very moderate letter suggests that Matthew's affection for his father was quite obvious and effective.

In November at Oxford Matthew was seen by Arthur Clough—who fervently hoped that Rugby School would "have the good fortune to be successful in Mat's Person,—for I suppose *he* only has a chance."[81] Then examinations began, and thirty-three men from the eminent public schools competed for two Open Balliol Scholarships through four days' classical paperwork. They learned from a Dean, in an exhausted assembly at ten o'clock on a Friday, that one star had prevailed. This candidate was James Riddell of Shrewsbury. "Then," says the London *Times*,[82] the Dean announced a "renewed struggle," in which four semifinalists competed in viva voce responses until it was nearly dark. The courts filled with gowned students in laughing, holiday mood and there were "rumours" and wagers, followed by shouting: for the second Balliol place had gone to an "Arnold." This news traveled fast. Apparently it was the sort one cannot credit: "I had not the least expectation of his being successful," wrote a father who had scarcely seen a Clough or a Stanley lurking in his lazy son. "The news actually filled me with astonishment."[83] Matthew was amazed too; he coasted, now, through several "grace terms" at school—for with the Balliol Scholarship he undercut complaints about his laziness and would have £30 extra, per year, for wine and clothes at Oxford.

He had studied as a schoolboy for the last time, and having slid along on his talent for construing and versifying, he might keep his feet up and continue to slide. He was a dilettante who beheld few terrors ahead. Clough felt university assignments were child's play —and he had been up at Balliol for two years and often reported back (Clough's failure to get a first-class degree in 1841 would seem inexplicable to Dr. Arnold). Matthew hadn't earned particular praise for anything he had done in logic or divinity classes; he accepted the ethical protestantism he heard in chapel and dramatized paternal doubts in his poems for *Fox How Magazine*. And he had hardly emulated his father's or Bonamy Price's habits of thought. He would never acquire much talent for careful definition, systematic thinking, or abstract speculation; he would turn handicaps into assets by proclaiming "radical mistrust" for modes of thought he couldn't handle.[84] His approach to ideas would be homespun, empirical, and intuitive in the unphilosophical sense—for all of his sophistication —though he would cast about widely for ideas.

The opening of a railway had brought a queer prelapsarian quiet to Rugby's streets. The staccato clatter of animal traffic had diminished and cobblestones were clean. In a rather antiseptic apartment, Matthew had sealed himself off from his father's social concerns by playing Prince Charming for his mother's benefit. His egotism at eighteen or nineteen was hardly of a kind that prompts self-inspection —and he was no more than dimly aware of certain paradoxes. He had unusual ambition but limitless capacities for being lazy and motionless; he hated to be alone for more than an hour or two, yet meant to be independent. He exulted in his glory, but needed Mamma's admiration of that glory to feel self-confident.

Everything pumped up the balloon of his ego now. Through a permitted eyeglass, he observed the Continent with "K," Tom, and their father in the spring of 1841—though rain and mists almost kept them from seeing the green Dordogne. Once he got out of the carriage to step across the French border into Irun, Spain, and found a weltering sea of mud so disgraceful that he retreated fastidiously to the carriage. Left alone at St. Jean-de-Luz, he "prowled on the shore," in lonely dignity, while the others wasted a whole afternoon looking for "the scene of Lord Wellington's victory."[85] Late one night at Tours, while Tom sang on a balcony, Matthew hung over a balustrade and peered into an avenue "swarming with people,"[86] and filled with incandescent shops and the exotic wonder of France.

As a minor addition to his glories, he won a very good Exhibition Prize after deeply pleasing the Cambridge examiner with a single, impeccable verse which he wrote in his own Latin:

Osculaque in mediis detque feratque rosis.

Matthew had decided to test his fine, quick, ready talent for translation on the rather haunting line,

And press her wanton in love's secret bower.[87]

Having left his family, this elegant young man found himself in satisfactory rooms at Balliol College on October 15, 1841. A stone's throw away from its many shops and noble façades was the convenient and delightful Broad Street, where the martyrs Latimer and Ridley had been burned alive.

3

GARDENS OF OXFORD
1841–1842

Adorable dreamer, whose heart has been so romantic!
who hast given thyself so prodigally . . . to heroes not
mine, only never to the Philistines! home of lost causes,
and forsaken beliefs, and unpopular names, and impossible loyalties!

—*Matthew Arnold on Oxford*

M ATTHEW meant to enjoy himself to the hilt for three years
under beautiful old towers and near luxurious grassy hills with
tantalizing, long views of the countryside. Free from the regimen of
assignments at school and away from his parents' eyes, he was to
expand emotionally and intellectually at Oxford. But there was
tenseness at the university when he reached Balliol College. Clerical
dons were arming in their tents for a war of extermination; in fact
there had been screams and casualties already.

The trouble involved John Henry Newman and Dr. Thomas Arnold.
Partly for that reason, Matthew tried to take no notice of the
controversy over Newman's "High Church" or Tractarian views. Yet it
is hard to shut one's ears in a battlefield.

In 1822 Newman had come to Oriel College with evangelical
opinions, which surprised no one; but in the eighteen-thirties, after
John Keble defended the Church of England against interference by a
secularized Parliament, Newman and Pusey and others wrote a series
of militant *Tracts for the Times*. Offering a "via media" between
Catholicism and evangelicalism, these were intended to strengthen
the sinews of the Church of England in a materialistic, scientific age.
The *Tracts* chided the clergy for lassitude, and emphasized the
importance of dogma, ritual, erudition, piety, and the doctrine of the
Apostolical Succession. Newman's High Church ideas stirred Oxford
and began to be felt throughout the kingdom and abroad. But in 1836,
he was strongly attacked (by implication) in a blunt, well-argued

48

"Oxford Malignants" essay by Dr. Arnold—the very title of which, though actually supplied by an editor, suggested the writer's feeling that Newman was deceptive and sly if not morally evil. Doctrinally, the Headmaster opposed the *Tracts,* for he was committed to the idea of an inclusive or latitudinarian Church of England, which, with a minimum of dogma, might welcome all Christians. Dr. Arnold was hailed as a champion at Oxford, where it seemed to many people that Newman and Pusey were leading the Church over to Rome.

While Newman chatted with his ardent followers, and delivered Sunday afternoon sermons at St. Mary's Church, his enemies despaired—until they read his *Tract 90* in 1841. People had suspected him of Romanism all along, and *Tract 90* seemed thoroughly Romanist! In the course of a somewhat arid review of their "propositions or terms," that tract endeavored to show that the Thirty-nine Articles of the Church of England were consistent with the "Catholic faith."

When the fat, ebullient, and intense William G. Ward of Balliol College (where he was a tutor and Fellow) went so far as to publish two pamphlets in defense of *Tract 90,* even the Master of Balliol became alarmed. Balliol's masters or governing officials over the years had intensely disliked controversy—ever since the medieval period when according to the historian of the college, its scholars had made a poor showing in street battles. Wycliffe the Reformer ruled over a hall in which "murder" and "adultery" were grounds for exclusion from every privilege, as were, under his wise and mild provision, "assault and battery upon the person of a Master."[1] From the Elizabethan age on, except when it became a tavern in the Civil War, Balliol College had been as blameless and quiet as any institution. In the eighteenth century its fellowships were bestowed on the logical basis of favoritism; its lectures were then almost soporific farces—which prepared undergraduates very well for their easy examinations. In the nineteenth century as the plan of "open" or competitive scholarships yielded results, the college revived. In the 1820s and 1830s its men earned the highest quality of B.A. degree and indeed appeared in First-Class lists more often than men from other colleges; its teaching staff or tutors included the most accomplished classicists in England. In fact, Balliol's quiet rebirth coincided with the mastership of Dr. Richard Jenkyns.

As head of Balliol, Dr. Jenkyns presided over its basic, decent harmony; he kept his eye on a quadrangle where tutors and students whisked to and fro in black gowns, and saw that morals and instruction were kept up. He certainly kept prostitutes *outside* the college gates, by day, and ensured that revelry would be quiet by night. He was a mild-mannered patriarch, with light sideburns and a mincing voice. Having watched a quadrangle before Matthew Arnold's birth, he would continue to watch it after the poet had married, conceived sons, and published *Empedocles* (1852).

In 1841, Benjamin Jowett became an assistant tutor at the College. He would himself rise to the mastership, but he never forgot his first greeting by Jenkyns—who swirled into the room where newly matriculating men came to pay their respects. "Do my eyes deceive me," Dr. Jenkyns began on safe ground, "or do I see a gentleman in my dining-room with his cap on?"[2] With his double chin, well-tied gown, and admirable voice, the Master in short kept the college peaceable and productive by being—probably without knowing it—a reminder of the human comedy. He kept pro-Newman and anti-Newman men on speaking terms by being a common subject of laughter. He "shed tears" after an interview with W. G. Ward, who, for his defense of *Tract 90,* had to give up his tutorship. The Master found nothing odious in Ward's pamphlets until objectionable passages "were pointed out to him"; then he was "deeply shocked."[3] In 1844, Ward, who three centuries earlier might have had a gunpowder sack tied to his throat, was treated to a formal "degradation" in Latin by Oxford's Convocation of Masters of Arts. Troublesome students, believing in free thought and free speech, were in sniping positions with snowballs awaiting the Vice-Chancellor, when a hall door suddenly opened and the huge, moonfaced Ward was seen plunging out into the November air. He had just told Convocation, rather grandiloquently in a peroration written by Arthur Stanley, what he thought of it in English, but he fell flat on his face in the snow —"pamphlets, paper, &c., flying in all directions."[4] What seems significant is that Ward's fiercest opponent at Balliol College, the slender dark-haired tutor A. C. Tait, was the man who accompanied the fat heretic back to Balliol's gates. Dr. Jenkyns had preserved kindliness in his Senior Common Room.

"Mr. Wickens," the Master of Balliol announced to a student, "I never stand at my window, but I see you passing."

The Master when meditating could be as motionless as yellowish Cotswold stone; Frederick Temple heard him muttering about "poor . . . Wycliffe . . . ."

"Indeed, Master," replied a dutiful student, "I never pass but I see you standing at the window."[5]

The Master now saw to his surprise fawn, scarlet, and rainbow-hued waistcoats; he saw men in leather breeches who carried riding crops instead of Aristotle in the quad, and one day, he summoned a new member of the "fast set." What transpired is unclear, but afterwards, while imitating his tones "in the most laughable manner," Matthew

Arnold let it be known that Dr. Jenkyns "considered his proceedings *desultory*."[6]

Matthew got through three weeks at college before it was "whispered" to Clough in Holywell that he was out with the most unstudious, wild set of men who hunted rabbits with hounds. From then on, Oxford became a country house. Matthew's formal achievements were unimpressive, but his clothes, laughter, antics, and minor feats were remarkable. People recalled his leap over Wadham's railings. They even remembered him naked. Capering on a riverbank one day, he made such a show of himself that a clergyman "came up to remonstrate," according to G. H. Lewes's diary. "Is it possible," Matthew replied while waving a towel, "that you see anything indelicate in the human form divine?"[7]

In the mornings, undergraduates dined on eggs or broiled ham and bitter ale in their rooms; and Arnold's scout, coming with breakfast, woke him up gently in rooms "at the top of the second staircase in the corner of the second quad."[8] Later in the day scholars dined under the vaulted stucco ceiling of Hall (now the old library)—and here Arnold put on a straight face. The four or five other resident scholars in 1841 and 1842 were serious men, especially James Riddell the classical scholar and Roundell Palmer, later Lord Chancellor, though little is known of C. S. Lock, who appears in 1842 as "a Blundell Scholar from Tiverton." Much of their talk was theological. Matthew was in a delicate position, because his father was the most redoubtable opponent of Newman and (without resigning from Rugby) would be coming up in December to lecture as Regius Professor of Modern History. "Dearest Crab," Dr. Arnold wrote on November 5, "the Professorship is all right . . . —Let Stanley and Lake know. . . . I must now begin to think in earnest about my inaugural Lecture.—Ever your loving Father, T. Arnold."[9] Matthew neither wished to embarrass his parent nor felt prepared to defend him; the year before, while waiting in the Vice-Chancellor's office for admission after the Balliol Scholarship exam, Matthew had fulminated against the Thirty-nine Articles; but he gave the impression now of being an "apostle of religious toleration in every direction." However, one fellow scholar heard him say that the "strict imposition of creeds" had done more to break up than to unite churches, nations "and families."[10] Clearly, Matthew believed in family unity.

Clough had almost died of boredom at college lectures. Matthew went to about fourteen each week. Most of the lecturers mumbled about books for the "Schools" or finals exam in *litterae humaniores*.

In Clough's surviving books there are plenty of marginalia, in pencil, having to do with textual exegesis and yet showing no trace of any larger view—possibly because he, like Arthur Stanley, thought the first year at Balliol a hundred times worse than the last at Rugby. Never known for cynicism, Stanley when lecturing over at University College told men to underline the Greek *Politics* in crayons as follows—"truths for all time, red; truths for the time of Aristotle, blue; and then," he added with a sad smile, truths for the final "Schools" exam, "black."[11] The examiners gave little credit for critical thought.

Rugbeians felt the college curriculum came up to almost Fifth-Form level. Some of Oxford's texts Matthew had read in childhood, others at school—but some no doubt were less familiar than were their authors' names. The list usually included the *Sermons* of Butler and the *Politics, Ethics,* and *Rhetoric* of Aristotle; Dr. Arnold's beloved Herodotus and Thucydides; the first ten books of Livy and three books of Polybius; and some standard Virgil, Horace, and Juvenal. Options were available from Homer and Pindar, as well as from the bucolic poets Theocritus, Bion, and Moschus on the Greek side, and Plautus, Terence, and Lucretius on the Latin. And in fact in his "Master's Book," Dr. Jenkyns records at least some of the readings assigned to "Arnold" during three college years. For "Divinity," Arnold was supposed to read biblical chapters, along with Butler's *Sermons* and the Church Articles; for "Math" and "Logic," he would start at Euclid. For "Greek," he was given Herodotus and Thucydides as well as Aristotle's *Rhetoric* and *Ethics,* and also Aristophanes' *Birds;* Aeschylus's *Eumenides, Agamemnon* and *Choephoroi, or the Libation Bearers;* and Sophocles' *Antigone, Oedipus,* and *Philoctetes*—the last of which he recalled ten years later when he wrote "Dover Beach." For Latin he had chiefly Plautus, Livy, and Cicero. Under "Morals," the Master tried to discern whether Matthew Arnold was really "desultory" or "respectable," "regular," or "irregular":

> Respectable but desultory in habits of reading—& not sufficiently attentive to the rules of the College.
>
> Respectable, but not uniformly regular or so satisfactory as might be expected.
>
> Improved in diligence & attention but still deficient in both. In part, concerning his studies good; in other parts irregular. Amiable & respectable but far from regular.[12]

Students wrote weekly essays. These were initialed by the senior tutor, or else by the Master, who liked to tell whether a legible essay showed "power & skill." Little was demanded of the essayist—sometimes not even an essay, for one could substitute "a copy of English verses," according to the Reverend Hay Escott, or, in special circumstances, a polite demonstration of one's ability to turn English into Latin. Dr. Jenkyns records that Matthew's "English Essays" evinced "considerable power & skill," and that he once did a "v. good" rendition into Latin, and even had a share in the "Rev. Dr. Richard Prosser's" special prize for work "In English." Matthew talked over papers with his young tutor, Ralph Lingen, later of the Education Office, who was said to be "flash about the waistcoats" but proved to be a "bore."[13]

However, there is evidence that he soon became a pawn in Oxford's and especially in Balliol's warfare against the Tractarians. At any rate, Matthew came under the eyes of Dr. Archibald C. Tait. As senior tutor, Tait was a powerful enemy of Newman. Though not apparently his assigned charge, Matthew sent Tait a letter the following August which suggests extra rigors may have been imposed by that senior tutor. "I hope if possible to get through my Histories in the course of this vacation," Matthew wrote. "I cannot but feel that the great trial will be the complete alteration of habits when I return to Oxford."[14] Tait, then, would not be returning to Oxford. Matthew was then grieved by a family loss, and his words may only reflect an impulse towards self-reform; but that Tait was one of "Four Tutors" of Oxford who publicly protested against *Tract 90* and that Matthew was deeply influenced by him are clear.

Like others then at the College, Tait rose to starry heights. At twenty-nine, he was a slim, Byronically handsome and black-eyed Scotsman with even a club-footed limp; a dry, proudly ambitious man who hated Newmanism as much as he loved the simple Church he knew. He had moderate talent for ideas, and a fine gift for feline maneuvering. Playing Iago to the Master's slow Othello, he outmaneuvered Ward and apparently switched the Sunday dinner hour to coincide with Newman's sermon. Having entered Glasgow University at fifteen and become a Balliol Fellow at twenty-two, he leapt avidly to the Rugby Headmastership at thirty—beating Dr. Arnold's precedent for youthfulness—and made the leap at least partly because the school was then in the limelight. Tait later departed for a northern deanery, where five of his young children died horribly from smallpox; he became Bishop of London in his forties and at the rather early age of fifty-seven, Primate of the Church. That he proved to be a humane administrator and "the most versatile of Victorian Archbishops"[15] may owe to softening he had had along the way, to personal tragedy and a wife's fortitude.

At Balliol he looked so much like the Vatican Apollo that people called him "Belvedere"—but he was a lonely man, too aware of his dignity and, perhaps, his lameness. He yearns in a diary for a closer "pastoral connection"[16] with students, whom he made participate more than was common at lectures. But he lacked the easy charm of Ward (who remained a college Fellow until his degradation in 1844). Whereas the fat heretic naturally called undergraduates "My darling," "My dear," and "Love"—a habit Matthew Arnold imitated—the limping Scotsman gave and inspired little affection; but did inspire respect and got undergraduates to read Aristotle and Butler with "faith in the classicality of their matter." He justified the wisdom of a short reading list and the virtue of "what is known familiarly and taught often"[17]—provided that the thing is great—and deepened a "desultory" young man's regard for books.

Responding to the intensity of Tait, Matthew saw a good deal of him. Perhaps he had to. Tait zealously, watchfully concerned himself with an Arnold because the name was so important. He must have *seen* Matthew going out to hunt rabbits and must have taken pains to ensure that the son of Newman's foremost enemy didn't become a disgrace. Everything was vital—for Tait—in an effort to scotch the effect of *Tract 90* and rid the air of Newmanism. Arnold may have remembered him—and certainly remembered Tait's felicitous translation of "dissociabili Oceano" as "with the estranging main," as Kathleen Tillotson[18] suggests—when he came to write one of his most haunting poems about isolation as a human condition. In "To Marguerite, in Returning a Volume of the Letters of Ortis," every individual is surrounded by an "unplumb'd, salt, estranging sea."

Matthew was now very happy. Tom, who visited his rooms in November, felt he was "one of the most popular men" and noticed that he didn't trample hard on toes. "Things"—of an argumentative nature—"which said by anyone else would have produced a deadly quarrel were said by [Matt] with such a bright playfulness . . . that the victim laughed before he had time to feel hurt."[19] Unfortunately, he was running into debt. One imagines why. The Snell Exhibitioners along with kilts imported whisky to the college; and the Etonians —who tended to be svelte and rich—brought in everything else for breakfasts and evening "wine parties." Having defied teetotalers in the bosom of his family, Matthew maintained a high, catholic regard for wines and liquors. He would drink gin neat on the Continent and ask for whisky at dry Oberlin in the States. He didn't offend the Snell Exhibitioners—who included a flamboyant, loquacious Scotsman named Campbell Shairp who became a friend—and some of his losses at vingt-et-un and at whist (which, later on, seem to have been re-corded in desperation) may owe to tipsy euphoria. One had to return hospitality, and a Balliol man at this time gave two or three parties a term. Moreover, his dressing table was beginning to look like Belinda's in *The Rape of the Lock*. It takes work and money, too, to be debonair. When Jane bounded up to see him, she could hardly believe her eyes! He perfumed his sideburns with Eau de Mille Fleurs, eau de cologne, "and twenty eaux beside,"[20] as she put it in the *Fox How Magazine*. (What did Dr. Arnold think?) Not that he reeked only of Paris, for she spotted on his table Rowland's red-rimmed labels. "ROWLAND'S MACASSAR OIL, KAYDOR, and ODONTO [or tooth powder]" emanating from a London shop near Matthew's eyeglass supplier—but sold by chemists at Oxford—combined the utmost in native "elegance and luxury."[21]

"I am in an awful state of want," he complained in his last college year, "with absolutely only one shilling and six pence in the world. . . . However," Matthew told his mother without forgetting *Pilgrim's Progress*, "the throats of all my great old Debts, Giants Pope & Pagan, are . . . cut."[22] This year at the end of Hilary term, either to humiliate or kill the giants, he sat for the Hertford Latin Scholarship. It paid well. Alas! The competition was keen. He lost out to Goldwin Smith at Christ Church but tied for second place with his old friend George Bradley of Rugby, who was now over at University College[23] with Stanley.

Swarms of big and little Rugbeians reminded him of Oxford's proximity to home. On December 2, 1841, his father came up in a divinity gown, rather like a visitation by Charlemagne to a holy city. Matthew went over to his cousin's home to wait. That congenial chess player Laura Ward had by now married an Old Rugbeian named Greenhill, who was studying medicine at Oxford. Matthew's parents reached the Greenhills; then they all went over to the Sheldonian Theatre, only to hear that the Vice-Chancellor was missing. Had he forgotten the time? Or the hall? "Very vexatious," thought Dr. Arnold. At last somebody led the Vice-Chancellor over from St. John's College and the lecturer began—skipping pages "vigorously" as his cap slipped down almost to his nose—and then there was a great ovation. Later "Mary & I," wrote the Headmaster, "walked up to Balliol to see Matt's rooms, & to call on Jenkyns, who had the Gout."[24]

Dr. Jenkyns recovered for the ensuing lectures in January 1842, by which time the Headmaster and his party were living in a rented house over at Beaumont Street. "Arnold's lectures," wrote Stanley with pride, "go on drawing . . . 300 or 400 every time."[25] Matthew in a large crowd heard his father expand on the apparent fact that "our English race is the German race"; on the affinities of Rome, Greece, and Israel with England; on the sociological importance of popular literature and on the need for moral and social reform in Europe—for her modern nations are the "last reserve in the world." Dr. Arnold was magnanimous, vivid, and moving. In one lecture, says Stanley, "he gave a most striking account of the horrors of the blockade of Genoa, at which the Master of Balliol is said to have wept." In reaction to these lectures perhaps, Matthew felt that "Papa's greatness" consisted "in his bringing such a torrent of freshness into . . . religion by placing history and politics in connexion with it."[26]

In the evenings, his father was affectionately wined and dined. And to the extent that Dr. Arnold became, in this season just before his death, a bulwark against the subtle, intellectual Puseyites and Newmanites of Oxford and a veritable royal presence in the town, Matthew perhaps felt himself to be the community's prince. He had been a black prince among the fry, then almost prince of Rugby School. Later he would play in his letters to Arthur Clough—self-consciously but congenially enough—Prince Hamlet. He merrily, grandly condescended to write for the *Fox How Magazine* in the holidays "The Incursion," partly to prove that he could burlesque Shakespeare's *As You Like It*, Milton's *Samson Agonistes*, and Wordsworth's *Excursion* all at once. Willy, Susy, and Edward Arnold become in their brother's farce a wild barbarian horde

in the heart of Oxford,
This great and awful university,

until, midway in the piece, there tragically enters

the SPIRIT OF PROPRIETY, *sick*

Spirit of Propriety
A little further lead me, good my friends,
That I may gaze on High Street ere I die.
. . . . . .
From Beaumont Street the frighted citizens
Rush in disordered crowds, and the pale Proctor
Arrays his Bulldogs at the accursed house door
That holds this strange, unmannered family.

"The Incursion" anticipates the family's invasion of Beaumont Street on January 25—and the presence of Willy Arnold with "lungs unconquerable" and Susy in "a brown garment half-way down her back"[27] in a Balliol dressing room. For their visit Matthew surely tucked away his eau de cologne. His younger brothers Tom, Edward, Willy, and Walter were mere Rugby School pupils—Walter, now six, was later to become a "Boy" sailor. His devoted sisters Jane, Mary, Susy, and Fan were in training with private tutors and *could* never go to university. Matthew felt immensely aloof from them all. Wrapped in a scholar's gown, he welcomed his relatives with an amused, superior graciousness, as Tom recalls. "Thank God you are in!" he reportedly announced at the start. And when "he had seen the last of us out on the staircase, 'Thank God you are out!' "[28]

By day, his father was busily and happily rediscovering the Cherwell. Dr. Arnold walked to Shotover with William Lake and up Headington Hill with Stanley, and he tramped through Bagley Wood and even up Elsfield's gray-green slope and found himself at Horspath and at Cumnor Hill again, and in the delightful valleys he had known as an undergraduate behind the Hinkseys. For a man suffering from circulatory problems—who had complained at night that his feet were cold and who at Rugby had been sleeping the sleep of the exhausted —these walks must have been as needful as pleasant. Except for a glimpse of him in June, his eldest son would not see him alive again. Through the years ahead, it seems, memories of this ardent walker were inseparable from the countryside.

And strange and vain the earthly turmoil grows,

Matthew wrote in "Thyrsis"—that tribute to the horrors of the Education Office and very lovely tribute as well to a landscape enriched by memories of his father and Clough.

And near and real the charm of thy repose,
And night as welcome as a friend would fall

. . . . . .

The white fog creeps from bush to bush about.[29]

Matthew breakfasted with his father on February 2, 1842. Later in the day, Dr. Arnold went over to Oriel Hall to dine with his old friend Hawkins. His arm was abruptly seized. "Arnold," began the Provost of Oriel, "I don't think you know Newman." Two mortal adversaries bowed politely and Dr. Newman said, with a certain slyness as he cheerfully admitted later, that he believed he had met Thomas Arnold already, for had he not "disputed" with him when the latter took his B.D. degree in "the Divinity School"?

"Oh," remarked Dr. Arnold, "I thought it had been Pusey."

Despite the minor contretemps, the schoolmaster got through an astonishing dinner without unpleasantness on either side. Matthew heard that his father and Dr. Newman settled on "the productions of North Africa," perhaps over the soup, as a safely noncontroversial topic, which may have baffled their two other dinner partners (Hawkins and Baden-Powell, who later contributed to *Essays and Reviews*). Newman spoke amiably of a great tree—"as big as a hill"—which the North Africans in their wisdom use "as an argument for the indefinite duration of the present earth."[30]

Matthew all this while had been appraising Newman himself. Perhaps his father knew it. At the risk of missing a meal, the most notable undergraduates had found their way over to St. Mary's Church from Balliol College in recent years—Stanley, Clough, and even William Lake had suffered crises of Newmanism. As a tutor, Lake was still very High Church. But Matthew seems to have been led over to St. Mary's by the son of one of his father's warmest college friends—by the most loyal, enduring of any of his own friends as time would show—young John Duke Coleridge.

Then in his third year as a Balliol Scholar, this veteran of Buckland's school at Laleham seemed to be dying. He resembled a long-jawed dressy skeleton in a Pall Mall shop. Six feet three inches high, he jingled faintly with strands and loops of golden chain, and his blue satin waistcoats hung loosely. In fact, he withdrew on account of illness in February, but returned to take a pass degree and win an Exeter Fellowship before settling industriously into the law. Like Tait, he became one of the most powerful and influential of men. As a boy he had listened in wonderment to his great-uncle—who may have been lucid when writing "The Rime of the Ancient Mariner" but seemed incomprehensible to little Coleridge and to little Coleridge's parents—and, having inherited some of the great-uncle's eloquence and capacity for monologue perhaps, he distinguished himself in Etonian debates and at the Oxford Union. One of John Duke Coleridge's speeches had been noted, with very little irony, in the London *Morning Post*. Later he would be noticed everywhere. As Solicitor-General in the seventies, he addressed the Tichborne-Claimant jury in a brief that took twenty-six days to recite. (His cross-examination of the bewildered Claimant had gone on inexorably for three weeks and a day.) Clearly he was destined for the woolsack. He became one of the most benignly anecdotal of Lord Chief Justices the nation has ever had, reading Virgil's *Aeneid* in his law chambers and looking like a Roman Emperor.

When Matthew found him at the Scholars' table, Coleridge was bursting with enthusiasm for "the glorious idea of the visible unity of the Catholic church."[31] Supporting the idea, he decorated his rooms in the first Balliol quad ("No. 2, pair right") with expensive line-engravings of the Madonna. As a wealthy student, he kept beautifully bound books and excellent port in the rooms. He had a semblance of an inward, passionate life too—for he wrote poems about sad theoretical love affairs and kept a notebook of privately approved universal truths. He tried to win the Newdigate Poetry Prize, even though the impossible topic had been "The Sandwich Islands."

> *Amid the vast Pacific's billowy flow,*
> *Here fruits unbidden, flowers untended blow.*[32]

No doubt there was much about this sentimental, generous, literal-minded and earnest young man that seemed to Matthew—even in 1841—rather comic. Yet there is evidence that the two were extremely close. Coleridge was desperately eager to be admired: "you are," one of his friends told him with justice, "rather in the *habit* of expecting people to like you . . . *hastily* . . . ; you would take affection by storm."[33] Matthew's closest friends were people hungering for affection, and he repaid John Duke with loyalty while protecting himself from this friend's overbearing need for confidences.

With a good family name and the prestige of a third-year man, Coleridge made the four o'clock escape to St. Mary's respectable. If Newman was rather dangerous, Newman's admirers were a little ridiculous. They "all hold their heads slightly on one side," writes Frederick Temple with the pardonable exaggeration of a future tutor. Newmanites "speak in very soft voices, all . . . make long pauses between their sentences, and fall on their knees exactly as if their legs were knocked out from under them."[34] Magnetizing hordes of undergraduates, St. Mary's rose in the middle of Oxford as big as an Irish cathedral. Its great bells, fine tracery, commodious wooden gallery, and tinted windows were designed to be impressive; on a saint's day the glittering parade of mace-carrying beadles escorting the Vice-Chancellor up to its front door so that he would not lose himself was magnificent.

Newman walked in alone. His tortoiseshell spectacles, emaciated ruddy face, and a certain leanness enhanced by a close-fitting tailcoat delighted cartoonists. Matthew would mimic Dr. Newman's *Tracts* —and he was ready to mimic scabrously. ("What a !!!Shite's!!! oracle," "I am . . . a very whoreson Bullrush," "what an enormous obverse that young woman . . . has," and "those Lombard republicans were s—s, if ever such there were"—are phrases that came easily to the son of a Headmaster whose journalism had shocked the educated public.) Newman's own brother, Matthew told Clough with a gratuitous "h" for the solemnity's sake, is "an hass. . . . One would think to read him that enquiries into articles, biblical inspiration, etc. etc. were as much the natural functions of a man as to eat and copulate."[35] But however ready he was to mock his father's opponent, he seems to have sat and even knelt in a mood to listen.

The preacher was acting out at least tangential scenes in an interior drama of the soul. Newman had seen that an emphasis on apostolicity and "strictness [in] matters of dogma and ritual" might be more than the Church could bear. The *via media* might disintegrate and he might find himself at Rome. Yes, but he wouldn't be impelled in any direction: he would test as objectively as he could in the course of theological studies and comparisons the ability of the established Church to come to grips with itself. What, then, did Newman want? Mainly a revitalized priesthood—deeply conscious of an apostolic role and of the importance of the sacraments—in a mystical and dogmatic Church. Matthew's father, as anxious as Newman about the life of the spirit, had preached and pamphleteered against doctrine and dogma. Dr. Arnold wanted barriers between Christians as low as possible so that Dissenters and Anglicans might unite, in a national and then in a world church, though he had no objection to crucifixes or wayside oratories or to the beauty and solemnity of ritual.

How beautiful now in the solemn light Dr. Newman's performance was! He seemed about to renew "for us . . . the Church of England," Matthew wrote many years later. "Who could resist the charm of that spiritual apparition, gliding in the dim afternoon light through the aisles of St. Mary's, rising into the pulpit, and then, in the most entrancing of voices, breaking the silence with words and thoughts which were a religious music—subtle, sweet, mournful?" And yet Newman was not an exalted priest in a Pre-Raphaelite mural—in or out of the pulpit.[36] He played the violin and had a wise horror of university committees. Reading *Mansfield Park* once a year to pre-serve his style, noticing the facing willow leaves in Christ Church meadow, he was a man haunted by ideas of nemesis and reaction. "With him," remembered Thomas Mozley, "neither person, nor rightful cause, nor just complaint, ever died."[37] Though moving from one doctrinal stepping-stone to another in a bleak agonizing field, he avoided historical theology in the pulpit; Newman "spoke to us about ourselves, our temptations, our experiences," says James Anthony Froude.

> He seemed to be addressing the most secret consciousness of each of us—as the eyes of a portrait appear to look at every person in the room. He never exaggerated; he never unreal. A sermon from him was a poem, formed on a distinct idea, fascinating by its subtlety, welcome —how welcome!—from its sincerity, interesting from its originality, even to those who were careless of religion. . . . These sermons were, I suppose, the records of Newman's own mental experience.[38]

In 1844, Matthew told his mother that Dr. Newman's system was "impossible."[39] But listening in St. Mary's, and listening again out on the London road at "dreary" Littlemore, where the preacher went into seclusion to await the death of his Anglican career, a young poet was deeply moved. Moved also by contemplating his own sensibility, as Jane noticed with amusement, Matthew took pleasure in trembling at the edge of a doctrinal precipice. "The Voice," which he seems to have written in 1844, refers to a speaker whose melancholy and lute-like tones

> Did steal into mine ear—
> Blew such a thrilling summons to my will,
> Yet could not shake it;
> Made my tossed heart its very life-blood spill,
> Yet could not break it.[40]

And perhaps only an experience approaching conversion, complicated by a sudden tragedy for all of the Arnolds and Matthew's deep bereavement, can explain a lifelong veneration. Arnold's feeling remained one of helpless, inexpressible gratitude—not that he didn't try to express it, for Newman was part of the "ineffable sentiment" of Oxford, a man of great "intellectual delicacy" from whom he had learned "habits, methods, ruling ideas, which are constantly with me."[41] He later read the sermons so intently that he confused what he had read with what he had heard, and pored over Newman's *Essay on the Development of Christian Doctrine* (1845) and the more haunting *Apologia Pro Vita Sua* (1864) in particular. There isn't a leading conception of Matthew Arnold's about culture, the nature of criticism, philistinism and liberalism, or the relation between poetry and religion that fails to reveal a Newmanic tincture—though he had a magpie's ability to pick up bits and pieces from everywhere, to fill out conceptions in his essays, and he may have culled from texts that influenced Newman. What the preacher offered was an illustration of a mental attitude—delicate and flexible, discriminating and urbane —that suggested all that a critical manner might be.

Dilettantism failed to prepare a freshman for tragedy—even for the experiences of waking in a perplexing nightmare that would not vanish. In June, his father was at Rugby. Matthew was to meet him in the north. Having sampled the very best things at college, and a few of the worst, Matthew found himself at Fox How with Jane on June 13. He was roused from bed in the morning to hear from Lake, who had come up from Rugby, that Dr. Arnold had died. On Saturday night, June 11, at a nine o'clock supper given for boys of Rugby School House who were leaving for the holidays, Dr. Arnold had been lively and happy. Since the whole school would be empty next day, he had remarked: "How strange the Chapel will look tomorrow." Having written in his diary, he had retired, and then had woken up after five o'clock on Sunday with severe, agonizing chest pains. He had not felt the pain of angina pectoris before. Dr. Bucknill's physician-son had come to the bedroom; he, Mrs. Arnold, and Tom had tried to aid the Headmaster, and laudanum had been given. After eight in the morning, however, Dr. Arnold sighed and stopped breathing. This news brought Matthew south to the curtained windows of his father's school—and there he heard some of the details an official biographer has given. "If," his father had told the physician, "the pain is again as severe as it was before you came, I do not know how I can bear it."[42] His father's death at nearly forty-seven was a blow to what remained of Matthew's simplistic childhood belief in a providential rule of the world. In an effort to understand the event, he later read the death-scene in Stanley's *Life of Dr. Arnold* "so often" that he sickened of it. "The part of the book I like least," he finally told his mother, "—it is the part most in the style of an ordinary religious English middle class biography, with (for my taste) too much detail, and too bourgeois in its character."[43]

In June he helped Stanley select a place in the school chapel for burial, and a night before the funeral went into his father's room. The first thing that struck him when he knelt at the coffin, he told Stanley, was that their "sole source of *information* was gone."[44] His family had consulted Dr. Arnold on everything. "So long as He lived," Matthew told parishioners at Whitechapel in 1884, the Disciples had "Him" to do "as one may say, all their thinking for them."[45] His own position, now, was like that of the bereft Disciples. Yet apart from a strong emphasis on Christian belief, his father had been definitive about little—chiefly about the need for wide reading, free inquiry, social concern and social action. Now, at any rate, there was a moving ceremony. Their eyes shining and their forelocks slicked down, the last Rubgy Fifth Form, the last "Twenty," and the last Praetorian Guard of a Rugby Sixth assembled from all over the nation for the obsequies. Two or three days after, Stanley read the service in chapel and "wavered," as he admitted, "in administering the wine to Matt and Tom . . . [standing] actually on [the] grave. I saw Mrs. Arnold directly afterwards," he notes, "for the first time since her widow's cap had been put on. She talked just as before but with greater calmness."[46]

Facing her loss with resolution despite her grief, Mrs. Arnold commissioned Stanley as a biographer that summer and gathered up sermons for an edition. Her eldest son at Fox How did little. "I had some hopes of receiving a few lines from Matt," Lake wrote thoughtfully to Mrs. Arnold, "to tell me how you all are. . . . I should like Matt's information to be about . . . his own reading, about all of you."

"I consider myself," Lake added for good measure, "as a kind of child of yours."[47]

Unnecessarily as Matthew perhaps felt, his mother struck up the childhood theme when Lake and Stanley arrived at Fox How. Arthur Stanley has "the simplicity of a child." Mrs. Arnold couldn't get over her delight in these two loyal Rugbeians and Oxford dons: Stanley and Lake are "so good as well as so superior in talent and reputation. They seem just as happy and contented as if we . . . had ever so much to amuse them."[48] To brooding eyes, they might have been suitors for her hand—or perhaps Rosencrantz and Guildenstern in the long vacation.

Matthew wrote Tait very formally in August about that don's elevation to the Rugby Headmastership. Most of his letter seems to say that apples ought to be red and the grass as green as possible at a "Christian school";[49] and its cumbersomeness and weary repetition of Dr. Arnold's views indicate that a still very immature young man was far from being at his best. He returned to Balliol in the autumn with a heavy heart. Arthur Hugh Clough, after badly disappointing the Balliol dons and almost starving for a year, was over at Oriel College with a fellowship. Still deeply in grief, Matthew turned to his old acquaintance for talk and friendship and poetry. Here was an old Rugbeian who felt the loss of Dr. Arnold as quietly and agonizingly as he did himself.

4

VERY SELECT COMPANY
1843–1845

> Who, if not I, for questing here hath power?
> —*"Thyrsis"*

M ATTHEW'S fondness for Arthur Clough ripened and deepened amid the clutter of breakfast trays and port bottles in congenial rooms at the top of old staircases. At twenty and twenty-four, the two men were united in an exuberant friendship. They soon accepted (in a small "Clougho-Matthean set") Todo or Theodore Walrond, a warmhearted Balliol Scholar who had been a football-captain despite his small size, and Tom Arnold who at nineteen was at University College. Matthew thought Todo a person of "feeling"—and Todo couldn't get over his own gratitude to Clough for the "simple grand humility with which he admitted to his intimacy one so much . . . his inferior."[1]

Clough was not only humble but facetious and merry: he called London University "Stinkomalee" and invented an official named "His Honesty the President of all Thieves."[2] But he could become an odd lymphatic whale of a scholar, with his piercing black eyes, heavy body, and florid brow (which became more Olympian as his hair receded). "I tried to talk with him," Mrs. Brookfield fretted in London, "but he had the most peculiar manner I almost ever saw. His eyes cut one through and through. . . . Mr. Clough sat at the foot of my sofa with this keen expression of investigation." Walter Bagehot mocked his outlook as that of reconciling everything with green peas, for "green peas are certain" and Arthur Clough was troubled by the invisible. He accepted the historicity of Jesus more easily than he did a living, invisible Jesus. Matthew noted his "morbid" vacillations and thought him "the most conscientious" of men—with justification, for Clough hardly wrote a love letter without cross-examining himself: "There, my dear Blanche," he later told his fiancée, "I have kissed the paper that is to go to you—what sillier piece of sentimentalism could I commit."[3] Skeptical about the mumbo jumbo of mesmerism, he once entrusted himself to a celebrated practitioner of that art: "Mr. Arthur Clough . . . assured me," the Reverend C. H. Townshend wrote, "that he knew

64

nothing about Mesmerism, but was willing to try. . . . I left my patient comfortably installed in an arm chair. . . . Suddenly, I heard a great kicking, and, going back, I found Mr. Clough in a most excited state, seizing whatever was next him, and hurling cushions &c. about the room. . . ." "It made me feel very ill,"[4] Clough said when he came to his senses. (Matthew would jot as the first title for a poem about his and Arthur Clough's Oxford walks: "The first mesmerist."[5]) Certainly, in what he himself called a "dim deceitful misty moonshiny night-time of existence," Arthur was a perpetual experimenter who longed, as Matthew noticed,[6] for commitment to ideals, while holding himself aloof in life with "disinterestedness." In the eighteen-forties he was maturing as a poet. Even his fragmentary drafts are eloquent. "Quiet, my sweet one," Clough jots with a line from *Hamlet* in mind—"But break, my heart, for I must hold my tongue"—

> *my heart*
> *Though it crack, it won't break*
> *Though break, not with thee.*
> *Though it crack, break it won't*
> *Though it break, break it won't with thee,*
> *Does it crack, it doesn't break*
> *Though it cracks,*
> *Though it breaks, it does not with thee.*[7]

His technical achievement was to develop a cadenced, conversational manner in verse, so "modern" that he is not yet fully appreciated, though his star has been rising in the late twentieth century. Clough's main theme is the difficulty of ascertaining truth in the world. In the *Bothie of Tober-na-Vuolich* (at first *Toper-na-Fuosich*)* he portrays the ebullient young Oxford men of Matthew Arnold's generation, out in the Highlands on a summer reading party; in *Dipsychus*, the typical Oxford man in his dazzling, psychologically engulfing, new urban setting:

> *I must sluice myself into canals*
> *And lose all force in ducts. The modern Hotspur*
> *Shrills not his trumpet of 'To Horse, To Horse!'*
> *But consults columns in a railway guide.*[8]

Ironic, implacable, funny, and subtle in his investigations of himself, he drew his own portrait in the person of Claude in *Amours de Voyage*. "Oh," that young Englishman writes from Italy to his friend Eustace,

> *and of course you will say, 'When the time comes,*
> *you will be ready,'*

*An older name for Dallungart on Loch Ericht; Clough heard that "Fuosich" had a lewd meaning in Gaelic and changed the title, inventing the word "Vuolich."

Ah, but before it comes, am I to presume it will be so?
What I cannot feel now, am I to suppose that I shall feel?
          . . . . . .
I am in love, meantime, you think: no doubt you would think so.
I am in love, you say; with those letters, of course,
          you would say so.
I am in love, you declare. I think not so; yet I grant you
It is a pleasure indeed to converse with this girl.
Oh, rare gift,
Rare felicity, this! She can talk in a rational way . . .
          . . . . . .
                    . . . 'tis
Song, though you hear in the song the articulate
          vocables sounded,
Syllabled singly and sweetly the words of melodious meaning.
     I am in love, you say: I do not think so, exactly.
          . . . . . .
I do not like being moved: for the will is excited; and action
Is a most dangerous thing; I tremble for something factitious,
Some malpractice of heart and illegitimate process;
We are so prone to these things with our terrible notions
     of duty.[9]

That originality helped Arnold to discover his own nerve. And Clough's view of the "whole world" as pictorial and hence as detached from the self, and his caution in crediting "anything" as a truth, made Arnold less eager to credit the truths of cultural heroes (ancient and modern) whose works he read in the 1840s, and helped him to become a realistic observer. During the ten years of their association Arnold evolved aesthetic creeds and wrote most of his important poetry: "The period of my developement (God forgive me the d—d expression!)," he told Clough, "coincides with that of my friendship with you."[10]

"That life of Oxford," he recalled, was "the *freest* and most delightful part, perhaps, of my life, when . . . I shook off all the bonds and formalities of the place."[11] Often with Arthur Clough, he walked after two in the afternoon to South Hinksey where Sybella Curr was an innkeeper behind the sign of the crossed keys. They went on to "Ferry" Hinksey, then a gray village with a haunted mansion, and climbed in a shaded tract known as Arnold's Field ("for it had been a favourite haunt of Dr. Arnold's"). Clough adopted an "ambling uphill motion,"[12] with heavy body bent forward. Above Childsworth Farm, they saw distant spires. They crossed in fields "waving deep with cowslips and grasses"[13] and headed for Boar's Hill plateau or the Cumnor Hurst, from which they could see across silent coombs the whole city in one direction, the valley of the Upper Thames in the west, and a line of green downs against southern sky. Clough stretched a "long time" before a good view, as Campbell Shairp noticed in 1843. On these occasions, his eyes narrowed. "Clough observed closely" but "did not speak often . . . or much less indulge in raptures."

Here will I sit and wait,

Arnold remembers with fidelity,

> *While to my ear from uplands far away*
> *The bleating of the folded flocks is borne,*
> *. . . . . .*
>
> *And here till sun-down, shepherd! will I be.*
> *Through the thick corn the scarlet poppies peep,*
> *And round green roots and yellowing stalks I see*
> *Pale pink convolvulus in tendrils creep;*
> *And air-swept lindens yield*
> *Their scent, and rustle down their perfumed showers*
> *Of bloom on the bent grass where I am laid,*
> *. . . . . .*
> *And the eye travels down to Oxford's towers.*[14]

Matthew wrote some of his best Virgilian school verses about hilltop perspectives. He jotted "Ball: Coll: 1843" in a new copy of Virgil and he translated the names of timeless plants in margins of the *Georgics* and probably reread the "quest" stories of Aristaeus and Orpheus in Book IV—which has more of his markings than any other section of his Balliol copy of Virgil.[15] Walrond referred lightly to "Orpheus-like" events; and Matthew was beginning to impose classical parallels on walks. The hilltop climb was a "quest" symbolic of the search for inspiration, for wide and clear sight, for ultimate truth.

> *Thin, thin the pleasant human noises grow,*
> *And faint the city gleams,*

he would write of a metaphorical ascent to sources of purity and truth, in a poem of 1846 with the Virgilian title "In Utrumque Paratus" (Prepared for Either Event)—

> *marvel not thou!*
> *The solemn peaks but to the stars are known,*
> *But to the stars, and the cold lunar beams;*
> *Alone the sun rises, and alone*
> *Spring the great streams.*[16]

In "Thyrsis," the setting would change from the "quest" landscape of Berkshire to that of

> *mountain-tops, in cloudy air,*
> *The mountain-tops where is the throne of Truth,*
> *Tops in life's morning-sun so bright and bare!*[17]

At present, Matthew escaped college formalities even when *not* out walking with intimate, "feeling" friends. "Matt utters as many absurdities as ever, with as grave a face," notes Manley Hawker, a fellow student and old Winchester companion.[18] His absurdities, lazy gambling, fly-fishing on holidays, and lack of reading disturbed the Balliol tutors; but he remained on easy terms with Jowett, Lake, and Temple because he met them as member of a debating club known as "The Decade," which included a few undergraduates from Balliol and other colleges. That club took up learned topics, prompting Dr. Newman to exclaim before he left for Littlemore: "Ah! that is a Balliol Society in which they discuss whether Saint Charles was a martyr or not."[19] Keeping his options open, Matthew frequented the hall behind Wyatt's picture shop where the Oxford Union met, and served a term or two as presiding officer.

Unable to master Euclid for Responsions, in his fourth or fifth term, he got permission to substitute Logic "at the last moment," and a day before the examination went to Jowett, who said that his "only chance" for survival was the rubicund and learned Frederick Temple. Having been a don for a short time, Temple believed in Oxford miracles and poured logic into his ears from nine in the morning till after two at night: "Arnold had been provided with paper, but took no notes. He lay back in his chair with the tips of his fingers together, saying . . . 'What wonderful fellows they were!' "[20] Next morning, Arnold answered every question in Responsions satisfactorily enough.

On Sundays, he listened to political editorials in the *Spectator,* which Clough served up with an Oriel breakfast. Apparently his interest in literature overshadowed his interest in politics. But the "Clougho-Matthean circle" was also reading Carlyle—and this lofty, acerbic prophet made an impression. Dr. Arnold had thought *The French Revolution* "delicious," and Mrs. Arnold recommended that work to her sisters with a shudder usually reserved for reports of hangings: "Get it . . . however you may dislike its taste."[21] Matthew found in Carlyle's *Past and Present* (1843) echoes of his father and of Newman: here was a work which gave the lie to political sophistries by condemning the gross materialism of the age, as well as laissez faire policies, and which exhibited the inwardness of a medieval community. Responding to the poet in Carlyle, he absorbed mannerism of style and useful ideas, and reacting perhaps to the injunction of *Sartor,* he read Goethe's *Wilhelm Meister's Apprenticeship* in Carlyle's translation and praised the book's large, liberal view of life. (Wordsworth, in contrast, threw *Wilhelm Meister* across the room in a pet of disgust at its seduction scenes, as Emerson heard.)

Certainly in 1843 he drew from Carlyle's account of the Lord

Protector of England in the Hero-Worship lectures. Professor Garbett, who perhaps won election to Oxford's poetry chair for the "purpose of excluding a follower of Newman and Pusey," had selected Cromwell as Newdigate Prize topic—thus aiming a timely blow at Oxford's Puseyite cult of King Charles the Martyr. Undergraduates scribbled poems about Cromwell the Soldier—and Matthew had been thrilled as a boy by soldiery: "See, Papa," he had said when holding out a red and a white rose in the Rugby garden, "here are York and Lancaster."[22] But he had trouble writing this poem. "As a boy, I used to write very quickly," he explains to Coleridge on March 2, "and I declare that . . . it was with an effort that I compelled myself to write more slowly and carefully, though now I am ready to confess that I could not write quicker if I would." As one suave writer to another, he confesses to a "great stiffness" in his poem—a fault ludicrously "united with . . . over-rapidity in the last part, which I had to finish in two or three days."[23]

"Cromwell" seems oddly entangled with memories of his father. Now twenty, Matthew celebrates the Lord Protector's youth in the flat fens, urbanely enough, by describing remote mountains and seas which teach to the soul "Freedom's mystic language." Poised to emigrate to New England, Oliver Cromwell at thirty-eight remembers his own

> *Youth stained with follies: . . .*
> *. . . . . .*
> *Repentant prayers, that had been strong to save—*
> *And the first sorrow, which is childhood's grave!*

Improved by nameless sorrows and a stern will, he falls into a Bunyanesque slumber. The allurement of America has tempted Matthew's Cromwell—as it tempted Matthew's father. But clairvoyance makes emigration unthinkable. He sees himself leading parliamentarians round the Royalist flank through gunsmoke at Naseby; beholds the hate-ridden eye of Pym, the fiery glance of Strafford. Archbishop Laud—whom Carlyle had described as a witless, nerveless "College-Tutor"—totters by. Milton and Falkland appear. Cromwell's enemies seem utterly benign and forlorn, particularly the "friendless" King Charles who awaits decapitation

> *like a lonely tree,*
> *On some bare headland, straining mournfully,*
> *That all night long its weary moan doth make*
> *To the vexed waters of a mountain lake!*[24]

Having invested King Charles with Lake District imagery, the poet treats the Lord Protector to a vision of his enfeeblement and death from overwork. Finally, Cromwell wakes up again beside the "dark ships," which are bound for America. And yet obviously he will not sail. Like Shakespeare's Macbeth and the Headmaster of Rugby, he will die in action.

Was his vigorous, chaotic, bloodstained, and tongue-tied existence praiseworthy?

> *A Life—whose ways no human thought could scan,*

Arnold writes hedgingly, invoking Carlyle's idea that "it was not to men's judgment" that this Hero appealed.

> *A life—that wrote its purpose with a sword,*
> *Moulding itself in action, not in word!*
> *Rent with tumultuous thoughts, whose conflicts rung*
> *Deep through his soul and choked his faltering tongue.*[25]

Though pardoning the poet Cowley, and employing the poets Marvell and Milton as secretaries, Oliver Cromwell would have been bored by poetic leisure in America. But, as "The Hero as King" proved, he had sincerity. At the end of the poem, one senses a conflict, mainly in a young poet's mind, between the ideals of self-possession and creative retreat on the one hand and responsible moral action on the other. One feels that a very gigantic paternal shadow darkens an otherwise lucid historical sketch; and that Matthew, in the process of writing, discovered that he sympathized with the ideal of responsible moral action more deeply than he had recognized.

With "Cromwell," he settled on poetry as his *vocation.* This was his calling, his star, his reason for being. His purpose in life was to compose new, beautiful, adequate lyrics. In this activity mere failures must not halt him; sleepless nights counted for little, and mean, low, distracting sensual desires could be purged. He reconciled this serious view of himself with his idle Oxford days, and though still looking for time-wasting pursuits he also wrote.

What worried him was that despite his jokes and gaiety, he couldn't write with exuberance. He lacked spontaneity. His father's social, hectoring views crept into his work or he was choked up, morally intense, when he should be free, vivid, lyrical. Or again he was false; something kept him at the surface of words, as he later told "K." It was odd, to him, that he found it difficult to be true to what he felt; his style was not his *own;* thus instinctively more and more he took *himself* as his chief topic in verse, and began to create his personality by writing about it. Conflicts were at the root of anything he felt; yet even his worried feelings about religion and love which he didn't discuss openly he would try to write about in verse, while drawing emotional support from his Fox How family.

In an approaching crisis—which would involve an "almost mania-cal" quest for what he called poetic "fulness," as well as romantic dilemma, and travel—Matthew would seldom forget his father. Stanley's *Life and Correspondence of Arnold,* published on May 31, 1844, hardly allowed anybody to forget the man. Freeing herself from editorial work, Mrs. Arnold was turning to the business of seeing that her children imitated her husband—who, she believed, was "in heaven." Her son Willy wrote a meaningful note: "Today is my Father's birthday. . . . Why do not people congratulate him or us upon his being in Heaven—For there he is." She looked for Arnoldian signs in Willy, and Matthew obligingly helped: "My dear son Matt thinks there are seeds of resemblance to his father in this dear Boy Willy—& this encourages me greatly."[26] In fact, Matthew's caustic remarks on Willy in his letters to his sister Jane, and the flatness of all but three stanzas (which concern himself) of his later elegy on his younger brother, "A Southern Night," have much to do with Mrs. Arnold's nervous, incessant veneration of her late husband and consequent pride in Willy; but she seems to have been as interested in Arnoldian qualities of her other children. After Willy went up to college she wrote to him worriedly, "Your Oxford life has never become a real thing to me—I do not know enough either of those with whom you most associate or what are your plans whether of work or recreation. . . ." Matthew, who was taking up billiards, must have been the object of that concern. "If only," she tells herself later, "I could cease to torment & harass myself with 10,000 misgivings about my dear ones and rest in my spirit in the faith that they are in hands infinitely wise and loving. . . ."[27] But it is clear that, insofar as thoughts and feelings about her children were concerned, she seldom escaped anxieties.

Winning the Newdigate Prize for "Cromwell," Matthew failed to recite the poem at Commemoration in June because the Sheldonian Theatre was in an uproar. Authorities were openly humiliating High Church clergymen—Pusey had been suspended from preaching and Ward's head was about to roll. As an apparent insult to Tractarians, a complimentary degree was being given to a mere Unitarian, who proved to be the innocent American ambassador. Incensed students, with their usual concern for the Vice-Chancellor, stamped and hooted through the "whole ceremony," so that it was impossible for anyone to recite "Cromwell"; but pleased no doubt with his prize, Matthew went off to Manley Hawker's home in Devonshire in a coach in July.

"We arrived," wrote Hawker as Matthew was in the act of pestering him, "after sundry displays of the most consummate coolness on the part of our friend Matt, who pleasantly induced a belief into the passengers of the coach that I was a poor mad gentleman, and that he was my keeper."[28] With further coolness, Matthew soon infuriated J. D. Coleridge, a native of Devon, by mocking the scenery of Devonshire.* The future Lord Chief Justice exploded: "The one-sided views of our friend Matt . . . urge one strongly to retaliate."[29] Coleridge got a letter of apology, ending with another insult. Arnold next made matters worse by taking Coleridgean nuptials too lightheartedly, and when that friend exploded again he sent him a revealing note: "Your last letter . . . is penetrated with that unfortunate error as to my want of interest in my friends," Matthew declared. "It is an old subject. . . . I laugh too much and they make one's laughter mean too much. However, the result is that when one wishes to be serious one cannot but fear a half suspicion on one's friends' parts that one is laughing, and, so, the difficulty gets worse and worse. . . . I know you are shaking your head."[30] If this laughter owed to a "wit that comes only of great intelligence," it proceeded too from a feeling of well-being, which depended on his pride of place in the family at Fox How. It operated as a thickening screen against arguments about religion and philosophy and also against inquiries into his own views. His closest friends were abandoning the faith of their school years—with painful consequences. Clough stated in 1844 that he couldn't feel the "power" of a Deity and later announced to his college provost, Hawkins, that Christianity was ethically deficient: "Is Xianity really so much better than Mohametanism, Buddhism . . . or the old heathen philosophy?"[31] demanded Clough, whose failure to sense the power of a Deity had led him, with a boldness typical of his former headmaster as well as his former tutor Ward, to question the practical social good of religion. Tom Arnold explained his own doubts in a series of anguished, detailed "Equator Letters," written in the middle of a sea voyage in 1847 to Campbell Shairp. Reviewing his Oxford years, Tom recalled feeling "very poor in thoughts." But then, he had read writers such as Carlyle, George Sand, and Emerson, who "seemed to stand apart from Christianity, and to owe their culture, and even their noble morality . . . to other sources." These writers testified to the weakness of the Christian ministry's response to art and beauty, to problems of social and economic inequality, and to the more universal problem of enslavement by unjust laws. Tom became an idealist, then a confirmed atheist. At University, he heard a voice rattling in Carlylean accents at his oriel window one dreary winter day: "Prate not any more of thy God and thy Providence, thou art here *alone*."[32] After hearing

---

*Arnold's mockery was *sui generis,* but he shared his parents' despair over dull landscape and their sensitivity to topography. J. D. Coleridge noted wryly in Devon: "Matt [said] . . . 'This is nice, *when* it has the sun upon it,' in a sort of patronising concession to me."

the voice, Tom became an idealist again, and then fell in and out of Catholicism before coming to rest in it at last and proving to be Matthew's affectionate "Popish Duck."

But Matthew, who gave up his belief in the Resurrection and in the Atonement by 1844, and probably in that year, was reluctant to discuss theology. A letter he sent home in June, after reading the *Life and Correspondence of Thomas Arnold,* is nonetheless revealing. For a paragraph, he explains that his letters are long but few: "As for Tom I have seen some of his letters . . . not their contents but their size, and I am sure they seldom contain more than half the writing of mine. . . . I repel complaints." Then he turns to Stanley's *Life:*

> I would have written in a moment if I could have known that . . . you wished me to speak about the Memoir, beyond what you had heard me say at Fox How.
>
> —There is not much for me to say—except as to the body of letters which I had not seen and which delight me: I did not know, even if I may have thought, that [Papa] had felt or entered upon many of the difficulties there discussed: and on whatever subject he touches he seems in these letters, above all other Places, to have got a free full expression of himself. . . . It often does happen that the rough sketch a man throws off says more about him than the same sketch filled up and transferred in all its fullness into a book . . . to us particularly who can supply what is absolutely necessary, from having known him, and no more than we want. On questions of Church, and of religious belief, (wishing only that he had sometimes begun a little further back) I could not have believed I should find anything to enjoy so fully and so fully to go along with. What I have always thought clean conclusive, as he would have said, against the completeness of Newman's system, making it impossible that it should ever satisfy the whole of man's nature, and which I have no doubt now I have heard him say, is most characteristically put out in the cxxxth Letter. . . . John Duke Coleridge abused one or two Parts [of the *Life of Arnold*] but his Criticism is generally SAD stuff. . . . Temple, a fellow and Tutor here, says he discovers in this Book the substance of all he has ever heard any Rugby man ever say. . . . only let me ask for my allowance to be paid as soon as possible: you shall have my Exhibition after June ends. . . . Prevail on the children to remember me by constant Pinches, and remember me to Henrietta, who I know admires my Beauty on Trust. I am very kind to Mary ["Bacco"]. Ever your most loving son
>
> *M Arnold*[33]

Though tactically reserved, he was seldom disingenuous with his mother. Here, Matthew cites a letter of Dr. Arnold's (sent to W. W. Hull on April 27, 1836) that is more political than theological. It was written by a schoolmaster then in difficult battle with old friends, High Church clergymen, trustees, and parents. It states (for reasons perhaps too obvious for Dr. Arnold to mention) that "the Roman

Catholic system has the legs right in number, the system is consistent; but it is based on one or two great falsehoods." Again, for reasons a broad clergyman need not specify, "the English High Church system" is "both false and inconsistent." However, one can be a Christian even if one's system is rather inconsistent and incoherent: "I would pray," wrote Dr. Arnold as a convinced latitudinarian in 1836, "that distinctions be kept up between Christians and non-Christians."[34] Dr. Arnold's letter—as one of the most offhand of those printed in Stanley's *Life*—is unimportant; but Matthew's citation of it is significant. His father's reduction of Christianity on occasion to a matter of nomenclature implied that one might be a Christian by styling oneself so. Matthew remained an outwardly dutiful Christian—in the vaguest possible sense.

But in 1844 he felt an obscure sense of loss, uncomfortable yearning, and a perplexity about himself and the world complicated by a sense that he couldn't come quite square with his family or himself. His draft for "Stagirius," "To a Gipsy Child by the Sea-shore," and his letters of 1845 and 1846 to his best friend reveal a poet unwilling to take refuge in mysticism, however vague, though taking refuge in aesthetic ideas and clever perceptions. The "Stagirius" draft of 1844 concerns a soul in a universe without Christ:

> *When the soul, growing clearer,*
> *Sees God no nearer,*

the soul becomes anxious, thwarted, and subject to flank attacks by the demon Pride:

> *The arch-fiend Pride*
> *Mounts at her side,*
> *Foiling her high emprise,*
> *Sealing her eagle eyes,*
> *And, when she fain would soar,*
> *Make Idols to adore,*
> *Changing the pure emotion*
> *Of her high devotion,*
> *To a skin-deep sense*
> *Of her own eloquence.*
> *. . . . . .*
> *Save, oh! save.*
> *From doubt, where all is double;*
> *. . . . . .*
> *Where faiths are built on dust,*
> *Where love is half mistrust,*
> *Hungry, and barren, and sharp as the sea—*
> *Oh! set us free.*[35]

In their rippling movement and polished ease, these lines are moderately frank. Of course Matthew at times enjoyed his romantic malaise. The lines indicate that he had scarcely begun to explore his intellectual pride, and yet they foreshadow the gravest theme in his letters to Clough, that the loss of a central faith is chilling to the poet's necessary warmth and intensity of feeling, damaging to "wide" vision.

Several sonnets published in *The Strayed Reveller* were drafted in 1844. They seem brash, and oddly heavy. "To the Duke of Wellington" originated in Matthew and Tom's visits to the House of Lords where they had seen the old Iron Duke, who was now castigating liberal peers. Wellington resembled Dr. Arnold in being "laborious" and "persevering," in the stylistically choked poem. Just as gravely, "Written in Butler's Sermons" attacks Dr. Tait's old hero—Joseph Butler, the eighteenth-century divine whose *Sermons* or *Apology* appeared regularly on the *litterae humaniores* reading list. Somewhat inadvertently, "Butler" suggests fragmentation of feeling in an undergraduate's innocent outlook. On the other hand, "Written in Emerson's Essays" is the first mark of a cautious devotion to the American sage: Arnold had read the 1841 and 1844 volumes of Emerson's *Essays* with mingled astonishment, approval, and doubt. Wondering if the Transcendentalist's feet were on the ground, he asked Clough if Emerson was "crazy" but decided that the insanity was one of Harriet Martineau's "d—d lies."[36] Emersonian ideas would indeed appear in his own work. In "The Poet" Emerson proved that mystics are inferior to poets: "Here is the difference between the poet and the mystic," wrote the author of so much good but nearly mystical American verse, such as "Brahma" and "Give All to Love"; "—[the mystic] nails a symbol to one sense, which was a true sense for a moment, but soon becomes old and false." Poets, who are "liberating gods," realize that verbal symbols are "fluxional" and indefinitely suggestive. Arnold in writing to Clough would denounce "mystics and such cattle,"[37] and in the sonnet "To a Friend"—and elsewhere—would see the poet as one whose powers are in Emerson's terms "in balance" and who "traverses the whole scale of experience, and is representative of man." Again, Emerson in "Prudence" foreshadowed a theme of *Culture and Anarchy:* "culture" aims at perfection of the individual "as the end." Emerson's essay on "Nominalist and Realist" has ideas about the subordination of poetic detail that appear in Arnold's Preface of 1853, and from the American's own *Poems* Arnold may have learned about argumentative lyrics with conversational lines and abstract titles.

But because Transcendental ideas appear in Carlyle and Coleridge, and reflect a disseminated tradition of philosophic idealism, one feels that Emerson less often formed than confirmed Matthew Arnold's outlook.[38] The sonnet "Written in Emerson's Essays" on the "voice oracular" suggests that Balliol men regarded the *Essays* so skeptically that he couldn't bear to show much early enthusiasm himself:

> *O barren boast, O joyless mockery,*

the sonnet concludes in manuscript with reference to Emerson's Transcendental optimism. If the manuscript draft is based on fact, one suspects the commonsense logic of Campbell Shairp, who often joined the Clougho-Matthean set and perhaps exuded scorn for the *Essays*. Walrond, too, was unimpressed by Emerson. Certainly Arnold, at this time, was reluctant to support any unfashionable idea very seriously in public.

In the summer of 1844, "Schools" (Oxford's final exams) were dreadfully near. Arriving at Fox How, Matthew observed as his mother's guests Julius Hare and "Miss Guy's Hospital Maurice" (a sister of F. D. Maurice), who required so little room it was said, "She sleeps in nothing." Of this saying, he remarked it "not quite decent."[39] Julius Hare was another of Mrs. Arnold's many friends who knew German ideas—like Christian Bunsen he had befriended Niebuhr, and like Crabb Robinson he had tasted coffee in Weimar with Goethe.

Mrs. Arnold was very "anxious" about her son's exams. She now asked Clough to tutor him at Patterdale, where an unlikely tutor tried to prepare an unteachable undergraduate in July, with Walrond along for ballast. "Matt is here," the tutor reports. "Should I relax in the least my yoke fellow would at once come to a dead stop." Arthur Clough's hatred for a demeaning system of examinations had contributed to his own failure to get a "First," but he did his best for a while. He had begun by dividing Matthew's day as follows:

> brkft 8 Work 9½–1½ Bathe, dinner, Walk and tea 2½–9½ Work 9½–11

"We have now revolutionized," Clough notes on July 31, "to the following":

> brkft 8 Work 9½–1½ Bathe, dinner 1½–3 Work 3–6 Walk ad. inf. tea d[itto]o.

Unfortunately, at four Matthew was out fishing. Still, it was raining and Clough rejoiced "to think that he will get a good wetting."[40] Some days, neither of the poets pretended to work. George Butler, a Rugbeian, recalls an all-day excursion this summer up Helvellyn. Matthew, the Bonamy Prices, and Butler scaled the peak from one direction and Clough and Walrond scrambled up from another. Meeting near the summit, they lunched in "full view of Striding

Edge." Somebody quoted a remark of Wordsworth's, to the effect that "his contemporary poets did not realise the sacredness and importance of their mission." Inevitably, this "gave rise to a discussion of poetry and poet's aim"[41]—topics which blended with a fine view of green valleys and blue lakes.

On August 1, when he should have been thinking of Schools, Arnold wrote the famous "Others abide our question" sonnet: he seems to have had in mind the distinction between subjective and objective poets, for on July 28, four days before the sonnet, he sent J. D. Coleridge a note explaining the difference between "the great class [of poets] headed by Milton as opposed to the other class headed by Shakespeare. . . . Our friend, young Germany [Schiller], would express the two classes by two words." In the poem, he draws on Carlyle's opinion of a "great, quiet, complete, self-sufficing" and "victorious" poet, whose works grew "as the mountains . . . shape themselves." The odd image of a peak planting "steadfast footsteps in the sea" suggests Carlyle's belief that Shakespeare's intellect was "unconscious"[42]—he had opened himself up to processes below the level of mere personality. Shakespeare is cloud-capped and mysterious to man, and partly submerged in a sea of the unconscious, and so perhaps mysterious to himself.

Despite one or two unintended ambiguities even in the final text, "Shakespeare" is powerful. Avoiding the loose sonorities and contortions of "Wellington" and other early sonnets, it anticipates the clear, bell-like manner of the "Chartreuse" and Obermann poems, and the terse, scene-setting opening of "Dover Beach." Antitheses in the octave create a tension which is resolved in very strong harmonies of meaning, sound, and sentence form at the close:

> Others abide our question. Thou art free.
> We ask and ask—Thou smilest and art still,
> Out-topping knowledge. For the loftiest hill,
> Who to the stars uncrowns his majesty,
>
> Planting his steadfast footsteps in the sea,
> Making the heaven of heavens his dwelling-place,
> Spares but the cloudy border of his base
> To the foil'd searching of mortality;
>
> And thou, who didst the stars and sunbeams know,
> Self-school'd, self-scann'd, self-honour'd, self-secure,
> Didst tread on earth unguess'd at — Better so!
>
> All pains the immortal spirit must endure,
> All weakness which impairs, all griefs which bow,
> Find their sole speech in that victorious brow.

Shakespeare is congratulated on a certain personal reserve, and on his good fortune in having avoided an Elizabethan Boswell. The line, "Didst tread on earth unguessed at. — Better so!" may rebuke Stanley's *Life of Arnold* published three months earlier, may even rebuke Dr. Arnold's outspokenness and bluntness. But Matthew had idolized his father's memory up to this point. He still did. In exalting the calm, intuitive, self-trained, objective artist rather than the forthright man of action as an ideal, the sonnet is a tribute to Arnold's best hope for himself.

By this time, it was terribly late to make up for three years' indifference to Latin and Greek philology. Oxford's finals began November 13. How can one do three years of work in a few weeks? Matthew saw handwriting on the wall, and as disaster approached he repeated a maneuver that had saved him in Responsions. He threw himself into the hands of the tutors. "He has had the wisdom," Clough notes in early November, "to be perfectly candid to his Doctors as to the amount of the disease, and both they and he have been very diligent during the last three weeks." Diligence might help. His case was not pressing or urgent—it was desperate. These examinations would determine his Oxford degree-class and perhaps his life. In a few finicky papers and in oral replies he would make to embarrassingly niggling questions, he *must* do well enough to earn a First Class degree. Long ago, John Henry Newman had sunk to a Third Class; but Newman wasn't a Balliol man. A Balliol scholar who sank to a Second Class through confusion (or any other cause) would disgrace himself, his school, college and family. Clough predicted he would get a second-class degree, though he might rise above it "in spite of all his ignorance."

The ignorance made Arnold lose the First Class expected of a Balliol Scholar. He shocked his examiners—though his second-class degree consoled Oxford and Cambridge graduates for the rest of the nineteenth century. Jowett grumbled about a Balliol "poet" (perhaps Matthew) lost in an Emersonian, Wordsworthian fog. Wordsworth himself, up at the Lakes, heard the news with a pang and remembered his own bitterness at Cambridge: "The Ven [erable] Poet at Rydal," Clough later wrote, had "taken Matt under his special protection as a 2d classman."[43]

Whatever Wordsworth's special protection meant, it didn't mean help. And Arnold needed help. His degree branded him as a shallow, lazy, silly man with a great name, who had thrown every chance to the winds and sunk to mediocrity. He had no money, no definite prospect: "my degree doing nothing for myself, and as Pupils avoided me as a suspected Person," he wrote to his uncle the following April, "I was by no means safe of a livelihood." Perhaps a poet might find a job, if the poet could part from whist-playing friends. Dr. Tait at Rugby offered to employ him, but only as a temporary master in place of Grenfell, who was ill. Matthew believed that teaching at the old school would please his mother, and that he might have time, when there, to read for an Oriel Fellowship he meant to sit for in the spring—though for that examination there would be, ironically, no set books.

He devoted his last few days at Balliol to a whist-and-billiards orgy. His laughter must have sounded a little hollow. Having lost more than two pounds, and borrowed money, he returned to Rugby on February 25, 1845—though not as a very glittering Old Boy. An Oriel Fellowship, as he told his uncle, would "in some measure atone for the discredit of a second class in the eyes of those who felt most discredit for it";[44] but at the moment he was an ex-Balliol Scholar who hadn't achieved much. Luckily for Matthew, Dr. Tait had fumbled with school disputes and alienated some of the staff, although nobody in Tait's position could look heroic, to men who had known the last, unforgettable Rugby Headmaster. Wryly, Matthew fancied himself as Hamlet in the court of Claudius: "But thou'dst not think, Horatio, how ill it is here," he tells Clough presently.[45] Clough visited the school to see how Matthew was doing. Gray Butler, a pupil there from 1844 to 1850 under Tait, reconstructed one of Clough's sudden arrivals in *Three Friends: A Story of Rugby in the Forties.* The account merges several occasions, but it catches typical expressions and seems fairly authentic. Matthew is out on the Rugby lawn, lolling in an easy chair, indolently stroking the head of a staghound and watching the clouds while complaining to a tutor of "these little creatures, whom I have the honour of teaching," when a strongly built and gravely thoughtful visitor appears.

> "Clough!" shouted the Tutor.
> "In the name of the Prophet, Clough!" said Arnold, "fresh from Oxford damps and metaphysics to breathe real youth and freshness at Rugby! Well! They have not killed me yet, dear, as you said they would: not even their whole schooldays and First lessons! Dear creatures! They are very kind to me, on the whole. . . . But a plague on pedagogy, when you are here! What is that under your arm?"
> "A new book of poems, Mat," said Clough, simply, "just out. It marks an era."
> "Yours," said Arnold inquiringly, "yours, beloved?"

After an indolent sigh, Arnold manages to murmur, "Ah, Clough, when we have that villa in the Caucasus we used to talk of—"[46] One's impression of Butler's accuracy, in the *Friends,* is supported by an anecdote told by the Bradley who became Dean of Westminster. It refers to a slightly later period. As a Rugby housemaster, Bradley introduced two parents to Matthew, who was then stopping overnight. Noticing his graceful tall form, "striking face and black whiskers," and very sophisticated manner, the parents watched as he waved dishes aside at dinner, and heard him explain to Bradley:

> "No thank you, my darling . . . I've just bitten off the tails of those three bull-pups of yours, and that does take the edge off one's appetite."[47]

However, he was earnestly, secretly intent this winter. Down the side of a diary page in March, he scrawled: "too much to record running every moment." In fact, he was running through a very heady reading list. Late in March he went up to Oxford; and then he recorded in triumph, tersely, six days later, before returning to Rugby: "got the Oriel."[48] Dr. Arnold had won that same distinction thirty years earlier. Matthew had become a Fellow of John Henry Newman's old college; and of course it was Clough's college!

He took leave of Rubgy, once again, as a satisfactory hero. He must have felt that the Oriel quadrangle, high-table elegance ahead, prestige of his Fellowship, and companionship of Clough would suit him. Gliding over cobblestones with his bags in a coach, he left the "little creatures" of the Fifth Form behind for the time being.

5

AN ORIEL FELLOW
"IN THE DEPTHS OF THE SEA"
1845–1847

To reflect—to turn the attention back upon a past
phenomenon or series of phonomena

We are plunged at birth into a boundless sea; crystal
clear, where all may be seen. . . .

You must plunge yourself down to the depths of the sea of
intuition

this starlit sea of life

—you damned pedants
                           —*from Matthew Arnold's notes*

Hasten, my soul! where *is* my soul?
                           —*Aristophanes*, The Wasps

T O a surprising extent Matthew had been carefree—despite the
loss of his father. He never lacked affectionate friends, though he
seemed lazy and irreverent enough to be taken lightly. He meant to be
a poet; and he feared that earnest dons might turn him into a grinding
student or a dull, arid pedant. He was "exceedingly glad" to be an Oriel
Fellow, as he told his Uncle Trevenen, but he was not a diligent
scholar: "I do not know why the getting this Fellowship should
increase my Confidence: for tho: it may in some measure atone for the
discredit of a second class . . . yet in real truth it leaves me, as to my
reading, very much where I was before: and the truth is that the
Examination was different, not that I deserved in April much more of
a literary success than in November." His election was bound to
delight people at home—and "it gives me a certain Prospect of
relieving Mamma of myself, tho: it is certainly not the first subject for
delight that occurs to her."[1] Mrs. Arnold was pleased indeed. Henry
Coleridge, a younger brother of John Duke, was elected to Oriel on the
same day as Matthew—and this news prompted another Coleridge,

one day at Ambleside, to stop Matthew's mother in the street. She was surprised to be quizzed by Hartley Coleridge, then reading German with the Claude girls at Broadlands. "Poor Hartley," noted Mrs. Arnold. "It was quite touching to me yesterday . . . he came up to me and congratulated me on Matt's success." Turning gloomily away, Hartley had remarked of his namesake Henry at Oriel: "*I hope he will have better fortune than some of the other Coleridges!*"[2]

Hartley had once collapsed in a drunken stupor inside Oriel's gates. Matthew himself was to gamble and drink whisky at Oriel, but he noted in his diary in April with great pride: "Chapel ORIEL morning."[3] Provost Hawkins had been an intimate adviser of his father and a firm opponent of Newmanism within the college—he was now on cordial terms with Mrs. Arnold and would take tea with her in June. Everything transpiring here would reach female ears, sooner or later, in Westmorland.

But spring was in the air—and life reasserts itself at Oxford. Out beyond the porter's lodge and over in the High, white-hatted dandies from Christ Church were sucking their ices outside Jubber's and Sadler's the confectioners; and the "fast set" was on the move.

Walking into a famous hall and sitting with polite dons and Fellows at the "pomp" of college dinners, Matthew seems to have been restless. Oriel had moved out of its eighteenth-century doldrums assuredly—from those bleak days when Joseph Butler, author of the *Analogy of Religion,* had thought of going to Cambridge. "Our people here," Butler complained bitterly at the college, "never had a doubt in their lives concerning a received opinion; so that I cannot mention a difficulty to them."[4] Provost Eveleigh had galvanized the common room; he helped to introduce the Honours Schools of Classics and Mathematics at Oxford in 1800, and moved Oriel to the intellectual front rank. The provostship of his successor—the famous Edward Copleston, a poetry professor at the age of twenty-six and a man of eloquence and presence—was even more brilliant. Fellows began to be elected on the *non res sed spes* principle (the basis of promise and not performance) and this had attracted remarkable talent: Thomas Arnold and John Keble met the shy Davison and the tireless Whately, who talked in tremendous paragraphs in the common room; Blanco White the former priest took up residence; Newman, as a third classman of Trinity, filled Thomas Arnold's vacated fellowship; and six years later when Edward Hawkins was elected Provost the college was ready to astonish Parliament and influence the future, for the *Tracts* emanated mainly from Hawkin's Oriel.

Edward Hawkins proved to be an interesting, strong-minded, and controversial Provost, with conscientious objections to Newman's and

Pusey's militant propagandizing. He certainly feared for their influence on undergraduates, deprived three Tractarians of their tutorships, and tried to fill vacant places with anti-Newmanists. "Fussy, jealous, meddlesome Hawkins," wrote the Rev. G. Tuckwell, who felt that the "decadence" began when the Provost secured a tutorship for a man who wore a white cravat. Hawkins "dragged Oriel down to the depths, having found it the first college in Oxford," declared Professor Morfill,[5] who proposed Dr. Arnold's name for the *Dictionary of National Biography*. Born before the storming of the Bastille, Edward Hawkins was still living in his nineties when Winston Churchill and Lenin and Stalin were infants; he was not only enduring, but farsighted and kindly—even if he gossiped. Having predicted Dr. Arnold's success as an educator, he welcomed Matthew to the university in 1841. He did his best to prevent riots, and expelled almost nobody. (Oriel students, now and then at night, attacked the rooms of High Church men and smashed holy effigies and some furniture. "I am sorry, Mr. ———," Clough consoled an undergraduate one morning, "that they have broken your teraphim.")[6] Though he detested Newmanism, Hawkins played fair but played hard: he was a product of Copleston's college, in which men were merciless in debate, disrespectful of donnish myopia and conventional views, but cordial to and respectful of one another: "I can say with a full heart that I love him," Newman himself declared of the Provost. "He provoked me very much from time to time, though I am perfectly certain that I have provoked him a great deal more." "I was very fierce," Newman added, of the Oriel period.[7]

If Newman and Pusey in the thirties were fierce, the evangelicals in the forties were fiercer. Outspokenness and free speech suffered all over Oxford when opinion turned against the tract-writers. By April 1845 a Balliol man was genteelly martyred—poor, fat Ward had been damned by Convocation and stripped of his Balliol tutorship on the day he fell in the snow; Keble was silent, and Pusey was banned from the office of university preacher on a charge of heresy—which oddly meant the Regius Professor of Hebrew could not preach on Ezekiel.

Sitting in his gown at dinners, Clough noted how dull the dons had become, and indeed Newmanists were under a cloud—with their leader out at Littlemore. Charles Marriott, the saintly ghost who inherited Newman's rooms at Oriel, appeared at supper in a veil or an eyeshade with a greenish cloak "made of two old M.A. gowns unequally yoked together" and seemed "silent, grave, and almost sleepy." "Lytton of evangelical opinions," Clough told his friend John Philip Gell, "is exceedingly grave, silent, and almost bashful." R. W. Church and J. F. Christie were "Newmanists better and worse." The latter was often scandalously out at Littlemore. The former remained a High Anglican and wrote an impartial history of the Oxford Movement; but after Newman's reception into the Church of Rome in December 1845, both Christie and the meek Henry Coleridge became Catholics.[8]

Bashful, silent older dons, and tense, preoccupied younger Fellows do not make for good common-room conversation, especially for a wit and a poet. "Then I know," Matthew writes to Clough in 1845 or 1846, and with college dinners partly in view, "what hideosities . . . what distortions, what Grimaces, what affectations . . . I shall hear and see amongst the born-to-be-tight laced."[9]

But Matthew made use of a bachelor's study. His desk-notes —which are undated—cover the period from the fourth or fifth term at Balliol to his earliest years as a School Inspector and many pertain to problems connected with his reading in the Oriel years and illuminate him. He jotted memoranda for a variety of reasons—to express impatience, to try out a writer's ideas and thus free his imagination, or to try to formulate a worldview and assemble ideas for his poems—and he valued what he jotted. The formal model for his notes was surely Goethe's *Maxims and Reflections*. Thinking deeply about life, Matthew "distanced" reflections so that they assumed the character of aphorisms, though he often descended to a "you" or an "I." The following notes were written either at Oriel or a little later in London:

A face hovers in mid-air, perhaps in a room already decorated with "Sea Pictures."

After all why am I restless [Matthew observes] because I have no one to say with tearful eyes to—I am wretched—& to be answered by—mon pauvre enfant—allons—sortons—dinons &c &c. [See the illustrations for the sketch of a lady's head.] Could we *imagine* a character we could be it—but we can only hope it: this is a bastard imagination: yet do young Geniuses thrive on it & its warmth, or on its absence & the liveliness of the constructive faculty?

So & so gives an opinion—how did he form it—penetrate yourself with the slight accidental way in wch A B C & D form & state opinions on all topics that do not vitally concern them, & do not in deference to authority your own inward uncertainty eternally [?] occasions in you, take their opinion for an absolute sentence.[10]

He exercised his "faculty" in an Oriel diary that is full of doodles, squiggles, X's, and lists of gambling losses (adjacent to a printed column of "FIRES, REMARKABLE"). He wrote:

They had not suffered yet they said we loved
Said we were happy—yet could shew no tears
Were hopeful having never yet despaired. . . . [11]

He faced an obvious problem in coming to grips with modern life. He knew little of life. His experience had been very restricted and conventional: but his early experience, at Laleham, had been vivid. Friedrich Schiller's essay "On Naïve and Sentimental Poetry," which associates Greek creativity with modern children and with men who are "children at heart," may have made him dwell on childhood; and Dr. Newman's conversion may have reminded him of his own early faith. "We would mould and educate," Matthew observes in an astonishing note,

> as if our wish could change the reality: as if in deference to the Protestant Parent's feelings Nature would keep high out of his child's sight all but the Protestant aspect of the Universe.[12]

"I would have others—most others," he confesses later to Clough, "stick to the old religious dogmas because I sincerely believe that this *warmth* is the great blessing." Had the Protestant Parent's religion failed?

> You find what answers to the yearning of your own inmost soul therein do you: my god, let us tell him that, for he cannot find what answers to that of his own in it.
>
> I cannot conceal . . . the objection which really wounds and perplexes me from the religious side is that the service of reason is chilling to feeling, chilling to the religious mood, and feeling and the religious mood are eternally the deepest being of man, the ground of all joy and greatness for him.[13]

"Stanzas from the Grande Chartreuse" suggests that he later wept at a Catholic monastery. Victorian gentlemen of unsettled faith wept easily in church: and Matthew wept unaffectedly and openly in the presence of his wife and once, understandably, before schoolchildren. His tears in "Chartreuse" interestingly occur in a passage that follows an appraisal of his early, influential instructors. "Rigorous teachers"—his own father and then Clough and Jowett at the "Decade" certainly, as well as Carlyle, Emerson, and Goethe—encouraged his skeptical habits, which destroyed his earlier faith and made him immune to religious dogma. They

> *Showed me the high, white star of Truth,*
> *There bade me gaze, and there aspire.*
> · · · · · ·
>
> *Forgive me, masters of the mind!*
> *At whose behest I long ago*
> *So much unlearnt, so much resigned—*
> · · · · · ·
> *I seek these anchorites, not in ruth*
> *To curse and to deny your truth;*

. . . . . .

Wandering between two worlds, one dead,
The other powerless to be born,
With nowhere yet to rest my head,
Like these, on earth I wait forlorn,
Their faith, my tears, the world deride. . . . [14]

The Friedrich Schiller essay, and his own notes, indicate that he deeply associated childhood and faith with the problem of creativity. For the child is endowed with an intuitive sense of oneness with nature and lives in a medium in which the imagination creatively perceives: "We are plunged at birth into a boundless sea," Matthew reflects, "crystal clear, where all may be seen, as the eye gets accustomed to the watery medium thro: which it is to look—but we are agitated and alarmed and by our struggles trouble the transparent medium." As adults we awake on a "starlit sea of life"; but before finding ourselves in an opaque sea or at the dimly lit ocean-surface of existence, we have lived in that "crystal clear" arena—which seems unclouded by willful thought and conventional time. "Time and the year," he reflects in another note reminiscent of Balliol days as well as of his boyhood, "are almost indefinitely prolonged for us in child-hood."[15] As an undergraduate, Matthew had defeated laws of purpose and consecutive time by doing the same thing over and over —throwing a line into a brook, repeating hilly walks or skiffing expeditions—or by turning logical discussions into circular ones by being solemn and absurd at once, as Manley Hawker noted, and he was still gambling. Gambling is the quintessential heaven for those weary of the clock: "No game is dependent on the preceding one," as the French philosopher Alain wrote later. "Winnings secured earlier are not taken into account . . . Gambling gives short shrift to the weighty past on which work bases itself."[16]

Time is the adult's bondage. In one of those retrospective moods so necessary for his significant work, Matthew once explained, with the help of Goethe and Schiller, how very little a beautiful city cared about time and how that city might save us from a human bondage: "Whispering from her towers the last enchantments of the Middle Age, who will deny that Oxford," he wrote, "by her ineffable charm, keeps ever calling us nearer—to the ideal . . . —to beauty, in a word. . . . What teacher could ever so save us from that bondage to which we are all prone, that bondage which Goethe, in his incomparable lines on the death of Schiller, makes it his friend's highest praise (and nobly did Schiller deserve the praise) to have left miles out of sight behind him;—the bondage of *"was uns alle bändigt,* DAS

GEMEINE!"*[17] Charmingly defying rules, writing poetry, fishing and boating, refusing to study philology but cramming at the last moment before examinations, Matthew at college had recaptured some of the spirit of his own boyhood.

Yet childhood, he considered, is unlike any other condition or age of man, for it is an unhurried period when intuitions and feelings dominate the mind—a cavernous green glimmering marine amphitheater where "all may be seen" because the "child's sight" is governed by instinct rather than preconceptions. Even after the agitations and alarms of our struggles, we have memories of the transparent "watery medium" in which we lived; and Matthew's submarine metaphor is related to his early experience. In Laleham years with "K," when he was scarcely more than four or five, he was not precocious enough to write poetry. But he acquired then an amusing, oceanic nickname and a fondness for the vicinity of the "pink acacia" and the garden nearest the house and later Crabby Arnold's father was so jocular. . . . "O Crabby the great . . . with all your Claws, reposing under the Shade of a large Sea Weed, and just going to catch the Gentleman as he comes near you.—Do not you think that you will make a beautiful Picture?—As for Prawn, he is half distracted with Joy from the double enchantment of Lempriere's Classical Dictionary, and Keightley's Mythology abridged . . . Crabby, my dearest . . . I am ever your own."[18] That marvelous oceanic identity lasted to the time when he and Tom were old enough to sink into mythologies, and classical fables, carrying men through the spray! In a year when he recalled "crooked legs," and vivid details of the green Campus Martius, he was delighting Mamma and "K" with clever compositions about naiads, whales, dolphins. He told Coleridge the early compositions were done "very quickly."[19] In the bleak summer after his father's death, when he could hardly speak, Mrs. Arnold found him deep in Herodotus—and yet having consoled himself with that book he found at Balliol he had astonishing trouble in writing! In "Cromwell," the themes about reflective withdrawal and social engagement are in unresolved conflict.

The trouble he had with writing in 1843 resulted in a letter about boyhood composition habits and probably made him *think* about creativity and the uses of rules and criticism for the first time. He told Coleridge pointedly: "There are faults in the construction [of "Cromwell"] which alarm Stanley terribly; and I should think that the construction of a Prize Poem ought to be conducted on certain fixed

*From Goethe's "Epilog zu Schillers Glocke": *What binds or enthralls us all,* THE COMMONPLACE!

principles, and would be, and very fairly, made a point of great importance."[20] In his reflections on the sea of childhood, in which all is pellucidly seen, he explored a deeper level of the composition problem. Creative power depends on psychic well-being or wholeness, on intuitive vision (which does not disturb the transparency of life), and on a calm underlying feeling of kinship with nature. "You must plunge yourself down to the depths of the sea of intuition," he notes insistently, for the adult world is hostile; "all other men are trying as far as lies in them to keep you at the barren surface."[21] Spiritually the poet must resemble the child, and Matthew would praise Clough as one of the "children of the second birth."[22] But without faith in a supernatural Power, he seems to imply, spiritual rebirth is arduous and nearly impossible.

In the long vacation of 1845, he declined an invitation to go walking in Scotland and accompanied "K" and his mother to the Isle of Man—where he must have drafted "To a Gipsy Child by the Sea-shore; Douglas, Isle of Man." That poem relates to his sight of a ragged child in its mother's arms at the Douglas pier: he and Tom, probably two years before, were watching "passengers land from the Liverpool steamer," as Tom recalls. At the head of a crowd stood a woman who "might have been a gipsy—she was looking down at the steamer, and the child in her arms was looking backwards over her shoulder. Its pitiful wan face and sad dark eyes" appealed to Matthew, who became "completely abstracted."[23]

Clearly, here was a subject for his theory of the intuitive power we have in early life. He addresses the child as if it were one of Wordsworth's promising outcasts, full of obscure but profound knowledge:

> *Who hid such import in an infant's gloom?*
> *Who lent thee, child, this meditative guise?*

Evanescent sails gleam on the horizon and water laps near a time-bound pier. To instruct "K" in the poet's detachment from his subject, he dissociates himself from the sad-eyed child:

> *Glooms that go deep as thine I have not known:*
> *Moods of fantastic sadness, nothing worth.*[24]

The gipsy infant cannot speak, yet its face is full of meaning. What accounts for its despair? Apparently the child has a grave stereoscopic view of its future—and even a sense of its exile in the world. Its appearance reminds the poet of philosophers he was then reading: "Epicureanism is Stoical," Matthew told himself in a confident desk-note, "and there is no theory of life but is."[25] He asks rhetorically:

Is the calm thine of stoic souls, who weigh
Life well, and find it wanting, nor deplore;
But in disdainful silence turn away,
Stand mute, self-centered, stern, and dream no more?

. . . . . .

Down the pale cheek long lines of shadow slope,
Which years, and curious thought, and suffering give.

The child has foreknown "the vanity of hope." Having dismissed hope, the poet appears to consider Christian teleology—but the poem is reticent at this point. With the help of fluid syntax, and beautiful images borrowed from more sensuous lines by Keats, he exclaims:

Ah! not the nectarous poppy lovers use,
Nor daily labour's dull, Lethaean spring,
Oblivion in lost angels can infuse
Of the soiled glory and the trailing wing.[26]

Though reminiscent of his Byronic melancholy in the *Fox How Magazine*, the lines imply that the gipsies—and by extension the human race—have fallen in a world that lacks a redeemer. Only the mutable beauty of a gipsy child is consoling. The poem testifies to a poverty in Arnold's philosophy and theology, to his lack of any animating idea that might encourage the spontaneity he wants. But it looks ahead to "Resignation," which treats the stoical gipsies and the poet's role in a more explicit, philosophically advanced manner.

"The Forsaken Merman" was written after he read Miss Howitt's translation of Hans Andersen's account of the Danish ballad "Agnete og Havmanden" (Agnes and the Merman) in 1847 or 1848, but Arnold follows a fuller version of the story in George Borrow's review, in 1825, of J. M. Thiele's *Danske Folkesagen;* and some details in the poem may relate to memories of Fledborough as well as to his long summer at the Isle of Man. Penelope Fitzgerald[27] suggests that wagonettes filled with Lancashire holiday-makers, and the presence on the Isle of Man of mid-Victorian clergymen—all jollily strolling, botanizing, and making Runic rubbings—may have entered into the unsympathetic picture of the land in the "Merman." Again, "little bays and ins and outs" he saw this summer and mermaid legends in guidebooks about the Manx traditions could have set his imagination working.

The poem aroused Tennyson's envy; but the story is very simple. Out at sea, the father of strange, beautiful mermaid children gazes from a bay towards the town which holds his human consort, Margaret, who has left him to save her soul in church and at a spinning wheel. Salt-tides move ineluctably and harsh winds blow, raking the spray, but there is a familiar world in green depths which the Merman describes:

Children dear, was it yesterday
We heard the sweet bells over the bay?
In the caverns where we lay,
. . . . . .
Sand-strewn caverns, cool and deep
Where the winds are all asleep.

The recollection of far-off sounds reminds the Merman of a loving, trusting past when he, his consort, and the children were united in the deep. The sea-arcades of the green underworld suggest the human past as well as a substratum of the psyche—an unconscious or semiconscious area where animals follow laws of their being in quivering, gleaming light:

Where the salt weed sways in the stream,
Where the sea-beasts ranged all round,
Feed in the ooze of their pasture-ground;
Where sea-snakes coil and twine,
Dry their mail and bask in the brine;
Where great whales come sailing by,
Sail and sail with unshut eye,
Round the world for ever and aye.[28]

Incantatory rhythms reinforce one's impression of an atmosphere profoundly harmonious—as in a domestic scene where the fiercest act is the brushing of a child's brilliant tangle of locks. "Once," the Merman recounts, Margaret

sate with you and me,
On a red gold throne in the heart of the sea,
And the youngest sate on her knee.
She combed its bright hair, and she tended it well.

She left at Eastertime to pray with her kinsfolk in the hillside church with its small-leaded panes and never returned to the sea, but with sorrow-laden heart she will sigh

For the cold strange eyes of a little Mermaiden
And the gleam of her golden hair.

More and more as he tells his tale, the Merman gains one's sympathy for his rich pagan values. *His* golden thrones are better than Margaret's spinning wheel; sea-stocks blooming in a shimmering emerald radiance are more compelling than the face of a "white-walled town" behind which there is endless routine of dull work. Why not live in the sea? Separated from parenthood, Margaret will not raise her head when, having led his infants through the cold night air to gravestones outside the church, the Merman pitiably calls:

'Margaret, hist! come quick, we are here!'

Her eyes are "sealed to the holy book,"

'Dear heart,' I said, 'we are long alone,
The sea grows stormy, the little ones moan . . .'

There are only the shut, dumb church door and the loud praying of the priest to his congregation.

Come away, children, call no more!
Come away, come down, call no more!

Down, down, down!
Down to the depths of the sea![29]

"You must plunge yourself," Matthew had counseled himself, "down to the depths of the sea of intuition";[30] but there is beauty and energy in the sea without the rational order of man. "Forsaken" because he cannot connect with the polity of the town, the Merman sings of coral caverns, and of the isolation and abandonment he will endure forever:

She will hear the winds howling,
Will hear the waves roar.
We shall see, while above us
The waves roar and whirl,
A ceiling of amber,
A pavement of pearl.
Singing: 'Here came a mortal,
But faithless was she!
And alone dwell for ever
The kings of the sea.'[31]

Plunging into the depths of the self may be necessary for the artist who seeks concentration of feeling, but Arnold implies that intensity of feeling or creative inwardness is not the same as spiritual wholeness. The artist isolates himself from his main source, humankind, in seeking the self-mastery he needs in order to create. Topically, the poem comments on the fragmented psyche at a time when neither religious certainty, nor, for many, theism was possible—and yet the divorce represented is very suggestive. A singer is divided from the land of civic duty and religious observance; love is sundered from faith, nature is divided from humanity, freedom is separated from work and community, the spontaneous imagination from the responsible will. There are of course imperial preferences: the author cares less for prayers than for the health of his imagination and describes the ocean-life with more gusto and approval than town and church.

Arnold seldom wrote as confidently about loss and divorce and being set apart. He uses the theme of alienation with superb effect, here and elsewhere, because he "felt it on the pulses." He had a splendid memory, a strong tendency to dwell on the emotional past—and his admiration for tradition, his elegiac gift, caution in making new friends, and preference for old Rugbeians such as Walrond and Clough manifest an emotional conservatism. Letters and journals his mother kept show that he *acted* in a manner that set him apart in the family from the time of his "crooked legs" until he went up to Balliol; and his jottings, for her, show plainly that he remembered the iron fetters ten years after he wore them. He remembered his exile to Buckland's—and details of the "detestable" playground, of "the really bad and injurious school," where he had survived, first, without Mamma, and then without Mamma's deliberately withheld letters —even when he himself was a middle-aged parent:[32] *You have got Malé twice in one week. . . . Whenever I hear of your dining in on Friday, I will directly give you the pleasure of a letter . . . write and tell me you have given proof of a week's diligence . . . vanity . . . I am very sorry for it, be it what it will. . . . You have therefore only to write . . . tell me you have given proof of a week's diligence & our letter shall be written. . . . As for little Nemi, she is the funniest and dearest little Thing you ever saw—she gets about very cleverly, and can all but walk alone.—Widda chooses now always to sit and wait for me to come up from the Hall. . . . And Bacco says that her Birthday is coming, and then she will be a great Woman . . . and then . . . the Death of poor dear Wixey the Gardener, who used to be so kind to you all.—It is so sad, dear Matt, to look into the Garden, where he used to work, and think that he is now under the Ground, never to work any more,—and this too, when it is only a Week to a Day, that he was first taken ill, and he died on Monday Morning, and today I have been with his Body to the Churchyard, where Mr. Page read the Funeral Service over him. . . . I was with poor Wixey the Night before he died, and . . . it was beautiful to see how patient he was, how ready to die, though he had so much in life to make him happy. . . . And so, my Boy, let us be as happy as ever we can . . . yet Christ has something better for us . . . then Hurt tried to knock Love, down with his club. . . .* [33]

Two experiences, that of being clamped into irons in a family of romping children and of needing years afterward to learn to walk properly, and that of being separated from the family because of his obstinacy about Latin, had given him the sense of exile from his mother's affections. In pain and bafflement, he had screamed at Laleham; Tom walked merrily to Chertsey and Matthew gashed his own head on an iron claw. The Buckland and Whately children tore pell-mell through the Campus and Matthew cried with his blister. His later letters to his mother would be full of adult wounds—eyestrain and face aches, biliousness and coughs, broken teeth and fevers; in a surviving photograph he calmly displays the hand, then covered with scar tissue, that he told his mother he once saw ablaze at Winchester. Mary never stopped adoring him: and Matthew understood perfectly that she was not only moved by the spectacle of any mortal in pain, but susceptible to the effects of charm—*When you see the Jura, think of me.*

> *Albania's mountains crowned with snow [she had written]*
> ......
> *The gallant ships that come and go—*
> *What wonder that so fair a sight*
> *Had power to charm a Lalehamite!*[34]

His success as a poet is greatest when he appeals through tragic themes and exquisite imagery to the sensitive emotions of that lady. "The Forsaken Merman" has a haunting appeal; in rhythms and imagery it is reminiscent of the Eaglehurst lines for Mrs. Arnold, and again of "The First Sight of Italy." It is also a perfect illustration of Schiller's essay on the naïve, so that it might complement almost any passage from that work.

> Genius expresses its most sublime and its deepest thoughts with this simple grace; they are the divine oracles that issue from the lips of a child; while the scholastic spirit, always anxious to avoid error, tortures all its words, all its ideas, and makes them pass through the crucible of grammar and logic, hard and rigid, in order to keep from vagueness, and uses few words in order not to say too much, enervates and blunts thoughts in order not to wound the reader who is not on his guard. Genius gives to its expression, with a single and happy stroke of the brush, a precise, firm, and yet perfectly free form.[35]

Searching for a new view of the world at Oriel, Matthew studied avidly. To cool his reactions to philosophic texts, he read grave refutations of the texts and constructed book-battles for his library forays. Having looked at Kant's *Critique of Pure Reason* early in 1845 and probably after hearing Temple's Balliol lectures on Kant, he began at Oriel Herder's *Metacritique* on Kant (1799)—a volume devoted to the gargantuan, somewhat myopic thesis that Kant's book is "Wortspielerei"[36] (word-jugglery). Along with Lucretius and the other ancient atomists, he read Cudworth's attack on the "Atmoic Atheists" —and along with Descartes' *Discourse de la méthode,* Bishop Stillingfleet's demonstration that "Mr. Des Cartes" was not after all "very clear and certain"[37] in his use of terms, a charge Arnold recalled when writing *God and the Bible.* Fascinated by Epicureans and the Stoic school, he considered the attacks on Epicurean and Stoic philosophies in Plutarch's anecdotal *Moralia.*

The synthesizing approach to religions in Bishop Berkeley's *Siris* (which begins with Rhode Island tar-water recipes before tracing the *anima mundi* in trim and lucid prose from ancient times to modern) and the eclectic interest in cosmologies and myths in that book and in the *Moralia* had a salutary effect on him. He must often have considered Plutarch's maxim,

> For nothing that is irrational or fabulous, or springing out of superstition (as some suppose), has been established in the religious rites but what has partly moral and salutary reasons, partly others not devoid of ingenuity in their bearings upon history and physics.[38]

He read Creuzer on ancient myths and symbols, Bunsen on Egyptian history and culture, Berkeley and Plutarch on the Egyptian nature deity Isis—and told Clough facetiously, "The true world for my love to live in is, a general Torpor, with here and there a laughing or a crying Philosopher. And while my misguided Relation [Tom] exchanges the decency God dressed his Features in for the deshabille of an Emotee, we, my love, lovers of one another and fellow worshippers of Isis, . . . will keep pure our Aesthetics."[39]

Tom, who was planning to reform the world along the lines of French socialism, recalls that Matthew seemed lost in a "vast sea of Goethe's art and Spinoza's mysticism."[40] Though misleading,* that comment suggests how little sympathy there was between brothers of the Clougho-Matthean set by about 1846. Goethe, among other factors, infected the set and divided the two Arnolds, for while Tom spoke of political activity, Matthew sought Goethe's detachment and inwardness. "Culture is to be distinguished from practical activity,"[41] that sage once informed Eckermann; and Matthew advised Jane to read Eckermann's *Conversations with Goethe* in the original German for her edification.

Although his "misguided Relation" even talked of revolution, he himself was not immune to a Rugbeian virus. "The strong minded writer" may "lose his self-knowledge," Matthew tells Clough, "and talk of his usefulness and imagine himself a Reformer, instead of an Exhibition."[42] Seeking a spacious, mature outlook that would keep him above the melée, he pursued the concept of the "World-Soul" (the

---

*Spinoza's name does not appear in Arnold's Oriel book lists, and his interest in this philosopher developed later in the decade. Properly speaking, there is perhaps no such thing as "Spinoza's mysticism"; Arnold's desk-notes reveal close attention to, and some disagreement with, Spinoza's "metaphysical formulas" and his subtle and difficult arguments in favor of a panentheistic Deity who may be worshipped.

anima mundi) from Plato down to the modern Germans and later used it metaphorically in "The Youth of Man,"

> *Murmur of living,*
> *Stir of existence,*
> *Soul of the world!*
> *Make, oh, make yourselves felt*
> *To the dying spirit of youth!*[43]

and with more literary tact and with a Wordsworthian echo in "Lines Written in Kensington Gardens" which he sent to his sister Jane in 1849:

> *Be others happy if they can,*
> *But in my helpless cradle I*
> *Was breathed on by the rural Pan.*
>
> . . . . . .
>
> *Calm soul of all things! make it mine*
> *To feel, amid the city's jar,*
> *That there abides a peace of thine,*
> *Man did not make, and cannot mar.*[44]

German philosophers arrested him for their Olympian breadth of view and concern with the inward world of the mind and the outward world of nature. Goethe and Schiller were indeed writers who decisively informed his attitudes to art and poetry, modern society, and the ancient Greeks—for all of Arnold's debt to Newman and to Carlyle (himself an interpreter of Germany).

From Jowett and Stanley at the "Decade," from Hares and Bunsens and the ebullient Crabb Robinson—who once told Mme de Staël how to interpret Kant and Schelling[45]—Arnold had his ears crammed full of German thought. Goethe and Schiller were familiar; Schelling and Hegel he read about now in the *Revue des Deux Mondes,* in a work by Charles de Rémusat, and in the Sorbonne lectures of Victor Cousin. Fortuitously, Goethe warned against the Germans' abstracting genius, since in the *Conversations* he derides his own countrymen as a "strange people" who make life "much more burdensome than is necessary" by their "deep thoughts and ideas." Schelling too, in page after page, assaults "pure reflection"[46] as an activity lethal to the spiritual life.

British philosophers of the eighteen-forties were suspicious of German thought, but family friends and men at Balliol and University College studied in Germany. J. D. Coleridge went over in the summers, and Jowett and Stanley, at Dresden and at Halle, improved themselves by "reading, analysing, and catechizing" Hegel and Kant.[47]

Though not finding clear Gallic logic in German transcendentalism, Victor Cousin and Emile Saisset—among Arnold's French guides —did at least take the Germans seriously. Saisset, in an article which Matthew certainly read in the *Revue des Deux Mondes* of 1846, praises the *"mouvements extraordinaires de l'esprit humain"*[48] to which Kant, Fichte, Schelling, and Hegel contributed.

Yet Matthew Arnold, whose deep affinities were with the Renaissance humanists, was cautious, and indeed he might have found himself at home with cosmopolitan, witty Erasmus or broad-minded More. At the bottom of his heart, he was even enough of a sensible Lockean empiricist to be wary of teutonizing his soul with too many a priori disquisitions; he felt that German systematizers offered no practical help:

> Shakespeare [he notes with condescension because the Germans were forever citing that playwright as an example of genius] suits the immoral-vulgar . . . ; but what does the poet's own conscience say to [Shakespeare] . . . —what would he say at seeing his easy morality erected by Germans and others into a system of life, & a thing to be held in view as an object for inward disciplining of oneself towards. He would say—you fools— . . . you damned pedants.[49]

Again, Arnold scoffs at pedantry, at the Germans' lack of worldliness:

> The Germans are so little in the full stream of life that they have full time to analyse and name all the fillets d'eau that come past them: hence . . . the ridiculous figure they cut. . . . Even in Goethe his language of freedom and head above water feeling in his theatrum mundi at Weimar seems astonishing to people used to think of a little German court as a hen coop.[50]

Clearly, Goethe was an exception to the teutonic pedantry. But how did that once aimless, half-dissolute young "Sparrow of Frankfurt-am-Main"—who had written in bad English a Cloughian poem called "Song over the Unconfidence toward Myself"—manage to become the confident author of *Faust* and *Dichtung und Wahrheit*? For an answer, Arnold looked into Gottfried Herder. Herder formed Goethe's mind at one point and even made him collect folksongs to learn about the origins of poetry. Arnold absorbed Herder's lessons in environmentalism and comparativism partly at second hand—but he would study Herder's *Ideas for the Philosophy of a History of Mankind*,* and he was already reading the *Metacritique* on Kant. Art for Herder is a prime shaper and symbol of cultures. Literatures are to be explored

---

*The *Ideen zur Philosophie der Geschichte der Menschheit* (1784–91), the first history of the world written with attention to man's astronomical, biological, and social conditions. It occurs on Arnold's reading lists for 1866, 1867, 1868, and 1869. At Oriel he probably stopped at the *Metakritik* (1845 Diary), but he took in Herder's ideas from Goethe and from modern commentaries on philosophical idealism and pantheism.

comparatively—as pupils had studied them at Rugby—and not without reference to national characteristics and geographical, social, and biological environments. The best that men have thought from ancient times to the present, according to Herder's idea of Time-Progress (the ineluctable *Zeiten-Fortgang*), remains in the human cultural tradition and is constantly growing and available to the individual. An English critic's later notion of "culture" is obviously indebted to Herder.

Presently Arnold jotted in one diary, "Schelling Bruno," and at the commencement of another diary, "Read or begin 1847 . . . Schelling's Essay on the Plastic."[51]

He may well have been led to Schelling by Coleridge's *Biographia Literaria*. In any case, Schelling's ideas often coincide with Wordsworth's, and a young Wordsworthian read with clear interest the lecture "Concerning the Relation of the Plastic Arts to Nature" (1807). That lecture of Schelling's introduced Arnold to Wincklemann—a modern source of Goethe's reverence for the Greeks and of Arnold's belief in them as models of artistic form and humane endeavor. Schelling elucidated the role of the artist's character and of forms of "firmly grounded beauty"[52] in modifying a very necessary passion in all art. ("We believe in the Universality of Passion as Passion," Matthew wrote to Clough, and later on: "If one loved what was beautiful . . . *passionately* enough, one would produce what was excellent without troubling oneself with religious dogmas. . . . As it is, we are warm only when dealing with these last.")[53] Attacking "shallow moralists" who deny the "positive" in man, Schelling richly appealed to a poet chafing over tight-laced friends, and led the chafing poet to attempt a sonnet on a picture.

Arnold had glimpsed one day an engraving of Cruikshank's picture, "The Bottle," a plea for abstinence. In "To George Cruikshank" he attacks the propagandistic artist with romantic German doctrines; for the "horrific," as Schelling had believed, is in art properly transmuted by the bewitching effects of beauty and charm, and even in the world no "external"[54] power—however malignant or horrific—can touch the soul. Reproaching Cruikshank, Arnold wrote:

> *Artist, whose hand with horror winged, hath torn*
> *From the rank life of towns this leaf! and flung*
> *The prodigy of full-blown crime among*
> *Valleys and men to middle fortune born,*
>
> *Not innocent, indeed, yet not forlorn—*
> *Say, what shall calm us when such guests intrude*
> *Like comets on the heavenly solitude?*
> *Shall breathless glades, cheered by shy Dian's horn,*

Cold-bubbling springs, or caves?—Not so! the soul
Breasts her own griefs; and, urged too fiercely, says:
'Why tremble? True, the nobleness of man

May be by man effaced; man can control
To pain, to death, the bent of his own days.
Know thou the worst! So much, not more, he can.'[55]

Despite the neutrality of its Keatsian imagery, the sonnet is almost as didactic as Cruikshank's engraving, but it marks Matthew's first attempt to counter a deficiency in his training: he had marine pictures on his wall and he had approved the "gigantic statues of Melpomene and Jupiter"[56] at the Louvre, as a fourteen-year old boy, but he was still ignorant of the fine arts.

Neither he nor Arthur Clough would have been what they were but for European idealism and romanticism. If Continental idealists offered no ultimate ideal for life, they suggested that one might be found. As Herder proposed the widest view of human societies, so Goethe proposed the cosmopolitan man of culture and avoidance of fragmentary ideas, and a search for the "whole" or the wide prospect. " 'Not deep the Poet sees, but wide,' " Matthew quoted himself for Clough's benefit, "—think of this as you gaze from the Cumner Hill toward Circencester and Cheltenham."[57] Matthew assiduously looked for panoramic perspectives on society and belief. He was now reading Sismondi's *Études sur les Constitutions des Peuples Libres,* on the broad subject of "public opinion" and comparative systems of government:

> La science sociale se divise en un grand nombre de branches [he read at a college where many of the dons appeared to be unaware of social science]. On peut en effet comprendre sous ce nom, l' éducation, qui forme les hommes pour la société; . . . l'histoire, qui représente, comme dans un grand miroir, aux sociétés à venir, les résultats de toutes les théories, de toutes les expériences des sociétés passées. . . . Une assez grande liberté spéculative régnait en France, pour les livres, dès avant la révolution. Là où Montesquieu, Rousseau, Turgot, Necker, les écono- mistes physiocrates, avaient écrit, on avait pensé sans doute avec profondeur sur l'ordre social.[58]

He put on his book list, "to be read or finisht, Lent Term, 1846," Montesquieu's broad classic of social and philosophical history, *Considérations sur les causes de la grandeur des Romains et de leur décadence* (1734). And in "In Utrumque Paratus," which he wrote at about this time, when he was reading Plotinus, he tried to express in forty-two lines the gist of the idealist and materialist views of man's cosmic setting, and of the origin of all societies.

O waking on a world which thus-wise springs!

—he wrote with aesthetic approval for the Plotinian view of the world as emanation,

> —*O waking on life's stream!*
> *By lonely pureness to the all-pure fount*
> *(Only by this thou canst) the coloured dream*
> *Of life remount!*

If the world emanated from an all-pure "Source of Intellection and of Being," one might through virtuous self-discipline achieve some of that purity oneself, and attain a vaster perspective. "In Utrumque Paratus" neatly balances the materialist or evolutionary view of the world's origin, against the Plotinian view, and subscribes precisely to neither; but Arnold would continue to see the path to *truth* as an ascent to a higher, less obstructed, grander observation point—and to this extent he remained on the side of Plato and Plotinus.[59]

In a cosmopolitan mood, he tackled the *Bhagavad Gita* in Sir Charles Wilkins' translation of 1785 and read it eagerly over the next few years. On the one hand he used Humboldt's German commentary as a guide; on the other, the appreciative comments of Victor Cousin. (To say what God is, Cousin regaled one of those vast tumultuous lecture-classes at the Sorbonne, Krishna *"est bien obligé d'être long, car il est toutes choses."*)[60] The *Bhagavad Gita* influenced Arnold's view of the poet's detachment, gave him material for "Resignation" and "The Scholar Gipsy," and certainly inspired meditations:

> The real central self [he wrote as a Rugbeian on the threshold of the East] is something exquisitely kind, fine tempered, liberal, in good taste, unenvious, comportable in itself.[61]

> The Indians [he told Clough] distinguish between meditation or absorption—and knowledge: and between abandoning practice, and abandoning the fruits of action and all respect thereto. This last is a supreme step, and dilated on throughout the Poem.

Clough was not very strongly attracted to the "Oriental wisdom,"[62] for he was eager to taste the world and not abandon it; and though Matthew would continue to read the *Gita* and other Indian classics, he found no practicable religion in the East. Evidently one does not become a disciple of Krishna overnight: "By meditation and observation we attain a faith," he tells himself in a relevant note, "and strike one day some good strokes in manner & behavior: ha, say we, what a power conviction lends to our practice: the next day the nerves are wrong, the manners full of blunder & despicability, and the conviction, metamorphosed into consciousness, riding us like a nightmare. Nor is it true that after repeated failures we stand." Directly after that he jotted: "—What pure spiritualists, & how unconcerned with cause

& effect, have we been in childhood."[63] His own idea about the "buried life" derives partly from his Oriental readings, but it must also have derived from his sense of disparity between the past and present. In early life, he had thought little, but *felt* much; and perhaps he had felt distinctly and insistently about a very few things, whereas in adulthood he was absorbing so many new viewpoints that he could feel quite overwhelmed: "But so many books thou readest," he wrote later in a manuscript draft for "The Second Best,"

> *such anxious*
> *But so many schemes thou breedest*
>
> *such furious*
> *But so many passions feedest*
>
> *That thy poor head almost turns—*
>
> *And (the world's so madly jangled*
> *Human things so deep entangled*
> *Nature's wish must now be strangled.*[64]

Questioning his own literary talent, he could at times question the wisdom of his own perspicacious German mentors, the value of the literary process, and the worth of striving to express oneself: "Goethe," Matthew observes, "on writing destroying thought—yes—and expression also—In that the two modes are incompatible—a total change takes place in the man passing from one to the other."[65] Again he considers that his guides have succumbed to the vice of too rationally managing themselves, and by implication accuses an age which is too rational and constricting to allow a great poet to breathe: "G[oethe] & S[chiller] in their correspondence & self-management make themselves what their reason prescribes: but for that reason they are not what the great free-operating poets Shakespeare and Moliere are."[66]

Feeling that he was losing his way, but that he had once perceived his "original course," he had an ally in Arthur Clough, who had written in a poem with a Wordsworthian title, " 'Blank Misgivings of a Creature moving about in Worlds not realised',"

> *How often sit I, poring o'er*
> *My strange distorted youth,*
> *Seeking in vain, in all my store,*
> *One feeling based on truth;*
>   · · · · · ·
> *Excitements come, and act and speech*
> *Flow freely forth; —but no,*
> *Nor they, nor ought beside can reach*
> *The buried world below.*
>
> *—Like a child*
> *In some strange garden left awhile alone,*
> *I pace about the pathways of the world.*

A "band of revellers"[67] in the form of joys and hopes and fancies interrupts the sadder part of Clough's litany. Like the phrase "the buried world," the "band of revellers" in " 'Blank Misgivings' " is interesting. Matthew was aware of Clough's phrases when writing later on, his own "Buried Life" and "Strayed Reveller"—but "revelling" had been one of the few ambiguous words in his own father's vocabulary. Dr. Arnold has used "revelling" to mean uproarious, unseemly conduct in the School House; but he also employed that very term when referring to the joys of reading in "Oxford's libraries."[68]

Alternating with Arnold's occasional moods of despair, and underlying those moods, was a sense of well-being. The self-confidence of his fine experiments in poetry and the strenuous efforts of his reading depended to some extent on emotional support he received from Jane and Mrs. Arnold.

Jane, his elder sister and closest friend since childhood, was no longer a worshipful muse with big eyes and a nervous tummy, but a slim, capable woman of twenty-four who had profited from home tutorials and served ably as her father's secretary. Also, she had recovered from a broken engagement to a Rugby master named George Cotton, who loved to dress Walter and Edward in silks and satins for theatricals. The engagement was terminated in 1842; Cotton admitted to having an alcoholic mother, and Jane tried to defend him against her father's fury. The situation produced enough strain and tension perhaps to contribute to Dr. Arnold's last illness. Relationships even in happy Victorian families, such as the Arnolds and Cloughs, were intense.

Brother and sister relationships could be unusually complex. The code prohibiting incest was at least as strong then as today. But the family was less embarrassed by sentiment, and since people did not blindly exalt sexual love, or fear that every kiss implies sexual desire, they permitted more physical contact between brothers and sisters and between heterosexual friends than we do. The family and school were safe, often sheltered arenas for developing the most complex feelings, aching loyalties and deep jealousies, intense arm-in-arm, exquisite, sentimental, clinging friendships. A brother might cradle his sister's head in his arms, or Anne Clough might imply how much she wanted to stroke Arthur's brow, and Matthew might hold his sister Jane in a long embrace—without a qualm. A people admiring sentiment, family loyalty, hugging, and kissing as much as the Victorians did, could explore much of the full range and complexity of human feelings. The difficulty was that although the worship of feeling helped novelists and poets in their art, that worship had its place too seldom before courtship in encounters between *un*related young men and women. One lived and felt *inside* the family—and one might feel most luxuriously and warmly adored by a brother or sister. At the risk of a brief irrelevance, Anne Jemima Clough's feelings for her brother Arthur may illuminate Matthew's deep regard for Jane Arnold. In June 1845, the paths of two brothers and sisters crossed: Arthur brought his sister Anne, who was then twenty-five, up to meet the Arnolds in Westmorland: Matthew was home, and Miss Clough's diary suggests that they made a tour of the estate. Anne notes the "roses and creepers" half burying the glinting, dark-blue façade of Fox How with its rough flat stones of varying sizes, which now and then emit reds and grays and greens. "Bacco's Brook" ran down the edge of a smooth lawn to the Rotha—only a few hundred yards beneath the symmetrical house itself, which is mild and gray from a slight distance. "There is a terrace, and the garden lies below. . . . Mrs. Arnold," as Anne Clough noted, "asked us to stop [for] dinner—They seem very nice friendly people, very sociable & easy to get acquainted with—Matt is very merry & facetious—Tom quiet—Miss [Jane] Arnold rather a decided sort of person—Mary very pleasing and amiable, as also Susan—Fanny a funny merry wild child—"[69]

Rather a decided sort herself, Miss Clough had begun to teach in Liverpool, and she soon launched a new small academy in the village of Ambleside. She became extremely friendly with the Claude girls whom she met in 1845. Eventually in the teeth of male opposition, she founded in 1871 Newnham College at Cambridge as one of the first institutions of higher learning for women and presided effectively as its first principal. In the eighteen-forties she was becoming critical of society, and exploring the meaning of a woman's—and a sister's—love in relation to the norms of the day. In a diary, she considers the possibility of premarital union with a lover, and with candor shows how willing she was to recognize the depth of her feeling for Arthur:

It seems to me that people have yet to learn what real purity is [Anne wrote early in 1849, when she was twenty-nine]. . . . In the still watches of the night or in the early morning he steals upon her unawares—Holy & beautiful doth she ever keep herself for him—The world may be knows but little of their intercourse [.] Why should they? Why cannot all this be a secret and a mystery between the two & the chosen friend of their hearts—This cannot be yet—The bands which hold society together must not be rudely & hastily snapped by individuals unless they are prepared to bear the consequences—which are mostly that they are cast forth & must for the most part cease to be workers. . . . Some of these days perhaps I shall say all of this is nonsense & untrue—but at least I will have recorded that once I did thus dream of Love & that this dream & the hope of keeping myself pure and beautiful for the unknown & imaginary Being has helped me to live—though I wd not say that the Being that has called forth my affections—is imaginary. No, far from it. My brother Arthur has been in a great measure all this to me—I have only wanted the certainty that he really does love me. How my heart has yearned for it. I feel so often I cannot be sure of it because I dont feel worthy of it—And yet last Wednesday when he went away I could believe it—Ah me. May our Almighty Father watch over him for good & the beautiful Angels be on his right hand & on his left.

If I have worshipped the creature too much may God forgive me.[70]

Anne always worshipped Arthur. He was only one year older than she: they were born on January 1, 1819, and January 20, 1820. (Matthew was one year and four months younger than his "K.") Literally in early life she sometimes had idolized Arthur from afar; but she had returned with her mother from South Carolina to the family home in Liverpool and found that the angel who won prizes and defended goalposts at Rugby was a flesh-and-blood mortal, subject to conflicts. She appraised Clough's troubles with his very overbearing tutor, Ward, with Newmanism, and with "German philosophers"—and she watched him suffer after Dr. Arnold's death: "This was to him a terrible affliction; he had ever felt the greatest reverence & affection for him. He came after hearing it as it were in a dream scarcely understanding or realising what had happened."[71] Not to love Arthur Hugh Clough with every fiber of her being would have been impossible—and even unsisterly—and yet her diary suggests that she may intelligently have understood some general causes for her daydreaming, worshipful love. The Victorian ethos exalted the family, and outside the family it tended to keep the sexes apart before marriage, almost ensuring that middle-class brothers and sisters—of about the same ages—might depend excessively upon one another.

Matthew's family relations were blameless, as were Anne Clough's; but he felt at least as intensely about Jane as his best friend's sister did about her brother. He had recited his earliest poems to Jane, had sent her the manuscript of "Shakespeare," would write "Resignation" and "A Question" for her; he shared much of his reading with her, confessed his doubts about his own poetry to her, told her that she was "almost" the only witness he had known ("other than Papa") to the possibility of "that abiding inner life"[72] he felt he needed. Jane in the forties and early fifties was his conscience, one of his main inspirations, probably his most significant critic, his principal confessor, and a woman he loved very profoundly—and loved without the fear that affected his relationship with his mother. Matthew Arnold always proves something about himself for "Mamma"—his diligence, or his manliness in the face of trouble and illness, his resemblance to the paternal ideal, his superiority or essential goodness of spirit and distinction of intellect—but he is candid, intimate, unaffected, modest, and at ease with Jane. "I have just read Goethe to Lavater," he tells her. "[Those letters] belong to his youthful impulsive time, before he had finished building the Chinese Wall round his *inneres*."[73] Matthew's almost gossamer "Chinese Wall" of levity and wit—which protected him even from Clough's grave assaults on religion—never became an obstacle between himself and Jane. A look of sadness, inexplicable to her adopted children, rarely lifted from Jane's face after her marriage to a good-natured and thoughtful politician; but she was a loyal wife and she must have influenced her husband, William Forster, in his work for the Education Act of 1870—the most important education bill of the century—for Forster's work reflects Dr. Arnold's principles relating to the state's involvement in the national life. Jane brightened normally when she referred to Matthew, and mused over him in her old age: "He was indeed a loving and beloved brother, and the days when we used to walk on Loughrigg together —he talking of, and repeating his poetry—and much else, come back."[74]

George Sand differed from "K" in being not only a prolific novelist, but a scandalous Parisienne whose life at the Quai Malaquais was so objectionable it was talked about everywhere. Matthew was to hear from the lips of her baby-faced confidant, Sainte-Beuve, about Alfred de Musset—who wore a maid's skirt to please her, emptied a water-jug on the philosopher Lerminier's head, and wryly versified:

> *George est dans sa chambrette*
> *Entre deux pots de fleurs,*
> *Fumant sa cigarette,*
> *Les yeux baignés de pleurs.*[75]

Even Clough was a little upset by Mme Sand, for though *Jeanne* was the most "cleanly French" novel he had ever read, the novelist's "actual life"[76] told against her. Rereading *Indiana* and *Jacques*, Matthew knew almost by heart the letter in which Indiana accuses her seducer Raymon (and by implication the whole age) of misinterpreting God. He knew the mordant "Sunday-Shoes letter" too, in which the suicidal Jacques damns the complacent, conventional Fernande (and by implication many churchgoers):

Voici la montagne, voici la mer, voici le soleil; le soleil brûle, la mer engloutit, la montagne fatigue. Quelquefois les bêtes sauvages emportent les troupeaux et l'enfant qui les garde: tu vivras au milieu de tout cela comme tu pourras; si tu es sage et brave, on te donnera des souliers pour te parer le dimanche.[77]

Mme Sand's early novels are essays on the post-Enlightenment condition of Western man: institutions such as the church and marriage appear to be moribund as formerly conceived and in need of renewal; society is often superficial, exploitative, and dull; and the most pretentious and foolish are often poetic souls, and lovers: *"Aujourd'hui, pour les âmes poétiques,"* George Sand's Lélia complains pointedly, *"le sentiment de l'adoration entre jusque dans l'amour physique. Etrange erreur d'une génération avide et impuissante!"*[78] One can hardly help but feel that Mme Sand wrote well, that she was generous and self-critical, and that her *affaires*—with few exceptions—have been accorded more significance than they merited. As the half-mystical tomboy Aurore Dupin, she had grown up near La Châtre in Berry, which Matthew Arnold was to visit, a region of holly and broom, small winding rivers and wide horizons. A romantic with medieval aspirations, she went to a Paris school run by English and Irish nuns, who partly account for Ophelias and Sir Ralphs who wander through her novels, and having inherited the estate of Nohant, she married Casimir Dudevant. Country life with a gross squire taught her that marriage was slavery; trial efforts with a pen convinced her that she could write fluently. She divided her life in two, spending half of each year as a bohemian in Paris, entertaining Balzac and contributing to the *Revue des Deux Mondes,* the other half as a provincial bourgeoise with her two children in Berry. In 1846 she was past forty, a restless celebrity with heavy-lidded eyes, an olive complexion, frank and simple mannish manners, and a low voice. Pestered by visitors, she avoided a young man from Paris by asking her plump maidservant, Bertha, to impersonate her at the interview.

Arnold later thought the best elements in her novels were "the cry of agony and revolt, the trust in nature and beauty, the aspiration towards a purged and renewed human society."[79] But she was associated with his youth—or, as he wrote in middle age, with "days of *Valentine,* days of *Lélia,* days never to return! How the sentences from George Sand's works of that period still linger in our memory and haunt the ear with their cadences! Grandiose and moving they come, those cadences, like the sighing of the wind through the forest, like the breaking of the waves on the sea-shore." It was after this recollection, in his essay on "George Sand" of June 1877, that he printed his translation of the final speech of Mme Sand's most formidable heroine:

Yes! yes! [Lélia cries in her cell on the mountain of the Camaldoli] I remember the cavern of truth . . . but I grope in darkness, and my tired arms grasp nothing save delusive shadows. And for ten thousand years, as the sole answer to my cries, as the sole comfort in my agony, I hear astir, over this earth accurst, the despairing sob of impotent agony. [J'entends planer sur cette terre maudite le sanglot désespéré du désir impuissant!][80] For ten thousand years I have cried in infinite space: *Truth! Truth!* For ten thousand years infinite space keeps answering me: *Desire, Desire.* O Sibyl forsaken! O mute Pythia! dash then thy head against the rocks of thy cavern, and mingle thy raging blood with the foam of the sea; for thou deemest thyself to have possessed the almighty Word, and these ten thousand years thou art seeking him in vain.[81]

Lélia was written in 1833, the year in which Sainte-Beuve introduced the novelist to Étienne Pivert de Senancour, who had composed a remarkable psycho-autobiography in the form of letters written by a wanderer in the Bernese Oberland, and entitled it *Obermann.* Significantly, much of Sand's novel is set amid the Italian Alps. Like her other early works, *Lélia* is a serious treatise disguised as a Gothic potboiler. Examining the despair of her soul, with the help of a poetic lover and a worldly confidant, majestic Lélia pricks a number of cultural balloons with tireless gusto and delight. Ascetic retreat is an irrelevance in the modern world; the romantic cult of nature is boring. The church is moribund or crazed. Sensual love is—at last —unsatisfactory as a replacement for religious faith. After much coquetry and several crushing embraces in her alpine chalet, Lélia flings her poet away: "*Laissez-moi, je ne vous aime plus!*"[82] She remains dissatisfied because the world has found nothing to replace a medieval ethos; nothing today appeals satisfactorily to the head as well as the heart; thus—as her poetic lover declares before his suicide —Lélia is reminiscent of Milton's defiant angels and of "*le pâle et ascétique visionnaire*" Prince Hamlet;[83] though of course she is even more reminiscent of Mme Sand. The book's themes appealed to Arnold's darker moods, and surely the gusto and delight of the style especially pleased him.

Intending to see the places in Berry George Sand had made so famous in *Jeanne,* he prepared for a journey to central France in June 1846. Would he understand modern France? Since the quick 1830 Revolution, the monarchy of a good, solid, bourgeois Louis Philippe had contributed to stability in Europe. Outwardly France was sunny, respectable, and dull—indeed, its king had the flair of a bored museum-keeper as he transported the body of the great Napoleon from St. Helena to the Invalides and stuffed Versailles "with pictures of all the battles of French history." His rigged, corrupt Parliament was filled with city entrepreneurs and country bourgeois; only a visitor familiar with French life in 1846, perhaps, might know that the underpaid, badly used working classes of Paris were *not* so cowed and dull as they seemed, might see the National Guard as rebellious and undisciplined, and might hear of mutterings on the left two years before the grand storm of 1848.

Matthew had read about a most enchanting hilltop view in France. First he looked up Toulx Ste. Croix "in Cassini's great map at the Bodleian Library."[84]

He selected his cousin, John Penrose, to accompany him on this trip to a fine hilltop vista. He left England with "J.P." in June; they entrained for a pleasantly warm Paris and then for a hot, airless, clammy Orléans, and took to rickety diligences when the railway tracks ended south of Orléans at Vierzon. On July 1, Matthew stood on the ramparts of medieval Toulx and surveyed, under a darkening horizon, as much of the earth as he had ever seen from Fairfield's high, rubblestrewn peak in the Lake District; one suspects he watched until the sky was black: "I stood at sunset on the platform of Toulx Ste. Croix, by the scrawled and almost effaced stone lions,—a relic, it is said, of the English rule,—and gazed on the blue mountains of Auvergne filling the distance, and southeastward of them, in a still farther and fainter distance, on what seemed to be the mountains over Le Puy and the high valley of the Loire."[85]

> *And faint the city gleams. . . .*
> · · · · · ·
> *The solemn peaks but to the stars are known,*
> *But to the stars, and the cold lunar beams.*[86]

An ascent to lookout point was a spiritual event for Matthew; and he needed this overview of George Sand's territory in order to bolster his confidence, for the day before, at Boussac, he had done an extraordinary thing. He was merely an unknown Englishman of twenty-three on holiday from the musty halls and bookstacks of Oxford; but he had sent to Mme Sand, with the plain intention of calling at her home, a letter conveying in "bad French," the "homage of a youthful and enthusiastic foreigner who had read her works with delight."[87]

He had no way of knowing whether she would reply, and the next few days he did some sightseeing. Having seen the problematical Druid stones of the *Pierres Jaumâtres*—which are near Toulx and are celebrated in Mme Sand's *Jeanne*—he went on with J.P. to visit Montluçon in the Bourbonnais, Clermont-Ferrand with its black cathedral, Mont Dore and the extensive view of the volcanic massif, and nearby Lac Guéris not far from basalt cliffs. On July 7 "J.P. left"[88] —either to return to Paris or to see the fashionable resort of Vichy with its new thermal establishment—and Matthew wandered about, redundantly seeing a few sights he had seen earlier in the month, but when he returned to Boussac a letter awaited him. Then at Nohant, with her children as well as her lover, Frédéric Chopin, who appeared to be dying, Mme Sand instructed him to call on July 14, 1846. He duly reached a handsome simple house not far from La Châtre at about midday and found "a large party assembled" at breakfast, which was not yet over. "I entered with some trepidation, as well I might, considering how I got there." Dressed in something that might pass for a Scottish outdoor costume and thankfully "not in man's clothes" as he remembered thirty years later, Sand put him at ease. She introduced him to her children and to the pale, thin, black-haired Chopin "with his wonderful eyes." Then she poured out *boisson fade et mélancolique* "for which English people are thought abroad always to be thirsting, —tea." Having discoursed of the local country, the peasantry and their mode of life, and of "Switzerland" and perhaps interestingly of Senancour,

> she touched politely, by a few questions and remarks upon England and things and persons English,—upon Oxford and Cambridge, Byron, Bulwer. As she spoke, her eyes, head, bearing, were all of them striking; but the main impression she made was . . . of *simplicity,* frank, cordial simplicity. After breakfast she led the way into the garden, asked me a few kind questions about myself and my plans, gathered a flower or two and gave them to me, shook hands heartily at the gate, and I saw her no more.[89]

Neither Sand nor Arnold is known to have recalled the conversation in further detail. Her Stenio in *Lélia* compares the heroine of that book with Milton's angels, and Mme Sand remembered Arnold flatteringly as "un Milton jeune et voyageant."[90] Perhaps she only meant that he was a handsome young English poet on his travels. His impression of her is more significant. Thrice, underlining the word, he recalled with still-remembered surprise her "simplicity." One remembers that Mrs. Arnold had been struck with that quality in Wordsworth,[91] though she had expected, before meeting that poet, to find him febrile and affected. Neither of Matthew's parents had any deep faith in the literary personaltiy; and their suspicion about the bohemian, complicated, eccentric, and careless morals of artists was shared by their son. In these years, Matthew appeared to be a harmless and aesthetically inclined dandy, with a touch of the fop that Crabb Robinson noticed, but he was in reality a complex bundle. The lyricist in him struggled elegantly with the moralist; the intellectual and critical parts of his brain responded with delight to his reading—but the amoral and emotional, creative and imaginative parts responded more often with protest. He was rational and intuitive by turns, and thus he especially prized his desk-notes, which altogether express many combinations and blends of "Arnolds." He told "K" significantly that his poems were only "fragments."[92] At times, certainly, his intellect good-naturedly and eloquently wrote in defense of his precious intuition:

> We have a fugitive delicate sense [he inscribed at a book-crammed table] thro: which we know all Things, & which needs only the slightest store of facts, etc: but this delicate sense is not in our power and while it slumbers we load the more mechanical sense with occupation but can never feel right in the centre of things.[93]

Unfortunately sightseeing is costly, and Matthew apparently taught at Tait's Rugby again to replenish his pocketbook in the autumn of 1846. One old friend—Shairp—wondered if he would ever leave the place: "Is Mat's employment in that capacity to be permanent?" he asked Clough in September.[94] Having stayed at the school from September 3 to the middle of October, Matthew made up for the drudgery by spending all of 1567 francs (about £62) in France again and indeed by having the time of his life in the theatrical capital of the world, in December 1846 and in January and February 1847 —altogether for six weeks. He said later that he simply "followed" the low-voiced Rachel, the tragedienne of the Théâtre Français, straight over to Paris in the holidays.[95]

Thousands of Englishmen and Frenchmen were enamored of Rachel. "She gesticulates little," wrote a critic, "and the distinguishing characteristic of her manner is calm determined self-possession."[96] Matthew projected his feeling for Mrs. Arnold and "K," to a certain extent, on two living French heroines. "What do you think of Rachel," he wrote to Clough, "—greater in what she is than in her creativity, eh?"[97] He had just filled his eyes and mind with George Sand; and he followed Rachel clearly for what she *was*.

Having boarded an early Folkestone boat, Matthew was in the French capital by December 29. The city was then in its glittering winter dress. Rachel and Rose Chéri and "Mademoiselle Nathalie" were saving the classical French drama from aridity and the avenues were jammed. Ladies and gentlemen night after night flocked to the Théâtre St. Antoine and the Théâtre Français, the Palais and the Odéon and the Variétés; and in fact an Oriel Fellow, dressed up "as the angel Gabriel,"[98] sat among them with his stick and monocle, no doubt applauding with discrimination. He observed the calm, self-possessed manner of Rachel and heard her deep sonorous voice ten times that winter. On his return from Nohant, he had seen her play twice in

London—first as Hermoine in Racine's *Andromaque*, at St. James's Theatre on July 20, 1846, and two days later at a command performance of Racine's most famous play, *Phèdre*, in the presence of the Queen and Prince Albert. In Paris, he heard and saw her depict, in the admiring words of Fanny Kemble, "the passions in the delineation of which she excels—scorn, hatred, revenge, vitriolic irony, seething jealousy, and a fierce love," as befitted the heroines of *Phèdre* and *Andromaque* (which he saw twice more) and other heroines in Corneille's *Cinna, Horace,* and *Polyeucte*.[99] She represented for him that profound emotional force and inward concentration he desired. In three retrospective sonnets to Rachel, written some years later, after her death at thirty-six, he recalled her as a radiant artist who triumphed over the conflicting cultural and spiritual forces of the entire Western heritage:

> *Sprung from the blood of Israel's scattered race,*
> *At a mean inn in German Aarau born,*

he declared in "Rachel III," with its curiously effective jolting lines and harsh rhythms,

> *To forms from antique Greece and Rome uptorn,*
> *Tricked out with a Parisian speech and face,*
>
> *Imparting life renewed, old classic grace;*
> *Then, soothing with thy Christian strain forlorn,*
> *A-Kempis! her departing soul outworn,*
> *While by her bedside Hebrew rites have place—*
>
> *Ah, not the radiant spirit of Greece alone*
> *She had—one power, which made her breast its home!*
> *In her, like us, there clashed, contending powers,*
>
> *Germany, France, Christ, Moses, Athens, Rome.*
> *The strife, the mixture in her soul, are ours;*
> *Her genius and her glory are her own.*[100]

"Rachel III" helps to explain why he later respected Lady de Rothschild, while flirting lightly with her. What Arnold would call the Hebraic and Hellenistic elements in Western culture are indicated in the sonnet: the most jolting line in the final tercet clashes within itself: for he himself was attracted to German ideas and French style and grace, to Christian emotion and Hebraic morality, Athenian beauty of form and Roman solidity and enterprise. He would find—in aspects of the large Western tradition—capacious mirrors and symbols of ingredients in the unique "mixture" of his own character.

In this bright entrancing winter, he made the most of Paris; he went to Embassy and Opera balls, dined alone and in company in sumptuous elegance, and ate so many bonbons apparently that he became ill on two occasions. He paid a call on Lady Elgin, and on the historian Michelet, who received him with especial warmth—for the historian was an admirer of the "travaux de mon pére" as Matthew later put it.[101] No doubt he was helped, too, by an introduction to Michelet furnished by Philarète Chasles, who had published new data in the *Revue des Deux Mondes* of 1846 concerning the life of Oliver Cromwell, and who had been a confidant of the Italian sentimentalist, Foscolo, author of *Letters of Ortis*. To put himself on better terms with the few notables he met, he brushed up his French with a series of lessons, and to understand what he heard in the music halls—and to enjoy irresistible cadences—he bought a copy of the *Chansons* of Béranger, who had tweaked the noses of the wealthy in Paris and made even Goethe laugh. "Take up Béranger," Goethe had announced to the adoring Eckermann,

> He has never been to a classical school or university; and yet his songs are so full of mature cultivation, so full of wit and the most refined irony, and there is such artistic perfection and masterly handling of the language, that he is the admiration, not only of France, but of all Europe.
>
> But imagine this same Béranger—instead of being born in Paris and brought up in this metropolis of the world—the son of a poor tailor in Jena or Weimar . . . and ask yourself what fruit would have been produced by this same tree grown in such a soil and in such an atmosphere.
>
> So I repeat: if a talent is to be speedily and happily developed, the great point is that a great deal of intellect and sound culture should be current in a nation.[102]

In Goethe's remarks in the *Conversations*, Arnold found a shrewd defense of culture, and many hints for the aspiring poet; in quieter moments in Paris he must have thought often of that theater-loving sage. Almost tunefully, the "Angel Gabriel" at last returned to England, reaching the monastic Oriel quadrangle on February 13, 1847.

Though enchanted to see him, Clough was astonished by his dress and deportment—let alone his voice and hair: "Matt is full of Parisianism; Theatres in general, & Rachel in particular," he reported to Campbell Shairp, who wore a bright plaid and kept an enormous hound. "He enters the room with a chanson of Béranger on his lips—for the sake of French words almost conscious of tune: his carriage shows him in fancy parading the rue de Rivoli;—& his hair is guiltless of English scissors; he breakfasts at 12, & never dines in Hall, & in the week . . . he has been to Chapel *once*."

Clough was unshocked, and exaggerated a little for the flamboyant

Shairp—while writing to his sister Anne that his friend was full of the "things of Paris—specially the theaters."[103]

Matthew knew, however, that his mother was worried. To her he seemed aimless, frivolous, and full of *Wanderlust*. As Clough put it in April, "his Mother was very anxious he should have something regular in the way of employment."[104] Months after he found employment, Mrs. Arnold fretted over every male Arnold with the exception of Walter—"so great a safety does there seem in his being so early placed under the salutary discipline of district duty."[105] (Walter, as a young midshipman, was so lonely he wrote home often.) There is some evidence she went so far as to set wheels turning: she may have thought of her late husband's magnificent Whig friends and pulled strings. Possibly she wrote to Lord Lansdowne, even when his own Whig party was out of office, about one of the new school inspector-ships for Matthew in connection with the government's Committee of the Privy Council on Education. It is certain that someone was in touch with the government's education committee on behalf of the Arnolds when its Lord President was the Duke of Buccleuch, in the last months of Peel's Conservative regime in 1846. Bureaucratic wheels were grinding and yet, as Matthew wouldn't become a school inspector until 1851, his confidant's report of the matter was propheti-cally correct: "Matt's inspectorship will not be decided for an age," Clough wrote to his sister at Liverpool on May 3, 1846.[106]

In accord with the tidal laws of politics, Whigs flooded back into office two months after Clough's report about the inspectorship. The energetic and diminutive Lord John Russell—who admired Dr. Arnold even while the Headmaster was alive—suddenly became Prime Minister. Benign faces sat around Russell's table. Lord Lansdowne himself was now Lord President of the Privy Council and head of the Committee of the Council on Education. Unable to offer an inspector-ship, but requiring a private secretary, he occasioned an entry in Arnold's diary of April 1847:

See to Ld Lansdowne.[107]

In April, Matthew must have considered very widely. He had been reading Lucretius, and he may have mingled ideas about the modern theater with some ideas about the *De Rerum Natura* and Lucretius himself. He would plan to interpret the modern world in the light of an ancient one, and this implied knowledge of the modern world. He was tensely ambitious, eager to observe from a vantage point and disin-clined to give up books, whatever anguish they might cause, and he clearly meant to bring his own poetry to a level of daring magnificence. After visiting London, he spent more than a week at Fox How, where he made ample opportunity to confer with his mother. Then he scurried back to Oxford. "Matt . . . suddenly appeared," noted Clough, who was beginning to lose track of his comings and goings. Many Oxford Fellows appeared to be almost stationary. "He is going away on Tuesday to London," Clough told Anne Jemima, "where he will probably now reside for some time, as he is to be Secretary to Lord Lansdowne, the President of the Council." His mother up at Fox How was foolhardy to sanction just that metropolitan employment: "Quite a mistake, I think," Clough wrote, perhaps thinking of the aristocrats and heavy carpets at Lansdowne House, ". . . but Matt does not seem to dislike the prospect, though he has no intention of making this his permanent line." Of course his departure from the college would create an unpleasant void, but, Clough wrote thoughtfully in a bookish chamber, "I did not expect him to stay here long."[108]

6

DISCOVERIES IN LONDON
1847–1848

Every man buried despondingly in his hands
His burning brow,
Even as I do.

—*Matthew Arnold,
in a discarded poem*

I T was not through a close, detailed consideration of his family
relationships that Matthew Arnold achieved insights into his own
nature. He feared probing into complex loyalties and cited Goethe's
theory of the demonic partly as an excuse for avoiding deep self-
analysis. Yet he needed a deeper understanding of himself. He found
his writing painfully slow and difficult, and wrote gloomy memoranda
to himself:

> Thou thyself . . . art perhaps to be one of those characters thou hast
> come across in thy reading, who *fail*.

> Thou beholdest George Sand, Musset, Bulwer, Jacobi, &c, and wishest
> to get out and uttered like them, even like most of them in a false
> strain—but never—

> Meeting a cockney on a Greenwich steamer, instead of laughing,
> say—does this gay unled varmint thing *succeed* with his accoutrements
> better than I do, or worse—

> The truth we saw intuitively we deal with mechanically—the work we
> conceived vitally we too often execute deadly. triste race humaine.[1]

The demon of creativity was strange: a writer might become "three-
parts iced over" and a man "might write a book through whose head all
manner of fruitful thoughts have passed: & yet the daemon shall not
allow him to put more than one of them into it."[2] His *Lucretius: A
Tragedy** soon lay on his table as so many disconnected, marbly

---

*The working title of his unfinished play. (Arnold in a motto for "Thyrsis" in 1867
called it "*Lucretius,* an unpublished Tragedy" to assert prior claim to the poetic subject
before Tennyson's "Lucretius" was printed in May 1868.)

chunks and scraps of verse. In one of his drafts for that play, he wrote
with Shelleyan vision and hope:

> *The Spirit of Man*
> *Moving over the face of the wide world,*
> *Free, disengaged, beholding from a height,*
> *Not hoodwinked in a dungeon—in one word*
> *Active and glad, not suffering and cast-down,*
> *Fills us with joy to see its power. . . .*
> *We too lay hold on all things with our mind,*
> *Not with our body; pain, therefore, and fear,*
> *Which are the body's part, have passed away.*[3]

But how much could one mentally grasp? The *modern mind* was a
problem. Having ransacked a library between whist games at Oriel, he
surely had found too much information and too many truths. "Had
Shakespeare and Milton lived in the atmosphere of modern feeling,
had they the multitude of new thoughts and feelings to deal with a
modern has," he informed Clough, they might have written more
simply. Or would they have written at all?—"the poet's matter being
the hitherto experience of the world, and his own, increases with every
century." What harm John Keats has done, with his sensuousness and
confusion. What a failure is Robert Browning, who obtains in his
poetry nothing but a "confused multitudinousness." One must begin,
Arnold solemnly advises Clough, "with an Idea of the world in order
not to be prevailed over by the world's multitudinousness . . . or at
least with isolated ideas."[4] But still, he wasn't certain that he had any
prevailing world view. He needed the distractions of a European
revolution, a Swiss journey, and a love affair in order to come to a
better understanding of himself; and an important part of his
education began in London.

In the spring of 1847, a poet of twenty-four went to work in a
beautiful building occupying all one side of Berkeley Square. He
would have attracted little notice on this first day of work. His wavy,
blackish-brown hair was brushed, combed, and no more than lightly
scented; he wore the smartest, most diplomatic black trousers and
jacket he could afford. He was to sit alone in an upstairs secretarial
room—undisturbed at a heavy teak desk—on weekdays for six hours
daily, and might read or write or gaze or twiddle. He must be available
for composing a few letters from drafts on personal matters, foreign
topics, or minor affairs of state for the Lord President of the
government, Lord Lansdowne, whose other secretary handled most
correspondence. Matthew might be required, too, to appear at
receptions, or at one of his employer's outlying estates. Lansdowne

House at Berkeley Square was set back from the street by a row of lilacs, a lawn dotted with crocuses in the spring, and a wide gravel forecourt. Carriages rolled up a drive by day and night—sometimes conveying important diplomats and visiting royalty to Lansdowne's entertainments.[5]

Along with Holland House at the west end of Kensington Gardens, this "backstanding lordly mansion" was a meeting place for Whig cabinet ministers, who came to discuss the fiscal crises and parliamentary strategy. In the curving gravel drive, they disembarked with brisk, socially polished young assistants. Young noblemen went into the government these days often through two narrow illuminated tunnels[6]—the celebrated "Eton and Christ Church, Oxford" route and the "Harrow and Trinity College, Cambridge" one—and more and more gentlemen entered government service, too. A professional class was rising in the ministries, but the aristocracy was still the hereditary ruling class. With parties in the House of Commons split three or four ways, the Prime Minister had to endure a squabbling, uproarious coalition. (The election of 1847 kept Lord Russell in the premiership while making his position in the Commons even worse, so that at times he despaired of leading the Whigs.) But noblemen in the cabinet guided a rich, energetic, and optimistic industrial kingdom, in which a million citizens were starving to death and half of the female population happened to be illiterate.

In a modestly opulent sitting room, furnished with a Rembrandt self-portrait and Sir Joshua Reynolds's painting of Lady Ilchester, the President of the Whig cabinet was relaxed and charming. Even the opposition liked Henry Petty-Fitzmaurice, the third Marquess of Lansdowne. At sixty-seven, he was well-preserved with a bald dome, heavy-lidded eyes, and a wide mouth. During and after the revolutions of 1848, he appraised France with typical mildness and good nature: "I wish the French," he told Lady Ashburton, "could produce something more useful to themselves though less amusing to others than the 'mobs' with which they contrive to season all their calamities."[7] With his confidential secretaries, he was anecdotal and delightful. Since he had a "person" to look after bills and letters he wouldn't "interfere often" with a private secretary's "time and occupations," although he might request "foreign letters, literary information, etc." Speaking in broken sentences, he could "scarcely state" what he really wished; but perhaps an observant employee "should find it out in the course of time." After a few hesitations, he probably told Arnold that he was glad to "enable" a confidential secretary "to be in Town and attend to [his] literary pursuits."[8]

As the "Nestor of the Whigs" and a patron of the arts, Lansdowne had turned his handsome Bowood estate in Wiltshire into an "abode of hospitality" for politicians and poets. Moore and Rogers once debated there as to whether their excellent host or another lord was "the more aristocratic in his habit of feeling." French *aperçu* and charming stories made the Marquess especially agreeable. He had derived wisdom from listening to Edmund Burke address Parliament—and some wisdom, too, in the past, from attractive Continental ladies. In youth, he had known the "famous beauty Mme. Taille." Once she observed that he was looking at her and said, *"Vous croyez que je rougis, je vous prouverai le contraire!"*—"and she rang for a basin of water and a towel and washed herself" before his astonished eyes! (Arnold heard that story at least once in 1847: "Had I the skill I had e'er Rudge flitted wormwards," he wrote to a fellow poet, "I would limn Bathsheba washing herself—bring up my gold in the paniers of an ass.")[9]

Arnold certainly heard one disconcerting note this year at Berkeley Square. Alluding to the Irish famine, Lansdowne said he expected "1,000,000 of persons would die before it was over."[10] The newspapers did not overlook the agony in Ireland; and it was common knowledge that Irish estate-owners wanted the government to reduce its famine-relief scheme and let the charitable societies feed the hungry. As a fiscal conservative and Irish estate-owner, Lansdowne adhered to the laissez faire principles of the *Wealth of Nations*. He believed in the efficacy of charity and his views weighed heavily in the cabinet. Long before, he had delivered a maiden speech on Ireland and served as a Chancellor of the Exchequer; he managed the Lansdowne properties (121,000 acres) in the Irish provinces creditably well. The Prime Minister "trimmed his Irish policy" to accommodate the views of Lansdowne and Palmerston in the cabinet. Relief was sharply curtailed—and a million citizens perished from hunger and related causes during the first twenty-four months of the Whig administration (up to July 1848).[11]

That Matthew Arnold was alarmed by an employer who *predicted* new famine horrors while recommending little to avert them seems clear: he repeated Lansdowne's prediction, up at Oxford, to Benjamin Jowett—who was scandalized. With "an income in this country of £300,000,000," the government might *avert* starvation, the Balliol don considered.[12] Matthew even wrote an angry, confused poem called "Horatian Echo," which certainly alludes to the Whig government in 1847:

> Mourn will we not your closing hour,
> Ye imbeciles in present power,
>   Doomed, pompous, and absurd!

And let us bear, that they debate
Of all the engine-work of state,
Of commerce, laws, and policy,
The secrets of the world's machine,
And what the rights of man may mean,
With readier tongue than we.

Only, that with no finer art
They cloak the troubles of the heart
With pleasant smile, let us take care.[13]

In mid-stanza he drops politics in order to explore the "dewy rose" of Eugenia's hair, and remind an Ambitious Friend of human mortality. But again, evidence of his revulsion over politics and feeling for Ireland appears in a letter of the following year, by which time the Irish provinces were on the verge of open rebellion and falling under the influence of the "Young Ireland" party of Smith O'Brien and Thomas Meagher. "And the newspapers—my God!" Matthew wrote to Arthur Clough.

> —But they and the H. of C. represent England at the present moment very fairly.
> I cannot believe that the mass of people here would see much bloodshed in Ireland without asking themselves what they were shedding it to *uphold*. And when the answer came—1. a chimerical Theory about some possible dangerous foreign alliances with independent Ireland: 2. a body of Saxon landlords—3. a Saxon Ch [urch] Estab [lishment] their consciences might smite them.[14]

With its enumerated points, this letter resembles an outline for a political pamphlet. But what young poet exists to write essays? Arnold in fact states in "Horatian Echo" (just before damning the Whigs) that politics is "no concern of ours."

"The Irish article is not to my taste," he further told Clough. Still, he adjusted with great care to his "hoary" employer,[15] and probably separated Lansdowne's charming personality from Lansdowne's adherence to Adam Smith's *Wealth of Nations*. Contriving to find in him an open mind, he later forgave the Marquess for supporting the money-saving and inhibiting "Revised Code" in education—while fighting against that code himself, tooth and nail.

Trying to neglect politics, Matthew experienced in London a deep tension, evident in many desk-notes. His father might have addressed a scorching pamphlet to the government, and his own college friends derided the ministries. The agonizing problem he faced was that of determining exactly what his own commitments and nature might be.

And we have been on many thousand lines,
And we have shown, on each, spirit and power;

> *But hardly have we, for one little hour,*
> *Been on our own line, have we been ourselves.*[16]

That problem became more exacerbated and strangely complicated.

Living in rooms at 101 Mount Street over the seamstress shop of a Mrs. Boag, he headed letters, "Boag's Baby-linen Warehouse, Mountstreet."[17] He dined with merry old college friends who were beginning professional careers: there was John Blackett, who wrote for the Whig *Globe* and who talked about the ministries. He later visited Blackett's sister Fanny in Paris after she became the attractive Mme Du Quaire. "Blackett wants me to pass the Nativity of our B.L. with him and his sister at Brighton," he told Clough this year. "But I am not earnestly bent on this. You talked of coming here."[18] He missed Clough; but he saw something of the wise Benjamin Brodie, a co-founder of the "Decade" who was lecturing on chemistry at the Royal Institution and courting the daughter of a Belgravia barrister.

In the summer he went up to Calder Park in Scotland to be with Theodore Walrond, that "feeling" man who had been so essential in the Clougho-Matthean set, and then he returned to Fox How. He seems calmly to have prepared himself for a shock that he knew was coming and for an intensification of his problems; and in the autumn he found comfort in a timeless sanctuary at Lansdowne House. He bought "Arts Books" in 1847 and he must have found the long front and main drawing rooms at his place of employment quiet in the mornings. From the walls, peasant girls and other women by Cuyp, Rembrandt, Guercino, Velázquez, and Gainsborough looked warmly down at the beholder. Upon pedestals or in niches, marble statues appeared: the Marquess told a secretary that they had been "dug up" at Hadrian's Villa. On exhibit were a Bacchus and a Juno Enthroned, an anonymous and rather smooth-featured emperor, a Jason untying his sandals, and a commanding and excellent *Marcus Aurelius as Mars.*[19]

Aloft in a secretarial chamber, Matthew almost dispensed with time. Here there was a musical clock. In one of his letters, he manages to jot down some softened reminders of his own childhood, his schooldays, and his college reading of George Sand, though he records little but what he sees and hears at the moment:

Here I sit [he wrote to Tom Arnold]; opposite a marble group of Romulus and Remus and the wolf; the two children fighting like mad, and the limp-uddered she-wolf affectionately snarling at the little demons struggling on her back. Above it is a great picture, Rembrandt's Jewish Exiles, which would do for Consuelo and Albert resting in one of their wanderings, worn out upon a wild stony heath sloping to the Baltic—she leaning over her two children who sleep in their torn rags at her feet. Behind me a most musical clock. . . . On my left two great windows looking out on the court in front of the house, through one of which, slightly opened, comes in gushes . . . soft damp breath. . . . The green lawn which occupies nearly half the court is studded over with crocuses of all colours—growing out of the grass, for there are no flower beds; delightful for the large still-faced white-robed babies whom their nurses carry up and down on the gravel court where it skirts the green. And from the square and the neighbouring streets, through the open door whereat the civil porter moves to and fro, come the sounds of vehicles and men, in all graduations, some from near and some from far, but mellowed by the time they reach this backstanding lordly mansion.[20]

In the heart of a ministerial building where parliamentary strategy is planned lies the citadel of art—in a chamber where time is told on a chiming clock and street noises from below are mellowed. When he wrote this letter, his brother Tom was far away. Probably Tom would enjoy the allusion to two brothers "fighting like mad" and would recall their father's treatment of Romulus and Remus in the *History of Rome*. In his own copy of that text, a few pages after the inked inscription ("M. Arnold—From his affectionate Father & Mother"), Matthew had read often how "Numitor was made king, and owned Romulus and Remus to be born of his own blood. The two brothers . . . loved rather the hill on the banks of the Tiber. . . . so they said, that they would build a city there; and they inquired of the gods by augury, to know which of them should give his name to the city."[21]

Though Tom Arnold had spoken recently of founding a whole new society, even a Coleridgean pantisocracy out among the Antipodean sheep, the young man had deepened. He had left Oxford with a first-class degree, studied law at Lincoln's Inn, suffered a terrible rejection in love by Henrietta Whately, and apparently settled down as a précis-writer in the Colonial Office under Lord Grey. Two Arnolds worked for the government in 1847. Baron Bunsen heard from Lord Grey at the Queen's soirée in the spring that Tom was doing very well, and Lord Lansdowne stepped over and announced to Bunsen in a beneficent tone: "And the eldest is with me as private Secretary, and does very well." ("I was glad to hear this, to me new, piece of intelligence," Bunsen wrote to Mrs. Arnold, "for a confidential place like that of private Secretary to Lord L. is exactly the place where a young man . . . finds that sort of steady intellectual employment, which I always thought so particularly desirable for your eldest Son.")[22] But Tom Arnold was furious over social poverty and inequality. When dining with the old Clougho-Matthean set, who sometimes still convened when Clough came to town, Tom played the role of the Rugbeian reformer very zestfully. He played it so well that Matthew

Arnold felt free to function as an "Exhibition." The two brothers complemented each other, Tom behaving as Matthew's alter ego. With Tom on hand, Matthew often delightfully threw every moral question to the winds. Once, the "set" dined out at Verrey's in Regent's Street. Matthew waxed eloquent over a work of Voltaire's, until Arthur Clough blurted out that the book was "licentious."

Matthew waved his hand as if to intimate that such a matter "had very little weight" with him.

"Well," Clough retorted, "you don't think any the better of yourself for that, do you?"[23]

Again, Tom praised Jenny Lind's "supersensual" singing and Matthew wryly pointed out to Clough that the Glorious Swede was not entirely beautiful because she had an "enormous obverse."[24] Tom's earnest language had its counterpoint in Matthew's "Shite's" and "s—s"; and Matthew's reaction to George Sand, so far, had been mainly aesthetic because Tom had taken her social message so deeply to heart. "We cannot accept the present," Tom had written gravely in April 1847, "and we shall not live to see the future. It is an age of transition; in which the mass are carried hither and thither by chimeras of different kinds, while to the few, who . . . have caught a glimpse of the sublime but distant future, is left nothing but sadness and isolation. . . . I shall remain here so long as I think honour and duty require . . . and then I shall go to New Zealand."[25]

Matthew "did not . . . care," Tom wrote later, "about reforming the world or any part of it."[26] Quite naturally, Tom found Clough more sympathetic. Yet even with the benefit of Clough's advice, Tom wavered over his New Zealand plans until an interview with James Stephen, the Permanent Under-Secretary of State for the Colonies, made up his mind for him. Stephen (Leslie Stephen's father) told him to resign from the Colonial Office at once, and emigrate. "This is so sudden," Tom wrote in October, "that I have not yet had time to think what I shall do."[27]

It turned out that the *John Wickliffe* was leaving for New Zealand the next month. Hearing that his brother would sail, Matthew escaped his presence and spent almost a fortnight at Oxford. "Matt has been up here," Clough wrote to Shairp on November 1. "His language has been as loose as ever, but I think on the whole he has behaved pretty well."

Fortified by Walrond and Clough, Matthew then returned to London to face the excruciating ordeal of seeing Tom depart. The New Zealand settler moved into the Mount Street rooms and packed up a forest of parting gifts for the long voyage. William Lake brought along an iron bedstead, Clough presented a copy of Spinoza, and Matthew some pots of marmalade from Fortnum and Masons. Late in November, a few companions stood on a windswept pier at Gravesend to see Tom off. "It was very cold," Edward Arnold recalled, "yet it was a brilliant sunset, and the river, with all its shipping is always beautiful." Tom bade adieux without difficulty, and then turned at last to the brother whom he called "the Emperor." "What he felt most, I think, was the parting with Matt. I saw the tears in his eyes when it came to that."[28]

His brother's departure affected Matthew's life. Always critical of Tom, he wrote to his mother that Clough was "Tom's superior" by far, and later on when the brother married overseas, Matthew declared to Jane: "What his relations with his wife are does not exactly come out. . . . I dare say there is no very deep-reaching sympathy between them."[29] Yet he missed Tom as a part of himself. That guileless, stammering, enthusiastic young man had been an émotif and a reformer, whereas he himself wished to be a coolly detached "Exhibition"; but reformers and Exhibitions were deeply mixed in Matthew Arnold's nature, and after Tom left, he began to quarrel with Clough and to fret with himself.

His tensions were increased by a sense of time passing, by the breaking up of that solid establishment the Arnold family, and even by a grave warning. Consulting a doctor, Matthew was blandly told in 1847 or 1848 that he had inherited his father's heart defect.

Three of his four brothers flung themselves out to the ends of the earth. The comical, low-pulsed and sluggish "Didu" or Edward was now in his last year at Balliol and thinking of taking holy orders; some of the tutors and fellows at Oxford were dull or sleepy enough for him; he was to be a Fellow of All Souls' and later, despite his lackadaisical temperament, a school inspector. Walter, the youngest brother, was already at sea as a "Boy" sailor. He was just twelve. He felt cruelly depressed because he was lost in an enormous ship and his squadron lingered in tatty, woebegone domestic and foreign ports. (Rum, prostitutes, and the language of his comrades disheartened Walter as much as "evil" ways of the sweaty, sunburned soldiers in India were to shock Willy.) Willy, who was thin and eager with dark fluffily piled-up hair and blue eyes, had got into trouble as a Christ Church student and faced Oxford's "penalties," and then, just when hungering for great actions and feeling that his soul was in danger, he enlisted as an ensign in the East India Company's Bengal Army. This frightened even Mrs. Arnold, since Willy was only nineteen and knew nothing about armies and nothing about defending himself—and had left the university without a degree. Willy looked boyish in his ensign's uniform with its stiffly flapping epaulettes over his narrow shoulders, its choked tunic collar, its brass buttons and sword, but he was intent on India. Before going out, he went to live with his older brother in London. The difference between his nineteen years and Matthew's sophisticated, worldly behavior at twenty-four seemed astronomical, at least to Willy. "Dear old Matt," Willy later wrote of the final month he spent in the Mount Street rooms before sailing for India, "I saw so much of him . . . there was the most entire absence of elder-brotherism on his part . . . yet our intercourse was that of man and boy; and though the difference of years was not so formidable as between 'Matthew' and Wordsworth, yet we were less than they a 'pair of Friends,' though a pair of very loving brothers."[30]

Matthew had no desire to open up mentally with Willy, but he was very solicitous about his younger sister Mary, who in April had married an assistant physician named Aldred Twining and moved to 9 Gloucester Road in London. Aldred Twining was a gaunt, pale man of about thirty with a stammer, and soon after his marriage he became as ill as any of his St. Bartholomew Hospital patients. Soon after he arrived in London, Matthew had breakfasted with them and heard news of the Wordsworths at Rydal Mount: the old poet gloomily had told Mrs. Arnold, "My daughter is dying, Mrs. Wordsworth will quickly follow and then I shall go."[31] Matthew was deeply affected by such news; but he considered that he was now virtually fighting for his survival as a poet. He screened his feelings from his family, and on occasion tried to mitigate the intensity of the feelings by laughing at disasters. After his brother Tom's *John Wickliffe* left port, the "Ship News" in the *Times* was filled with listings of "crews lost" and maritime wrecks. An unpredicted hurricane in November had struck the English Channel. Matthew told Clough: "I think it possible Tom may have trotted into Arthur's Bosom in some of the late storms; which would have been a pity as he meant to enjoy himself in New Zealand."[32]

But he became ill after Tom left. Even when he knew the *John Wickliffe* was safe, he was inflicted with "a thousand" bodily complaints. Having praised a Clough poem in which the feeling ran "deep," he suddenly posted a letter insulting Clough's poems and damning the work of his collaborator Burbidge for good measure.

He was "rasped"[33] and morose. After gaps of blank space, one finds at the end of his diary of 1847 a scribble—not unlike that of an Arctic explorer or mountain-climber writing a dramatic last entry:

ended at Laleham

That entry is certainly an ending and a beginning. For November 1847 was a turning point in his life. He was beginning that rather short period—of five or six years—during which he perfected his theories of the lyric and of the long dramatic poem and wrote some of the most significant English poetry of the nineteenth century.

For a few days, he recovered his health and spirits beside a familiarly clear and swift river. "I never go along that shelving gravelly road up towards Laleham without interest," he wrote to his mother, "from Chertsey Lock to the turn where the Drunken Man lay. . . . Yesterday I was at Chertsey, the poetic town of our childhood as opposed to the practical historical Staines." The *poetic* and *practical* towns had vied over his cradle, apparently, and the poetic one is backed by a narrow fascinating lane that leads—"nowhere, but to the heaths and pines of Surrey." "How unlike the journey to Staines and the great road," he observes. Laleham Village reminds him of Jane Arnold, "only I am afraid she falls more and more out of sympathy with the Bucklands," he adds, "while I blend them more and more with the place: and with persons as well as things gone to venerate the tie of attachment in preference to that of passion, admiration or common interests."[34]

A reduced esteem for "passion" in a keen admirer of Schelling is interesting at the time, for he wrote this report of his Laleham trip on January 2, 1848. Eleven months later, "Matt's romantic passion" for a neighbor from Ambleside who was born on the Continent and baptized in the French Reformed Church—the pale, blue-eyed Mary Claude*—was to amuse all of his family.[35] His veneration for "persons gone" is illuminated by the rest of the letter: at Laleham he sought out charwomen who remembered his father, and lingered in a familiar garden by the "pink acacia." Having turned twenty-five, and lost Tom's presence, he needed that spontaneity of consciousness and intensity of purpose he recalled in his father, for he was struggling for self-possession.

He found it hard at present to compose verse at all. "I write a good deal easier than I did—tho: not much in quantity," he told Jane later—by which time he was getting over an "obscure" style.[36] Peculiarly, his most obscure and contorted poems of the late 1840s seem to illuminate him the most clearly. Despite the involuted style of

---

*The factual story of Arnold's "Marguerite," or Mary Claude, is told for the first time in Chapter 7 of this biography. One may say, here, that her "paled" features and "blue eyes" were familiar to Arnold by January 2, 1848. A descendant of French Protestant exiles, related through her aunt J. S. E. C. Reclam to exiles in Geneva and through her mother to the Chambeau family of the French community of exiles at Berlin, Mary Claude had been taken from Friedrichstadt to Liverpool as a child. She summered at Rothay Bank and then at Broadlands at Ambleside, and was drawn into the Clougho-Matthean set in 1847. "Matt's romantic passion for the Cruel Invisible, Mary Claude" became a topic for laughter, among Arnold's friends and family, in November 1848.

the verse, the Chorus in "Fragment of an 'Antigone'" expresses a theme rather emphatically. The individual who has left home remains "unguided":

> In little companies,
> And, our own place once left,
> Ignorant where to stand, or whom to avoid,
> By city and household grouped, we live; and many shocks
> Our order heaven-ordained
> Must every day endure:
> Voyages, exiles, hates, dissensions, wars.[37]

The numbing shocks of "voyages" and other vicissitudes reduce one's sense of purpose in life by weakening the consciousness of family-connectedness, and therefore they perhaps diminish one's sense of identity. A man's experience may be "opulent"—presumably he may live or work among the wealthiest, most interesting, and most powerful of men in society. But nothing is given to us quite freely. Life is perhaps a conspiracy against the self-possession of every individual. Baffled and misled by the world, we may follow a precious "clue" and obey the "primal law":

> Him then I praise, who dares
> To self-selected good
> Prefer obedience to the primal law
> Which consecrates the ties of blood: for these, indeed,
> Are to the Gods a care.[38]

These five lines remind one of his Laleham letter to Mrs. Arnold, of January 2, in which he venerates the "tie of attachment" with persons gone. But in "Fragment of an 'Antigone'" there is an emphasis upon daring and hardihood required of one who would prefer "ties of blood" to other associations since the special family bond, "deep-inwound," is not easy to bear. Moreover, there is in Arnold's treatment of the legend of Zeus snatching Hercules from a funeral pyre, near the Thessalian crags, a suggestion that death is a welcome release from the earthly phase of a bondage:

> But he preferred Fate to his strong desire,
> Nor did there need less than the burning pile
> . . . . . .
> To achieve his son's deliverance, O my child![39]

In a somewhat different mood, he wrote and later rejected for publication an untitled poem beginning, "And every man relates. . . ." Treating the theme of the wanderer in this work, he omits any mention of blood bonds and parental guides. Here the expression is more lucid, and the dilemma of the speaker, perhaps more acute. In anticipating the style and imagery of T. S. Eliot, Arnold carries one into a rather flowering wasteland. No contemporary can explain his purpose; all men have wept, raved, desponded, and at last mutely accepted fate. A missing father and a missing Deity have become nearly one and the same:

> And every man relates
> The history of his life
> So far as he has yet gone,
> . . . . . .
>
> And every man has wandered,
>   Every man wept,
>   Every man raved,
> Every man buried despondingly in his hands
>   His burning brow,
>   Even as I do.
>
>   . . . . . .
>
>   On rocks, by rivers,
>   In cities, in fields,
> . . . they have struck root and planted themselves,
>   Given over their wanderings. . . .
>
> Who led you, O men, who counselled you?
>   By this rock, by this river,
>   In that city, on that field,
> Wherefore did you strike root there and plant yourselves?
>   Why cease your wanderings?
> Long you wandered, I know, but why
>   Rest you now here?
>
> You know not, you cannot answer.[40]

Having rejected dogmatic creeds, Arnold was left with the memory of a childhood faith intricately bound up with a memory of his father's intensity and commitment. At twenty-five, he required his father's inwardness in order to succeed as a poet. The alternative would be to be without inner strength and wholeness, to wander in a superficial aimless freedom until one's creativity exhausted itself. But in venerating Dr. Arnold the man of inwardness, he drew closer to the militant social critic and formidable public-school reformer. The "ties of blood" and the "tie of attachment" to persons gone apparently made him feel, at times, that his brow was "burning."[41] He hardly felt restored to himself as a creative poet by contemplating his father, and while attempting to achieve a new and richer "inward life," he jotted such a notation as this:

The misery of the present age is not in the intensity of men's suffering—but in their incapacity to suffer, enjoy, feel at all, wholly & profoundly—in their having their susceptibility eternally agacée by a continual dance of ever-changing objects . . . in their having one moment the commencement of a feeling, at the next moment the commencement of an imagination, & the eternal tumult of the world mingling, breaking in upon, hurrying away all. . . . The disease of the present age is divorce from oneself.[42]

Such a note reveals his reading of the "Ancient Atomists," and particularly of the *De Rerum Natura;* and it also indicates that Matthew lived at times in the psychological atmosphere of the Heraclitian flux. The misery and disease of the age are "divorce from oneself." In drawing close to Dr. Arnold the reformer, he aggravated a conflict in himself between the creative poet and the practical activist, the lyricist and the puritan, the imaginative man and the ethical man, a conflict that he never would quite resolve.

But the conflict was productive. He drew from his father's memory a sense of the importance of one's chosen calling: surely, nothing but extinction would keep him from achieving success as a poet. He would wage such a campaign! In his notebooks, he quoted Goethe's maxim, again and again: *Es ist besser das geringste Ding von der Welt zu thun, als eine halbe Stunde für gering halten.* He would lose not a half hour; and apparently he contemplated his poetic projects wherever he happened to be. "I hear Matt was seen walking about his own domain at the Lakes," Campbell Shairp reports to a friend.[43] On holidays in Westmorland, he did much contemplative strolling. "While walking up and down on a soft bloomy day in the field by the Rotha," below Fox How, he soon composed "The New Sirens." The chief source for this poem seems to have been the debate in George Sand's *Lélia* between that novel's heroine, who represents romantic passion and ennui, and her sister Pulcherie, who embodies the ideal of sensual beauty. Matthew's friends failed to understand the poem, and his family was mildly derisive: "If Matt *has* accomplished the Feat of producing anything more unintelligible," Willy wrote, "I shall expect to hear soon of his squaring the Circle."[44]

"The mythological Sirens were, as you know," Matthew wrote to C. E. Swinerton,

> beautiful and charming creatures, whose charm and song allured men to their ruin. The idea of the poem is to consider as their successors Beauty and Pleasure as they meet us in actual life, and distract us from spiritual beauty, although in themselves transitory and unsatisfying.[45]

The last sentence is reminiscent of a boy's homilies in "Alaric at Rome"; and "The New Sirens" is darkly obscure—and full of energy—because it concerns autobiographical problems. Having tried to clarify the text, and "doctored" it so much that he couldn't bear to look at it, Arnold devised a prose précis for Clough. Years later, he admitted with pride of this poem: "Rossetti and his school say it is the best thing I ever wrote."[46]

"The speaker (one of a band of poets) stands under a cedar, newly awakened from a sleep," Matthew carefully explains in the précis. The poet is surrounded by an exhausted and beautiful company of females, or the New Sirens, who he had dreamed were "the fierce sensual lovers of antiquity." Having come from an Oxford-like region,

> dragon-warded fountains,
> Where the springs of knowledge are,

and tired himself with books, the poet imagines arguments against self-restraint that "fierce" female lovers would put to him:

> 'Come,' you say, 'opinion trembles
> Judgment shifts, convictions go;
> Life dries up, the heart dissembles—
> Only what we feel, we know.
> Hath your wisdom felt emotions? . . .'[47]

At first the poet cannot respond. "And," as Matthew explained, "he says, I cannot argue against you: for when about to do so, the remembrance of your beauty and life as I witnessed it at sunrise on these lawns . . . stops my mouth."[48]

With moral and philosophical arguments against beauty and love "stopped," the poet sings superbly well. He imitates the vague and sonorous movement of Shelley's "Sensitive Plant" and "Adonais" and the sensuality of Keats's odes. The autobiographical time is at first that of boyhood: the young poet has seen modern Homeric sirens in an "upland" valley—just as Matthew might have imagined them by looking out a bedroom window at Fox How. In that "upland" view, he could see cedars, and across the Valley of the Rotha, the long slanting edge of Wansfell protecting one side of the valley like a woman's glittering arm.

Females with showering hair had stepped through yielding woods at dawn to meet godlike creatures who beckoned them with "golden horns." Images of water and gold suddenly suggest the sunken world of "The Forsaken Merman." "For me," says the poet,

> my thoughts are straying
> Where at sunrise, through your vines,
> On these lawns I saw you playing,
> Hanging garlands on your odorous pines;
>
> When your showering locks enwound you,
> And your heavenly eyes shown through;
> When the pine-boughs yielded round you,
> And your brows were starred with dew;

> *And immortal forms to meet you,*
> *Down the statued alleys came,*
> *And through golden horns to greet you,*
> *Blew such music as a God may frame.*[49]

From this point on, lyrical beauty drowns out everything else. The poet's assumption is that sensual love exhausts the spirit. But as the "sombre day" advances, he shows only that the New Sirens lack diversion. Clearly a few books, or copies of the *Illustrated London News*, might have comforted the Sirens between bouts of lovemaking. Even the weather is sensual in its gloominess:

> *And if the dawning*
> *Into daylight never grew,*
> *If the glistering wings of morning*
> *On the dry noon shook their dew,*
> *If the fits of joy were longer,*
> · · · · · ·
> *No weak nursling of an earthly sun . . .*
> *Pluck, pluck cypress, O pale maidens,*
> *Dusk the hall with yew!*
> · · · · · ·
> *For the eye grows filled with gazing,*
> *And on raptures follow calms;*
> *And those warm locks men were praising,*
> *Drooped, unbraided, on your listless arms.*
>
> *Storms unsmoothed your folded valleys,*
> *And made all your cedars frown;*
> *Leaves were whirling in the alleys*
> *Which your lovers wandered down.*
> *—Sitting cheerless in your bowers,*
> *The hands propping the sunk head,*
> *Still they gall you, the long hours,*
> *And the hungry thought that must be fed!*[50]

In the end, the New Sirens reenter a Palace of Love, and the poet is left musing in the chilly gloom under his cedar. In the prose précis, lovemaking is implicitly associated with a "revel," and the poet moralizes hypothetically:

> —That is right, he continues [after the New Sirens have "re-entered the palace"], away with ennui. . . .
> —But (after a pause he continues), I, remaining in the dark and cold under my cedar, and seeing the blaze of your revel in the distance, do not share your illusions: and ask myself whether this *alternation* of ennui and excitement is worth much? Whether it is in truth a very desirable life?
> And, he goes on, were this *alternation* of ennui and excitement the best discoverable existence, yet it cannot last: time will destroy it: the time will come, when the elasticity of the spirits will be worn out, and nothing left but weariness.[51]

But the poet has neglected good arguments he put in the New Sirens' mouths. Time exhausts "the elasticity" of the spirit—but time exhausts everything. That the heart dissembles, that wisdom without experience is shallow, that the brain may defeat the spirit, and that it is wrongful to deny love—all are unrefuted.

Arnold's clearest poetry is retrospective—and he was too much absorbed in his "romantic passion" for a blue-eyed lady when, in 1847 or 1848, he composed this poem. Still, the structure allows him to dismiss moral values for stanzas at a time and to express aesthetic ones. "The New Sirens" succeeds in its imagery and movement, and draws upon that devotion to "actual" beauty which led him, as a boy, to Shelley and Keats, and which he had expressed in the un-Rugbeian stanzas of "Alaric" (before the concluding homilies). It attempts to illustrate Goethe's advice of renunciation in love for the young poet, and borrows from the strong antisensual thesis in *Lélia*, but its moral argument is at odds with its imagery and feeling.

Arnold was extremely sensitive to a threat romantic passion posed to him; he drew inspiration from beauty while fearing that sensuality would endanger his self-possession. He would preserve his creative vitality by cleaving to his Fox How family. As a man of the world, steeped in the novels of Disraeli and Edward Bulwer, let alone the whole corpus of Byron, he knew the world can rob one's *capacity* to feel. "To mock at feeling, . . . to enter a mauvais lieu at your ease . . . implies only the total absence of all youth and richness of soul—and the presence of a dead barren negative callosity," he tells himself. As a reader of "books of sentiment" including those of Jean Paul Richter (whom all the Clougho-Mattheans read at Oxford), he adds a note in which even the syntax dies away: "—The feeling with which a man of the world read in books of sentiment and its graduall [*sic*] suffocation in the world, after he himself has had his suffocated."[52]

Meanwhile, fragments of poems and obscure MSS. lay on his Mount Street table. Lately he had received a large bundle of manuscripts written by Clough and by Thomas Burbidge, who were collecting their works for *Ambarvalia*. Burbidge was a patently hopeless poet, who had written of Dr. Arnold (no doubt with laudable intentions),

> Yes, noble Arnold, thou didst well to die!
> • • • • • •
> But now thou art on high
> Among the Immortal and Invisible Quire.[53]

But instead of demolishing Burbidge, Matthew replied to Arthur Clough that he was reluctant to read Clough's own work: "I have abstained from all general criticism. . . . But on the whole I think [your poems] will stand very grandly, with Burbidge's 'barbaric ruins' smirking round them."[54]

Clough sent back an "explosion," and Matthew quickly apologized: "I sent you a beastly vile note the other day; . . . all the exacerbation produced by your apostrophes to duty . . . put me quite wrong." But he is reluctant to draw in his horns. In a remarkable paragraph which developed into a theory of the brief lyric, he pirouettes on "tho" and "yet" clauses to contradict every statement he makes—while holding his great friend at bay:

> I do think however that rare as individuality is [he advises Clough] you have to be on your guard against it—you particularly:—tho: indeed I do not really know that I think so.

Shakespeare in *A Midsummer Night's Dream* had declared that "if imagination would apprehend some joy it comprehends some bringer of that joy"—and in poetry that joy-bringer must be *beauty*. This operation, in his opinion, Arthur Clough despises. And how is vital beauty to be achieved in verse?

> To solve the Universe as you try to do [Matthew continues with emphasis] is as irritating as Tennyson's dawdling with its painted shell is fatiguing to me to witness: and yet I own that to *re-construct* the Universe is not a satisfactory attempt either—I keep saying Shakespeare, Shakespeare, you are as obscure as life is: yet this unsatisfactoriness goes against the poetic office in general: for this* must I think certainly be its end. But have I been inside you, or Shakespeare? Never. Therefore heed me not, but come to what you can. Still my first note was cynical and beastly-vile. To compensate it, I have got you the Paris diamond edition of Béranger, like mine.[55]

His reading of Aristotle and Coleridge lie behind his notion that poetry must exhibit more than a decorative beauty. Indeed there are two grave poetic faults. Both defeat lyric beauty. One of them is mere analysis of the world (Clough's fault, which excites "curiosity and reflection" but which leads to aridity and does not give "pleasure"), and the other is mere decorative painting (Keats's and Tennyson's fault, with which one cannot produce "the truly living and moving"). Clough's diligent, heady attempt to solve the universe is as mistaken as Tennyson's dawdling with its painted shell—for neither poet "groups" objects. Arnold explained later with a trace of gentle

---

*That is, "to re-construct the Universe" or to recreate life through the artistic imagination.

Olympian exasperation: "Trying to go into and to the bottom of an object instead of grouping *objects* is as fatal to the sensuousness of poetry as the mere painting, (for, in *Poetry*, this is not *grouping*)."[56] Behind his theorizing lies much intellectual confidence, and also an awareness that he needs a cooler and steadier objectivity—much greater detachment from his own emphatic feelings—if he is to survive as a poet. Shakespeare is a model of cool objectivity, but then, Shakespeare's ornateness in *style* will not do. To style, Matthew attached a key importance, though his conception of style was as fluid and evolving as his later conceptions of culture and religion. In Sophocles' grand style, he announced to his friend the next year, "grand moral effects are produced by *style*. For the style is the expression of the nobility of the poet's character, as the matter is the expression of the richness of his mind: but on men character produces as great an effect as mind."[57] His almost fanatic attention to verse style prompts one to feel that Matthew Arnold's poetic clichés and cacophonies are sometimes very functional—and indeed his stylistic faults appear in brilliantly effective works: "To a Friend" and "Memorial Verses" and the Obermann "Stanzas." He implies that harsh and smooth styles may be of use in "grouping" images—and he explains later that a "heightened and difficult manner" and a "counter-balance means" in verse are permissible.[58]

This year, he addressed to Clough one of the most impressive sonnets he ever wrote. Illustrating his theory of "grouping" and his "counter-balance means," a tonally harsh manner at the outset of "To a Friend" supports an image of modern discord:

> *Who prop, thou ask'st, in these bad days, my mind?*

Two guides for the present are a blind poet whose lucidity of soul had helped him to see, and a crippled slave whose Stoicism had helped him to endure. By not naming Homer or Epictetus in the sonnet, he makes two very formidable figures step out of their books. They become associated with the grandeur of their locales, the "Wide Prospect" or the European continent, Asia and Rome, and Mount Tmolus with Smyrna Bay at its foot:

> *He much, the old man, who, clearest-souled of men,*
> *Saw The Wide Prospect, and the Asian Fen,*
> *And Tmolus hill, and Smyrna bay, though blind.*
>
> *Much he, whose friendship I not long since won,*
> *That halting slave, who in Nicopolis*
> *Taught Arrian, when Vespasian's brutal son*
> *Cleared Rome of what most shamed him.*

The four lines about the "halting slave" are of great importance, inasmuch as the talks of Epictetus—recorded by his pupil Flavius Arrianus, around 95 A.D., in a school of philosophy at Nicopolis —were to be the ethical substratum of Arnold's thought for the rest of his life. Certainly Epictetus would have been at home in Dr. Arnold's Rugby. In succinct Greek, with great wit and pathos, Epictetus had told his pupils why they must "run risks," why they should have "no master" and no fear of events, why they should "show confidence in things that lie outside the province of the moral purpose, and caution in things that lie within the moral purpose."[59] Any attitude that can withstand the test of life was, in Arnold's view, Stoical; and Epictetus was a dazzingly incomparable Stoic.* But in 1848 he felt that Sophocles, like Goethe, offered a model of the man who lives in society while retaining a superb detachment; and also that the author of *Antigone* and *Oedipus at Colonus* after all had the steadiest vision through a long, creative life. "But be his," he concludes in the melodious sestet,

> *My special thanks, whose even-balanced soul,*
> *From first youth tested up to extreme old age,*
> *Business could not make dull, nor passion wild;*
>
> *Who saw life steadily, and saw it whole;*
> *The mellow glory of the Attic stage,*
> *Singer of sweet Colonus, and its child.*

For its fine technique, its depth of feeling, and its quality of being a natural reply to an academic man, "To a Friend" contrasts with three other sonnets he sent Clough in 1848. The two with the title "To a Republican Friend" and "Religious Isolation" are attempts to clear mental room, to rid himself of political obsessions. They are at once hectoring and defensive, whereas "To a Friend" is confessional and inevitable.

By February 1848, Arthur Clough had become a stalking horse in the field of poetic theory, and indeed he had been pushed out of the field of poetry, by his friend, more than once. Arnold needed strong opposition to define his views; lacking opposition, he created it. "It is necessity not inclination that ever repels me from you," he informs Clough. "A growing sense of the deficiency of the *beautiful* in your poems . . . made me speak as I did. . . . No—I doubt your being an

---

*Epictetus's Greek has been translated well into English by W. A. Oldfather, for the two volumes printed by the Loeb Classical Library in 1925. After years of reading the Greek, Arnold bought George Long's translation of 1877, which though scholarly and exact misses the succinctness, informality, lightness, and pathos which mark Epictetus's exceptional style of delivery. Arnold, in "Marcus Aurelius," faulted Long as a translator, and was sensitive to the brilliance of Epictetus's style.

artist: but have you read Novalis? He certainly is not one either."[60] Trading insults, Arnold and Clough behaved like the rattlesnake and porcupine. Clough was a hard-working poet and an embattled spirit who was thinking of giving up his Oriel Fellowship—no matter *what* the Provost of Oriel said to dissuade him—and he had nobody to turn to for advice. ("You being away," Clough wrote plaintively to Tom Arnold, "I don't know who to ask.")[61]

But very happily, the European Continent now began to explode, distracting two fervid friends from minor insults and explosions. Telegraph keys had been installed lately in London. At Lansdowne House Matthew was able to get "later news than any of the papers"[62] —and thus, quite suddenly, he became a political oracle.

What Matthew heard, on February 22, was that Paris crowds had rioted and lit bonfires on the Champs Élysees. Fourierism, Saint-Simonism, and other exciting ideologies were in the French air—and two tireless opposition newspapers, *La Réforme* and *Le National,* had whipped up feeling against the dull constitutional monarchy of Louis Philippe. On February 23 the Red Flag appeared in the Boulevard des Capucines. By then, crowds in the faubourgs wouldn't have been satisfied with the King's head—or with that of his chief minister, Guizot. National Guard legions defected, and an intrepid Guard captain and a number of École Polytechnique students walked into the Hôtel de Ville and took it without a blow. When a provisional government was announced, France's great romantic poet, Lamartine, appeared at the head of it!

Lord Lansdowne's mouth dropped open. "My man remarks that Poets should hold up their heads," observed a debonair secretary in London, "now a Poet is at the head of France. More clergyman than Poet though," Matthew adds, apparently oblivious to the fact that Lamartine had spoken bravely to crowds who leveled muskets at him.[63] Quite uncertain as to what he ought to feel about Lamartine and the Paris Revolution, Matthew was victimized by his moods. He was "really heated to a very fervid enthusiasm," as Clough noticed, and evidently depressed to a very glum despair. The French were foolish, and they were "fine."[64] Lamartine was a dull clergyman, and a prophet. What was plain was that the French were responding to *ideas* concerning universal suffrage and social equality, national workshops for the unemployed, and even the future confederation of Europe —and in this they differed vastly from the British. "Social changes are *inevitable* here," the eldest son of the late Dr. Arnold considers. "And such is the state of our masses that their movements now can only be brutal," he continues in a letter to Jane. "There is no one, as far as one sees, to train them to conquer by their attitude and superior conviction: the deep ignorance of the middle & upper classes, and their feebleness of vision becoming . . . daily more apparent. . . . See what people mean by placing France *politically* in the van of Europe: it is the *intelligence* of their idea-moved masses which makes them politically as far superior to the *insensible masses* of England as to the Russian Serfs. —And at the same time they do not threaten the educated world with the intolerable *laideur* of the well-fed American masses."[65] Matthew's fervid relationship with the United States had begun: the Americans were uncivilized because they overthrew the aristocratic principle, and vigorous because they responded to ideas. He now taunts a "Tom Yankee" friend. Unbelievably, the American Ambassador had congratulated the new Paris regime without orders from Washington! "I wish you could have heard me and my man," Matthew tells Clough who must have regretted that he had ever lived in South Carolina, "sneering at the vulgar officiousness of that vulgar fussy Yankee Minister at Paris."[66] More seriously he asks himself where England will be in the twentieth century, if she is inhospitable to ideas?

> How plain it is now [he wrote to Jane], though an attention to the comparative literature for the last fifty years might have instructed any one of it, that England is in a certain sense *far behind* the Continent. In conversation, in the newspapers, one is so struck with the fact of the utter insensibility, one may say, of people to the number of ideas and schemes now ventilated on the Continent—not because they have judged them or seen beyond them, but from sheer habitual want of wide reading and thinking. . . . Our practical virtues never certainly revealed more clearly their isolation. I am not sure but I agree in Lamartine's prophecy that 100 years hence the Continent will be a great united Federal Republic, and England, all her colonies gone, in a dull steady decay.[67]

The February Days encouraged the critic and the ethnographer, the Francophile and internationalist—and even the poet in him, for his view of England's "isolation" illuminates "To Marguerite—Continued" and "Dover Beach."

The revolution stirred the patriotic side of his soul, too, and he would sacrifice "half of his life" for his nation in the end. On March 6 and 7, he observed the Trafalgar Square riots, which developed out of meetings on the income tax; and a month later he was with the Chartists at Kennington Common ("braggarts as they are, says my man").[68] Meanwhile Mrs. Arnold's excitement promoted his own activism. She had recited from the newspapers in 1830—when Charles X issued the fatal five ordinances—and her eyes opened widely over a revolution now. What would calm her Celtic eyes? "Paris seems ready to boil over at fever heat," Mrs. Arnold writes on March 20. It will be a pity if "anarchy" mars "the wonderful example we have had of how a total revolution in the established order of things can take place. . . . As dear old Wordsworth said to-day, it seems like a state of suspended animation. You may suppose with what almost breathless interest we await the news from France."[69] Matthew sent home detailed "general chronicles"[70] to pacify her.

Amazingly, the revolution was spreading. During March every German king, prince, or princelet swore to a liberal constitution or appointed a new liberal assembly. Professors became premiers, students sat with shopkeepers in elected assemblies, and Rachel sang the *Marseillaise* thirty-four times in a day—and survived. Clough was ecstatic: "The Red Flag flying at Paris. And so my dear Vive La Republique, Vive le Drapeau Rouge!" he wrote to Tom. And with remembered enthusiasm in *Amours de Voyage:* "I, who nor meddle nor make in politics," Clough wrote happily,

> *Never predicted Parisian millenniums, never beheld a*
> *New Jerusalem coming down dressed like a bride out of heaven*
> *Right on the Place de la Concorde.*[71]

Perhaps the New Jerusalem *was* arriving—but in the face of it, what should one do? Matthew resorted to comedy. He heard with great delight that a revolt was called off at Rugby School because the Headmaster was ill. Monckton Milnes peremptorily "refused to be sworn in a special constable that he might be free to assume the post of President of the Republic at a moment's notice," he told his mother. "Tell Edward," he asks Clough to inform Didu, "I shall be ready to take flight with him the very moment the French land, and have engaged a Hansom to convey us both from the possible scene of carnage."[72]

After sending a facetious note to "Citizen Clough, Oriel Lyceum," he received from Oxford an appropriate broadside:

LIBERTY!   EQUALITY!
FRATERNITY!

CITIZEN ACADEMICIANS,

The cry of reform has been too long unheard. OUR INFATUATED RULERS refused to listen to it. The term of their tyranny is at length accomplished.

The VICE-CHANCELLOR has fled on horseback. . . .

The UNIVERSITY is no more. A REPUBLICAN LYCEUM will henceforth diffuse light & civilization. . . .

A PROVISIONAL GOVERNMENT has been established. The undersigned Citizens have nobly devoted themselves to the task of Administration.

> (Signed) Citizen CLOUGH
> *President of the Executive Committee*
> SEWELL
> BOSSOM (Operative)
> JOHN CONINGTON
> WRIGHTSON (Queen's)

FLOREAT LYCEUM[73]

But there were dreary signs before the summer that the New Jerusalem was in trouble. Wearing himself out and becoming cynical, Lamartine presently declared that the February Days occurred because France was bored. Economic difficulties plagued Paris, and reactionary forces all over Europe licked their wounds and ominously counted muskets. Arnold heard that the beautiful new government was split—with the radicals Ledru-Rollin and Louis Blanc and the moderate-conservatives on opposing sides and France's illustrious poet desperately "neutral." The news was "sad—yet with a radiance in it like that of the stars," he read in a passage of Carlyle in the *Examiner;* "sternly beautiful, symbolic of immortality and eternity!"[74]

"How solemn, how deeply *restful*,"[75] he wrote to Arthur Clough about this, and repeated almost the same sentiment to his mother. He was probably reminded in March of an earlier essay, "Goethe's Works," in which Carlyle had translated an epigrammatic lyric of Goethe:

> *Wie das Gestirn,*
> *Ohne Hast,*
> *Aber ohne Rast,*
> *Drehe sich jeder*
> *Um die eigene Last.*
>
> *Like as a Star*
> *That maketh not haste*
> *That taketh not rest*
> *Be each one fulfilling*
> *His god-given Hest.*[76]

Probably Carlyle and Goethe together, as well as his memory of the "one lesson" in Wordsworth's "Hartleap Well," inspired now the important sonnet which he used as the introductory piece in *The Strayed Reveller.* The sleepless ministers in "Quiet Work" appear to be the unhasting stars which teach the meaning of "toil unsevered from tranquillity." They suggest that within the divided self there is a potential unity which enables a gifted man to produce great work. The poem embodies Arnold's hopeful intuition of a quiet source of being in himself from which poetry "too great for haste, too high for rivalry" might come; and yet all of his best poetry is a tissue of unresolved contradictions. "Yes, while on earth a thousand discords ring," he wrote in "Quiet Work," and his own discords seem to ring in the revisions he made in the poem's printed text:

> *Two lessons, Nature, let me learn of thee . . .*
> *One lesson, Nature, let me learn of thee . . .*
> *Two blending duties, harmonis'd in one . . .*
> *One lesson of two duties, kept at one . . .*[77]

He "doctored" his work incessantly and wrote fewer poems than Tennyson or Browning because he couldn't satisfy an inner censor with conflicting demands. His deepest problem was psychological as well as artistic: how could he express himself fully? No idea gave him a fully satisfying notion of the modern world or of himself; and this spring he apparently experienced that quiet crisis which is implicit in "The Buried Life" and in "A Summer Night." "I . . . walked the streets," he wrote to Jane at one point.[78]

> *But often, in the world's most crowded streets,*
> *But often, in the din of strife,*
> *There arises an unspeakable desire*
> *After the knowledge of our buried life, . . .*
>
> . . . . . .
>
> *And many a man in his own breast then delves,*
> *But deep enough, alas! none ever mines.*[79]

His large, usually generous comparativist interest in nations, peoples, and races is related to that desire for a deeper self-definition; and indeed his most autobiographical prose work takes a personal view of the problem of race. Writing in 1866, he protested on almost every page of *The Study of Celtic Literature* that he was a calm, dispassionate observer of the Celts. "Why," Matthew assured the reader in a delightful way, "my very name expresses that peculiar Semitico-Saxon mixture which makes the typical Englishman."[80]

Yet he included this memory of his father:

With the stream of my brother Saxons . . . I part company. . . . I remember . . . I was taught to think of Celt as separated by an impassable gulf from Teuton; my father in particular, was never weary of contrasting them; he insisted much oftener on the separation between us and them than on the separation between us and any other race in the world; in the same way Lord Lyndhurst . . . called the Irish, "aliens in speech, in religion, in blood." This naturally created a profound sense of estrangement. . . . Such was the sense of antagonism, making it seem dangerous to us [that is, to Englishmen generally] to let such opposites to ourselves have speech and utterance.[81]

The danger of letting "opposites to ourselves have speech and utterance," a "separation," "an impassable gulf," and "a profound sense of estrangement" are phrases that apply to Matthew's underlying mood in 1848 and throughout the next few years. Unwilling to review the manner in which he had appealed to his father, by being active and earnest at crucial moments in a Saxon school, and the manner in which he had appealed to his mother, dazzling and surprising her with his wit, his very sad poems, his acting, his pathos, even his shameless indolence and his "admiration of rank & fashion," he looked instead at the outward spectacle of the world and also sought in books for self-understanding. He found his nights extremely long. "In the watches of the night," he knows that he has no "profound stirring" for politics.[82] Poetry is his metier—though his desire for fullness in it is nearly maddening. Later he finds a letter of Jacobi's to Goethe which reminds him of Clough, whom he continued to treat as a stalking horse in the field of life. "Now for my best hand," Matthew wrote, and then transcribed these words in German for his friend's edification: "What I was I still am, troubled from my childhood up with a secret unconquerable disgust with myself, a nobody, so that I, always more impoverished in hope, often can hardly suffer the thought of the thing I am: a lie among nothing but lies, a thing of dreams among dream-things, and whenever I think I am awake I am still less than that."[83]

> And what we say and do
> Is eloquent, is well—but 'tis not true!

Perhaps, if what one does and says is "not true," then, as Jacobi declares, one is a "lie" or a "nobody," and self-disgust is inevitable. But what, then, are other people? One may be only a "lie among lies, a thing of dreams among dream-things"—and the human will is doubly paralyzed, for the world is a ghostly lie. "And then," Matthew continued in "The Buried Life,"

> we will no more be racked
> With inward striving, and demand
> Of all the thousand nothings of the hour
> Their stupefying power;
> Ah yes, and they benumb us at our call!
> Yet still, from time to time, vague and forlorn,
> From the soul's subterranean depths upborne
> As from an infinitely distant land,
> Come airs, and floating echoes, and convey
> A melancholy into all our day.[84]

Arnold's apparent sense of futility and declared sense of melancholy were illuminated for him, this year, by two extraordinary works. One of them was Senancour's *Obermann* (1804), which sent him to Switzerland in the summer. The other, which may account for his spelling the word "literature" as "litterature" this year and which he was reading in March, was the *Cours de littérature dramatique* (1843), by a politician and Sorbonne lecturer of the day named Saint-Marc Girardin. Endowing fashionable topics with rather dire significance, Girardin at least is suggestive. In one lecture, he discusses the "theme of maternal love" in plays about Merope, and compares dramatizations of that Euripidean heroine by Torelli, Maffei, Voltaire, and Alfieri. In another, he discusses the fourth-century monk Stagirius, who suffered incurably from the nineteenth-century complaint of *mal de siècle*. To be sure, the lecturer explains that Stagirius is the historical prototype of Shakespeare's Hamlet, as well as of Chateaubriand's René and Goethe's Werther. His disease is "sadness," he explains, "or rather *l'athumia* (accidie) since the Greek word is a thousand times more expressive than the French; it is the failure of energy and resilience; it is depression . . . it is the nothingness of the soul."[85]

Girardin gives perspective to the pessimism one finds in Melville's *Bartleby* or *The Encantadas* or indeed in such works as *René* and *Obermann*. The piece on Merope suggested to Matthew Arnold the subject for a tragedy, and the one on Stagirius suggested the title for a lyric—and perhaps confirmed a historical thesis which much of his Oriel reading had pointed towards. Girardin shows that brilliant representative modern figures suffer from lassitude and self-doubt, which thus may be related to historical causes. Arnold perceived that a chief fact about modern Europe was the final disintegration of the medieval world view. That dissolution, he came to realize, had begun with the Reformation and had ended in the French Revolution of 1789, of which the February Days of 1848 could be seen as reminders. The power of aristocracies and monarchies was gone: the present belonged to the ignorant middle classes, and the future to the masses. Since no Christian church could reassert its authority or enforce its dogma,[86] a psychological vacuum remained. In consequence, Arnold concluded, man lacks a deep identity; he suffers from disorientation and ennui, shifting and unsatisfying feelings, shallowness of being, dissatisfaction with his own endeavors—from debilities caused by the lack of any compelling authority for the spiritual life. Arnold's Obermann poems, "Dover Beach," and "Stanzas from the Grande Chartreuse" explore what was lost in 1789. That Arnold's poetry is not depressing owes to his temperamental ebullience—he is never known to have depressed a friend—and to his recognition that a historical ending implies a historical beginning. If the medieval view is dead, what can replace it? Even his most introverted and withdrawn characters, the most impressive of his dramatis personae—the poet of "Resignation," Empedocles, and the Scholar-Gipsy—contain the seed of that optimism one finds in his most autobiographical essay. "When," Matthew Arnold wrote in 1866,

> Goethe came, Europe had lost her basis of spiritual life; she had to find it again; Goethe's task was,—the inevitable task for the modern poet henceforth is, . . . to interpret human life afresh, and to supply a new spiritual basis to it.[87]

Far from having a picture of "the poet's task" this spring, he became calmer and steadier as revolutionaries bickered. He purged himself of politics in the "To a Republican Friend" poems—one of which mildly insults France, while the other looks for a trace of sanity in that "social fanatic" Arthur Clough.

This heavy-set, balding Rugbeian with his grand forehead, piercing eyes, and modesty and brilliance was now twenty-nine. The Paris Revolution had touched Arthur Clough. In the spring Clough saw Paris with Emerson, and exulted over the graffiti of the revolution on Vincennes's walls and enjoyed himself in the sun; indeed at Easter up at Oxford, he even resigned his Oriel tutorship because of religious scruples. Clough wouldn't subscribe to the Thirty-nine Articles as required of a Tutor, or sign "oaths" any longer. However, he had spent his adult life at Oxford. If Clough now left those emotionally supportive halls, what would he do? He not only lacked money and a job, but was too beset by scruples to make firm, hard-headed, practical commitments. Arnold worried over him far more than might seem, and would send him tactful, careful advice even after Clough moved to London and tried to support himself there. Close, creative friendships are likely to be selfish: neither poet could afford to sympathize too intently with the other's work. Both benefited from a unique, warm, and very intense intimacy which included an ongoing, indispensable debate over poetry and poetics. When Clough was in trouble, Arnold at least moderated the ferocity of that airy debate, and showed his friend clearly enough that he loved him. He could appreciate the energy, freshness, and sincerity of Clough's poems—and he seems to have understood in 1848 that this poet's ironic and comic talents, social vision, and interest in landscape, cities, people, and the vagaries of modern feeling had not yet found their fullest expression. Clough was soon to write the *Bothie, Amours de Voyage,* and *Dipsychus.* These fine works with their free exploration of the modern psyche owed much to Arnold and the liberating mood of 1848. Arnold, for his part, tried to praise one or two of them as he could; but the embarrassment and warfare that preceded the ending of a friendship was soon to come.

One weekend after listening to Wordsworth snort over politics up at Rydal, Ralph Waldo Emerson came to town. Emerson in the flesh was round-shouldered, bland, and almost humble, or not at all like the prophet of "Self-Reliance." Clough nervously introduced him to Matthew and a "pleasant" interview took place,[88] though Emerson preferred Clough's grave earnestness and frank smile. In bidding the American goodbye later at the Liverpool docks, Clough said, "Think where we are. Carlyle has led us all out into the desert and he has left us there." Whereupon Emerson naturally put a hand on his escort's smooth brow and replied, "Clough, I consecrate you Bishop of all England."[89] What is interesting is that Arnold praised Emerson's viewpoint highly in "Religious Isolation" while remembering him, in person, as "thin and ineffectual, and self-defensive only."[90]

By summertime, he could see that Clough needed tactful prodding and cheering up. Clough was truly leaving Oxford because he couldn't sign the Thirty-nine Articles, and he had no job. "My dear love," Matthew wrote gently and forbearingly, "I desire you should have some occupation—I think it desirable for everyone—very much so for you." Perhaps he could tutor the little Rathbone Greg children at Esher, a heaven for beauty, or else could join Ralph Lingen in the education office? "Eh? . . . [only] I don't think you'd stand that—and then when you have begun the work is very hard . . . but efforts might be made if you liked: £500 a year and no oaths."[91]

While offering vocational advice, Matthew threw himself into language preparations for a journey. "It is now said that Parliament will be up in the middle of August," he tells his mother on July 16, and this will give "longer days" for visiting Switzerland—which he often desires. Apart from twelve Italian lessons, he is polishing up German and this effort is "almost breaking" his heart.

"They are lumbering old cart-horses, the Germans," writes a poet who followed Goethe like the northern star. "Their endless chatter about minutiae would make me furious, if I did not remember that they have had recourse to this because they have no practical life, . . . and the mind must be occupied."[92] Why was he so furious over the Germans? His sisters knew of his passion for German-born Mary Claude, who was collecting and translating German fables. Mary, who was traveling this summer, had relatives in Geneva. His petulance may reflect uncertainty about his feeling for her. He left prepared for various moods at any rate, and took along a copy of Epictetus and a copy of Béranger for Switzerland. Epictetus the crippled slave counseled Stoicism, and the lyric poet offered laughter and song for "highly cultivated désillusionés roués."[93]

Also, Matthew took along Murray's *Handbook for Travellers in Switzerland,* to see where he was going in summer regions of ice and snow in the Bernese Oberland, among those "dreams within dreams," those very great mountains which he wrote about so romantically:

> *Hark! the wind rushes past us!*
> *Ah! with that let me go.*
> ⋯⋯
> *There to watch, o'er the sunk vale*
> *The frore mountain-wall,*
> *Where the niched snow-bed sprays down*
> *Its powdery fall.*
> *There its dusky blue clusters*
> *The aconite spreads;*
> *There the pines slope, the cloud-strips*
> *Hung soft in their heads.*
> *No life but, at moments,*
> *The mountain-bee's hum.*
> *—I come, O ye mountains!*
> *Ye pine-woods, I come!*

7

THE INTENSITY OF LOVE
1848–1849

Forgive me! forgive me!
  Ah, Marguerite, fain
Would these arms reach to clasp thee!
  But see! 'tis in vain.

. . . . . .

Far, far from each other
  Our spirits have grown;
And what heart knows another?
  Ah! who knows his own?

—*"Parting"*

ARNOLD'S journey to Switzerland implied an adventure in time, for even as a boy on the northern hills he had known the Bernese Oberland. The Swiss peaks, prodigious and exciting, loomed in his father's wall prints and he was familiar with quaint German names such as the Jungfrau and the Eiger and the Schreckhorn . . . the "Maiden" and the "Ogre" and the "Terror Pike"! A vivid portion in his father's *History of Rome,* as a matter of fact, concerned Hannibal's exploit in taking a southern army over the winter Alps when the commander faced annihilation.[1]

Matthew still minimized his father's work in holding a public school "together"; but Hannibal's heroic Alps were his father's Alps—and he saw the fine peaks and the green, misty Rhône in the lonely early autumn. For a day or two over Switzerland the sky was brilliantly blue. He watched a high, jagged impossible Oberland ridge as sunset caught it in a "rosy glow," and climbed the Faulhorn: "8300 above the sea, my duck," he wrote to Clough.[2] With a "good Christian and a family man" as a guide, he took a charabanc over the Simplon into northern Italy, but the weather reports at Domo d'Ossola were as forbiddingly bad as the skies. "*Coupons court à notre voyage.*

Revenons en Suisse," he told his guide, a keen appreciator of the dark Italian girls (who lacked British *female hardness,* as Matthew later informed Jane).

The route from Isella to Simplon was "glory to God," and when mists enveloped him, he might have been in a chariot with the Merman. In "freezing" weather he warmed up, as best he could, at a "vast hotel" at Leukerbad on September 29. He had planned to reach Leukerbad as late as possible, for now, though this health resort above the Rhône was unaccommodating, it was better than it appeared to be during the tourist season.[3] As late as August, Leukerbad confirmed what the British journals advised: that a good deal of Switzerland was a health resort for madmen, or a home for cretins and imbeciles. "To the unstrung frame and the jaded brain 'sweet are the uses' of a walk in Switzerland," the *Athenaeum* commented,[4] before discoursing on Dr. Guggenbühl's home for cretins near the Lake of Thun. "The stranger will be amazed," wrote Murray in the *Handbook,*

> on entering [a large wooden shed overlooking the Leukerbad valley] to perceive a group of some 12 or 15 heads emerging from the water, on the surface of which float wooden tables, holding coffee-cups, newspapers, snuff-boxes, books, and other aids. . . . A motley company, of all ages, both sexes, and various ranks, delicate young ladies, burly friars, invalid officers, and ancient dames, are ranged around . . . while a solitary sitter may be seen reviving in the hot water a nosegay of withered flowers.[5]

But now Arnold was "all alone" in a frigid isolated hotel, and his mind certainly was free to focus on a romantic meeting arranged for the next day. Sitting at a log fire that night, in his hotel, he became tipsy with champagne (which he drank "to guard against the cold"). "Tomorrow," he tells Clough, "I repass the Gemmi and get to Thun: linger one day at the Hôtel Bellevue for the sake of the blue eyes of one of its inmates: and then proceed by slow stages down the Rhine to Cologne, thence to . . . England."[6]

The notion of "blue eyes" makes him restless. He conjures up "raw mammoth-belched half-delightful objects the Swiss Alps," before alluding resourcefully to Horace: *What are lovely white ladies at top, terminate below the waist as black fish.* The glaciers of the "Maiden" and the "Ogre" and the "Terror Pike" are hideously, horrendously alive in the night! "Above all," he insists with some dignity in a lewd joke, "the grand views being ungifted with self-controul . . . desinunt in piscem [end as fish]. And the curse of dirty water," he continues with moral fastidiousness, "—the real pain it occasions to one who looks upon water as the Mediator between the inanimate and man is not to be described. I have seen clean water in parts of the Lake of Geneva."

But the whole area around Geneva, where his foreign-born summer neighbor Mary Claude, the blue-eyed and pale exile from Friedrichstadt, has relatives, is "spoiled by . . . that furiously flaring bethiefed rushlight, the vulgar Byron."[7]

Arnold has been reading Béranger's witty poems about lust. In the spring he had told his mother to "show to Wordsworth" the piece in the *Examiner* in which Béranger, when urged to enter the French Assembly, declared he was "following his own course."[8] But hasn't Béranger been corrupted by Parisian readers? "Voila pourquoi . . . there is something 'fade' about Béranger's Epicureanism," he tells Clough now. "Perhaps you don't see the pourquoi, but I think my love does and the paper draws to an end. In the reste, I am glad to be tired of an author. . . . More particularly is this feeling with regard to (I hate the word) women. We know beforehand all they can teach us: yet we are obliged to learn it directly from them." He has learned everything about women by reading George Sand and the male philosophers and yet he has hardly lived. Suddenly, he imitates for Clough's benefit the mocking style of Hamlet: "Why here is a marvellous thing. The following is curious," he pens in a cool and offhand manner before jotting pseudo-Elizabethan verses.[9] Perhaps the champagne goes to his head; and yet he is troubled by a blue-eyed Ophelia. A letter Matthew sent from Thun, later on, suggests that he tries to sink into a unified melancholy mood in the Alps to recover his past and see the future. Intent on finding his way as *a poet,* he needs self-possession —or the true "besonnenheit"* —and his "one natural craving" isn't even for "profound thoughts, mighty spiritual workings etc. but a distinct seeing of my way as far as my own nature is concerned."[10]

Why, then, has he arranged to see "blue eyes" at Thun? He had met heroic, artistic ladies on the Continent. He had drawn strength from Mme Sand and Rachel, both so defiant in aesthetic passion. A meeting at the Hôtel Bellevue may do him good, for he will be near the limpid River Aar and the turquoise Lake of Thun and not far from the white Blumlisalp; he may sail down the Rhine, later, with fresh resolution, or with memories of a lovely Friedrichstadt exile who reminded him of his boyhood. And yet once, with two smiling, beguiling, damned, doomed, false, lying friends, a prince had left on a journey and returned home with resolution. Arnold played that sad prince face-

---

*For Herder, *Besonnenheit* was a key term, meaning "reflection" and defining that distinct grasp of things which separates man from animals. For Goethe, it usually meant "self-possession." Matthew Arnold—writing from the Swiss German-speaking town of Thun to Clough—meant by it "deep self-possession." He was aware that in German romanticism of the 1770s the term is related to what the *Stürmer and Dränger* (Herder and his followers) felt to be the central importance of expression, of art, and of feeling in man's life.

tiously, and, knowing how the tragedy ended, later wove references to *Hamlet* into his "Marguerite" or *Switzerland* lyrics. The conspiracy against him was not that of a lecherous King Claudius, but really something worse: it was *all* of modern life and society.

A poet struggling for inwardness and self-command is a ludicrous phenomenon (and the urgent, ironic tone of his letters shows that he was aware of this). But his position was worse than that of a tragic hero: "These are damned times," he writes later from a modest hotel near the limpid River Aar. "Everything is against one—the height to which knowledge is come, the spread of luxury, our physical enervation, the absence of great *natures,* the unavoidable contact with millions of small ones, newspapers, cities, light profligate friends, moral desperadoes like Carlyle, our own selves, and the sickening consciousness of our difficulties." Modernity conspired against one's feelings and robbed one's faith in the poetic imagination. Yet to whom would it be tragic if he abandoned his art? His chance for success as *a poet* might be a deep self-assessment that would put him profoundly in touch with his emotions, but he felt *"faussé"* or on the wrong track in "all intellectual and poetical performance,"[11] and his letters from the Alps reflect some despair.

He could not achieve the "calm" he required to tell why he was intellectually *"faussé."* Several of his memories perhaps were irritating: one of his father's commandments recorded in the *Life of Dr. Arnold* was ironic in its very simplicity: "Forwards, forwards, forwards, —should be one's motto."

"Forwards, forwards," Matthew echoes in "Self-Dependence," written after he had seen the Alps. Existence bore him forwards while he searched for precious self-definition:

> *Weary of myself, and sick of asking*
> *What I am, and what I ought to be,*
> *At this vessel's prow I stand, which bears me*
> *Forwards, forwards, o'er the starlit sea.*
>
> *And a look of passionate desire*
> *O'er the sea and to the stars I send:*
> *'Ye who from my childhood up have calmed me,*
> *Calm me, ah, compose me to the end!'*[12]

Here is the same quest for a sense of identity that one finds in Senancour's elegant letters, *Obermann.* Senancour's hero is a young postrevolutionary wanderer who asks "Qui suis-je donc?"[13] because lack of faith makes him unsure of himself and his purposes. After finding an answer to the question "Who am I then?" by submitting to dull work, he quits society to ponder his life in alpine solitudes. That effort makes him a philosopher of the "sentimental school," who seeks an epistemology of "feeling" and a discipline of spiritual rebirth while trying to rid himself of a tension between monkish instincts and his sense of the goodness of desire. Obermann even wonders at moments, like the young Senancour in the Alps, how he can bear to live.

In "Stanzas in Memory of the Author of 'Obermann,'" Arnold sympathizes with the sensibility of Senancour—whose own perplexities are reproduced in Obermann's letters. "Yes," he salutes the author with felt emphasis,

> *I hear thee saying now:*
> Greater by far than thou are dead;
> Strive not! die also thou!
>
> *Ah! two desires toss about*
> *The poet's feverish blood.*
> *One drives him to the world without,*
> *And one to solitude.*[14]

Obermann thinks of suicide, but continues to live as he hopes to find serenity by dying to the will. As an anguished young man who finds only rare moments of peace, he hardly controls the willfulness of his thought or the nagging of his desires; his companions remain the sublime white Finsteraarhorn and Schreckhorn which suggest to him only time's eternity. He looks forward to natural death—when he will have near him the magical alpine daisies, or *marguerites des prés,* which he loves because they evoke the past so vividly (*"les souvenirs qu'elles suscitent ramènent fortement au passé"*).[15] The *marguerites* may recall for him the lost illusion of God.

Senancour offered to Arnold a good model of inwardness and of strong, impassioned symbolism, as well as a difficult example of the epistemology of "feeling" which he was to consider before writing *Switzerland*. His need for self-possession implied an Obermann-like effort in "prayer," and he was to return to Thun in 1848 "more snuffing after a moral atmosphere to respire in than ever before in my life"; but he could not accept, any more than Obermann could, the idea of rebirth through Christian faith—despite his ironic piety with Clough: "Marvel not that I say unto you, ye must be born again." Discouraged by faith and abstract philosophy, he might contemplate great individuals as his guides. In the Obermann "Stanzas," he exalts Wordsworth, Goethe, and Senancour as men of guiding sensibility, before dismissing Senancour on the charge that he was "unstrung." (Perhaps as the *Athenaeum* suggested, anyone who had to wander for long in the Alps must be mad.) Indeed Arnold could imagine scholar-gipsies vividly, but he seldom praised an intelligent man for being one. He was to consult *Obermann* earnestly, while removing

himself from the book's author, Senancour, whom he salutes as a
gently deranged failure in the "Stanzas":

> *I in the world must live; but thou,*
> *Thou melancholy shade!*
> · · · · · ·
>
> *Farewell!—Whether thou now liest near*
> *That much-loved inland sea,*
> *The ripples of whose blue waves cheer*
> *Vevey and Meillerie;*
>
> *And in that gracious region bland,*
> *Where with clear-rustling wave*
> *The scented pines of Switzerland*
> *Stand dark round thy green grave,*
>
> · · · · · ·
>
> *Or whether, by maligner fate,*
> *Among the swarms of men,*
>
> · · · · · ·
>
> *Farewell! Under the sky we part,*
> *In this stern Alpine dell.*
> *O unstrung will! O broken heart!*
> *A last, a last farewell!*[16]

At Thun he was to elevate Clough as a spiritual model in life. "While I
will not much talk about these things [such as the subject of spiritual
rebirth]," he wrote later to his modest fellow poet, "yet the considering
of them has led me constantly to you the only living one almost that I
know of:

> *The children of the second birth*
> *Whom the world could not tame—*

for my dear Tom has not sufficient besonnenheit for it to be any *rest* to
think of him any more than it is a *rest* to think of mystics and such
cattle."[17]

Though halfway round the world in the Antipodes, his brother is
upsetting, for he has not "a 'still, considerate mind.'" For calmness,
Matthew is to fall back upon a prudent morality: "Thou fool," he later
told the amused Clough, "that which is morally worthless remains so,
and undesired by Heaven, whatever results flow from it."[18]

On both of his brief autumn visits to the Alps, in 1848 and 1849, he
had the uses of romantic love to think about. *"La recherche de sa
véritable identité, voilà bien la préoccupation maîtresse d'Arnold,"*
Louis Bonnerot[19] comments on Arnold in love—in a study that is the
more impressive because it was written before the Claude letters,
Anne Clough's diary, and Tom Arnold's remarks on "Matt's romantic

passion" came to light (during an investigation which confirms the identity of Arnold's "Marguerite" beyond any doubt) in the 1960s and 1970s. Could *love* help him to understand the "damned times" and himself? Beneath his theatrical manner and ambivalent feelings and down among his memories there might lie a principle that would show him his "way." For months, he had been in love with a bewitching, slender exile—his own holiday neighbor at the Claudes' Rothay Bank at Ambleside. Mary Claude was supposed to see her relatives, the Reclams, at Geneva this summer. Might not his "passion" for her illuminate his mind, his view of the past and deepest commitments and yearnings? Love for Matthew, at twenty-five, is not so much an exciting sensation as a way of knowing; less a palace of delights than a window opening on himself and the world.

On the night of September 29, he feared the beauty of a pale exile with blue eyes. In hotel firelight at Leukerbad, he predicts his "Marguerite" lyrics in his rather pseudo-Elizabethan lines for Clough:

> 'Say this of her:
> The day was, thou wert not: the day will be,
> Thou wilt be most unlovely: shall I chuse
> Thy little moment life of loveliness
> Betwixt blank nothing and abhorred decay
> To glue my fruitless gaze on . . .?'[20]

His view of poetry is the reverse of Baudelaire's—a *poem* cannot save a lady from the worms, but may save a poet from a worm-bound lady. Time will remind him of the transience of his lovely Ambleside neighbor's blue eyes.

On September 30, he walked out of his hotel into white, freezing mists. They lay along the valley concealing the Rhône. Climbing the Gemmi Pass near the shale avalanches, he looked back over a magnificent autumn scene, and, after a second look a year later, he depicted the view in the "Stanzas"—in a manner suggesting canvases by Caspar David Friedrich (1774–1840), who like Arnold rejected the optimism of transcendentalists.

He used the severe, nominal style with more restraint in "Dover Beach," but here it lends dignity to the natural scene and beauty to his passionate identification with Obermann:

> Behind are the abandoned baths
> Mute in their meadows lone;
> The leaves are on the valley paths,
> The mists are on the Rhone—
>
> The white mists rolling like a sea!
> I hear the torrents roar.

Yes, Obermann, all speaks of thee;
I feel thee near once more!

. . . . . .

Yet, through the hum of torrent lone,
And brooding mountain-bee,
There sobs I know not what ground-tone
Of human agony.

. . . . . .

Away the dreams that but deceive
And thou, sad guide, adieu!
I go, fate drives me; but I leave
Half of my life with you.[21]

These lines are German in feeling. In 1848 he intended to meet a lady who read and—in her own stories—imitated the sentimental German Richter. Born in Berlin, Mary Claude still read enough of the Germans to be called "a good German." Anne Clough, her friend, had lately visited the town of Thun, known for its folklore and Minnesinger legends. Mary was now collecting German folktales, and she probably meant to reach the Hôtel Bellevue, Thun, for a meeting with Arnold. If Arnold's heart raced as he reached the hotel he had time to admire the lobby, even to feel vexed, outraged, jilted, and stoical and half-relieved, too. Mary had returned home earlier than planned, and Arnold simply cooled his heels on the Hôtel's Hofstettenstrasse. Later, he made his way down the scenic Aar Valley to the Rhine, and sailed towards England by "slow stages."[22]

Back at home, he talked to his most worldly sister Mary or Bacco, and, on November 25, 1848, she wrote a "long letter" about "Matt's romantic passion for the Cruel Invisible, Mary Claude."[23]

Matthew had laughed at everyone else's romances. Now, his family and friends were amused to learn that he had gone to Switzerland to see a "neighbouring" girl who hadn't appeared! "Matt's romantic passion" delighted Tom in New Zealand "beyond everything"[24]—and Walrond, Shairp, and Clough "ridiculed" him at home.

His situation was bad and becoming worse. His humiliation and perplexity were only beginning. As his friends pressed for exact details, he began to look foolish. His romance in the Alps was *worse* than farcical: it now destroyed his pose as the easy Emperor who was more coolly witty and sophisticated than anyone else. Whatever he said, the joke was on *him*; for the story was too good; he appeared to have waited like a hot schoolboy for a princess—as if she would sexually succumb!—and the princess or the girl from Broadlands near Fox How had snubbed him! A letter of November and remarks of his friends suggest that Matthew's veneer of foppishness dissolved and deserted him, leaving him as a moodily irritable man in his twenties with a monocle, and a look of misery. With detachment he might have found a neat formula to combat this—but his emotions were engaged. Six feet tall and overbuttoned and overdressed, he seemed obscurely pierced, struck in his Achilles' heel: indeed since his childhood days in leg-braces he had feared being taken as *less* than other people, as less wanted, less personable and engaging. He admired ridicule, but not when directed at his own head: Matthew in his twenties could not have people laughing *at* him. His friends clearly attacked him, and after a while Matthew struck back.

With quiet fury, he accused Walrond and Clough of not being "worldly" enough and of lacking in "tact." "That fool Shairp" surely came under fire, since Shairp took months to get over referring to "the said Hero—Matt."[25] In November, when he heard that the Oriel dons approved Clough's just-published *Bothie of Toper-na-Fuosich,* he struck back rather hard at Clough. (The *Bothie* was Clough's first book and he longed above all for Matthew's approval.) "I have been at Oxford the last two days," Arnold writes in a suave, lethal manner as if to demolish Clough's self-confidence,

> and hearing Sellar and the rest of that clique who know neither life nor themselves rave about your poem gave me a strong almost bitter feeling with respect to them, the age, the poem, even you. Yes I said to myself something tells me I can, if need be, at last dispense with them all, even with him: better that, than be sucked for an hour even into the Time Stream in which they and he plunge and bellow. I became calm in spirit, but uncompromising, almost stern. More English than European, I said finally . . . and took up Obermann, and refuged myself with him in his forest against your Zeit Geist.[26]

Though shaken, Clough accepted an apology for this letter—and Arnold kept on apologizing for it. Arnold ranted, too, about "intellectual dietetics." Actually his severe words reflect, in part, a new poetics, for he was turning for models of inwardness to the "sentimental school" of Senancour, Richter, Chateaubriand, and Foscolo. He was to practice the sentimentalists' *passion réfléchissante* in *Switzerland, Tristram and Iseult,* and *Empedocles on Etna.* Inward-seeing and wide-seeing, the reflective passion depends on feeling as a guide to knowledge. He believed his friends lacked the fine sensibility to *feel* and called them "more American than English," while warming himself over the refinement of Obermann—who is sensitively devoted to death, quite unlike Matthew's friends. "The living and the dying," Matthew jots, "—those who are to live must be vulgar like Napoleon —those who are to die may hang over Nature, like Obermann." Appropriately, he soon watched the faces of ladies and gentlemen in the London parks and found only "stupidity and hardness." He was becoming European with a vengeance; and after "agitation" he reported that he'd read Keats's letters without finding an "Idea" or even "isolated ideas."[27]

But he couldn't bear to be estranged from friends. Arnold was not a cold or vengeful man at twenty-six, or at any other time. He was sentimentally affectionate and loyal; he played the worldling lightly, on the implicit understanding that as Lord Lansdowne's secretary he really *was* superbly informed, serene, worldly, and chic. He vexed his friends, but at least those such as Clough, Shairp, and Walrond had no wish to destroy or humiliate him. The friends heard either from Anne Jemima Clough or through Arthur enough to know that his case was complex. Arnold was genuinely in love with Mary Claude. This complicated matters. If Mary had come on from Geneva to the Hôtel Bellevue without her mother—as had been possible—Arnold might have made love and kept her more than "one day" at the Bellevue. And if while waiting he half-expected her to appear unchaperoned, then his disappointment *was* crushing. Certainly by December the friends were anxiously looking for a way for him to save face, with *them;* and next month Arnold found a good way. In January 1849, when still insulting Clough in letters going overseas to Tom, he wrote "To my Friends, who ridiculed a tender Leave-taking."

This is a fine propaganda-effort. The poem is fascinating as a literal portrait of Mary Claude and as an exercise for better *Switzerland* lyrics ahead. So timid that she refused to attend a *"point de réunion"*[28] with her own mother, Mary had disappointed him by failing to meet him, he implies, *before* their parting in Westmorland:

> Many a broken promise then
> Was new made—to break again.

Hence he was not dejected or surprised, at all, to miss her in a pleasant hotel in the Alps. He grandly forgives lecherous friends:

> Laugh, my friends, and without blame
> Lightly quit what lightly came.

More suave and worldly than anyone else, he used to be a light fool like Todo Walrond and Campbell Shairp:

> But my Youth reminds me—'Thou
> Hast liv'd light as these live now.'[29]

To display the "memory picture" he had while waiting for his lady at the Hôtel Bellevue, he portrays her in harmless pastels. She is "Marguerite," a name chosen for her sympathy with European sentimentalists. Doubtless, up in the Lake District before they parted, the very beautiful Mary Claude had promised in June or July of 1848 to embrace him again:

> *Ah, I hope!—yet, once away,*
> *What may chain us, who can say?*
>   . . . . . .
>
> *Paint that lilac kerchief, bound*
> *Her soft face, her hair around:*
> *Tied under the archest chin*
> *Mockery ever ambushed in.*
> *Let the fluttering fringes streak*
> *All her pale, sweet-rounded cheek.*[30]

Mary Claude's mockery, her "power of . . . ridicule" and "wit" and "abuse" and "spleen," were almost as famous as her "paled" features. Hartley Coleridge felt she was "as beautiful a creature" as he had ever seen, but apparently feared her temper.[31] Having described her mockery as arch, Matthew conjures up a parting scene:

> *Paint that figure's pliant grace,*
> *As she toward me leaned her face,*
> *Half refused and half resigned,*
> *Murmuring: 'Art thou still unkind?'*
> *Many a broken promise then*
> *Was new made—to break again.*[32]

Her underlying "sadness" or "pensiveness"[33] were, in fact, well-known among the Friedrichstadt exiles in England. Matthew paints her with exactness, as his friends Walrond and Clough know her well:

> *Paint those eyes, so blue, so kind,*
> *Eager tell-tales of her mind;*
> *Paint, with their impetuous stress*
> *Of inquiring tenderness,*
> *Those frank eyes, where deep I see*
> *An angelic gravity.*[34]

His refrain suggests a gauche view of kissing, but alertness to Shakespeare:

> *Ere the parting kiss be dry,*
> *Quick, thy tablets, Memory!*

"My tables, meet it is I set it down," Prince Hamlet vowed when recalling the Ghost and trying to forget Ophelia.[35] Matthew would recall his own Ophelia, who has walked with him in "moonlight"—but alas! he forgets her already:

> *What, my friends, these feeble lines,*
> *Show, you say, my love declines?*
> *To paint ill as I have done,*

Proves forgetfulness begun?
Time's gay minions, pleased you see,
Time, your master, governs me;
> *Pleased, you mock the fruitless cry;*
> *'Quick, thy tablets, Memory!'*

Ah, too true! Time's current strong
Leaves us fixed to nothing long.[36]

But he never forgot Mary Claude. "About her," he wrote in October 1886, "I have a sentiment and her looks as I remember them."[37] Her tension between mockery and gravity, her baptism in a small, close-knit, ardent French-speaking community at Friedrichstadt, in March 1820, and her connection with French exiles at Magdeburg, Berlin, and Geneva—all would be remembered. "Tall and beautiful" in the eyes of one of her friends, and *"beautiful exceedingly"* even in "mind" to another, she was an author in her own right. "Intense" and candid in manner, she was more than a slender Continental heroine; and yet, but for the tangible evidence of Claude letters and Anne Clough's diary,[38] one might imagine she had stepped out of *René* or *Werther*.

Having emigrated from the French community at Berlin, Mrs. Claude with her four daughters and her son, Louis, summered at Rothay Bank when the Arnolds moved into Fox How. Gradually, the Arnolds discovered that the Claudes belonged to an international network of French Protestant exiles; Claudes and Reclams and Chambeaux had left France for Switzerland after the Revocation of the Edict of Nantes; an Adolph Claude had married a Jeanne Reclam and emigrated to Valparaiso—and as an emigré "Marchand à Liverpool," Adolph's brother had moved from Berlin to Liverpool in the 1820s, with the young and pretty Mrs. Claude. Widowed in England in 1828, with five young children, Mrs. Claude had come under the protection of the wealthy James Brancker and then had taken a summer house—Rothay Bank—to be near Brancker's garish summer home at Clappersgate.

A vivacious woman with an accent, Mrs. Claude often chattered in strange tongues with her four beautiful daughters—Anne Lucrèce, Mary, Jane, and Louise. (Even as a child, Mary Claude was an eager linguist; she later fretted because her Valparaiso cousin Jeannette at eleven knew only German, French, Italian, Spanish, and English, "besides what a child is generally taught at school.")[39]

On the other hand, Mrs. Claude quite meant to become an "english" woman herself. At Ambleside in the summers, she let her only son Louis keep a pistol, and urged him to play with the Arnold boys. Louis was "occupé a faire *des riens*," as she wrote,[40] but she laughingly approved of Louis's young friend "Matthew"—and Louis Claude, in fact, was to send Matthew Arnold a letter about "old times" and meet him in 1884 at Madison, Wisconsin. In the 1830s Matthew and Louis had shot together; they perhaps explored the circular path and hidden house at Curwen's Island—one model for Circe's Isle in the "Strayed Reveller"—and scrambled on the slopes at Wastwater, which Matthew revisited before writing "Dover Beach."

Matthew remembered young Mary Claude as a dream-child or slender "vision"; her birth in a French community, in Germany, must have made her irresistibly entrancing in his boyish view.[41] In her mother's eyes the girl was only a gangly, headstrong creature with a tongue. "We go on abusing Liverpool," Mrs. Claude wrote one winter in improving English to her admiring friend Hartley Coleridge. "Mary remains as vigorous as ever . . . and looks forward to spring and the hope of visiting Ambleside as her only comfort." Mary acted out Friedrich Schiller's plays with Anne Lucrèce, and took dancing lessons "in defiance of the godly."[42] At Rothay Bank she was in her element: she esteemed Frederick Faber the poet and became disenchanted only when she read his verses—instantly, he ceased to be "something more than mortal." Often she led her sisters on picnics and climbs: the girls "love Fairfield and Loughrigg better than anything else in Westmorland," wrote Mrs. Claude. In a long dress, Mary led a company of pretty sisters on a delightful "short cut"[43] to Rydal near the Fox How meadow where, on a "soft" day, "The New Sirens" was composed.

When Rothay Bank was sold, in 1839, the Claudes vanished. Hartley, meanwhile, spoke of their tragedy. It seems that Mrs. Claude was the first to recover after the death of Mary Claude's frail elder sister, Anne Lucrèce: "short as it was," wrote the mother, "her life had been useful—why should I grieve:" But Mary grieved for Anne Lucrèce. On a trip to London she denounced St. Paul's and some of the other churches and then one night at Dulwich Wood she wept while the nightingales were gloriously singing. "Mary was much disappointed in the song of the nightingale, not in the beauty but in the character," Mrs. Claude told Hartley. "In poetry they are always (she says) connected with despairing hours . . . & she is much amazed to find them so joyous—so exulting." Hartley, as a talented son of S. T. Coleridge, was touched and charmed by this news. "Still more should I have been delighted," Hartley wrote to Mary Claude, "had my Father been alive, in as much as he was the first modern Poet to explode and defy the old fancy of the Nightingale's *melancholy song*."[44]

If the story about Mary Claude and the nightingales reached Fox How, it would not have been lost on the young poet there. Matthew felt that Mary's temperament was "inextricably allied" with sadness[45] —and yet she returned to bright, aggressive moods in 1842 when the family resettled at Broadlands on the plain of the Rotha and Brathay. Taken to an exhibition by her mother Mary Claude was so bored that she allowed herself to be shocked by a "galvanic battery" on display and exclaimed loudly, "Try it on the dead reptiles in the next room!" She upset friends by mocking the ugliness of commerce, and congratulated Hartley on going to Plymouth where he might see "Men of War instead of men of business."[46]

Slender enough to have stepped out of *René,* she was reading romances and even writing them. In the spring of 1845, she met Anne Clough; the two women became good friends; and when Anne stayed at Broadlands, she drew Mary into the Clougho-Matthean set. Mary was then surrounded by fascinating young men, with whom she quite lost her timidity: "Mary C. and I rode the poneys most of the way to Skelwith and had Arthur as a companion," Anne notes with pleasure in June 1847. Later, "Mr. Walrond came. We went on the lake in a boat down to the Ferry house and had the most beautiful views of Fairfield and Troutbeck and in Langdale. . . . We lay between Curwen's Island and the shore." Moonlight walks agreed with Mary Claude: "In the evening walked by moonlight by the waterfall. . . . Brothers' Water . . . and Mr. Arnold joined us there. . . . We scrambled up the waterfall and among the rocks in the stream. Dined under the trees by the stream." After an evening at the Arnolds', Mary it seems was among those "lost" on the fells on a "beautiful moonlight night."[47]

Yet if Matthew feared her "dark blue eyes" and anguished over the "tie" of passion, how did his "romantic passion" for her develop? Clearly, he valued her feeling for Foscolo and Richter and esteemed her writing. Books circulated in his set. (Hartley's books, as we know from Mrs. Claude's and Mrs. Arnold's notes, went from Nab Cottage to Fox How to Broadlands and back.) In her own *Consideration* (1847), Mary Claude refers to the "impotency" of mind, to the "littleness of the human understanding" and to that in nature which is "far beyond the comprehension of human reason."[48] Written at twenty-six, that little tract led her to deny the value of abstract reason, and she plunged defiantly into European literary sentimentalism. Her fondness for Novalis and Richter, moreover, reinforced her impatience with church going: "Mary and I," Anne noted, "staid at home while the others went to church. . . . There is in Mary Claude such an intense degree of feeling for suffering. . . . We agreed that church going in a general way did not tend to excite, at least not in our own case. . . . [Mary Claude] spoke too of the weariness and painfulness of thought."[49]

Mary found some "relief" from thought by imitating Foscolo and

Andersen. Foscolo had written of man's bitter, total isolation and of the consoling moon, and Mary expands a page of his sentimental *Letters of Ortis* in her own allegory, "The Moon." Andersen had written fables of the sea; and Mary, in her poem "The Sea," calls for prayer but implies that beauty and power in the "red and green"[50] deep are alienated from the Christian order. "The Forsaken Merman" (1849) is not unlike "The Sea" (1847), with its red and green imagery, and Arnold admitted he found in Mary Claude's fables "the soul of Northern Europe" and the genius of the "Germany of Jean Paul Richter" and the "Denmark of Hans Christian Andersen."[51] He admired her use of the daisy as a symbol of modern isolation; he thought well of Mary's interest in Foscolo, and preferred her sentimental Germans to the skeptical, excoriating Heine, who quite "disgusted" him, as he told his mother.[52] Mary Claude's authors yearned for that *wholeness* of mind and feeling existing before the shocks of the Reformation and French Revolution. Tieck, Novalis, and Richter, as Arnold felt, were "rivers" or "courses of spirit" detectable in Goethe and might offer clues for a new art, and Mary was Matthew Arnold's ally in the Clougho-Matthean set from 1847 to 1849. While he admired her authors he wrote his most successful poetry; and when he came to believe that Heine had quite destroyed the German sentimental school, his best days as a poet were over.[53]

"To Meta" shows that he was eager to treat a lovely exile's views with respect. "The daisy," as Charlotte Yonge explains in *History of Christian Names,*

> = symbol of humility = marguerite. . . . German forms: . . . Mete, in the time of Klopstock's sway over the lovers of religious poetry was very fashionable; and Meta almost took up her abode in England.[54]

"Meta" is romantic German equivalent of "Marguerite"; and in "To Meta," Arnold allegorizes one of the choice themes of that "good German" Mary Claude by recreating a special moonlight walk. Strolling in an upland valley with a beautiful young woman who admires Novalis's yearning for the cloister, the poet observes

> *the sweet and moon-bathed land.*
> *Softly gleam the far blue mountains,*
> *Dark the valley sleeps in shade.*

Suddenly he and his lady are not watching "Curwen's Island" or the "Ferry," but the pallid walls of a medieval cloister. With mild alarm, Meta turns to him:

Meta, with a vague misgiving
Your sweet eyes are turned on me.[55]

Perhaps the idea of the "cloister and life liveable" is a distinct possibility, a choice lovers might make. Arnold hardly needed to feign sympathy with Mary's views for he could understand the need for cloistral withdrawal from the world, especially when in love. He jotted in one diary of his late twenties:

> [Mme de Staël's] Delphine says—
> Malgré mon gout pour la société de Paris, je retirerai ma vie et mon coeur de ce tumulte.
>
> In der Liebe ist es anders. Du verdienst sie weil du dich nicht darum bewirbst—und die Leute erhalten sie auch meist allein die nicht danach jagen. (In love it is otherwise. You deserve it because you do not strive for it—and for the most part those only gain love who do not hunt for it.)
>
> After dinner walked alone to Brathay churchyard and sate there till dark. . . . Thorough bad day: & could never collect myself at all.[56]

But on the other hand he was too fascinated by the world and addicted to theatres and bachelor supper parties with barristers to see himself in a retreat, even in a love nest forever with a pale lady. Meta asks him to make a choice. "Where," she demands as they approach the shimmering cloistral walls,

> *is assurance*
> *Of a spirit softly clear,*
> *Of calm wishes, mild endurance,*
> *All the heart enjoins, but only here?*[57]

In argument he usually let himself off the hook with light non sequiturs, but he is grave with his lady:

> *Spare me, Meta. Question rather*
> *That lone gazer leaning near.*

The question he asks her to put to the medieval "lone gazer" at the cloister, "Tell me, is it quiet here?" is tendentious, for he knows the answer. In fact, he makes love to Meta's deliciously parted lips through the eyes of the monk, even as that figure rises slowly

> *From the pillar where he leans,*
> *In your gentle melancholy*
> *All your spirit's history gleans;*
> *Scans those parted lips, that purely*
> *Pleading gaze, that forehead clear,*
> *Signs the cross and answers, 'Surely*
> *You say true, my daughter, peace is here.'*[58]

Arnold refused to print "To Meta," perhaps because he saw that having written it in the stanza of "The New Sirens" he had disguised a love lyric as a treatise on German sentiment for the abbey. He may have sent it as a peace offering to Mary Claude, after she failed to appear at Thun. Anyway, their romantic understanding hardly survived his being ridiculed by his intimate friends. The fact that he printed "Tender Leave-taking" about her kisses, in *The Strayed Reveller,* suggests that their romantic intimacy ended in 1849.

Returning to Thun in September of that year, he further considered love's uses. Matthew certainly had found that the doctrine of correspondences teaches Obermann that the "complement of everything is outside itself" and that love is valuable, if illusory.[59] As for sexual love, Obermann says that "morality would be substantially the gainer by abandoning the support of an ephemeral fanaticism in favor of dignified dependence upon indisputable evidence."[60] The commands *thou shalt* and *thou shalt not* are fanatical and degrading because we do not know who we *are.* But Obermann insists that love may be a phantom and that its sensations cannot lead to truth about the self, or to peace which is in the heart "inaccessible to illusions." Obermann's ethical sponsorship of love is at odds with his quest for truth. Arnold seems, however, to have found in Mme de Staël a clue as to how love, strongly approved by European sentimentalists, may become an avenue for self- and even world-knowledge. In the tragic love in Goethe's *Werther,* Mme de Staël had stated, the hero's feeling is that of *"la passion réfléchissante, la passion qui se juge elle-même."*[61]

Passion which exists to *judge itself* depends on the extreme isolation of the hero. In Chateaubriand's *René,* for example, the hero's incestuous love for his sister Amélie drives him guiltily up Mt. Etna's charred, bleak rim, where he sees at one glance the world below maplike and ordered, and at another glance an image of his soul *"dans le cratère de l'Etna."*[62] Doubtless the *"passion réfléchissante"* is arduous. In 1849 Arnold was carried emotionally up to Mt. Etna's crater with poor René, and again left at an "abyss" with Obermann who cries, "But on what shall disillusioned thought repose?"[63] If the reflective passion requires that one shall learn about the self and the world by impugning analytic thought and detaching oneself forcibly from society, then from what source is joy needed for creativity to come? He was to approach that problem among others in *Empedocles on Etna.*

In the Alps, he set to work on lyrics of *"passion réfléchissante"* for *Switzerland*—a sequence of poems which have little relation to English love lyrics and are by far the most European works he ever wrote. "Meeting" and "Parting" were certainly drafted at Thun. "A

Dream" and "A Farewell," as well as "Isolation. To Marguerite" and "Letters of Ortis" may belong to 1849. "Absence, which involves Miss Wightman as well as Mary Claude, may have been written in 1850. Five of these lyrics appeared with his *Empedocles on Etna* in 1852, and then in the *Poems* of 1853 he first arranged seven in a coherent story-telling *Switzerland* sequence. In later editions, he changed number, order, and titles of the lyrics until, in 1877, he settled on the arrangement we have today.[64]

He first seems to transfer Mary Claude, boldly, to a region of 125 square miles of blue ice, in "Meeting," where she appears near the Lake of Thun:

> *Again I see my bliss at hand,*
> *The town, the lake are here;*
> *My Marguerite smiles upon the strand,*
> *Unaltered with the year.*
>
> *I know that graceful figure fair,*
> *That cheek of languid hue;*
> *I know that soft, enkerchiefed hair,*
> *And those sweet eyes of blue.*[65]

There is no unfeeling sterility here—nor self-satisfaction. The nominal style turns everything into an emphatic substantive: the town, the unchanging lady suggest a fixed "memory picture" and a mind in quest of permanence and stability. On "moonlight" walks near home, he must have considered what he would do if his lady were willing to yield herself wholly to him:

> *Again I spring to make my choice;*
> *Again in tones of ire*
> *I hear a God's tremendous voice:*
> *'Be counselled, and retire.'*
>
> *Ye guiding Powers who join and part,*
> *What would ye have with me?*
> *Ah, warn some more ambitious heart,*
> *And let the peaceful be!*[66]

Pride goads him to sexual conquest, but pride defeats him as a poet by inhibiting his imagination. Trying to reform himself he has told Clough, "We have the common quality, now rare, of being unambitious, I think." He now mocks pride with an allusion to Homer: when Patroclus in the *Iliad* stormed the Trojan gates the shining god, Apollo, appeared over the gates to tell him to retire. That Apollonian voice seems to reflect his need for authority—for a comforting release from the dictates of an imperious will. Behind his words, "I will have a real effort at managing myself"[67] (Matthew swore off reading newspapers on one day and conscientiously read them the next), one sees a poet who had exalted volition's role in trying to be true to noble ideas and strong desires by willing himself to act on them. When they conflicted he was torn apart by his own moral and idealistic mind.

In "Parting," he invokes the congenial and pure autumn storm-winds that symbolize his passion for a lady:

> *Ye storm-winds of Autumn!*
> *Who rush by, who shake*
> *The window, and ruffle*
> *The gleam-lighted lake;*
> . . . . . .
> *Ye are bound for the mountains!*
> *Ah! with you let me go*
> *Where your cold, distant barrier,*
> *The vast range of snow,*
> *Through the loose clouds lifts dimly*
> *Its white peaks in air—*
> *How deep is the stillness!*
> *Ah, would I were there![68]*

The winds would drive him from his lady to a region of ideal calm and stillness—but they are inimical to life in defoliating the alpine valleys and freezing the land. In the stillness he may find only aridity, a separation from friends who give him after all the best sense of himself; and he recognizes that he cannot live within the framework of his view of the soul's contemplative retreat, the soul's purity of being and knowing. When most in retreat, he genuinely aches for a lady. Arnold recalls her voice in a vignette suggestive of his earliest visits to the wide, wet lawns of Rothay Bank—where the beautiful young sisters of Louis Claude so often chattered in French and German:

> *What voice is this I hear,*
> *Buoyant as morning, and as morning clear?*
> *Say, has some wet bird-haunted English lawn*
> *Lent it the music of its trees at dawn?[69]*

But a succeeding vignette of strangled sounds and thundering cataracts drowns out the temptations of love and society. Like Faust, he would seize the unconscious, martial up a beautiful spirit when it might serve:

> *Ah! they bend nearer—*
> *Sweet lips, this way![70]*

He achieves only a perspicacious sense of bewilderment in the face of life's choices. Desires and ideals swing him to and fro. With its unlinked interior monologues following in a rushing contradictory sequence, "Parting" suggests that truth for the individual lies in a continuum of psychic states. The poem must have been written in a fine impulsive rush of feeling and polished in tranquillity: its structure might be that of the unconscious. Arnold here opened a door to the future in predicting dramas of the experiencing psyche from his own *Tristram and Iseult* and *Empedocles* through Clough's *Dipsychus* and Tennyson's *Maud,* to later combinations of interior monologues in Pound and Eliot.

The coda of "Parting" has a temporal as well as a spatial reference. Mary Claude reminds him not only of European sentimentalism, but of the time when she herself was a "vision" in the creative "Westmoreland of Wordsworth and Hartley Coleridge" (as he wrote of her).[71] She is like Obermann's *marguerites des prés,* which have the power of uniquely evoking the past. In the coda, he traverses a time span from the analysis-ridden present to his childhood past, with its simple nature worship and its accustomed family prayer bells (which he had taken very easily for granted). In those days he had encountered Shelley's poems, and there are Shelleyan echoes in his verse:

> *Forgive me! forgive me!*
> *Ah, Marguerite, fain*
> *Would these arms reach to clasp thee!*
> *But see! 'tis in vain.*
>
> *In the void air, towards thee,*
> *My stretched arms are cast.*
> *. . . . . .*
>
> *Far, far from each other*
> *Our spirits have grown;*
> *And what heart knows another?*
> *Ah! who knows his own?*
>
> *Blow ye winds! lift me with you!*
> *I come to the wild.*
> *Fold closely, O Nature!*
> *Thine arms round thy child.*
>
> *To thee only God granted*
> *A heart ever new—*
> *To all always open,*
> *To all always true.*
>
> *Ah! calm me, restore me;*
> *And dry up my tears . . .*[72]

He is much less successful in "A Farewell," in which he tries to imagine what a real love affair might be like in the Alps; but he succeeds when the evoked feeling ranges back to childhood. His greatest Switzerland lyric replies to Foscolo's *Ortis* and gestures towards Mary Claude's "Letter Addressed to a Friend in Returning a

Book" (and reflects the isolation theme of her stories) but also contains echoes of the reading he had done long in the past, beginning with Keble's *Christian Year* (which he knew when in leg braces at Laleham). The first value of Mary and the sentimentalists to him, as a poet, was that they helped him to concentrate large, important spans of his emotional life in brief lyrics.

Mary Claude's volume of fables, *Twilight Thoughts* (1848), begins with an epigraph from Jean Paul Richter, which perhaps led Arnold back to Carlyle's quotation from Jean Paul, where he found a compelling image for modern isolation of the spirit:

> Isolation is the sum-total of wretchedness to man. To be cut off, to be left solitary; to have a world alien, not your world. . . . Without father, without child, without brother. Man knows no sadder destiny. "How is each of us," exclaims Jean Paul, "so lonely, in the wide bosom of the All!" Encased each as in his transparent "ice-palace"; our brother visible in his . . . , visible, but forever unattainable; on his bosom we shall never rest, nor he on ours. It was not a God that did this; no![73]

Having used the Endymion and Luna myth rather perfunctorily in "Isolation. To Marguerite," Arnold substituted, for Jean Paul's "ice-palace" metaphor, the vivid imagery of sea and islands in his next poem. He now contradicts Carlyle's opinion about God's noninvolvement in man's fate and fashions his title from Mary Claude's "Letter Addressed to a Friend" as well as from Ugo Foscolo's *Letters of Ortis*—the tale of a gloomy Werther-like Italian who kills himself after disappointments in politics and love. Wordsworth, who debated with the red-haired exile, Ugo Foscolo, at a soirée at Benjamin Haydon's in London, was perhaps correct in detecting cynicism in Foscolo. On that occasion Wordsworth had defended the value of "disinterestedness" as against Ugo Foscolo's angry tirade to the effect that selfishness was the basic human motive.[74] Drawing Wordsworth out on "Italian" subjects, Arnold perhaps heard his opinion of Foscolo—and Wordsworth may have repeated it at the Claudes' Rothay Bank where he called with Crabb Robinson. In any case Arnold's "To Marguerite, in Returning a Volume of the Letters of Ortis" aims to engage with Foscolo, Richter, and Carlyle, and to enlarge upon them.

The thoughts of Ortis about his estrangement proceeded from that hero's bitter unhappiness: he failed to see isolation as *inevitable*. Since Arnold sees it as a principle in life, his manner is properly emphatic: *Yes, Ortis was isolated—and so are we all:*

> *Yes! in the sea of life enisled,*
> *With echoing straits between us thrown,*
> *Dotting the shoreless watery wild,*
> *We mortal millions live alone.*

The sea and islands are severe and reconciling—for as Nature reflects, symbolizes, and participates in man's condition its beauty may reconcile men and women to life. The islands have a separate, interior, Spinozan reality, and so they suggest a universal estrangement:

> *The islands feel the enclasping flow,*
> *And then their endless bounds they know.*
>
> *But when the moon their hollows lights,*
> *And they are swept with balms of spring,*
> *And in their glens, on starry nights,*
> *The nightingales divinely sing;*
> *And lovely notes, from shore to shore,*
> *Across the sounds and channels pour—*
>
> *Oh! then a longing like despair*
> *Is to their farthest caverns sent;*
> *For surely once, they feel, we were*
> *Parts of a single continent!*

Recent themes in Arnold's experience meet here: his awareness of the lost medieval religious unity and of England's separation from the necessary social thought of revolutionary France. More deeply the lines reflect memories of a time when he was isolated by a boy's pride at Laleham.

He replies to Richter and to the "sentimental school" Mary Claude championed: the sentimental moon and nightingales only deceive in suggesting that souls meet in high feeling, when our isolation is total. Lovers sense they might once have constituted a unity and in spirit remain apart:

> *Now round us spreads the watery plain—*
> *Oh might our marges meet again!*
>
> *Who ordered, that their longing's fire*
> *Should be, as soon as kindled, cooled,*
> *Who renders vain their deep desire?—*
> *A God, a God their severance ruled!*
> *And bade betwixt their shores to be*
> *The unplumbed, salt, estranging sea.*[75]

Since there is no longer a universal belief in a merciful God, the modern pagan deity of fate is mysterious, uncompassionate. The sea he has decreed between individuals is uncrossable, bitter to taste, measureless. That water is "the Mediator between the inanimate and man"[76] is man's dream; but we shall live in isolation without end until there is a spiritual basis again for life, and the poet returns to a thesis Girardin and Senancour pointed towards. Arnold's pessimism would not last; but he felt a rift opening between himself and others. He told his sister Jane that it was strange how life in subtle ways detached one from those unlike oneself: "I feel this," he enlightened Jane not long after she married, "in my relations to all of you. I am by nature so very different from you, the worldly element enters so much more largely into my composition, that as I become formed there seems to grow a gulf between us, which tends to widen till we can hardly hold any intercourse across it."[77] He had experienced the gulf when he attacked friends for mocking his romantic behavior. Another experience had come with his "intellectual dietetics," and a retreat into Obermann's lonely intuitive forest of perception. (He had patched up matters with Clough, but was seeing less of him).

It was his "worldly element" too, that divided him from Mary Claude, although her impatience with Arnold's egotism and her French "mockery" perhaps helped to end their "moonlight" walks. He is convincing when alluding to her guileless innocence and unworldliness:

> . . . the soft, ash-coloured hair—
> The cheeks that still their gentle paleness wear—
> The lovely lips, with their arch smile that tells
> The unconquered joy in which her spirit dwells.[78]

To be sure, *Switzerland* forces her back towards her role as a child-exile and neglects her intellectual and artistic life. Arnold never seems to have acknowledged that her skeptical attitude to abstract thinking was based on wide reading and earnest discussion. And yet his boyish "passion" for her helped, at least, to loosen the strong, deep hold that Jane Arnold had on his feelings and prepared him for fulfillment in love. Mary Claude's sentimentalists also helped him to rid himself of English literary influences and encouraged a confident inwardness of viewpoint in his work. Even "A Dream"—though not one of his best lyrics—suggests that the strong symbolism of the sentimentalists impressed him. That poem suggests a dream-fragment recorded impromptu. Sailing down an alpine stream, a young poet and his friend, Martin, pass a balcony upon which Marguerite and Olivia appear. The women wave and beckon as in a dream—

> Clad were they both in white, flowers in their breast;
> . . . . . .
> And more than mortal impulse filled their eyes.[79]

But the navigators drop under black cliffs, through racing alpine cataracts to the scorching plains of the arid, defeating spiritual present and then to a release in a sea of death. The poem illustrates the fate of talented men who have knowledge but, being crippled by it, are powerless to act; for they are, as Arnold's father stated in his last Oxford lecture, very much like men "embarked upon the rapids of fate, which hurry us . . . while all the while, there are banks on the right and left close in sight, an assured and visible safety if we could but reach it, but we try to steer and pull our boat thither in vain; and with eyes open, and amidst unavailing struggles, we are swept away to destruction."[80] The assured symbolism of the poem indicates that Mary helped Arnold from 1847 and 1849, in escaping from those inhibitions upon feeling that "A Dream" nightmarishly portrays.

Because Mary Claude neither married nor returned to the Berlin French community, references to Matthew's intimacy with her were suppressed after his own marriage. With much effort, he brought *Switzerland* to an end in 1863, with his awkward "Terrace at Berne," in which his romantic friend is symbolically reduced to prostitution and left as a corpse:

And Marguerite I shall see no more.[81]

He thus saved his friend from gossip, and kept the world from guessing at any connection between himself and Mary Claude, who in fact lived within a mile or two of Fox How until she died in 1912. But he wrote a much truer valedictory, in a few lines of "A Farewell," which recall *Traumdichtungen* or dream-passages by her own favorite author Jean Paul Richter. Arnold here borrows a phrase or two from Clough, and the main idea from Richter:

> *We shall one day gain, life past,*
> *Clear prospect o'er our being's whole;*
> *Shall see ourselves, and learn at last*
> *Our true affinities of soul.*
> . . . . . .
> *And we, whose ways were unlike here,*
> *May then more neighbouring courses ply;*
> *May to each other be brought near,*
> *And greet across infinity.*[82]

His romance with Mary Claude was agonizing, if not quite mortifying, to his ego, with long intervals between meetings in Westmorland and nervous kisses in the moonlit dark—but Mary became his effective "Marguerite," for he could recall her, so well, from their Lake District childhood. She proved to him that the bold, intuitive feelings of his early youth were unrecoverable. He was now concerned with a brighter underlying theme of *Switzerland:* the difficulty and necessity of a sustained relationship in love. And he was coming before the world as a poet.

8

"THE STRAYED REVELLER"
1849–1850

Consider whether you attain the *beautiful.*
> —*Arnold to Clough*

O NE of the best sports of the Arnolds at Fox How was Matthew-watching. "Matt," Jane writes to her brother Tom in an amusing letter, "is stretched at full length on one sofa, reading a Christmas tale of Mrs. Gaskell's which moves him to tears, and the tears to complacent admiration of his own sensibility."[1] Early in 1849, the Arnold sisters found an even more sensational topic than Matthew's "romantic passion" for Mary Claude. Matthew was to appear in print with a collection of lyrics!

Matthew awaited his debut before the public with the sense that he had fiddle-faddled away his youth. He was twenty-six. Perhaps he must succeed as a *poet* now or never. As publication day drew near, he used Clough as a stalking-horse or alter ego once again, putting many of his doubts about the introspective quality of his own lyrics and about his own failure to attain the "beautiful" and achieve "PLEASURE" into paragraphs that implied Clough was not advancing. "Dear Clough," he wrote from Lansdowne House in February, "If I were to say the real truth as to your poems in general, as they impress me—it would be this—that they are not *natural.*"[2] Clough dismissed this outburst as a reflection of Matthew's nerves.

Concerned with not disgracing the family name if he should fail, Matthew printed not under his own name, but as "A." (His father had used that initial when writing social criticism for the *Englishman's Register.*) Getting copies of his new book from his father's publisher, B. Fellowes, he sent them modestly to friends as "From the Author." When J. D. Coleridge remarked that he had got, in the post, a book by a strange "A," Matthew quickly told him: "Ah, yes, by an American."[3] A small dark green volume, *The Strayed Reveller, and Other Poems* by "A" appeared on February 26, 1849. The publisher apparently bore the cost of the imprint of 500 copies. "His doing everything at his own risk," as Matthew later remarked, "is a great thing."[4]

The Strayed Reveller seems a great thing—and a valuable rarity today—because for sheer lyrical beauty it is the best first collection of lyrics by an Englishman from Arnold's time to ours. Its twenty-seven poems—including the Balliol sonnets, the "Gipsy Child," "The Forsaken Merman," "Mycerinus," "The Sick King in Bokhara," "The Strayed Reveller," and "Resignation"—answer one or two Goethean questions that Matthew had thought about ever since his university days. At a time of false optimism and spiritual malaise, how is *any* poet to preserve himself? What should one accept or reject, and what is the proper attitude for creativity?

One understands why the volume seemed gloomy to an optimistic nation pleased with its industrial plant and new railways. Arnold implies that the modern poet is a representative man, and that man is as spiritually isolated as the Hayswater Boat in its black mountain tarn—

> *A region desolate and wild.*
> *Black, chafing water: and afloat*
> *And lonely as a truant child*
> *In a waste wood, a single boat.*
> *. . . . . .*
> *It moves, but never moveth on:*
> *And welters like a human thing*
> *Amid the wild waves weltering.*[5]

Fluctuations of the modern spirit in its moods and perceptions work against inner warmth, concentration, steadiness, strength, and hope. Clergymen, it seems, tell the same lies one reads in *The Times*'s leaders; and even the optimism of a Wordsworth or Tennyson is suspect, for in fact

> *Joy comes and goes, hope ebbs and flows*
> *   Like the wave;*
> *Change doth unknit the tranquil strength of men.*
> *   Love lends life a little grace,*
> *   A few sad smiles; and then,*
> *   Both are laid in one cold place,*
> *   In the grave.*
>
> *Dreams dawn and fly, friends smile and die*
> *   Like spring flowers;*
> *Our vaunted life is one long funeral.*
> *   Men dig their graves and bitter tears*
> *   For their dead hopes; and all,*
> *   Mazed with doubts and sick with fears,*
> *   Count the hours.*[6]

The pathos and truth in *Strayed Reveller* derive from the modest amount of Arnold's "action and suffering"[7] since his father's death —and the volume at the deepest level is a report to the Headmaster of Rugby. Thus "Mycerinus" is an allegory about a poet's behavior at Balliol and Oriel. The poem uses the story, in Dr. Arnold's beloved Herodotus, about the Egyptian Pharaoh who has reigned so well that the jealous gods tell him, through an oracle, that he must die in six years. With the irony of an undergraduate whose faith has been destroyed, Mycerinus comments on his only "crime":

> *My crime—that, rapt in reverential awe,*
> *I sate obedient, in the fiery prime*
> *Of youth, self-governed, at the feet of Law;*
> *Ennobling this dull pomp, the life of kings,*
> *By contemplation of diviner things.*[8]

Why live a virtuous life, if the heavens are cruel and unjust? Indignantly, Mycerinus leads a band of revelers to the cool palm groves of the Nile where he carouses for "six long years." His revels are interesting. Unlike the Pharaoh in Herodotus, he does not try to cheat the gods by drinking day and night to turn six years into twelve, but instead forgets the element of time:

> *His brow was smooth,*
> *And his clear laugh fled ringing through the gloom,*
> *And his mirth quailed not at the mild reproof*
> *Sighed out by winter's sad tranquillity;*
> $\cdots\cdots$
> *No, nor drew dark when autumn brought the clouds.*[9]

Like Arnold the drinker and gambler and laugher, he escapes from the consecutiveness of work—and thus becomes attuned to and a part of the eternity of nature. Implicitly, the poem associates drinking and eating with creativity, and even illuminates Matthew's later delight in his "Drinking Anecdotes":

Sophocles said to Aeschylus, alluding to his habit of drinking [Matthew wrote at the Athenaeum Club]—If you write what's good, Aeschylus, you write without knowing it. He composed his tragedies under the influence of wine—so did Alcous and Aristophanes.

Persians and Scythians great drinkers—The Scythian woman drank as well as the men.

The Thracians the beer-drinkers par excellence. The Aegyptians drink it. . . .

Cantibaris, a Persian, ate till his jaws were tired—then sate with his mouth open for his servants to cram him.

Cambes, king of the Lydians—a great glutton—one night cut up his
wife and ate her . . . the thing got known. . . .[10]

He was eventually to have his "weight problem"; and it was the
hedonist in him that helped to produce his best work.

His Egyptian poem refrains from describing Mycerinus's death
—and at the end leaves the reader with echoing sounds of the
Pharaoh's revels, which tell

> *his wondering people of their king;*
> *In the still night, across the steaming flats,*
> *Mixed with the murmur of the moving Nile.*[11]

Perhaps in contrast to the eternity of nature, the unmerited doom of a
king does not matter.

The title poem, "The Strayed Reveller," is a more complex and
oblique work. Arnold took its setting and two characters over from
Book X of Homer's *Odyssey* and gleaned material for the youth's
vignettes from Captain Alexander Burnes's *Travels into Bokhara*
(1834) (a source as well for "The Sick King in Bokhara" and "Sohrab
and Rustum") and from De Guérin's delicate fable "Le Centaure,"
which Mme Sand first published in 1840 in *Revue des Deux Mondes*.
In fact, the "Centaure" so haunted Arnold that he went about
breathing into his friends' ears "with the strangest pronunciation
possible," in 1847 or 1848, such lines as

> *Mais au bord de quel Océan ont-ils roulé la pierre qui les couvre, ô*
> *Macarée!*[12]

Further, the youth's vignettes are indebted to Goethe's idea in
"Grenzen der Menschheit" that the mortality of a beholder must affect
his mode of perception:

> *Was unterscheidet*
> *Götter von Menschen?*
> *Dass viele Wellen*
> *Vor jenen wandeln,*
> *Ein ewiges Strom:*
> *Uns hebt die Welle,*
> *Verschlingt die Welle*
> *Und wir versinken.*[13]

(How are the gods different from men? It is that the gods see before
them an endless flow of innumerable waves; but we are swept up and
devoured by the waves, and we sink to our deaths.)

But certainly, too, Matthew Arnold's memories of his *experience* of
reading romantic poetry, and of his parents' own poetry and of their
poetical theories, are apparent in "The Strayed Reveller."

At dawn a youth has left his hut among high chestnut woods, and while descending into a valley to join a throng of revelers at Iacchus's temple, he strays past the sleeping lions into Circe's palace. Having drunk of her magical wine, the youth awakes at dusk and speaks as loftily and beautifully as any character in Milton's *Comus:*

> *I see the night-dews,*
> *Clustered in thick beads, dim*
> *The agate brooch-stones*
> *On thy white shoulder;*
> *The cool night-wind, too,*
> *Blows through the portico,*
> *Stirs thy hair, Goddess,*
> *Waves thy white robe!*[14]

Naturally, Circe is amused by him. Why has he strayed from a world of revelers into a palace of art? "Trembling, I entered," he explains of his morning's visit; and one thinks of Arnold's straying from whist tables into the breakfast room of George Sand at Nohant.

Suddenly, the youth is seen by Ulysses, who in his cordial regard for boyhood and naiveté about poetry indeed resembles Dr. Arnold. "Ever new magic!" exclaims the Greek commander, stepping across Circe's portico like a sunburned ghost from Valhalla with "one arm bare."

> *Hast thou then lured hither,*
> *Wonderful Goddess, by thy art,*
> *The young, languid-eyed Ampelus,*
> *Iacchus' darling—*
> *Or some youth beloved of Pan,*
> *Of Pan and the Nymphs?*
> *. . . . . .*
> *What youth, Goddess, what guest*
> *Of Gods or mortals?*

"I lured him not hither, Ulysses," replies the goddess in her white gown.[15] The boy with vine leaves in his hair has wandered deliberately into her palace. To correct Ulysses' assumption that a poet is someone who picks up a trade, the youth now tells what he has seen when drunk with magic wine. He discourses very vividly on two distinct modes of poetry, and repeats Dr. and Mrs. Arnold's early theories. There had been for Dr. Arnold a kind of poetry that is superficial, charming, and luminous, as he had explained in his wife's journal:

> *Then so should Verse be but a passing Charm*
> *Or sing responsive but to outward Shows.*[16]

This poetry of "outward Shows" befits the "golden opening prime of Youth,"[17] as Dr. Arnold had thought, and Mrs. Arnold often composed "outward" poems. But, for both parents, there had been a serious, sincere, *inward* poetry, too, which truly means what it *says*. If the topic is an inward one, as Mrs. Arnold once duly explained,

> *I would not utter idle lays*
> *Like poets use to those less dear*
> *In verse which means not what it says.*[18]

Mrs. Arnold's inward poems are conventional enough, but Dr. Arnold had achieved a very simple, moving eloquence in the inward mode:

> *Servants of God!—and shall I say*
> *That ye as blind have gone astray?*
>
> *Where shall the River end, and who can stem*
> *The boundless Sea wherein its Stream is lost?*
>
> *What boots it though his early years*
> *Were wreathed with more than Childhoods flowers.*
>
> *Go my Friends & dig my grave*
> *For I would from wandering cease.*[19]

The simple, illustrated family poetics had been one basis for Arnold's early lucubrations on poetical theory. Contrasting two kinds of verse in "The Strayed Reveller" the youth now depicts several objects, real and fabulous, as seen by the happy Olympian "Gods" and again by the "wise bards." The visions of gods are superficial, charming, painterly, and beautiful. Turning "on all sides their shining eyes," the gods behold the blind prophet Tiresias, or the proud, snuffing Centaurs in Pelion's glens:

> *They see Tiresias*
> *Sitting, staff in hand,*
> *On the warm, grassy*
> *Asopus bank,*
> *His robe drawn over*
> *His old, sightless head,*
> *Revolving inly*
> *The doom of Thebes.*
>
> *They see the Centaurs*
> *In the upper glens*
> *Of Pelion, in the streams,*
> *Where red-berried ashes fringe*
> *The clear-brown shallow pools,*
> *With streaming flanks, and heads*
> *Reared proudly, snuffing*
> *The mountain wind.*[20]

Here is the spontaneous, pure poetry of the childlike sensibility that was so praised by Richter and Schiller. One may say that in our own century in English poetry only T. S. Eliot has equaled its intensity —and indeed *The Waste Land* reminds one of vignettes in the "Reveller." The gods' cameos, however, are restricted to isolated moments in time and satisfy as renditions of single viewpoints. But "Tiresias" and "the Centaurs" may effectively be seen in different ways; in fact, these very same objects, as the youth tells Ulysses,

> *The wise bards also*
> *Behold and sing.*
> *But oh, what labour!*
> *O prince, what pain!*[21]

Ulysses (and Matthew's father) have underestimated the artist's needful suffering and work. Dr. Arnold belittled verse that responds "but to outward shows," and felt that even worthy, inward poetry is only a matter of inspiration. Holding that inward poetry results from "labour" and "pain," Matthew bridges a gap between his aestheticism and his family's work ethos—and moves closer to Dr. Arnold.

The "wise bards" know how the Centaurs feel in combat with the Lapiths, in that fierce struggle in which the Greeks found a symbol of the defeat of barbarism by civilization. Sympathizing not merely with the rational Lapiths, the bards must also feel the heavy Lapithian spears that drive crashing through the Centaurs' bones—and know the terror inflicted by Theseus and by Alcmena's "dreadful son" Hercules:

> *They see the Centaurs*
> *On Pelion;—then they feel,*
> *They too . . .*
> *. . . . . .*
> *They feel the biting spears*
> *Of the grim Lapithae, and Theseus, drive,*
> *Drive crashing through their bones; they feel*
> *High on a jutting rock in the red stream*
> *Alcmena's dreadful son*
> *Ply his bow;—such a price*
> *The Gods exact for song:*
> *To become what we sing.*[22]

The price of the artist's humanity is to become what he sings; in Arnold's view of the imaginative life the poet cannot escape the pain of the human lot.

But how is Arnold's youth to become a "wise bard"? Arnold's failure to say how, in "The Strayed Reveller," is more than a deficiency: the poem leaves the youth simply wondering about his experience. Yet the youth touches on the mystery of creativity. If "labour" and "pain" are conditions of life, then dreams, laziness, childhood, timelessness, the unconscious—even drunkenness—may be the conditions of poetry. The youth in the end knows that Ulysses is as subject to illusions in the flux of experience as anyone else. "And thou," he finally cries out to the Greek commander,

> Wave-tossed Wanderer'
> Who can stand still?[23]

Certainly the youth has benefited from Circean wine. The poem implies that visions of Circean or romantic poets may help any new poet (though the youth must escape from romantic indiscipline). Arnold even implies that the vaguest, indulgent images in Keats or Shelley may be helpful to the neophyte poet; he only fails, perhaps, to indicate his own *comparativist* method of detaching himself from those poets. Unlike the Strayed Reveller, Arnold played England and the Continent off against each other, freeing himself from the spell of English romantics by adopting German and French romantic literary guides, and criticizing those guides ("lumbering old cart-horses") in the light of English literary graces.[24] He used and borrowed from the romantics, but was not deeply in thrall to them—and indeed he usually underrated Keats's and especially Shelley's ideas.

Less suggestive than "The Strayed Reveller," "The Sick King in Bokhara" was the first of his poems that "dear old Clough thoroughly liked,"[25] and here Arnold comes to terms with Rugby School's humanitarian social ethic. A Tamburlaine with a gnawing social conscience, the Bokharan King is "sick" because his pity cannot save the virtuous Moollah, or priest, who during a drought in Bokhara has cursed his family for stealing his drinking water. In Mohammedan law, it is a capital crime to curse one's family. Racked with guilt, the Moollah begs the King to try him for his crime and have him stoned to death.

After the Moollah is killed, the wise old Vizier—a Lord Lansdowne who believes that pity has its limits—points out to the King that charity ought to begin and end at home. As for the lepers, the sick, and the poor, exclaims the Vizier,

> All these have sorrow, and keep still,
> Whilst other men make cheer, and sing.
> Wilt thou have pity on all these?
> No, nor on this dead dog, O King![26]

Here is the good sense of Whig conservatism in opposition to the idealism of Rugby men such as Tom and Willy Arnold—as represented in the distraught, conscience-ridden Bokharan King. Why not "sing" as one can, rather than weep for the dead or the poor whom one cannot help? The dialogue between Vizier and King instructs those who would paint a man's role in stark primary colors, rather than see that loyalty to the self and loyalty to society demand a compromise. And what is the King's compromise? He will wash the dead Moollah's wounds and bury him, in state, in a beautiful "fretted brick-work tomb" on the Samarcand road.[27] The tomb is a symbol for aesthetic poetry, which may draw society's attention to some of its stoical and moral heroes.

In no other poem of 1849 does Arnold come closer to the true realities of industrial life and poverty than in the "Sick King," in which London is orientalized as dusty Bokhara. He hardly knew how to poeticize starvation and wretchedness, and his feeling that he *ought* to help his nation gave him sleepless nights and made him feel that his head was burning. What is impressive is the candor with which he expresses his own guilty social conscience in the King, and the ingenuity of the aesthetic compromise.

In "Resignation," set in the congenial Lake District, he makes a direct appraisal of the intellectual and spiritual legacy of his father. His sister Jane now becomes his alter ego; she is the half-bored, smiling, undisciplined Faustian activist in his own nature, who seems to desire "poignant experience," as Lionel Trilling[28] points out; but she is also important as a critic who punctures Arnold's complacent rhetoric and causes him to refine his ideas. The poem concerns essential similarities between his own walk with Dr. Arnold and Jane over the Armboth Fells in 1833, and the same walk with Jane a decade later. More sharply than in eighteenth-century landscape poems about two experiences of the very same scene, such as Goldsmith's "Deserted Village" or Wordsworth's "Tintern Abbey," this poem heightens its narrative content, so that one difference between the two walks stands out. On the second trudge, the Arnold children lacked their original guide. Boyish opening images of Huns who crouch in saddles, files of Goths, and warriors "scarfed with the cross" underline the militant aspect of the first walk; and at once the reflective Matthew criticizes that walk. Whereas, he says, the activist struggles to reach a goal, the "milder" poet demands freedom

> *from passions, and the state*
> *Of struggle these necessitate.*[29]

But the second walk reveals how little anything has changed. Matthew and Jane see the same stream, the same stones, and become simply "ghosts" of a spiritually boisterous company.

As the more loquacious ghost, Matthew muses on the gipsies he and Jane have just seen in the valley below, and defines an ideal of instinctive endurance. He admires the "hereditary" stoicism of the gipsies which saves them from disquieting ideas, but he denies them rationality as he introduces a long definition of the superior, all-perceiving poet. Unfortunately, there is so much braggadoccio in the long speech beginning,

> The poet, to whose mighty heart
> Heaven doth a quicker pulse impart,[30]

that Jane punctures his rhetoric with a smile at line 199—and he begins his reflections on the poetic nature all over again.

Jane's interruption, moreover, contains an important criticism of his own behavior and outlook. He reads her viewpoint apparently in the very curve of her lips:

> But that wandering smile,
> Fausta, betrays you cold the while!
> . . . . . .
> Those gipsies, so your thoughts I scan,
> Are less, the poet more, than man.
> . . . . . .
> Deeper the poet feels; but he
> Breathes, when he will, immortal air,
> Where Orpheus and where Homer are.
> In the day's life, whose iron round
> Hems us all in, he is not bound;
> He leaves his kind, o'erleaps their pen,
> And flees the common life of men.
> He escapes thence, but we abide.[31]

These lines probably offer the gist of comments on himself that he heard from the women in his family. As Arnold fled from work by escaping into a sinecure at Lansdowne House, so in his art he "o'erleaps" the day's tedium and exalts in the Homeric and Orphean ozone. His sisters felt that his ideas about life had no pertinence to ordinary men and women, from whom he held aloof. His sister Jane would not deny his talent, but she had a manner of contrasting him very unpleasantly with Wordsworth: "Matt's philosophy holds out no help," Jane in fact wrote pointedly to her brother Tom. "Wordsworth's poetry . . . did speak the word that was needed. . . . In a most artificial age, he led men back to Nature." But while common men are struggling for their own "spiritual, social or political life—and conscious that they must sink unless they find some mighty Helper, surely language [such as Matthew's] which tells them of a dumb unalterable order of the universe . . . will seem too unreal and too hopeless." Matthew has "a good deal of the Eastern philosopher about him" and that really doesn't "suit the European mind."[32]

Arnold, now, seems to reply to his sister's amiable viewpoint. Man, he firmly declares, inhabits a cosmos which outlasts every human interest, hope, grief, or joy: and if man could perceive farther in the macrocosms of his universe he would still see

> *and see dismayed,*
> *Beyond his passion's widest range,*
> *Far regions of eternal change.*[33]

Hence a poet judges "vain beforehand human cares" and approves the *resignation* which is recommended by Epictetus and especially by the Hindu *Bhagavad Gita:* "A disinterested mind and conquered spirit who in all things is free from inordinate desires, obtaineth a perfection unconnected with works, by that resignation and retirement which is called Sannyas."[34] To be sure, Matthew read the *Bhagavad Gita* with a mind qualified by Goethe, Coleridge, and the romantic poets generally, for his own "resignation" is a preparation for high achievement. At twenty-six, he "resigned" only from what he disliked (sexual love which might distract him from poetry and divide him from his family; the common herd; a dull profession) and accepted only about as much mysticism as he found in "Tintern Abbey." Upon the latter work he leans rather heavily, before using it as a foil. "They, believe me," he assures Jane near the end of the poem,

> *who await*
> *No gifts from chance, have conquered fate.*
> *They, winning room to see and hear,*
> *And to men's business not too near,*
> *Through clouds of individual strife*
> *Draw homeward to the general life.*[35]

The "general life" is that of nature, as presided over by a semipantheistic Wordsworthian Deity. Arnold was later to criticize the mystic, Amiel, of the *Journale Intime,* in a manner that suggests his own revulsion against confounding personal life with the "general life." Though forty years separate "Resignation" from his "Amiel" essay, there is only a slight shift of emphasis between them; in the former he would draw close to the natural life congenial to his pen; in the latter, avoid "bedazzlement with the infinite" enfeebling to *any* pen. Amiel let the bedazzlement "paralyze" him.[36] Far from being bedazzled by Wordsworth's mysticism, Matthew finds in rocks, hills, streams, and the "lonely sky" a Greek Stoical message. All these, he tells Jane,

> *If I might lend their life a voice,*
> *Seem to bear rather than rejoice.*[37]

His only original mystical note in "Resignation" is negative. The "something that infects the world" in the final couplets is a force of disquietude or a ubiquitous disease of the divided spirit in modern life, a tension in the individual who is at the mercy of the analytic *Zeitgeist* and far from being at one with himself. "Not milder is the general lot," Arnold concludes,

> *Because our spirits have forgot,*
> *In action's dizzying eddy whirled,*
> *The something that infects the world.*[38]

If he sees the resignation a creative poet needs, he has not achieved it; thus in the "dizzying eddy whirled" he is perhaps a neophyte Strayed Reveller rather than a Wise Bard or an Olympian.

What would friends and the public make of such a personal poem? Arnold now waited for everyone's opinion of the whole *Strayed Reveller*. "I have not heard from you my darling," he reminded his sister in March just after the volume appeared. "I hear from Fellowes that it is selling very well . . . I hear interest expressed about it, though everyone likes something different (except that everyone likes the Merman)."[39]

City men such as Brodie and J. D. Coleridge liked most of the poems; but his Oxford friends failed to see the volume's beauty. They complained that Arnold's "subjects"[40] didn't interest them. James Anthony Froude, whose novel *The Nemesis of Faith* lately had been burned in public by the Rev. William Sewell at Exeter College, was in no mood for lyric beauty: "I have *resigned*," Froude had just written to Arthur Clough. "I was *preached* against Sunday in chapel, denounced in Hall, and yesterday *burnt* publicly (by Sewell) before two Lectures." "I admire Matt," Froude wryly continued, "—to a very great extent. Only I don't see what business he has to parade his calmness and lecture us on resignation when he has never known what a storm is and doesn't know what he has to resign himself to. . . . I go to Bath the end of the week and will give Matt['s book] to [a friend]. I wish M. didn't so utterly want *humour*."[41]

Clough, who later spoofed "Resignation" by writing a "Resignation: to Faustus" with references to dung and urination,

> *True brother of the bipeds there,*
> *If Nature's need requireth,*
> *Lifts up his leg with tranquil air,*
> *And tranquilly retireth,*[42]

probably agreed that *"humour"* would have helped Arnold's book, and may have told him about Froude's reaction. If Arnold turned a deaf ear to critics such as Froude and Clough, he was most affected when his sister complained about the volume's unevenness. "Like what you can my darling," he replied to Jane. His faith in the volume began to crumble: "The poems stagger weakly & are at their wits end. . . .

Meanwhile change nothing, resign nothing that you have in deference to me or my oracles; & do not plague yourself to find a consistent meaning for these last."[43]

Clearly, he needed some praise. Actually he read more than a little in 1849. Seven prominent journals noticed the book; they were about equally divided on its merits and faults, yet even the more hostile virtually agreed with the *Guardian* that he had a "bold yet delicate touch," or with the *Spectator* that he showed "poetic power, and occasionally depth of thought." Most ranted against his metres while praising the "Merman." In an unsigned notice in *Fraser's*, Charles Kingsley observed the "delicate finish" and severity of language in Arnold's poems, finding in "Merman" a very healthy pathos. But Kingsley sounded a political note: "To what purpose," he asked in his review, was "all the self-culture through which the author must have passed[?] . . . When we have read all he has to say, what has he taught us?"[44] W. E. Aytoun in *Blackwood's,* a journal with weight in literary circles, nodded at his fine "painter's gift" and "promise," but seemed heavily facetious: "A" is gloomy for no reason at all, or rather because it is fashionable "to maunder so incessantly about gloom."[45] Puzzled as to whether the author, "A," is a grown man or a stripling, Aytoun finds him mainly a perverted imitator of Tennyson.

The Gentleman's Magazine found Arnold correct but insipid; the *Spectator* despite its kindness wondered if he had a "subject"; and the *Literary Gazette* blamed him (as some of his friends did) for imitating the classics.[46] Unable to make up its mind, *The Athenaeum* gave three-fourths of its review to quotations from his poems—itself a tribute. "He reminds one," wrote the *Guardian* handsomely, "of the picturesqueness of Homer and the pellucid depth of Sophocles, and yet never loses his individual existence." His "Strayed Reveller" and "Antigone" fragment, added the reviewer, convey the beauties of "Greek poetry" more fully than any other poems in English. This reviewer had an inkling, at least, of the importance of his metrical experiments in free verse in the "Reveller" itself. Having adapted from Greek choric meters and Goethe's experiments, Arnold in fact was helping to move English verse *technically* in a new direction.

Arnold waited a year before reading an even better notice by William Rossetti in the obscure, Pre-Raphaelite *Germ*. Rossetti saw that his self-conscious, intimate manner was one of his appeals and that "throughout" the volume he subordinated "the parts to the whole" and achieved rich beauty and gave pleasure. Rossetti said what the author wanted to hear. "Can you," Matthew later asked a friend, get "the address of one William Rossetti for me?—an ingenious youth who used to write articles in a defunct review."[47] But in 1849, he felt he had failed. He refused to credit the best reviews since Jane and trusted friends were lukewarm in his poems. Perhaps he was at war with himself. Although he hungered for Clough's and Walrond's praise, he had insulted both of these friends lately; and having damned Clough's *Bothie* in a bitter mood, he couldn't expect Clough's raptures now. Up at Fox How, Mrs. Arnold clearly sensed an emergency and sent Matthew a whole file of letters (including one from Miss Fenwick, who thought Tom had written the volume). Matthew replied that the letters were mainly kind, "though one's vanity desires instant trumpet-blowings in all the newspapers." Then he told Jane he had got "absolutely to dislike" *The Strayed Reveller*.[48]

The critics kept him in torment (as they never did in his late life) not because they wounded him, but because Arnold looked at their notices for a stamp of authority, that sanction or assurance which would tell him it was right for *him* to be a poet. Perhaps only the voice of his father would have given the full, calming assurance. He might go abroad, he told Jane later, to live at Rome in the manner of Goethe and "see no English" and "hear nothing more about my Poems. It does me no good hearing the discussion of them—yet of course I cannot help being preoccupied by it. I intend soon to try and make some strong resolution in this respect—and *keep it*."[49] He made up a list of approved critics: "You—Froude—Shairp," he told Jane, "I believe the list . . . stops there"; and then Froude and Shairp were crossed off and replaced by a better name. "You and Clough," he told Jane, were the critics he tried to please.[50] Of course, he could hardly write poems without Arthur Hugh Clough's *encouragement*, which was almost symbolized by their favorite tree in the Cumnor Hills! "Hear it," he was to write in his last report about that tree, in "Thyrsis," in which he apostrophizes his great friend,

> *from thy broad lucent Arno-vale*
> *(For there thine earth-forgetting eyelids keep*
> *The morningless and unawakening sleep*
> *Under the flowery oleanders pale),*
> . . . . . .
> *There thou art gone, and me thou leavest here*
> *Sole in these fields! yet will I not despair.*
> *Despair I will not.*

Whatever happened, he would have Jane Arnold as a reader. Jane, surely, would not fail him. Perhaps, indeed, his "esoteric" poems were "calculated to interest none but the writer and a few "esprits maladifs": Jane was "not an esprit maladif,"[51] as he quickly assured her; and surely, surely that dear sister would read his esoteric poems for his sake?

Not long before *The Strayed Reveller* appeared, he hopefully had jotted an interesting list of short poems to write in 1849:

Compose

 1. Empedocles—refusal of limitation by the religious sentiment.
 2. Eugenia—refusal of d[itt]o by the sentiment of love
 3. To Antonia—a system of the Universe.
 4. To Meta—the cloister & life liveable.
 5. Kantire & the net driers
 6. Thun & vividness of sight & memory compared: sight would be less precious if memory could equally realize for us.
 7. An Eastern court—dancing—consciousness—one bayadère appearing behind the other.
 8. Shelley—Spezzia—ah an eternal grief. The Alexandrian pessimism.
 9. Narcissus—some wish to be thy lover.
10. 5 sonnets—outthunder—So far—When I have found.—It may be true that men *cannot* do the best they can *devise* [desire?]: it is equally true they have never yet done it—5—
11. —religious yearning—an education by a chapel—youth—marriage —children—death   the religious yearning never quenched.
12. The first mesmerist.
13. The bête northern invaders turned back by the iron shoe trick.[52]

So far he had written No. 4 ("To Meta") as well as No. 6 ("Tender Leave-taking," about his reflections on the theme of "sight & memory compared" while waiting for his lady at Thun). Apparently No. 8 was to combine with No. 11 as "Stanzas from the Grande Chartreuse," and No. 12 after much work was to be "The Scholar-Gipsy." Among the projects which forever languished was No. 13, which was to be about a traveler who discourages a whole army from reaching Rome by holding up two pairs of broken iron-soled shoes, "new when he left Rome."

Early reviews of the *Reveller* decided him against printing "another volume of poems" the next spring. "I shall leave the short poems to take their chance, only writing them when I cannot help it," he told his mother in March, "and try to get on with my Tragedy."[53] He usually referred to his "unfinished Tragedy," Lucretius, in the future tense. This spring, political bickerings between ancient Milonians and Clodians, "events at the end of 53 B.C.," and the gloom-weighted figure of Lucretius quite depressed him.

What great subject would impress Jane Arnold and the critics—and give him free scope? In *De Rerum Natura,* Lucretius refers with cavalier respect to an earlier, very Goethean and wonderful figure, the Sicilian-Greek scientific theorist and poetic philosopher, Empedocles, of whose hymns and poem on nature less than 1,000 lines survive. His name came first on Matthew's composition list. In Diogenes Laertius's gossipy *Lives* (a book which once charmed Montaigne) he found several accounts of the proud young Empedocles who, with his friends and teachers Parmenides and Zeno-of-Elea and Xenophanes, had lived the exuberant philosophical existence of the Clougho-Matthean set. In the second volume, *Empedoclis Agrigentini Carminum Reliquiae,* of Simon Karsten's *Philosophorum Graecorum veterum, praesertia qui ante Platonem floruerunt,* published in Amsterdam in 1830–38, he found insights into Empedocles' career, character, and alleged suicide on Mt. Etna. Empedocles was a grandson of a victorious charioteer in the Olympic games. Born into an "illustrious family" at Agrigentum in Sicily around 490 B.C., he "swam" as a young man "in a swelling consciousness of his superiority." While exchanging witticisms with his friends, he wore "long waving hair" and a golden circlet and a purple robe to show that he was a *poet.* Having found many new medical cures and invented Greek rhetoric, he charmed the winds and played the lyre so well that his music restrained "a young man who [was] . . . intent to kill a judge."[54]

"He is a philosopher," Matthew jotted. In fact Empedocles had observed the narrow fragmented quality of perceptions and had emphasized bold, wide, realistic vision:

> He has not the religious consolation of other men, facile because adapted to their weaknesses, or because shared by all around. . . .
>
> He sees things as they are—the world as it is—God as he is: in their stern simplicity.
>
> The sight is a severe and mind-tasking one: to know the mysteries which are communicated to others by fragments, in parables.[55]

All of his life, Matthew might have been preparing to celebrate Empedocles. How often he had considered the "historical knowledge" symbolized in the rich horde of foreign and ancient coins, at home, in the "Mt. Etna Cabinet." "You have often felt amused & interested," Mrs. Arnold had told her children in the 1830s,

> by your father's coins—and I hope will be more so as you get more historical knowledge. . . . Mr. Cureton came down from London to value them. They were collected by my Uncle Sir Charles Penrose, whose different commands abroad had given him good opportunities —and it was very gratifying to me that they should thus be continued in our branch of the family. The old cabinet in which they are placed was made of wood that grew on Mt. Etna.[56]

Even as Dr. Arnold's pictures of the Schreckhorn and Finsteraarhorn at first brought Switzerland into Matthew's life, the Mt. Etna cabinet had given him a sense of another domain—the rich, historic past. His mother's interest in the cabinet's coins was paralleled by her excitement over panoramas and dioramas—and Matthew inherited that excitement. "To Panorama of the Tour of Europe with Clough and Slade,"[57] he jotted in a diary. He may have noticed the advertisements in London, all through the late summer and early autumn of 1848, heralding a new exhibit—"Mt. Etna. A Diorama."[58]

What apparently struck him most in 1849 was the interesting ambiguity of Empedocles' dramatic leap into the volcano of Etna. Why had this great man killed himself? The philosopher-poet was "filled . . . with joy": he had "friends who shared his hope and joy and communicated to him." But in middle age Empedocles lost his friends, the world was against him and incredulous of truth, and he fell on a barren time. Clouded and oppressed, he was still capable of intelligent action, and his suicidal leap into Mt. Etna's crater was *affirmative*. It was an action such as an honest René on Mt. Etna, or even the joy-seeking Obermann in the Alps might take. "Before he becomes the victim of depression," Matthew wrote in his working notes,

> and overtension of mind, to the utter deadness to joy, grandeur, spirit, and animated life, he desires to die; to be reunited with the universe, before by exaggerating his human side he has become utterly estranged from it.[59]

Indeed, like René and Werther and the Gipsy Scholar, Empedocles would remain young and "human" forever.

For a few weeks, after "fermenting too much about poetry in general to do anything satisfactory,"[60] Matthew surely found that *Empedocles* wrote itself. Before bogging down, he was seen by Campbell Shairp, who notified Clough exuberantly that "the said Hero—Matt" was "working on an 'Empedocles'—which seemed to be not much about the man who leapt into the crater—but his name and outward circumstances are used for the drapery of his own thoughts."

Matthew, it seems, was versifying his own sardonic desk-notes for his "Greek" poem. "I wish," sighed Campbell Shairp, "Matt would give up that old greek form but he says he despises all the modern ways of going about the art and will stick to his own. . . . He thinks he sees his way."[61] In the summer, however, he obviously lost his way. He was distracted now by Clough's absence in Rome, where that friend was looking at the siege of Mazzini's patriots by the French Army and seemed likely to have his head blown off. "Dear Matt," wrote Clough in a journal-letter from behind the bombarded Roman lines on June 23 and July 3, 1849.

> Why the d—l I shld write to you he only knows who implanted the spirit of disinterested attention in the heart of the spaniel—. . . . Our orbits

... early in August might perhaps cross. ... —Not that I particularly desire or any way urge such an event—but I advertise you that I hope to be in the Geneva country about that time—reposing in the bosom of Nature from the fatigues of Art and the turmoil of War!!!!

Quid Romae faciam? What's Politics to he or he to Politics? But it is impossible to get out [of Rome], and if one did, Freeborn, [the] Vice Consul, who however is a *Caccone*, says the French *avanposti* shoot at once.

What if Clough were killed?

Well, we are taken; the battery immediately to the left (as you go out) of San Pancrazio was carried by assault . . . while we in this corner got bombarded by way of a feint.—The Roman line in several cases has behaved ill. . . . I believe they meant to bombard us *really*.[62]

While Clough dodged the bombs of San Pancrazio, Matthew wrote his rather Spinozan "Consolation," to remind himself that man belongs to a universal rather than a political order:

> *Mist clogs the sunshine.*
> *Smoky dwarf houses*
> *Hem me round everywhere;*
> *A vague dejection*
> *Weighs down my soul.*
>
> *Yet, while I languish,*
> *Everywhere countless*
> *Prospects unroll themselves.*
> . . . . . .
> *Two young, fair lovers . . .*
> *Stand, tranced in joy.*
> . . . . . .
> *'Ah,' they cry, 'Destiny,*
> *Prolong the present!*
> *Time, stand still here!'*[63]

But this manner would not do for *Empedocles*. In July he published in the *Examiner* the sonnet "To the Hungarian Nation," but felt that his enthusiasm for the Hungarians under Kossuth (then resisting both the Austrians and Russians) was too trivial even to send Mrs. Arnold, who loved the newspapers.

Trying to regain concentration, he pored over biographies of Goethe and of Goethe's English heroes, Byron, Scott, and Burns, and also read Comte de Las Cases's *Mémorial de Sainte Hélène*. But it was while reading a life of Napoleon that he was truly "penetrated with admiration." What he admired in that hero was not so much "calm," but a "recklessness of assertion."[64]

Dropping *Empedocles*, he began to assert himself in a freer and easier manner; he spent more time in the company of barristers in town and on one occasion he was led into the presence of a dignified legal dragon—a justice of the Court of the Queen's Bench named Sir William Wightman.

Among Matthew's new friends was an easygoing, hilarious young Etonian named Wyndham Slade, who after attending Balliol College and taking a degree in 1848 had begun to drudge at law at the Inner Temple. Slade inherited his charm from his young Irish mother—who married the sixty-year-old General Sir John Slade. The General was a worldly man who sired fifteen children by two wives, begetting Wyndham during a long crisis of boredom after Waterloo.

Wyndham Slade loved good parties, fishing and hunting, and tours on the Continent: he was to rent Arnold's rooms at 101 Mount Street and lend that perennial bachelor's retreat to him as a storeroom for books and as a hideaway from Arnold's in-laws. Together, in 1849 and 1850, they went to fashionable balls and soirées. One evening Matthew "wonderfully" agreed with the physicist William Grove, who "likes and disapproves of modern existence," as he wrote home to his mother, "and . . . sighs after a paternal despotism."[65]

Another time, arm in arm with Wyndham Slade and J. D. Coleridge apparently, he was taken to a party for barristers and students of the Inner Temple given, in the fashionable Belgravia district, by a justice of the Queen's Bench. Sir William Wightman lived at Eaton Place.

The architecture of Belgravia—Matthew later felt—expresses only "the impotence of the architect to express anything."[66] Going into a room filled with polite law students and autocratic Western Circuit judges, he was at a far remove from poetry. J. D. Coleridge thought that Mr. Justice Wightman was "a real character."[67] At sixty-four, the Judge was famous for "accuracy and caution"[68] and for his short, horrid outbreaks of temper at murder trials. His personal motto was *Aequam servare mentem* (Preserve equanimity). As if to hint at the crotchetiness he tried to conceal, his family crest displayed a leaping buck, collared and attached by chains to a tree stump.

In literature the Judge's tastes stopped just after Pope and Fielding. The latter, he observed, had spent eight years as a barrister on the Western Circuit while writing *Tom Jones*. One of Wightman's very good friends—who in fact was to sit *"cum Judice"* at Arnold's wedding[69]—was the notorious Tory reviewer, John Wilson Croker, who had reviewed Keats's *Endymion* harshly enough to inspire Shelley's mordant lines—

> *Who kill'd John Keats?*
> *"I," says the Quarterly,*

So savage and Tartarly;
  " 'Twas one of my feats."[70]

Failing to discourage such liberals as Hunt, Shelley, and Keats, Mr. Justice Wightman's friend had had better luck with young Tennyson. Croker's niggling review of the latter's *Poems,* of 1833, helped to depress young Alfred Tennyson for ten years. The publisher of the Judge's friend hoped Wilson Croker might yet get his "critical claws and beak"[71] into the veins of some new, liberal, vainglorious poet.

The demolisher of poets seems to have been ill this evening, but Arnold assessed other faces at the Judge's party. He saw one lady as beautiful as a cut-glass chandelier. Frances Lucy, one of the host's three daughters, was so petite she seemed hardly mortal. She was dazzling in pink or lavender satin with every ruffle and curl in place, "so small, so delicate, so dainty," as an admirer put it, that "she looked something like a Fairy Queen and something like a Dresden Shepherdess."[72] Her soft eyes were unlike the Judge's, but in certain ways she resembled her Papa. Fanny Lucy was "a zealous and consistent High Churchwoman of the Tractarian School" who worshipped at St. Paul's, Knightsbridge, where she heard that admirable High Churchman Mr. Bennett. Yet, if she memorized psalms and lessons, she did not let religion utterly ruin or dictate her life. Her taste was expensive, her fondness for pretty carriages keen; and in almost everything she deferred to Papa's will. Though "entirely free from the taint of letters," she was the stiffest of Tories.[73]

Having watched this pretty young lady, Matthew thought a good deal about her. She was the antithesis of the timid Mary Claude, who would have been lost in the world of a baronet; seemingly the Judge's daughter was as indifferent to literature and ideas as any other handsome young Tory belle. She had the confidence of wealth and beauty; and if she expressed perhaps only the vacuity of inexpressiveness—or the Toryism of her father and the banalities of St. Paul's —she was ravishing to look at.

Would it harm him to pursue her? Matthew keenly admired "rank & fashion."[74] He needed the stimulus of love; he felt book-weary and stuck in the manuscript of *Empedocles*. Here was a lady who could guarantee his entry into society. In an early letter about Miss Wightman, he suggests however that he finds her fascinating because she is so hateful.

Her prettiness, hard Toryism, and above all her High Church religion would, perhaps, make her hateful to Jane. His "darling" sister—after writing so disapprovingly of *The Strayed Reveller*—was striking a new blow at his life as a poet. Jane was now engaged to marry William Forster, a lean social activist and a gaunt shrill Quaker, who had spoken to the workers at Bradford about communism and Saint-Simonism and who felt that the British government ought to educate poor children and feed the hungry. There is clear evidence of Arnold's early dislike and distrust of Forster (despite certain attempts of his family to obliterate the evidence). If Jane married Forster, she might sympathize even less with a debonair, inactive poet at Berkeley Square.

Arnold warred with himself because he was *susceptible* to his family's activist ideas. He depended upon his sister Jane as an inspiration and link with his youth and found her sympathy for him rather incomplete. In turning to a Tory belle, he in a certain sense turned back to his early days when he had won the applause of his sisters (especially of Jane) by playing Lord Byron, by admiring "rank & fashion" and courting Sir Grey Skipwith, and even by mimicking the family's liberal earnestness. To be sure, he found Miss Wightman sexually appealing and he yearned for her.

In "Absence," he portrays some of his conflicting feelings. In this lyric, Miss Wightman has the demure "eyes of grey," and Miss Claude—that *amour* of his Lake District summer days and living symbol of his childhood—has the eyes of blue:

> *In this fair stranger's eyes of grey*
> *Thine eyes, my love! I see.*
> *I shiver; for the passing day*
> *Had borne me far from thee.*
>
> *This is the curse of life! that not*
> *A nobler, calmer train*
> *Of wiser thoughts and feelings blot*
> *Our passions from our brain;*
>
> . . . . . .
>
> *I struggle towards the light—but oh,*
> *While yet the night is chill,*
> *Upon time's barren, stormy flow,*
> *Stay with me, Marguerite, still!*[75]

Love is consoling and useful in offering his mind an organizing center, and yet baneful in keeping him in turmoil. The second stanza might be an epigraph for his *Tristram and Iseult*. Having tried in vain to meet Miss Wightman formally, he sent Wyndham Slade a revealing letter about her—probably in the spring of 1850. "Last night for the 5th time," Matthew writes, comparing himself neatly with the South African, zebra-like quaggha,

the deities interposed: I was asked specially to meet the young lady—my wheels burned the pavement—I mounted the stairs like a wounded quaggha, the pulsations of my heart shook all Park Crescent—my eyes devoured every countenance in the room in a moment of time: she was at the opera, and could not come. At the last her mother had had tickets sent her, and sent a note of excuse.[76]

Oh misery! Indeed he had shown "Spartan fortitude" the night before, but in the morning "dejection and lassitude" forced him to considerations unflattering to a baronet's daughter. "How strange," he tells Slade, "about die unerreichbare schöne [the unattainable beauty]! To have met her, to have found something abstossend [repugnant], and to have been freed from all disquietude on her account, voilà comment je comprends [this is how I understand] a matter of this kind. But all the oppositiveness & wilfulness in the human breast is agaçée [annoyed] by a succession of these perverse disappointments."[77] Fate kept him from seeing enough of Miss Wightman to tell how unpleasant she might be.

"I suffer," he told Slade; but Matthew went to her parties. Miss Wightman saw him as a tall, slightly foppish, well-tailored young man of twenty-seven with dark, trimmed side-whiskers, a broad and handsome mouth, clear blue eyes, and wavy blackish hair. He leaned this way and that among his male friends, chatting in French, dropping a bland and harmlessly witty remark as he veered into English. He was obviously a lord's private secretary on leave from an Oxford Common Room. He was so completely at home in rooms filled with barristers and judges that she was, perhaps, impressed. More certainly she was impressed by Arnold's rather famous surname, by his dark good looks and gentle, graceful manner as he turned on a heel to smile at her mother or sisters. He magnetized young men and attracted *her*—but then she had many admirers and confidantes. With her delicate but vivacious form, her tiny arms and ankles, pinched waist in a yellow dress, petite features, and keen, busy and absorbing friendships, Fanny Lucy often seemed to be in the midst of a swarm of people. Ladies and young gentlemen gushed over her; and if the idea of "Mr. Arnold" disturbed her ever so slightly, it was the idea she had of him as an unusually charming but complacent man-about-town. She finally encouraged him just enough to keep him on the boil. Later she may have noticed something troubled in his amusing and witty chatter, something perplexed and ill at ease and even lugubrious, and felt that he was afraid to commit himself in love.

When apart from her, he had many occasions to be moody about his dejection and lassitude. The gravity of his situation was becoming clear to himself; love unsettled and stirred his self-command, even his absurd pretense of cool, witty composure with his friends, and it unlocked rebellious desires he could hardly name. He thought more intensely of Miss Wightman and fell in love with an "unattainable" image even as he ran off to the Wightmans' parties, and his heart beat all the faster perhaps because to her parents the name "Arnold" conjured up a distasteful liberalism. His foppish smiles and grimaces, too, doubtless alarmed the Judge. (They were to alarm Miss Brontë.) "Matt," Clough informed Tom Arnold at last in July, is "deep in a flirtation with Miss Wightman. . . . It is thought it will come to something, for he has actually been to Church to meet her."[78] How delectable, how ravishing she looked in her cloak and demure dress with a prayerbook on Sunday mornings! But how long could one converse with a Tory belle, about nothing at all, in church vestibules?

Matthew's happiness became most precarious. Mr. Justice Wightman never sentenced a sheep-stealer to death without prima facie evidence, for he was fair; but if Arnold *ever proposed marriage* the Judge would sentence him to misery—and forbid Fanny Lucy from ever seeing him.

He was bewilderingly but deeply in love and most uncertain as to the future. The elegance of his clothes cheered him very little; he could easily drink too much and lower his head on a writing desk. But he could find rhythms, and make poems out of his worst problems. To relieve his torment he scribbled "Destiny"—a poem that might have surprised the boy Thomas Hardy, then in Dorset:

> —*Ask of the Powers that sport with man!*
> . . . . . .
> *They yoked in him, for endless strife,*
> *A heart of ice, a soul of fire;*
> *And hurled him on the Field of Life,*
> *An aimless unallayed Desire.*

He also wrote "Youth's Agitations" in which he peers "ten years hence"[79] to conclude that youth and age share discontent in common. In a darker mood, he wrote "Courage," in praise of that Cato who stoically stabs himself to avoid being Caesar's captive. Despite a portentous title "Human Life" perhaps seeks out a deeper level of his bewilderment. Anticipating images in "Dover Beach," Arnold imagines each man as a ship in "the sea of life by night," sailing before a wake that creates a "long-drawn roar." If, in the sea, Fate carries one past the "unsuiting consort,"[80] then human action in the world is circumscribed if not illusory. How can we accommodate *love* to our deliberate plans in life, if we are so controlled by Fate?

Fearing marriage as much as he desired it, he knew that his salary from Lord Lansdowne—£72 a quarter—wouldn't support Miss Wightman. And he had little confidence that the daughter of a Tory judge would make an ideal wife. "I think," he had told Clough late in 1849, "I shall emigrate: why the devil don't you."[81] But at least, while lounging in a scenic hotel in Switzerland, he had found a legend that really illuminated his perplexity. Turning through issues of *Revue de Paris* at Thun, he had read La Villemarqué's vivid account of Tristan and Iseult.

Arnold found himself quite absorbed by the legend of Tristan—who once swallowed a potion causing him to love Iseult of Ireland and Cornwall (the first Iseult), and then in Brittany married Iseult of the White Hands. La Villemarqué had followed the medieval spirit of the legend in depicting Tristan's disguises, the trickery of his adultery at the court of King Marc, and the cruel jealousy of the second Iseult. Dunlop, in *History of Fiction*,[82] was yet more medieval—as in the statement that Queen Iseult gulled her husband on his wedding night by making the virgin, Brangien, share his bed, and then turning Brangien over to murderers.

Taking his main inspiration from La Villemarqué, Arnold drafted a poem about Tristan. The legend "fastened upon me," he told Herbert Hill later. "When I got back to England I looked at [Malory's] Morte D'Arthur and took what I could, but the poem was in the main formed, and I could not well disturb it."[83]

Treating materials then nearly unknown in England, he wrote the first modern version of the story: for Arnold's *Tristram and Iseult* precedes Wagner's opera *Tristan und Isolde* by thirteen years and Tennyson's "The Last Tournament" by twenty. The best poems he wrote before his marriage might be footnotes to *The Tragicall Historie of Hamlet* and this one relates to Shakespeare through inversions: King Marc as King Claudius recedes into the background and the hero steals away his uncle's bride at court not because he wishes to, for the hero is no longer himself. Indeed as *Switzerland* comments on *Hamlet* of Acts I and II, *Tristram and Iseult* seems to elaborate on the lines in Act V, in which a victimized Hamlet claims to be innocent of Hamlet's crime:

> *Was't Hamlet wrong'd Laertes? Never Hamlet:*
> *If Hamlet from himself be ta'en away,*
> *And when he's not himself does wrong Laertes,*
> *Then Hamlet does it not, Hamlet denies it.*
> *Who does it, then?*[84]

If, as Arnold appears to reason, man is victimized neither by Fate nor by an uncaring God, then man is betrayed by conditions inherent in life. La Villemarqué had suggested that the medieval hero is hardly ever culpable or in moral error, for Tristan is hardly ever Tristan. His mind is affected by a poisoned dart and again, after his cure, by a magic love potion. Arnold's poem emphasizes the hero's suffering and lack of culpability by making little of his adultery and by telling the tale at its tragic end. In part I, Arnold's hero is a dying poet with a gold harp at his elbow and also a man in delirium recalling earlier moods of delirium—for he reflects on phantoms he saw in his deranged, tormented periods of longing for Queen Iseult. Tristram has lived a life in which actions have meant little and memory-pictures, almost everything. His first lady has haunted him ever since they parted at King Marc's court. Once, he saw her gliding through spears, above a river of blood near Rome:

> All red with blood the whirling river flows . . .
> 'Up, Tristram, up,' men cry, 'thou moonstruck knight!
> What foul fiend rides thee? On into the fight!'
> —Above the din her voice is in my ears;
> I see her form glide through the crossing spears.
> Iseult! . . .[85]

Queen Iseult is a faint ghost, in moonlight. Her image speaks to him from the surface of spring water Tristram would drink:

> —Mild shines the cold spring in the moon's clear light;
> God! 'tis her face plays in the waters bright.
> 'Fair love,' she says, 'canst thou forget so soon,
> At this soft hour, under this sweet moon?'
> Iseult! . . .[86]

As he dies Queen Iseult comes to him; but part II treats their meeting in a strange, surrealistic fashion in which the living behave as *objets d'art* while an *objet d'art*—the huntsman who is only green fabric in a wall tapestry—magically behaves as if alive. As in the "Marguerite" lyrics Arnold had reduced and formalized real people to serve through time as symbolic figures, so in the meeting scene he reifies the love of Tristram and Iseult by locking it into the stately decorum of their rhymes. Passion is becoming modulated as that which is to endure forever in the realm of European art:

TRISTRAM

> Raise the light, my page! that I may see her.
>   Thou art come at last, then, haughty Queen!
> Long I've waited, long I've fought my fever;
>   Late thou comest, cruel thou hast been.

ISEULT

Blame me not, poor sufferer! that I tarried;
Bound I was, I could not break the band.
Chide not with the past, but feel the present!
I am here—we meet—I hold thy hand.

. . . . . .

TRISTRAM

Thou art paler—but thy sweet charm, Iseult!
Would not fade with the dull years away.
Ah, how fair thou standest in the moonlight!
I forgive thee, Iseult!—thou wilt not stay?

ISEULT

Fear me not, I will be always with thee;
I will watch thee, tend thee, soothe thy pain;
Sing thee tales of true, long-parted lovers,
Joined at evening of their days again.[87]

The Keatsian "always with thee" suggests that their love is to be eternalized. As in "Ode to a Nightingale" the blending of the mortal and artistic may be only a fancy. However, the time scale remarkably changes in the scene: as the green tapestry huntsman drowsily awakes and the lovers lie quiet as statues, a medieval narrator speaks of lovers who lived "a thousand years ago," so that the *time* in part II comprises a thousand years before and after the *Liebestod*.[88] Tristram and Iseult's legend—revived in the poem—is proof that the transmuting process of their cold, formal speeches has succeeded.

Part III is even bolder in artistic design. Iseult of the White Hands now recounts the tale of Merlin and Vivian—which seems an imposition on her small children, though her theme of love as victimization extends to them. The innocent, small children as well as the natural setting in which Iseult is seen have, in fact, the peculiar effect of making her story chilling. She tells how the slender Vivian, with mocking blue eyes, led the entranced, hapless, lovesick Merlin to a spot under a thorn. There he became fixed and paralyzed forever by Vivian's spell:

> *Nine times she waved the fluttering wimple round,*
> *And made a little spot of magic ground.*
> *And in that daisied circle, as men say,*
> *Is Merlin prisoner till the judgment-day.*[89]

Arnold chiefly objectifies his fear of commitment to any woman, in the Tristram and Iseult and Merlin and Vivian tales. It is possible to find hints of Mary Claude in the first Iseult as well as in Vivian; for *Tristram and Iseult,* after all, was planned as he composed his "Marguerite" lyrics. Importantly he depicts Iseult of the White Hands very kindly as if she were a guardian of the creative spirit—though one cannot be sure that she is Miss Wightman of Eaton Place. Nevertheless, by the time he finished the poem, he had met his Tory belle.

Dr. Thomas Arnold, Headmaster of Rugby School and Matthew's father. He had survived the Rugby trustees' motion of censure by one vote when Thomas Phillips painted him in 1839. (*National Portrait Gallery*)

LEFT: Lydia Penrose's sketch of the Arnold family in their drawing room at Fox How, 1835. A governess sits among eight Arnold children. Mrs. Arnold is in the foreground between Dr. Arnold at left and Matthew, aged twelve, on her right. (*Courtesy of Mrs. M. C. Moorman*)

ABOVE: Visitors arrive on the lawn at Fox How, under Loughrigg Fell. In this posed but remarkable photograph, Mrs. Arnold and Fan are at the left. Matthew's brother Willy is believed to be the young man lying on the grass. (*Courtesy of Mrs. M. C. Moorman*)

LEFT: Fox How, the Arnold family's home in the Lake District. (*Photograph by Herbert Bell*)

Jane Arnold or "K," after her marriage to William Forster. (*Courtesy of Mrs. M. C. Moorman*)

Matthew Arnold. An early photograph, taken around 1860 when he and Clough were employed in London. (*Wordsworth Library, Grasmere*)

Arthur Hugh Clough at about thirty when he left Oxford to work in London. From a crayon portrait. (*Courtesy of Miss Katharine Duff*)

Henry, Third Marquess of Lansdowne, who employed Arnold as a confidential secretary with little work to do. (*From a photograph in* An Italian Englishman *by Charles Lacaita* [*London, 1933*], *Grant Richards*)

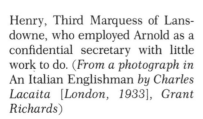

Thomas Arnold, Matthew's brother, who taught with Newman at the Birmingham Oratory and later befriended Gerard Manley Hopkins. From an early daguerreotype, 1847. (*Courtesy of Mrs. M. C. Moorman*)

Susanna or Susan Arnold, the sister to whom Matthew recited "Yes! in the sea
of life." (*Courtesy of Mrs. M. C. Moorman*)

9

"EMPEDOCLES ON ETNA"
1850–1851

By England's lakes, in grey old age,
His quiet home one keeps;

      . . . . . .

But Wordsworth's eyes avert their ken
From half of human fate.
> *—Arnold on Wordsworth,*
> *November 1849*

A RNOLD'S courtship of Miss Wightman helped him to revise his feelings about Wordsworth. Courting the "stiffest of Tories," he seems to have lost his objections to the gray poet of Rydal's Toryism. He even reversed his very Cloughian opinion that the elderly poet avoided the "actual world" or screened his "ken" from "half of human fate."[1]

Wordsworth could be seen as heroic—and certainly the eyes of many Arnolds misted when anyone spoke of him. Great sorrows had failed to crush Wordsworth. Even after Dorothy's illness began, he heard sounds that once informed the *Lyrical Ballads:* he listened to the owl at Rydal, and recited perhaps at the Arnolds' in the 1830s just how

> *mid the gleam*
> *Of unsubstantial imagery—the dream*
> *From the hushed vale's realites transferred*
> *To the still lake—the imaginative Bird*
> *Seems, 'mid inverted mountains, not unheard.*[2]

Yet Wordsworth broke down when his daughter Dora died; when the Arnolds called on him in the winter of 1847, he still sobbed heavily and sat close to fires. Early in 1849, he lost Hartley Coleridge and after Mary Wordsworth kissed the face of the corpse at Nab Cottage, her husband went out to Grasmere and, bending over, sketched three graves in the ground. Of the inebriate Hartley, he said: "Let him lie by us, he would have wished it."[3]

Perhaps his wish to keep the railways out of the Lake District was silly—but the "iron tide" made him eloquent. Mrs. Arnold was at his door when he announced, deeply, "I have been writing a sonnet" and recited "Is there no nook of English ground secure."[4] At a meeting about the new railways, however, he ranted so much that the chairman called him to order twice.

A year or two before he died, he came to Fox How. He had taken Matthew "under his protection"—and the younger poet drew him "out" well, as Wordsworth sat on a fireside stool and talked on everything from Italy to Coleridge. He wore "a loose brown frock-coat, trousers of shepherd's plaid, a loose black handkerchief for neck-tie, a green and black plaid shawl around the shoulders," as well as a hat with a blue veil or a "Scotch bonnet." His features seemed sensitive, and his hair looked "rather long behind." Wordsworth spoke in bass tones as if under oath, without a trace of irony. In poetry, he told Arnold with emphasis, "Goethe was not inevitable enough."[5] (Matthew accepted this verdict.) Touching England, he seems to have expanded on the text printed in 1845 as a note to "Love Lies Bleeding." Arnold often repeated phrases from that note—which ranks with passages that most influenced him in Epictetus and Goethe. "It has been said [of] the English," Wordsworth declared,

> though their country has produced so many great Poets, [it] is now the most unpoetical nation in Europe.

("Reflect," Arnold told Clough, "in spite of all the nonsense some people talk, how deeply *unpoetical* the age and all one's surroundings are. . . . Not ungrand, not unmoving:—but *unpoetical*.")[6] Wordsworth touched also on the "disinterested imagination." "Trade, commerce, and manufactures," he insisted,

> have made our countrymen infinitely less sensible to movements of the imagination and fancy. . . . How beautiful were, in most instances, the names our forefathers gave to our indigenous flowers! . . . Will their botanical names ever be displaced by plain English appellations, which will bring them home to our hearts by connection with our joys and sorrows? It can never be, unless society treads back her steps towards those simplicities which have been banished by the undue influence of Towns spreading and spreading in every direction, so that city-life with every generation takes more and more the lead of rural. . . . Inhumanity pervades all our dealings in buying and selling. This selfishness wars against disinterested imagination . . . and barbarism spreads.[7]

Wordsworth felt that the "undue influence" of towns and trades would increase man's capacity to think selfishly, unfitting the psyche for its free play. The "disinterested imagination" arises when unselfish feeling is quite as strong as directed thought. Two social classes seemed to him guilty of atrophying man's "movements of the imagination." "I was brought up," as Arnold later recalled, "under the influence of a poet who was very much dissatisfied with the proceedings of the middle and upper classes among us. . . . That poet convinced me, and therefore I have spent most of my leisure time in preaching . . . to those classes."[8]

Arnold was not turned into a social critic by what he heard, but Wordsworth persuaded him that an *unpoetical* age might lead to a bleaker future. Arnold could see that man's thinking and feeling might be balanced through a strengthening of man's capacity to feel and an attack on selfish activity. Even Wordsworth's verse could be seen as a corrective. What was "Michael" or "The Solitary Reaper" but an attempt to praise rural feeling and connect "our joys and sorrows" with a healing, restoring "nature?"

On April 23, 1850—Shakespeare's day—two of Matthew's sisters happened to be out walking near Rydal Mount when they saw a hand drawing the curtains across the cottage window. A fortnight after his eightieth birthday, the greatest English poet of the nineteenth century was dead.

Coming north at the time, Arnold was greeted by the poet's son-in-law Edward Quillinan, who had found a few virtues in *Strayed Reveller*. "You and I can see," Quillinan enthused to a friend, "through all that affectation of mystification & all that uneasy labour to be quaint & brilliant . . . that [Matt Arnold's] a man for a' that." Hoping not to stunt Arnold through injudicious "flattery,"[9] Quillinan now proposed an elegy on Wordsworth.

Certainly Quillinan was amazed, a month later, to find that Arnold had linked Goethe and Wordsworth in a "triple Epicede" with Lord Byron. To link the poet of Rydal with an adulterous sot! "Leaving other objections out of the question," he felt, Byron was "not tall enough for the other two."[10] Quillinan perhaps noticed that "Memorial Verses: April 1850" defines the poets against a wide backdrop of the Europe of Wordsworth's day. Arnold actually praises Byron mainly for defiance. ("There is the Titanism of the Celt, his passionate, . . . indomitable reaction against the despotism of fact," Arnold was to declare, "and of whom does it remind us so much as of Byron?")[11] Byron is to be felt rather than heard:

> He taught us little—but our soul
> Had felt *him* like the thunder's roll.[12]

Here was the force that made a poet *succeed*, if a thousand factors militated against the harmony of the inward life. Goethe, on the other hand, had tried to analyze factors that destroyed man's inward harmony. Arnold sees him in Novalis's term as the iron age's "physician":

> *He looked on Europe's dying hour.*
> . . . . . .
> *He said:* The end is everywhere,
> Art still has truth, take refuge there![13]

Yet Goethe became an undertaker; he never relieved the distress caused by the dissolution of the medieval order after 1789 but simply played the chorus in a gigantic tragedy, as religion became moribund by externalizing itself in formalities. Wordsworth in contrast was a sentimentalist; he did more to touch man's capacity to feel than even Chateaubriand or Senancour or Richter, and thus he alone is indispensable:

> *But where will Europe's latter hour*
> *Again find Wordsworth's healing power?*
> . . . . . .
> *Others will strengthen us to bear—*
> *But who, ah! who, will make us feel?*[14]

That poet's success lay in his elegiac manner of carrying one back to youth or childhood, when the mind is immune to "trade, commerce, manufactures, physical science and mechanic arts," which curl up imaginative feelings. In fact, Arnold's mentor linked him with his own days on Loughrigg. Had not Wordsworth peered over the parapet of a wintry fort, in 1837, and walked with him and his father on the fells? "He too," Arnold writes in his most deeply felt tribute to an elderly friend,

> *upon a wintry clime*
> *Had fallen—on this iron time*
> *Of doubts, disputes, distractions, fears.*
> . . . . . .
> *He spoke, and loosed our hearts in tears.*
> *He lay us as we lay at birth*
> *On the cool flowery lap of earth,*
> *Smiles broke from us and we had ease;*
> *The hills were round us, and the breeze*
> *Went o'er the sunlit fields again;*
> *Our foreheads felt the wind and rain.*
> *Our youth returned; for there was shed*
> *On spirits that had long been dead,*
> *Spirits dried up and closely furled,*
> *The freshness of the early world.*[15]

"Memorial Verses" is emotive and suggestive; "The Youth of Nature" is existential, inquiring, scenic, and rather more unified than its critics have believed. Sitting in a boat on a June night, when the lyric perhaps was written, Arnold's Lake District speaker alludes to elegies by Wordsworth and Collins in which oars rise in final tributes:

> Raised are the dripping oars,
> Silent the boat! the lake,
> Lovely and soft as a dream.

Under the moon and the stars, the speaker muses on noble landmarks:

> Rydal and Fairfield are there;
> In the shadow Wordsworth lies dead.

In very beautiful lines, he alludes to the rock of the Pillar and town of Egremont in Wordsworth's "The Brothers" and the cottage of The Evening Star in "Michael:"

> The Pillar still broods o'er the fields
> Which border Ennerdale Lake,
> And Egremont sleeps by the sea.
> The gleam of The Evening Star
> Twinkles on Grasmere no more,
> But ruined and solemn and grey
> The sheepfold of Michael survives.[16]

Why, then, is the speaker filled with "pain and dejection?" Possibly because the rural "social order" forming Wordsworth's sensibility had dissolved while he lived; he grew "old in an age he condemned." [17] The speaker now asks if beauty exists independently of its interpreter, and concludes that it is set in the world but that those with the deepest self-knowledge are most alert to it; hence even Wordsworth's egotism made him the "priest of us all"—if his integrity made him a lonely priest who, in old age,

> Felt the dissolving throes
> Of a social order he loved;
> Outlived his brethren, his peers,
> And, like the Theban seer,
> Died in his enemies' day.[18]

In a fairly objective poem, Arnold thus refashions his mentor as a type of the "Theban seer," Tiresias—even as a type of the estranged, isolated Empedocles.

The theme of Wordsworth as an isolated seer was clear to him by the time he finished "Memorial Verses," which satisfied Matthew himself: "I have at Quillinan's sollicitation dirged W. W. *in the grand style*," he told Clough in May 1850, "and need thy rapture therewith."[19] A reunion at Rugby had improved his relations with Clough. With this friend he was again intermittently stating, testing, probing, and placing together a still inchoate critical manifesto for poetry. By-products of their debate were just those witty insults, affronts, slanders, and angry or agonizing silences which seemed to be forgotten when they met at the house of a Rugby master. Behind lace-curtained windows and amidst Arabian carpets, books, school lesson-plans, bottles, glasses—quite out of sight of beastly Rugby schoolboys—Arnold and Clough, having come up from London, would rediscover their affection with the help of Walrond's port or Shairp's Scotch.

Since leaving Oriel College, Clough had lived at his mother's house in Liverpool for three months while writing lyrics, reading, and translating. He had visited Rome and lingered indecisively in Italy for some weeks, before finishing his *Amours de Voyage* in October 1849. Now in 1850 Arthur Clough was trying to survive in London —though hardly reconciled to the metropolis. He was Head of University Hall, a hostel for University College students, but the salary was only £30 a year. Clough not only disliked Bloomsbury but hated the stuffy, middle-class air of religious Dissenters infesting the college at Gower Street. He seemed a whale in a new millpond—and the minnows round him were quick, skittery, and alarmed. Clough failed to recruit students for the hall, wrote strange replies to official letters, and seemed so taciturn that colleagues hardly knew what to make of his tall, bulky form, slow gait, enormous brow, and solemn black eyes. University College authorities were displeased, since he refused to throw himself boldly into lecturing or running a men's residence. He was living out the theme of *Amours de Voyage,* or trying to adjust within himself the urge to plunge into the bourgeois world and the urge to pull out; the desire to commit himself to dull, civic responsibilities and the desire to remain aloof and psychically free. More than one friend felt that he was headed for vocational disaster at the men's residence and a nervous collapse. Arnold tried to cheer him up by joking, bullying, and prodding—but Clough's gloom and trouble to an extent were contagious. The plight of Clough entered into just that unusual examination of the modern spirit Arnold was making in *Empedocles.*

The most immediately obvious, thickening, blackening cloud over Arnold's own head was his sister Jane's engagement. He could feel far too dispirited and restless for days at a time to do anything about Clough. Jane depressed him; her fiancé sickened him. He could see but not accept that it was fitting for her to marry Forster, who wanted to feed and educate the kingdom: "I must write to you," he tells his sister urgently, "—I have been in a kind of spiritual lethargy . . . —but I feel quite sure my darling that when I can sink myself well down into the consideration of . . . your circumstances . . . then will you be truly

set right in my mind in respect to your engagement. . . . My objections are not based in *reality*, that I feel."[20]

His meditations on an elderly poet made him look at his surroundings for clues to uneasiness. He needed to get *inside* the dilemma of
time; of history: "I am subject to these periods of spiritual eastwind
when I can lay hold only of the outside of events or words," he tells
Jane. London has become a desert. Clough is remote. The "material
eastwind" at horrid Berkeley Square "has something to do" with his
"spiritual eastwind" and with "the strain and uneasiness in which in
these days & in London it is so hard not to live."[21]

Surely Jane, who sustains him in his "dryest periods," will never be
false to herself; and as if to display his candid, claiming love he insults
her fiancé. Matthew has met an abominable Forster relative, who "said
quite seriously—'I congratulate you Mr. Arnold—your sister is going
to marry a cousin of mine.' . . . *Quelle bêtise!*"[22] Matthew cries out.

Sensing that Jane slips away from him and needing help from his
family, he turns to his young, widowed sister Mary Arnold Twining or
"Bacco," who lives in town on a heady diet of F. D. Maurice and
Christian Socialism. On the forehead of poor lonely Bacco—who
refused to live at Fox How and who was to marry twice again—he
finds the iron gray mark of doom. Bacco "was at the Bunsens—very
quiet in manner," he informs his sister Jane; "the gods as Schiller says
have fastened an iron ring round her forehead—& this gives her a
separated look in company, poor poor thing. I shall . . . try if I cannot
be of help to her." [23]

Possibly Bacco helped *him,* iron ring and Schiller's gods and all. At
any rate, Arnold now turned a bitter sense of foreboding into the
magnificent despair of Empedocles on a charred wasteland of Etna.

He probably had done little more for *Empedocles* so far than versify
his desk-notes—which bring Stoical skepticism to bear on popular
religious assumptions. In May 1850, when, it seems, he returned to
the poem, he was very scornful of a work called *Phases of Faith,* by
Francis Newman (a brother of the Roman convert). He may have seen
Clough's review of that writer's *The Soul,* in which Clough hails
Francis Newman and sneers at Dr. Arnold. "This beast," Arnold writes
to jar Clough, "bepaws the religious sentiment so much that he quite
effaces it to me." The *Phases* is "a display of the theological mind,
which I am accustomed to regard as a suffetation. . . . This sort of
man is only possible in Great Britain and Northern Germany, thanks
be to God for it. Ireland even spews him out."[24]

And indeed—as Tom Arnold noted—*Empedocles on Etna* was to be "full of sardonic refutations of moral and religious platitudes." [25] The poem's hero is a pagan Christ, who offers a creed for a world devoid of religious or ethical meaning, before ascending a wasteland to Calvary.

Empedocles is also a sentimental hero who exists in Arnold's version of Prince Hamlet's world. "Shakespeare," Arnold commented on that world in the essay "Hamlet Once More,"

> conceived [*Hamlet*] with his mind running on Montaigne, and placed its action and its hero in Montaigne's atmosphere and world. What is that world? It is the world of man viewed as being *ondoyant et divers*, balancing and indeterminate, the plaything of cross motives and shifting impulses, swayed by a thousand subtle influences, physiological and pathological. [26]

This "physiological and pathological" world is our own, and elements of Hamlet's—or even Clough's—personality might define an ideal inhabitant of it such as the critic:

> The critic of poetry should have . . . the most free, flexible, and elastic spirit imaginable; he should be the 'ondoyant et divers,' the undulating and diverse being. [27]

Even in 1850, his meditations on Clough and on Hamlet's psychology seem to have led him to a theory of personality and a theory of history that give *Empedocles* its depth of meaning. Empedocles is a brilliant teacher and healer who disintegrates because his epoch is inhospitable; and yet it is a condition of life that he should be subject to a thousand splintering "influences, physiological and pathological." In men of talent, in Arnold's view, "pathological" tensions divide the psyche. In ages of faith, religion unites the torn psyche. *But we kill our Gods:* we attribute our weaknesses to them and reduce the divine through a scientific means of apprehending reality—until, in ages of unbelief, we observe our own suffering in Werther or Obermann or Hamlet, or indeed in a pagan Christ who on a "blackened, melancholy waste" walked to his death.

Arnold meant his Act I to illustrate "Modern Thought," and Act II, "Modern Feeling." [28] Empedocles now haunts the forbidding slopes of Mt. Etna, rather as Clough haunted Gower Street and University College, with the air of a man abandoned by friends and scorned by enemies. He has two concerned friends. The physician Pausanias and the harpist Callicles await him on Etna's lower wooded slopes. Callicles may charm him out of his illness:

> *I have my harp too—that is well. Apollo!*
> *What mortal could be sick or sorry here?* [29]

Pausanias attributes Empedocles' decline to external causes and thinks "sophists" in the schools have driven him mad with mockery;

he wishes, while he can, to learn the secret of Empedocles' "miracle" cure of a woman who lay in a deathlike trance. Here, again, is a hint of the dilemma of Clough, who couldn't tell his friends from his enemies and admired that *beast*—the evangelical Rev. Francis Newman. Pausanias represents British evangelical churchmen, and the sophists are new rationalists who rival the clergy. As Callicles knows, the sophists are admiring of Empedocles, not his enemies.

But if the admiring rationalists do not help Empedocles, the representative modern intellectual, than who *can* and *will*? Callicles, his other friend, is a boy with charm and insight; for him the inward world of the mind and the world of nature are consistent and beautiful. Representing the power of art, he offers hope to Empedocles in Act I, before turning unwittingly into a nightmare boy and an inventor of lethal myths in Act II. He knows that Empedocles' sickness has complex, inward causes:

> *He is too scornful, too high-wrought, too bitter.*
> *'Tis not the time, 'tis not the sophists vex him;*
> *There is some root of suffering in himself,*
> *Some secret and unfollowed vein of woe,*
> *Which makes the time look black and sad to him.*[30]

At the end of scene i, the situation is almost that of Browning's *Saul:* while Pausanias waits, Callicles hides in the "brushwood" of Etna to charm Empedocles back to health with song.

Scene ii is a fine tour de force, with a reversal. As an amalgam of Arnold and Clough, the poet-philosopher Empedocles now discourses on illusions about religion and life. In his long, unpleasant chant, he describes a frightening epoch of lost faith:

> *The Gods laugh in their sleeve*
> *To watch men doubt and fear,*
> *Who knows not what to believe*
> *Since he sees nothing clear.*[31]

The modern soul inhabits an arid, threatening, giant wasteland. Here Arnold's dismal privately confessed "spiritual lethargy" and "strain and uneasiness," his sense of London as a desert and his headaches and worries over a sister's engagement mingle in a panorama in which the living are dead, and a dead father and Headmaster of Rugby School is alive but powerless. These personal experiences are universalized in verse that seems to apply to a factory-and-tenement Victorian city and beyond. This is the index of our condition, the landscape of the European soul in its busy, brittle, hollow age of disbelief:

> *Heaven is with earth at strife,*
> *Signs make thy soul afraid,*

The dead return to life,
Rivers are dried, winds stayed.

In this situation, one's only response must be to examine one's feelings, to plunge into one's own bosom:

Man gets no other light,
Search he a thousand years.
Sink in thyself! there ask what ails thee, at that shrine!

Mixing Stoical ethics with Epicurean theology, Empedocles blends the very cheerful Epictetus with the sad Lucretius; he mixes ideas of Emerson with Senancour, even Carlyle with Spinoza. His chant has the bitter gusto of a bored undergraduate, the neat snippety effect of Arnold's most exaggerated pronouncements to Clough:

Nature, with equal mind,
Sees all her sons at play;
Sees man control the wind,
The wind sweep man away.[32]

Modern man is a "cheat" or a fool, or both; his activities are so oppressive he imagines deities who know the "all" he fails to master, as Empedocles declares with ever more scorn and acerbity:

We map the starry sky,
We mine this earthen ball,
We measure the sea-tides, we number the sea-sands;

We scrutinize the dates
Of long-past human things,
The bounds of effaced states,
The lines of deceased kings;
We search out dead men's words, and works of dead men's hands;

We shut our eyes, and muse
How our own minds are made.
What springs of thought they use,
How rightened, how betrayed—
And spend our wit to name what most employ unnamed.

. . . . . .

Fools! That in man's brief term
He cannot all things view,
Affords no ground to affirm
That there are Gods who do.[33]

In brief, all idealisms, all notions about the existence of Heaven and the benignity of nature wither in the outlook of an estranged philosopher-king. Trying to remove the mist from Pausanias's evangelical eyes, Empedocles at last reveals what especially embitters and numbs. Arnold combines his own experience at Oriel and love-and-hate attitude to books, with the elderly Wordsworth's sadness and bitterness:

> *But still, as we proceed*
> *The mass [of learning] swells more and more*
> *Of volumes yet to read,*
> *Of secrets yet to explore.*
> *Our hair grows grey, our eyes are dimmed, our heat is tamed.*[34]

Empedocles—divided from the spontaneity of his youth—is victimized by whole libraries. Having started as a poet, he has become an intellectual in an emerging historical epoch which, as Arnold wrote about "one of those ages which calls themselves modern," exhibits to the dazzled beholder "the spectacle of a vast multitude of facts awaiting and inviting" comprehension. "And everywhere there is connection," as he was to explain in his "Modern Element in Literature,"

> everywhere there is illustration: no single event, no single literature, is adequately comprehended except in its relation to other events. [To understand these connections and ourselves] that we may correct our mistakes and achieve our deliverance—that is our problem.[35]

Yet Empedocles—despite his eclecticism—finds no clue to his *own* deliverance, since underneath his bookish malaise is another malaise or his "secret root of suffering." In earlier days, as he declares in a Wordsworthian passage that quite belies Wordsworth,

> *we received the shock of mighty thoughts*
> *On simple minds with a pure natural joy;*
> *And if the sacred load oppressed our brain,*
> *We had the power to feel the pressure eased,*
> *The brow unbound, the thoughts flow free.*[36]

In youth he had felt "oppressed," for the "sacred" load of new ideas had combined with psychic "pressure" to make his head swim. Yet loving companions helped him to "feel the pressure eased." One recalls the value Matthew placed on Jane's love; he may have felt that in losing her in marriage, he was being divided from a prime agent who had kept him *not* on "the outside of events" and "words," but inside, seeing, unperplexed, and unchoked; and indeed Jane's presence and love were what he mainly recalled of his earliest years. Empedocles was subject to "pathological" tensions, presumably, even in early youth. But the easy, loving comradeship which once kept his mind in balance, he has lost. A harsh, fact-ridden "modern" epoch has combined with tensions to shatter his intellectual personality. He has become only a "flame of thought," nothing but an eternally "restless mind."[37]

His suicide is as revealing as it is impressive. If Callicles' songs relieve his throbbing head, they add to his despair. The boy's limpid voice rising from the woods prompts him to move up through dark, billowing smoke to the tongues of orange fire at Etna's crater. The beautiful song about Cadmus and Harmonia—who became bright snakes after their "Theban woe"—only reminds him of his own mental decline. The song about Typho who was pinioned under Etna after a war against Zeus reminds him that, as a philosopher, he is chained by a host of little men who call him a necromancer. "The brave, impetuous heart," cries the philosopher on Etna's rim,

> *yields everywhere*
> *To the subtle, contriving head;*
> *Great qualities are trodden down,*
> *And littleness united*
> *Is become invincible.*[38]

Having predicted Yeats and the twentieth century, Empedocles in a fit of disgust hurls down his robe and golden circlet, and repudiates the world.

The bloodiest song of Callicles that drifts up from below concerns the woodland fawn, Marsyas, who challenged Apollo to a musical duel and for his presumption was flayed alive: "Ah, poor Faun, poor Faun! ah, poor Faun!" sings the nightmare boy.[39] The tale of Marsyas illustrates that service to the god of poetry *is too hard to bear,* the poet's unavoidable self-dissection too painful. This nightmare of being torn apart for lyric presumption, brain from the mottled skull and heart from ribcage, was Arnold's own—even if it comes from his reading of Goethe's letters and he indulged it self-consciously. Arnold, again like Empedocles, was a dramatic *poseur* who did indeed suffer as he tried to save his talent and find his way as a poet. He told Jane rather movingly what a "temptation" there was,

> if you cannot bear anything not *very* good, to transfer your operations to a region where form is everything. Perfection of a certain kind may there be attained, or at least approached, without knocking yourself to pieces, but to attain or approach perfection in the region of thought and feeling, and to unite this with a perfection of form, demands not merely an effort and a labour, but an actual tearing of oneself to pieces.

Even Goethe, he assured Jane, said "he might have produced half a dozen more good tragedies; but to produce them, he says, I must have been *sehr zerrissen.*"*[40]

A poet "choked" by an unpoetical time experiences pain as he

---

*completely ripped apart.

dissects himself in order to write. Arnold's cry, *"Congestion of the brain* is what we suffer from . . . I . . . cry for air like my own Empedocles,"⁴¹ was genuine enough. What he reviewed as he completed *Empedocles* were years in which he had tried to find ways to unite his intellectual and lyric gifts. "I feel immensely," he said, appealing to Clough's sympathy, "what I have (I believe) lost and choked by my treatment of myself and the studies to which I have addicted myself. But what ought I to have done in preference to what I have done? there is the question." He rightly believed his own allies had been few, his real life almost totally occupied with poetry: "I doubt," he told Clough, "I shall ever have heat or radiance enough to pierce the clouds that are massed around me. Not in my little social sphere indeed, with you and Walrond: there I could crackle to my grave—but vis à vis the world."⁴² If he exaggerated his troubles in Empedocles' suicide, he *felt* what Empedocles felt. In the first part of the poem, Arnold gives a good specimen of his own views except that he makes Empedocles describe a cosmos ruled by hostile, or indifferent, gods. Arnold viewed the cosmos with eyes trained by Berkeley and Spinoza. These writers posit inconsistent, multivalent notions of Deity—Spinoza for example believed in a pantheistic Deity who can yet be loved and worshipped. "There is a God, but he is not well-conceived by all," Arnold held with perfect sincerity; and again, in 1850: "In all religions the supreme Being is represented as eternally rejoicing."⁴³ Empedocles is "dead" to faith—his grand comparativism extends to ethics and not at all to Gods of believers. Arnold, viewing man in a sacramental light, maintained Spinozan belief in a prime deity until he died.

Yet the paradox of modern faith, he felt, was just this: intellect is needed to bolster or to *keep up* our beliefs. Faith is not instinctive or natural for many of us; thus even in religion, mind or thought may take possession and unbalance us. When Empedocles imitates Chateaubriand's René and advances to Etna's brink, he utters one of the finest speeches in modern literature—and it is here that Arnold injects his best insights into Clough's and his own dilemma, his sense of the divided self, his feeling of what he had "lost and choked" in himself by studies, his awareness of his restless intellect, his dissatisfied self-centered mind, and his knowledge that each mind can only try to solve the problem of its disjunctions.

Empedocles must kill himself. If his body returns to earth, his blood to water, heat to fire, and breath to air, which parent element will receive his *mind or thought*? Portraying the intellectual of our own time, he tries to imagine the fate of his "mind or thought" after he dies:

And we shall be the strangers of the world,
And they will be our lords, as they are now;
And keep us prisoners of our consciousness,
And never let us clasp and feel the All
But through their forms, and modes,
        and stifling veils.
And we shall be unsatisfied as now;
And we shall feel the agony of thirst,
The ineffable longing for the life of life
Baffled for ever; and still thought and mind
Will hurry us with them on their homeless march,
Over the unallied unopening earth,
Over the unrecognising sea; while air
Will blow us fiercely back to sea and earth,
And fire repel us from its living waves.
And then we shall unwillingly return
Back to this meadow of calamity,
This uncongenial place, this human life;
And in our individual human state
Go through the sad probation all again,
To see if we will poise our life at last,
To see if we will now at last be true
To our own only true, deep-buried selves,
Being one with which we are one
        with the whole world;
Or whether we will once more fall away
Into some bondage of the flesh or mind,
Some slough of sense, or some fantastic maze
Forged by the imperious lonely thinking-power.
And each succeeding age in which we are born
Will have more peril for us than the last;
Will goad our senses with a sharper spur,
Will fret our minds to an intenser play,
Will make ourselves harder to be discerned.
And we shall struggle awhile, gasp and rebel—
And we shall fly for refuge to past times,
Their soul of unworn youth,
        their breath of greatness;
And the reality will pluck us back,
Knead us in its hot hand, and change our nature.
And we shall feel our powers of effort flag,
And rally them for one last fight—and fail;
And we shall sink in the impossible strife,
And be astray for ever.[44]

"She spoke too of the painfulness of thought," Clough's sister had noted of Mary Claude, "and what a relief any employment was which could make one think less."[45] To be sure, the hegemony of modern thought had been condemned very powerfully by Newman, by Wordsworth. Yet the force of Empedocles in Act II is undeniable and with Callicles' subtle lyrics in a structure that is a triumph in itself, *Empedocles on Etna* is perhaps, as critics have said, the finest work of its length in Victorian literature.

By the time he wrote its ending, Arnold had rejected much of Carlyle, who in *Sartor* denounces the quest for joy. Empedocles steps up to the orange lava in a moment of pure joy; cheered to be a witness to the truth he leaps into a "sea of fire," even as Callicles' voice rises from the woods below:

> *Not here, O Apollo!*
> *Are haunts meet for thee.*[46]

Rejecting Empedocles' whole story as being unfit for verse, as if to anticipate Arnold's Preface of 1853, the nightmarish Callicles explains what the proper topics for Divine Muses may be:

> *—Whose praise do they mention?*
> *Of what is it told?*
> *What will be for ever;*
> *What was from of old.*
>
> *First hymn they the Father*
> *Of all things; and then,*
> *The rest of immortals,*
> *The action of men.*
>
> *The day in his hotness,*
> *The strife with the palm;*
> *The night in her silence,*
> *The stars in their calm.*[47]

Beautiful as these lines are, they suggest Callicles would deny the role of any artist—for he would "hymn" rather than sing. "You succeed best you see . . . in the hymn," Arnold had berated Clough, "where man, his deepest personal feelings being in play, finds poetical expression as *man* only, not as artist:—but consider whether you attain the *beautiful,* and whether your product gives PLEASURE."[48] The poetic hymn is inartistic and designed for man's improvement —whereas the true poem is artful and designed to give pure beauty. To "hymn the Father" is to indulge in a socially useful act; but to write honestly of Empedocles is to create what is permanently useless but true and beautiful. Arnold knew that his treatment of Empedocles was artful and moving. But he suffered to write this poem; he associated himself with the tragic Wordsworth who stared into hearth-fires with the insane, ruined reminder of youth—Dorothy—and indeed he described Clough's disjunction and his *own* disjunction between mind and feeling and implied that it represents a general condition, which is the true cause of our sense of "isolation" in modern times. Frank

Kermode is right in saying that the way ahead for Arnold as a poet, now, "lay in the cruel effort and continued self-expenditure of a series of Empedoclean victories."[49] The solution to Empedocles' dilemma —indeed his only victory—was for him to await a moment of joy, when he could end his dividedness by embracing the "sea of fire" with his whole soul.

Empedocles' joy is brief. He symbolizes a poetry of truth costly to the artist. Callicles' joy is lasting: he symbolizes a poetry of morality— consoling to those who create and receive it. Arnold wavered between the two kinds but wrote in his true Empedoclean mode in works such as the two Oxford elegies, again in "Dover Beach" and "Grande Chartreuse," "The Buried Life" and "A Summer Night," and in other lyrics including those about growing old. His prose is an adjunct to his best poetry—and especially to *Empedocles on Etna*—since in his social and literary essays he seeks a middle ground between the aridity of fact (or the world of scientific positivism which really destroys Empedocles) and the truths in religion and myth (or the world implicit in the songs of Callicles, the nightmare boy myth-maker). *Empedocles* concerns the modern information explosion and makes a valid comment on our own age, while stating Wordsworth's earlier problem. In an age of facts and science, how can we keep thought and feeling in balance? How can we nourish the capacity to feel as well as our capacity to know? We may by sheer thought achieve great results, but what are they worth without the feeling which humanize them?

Carlyle, a man of deep feeling, is a withdrawing and diminishing presence in *Essays in Criticism* and *Culture and Anarchy,* and in all Arnold's writing after *Empedocles*. The spiky, puritan works of that prophet charmed him—but not the Carlylean gloom and bitterness. As early as the spring of 1850 Matthew had rebuked Carlyle's decrees against happiness; he keenly wanted happiness and found it available, for he certainly suspected that his love for Lucy Wightman was returned. He learned that his lady's worst fault was her timidity; though adventurous she was easily frightened. For Arnold, she was a canary in a mine shaft. When she smiled he apparently never feared his demons—his deep, productive tensions—and could face life with confidence. Her worries prompted him to look for a cause in his own temperament. Her wonderful normalcy was consoling.

Fanny Lucy was connected through her family and friends to a rather large complicated network of social affairs at Hampton and London, and was constantly busy. She went to the theater, appeared at formal balls, and spent weekends at estates which Matthew never visited. Socially her niche was higher than his—though her father's parties for barristers had given Matthew a chance to meet her. She was elegant, diminutive, self-assured, and as pretty as could be —whether in her riding costume, her spring attire with the light, pastel hat, her summer veil and green shawl, or her formal ballroom dresses. She magnetized her share of adorers, surely, too: she attracted barristers and kept them at bay. Nearly all young ladies in her set were expert at light flirtation. What did she see in Arnold?

He exuded his Oxford background and his debonair bachelorhood, as he laughed with male friends and spoke blandly to ladies. But on closer acquaintance, he must have revealed how little he understood ladies. Not much had prepared him for serious flirtation in courtship. When one makes every allowance for Matthew's facetiousness—and it must be a large allowance—one comes up, again and again, next to the hard evidence that as a young man he did not *like* women. He didn't comprehend them. They were things, distractions, objects which teach men only what men already know; they were vain, inconstant, mentally inferior, less able than men as lecturers and classroom teachers. To be sure, living or dead, if they were French, their sexual infidelities were excusable and their artistic or intellectual feats might be inspiring. He admired Frenchwomen who were larger than life such as the Marquise de Sevigné or Mme de Staël, Rachel or George Sand. From a French text by a female, he could always learn. With young Englishwomen, he was always on guard. Few of them were like his frank, outspoken, mountain-climbing sisters. He could be wincingly affable, correct and polite, without enjoying or even understanding the nuances of a relationship. He hated *silences*. No sooner did he become sexually interested in a woman, than he complained of her mockery or inattention.

As her letters and diaries show, Fanny Lucy was intelligent and observant as well as sensible and ironic. She perceived bores; she disliked publishers and literary men because they were loud and pretentious. As a woman who had traveled on the Continent and met in her father's company the most able and worldly barristers, she may have found in Arnold the very reverse of worldliness. His naiveté in personal relationships she could not have missed, since any week now in her adult life she saw gentlemen who behaved with more unaffected ease in the company of young ladies. During courtship, she found him oddly affected by *her* irony. He was easy to torture. He perhaps fancied himself tortured even when she tried to be kind, but she had to be cautious and cool-headed for a number of reasons: for example, she had heard about his sisters. Young men of his class and background were close to their sisters, but Matthew was inordinately fond of his. If *they* objected to her, might he not withdraw his attentions from herself? And if he proposed and she accepted, what assurance did she have that he would get round her father? (The Judge wouldn't hear of her engagement to a man without money, career, and solid prospects.) She encouraged Matthew because she was attracted by his simplicity, his innocence and vulnerability, his heavy emotional loyalties, even by his desperate gratitude. He was a handsome, brilliant man, but clear and plain in all that counted, as she always felt. Exactly because he was not at ease, not superficial, not worldly and smooth and smug, she felt that he would try to be exceedingly gentle and would think of her always as first in his heart. She waited for a final sign this summer that he would never draw back. As solicitous as he was, she tested him with her light remarks and composure—her folded, gloved hands or her trifling attentions to her costume.

Arnold noted, on their honeymoon, her claustrophobia and fear of heights and suffering over the bitterly cold weather in the Alps—and yet she endured hard travel and was to face tragic hardships. He may have been very grateful that she was not terrified by the Judge; but early in August he had much to worry about. Profoundly disturbed by Jane Arnold's engagement, he wondered it seems how he could *bear* to wait for Jane at Rydal Chapel on August 15, to give her hand away. Jane seemed to be abandoning him—while Fanny Lucy was unattained! Indeed his romance, meanwhile, was eerie. The Wightmans were dead silent—and silence seemed meant to ensnare him. Perhaps the Judge calculated that if he could get him to declare himself, he could get rid of him for good.

Brooding on his own Empedocles, Arnold received an invitation from out of the blue, and went out to Mr. Justice Wightman's house at Teddington near Hampton. The chief record of his visit is "The River," the most literal of those *Faded Leaves* lyrics inspired by a sudden crisis.

Stillness was now in the air, and he disliked hot, clammy days. The Judge's house overlooked lawns that plunged—under admirable shrubbery—down to the cool Thames. The river invited the lovers and Arnold turned one boat ride into a poem about love and death: one sees Fanny Lucy prettily seated astern as Matthew watches her. A cool breeze comes near evening:

> *On the broad-bosomed lordly Thames*
> *Down which we glide, the August sun*
> *In mellow evening splendour flames;*
> *Soon will our voyage all be done.*
>
> *Wrapped in thy shawl, in still repose*
> *Back in the stern-seat soft-reclined,*
> *Round thy sweet form the cool air blows,*
> *And thy veil flutters in the wind.*

His reflections become more urgent, imploring as his lady's head is averted:

> *I only see those fingers small*
> *Flit charmingly in careless play*
> *Through the green fringes of thy shawl . . .*
> *Let the shawl be. . . .*
>
> *. . . . . .*
>
> *Silent the swans beside us float—*
> *None speaks, none heeds; ah, turn thy head!*

The indifference of nature and his unheeding lady prompt him to speak boldly, at least in the poem:

> *My pent-up tears oppress my brain,*
> *My heart is swollen with love unsaid.*
> *Ah, let me weep, and tell my pain,*
> *And on thy shoulder rest my head!*
>
> *Before I die—before the soul,*
> *Which now is mine, must re-attain*
> *Immunity from my control,*
> *And wander round the world again.*[50]

As a matter of fact his "pent-up" feelings and some calculations made him speak—directly. Whether or not Fanny Lucy heard anything metaphysical in what he said, she wonderfully consented to marry him—and her consent ended his bliss. Fanny Lucy spoke to her father; and the Judge, who was *not* "sure that Arnold could support a wife" on a secretarial income, ended months of quietness with a judicial sentence. He very simply forbade "any further meeting"[51] between Matthew and Fanny Lucy.

And that was that.

Not long after the Hampton visit, Matthew sent a note about these dreadfully unhappy circumstances to his family up at Fox How. Even Tom heard of a terrible "counterblast" and learned that "it was not all prosperous sailing" in his brother's courtship.[52] Circumstances were now forcing Arnold out of England, and so he couldn't be "best man" at Jane's wedding, alas! Mrs. Arnold surely replied to her son that his pig-headedness was amazing—for Jane urgently needed his loving support at Rydal Chapel. Still, Edward, or "Didu," was to give Jane's hand away. Since Mrs. Arnold with normal clairvoyance invited no wedding guests from outside the family, Matthew's disgraceful piggish absence might be concealed. Seventy years later, Mrs. Humphry Ward (Tom's daughter) claimed that the happiest features of Jane Arnold's marriage to William Forster on August 15, 1850, were Jane's "radiant look" and "Matthew Arnold giving his sister away, with the great fells standing sentinel."[53]

Matthew's sister Mary, who stood sentinel, gives in 1850 a truer picture in a letter to Tom. Quite clearly, at neither wedding breakfast nor the wedding party at chapel was Matthew in evidence:

Picture to yourself [the] 15th August, 1850. . . . Look into the dining room at the usual breakfast hour, and you will see the table at its usual size, with the old green and white china, and large white cake of that peculiar aspect which belongs to one occasion. The cake, however, is uncut, and the small party, consisting of Mamma and your four sisters, Edward, and one other [William Forster] who, though not related, seems to have some near and very significant claim, are gathered around the table. . . . After breakfast, however, things do not take their usual course—something different from common is astir. The sisters go upstairs, and there is some special dressing. It is a very simple affair, however—no maids in attendance, but K's little dressing-room door is shut, and something is going on within. Presently the door opens, and the dear K. comes out dressed differently indeed, very differently from usual, but scarcely less simply—so gracefully becoming is the plain white silk dress and the lace veil which entirely covers, though it does not conceal the sweet modest face and head with its wreath of orange-flowers and myrtle. About ten o'clock, in three carriages only, we went to Rydal Chapel. William went first with Edward, then Susy and Fan, (the two bridesmaids), and Rowland and I followed—and Mamma and K., came last. Some little girls, the children of Dr. Christopher Wordsworth, were dressed in white and scattering flowers in the churchyard.

Dismally Edward waited "at the gate to lead K. into church."[54]

With great care, Matthew had made his calculations. Within a day or two of losing Jane, he won Miss Wightman's heroic consent. He irritated the Judge just as the Wightmans were planning a tour of the Continent; and the Judge's awful prohibition upon his seeing Fanny Lucy, or "counterblast," gave Matthew the excuse of being too bewildered to attend Jane's wedding. He humiliated Jane by finding it inconvenient to be her "best man," and now had the pleasure of following Fanny Lucy about in the Rhineland while keeping out of sight—even managing to sleep chastely one night in a hotel in which she stayed. He composed a series of ardent little conventional lyrics for *Faded Leaves*, in all of which he is the suffering, frustrated lover. In "Excuse" and more aptly in "Longing," he blends Fanny Lucy's image with that of the Uranian Aphrodite, the goddess of ideal love:

Come to me in my dreams, and then
By day I shall be well again!
* * * * * *

Come, as thou cam'st a thousand times
A messenger from radiant climes,
And smile on thy new world, and be
As kind to others as to me!

Or, as thou never cam'st in sooth,
Come now, and let me dream it truth;
And part my hair, and kiss my brow,
And say: My love! why sufferest thou?

"I have no one to say with tearful eyes to—I am wretched—& to be answered by," he had mused dreamily, "—mon pauvre enfant— allons—sortons—dinons. . . ."

Come to me in my dreams, and then
By day I shall be well again!
For then the night will more than pay
The hopeless longing of the day.[55]

He was postponing his reckonings. He was postponing expiation of the deep guilt he felt over hurting Jane, just as he postponed expiation of his guilt at being so little of a social activist. He had no definite idea as to how he might support a wife. He may have foreseen, dimly, that purgatory lay ahead; but in the autumn he spent what was meant to be a carefree hunting week with Slade. They took guns into the Lake District. What Matthew chiefly rememberd was the rain; young Slade would "blaspheme," under the blackened skies, as the "daily satura- tion" of his pitiful and un-waterproof coat "commenced on some lonely mountain or other."[56] Thunder smashed overhead; lightning split up the heavens, and the rain was endless and very hard.

10

"FANCY 'THE EMPEROR' MARRIED!"
1850–1851

Surdum te amantissimis tuis praesta; bono animo mala precantur. Et si esse vis felix, deos ora, ne quid tibi ex his, quae optantur, eveniat. Non sunt ista bona, quae in te isti volunt congeri; unum bonum est, quod beatae vitae causa et firmamentum est, sibi fidere.

(Be deaf to those who love you most of all; they pray for bad things with good intentions. And, if you would be happy, entreat the gods that none of their fond desires for you may be brought to pass. What they wish to have heaped upon you are not really good things; there is only one good, the cause and support of a happy life,—trust in oneself.)

—*Seneca,* Ad Lucilium Epistulae Morales,
Epistle XXXI ("On Siren Songs")

MATTHEW Arnold wickedly had offended his "darling" Jane by insulting the lean, hòarse William Forster and then missing her wedding. When hardly on speaking terms with Jane, and forbidden from seeing his "fiancée" by a Justice of the Court of the Queen's Bench, he wrote to Clough. *"Mut verloren alles verloren,"* Matthew scribbled.

Splendid, sage advice rang in his ears, in immortal cadences of Goethe's:

Ehre *verloren—viel verloren!*
Musst Ruhm gewinnen.
(Honour *lost—much is lost!*
You must win fame.)

Mut *verloren—alles verloren!*
Da wär es besser, nicht geboren.[1]
(Courage *lost—all is lost!*
Then it were better not to have been born.)

He needed rational courage to decide what to do. Could he afford to stay at Berkeley Square on a salary of £72 a quarter? Reaching his secretarial desk under Rembrandt's *Jewish Exiles* these days at eleven, he read Locke and Spinoza and wrote letters for the Marquess of Lansdowne until four or five. The job was a sinecure that kept him from the fringes of his employer's affairs, and the letters called for no thought. Matthew livened them up with Frenchified spellings—as when he dropped the 'u' in 'favourably' and 'favourable' (though in official letters he did not write 'peu favorable' as he did for friends).

"Berkeley square," he indited very typically at a handsome teak desk.

Sir
   I am directed by the Marquis of Lansdowne to acknowledge your letter to him of the 8th inst. . . . He will be happy to present to the House of Lords the petitions, praying for the enfranchisement of copyholds, to which it relates, as he is very favorably disposed towards such a measure.
   I remain, Sir,
   your obedient servant,
   M. ARNOLD.—²

James Peachey Esq:ʳᵉ

His present work was easy; but if he married he would lose an Oriel stipend of about £120 a quarter. And there was the rub. How could he persuade the Judge that £72 a quarter from Lord Lansdowne would even keep Fanny Lucy alive? On the other hand if he took a job with better pay, he might lack energy for reading and poetry. "Hard dull work, low salary, stationariness," he felt, "and London to be stationary in . . . do not please me."³ Travel might be exhilarating. But to be cooped up in a fixed, dull job! At Lansdowne House his *stationariness* irked him.

In 1846, Mrs. Arnold had wanted him to be a School Inspector. The Inspectors, or "H.M.I.s," were gentle academic men; one of them, an optimist named Morell, had prepared for the job by studying philosophy at Bohn under Fichte. (Perhaps that training helped Morell in England, when in schools he saw hungry thin boys; or when he met Pupil Teachers of fifteen and sixteen who taught eighty children in freezing rooms with cracked windows and no heat.) The H.M.I.s reported on the "elementary schools" for poor children between the ages of four and thirteen.

Arnold's horrors were ahead of him. He lacked demographic data, but knew of Lord Lansdowne's worries and estimates. The growing population of England and Wales in 1851 would total 17,927,609. Three-quarters of these people belonged to the "manual labour class" and perhaps 15 percent earned as much as £1 or £2 a week. For their millions of children—many of them now employed as child mineworkers, child factoryhands, child beggars, or even child prostitutes—the British government had no plan, idea, or scheme, no national or local system of education whatever. When W. J. Fox, the M.P. for Oldham, introduced a bill to establish a national system of education in 1850, his motion was defeated in the House of Commons by 287 votes to 58. Yet Holland had a state system of schools, the finest in Europe. France and Prussia had intelligent, humane, centrally organized school systems—and the United States was not far behind. Massachusetts had set up a state board of education in 1837, under the vigorous secretaryship of Horace Mann. In England the state merely allocated a small sum of money each year to schools run by churches and charities—and employed a few clergymen, dons, and philosophers to see how it was spent. These were the H.M.I.s.

In 1850 for Matthew, the stars might have been conjoining in bureaucratic heavens; Lord Lansdowne headed the education committee, and an old Balliol tutor, Ralph Lingen of the bright waistcoats, of all people, was in charge of the genteel School Inspectors. "Lingen, who is Education Secretary, and was once my tutor at Oxford, and a genius of good counsel to me ever since," he casually wrote to Fanny Lucy in December, "says he means to write me a letter of advice about inspectorships, applying to Lord Lansdowne, etc. Shall I send it on to you?"[4]

Lingen determined his life for the next thirty-five years. Unlike his father, Arnold had no interest in schools. But he had a guilty social conscience and enjoyed trains and travel. The inspectorship would open up the nation to his unusual comparativist's eyes; it would connect him with his father's ideas—even to a Headmaster's remembered energy and ambition. In 1850 Matthew felt that Lansdowne House had become a dull replica of Oriel College; he yearned for something new and needed money to marry. And yet some lines in Coleridge's "Ancient Mariner" might have applied to *a poet* seeking an inspectorship just then:

> *(Heaven's Mother send us grace!)*
> *As if through a dungeon-grate he peered*
> *With broad and burning face.*[5]

The education office was understaffed and underpaid; scholarly men were working so hard they fainted in the office. Arnold, as a School Inspector, was to cry out in a note to Fanny Lucy, "I am too utterly tired." In a "positive purgatory,"[6] while his son Basil Arnold was dying, he was to work into the night with school papers. He was to talk to more working-class children than any other poet who has ever lived, and begin with a positively gigantic school district of 104 schools, in the counties

of Lincoln, Nottingham, Derby, Stafford, Salop, Hereford, Worcester, Warwick, Leicester, Rutland, Northampton, Gloucester, and Monmouth, with all those of North Wales except Flintshire and Denbighshire, and the whole of South Wales.[7]

Lingen described the job in rather general terms. Relieved that his future was settled, Matthew boasted about going into debt to marry —and paraded his unique boldness and nerve at home (though Tom was already a married School Inspector at the end of the earth, in Tasmania, and Willy was risking his life in an Indian hill station). "Marriage with a narrow income and precarious future," Matthew assured his mother, "is a sort of gambling state which can only be supported by those of firm nerves."[8]

Up north at Christmas, the "firm nerves" of this Oxford gambler were appraised by one of the most intuitive women in England. One may be pardoned for dwelling on his meeting with the author of *Jane Eyre,* nearly on the eve of his twenty-eighth birthday.

On December 21 he was invited over to Quillinan's Loughrigg Holme, with its smoky old ceiling beams, to see two famous ladies. The first he knew: "At seven came Miss Martineau and Miss Brontë (Jane Eyre)," he told his fiancée in a letter that night. He perhaps knew that when these two ladies had called in August at Fox How, when the Forsters were there, the author of *Jane Eyre* and his mother had *not* hit it off well (Miss Brontë thought his mother lacked "genuineness and simplicity");[9] but Jane and the novelist had responded to each other's quiet manner, and in October Jane and William Forster had paid a call at the Brontë parsonage in Haworth, from their own first home in Rawdon.

For a few minutes this evening, Matthew was cornered by Miss Martineau who, despite her atheism, was admired by his whole family except for the pious Jane herself. "Talked," he noted, "to Miss Martineau (who blasphemes frightfully) about the prospects of the Church of England, and, wretched man that I am, promised to go and see her cow-keeping miracles . . . —I, who hardly know a cow from a sheep." Miss Martineau ran an experimental farm near her home, the Knoll, Ambleside. Extracting himself from that lady's blasphemies, he met the tiny novelist, who had lost her sisters Emily and Anne and was thinking about her Brussels experiences for *Villette.* Gazing at her "expressive gray eyes," he smirked and grimaced and clutched a monocle—in a manner that led another friend to despair over the way he "puckered into elaborate grimaces." He talked with the shy, brilliant woman about her "curates" in *Shirley* and then some "French novels" (probably those of George Sand) and then her "education in a school at Brussels," before the two ladies rose to leave and he "sent the lions roaring to their dens."[10]

The greatest lion, that night, must have shaken her head under the stars, as she walked home with Miss Martineau. "It is observable," Miss Brontë felt,

> that Matthew Arnold, the eldest son . . . inherits his mother's defect [of insincere manners]. Striking and prepossessing . . . [he] displeases from seeming foppery. I own it caused me at first to regard him with regretful surprise. . . . I was told however, that 'Mr. Arnold improved upon acquaintance.' So it was: ere long a real modesty appeared under his assumed conceit, and some genuine intellectual aspirations, as well as high educational acquirements, displaced superficial affectations.

Charlotte Brontë adds that his "theological opinions" were "vague and unsettled,"[11] but she perhaps hardly dreamed how unsettled he was. The praise of defiant feeling in her novels upset Arnold, as he tried to face up to his inspectorship and persuade Jane that he was most responsible. In his timely poem on Charlotte Brontë and premature elegy on Miss Martineau, "Haworth Churchyard," he finds a masterly accent in *Jane Eyre* and praises Emily Brontë—whose "too bold dying song" in "No coward soul is mine" had shown scorn for the vanity of religious creeds that have shaken men's hearts. Arnold was much taken by Emily Brontë's work:

> *And she*
> *(How shall I sing her?) whose soul*
> *Knew no fellow for might,*
> *Passion, vehemence, grief, . . .*
> *Whose too bold dying song*
> *Stirred, like a clarion-blast, my soul.*[12]

Yet even so, the Brontë sisters, it seems, made him sin against his critical sanity. When Charlotte's best novel appeared, he told Jane that *Villette* indeed was "disagreeable" because Charlotte's mind contained only "hunger rebellion and rage." In contrast he praised one of Bulwer-Lytton's tepid, unfelt works for its "gush" and "better humour" and "mellowed constructive skill—all these are great things."[13] Appealing to his feelings and exciting his anarchical, defiant attitude towards the genteel world of middle-class England, the Brontës "stirred" him too much.

Even now, he struggled to master *his feelings*—and campaigned to regain Jane's love and approbation. Matthew's purely selfish, aching desires had led him to be furious with Forster for taking Jane away.

During her engagement he had sent her a copy of Tennyson's *In Memoriam,* as a sign that their old intimacy was much lamented; but Jane had not replied. "Since you do not write," Matthew addresses her now in January 1851, "I must be the first." He has "heard" Jane's letters read aloud at Fox How, even if she wouldn't write to him. And now, though he doesn't mention her wedding, he vows to make war on his "worldly" element until it "ceases to isolate him" from Jane. He becomes wiser and saner, it seems, every day at twenty-eight. The "open and liberal state of our youth," he tells Jane as he generalizes his dilemma,

> we *must* perhaps all leave and take refuge in our morality and character: but with most of us it is a melancholy passage from which we emerge shorn of so many beams that we are almost tempted to quarrel with the law of nature.

If he abandons the life of intuitive feeling, upon which his poetry depends, he may make that sacrifice for darling *Jane,* his own "K." Then she will forgive him, adore him so much. To melt her heart he says he has influenza and that "the Judge still absolutely prohibits"[14] him from seeing Miss Wightman. (He doesn't admit that he hears from Fanny Lucy every day or that he is writing, one by one, ninety letters to her.)

How could he persuade the pious Jane of his closeness to her? He sends her a gift of Tasso's poems (as if *Jerusalem Delivered* might cancel in her mind the dolorous effect of Tennyson's *In Memoriam*). And anyway, he is reading unworldly things she likes such as Thomas à Kempis's *Imitation of Christ* and "Ecclesiasticus," though he forgets to say that he is taking down fashionable quotations from Mme de Staël's *Delphine,* and has other, elegant "French books" on his reading list such as:

Mme. de Kruder's Valerie
Mme. de Souza. Romans choisis.
Mme. Charrière. Caliste où lettres écrites de Lausanne.
Mme. de Rémusat. de l'éducation des femmes.[15]

With half of his mind he was sincere in telling Jane of his earnestness and scorn for fashion and newspapers—but with the other half he followed gossip and the newspapers. If his name came before the education committee when the Whigs and Lord Lansdowne were out of office, he might not *get* an inspectorship—and thus couldn't marry! "I . . . retire more and more from the modern world and modern literature," he assures his beloved "K," "which is all only what has been before and what will be again. . . . When I hear of some new dispute or rage that has arisen, it sounds quite historical; as if it was only the Smiths at Ephesus being alarmed for their trade." And now he imagines what would happen if both Miss Wightman and Jane's husband were to die. Jane is "what no one else" can "exactly be again,"

> unless indeed we were both to lose what we have dearest, and then we should be drawn together again, I think, as in old times. [16]

In his diary of 1851 and letters to Jane, he is on the other hand condescending about the pretty woman he is to marry. Miss Wightman is "sweet." He refers to his fiancée pityingly, in the tone he had used in "A Farewell," in the *Switzerland* series, when describing young women as "things." "She is so loveable," he writes as if Miss Wightman were a kitten or a pet mouse. "I am more inclined sometimes to cry over her than anything else: it is almost impossible to be soft and kind enough with her."[17] He was *not* about to let Miss Wightman take that special place in his heart reserved for "K." He vowed not to recite his poems to his bride. Even after Fanny Lucy began to attack his ignorance of music and art, he kept up for his family's sake a bantering, condescending mode in referring to the woman who happened to be his wife but who hadn't "a trace of literature." (She knew more about modern novels than *he* did.) "I always find," he remarked of Fanny Lucy, "that she thinks as a great many people think."[18] He pretended that she was too dull, again that it was impossible that she could fathom his writing or know his aims: "Flu" is "always thrown into a nervous terror," he told his family, "by my writing anything which she thinks likely to draw down attacks on me." He regretted his "mistake in not consulting her more, & reading things to her. . . . But," he told his mother, "my poems I am less and less inclined to show or repeat—though if I lived with K, I dare say I should never have got out of the habit of repeating things to her."[19]

He loved Fanny Lucy more than he admitted to his family; yet it isn't surprising that as Willy put it, he seemed the last soul to be "happily married—or rather happy in matrimony." The idea utterly boggled Tom Arnold's mind: "Fancy 'the Emperor' married!" [20]

Nervous about sex, his "engagement," his vocation, his sister, and his future, Arnold jotted hectic and confused diary entries in 1851. Despite the Judge, he met Miss Wightman at the "Eastern Counties station" and felt "almost happy."[21] He heard from her sister, "Baby," that the Judge wouldn't permit a wedding, until he had the inspectorship. And now that prize slipped through Arnold's fingers!

The Whig "ministers have managed to get beaten by forty-eight tonight by the Radicals on a motion to enlarge the franchise," Arnold wrote desperately to Miss Wightman on February 21. If the Whigs resigned, his inspectorship couldn't be approved.

Next day he drove to Laleham with an aching head. Returning to town, he "drove straight to Lansdowne House" and heard, that night or at breakfast, that the Whig regime *had* fallen. "Postponed interview with the Judge," Matthew miserably recorded. He spent a "wretched nervous" time pacing to Hampstead with Clough and sent three political love letters to "Flu" in twelve hours. His marriage hung on the complex workings of politics; feeling "anxious" and "uncomfortable," he began to read Milton's *Paradise Regained,* when he heard the news: "Ministers in again"! Russell and the Whigs had risen like phoenixes from political death! Next day he flew like a shuttlecock between judicial chambers and Lansdowne House and finally "saw the Judge"—who believed that the hateful Whigs hadn't *yet* given Arnold a job. Now he read "Milton at breakfast"—as if *Paradise Regained* would bring blessings from heaven. His fiancée most effectively pleaded with the Judge. "Went to the Judge at Chambers," Arnold wrote after a nauseous time on March 7, and "settled our engagement."[22]

And now, for the first time, he perused "blue books" about official education policies, and he perhaps heard about his gargantuan inspectorial district. Still, he felt that railway journeys wouldn't unnerve him: *A cramp'd pis-aller life has produced a cramp'd pis-aller poetry,* he jotted.[23] On March 23, 1851, he noted in his diary,

L^d L[ansdowne] appointed me Inspector

—and then he agreed with the Judge as to finances and a spring wedding.

Yet with his future all aglow, Matthew felt "restless and unsettled" even as he reread the peerless Epictetus. With one "very bad night" after another, he noted ominously in March: "mostly quite unsettled, roaming about" and "feverish and uneasy" and "languid and unwell."[24] He was "languid" when he became an inspector—and an interview with an old friend (who managed a training school with the future anthologist F. T. Palgrave) only made him feel, it seems, that his "talk with Temple about the inspectorship" was useless. Thereafter Arnold put the job out of mind: "I ignore my future," he quoted in his diary from Chateaubriand's French: "Is there today a clear future for anyone?" Chateaubriand had predicted the death of Western culture with Europe sinking decrepitly in a "powerless anarchy" ("une impuissante anarchie")[25] of passions and mores—and clearly the ideas of culture and anarchy for Arnold in 1851 were not what they would be in *Culture and Anarchy.* To believe the death of culture "could be" is to minimize one's sense of obligation to society. In future he kept detached to an extent from the social scene by imagining *no* conscious effort could affect history; indeed in his diaries, he was to jot with approval four times:

> Society is a sort of organism on the growth of which conscious efforts can exercise little effect. Karl Marx.[26]

He hadn't yet discovered Marx. But he embraced European social pessimism this spring to gain a deeper purchase on his anxieties and slowly returned to one thesis: he was beset by *pride*. What were ups and downs of his moods really but evidence of *conceit*—which made him panic when life went well? On April 23, he humiliated his pride in a long stroll in green "Cumnor country" with William Yonge Sellar ("Sellar and the rest of that clique," he had fumed to Clough, "who know neither life nor themselves"). He even cut poor Clough, who believed Miss Wightman with her small "aquiline nose" had the look of a "natural enemy."[27] But he also avoided Sir William Molesworth and Baron Monteagle, among Whig nobles who were inviting him to dinners. All of this perhaps gratified a Tory Judge, who promised a fine "marriage settlement."

A deeper reason for Matthew's avoiding liberal friends and politicians just before his wedding is evident, however, in his friendship for Melville Portal—a young M.P. who had given his maiden speech in Parliament on Ecclesiastical Titles. Portal was a Tory. At Christ Church during Arnold's early Balliol days, Portal had defended John Henry Newman and the "High Church" party. "Dined with Portal at the Alfred [Club]," Matthew noted—during a week in which he had no time for Clough. And again in May: "dined with Portal at club" and "breakfast with Portal."

One night Arnold went alone to Eaton Place and secretly watched "Flu." Twice again in May, he walked the streets to cold, silent cobblestones of his fiancée's Belgravia, "to see Flu at the window." [28]

During these *voyeur* episodes, he perhaps thought of his very remarkable notes on pride. On a sheet actually labeled "M. Arnold, Ball: Coll: 1843," he had over the past four years, from 1847 to 1851, been carefully annotating the idea that *"pride is madness"*:

Stephens
A. de Vere   P.P. p r i d e   i s   m a d n e s s
G. Planche & Barbier

> Gott hat den Menschen einfach gemacht
> aber wie er gewickelt wird & sich
> verwickelt, ist sehr [schwer] zu sagen.[29]

Standing in the chill, empty street at Eaton Place—and seven or eight years removed from Balliol College—Arnold looked forward to a new career and a honeymoon; but he was far from content. Obsessively, he seems to have turned over in his mind the substance of his allusions to overweening pride: his note on "Stephens" refers to the mad dramatist George Stephens, whose incoherent plays had appeared in 1845; and again, "A. de Vere" refers to Aubrey de Vere's lucid analysis of an artist's presumption and madness in the poem "Tale of the Modern Time." "G. Planche & Barbier" reflects Arnold's avid, continual reading of *Revue des Deux Mondes:* in that journal he had found Gustave Planche's review of Auguste Barbier's surrealistic *Lazare,* a poem in which London is a vast, infernal, phantasmagorical city in which pride has reduced everyone to incoherence or madness. "God has made man simple (*einfach,* composite, not-fragmented)," Goethe had told Mme von Stein in Arnold's German quotation, "but how man became wound up and entangled himself is difficult to say."

The *pride is madness* notes combined apparently with memories of his earlier nighttime walks back in 1848 to help Arnold finish, in 1851, "A Summer Night" and "The Buried Life," themselves preludes to his honeymoon works "Dover Beach" and "Stanzas from the Grande Chartreuse."

In these four lyrics—among the most powerful he ever wrote—he very candidly explores his own plight and feelings and those of urban people. He is more intimate with the reader and more modern in technique than Tennyson or even Hardy; and as he lets archetypal images of prisons, seas, and rivers as well as prosaic phrases carry the burden of his meaning, he achieves universality with literalness and intensity.

Occasionally, one may say, Arnold gains an effect of sincerity by writing indifferent lines. "A Summer Night" may have begun with a bad couplet:

> *The dropping patter of a child's small feet*
> *Did fall like rain in the deserted street.*[30]

But in the better final version, he places *himself* beneath windows which express only the horror of inexpressiveness:

> *In the deserted, moon-blanched street,*
> *How lonely rings the echo of my feet!*
> *Those windows, which I gaze at, frown,*
> *Silent and white, unopening down,*
> *Repellent as the world.*[31]

Taking "Flu" home one night in May after his vigils, he perhaps talked as idly as his speaker has done in "The Buried Life." He had spent a very pleasant day, introducing her to friends and joining them all at the Royal Italian Opera Company's showing of Meyerbeer's *Les Huguenots*. But of his walk to Eaton Place he records only the phrase, "bitter cold moonshine";[32] and in "Summer Night" the moon becomes a symbol of a calm, Newman-like lucidity searching the innermost heart:

> And the calm moonlight seems to say:
> Hast thou then still the old unquiet breast,
> Which neither deadens into rest,
> Nor ever feels the fiery glow, . . .
> But fluctuates to and fro,
> Never by passion quite possessed
> And never quite benumbed by the world's sway?[33]

The horrors in life for Arnold were those he discovered in himself and intuited in others. He felt that we are fragmented: we are neither this nor that. We fluctuate: our inner lives are seldom constant. And finally we *think* we have goals and sufficient rules for living but we know so little about ourselves that we err morally, to die in spirit before we die in flesh. Since the mass of men are too numbed to care about inward vitality, he was tempted by pride to set himself over the crowds; but *pride is madness*—"And," he continues,

> I know not if to pray
> Still to be what I am, or yield and be
> Like all the other men I see.

What *are* the "other men"? Men alternate between languor and passion: the mass are clerks and drones existing as slaves in the soul's hot prison, and the so-called independent few, or intellectuals, are madmen on a sea of moral experiment flying before despotic winds. Not that he would place himself among intellectuals. These slaves who "their lives to some unmeaning taskwork give" will soon, he realizes, include himself; and his lines especially in their tone depict the souls of a thousand million city people from his time to ours, from Leningrad to Sydney, London to New York to Tokyo:

> Most men in a brazen prison live,
> Where, in the sun's hot eye,
> With heads bent o'er their toil, they languidly
> Their lives to some unmeaning taskwork give,
> Dreaming of nought beyond their prison-wall.
> And as, year after year,
> Fresh products of their barren labour fall
> From their tired hands, and rest
> Never yet comes more near,
> Gloom settles slowly down over their breast.[34]

The "few" who escape from economic necessity and social conformity, the proud intellectuals, are like the mad helmsman,

> Still bent to make some port he knows not where,
> Still standing for some false, impossible shore. . . .
>
> Is there no life, but these alone?
> Madman or slave, must man be one?[35]

The only sane alternative in life is Newman's "plainness and clearness without shadow of stain!/Clearness divine!"[36]—which seems as remote and unattainable to a poet on the eve of his wedding as the stars over urban housetops.

An even more powerful poem, "The Buried Life," actually suggests the Tractarian poetics of Newman, Pusey, and Keble—especially in the ambiguity of its imagery. By its "indefiniteness," Pusey once declared at Oxford, a biblical symbol gains "reality, comprehensiveness, energy. . . . No deep saying was ever uttered which was not capable of many applications and a variety of meanings."[37] Arnold admired the biblical symbols in Isaiah which as a boy he repeated to his father:

> When thou passest through the waters, I will be with thee.
>
> I give waters in the wilderness, and rivers in the desert. [38]

Isaiah's rivers suggest God's grace. In his poem the Deity is not mentioned but the speaker has a "thirst" or an "unspeakable desire" or an ardent "longing" to discover the "soul's subterranean depth"[39]—or that inner Arnoldian reservoir of tantalizingly sweet sounds and hauntingly faint memories—and so, perhaps, he has an attitude of faith. As Arthur Clough declared, the true locale of the modern muses is the "midnight city," where Faith walks "in the garb of Doubt" and a man hunts himself.[40] In that midnight city, or even in the insane town of Barbier's Lazare, Isaiah cries out for the river of the true self.

In one desk-note after another, Arnold had thought about the true self in relation to medieval Catholicism, plural identities, and modern feeling and expression:

Why are we so interested in origines, and in the dark ages. Because man had in one case not overexcited himself—and in the other had succeeded in forgetting—had thrown off the burden of his over-stimulated, sophisticated, artificialized, false-developed miserable nervous sceptical self and begun life anew.

—We have been on a thousand lines & on each have shown spirit talent even geniality but hardly for an hour between birth & death have we been on our own one natural line, have we been ourselves, have we breathed freely.

The spirit of life pours itself into this or that man, and the power and veracity of his operation makes the feeble ghost-like mass of mankind adore him, and follow his oracles as if the Spirit of Truth had dictated them; but it is not so: Caesar, Goethe, Napoleon are mightily enstrengthened by the indwelling Spirit of life: but the Spirit of Truth incarnates itself seldom or never in man—if ever, in the still and hardly known.

—It is so all are born to feel—some to express—tho: every feeling has its word, every one who has the feeling cannot seize the word, and yet we live at a time when expression is so universal and appears so facile that all who have the feeling imagine they can find the expression too—but it is not so.[41]

Always uncertain of one's deep nature, how can one expect to be truly happy?

Man has an impulse for happiness: he sees something of it, hears traditions of much of it: he thinks therefore he *ought* to have it: what is true is, he *may* have it if he *can*.[42]

In the "dark ages" or during the medieval ethos man was made happy and whole by a faith which united reason and emotion. The *Zeitgeist* favored belief: a "Sea of Faith" was at its height. But as faith retreated, the buried self lost touch with the rational self; a man is now cut off from adequate words because he is divided from the deepest feelings. When are we even natural? "To desire to be *natural* in conversation," Arnold wrote, "and not to have the force necessary to supply the demands this desire makes on your collectedness, invention & spirit"[43] is one sign of the new alienation-from-the-self.

"The Buried Life" opens in the middle of talk which is quite uncommunicative, or banter which says utterly nothing—and as also in the Hampton poem "The River," light flow of talk with a lady precedes a poet's tears:

> Light flows our war of mocking words, and yet,
> Behold, with tears mine eyes are wet!
> I feel a nameless sadness o'er me roll.
> Yes, yes, we know that we can jest,
> We know, we know that we can smile!
> But there's a something in this breast,
> To which thy light words bring no rest,
> And thy gay smiles no anodyne.[44]

If love is a means through which he might see himself, he is quick—almost too quick—to see it as a symptom of estrangement:

> Alas! is even love too weak
> To unlock the heart, and let it speak?
> Are even lovers powerless to reveal
> To one another what indeed they feel?

The mass of men, including himself, live and move

> Tricked in disguises, alien to the rest
> Of men, and alien to themselves—and yet
> The same heart beats in every human breast![45]

It is this paradox, that of the alienation of men despite their generic similarity, that inspires an urgent discourse on "the buried stream." The poet eddies "at large in blind uncertainty" and is on a "thousand lines" as a role-player but never on his own, and finally is divided from meaningful words because he is severed from deep and certain feeling. Even to moritify pride and

> no more be racked
> With inward striving, and demand
> Of all the thousand nothings of the hour
> Their stupefying power,[46]

is by no means proof against atrophy or even madness. Arnold had found no answer to the problem of the *unity* of the self; and yet he believed that the heart of the lover is changed by a clarifying impulse, which (in "Memorial Verses") he had credited to the power of Wordsworth's poetry. If love cannot at all substitute for religion, it may unlock the heart. "Only," he writes with caution,

> —but this is rare—
> When a beloved hand is laid in ours,
> When, jaded with the rush and glare
> Of the interminable hours,
> Our eyes can in another's eyes read clear,
> When our world-deafened ear
> Is by the tones of a loved voice caressed—
> A bolt is shot back somewhere in our breast.[47]

The ritualistic erotic act (before the final sexual act) stirs a "lost pulse of feeling" and the eye sinks inward,

> the heart lies plain,
> And what we mean, we say, and what we would, we know.
> A man becomes aware of his life's flow, . . .
> And an unwonted calm pervades his breast.
> And then he thinks he knows
> The hills where his life rose,
> And the sea where it goes.[48]

"Buried Life" changes one's view of love as one reads the poem; the love relationship is finally seen as a means of self-discovery and of help to the problem of each individual's deepest identity. Arnold makes a more serious case for the value of sexual love than do his contemporaries. He found the best reasons to be happy on his honeymoon; and indeed in June, he faced his wedding evenly. He had a gallant attitude to Fanny Lucy—without any deep understanding of her. And Fanny Lucy, who was to become hysterical during the French Alpine part of their honeymoon, clearly believed that he was gentle, loving, and attentive. A woman less in love, perhaps, might have understood that marriage with him was likely to be disastrous; he had little experience with women outside his family. He was slow, uncertain, clumsy, tactless in forming friendships, inconsiderate with Rugby and Oxford men who loved him.

He was even careless. Borrowing money from four people, Matthew had £2 "stolen" just before the ceremony.[49] He was cool and neatly dressed at the right time; but then he referred jauntily to Flu Wightman as a "charming companion," in his condescending way, when he mingled with friends at Teddington on Tuesday, June 10, 1851.

Crowds of Tories and heaps of flowers filled the Wightmans' downstairs rooms. The Judge had got Wilson Croker, the jaundiced reviewer, out of a sickbed for the happy day. Swirls of rain kept the wedding party indoors—so that smartly dressed, polite, correct barristers and their wives mingled with odd, scruffier-looking Arnold guests. Among the latter was a balding, stooped, but formidable personage whom Matthew clearly liked and patronized: Arthur Hugh Clough must have kept himself from knocking over potted flowers, even in his misery. He was about to be fired from a job. (His employers at London University, where he was Head of University Hall, condemned him for slackness in recruiting students to the hall.) Arnold's mother kissed him before he climbed into a carriage, and Clough at last perhaps smiled in the rain. "Matt is married," that friend sighed. "Nobody cried; Matt was admirably drest, and perfectly at ease—it rained, but we did well enough—they went off before the breakfast."[50]

Driving in gray rain to Hampton station, the bridegroom left behind much of his life. He must have thought about Todo Walrond and Campbell Shairp who were still on Rugby's staff. Walrond was going to Balliol, to lecture on "Philology" en route to the civil service in London; Shairp was soon to rise to St. Andrew's University's Chair of Latin; and Melville Portal (much to everyone's surprise) was to marry a lady in the Whig premier's family. Though Arnold did not know it in June, little Arthur Stanley this year was to emigrate from Oxford as Canon of an historic old cathedral. Dr. Arnold's star pupil and elfin biographer was thus the first of Matthew's friends to rise to genuine prominence. Still, an old crony found that friend positively cowering in his rooms in 1851: "Think of me," remarked the new Canon of Canterbury, "lost in that huge Cathedral."[51]

Marriage divided Arnold from his friends more sharply than all of his airs and insults and antics. He missed Clough and Walrond more unbearably than he let on.

In the carriage in her traveling costume, Fanny Lucy looked petite and delicate. Arnold had wept over her while referring to her mockery. One notes an ironic tone in her own diary; and in her honeymoon letters to Lady Wightman a cheerful, rational, plausible, calm-after-the-storm reportorial manner, as if everything were well after a riot in an asylum. If her head darted this way and that as if she were bored with Matthew already, she lessened the tensions they both felt over a wedding night ahead.

The paradox of her character was that she enjoyed excitements, ordeals, and uncertainties that she feared. She could imagine mishaps in every lurch, shudder, and scream of a locomotive at Hampton Station, every jolt in a railway carriage—yet she liked to travel. Her upbringing in late stages had been adventurous. She had gone to Paris for the museums and art galleries and discovered a taste not only for painting and sculpture, but for foreign travel. She was readier, neater, and tidier, and more businesslike than the slow, dilatory Arnold; and apart from her interest in the Anti-Vivisectionist cause, and her strong approval of Keble and Pusey, she had a moderate, calm, detached view of her world. Far from being unliterary, she was "a very good judge of all prose," as Arnold admitted on December 18, 1861, at least three years after he began to profit from her criticism of his own work. Her mind was more logical than the minds of most of the men he knew, and troublingly able to show him his faults in argument. Flu's "good sense is so great," as he knew, and at least as great was her confidence. As a realist, she had not married with her eyes shut or failed to imagine itinerant lodging-house days ahead. Arnold had *no* prospect of buying a house or settling down immediately: she knew this well. At the Wightmans' balls and soirées she had been decorative, a star round which her sisters and admirers turned. But in marriage, she was to be outspoken and intelligent, compact and practical, busily attentive to Matthew's colds and sleepless nights, as well as to grave illnesses of her children—and the desperate needs of her thin, asthmatic, gasping Tommy, a sensitive boy with a cardiac complaint. Neither she nor Arnold foresaw terrible and pitiable troubles with their children; but it is important that she was a very pretty woman, a baronet's daughter, who could *imagine* herself in heavy unbecoming winter shawls in northern cities, traveling from place to place without a permanent roof over her head and taking small children with her.

Why is it, to judge from Arnold's diary, that their journey threatened to turn into a shopping expedition to keep her gown in trim? The terrors of marriage for any Victorian gentleman involved learning to protect his wife's clothes. But Fanny Lucy clearly stressed this requirement: she feared the wind might disturb her ribbons or hat: her little arms went here and there about her costume, and she excluded him from these attentions. What did Matthew know about female finery? She thus made him even more gallant, solicitous, and worried. How could he manage the wedding night?

A certain psychological game—or a set of games—is played by every married couple, in every age, and it is curious that we still lack adequate comparative data about these games. In the Victorian age, males among the gentry emphasized the fragility and delicacy of their wives. A wife's sexual attractiveness might thus be enhanced, and if she became less a person than a pretty object, she ensured that her husband might be gentler, softer, kinder, and more attentive than otherwise. Arnold began this game when, in courtship, he wept over Flu and imagined (as he told "K") that he couldn't be gentle *enough* with her. And one may add this: Fanny Lucy played the game, long after their wedding night, not only to make him gentler but to educate him in her requirements and her rights. Her later hysteria in the Alps, fright in the Catacombs, despair over a snow-bogged carriage, and misery in cold climates may be too easily dismissed as temperamental. She was a strong, compact, neat, alert, and finely observant person married to a man who had been overindulged by his sisters and mother. She knew that Matthew adored her; she loved *him*. But his selfish egoism would have to be reduced if she were to enjoy their life together. Certainly, Victorian handbooks for young brides might dictate that she hang upon her husband's every word; but at least since Jane Austen's time the gentry had been hearing about women's rights, too. One pauses over the fact that Fanny Lucy—who hadn't a trace of literature in her mind, as Matthew put it—was a reader of that same Jane Austen, who for example in *Persuasion* had written with fury about the social inequalities of the sexes. We often still misread Jane Austen as though her Anne Elliot suffered and perceived nothing, or as if "sensible Jane" had nothing to do with the revolutionary climate in which she lived; but it is doubtful that intelligent Victorian women read her with minds just so dull, unfeeling, and complacent as modern critics often do, and the note of irony in Fanny Lucy's diaries and letters suggests to us, I think, that *she* found a sympathetic soul in that writer. Arnold's friends agreed that his worst, egotistical, selfish traits began to disappear after he married. One of his undeniable virtues was that he was always capable of changing his outlook, of getting out of narrow ways of thinking and feeling, and it is clear that his wife found that he *could* be made to open his eyes. She was not to nag him, but to help him to find more in English women than he sensed at the start of a nervous honeymoon journey.

Despite his debts, he planned a honeymoon at Alverstoke by the sea—and hoped to afford a Continental tour. Fanny Lucy completed her shopping when they left the train and they went to a hotel. On the strait which divides Hampshire from the Isle of Wight, the newlyweds spent six days.

His wife seems to have been surprised by his gentleness; in any event her really ironic note of protest does not begin, in her surviving honeymoon letters, until after their later arrival in Paris. Even then, Fanny Lucy is at first so self-effacing and apologetic that one suspects Matthew *began* as a very considerate husband indeed.

They loved their surroundings at Alverstoke. Gulls flying up from hunting and jagged rocks and little caves and shallow clear water all fascinated them both. If they were inexperienced in a bedroom they were also deeply in love: discovering sex for the first time, Fanny Lucy and Matthew enjoyed their security. One day they took an embattled ferry in rough, choppy water to the Isle of Wight and back and on other days paced the shore. To the south of their hotel was the famous Spithead anchorage. Within walking distance was the debris of the sea's threshold—thongweed and ribbonweed and cowries, blackened and stiff strands of the channeled wrack, or brown and olive fronds of seaweed with its branches swelling into bulbous, heart-shaped structures. The sounds of falling and rising tides must have reminded Arnold of his summer at the Isle of Man when he had written "To a Gipsy Child" as a comment on spiritual isolation and loneliness. His sense of well-being, of nearness to a loved person sometimes released his elegiac talent. Though enthralled with Fanny Lucy, he heard in the music of breaking waves on a beach the note a tragedian had heard "long ago on the Aegaean."[52] The theme and imagery of Sophocles' *Philoctetes* occurred to him now, if not also later, when he and Fanny Lucy spent a night at Dover. What is so interesting is the likelihood that he discussed the *feelings* aroused by this play with his wife, that this important experience he shared with her; perfection, intensity, and beauty of the poem he was about to write contrast sharply with a certain stiffness in "A Summer Night" and "Buried Life." Rather, "Dover Beach" has an inevitability and an easy, free, natural conversational quality that suggest it has been "talked out." It concerns not only two lovers, but our modern predicament in friendship and all human relationships. It is in keeping with Fanny Lucy's High Church views and it expresses a certain trust in the intimate, unlocking, saving, and special goodness of sexual love in a way that does *not* suggest a man's isolated reflections. Sophocles' play, its main literary source, might be a comment on Matthew's recent difficulties with his friends. In the play Philoctetes is abandoned by friends on the desert island of Lemnos—where he hears the melancholy sea. The Greek word *amphiplakton* ("beating all round") might be an auditory image for the sadness of his predicament: "I know of no other," one reads in Sophocles' tragedy,

> *by hearsay, much less by sight, of all mankind*
> *Whose destiny was more his enemy when he met it*
> *Than Philoctetes.*
>   . . . . . .
> *There is wonder, indeed, in my heart*
> *how, how in his loneliness,*
> *listening to the waves beating all round,*
> *how he kept hold at all*
> *on a life so full of tears.*[53]

A manuscript of part of "Dover Beach" dates from the time of Matthew Arnold's honeymoon, and his diary shows that even after he and Fanny Lucy set up housekeeping at Hampstead they planned a return to the coast. Late in June, in fact, they journeyed to a hotel at "Dover."

"Dover Beach"—not surprisingly—opens with images of confidence and beauty and profound security. The speaker might be talking to his bride in a moonlit city near glimmering chalk cliffs:

> *The sea is calm to-night.*
> *The tide is full, the moon lies fair*
> *Upon the straits; on the French coast the light*
> *Gleams and is gone; the cliffs of England stand,*
> *Glimmering and vast, out in the tranquil bay.*
> *Come to the window, sweet is the night air!*[54]

The lover's ear picks up a sound:

> *Listen! you hear the grating roar*
> *Of pebbles which the waves draw back, and fling,*
> *At their return, up the high strand,*
> *Begin, and cease, and then again begin.*[55]

In the Lake District Arnold knew the severity of one fine, plunging line of mountainous gray "scree" running into translucent depths of water as though falling to the middle of the earth. Wastwater on dark days is metaphysically severe. He had seen that line of scree in the rain lately, and it is possible, though not certain, that his memories of

Wastwater and Dover's beach combine in an image of "vast edges drear." The sadness he "hears" is ontological; the ebb and flow of misery is eternal or set in life's conditions. A Greek playwright had heard that sound:

> Sophocles long ago
> Heard it on the Aegaean, and it brought
> Into his mind the turbid ebb and flow
> Of human misery.

An auditory metaphor of water now expresses a sense of the retreat of faith; and the poem ends with the most deeply felt seventeen lines ever written by a modern English poet:

> The Sea of Faith
> Was once, too, at the full, and round earth's shore
> Lay like the folds of a bright girdle furled.
> But now I only hear
> Its melancholy, long, withdrawing roar,
> Retreating, to the breath
> Of the night-wind, down the vast edges drear
> And naked shingles of the world.
>
> Ah, love, let us be true
> To one another! for the world, which seems
> To lie before us like a land of dreams,
> So various, so beautiful, so new,
> Hath really neither joy, nor love, nor light,
> Nor certitude, nor peace, nor help for pain;
> And we are here as on a darkling plain
> Swept with confused alarms of struggle and flight,
> Where ignorant armies clash by night.[56]

The poem's discourse shifts literally and symbolically from the present, to Sophocles on the Aegean, from medieval Europe back to the present—and the auditory and visual images are dramatic and mimetic and didactic. Exploring the dark terror that lies beneath his happiness in love, the speaker resolves to love—and exigencies of history and the nexus between lovers are the poem's real issues. That lovers may be "true/To one another" is a precarious notion: love, in the modern city, momentarily gives peace, but nothing else in a postmedieval society reflects or confirms the faithfulness of lovers. Devoid of "love" and "light," the world is a maze of confusions left by "retreating" faith.

The Thucydidean image of the night battle—in the oddly satisfying ending—had been used once by Newman when he defined controversy as a "sort of night battle, where each fights for himself, and friend and foe stand together." That image also occurs in Clough's *Bothie of*

Toper-na-Vuolich which Arnold had slandered; and the ending of "Dover Beach" may convey an apology.[57] If Clough, in "Dover Beach," is chastised for optimism about love, Arnold implies too that in his own struggle to find himself as a poet he has attacked his friend and ally. His contrition is qualified perhaps by his discovery of a good, ontological reason for loss of camaraderie in a circle of friends: the modern life of the spirit is that of blind contest and error.

"Dover Beach" satisfies because it explores the suspicion we justly have of ecstatic, "perfect" moments; at the same time, it frees the lover's guilt over his own sensuous ecstasy—as he stands at the window on a fine night—so that he may enjoy himself. Matthew was rapturously in love; and his bride returned his love while eyeing him askance. He ate and drank very much while her appetite left her satisfied with a cup of coffee and one roll. She noted later with justice in her Dresden doll manner, that "men are such pigs about their dinner."[58] "It is a great thing in my favour," Arnold felt, "that I am utterly indifferent about the time of my breakfast."[59] Not that he was in danger of starving on his honeymoon. What he craved was anything at all to cool his torrid brow: he bought "sarsparilla" this summer and went to great lengths to ice it. "The greatest luxury of modern times," he admitted later at Brighton (a town he hated and Fanny Lucy loved) was "ice." Threepence might buy enough "to cool all one drinks at dinner."[60]

Fanny Lucy was to marvel over his predilection for cold days, cold houses, cold rooms; Matthew dressed in the iciest room in his house where his sponge in the winter was "frozen to the marble of the washhandstand"[61] and his jug, in the mornings, was full of ice. Again he enjoyed ice-skating; he glowed when his mother, then nearly eighty, laced up *her* iceskates at Rydal Lake. But his wife detested the cold. She was "most pinched" by it.[62] She couldn't find a climate warm enough. She longed for him to take her to Italy; he did so, while calling her a "born cockney" who understood "London sightseeing" best.[63] In Italy, Matthew swilled wine and thought of ways in which a baronet's daughter might improve herself: "I have rather wished you wore ear-rings," he later told her, "—the great gold ear-rings of [Italy], in such a variety of styles, please me so much."[64] If she adorned herself with those garish, barbaric trinkets, she chided *him* on other aesthetic matters. Her husband was tone deaf to music, to opera! What could one *do* with a poet who found Turner's paintings "insane" and the Elgin Marbles in the British Museum "a little beyond" him?[65] (Fanny Lucy forced him to hear Wagner's operas, made him look at art galleries, and connived later with a daughter to put modern novels under his nose.)

Physically, he towered over her. With rich amusement, the Cloughs noted that when he took her hand to leave a soirée, little Fanny Lucy flew over the carpet. Matthew callously abandoned her to gamble at whist with the Lingens, and felt that her delight in her parents' large, warm rooms at Eaton Place was folly. Irascible as Mr. Justice Wightman was at the assizes in the southern or Welsh counties —where Arnold served, now and then, for a fee as his legal "Marshal"—he was even more irascible at Eaton Place. When forced to stay with his in-laws, Arnold dreamed of bachelorhood and often fled secretly to Wyndham Slade's rooms. Not that he found fault with his in-laws' *largesse,* for they paid him £50 quarterly (as the "marriage settlement") whether he served as the Judge's legal Marshal or not. But Matthew was irritated by the fuss at Eaton Place; again he derided his wife's connection with the minor aristocracy.

Slowly, Fanny Lucy wore down his egocentricity. She was *not* swept off her feet by Rugby and the Dr. Arnold legend, or by Matthew's usually inchoate liberal views. She sensed in him, however, a paradoxical austerity, an inner area of mind that her love could not penetrate—and this made her curious about his verse. His poetry seemed rather gloomier by far than the delightful man who wrote it: "From the austere tone of some of the poems," she felt, nobody could imagine his "loveable nature, and that he, indeed, was 'Consoled by spirits gloriously gay!'" This woman was his chief consoling spirit: "beautiful & graceful as his prose is," she wrote generously, "he will be best remembered by his poetry." Though he wouldn't recite from manuscripts, she became aware of his habits and perhaps observed him working at "Dover Beach." "Matt," she later told Mrs. Clough, "never wrote until the last moment & when his subject had thoroughly been formed in his mind."[66]

Perhaps even while watching the faint gleam "on the French coast" from Dover, Arnold had thought of his planned tour abroad. A Continental honeymoon might have, for him, a sacramental aspect; he planned to see a famous monastery.

In fact, his Continental honeymoon in September began with a comic parody of "Dover Beach." The Arnolds took a night train to Dover. Alighting at the port on a thick, close, starless night, they joined a moving throng of Frenchmen and Germans: "Pitch dark," noted his wife, "and the getting of all the luggage from the railway to the steamer was [difficult] . . . as the truck . . . gave way & everything was quite scattered on the ground; then the noise and confusion of tongues was quite astonishing."[67] Ignorant of friend or foe, "Matt" battled by night for the luggage. He meant this journey to be a very dramatic and spiritual one, to an eleventh-century monastery in the Isère; and after bundling his wife and their valises on the Channel boat, he seems to have become reticent. Even the thickness of the night one suspects was important to him: "Close still dark night," he noted of the crossing to Calais, and "heaps of foreigners on board." At 2 A.M. they revived with cups of tea at Calais, and then continued to Paris, where Fanny Lucy fell into a hot bath on the *quatrième* of the Hôtel Windsor. After dining salubriously and taking her to the Louvre, Arnold noted: "Strolled alone to the rue de Bac & the river."[68] He may have found something irritating in her hearty, prosaic, "Here we are in dear old Paris."[69] His diary reveals him as rather more interested in moments when he is "alone" than in those with his wife. He left her—only to rush back to her arms—but in the deepest sense, he was isolated.

One day they sailed in rain and mist down the cool Saône. From Lyons, they took a carriage to the junction of the Saône with the Rhône—which at that point has tumbled down swiftly and turbulently from heights in Switzerland's Bernese Oberland. "Saône not so slow," Matthew jotted equitably; and later in the day: "to a café by the theatre alone." They journeyed on. Now they stopped at the Hôtel des Trois Dauphins, at Grenoble, in the high Isère; and then on Sunday, September 7, 1851, Matthew records in his diary very simply and briefly, "Grande-Chartreuse."[70]

Set under limestone hills in a rocky "Désert," which St. Bruno chose in the eleventh century as a site for his ascetic experiment, the monastery of the Grande Chartreuse connected one with the middle ages. Its buildings often had been rebuilt over the centuries but its way of life had seldom changed—and with marvelous consistency Carthusians were scorned by the worldly. When the English Carthusians offered corporate resistance to Henry VIII, priors and monks had been racked and killed. The monks in the Isère were summarily expelled from their monastery in 1783 and forced to pay heavy rent when allowed to return to it. Profits from the famous chartreuse liqueur never alleviated their meager lives—for the ascetics, here, drank diluted wine, lived in rough hair shirts under white tunics, and gave away their wealth to charities.

"Stanzas from the Grande Chartreuse," as the Rev. Dom Andrew Gray has shown, is hardly a reliable guide to their customs and ceremonies. Arnold confuses a mass with the Service of the Pax and implies that dead Carthusians are buried in wooden beds (rather than on a spare wooden plank); moreover, an image of organ music occurs very oddly in his poem. But he spent a night at the monastery and his poem is the result of a complex experience. He and Fanny Lucy approached the Désert on a gray, forbidding day. "The weather was bad," Fanny Lucy noted. "There was a fog."[71] Raw, bitter cold pierced them as they rode up a trail on mules and wondered if they might not themselves fall into the River Guiers Mort. In the "Stanzas," the poet is an Orpheus who passes "dark forges long disused" and then a River of Death:

> *The autumnal evening darkens round . . .*
> *While, hark! far down, with strangled sound*
> *Doth the Dead Guier's stream complain,*
> *Where that wet smoke, among the woods,*
> *Over his boiling cauldron broods.*[72]

Debemur morti nos nostraque, Arnold had read in Horace.[73] Death divides man and wife even if they die together, and perhaps in the cold he had a foretaste of death. When through mists, he saw the Aiguilette and the high roofs of dark slate, turrets surmounted by bare reminders of the Crucifixion, he was stopped at a gate and divided from his wife. Grief changes one's features. His wife had not known grief—but by now her features had altered for she was "pinched" by the weather. She had a very "uncomfortable time" she noted, "as it was bitterly cold. Matt was allowed to have supper with me, but at ½ past seven he was turned out." Then she was alone "in a small house."[74]

Arnold was shown the library, chapel, and cloisters before he was led to a row of dark huts:

> *The cells!—the suffering Son of Man*
> *Upon the wall.*[75]

He was duly given as his wife records, "a cell to sleep in. He got up at 11 & went to the Chapel & heard midnight mass. . . . the monks chanting the service in a low monotonous tone, each holding a taper: indeed every man had one and the Chapel was lighted in that way."[76] With morbid fascination, he observed the circulation of the tablet of the Pax, and the white complexion of the monks in flickering candlelight:

> *With penitential cries they kneel*
> *And wrestle; rising then, with bare*
> *And white uplifted faces stand,*
> *Passing the Host from hand to hand.*

The ceremony had an aspect of death. Arnold half-observed, half-participated in it; and the main question in his poem arises inevitably after he describes the Pax service:

> *The House, the Brotherhood austere!*
> *—And what am I, that I am here?*[77]

What, he imagines his father and other sages asking, is he doing now "in this living tomb?" Trained to be rational, he had noted the "Protestant Parent's wish" that "Nature would keep high out of his child's sight all but the Protestant aspect of the Universe." In the "living tomb" he is at the center of the traditional faith of Europe and he, like the sentimentalists, feels its force and sanity:

> *Take me, cowled forms, and fence me round,*
> *Till I possess my soul again; . . .*
> *Last of the race of them who grieve,*
> *Here leave us to die out with these*
> *Last of the people who believe!*[78]

For Arnold the Roman Catholic faith, though unpurged as he felt from inadmissible features of doctrine and dogma, was one measure of the *adequacy* of a world outlook: in uniting the heads and hearts of many believers it had united a continent. He was compelled to agree with the "world" that the faith of the Carthusians is anachronistic—"a dead time's exploded dream." But Niebuhr's historicism and especially Vico's cyclical view of change taught him that an age of faith was destined to come again in future. Meanwhile there has been no adequate substitute for the medieval outlook, and so one waits "forlorn," "melancholy," and "wandering,"

> *between two worlds, one dead*
> *The other powerless to be born.*[79]

Rationalism has left beyond only restlessness and pain for those acutely conscious of the need for faith. And what, indeed, have recent thinkers done to bring about a viable world outlook?

> *Achilles ponders in his tent,*
> *The kings of modern thought are dumb.*[80]

Arnold was not to escape from the influence of English romanticism; and as we have seen he had come lately under the influence of French and German romantic sentimentalists who aspired to an earlier Christian outlook. The ontology of Richter and Novalis and even Senancour is medieval, for they view the conditions of existence as requiring *something like* the medieval unified sensibility for our survival. Since these "sufferers," as well as Byron, Shelley and other romantics, have done nothing to bring the future nearer, however, Arnold accuses them in three of the loveliest stanzas he ever wrote:

> *What helps it now, that Byron bore,*
> *With haughty scorn which mocked the smart,*
> *Through Europe to the Aetolian shore*
> *The pageant of his bleeding heart?*

> *That thousands counted every groan,*
> *And Europe made her woe his own?*
>
> *What boots it, Shelley! that the breeze*
> *Carried they lovely wail away,*
> *Musical through Italian trees*
> *Which fringe thy soft blue Spezzian bay?*
> *Inheritors of thy distress*
> *Have restless hearts one throb the less?*
>
> *Or are we easier, to have read,*
> *O Obermann! the sad, stern page,*
> *Which tells us how thou hidd'st thy head*
> *From the fierce tempest of thine age*
> *In the lone brakes of Fontainebleau*
> *Or chalets near the Alpine snow?*[81]

He himself—or his narrator in the "Stanzas"—is actually poised between a wish to celebrate the "sufferers" and a wish to see the new future dawn, and even to assist at that dawn. He interestingly defines the new age, while begging the reader's permission to weep with the failed romantic sufferers:

> *Years hence, perhaps, may dawn an age,*
> *More fortunate, alas! than we,*
> *Which without hardness will be sage,*
> *And gay without frivolity,*
> *Sons of the world, oh, speed those years;*
> *But, while we wait, allow our tears!*[82]

But is *he* not one of the "Sons of the world"? More and more, his poem turns into an exercise in self-definition. While treating the monastery at Isère as a symbol of Europe, Arnold has described tensions within himself. He would aspire as an intellectual to the austere, lonely "high white star of Truth;"[83] he would attempt, as an elegiac poet, to lament the wholeness of the past and the failures of visionaries; and again he would shelter himself in faith to unite his feelings and intellect. But he cannot do all three.

In the final stanzas, the Grande Chartreuse becomes a more manageable, personal symbol. The monastery, now, suggests his own childhood. "We are like children reared," he writes, "beneath some old-world abbey wall." In his mind's eye, he glimpses the shining lances of a passing army—an army of recognizable activists:

> *Forth to the world those soldiers fare,*
> *To life, to cities, and to war!*[84]

The activists appeal from one direction. From another, he hears bugle notes and laughter—and one is reminded of sportsmen of the Lake

District, such as the bugle-playing fisherman Joe Winn and the laughing truant Louis Claude. "Action and pleasure" are alike impossible for those reared in a "shadowed nave" who have watched "yellowed tapers" in the "high altar's depths divine." Three stanzas at last underline a distinction: though reared in an atmosphere of faith, Arnold has been subject to varying influences and may choose among withdrawal, action, and pleasure. He is thus unlike the monastics who protest:

> 'Fenced early in this cloistral round
> Of reverie, of shade, of prayer,
> How should we grow in foreign ground? . . .
> —Pass, banners, pass, and bugles, cease;
> And leave our desert to its peace!'[85]

Neither benumbed, monastic, nor pleasure-seeking, he may even take command of an invisible "army" and struggle with intellectual weapons to help create a new age. "Man is born with a 'turn for being a sovereign prince,' "[85] Matthew reminded himself; but what is a prince who *does nothing*? "What are you?" asks Epictetus. "If you regard yourself as a man and as a part of some whole, on account of that whole it is fitting for you now to be sick, and now to make a voyage and run risks, and now to be in want, and on occasion to die before your time."[87] The Stoic spirit of Epictetus and the rational spirit of Voltaire brood over the end of the poem—and perhaps informed Arnold's thoughts on his night at the monastery. If the *siècle de lumière* ended monasticism, the only choices for the modern spirit are action, pleasure, or death-in-life. He would never choose pleasure and no one with ambition and energy chooses death-in-life. In the French Isère he seems to have detected his affinity with the insolent eighteenth-century humanists and especially with the active Voltaire. Later he was to quote a remark on Voltaire which catches the very spirit in which he himself meant to face the world:

> "advancing," as Michelet finely says, "in every direction with a marvellous vigour and with that conquering ambition which Vico calls *mens heroica*."[88]

He wrote "Grande Chartreuse" after his journey in the Isère—and polished it before it saw the light of day in *Fraser's Magazine* in 1855: "I think in the first stanza the comma will not do," he told the *Fraser's* editor J. W. Parker, and "if it is not giving you too much trouble, will you substitute *boiling* for *black-worn* as an epithet for the cauldrons of the Guiers Mort?"[89] But the insights into his conflicts, the final separation of himself from the ascetics, and his choice of moral action were perhaps clear to him on Monday morning, September 8, 1851.

On that refreshing morning, he was eager to start for Chambéry. His wife shivered; in the bitter cold she had "heard mass, the Père Superieur of the Chartreuse officiating." Matthew was full of *his* "very striking" ceremony.[90] Fanny Lucy wondered if she could ever again get warm. She perhaps felt that Arnold's optimism was worse than his meditative silences, for out beyond Albertville—that very afternoon —he thought nothing of asking her to walk "for about 3 hours & a half" in the company of two guides, when they couldn't find mules. Night was then coming on. They were in the high Alps. At a roadside chalet, she pleaded exhaustion; but, having hired a mule, Matthew helped his wife up onto its broad back and found a guide willing to take them on to Les Chapieux—though the narrow path ahead was dangerous. "Quite dark," Fanny Lucy noted. Suddenly they were in the middle of nowhere. Alpine peaks glistened and in starlight she observed that the ground had vanished: "It was so dark," she recalled of her terror, "& I was perched on this enormous mule, with no saddle, only a kind of pack made up with hay & my shawl." Feeling "very insecure," she could see the guide about two yards ahead of the mule, where he walked "holding the end of a long rein." Matthew was behind. They seemed to be "crawling" at the edge of a precipice: "I had my legs dangling over the edge at a most frightful height, with nothing for hundreds of feet below."

The newlyweds didn't fall off the precipice—but they came through this adventure scathed. Fanny panicked: "I never was more alarmed & I altogether lost my nerve." Matthew tried to calm her—without losing his balance or frightening her great mule—but (as she herself put it) she "behaved most dreadfully."[91] He had made a change in their plans: instead of taking the good road to Chamonix where letters awaited them, he had made a Hannibal-like maneuver and tried to take them over a little-used *col* directly into Aosta in the Italian Alps. Matthew was thinking perhaps of the view he would have next day of Mont Blanc, but he egotistically neglected the plainest of facts. Knowing that she was sensitive to cold, he had kept his wife at a freezing monastery; and knowing she was fearful he had begun a steep ascent in the lethal dark. He couldn't reach her side, now, on the trail to Les Chapieux, and for three hours, "till past 10" when they saw lights, he tried to soothe her as he tramped behind her mule. Marriage was to give him further insights into the smug, male depths of his egotism.

After a night at Les Chapieux they saw gleaming Mont Blanc; and in a low bumping *charabanc* reached Aosta. From then on they braved rain and crowds to see what they could of Milan, Verona, and Venice. "We came here by railway," Fanny Lucy observes in a fine Venetian hotel:

We have been over the Doges' palace & seen every part, including the Bridge of Sighs and the dungeons. The last I was very glad to get out of. Then we went to St. Mark's. . . . The gondolas are quite delightful & we both like going about in them immensely.[92]

By this time they were exhausted, and Fanny Lucy's impatience with his easy optimism became evident. He made her bitterly cold by taking not the safest, but the most scenic pass back through the high Alps. She watched him in his "wretched work" helping to push their snow-bogged public carriage up St. Gotthard's. "Wretched work" did not relieve her cold hands and feet. Cruelly bitten by the cold, she taunted him over his slowness in getting them to Paris: Lake Lucerne she liked as a lake, all "very fine but still cold." God, perhaps, might get her home to Lady Wightman.

"Far on our road home," she writes with relief on October 1, "and hope (D.V.) to be there about Tuesday next. May we go to Eaton Place," she asks her mother. "Matt wants to be in London for a day before he goes to Manchester."[93] She was relieved to be in Paris. Though eager to begin work, Matthew delayed in the French capital before the future swallowed him. At this time, he surely brooded on events. He was very able with ideas, but weak and naïve in the realm of human relations. Lately, he had tried to please his own family. Despite a few *contretemps*—and her susceptibility to panic, to the cold—he nearly pleased Fanny Lucy; he had made amends to his sister Jane and delighted his mother by becoming a School Inspector. Had he acted wisely? "Be deaf to those who love you most of all" was a Senecan text unlikely to occur to him at Paris; but he was soon to feel he had plunged into work for which he was "not born."[94]

He parted from his wife on October 11. Next day, John Morell, an optimistic Inspector, showed him Manchester. His own optimism survived for several days. He "might get interested in the schools after a little time," as he wrote to his wife: after all "their effects on the children are so immense." Even if the masses are ignorant, the future effect of schools "in civilising the next generation of the lower class. . . . may be so important. What a fine, triumphant sight in Manchester to see people who cared about reading!" So far he had seen only a few model schools. "We shall certainly have a good deal of moving about," he tells Fanny Lucy, "but we both like that well enough."

And then four days after beginning work he anticipates withdrawing from it: "we can always look forward to retiring to Italy on £200 a year."[95]

PART TWO

I remember, only the other day, a good man looking with me [at children in] London,—children eaten up with disease, half-sized, half-fed, half-clothed, neglected by their parents, without health, without home, without hope.

—*Culture and Anarchy*

Surely you have some better programme than this your present one,—*the beatification of a whole people through clap-trap.*

—*Friendship's Garland*

Goethe's profound, imperturbable naturalism is absolutely fatal to all routine thinking; he puts the standard, once for all, inside every man instead of outside him; when he is told, such a thing must be so, there is immense authority and custom in favour of its being so, it has been held so for a thousand years, he answers with Olympian politeness, "But *is* it so? Is it so to *me*?"

—*Essays in Criticism*

11

LORD RUSSELL'S "BASHAWS"
1851 AND 1839–1852

Strive not about little things, lest you lose the sight of the mark of your high calling.
—*Thomas Wilson, Bishop of Sodor and Man*

Steam and iron are making all the Planet into one Village.
—*Carlyle*

"OF all the Inspectors," wrote Arnold's contemporary John Snell, "I do not know one who has attained his appointment because of his experience, his love of the work, or his peculiar fitness for it." In principle John Snell does not exaggerate in his appraisal of Victorian School Inspectors. At twenty-eight, Arnold had put on "laced boots of a very stout make" with tweedy clothes and become and H.M.I. or "one of Her Majesty's Inspectors of Schools." He was a tall, handsome, and intelligent poet—but would his striking presence and creative sensibility help him in classrooms full of terrified, undersized children? Matthew was bored by routine details. Would his knowledge of Laleham School, Winchester, or Rugby, do him any good? Those schools were astronomically far removed in quality from any of the desperate classrooms he would have to inspect. He was appalled by dingy squalor; he knew nothing about teaching illiterate working-class children. Would even his acquaintance with teachers such as Dr. Arnold, Tait, or Temple help? He was to see pupil-teachers, fifteen years old, trying to keep order in classrooms packed with child factory workers.

He hated education bureaucrats and committee work; he never had written reports on drainage, ventilation, floors, heating, or school equipment; he knew only vaguely of the enormous struggles of the Committee of Council to get desperately needed money from Parliament. At first he wrote and quite probably thought as little as possible about banal duties ahead. He had to look fixedly at "elementary

247

schools" in nearly a third of a kingdom and fill up "six sheets and a half" of paper for every school he saw.[1]

After a few days with Inspector Morell, he did however rediscover *one* love of his life: that is, as when he was about to leave for Toulx or Bernese Oberland, he bought maps. He filled his pockets with them and must have pored over them when sitting alone, on the edge of his bed, in a lodging house. As a child he had spent mornings with "dissected maps" and as a poet he had brought beautiful, topographical features into his imagery to render complex moods and blends of feeling and idea. This was one of his lasting passions. In his essay "Ordnance Maps," he declares himself a "lover of maps" who sees in the map a complex "picture" with "nomenclature."[2] The map mediates between verbal and graphic symbols, bridging between a linear enchainment of words and the multiform world of natural beauty. As a student of maps with a sense of the gap between words and nature, he was pleased by one aspect of his new job. (He was soon to write in "Scholar-Gipsy" a topographical poem with an interesting map myth.)

Travel caused him to study the map of England; and the nation mapped at his knees had changed in a decade. Quite suddenly, the colossus was threaded with configurations of black lines connecting the manufacturing quadrangle with the midlands hub—and that quadrangle and hub were "the workshop of the world." Lines snaked between Preston, Liverpool, Leeds, and Sheffield—and south to the massive hub of Birmingham and Wolverhampton. They arched into maritime and farming counties, spiraled in the richly endowed iron and coal-mining regions of the north and west, and plunged headlong from ten directions into the vast vortex of London—which besides ten railway termini had seven elegant passenger station buildings in 1851.

Who were the Lilliputians who put threads over this map? "Railway barons" in a decade had quadrupled the network of operative track. Rail companies in a laissez faire age even greedily built parallel sets of track; there were soon to be 476 separate, competing rail companies in the British Isles. Speeds of locomotives had risen from twenty up to fifty, sixty, and sixty-seven miles an hour and hence, despite nine derailments in one week in August, travel was magically rapid and almost safe. A traveler getting from London to Birmingham entered the splendid, high Doric portico of Euston Station amid columns five-and-a-half feet thick and seventy feet tall; at elaborate booking offices he bought a ticket and at ornate, vast stalls, a newspaper or a book of poems (Arnold's *Empedocles on Etna* itself came to railway bookstalls). Again in a new age of pictorial journalism, he might buy the *Illustrated London News* or *Pictorial Gazette*—which as ancestors of film and television were already reducing the serious readership for books—or, if he were still literate, a copy of the London *Times,* which contained 210,000 words and came wonderfully from an Applegarth steampower press at 2,000 copies an hour. With an antimacassar at his head, he settled back at Euston in a pandemonium of hissing steam and clanging bells. He heard high-pitched cries of porters, the shout of engineers, the crash of metal on metal. Two or three brass-ribbed monsters in tandem exploded in quickening, even rhythms, thundered and hooted now in the open air near Gothic signal towers and castellated engine houses, filled the sky with soot and fire and screamed demonically at crossways, churned and gained speed in the blurred flatlands. A swirl of rain brought soot against his window, but the battering steady rhythms continued. (He hardly had a chance to finish *The Times!*) Three hours and a hundred miles later, he alighted in a city which had quadrupled in size in fifty years and boasted the largest steam-engine factory on earth. Producing electroplated goods, firearms and iron sheeting, tools and steel pens in red brick palaces that used 377 tons of coal in a day, Birmingham was a marvel of the world.

"Next to Liverpool," Matthew Arnold told his pregnant wife in December, "[Birmingham is] the finest of the manufacturing towns: the situation high and good, the principal street capital, the shops good, cabs splendid, and the Music Hall unequalled by any Greek building in England that I have seen."[3] Most of his fine adjectives applied to his mood. Freed from introspective self-conscious work on poetry, he was moving about more rapidly than any other British literary man before him, and thanks to the rails, he was one of the first to compare many English and Welsh towns within a single week. He was too excited to know he was tired. He had become a fairly ecstatic sightseer after leaving Her Majesty's Inspector John Morell. Having seen a school at Oundle, Arnold had swung up in a northeast trajectory to market towns of Bridlington and Filey on the North Sea, plunged to cotton mills of Milford and Belper, and gone on to the porcelain and hosiery center at Derby and finally west to Birmingham. From central Birmingham he took a train to the industrial warren of West Bromwich, where he saw three schools, and went on to Audley and the Staffordshire potteries.

At Fox How with his young wife at Christmas, he was in good spirits but exhausted. Despite her pregnancy, his wife wanted to join him on his rounds in the new year. Still in debt—though he had repaid some of the £400 he had borrowed to marry—he perhaps wondered how he could pay hotel bills. Spending more than he earned, he was to earn slightly less each year in the next few, trying years.

He complained a little of frustrations. On some days, he had begun so early he missed breakfast and often missed luncheon too. He had tried to see schools that didn't exist; schools that had closed for lack of funds, others that lacked chairs, textbooks, teachers. The Council Office kept him badly informed. *"List of Schools,"* Arnold appealed to his employers. "Sir," he now urged the education clerks in London, "I should be much obliged if you would give direction for my being supplied with a [complete] list of schools. . . ."[4]

Already out on the road, "M. Arnold" it seems lacked a complete list! The first clerk scrawled on the back of his letter:

Inspector
_____

29 December 1851
_____

M. Arnold Esq
Applied for a list of
Schools in his district
liable to inspection.

Exhausted by this effort, the first clerk passed his request to another who noted:

l[etter] Ack. The list which
you desire will be prepared
& forwarded to you as soon as
possible—J.M. Jackson
to prepare list.
          30/12/51

The third clerk woke up and signed in bright red ink:

done
J.J.

The first clerk observed that Arnold's request was the 8,374th piece of inspectorial business of the year.[5]

The education office was harassed. It was a tedious bureaucratic outpost in a hopeless war. The previous Secretary had noted three years earlier of its employees, who sometimes worked till they dropped: "Mr. Armytage is the victim of chronic congestion of the brain and practical paralysis. . . . Mr. Harrison had a very sudden attack of congestion of the brain threatening paralysis. . . . Mr. Lingen has recently left the office in a state of great nervous exhaustion."[6] A month later, the valiant Secretary fell to the Council Office floor, "and remained unconscious for a quarter of an hour." A slight, hollow-eyed man with a bald dome, he was carried to his home and put to bed—but inasmuch as the next day, a Sunday, was an ordinary working day for him, he dictated a note with normal unction:

> Mr. Kay-Shuttleworth presents his compliments . . . and not being al-
> lowed to write, begs that Sir Robert [Peel] will excuse his employing
> another pen to say that he was prevented from completing a letter . . .
> yesterday by very sudden indisposition.[7]

Kay-Shuttleworth had by then worked thirteen years in the struggle over elementary education; he was retired in bad, shattered health and replaced when Arnold's old tutor, Lingen, recovered from "great nervous exhaustion."

The health of men at the Council Office had a long history. Briefly what was the background of the elementary education struggle and what were Her Majesty's men appointed to do? Education is the Cinderella of English politics and now and then, it seems, attempts are made to humiliate, embarrass, or starve her. In Victorian England the only schools ever directly aided by the state were "elementary schools" offering mainly rudimentary training for children of the lower middle class and working class up to the age of thirteen or fourteen. (Arnold seldom "inspected" an older pupil, though he quizzed older "pupil teachers.") Seven or eight hundred endowed grammar schools and a handful of public schools existed for the elite, but apart from these, which were in touch with universities, the scene was chaos. Arnold wrote that the poor were not educated at all and the English middle class was "nearly the worst educated in the world."[8] England, as Horace Mann noted with fine Yankee disgust,

> is the only one among the nations of Europe, conspicuous for its
> civilization and resource, which has not, and never has had, any system
> of education for its people.[9]

Why was there no "system"? With traditions of self-help even reformers in mid-Victorian England feared that too much schooling would coddle the working class or drive it to revolt. Factory owners wanted the state *out* of education entirely, and Anglican and Dissenting churches, while running schools, feared the godless House of Commons and feared each other more.

When in 1833 the state offered a grant of £20,000 to be administered by two religious societies for building new schools, surveys were made. Only one in seventeen persons in towns seemed to be undergoing education; a few towns of 25,000 lacked a school. Apparently thirty-four percent of children then at York, fifty-one percent in Birmingham, and sixty-four percent at Westminster never saw a class in their lives.[10] Children working at power looms in 90 degree heat hardly had time for class—though the Factory Act of 1833 limited thirteen-year-olds to sixty-nine hours of work a week. Girls of ten, fourteen, and sixteen, working stripped to the waist beside half-naked men in underground mines, did not think of textbooks and blackboards; nor did child workers of four, five, and six who were stunted, crippled, suffering from "black spit," spine and lung diseases. Children who went to school (often for twelve months in their lives) might find themselves in unsalubrious charity day schools exhibiting "every vice,"[11] from drunken teachers who could pull the ear off a boy, fracture a skull, or cripple a child with the swing of a stick, to cellar-holes lacking a single window.

Because of the shortage of teachers a northern doctor who had written on Manchester cotton workers, one James Phillips Kay (later Kay-Shuttleworth), obtained in 1838 a grant of £500 to train "pupil teachers" in a Norwood workhouse-school. Kay's "Norwood experiment" became the first state-sponsored elementary school and Kay was to advocate a national system and direct Her Majesty's Inspectorate. Arnold disliked James Kay partly because he lacked "high cultivation" and "was not a good writer." (Kay's loquacity was to be tempered by Lord Lansdowne's severe, classical hand when the Education Secretary sent out 174 questions to inspectors.) As Education Secretary, Kay "did not attract by person and manner," as Arnold (who made his acquaintance in 1846) later recalled. "His temper was not smooth or genial, and he left on many persons the impression of a man managing and designing." Kay avoided simple or monocausal explanations of evils and was not doctrinaire, and yet he built in the elementary schools a system for controlling the poor. But Arnold paid a tribute to him that no social historian has challenged: his "faith in popular education" was "heroic."[12]

"The pauper children assembled," Kay wrote of his Norwood experiment, "from the garrets, cellars, and wretched rooms of alleys and courts in the dense part of London are often sent [here] . . . covered only with rags and vermin; often the victims of chronic disease; almost universally stunted in their growth and sometimes emaciated with want. . . . This is the seed from which the elementary school grew." The 1,100 ragged children at Norwood had been beaten for petty thieving, and made to sort out bristles and henna for "education." Kay forbade the beatings and made his staff show concern for stunted, ragged pupils. Thieving stopped at Norwood. "The children now at least display in their features evidence of happiness," he wrote of Norwood; "they have confidence in the kindness of all."[13] Elegant visitors to the school noted that waifs in rags greeted them with civil respect.

Impressed by Norwood, Lord Lansdowne appointed James Kay Secretary to the Committee of Council on Education, in 1839. The bill proposing the committee had passed in the House of Commons by two votes. It was crushed in the House of Lords, but the Lords were admonished by Queen Victoria and the bill became law—perhaps partly because it raised the annual education grant to only £30,000, less than the amount voted that year for the Royal stables.

Controlling the purse strings for education, Parliament thus set up the first education office, under the protection of the prestigious Privy Council. (Since any Order in Council was irrevocable by the Queen's prerogative, the education office was not likely to be abolished but it could be starved.) Lacking funds and opposed by *The Times* and more than half the nation's Church leaders, and hardly supported by public opinion, the Secretary set to work. He opened a normal school at Battersea and lived and lectured there while running the Council Office. He developed the "pupil-teacher" system whereby candidates learned by teaching and apprenticing themselves to qualified school masters. He followed the fortunes of his graduates when they took low-paying jobs, defended them when they were in trouble. Also he minutely guided his elite shock troops, the first inspectors.

Inspectors were required to find out how exchequer grants were being used, and "to visit schools to be henceforth aided by public money . . . to collect facts and information, and to report the result." [14] Construing "facts and information" as broadly as Arnold would do, Kay encouraged inspectors to report on *all* social conditions operative on schools and not to mince words. The best of his men, Seymour Tremenheere, wrote descriptions of child workers, and in a report on Greenwich schools run by a church-affiliated society, stirred up clerical wrath.

There was an angry explosion. Obliged to dismiss Tremenheere for seeing too much and writing too clearly, Kay fell to his knees before strong enemies. Edward Baines, editor of the *Leeds Mercury,* and the Congregationalist Edward Miall formed the Voluntaryist party—a pressure group drawing Nonconformist schools from the state's orbit by causing them to refuse grants and inspection. [15] When church-affiliated groups gained the right to approve the choice of H.M.I.s, the inspectorate developed on denominational lines, to Kay's anguish. There had to be one set of inspectors for schools run by an Anglican-affiliated "National Society"; another for those run by the Dissenter-affiliated "British and Foreign School Society"—which approved Arnold's right to be an H.M.I.—and yet another for Catholic schools. Concordats with church groups led to delays, waste, rivalries, handicapping the state's role for twenty-five years. Arnold found that religious schism and the pride of middle-class Dissenters and their animosity to the state all meant the poor would suffer.

Yet if a church group approved an H.M.I., that man followed government orders. Kay kept his inspectors too busy to forget they were responsible first to the state. By 1848, he had made inroads in public opinion—had won *The Times,* for example, to his side—and had selected eight clerical inspectors for Anglican schools, two lay inspectors for Wesleyan and other Dissenter-run schools, and a Catholic inspector—and the office by then had set a pattern for inspecting as well as an inchoate model for Arnold's social criticism. Kay's H.M.I.s had picked up their pens. Ignorant of the working class but horrified by what they saw and used to Senior Common Room talk, they wrote poetically about suffering. In reports they used classical or Miltonic allusions. The Rev. Mr. Brookfield, of Kay's southeastern district, cajoled Carlyle to help him look at classrooms and used witty conceits with double entendres that mystified and irritated Members of Parliament who read his "annuals." Joseph Fletcher, for Wesleyan and British schools, whose death was caused partly by overwork and whom Arnold was to replace, turned a report into a survey of education since the Reformation, with statistical tables, maps, and a fine patch in which he blamed capitalists for not aiding the proletariat—"even if only to relieve their own pockets when the poor came on the rates."[16] (M.P.s felt that Fletcher's annuals were almost too costly to print.) The best inspector after Tremenheere's dismissal was perhaps the Rev. H. Moseley (1801–1872) of the midlands district, who had held an Oxford chair of philosophy at thirty. With rare humility, he saw that he and his colleagues could never penetrate "the inner life of the classes below us in society," for the "springs of public opinion, the elements of thought and principles of action" that animate the workers are *not known.*[17] Because neither Kay nor his other staff attained to this humility, Arnold took a lofty view of the lower orders and never fully credited the distinctive values of working-class culture. In Kay's ignorance, one sees reflected the only weakness in certain brilliant arguments in *Culture and Anarchy.*

Filled with sympathy for the happiness of the poor, the Secretary did encourage his men to report boldly after Tremenheere was dismissed —and they still followed Kay's lead. The Rev. Mr. Allen reported that 48 of 116 midlands schools were "good," that landowners in a "voluntary" age were indifferent to education, and that clergymen in his district begged like mendicant friars for schools—one desperate clergyman, with an income of £135, gave £20 a year to support the impoverished school where he taught.[18] F.C. Cook reported from the east that parents who refused to let their boys scare off crows for farmers, seven days a week, could be dismissed from *their* jobs and starve. Terrified parents kept boys in the fields.[19] All inspectors found *some* church schools well-taught and well-equipped, but too often they found misery in classrooms dependent on charity:

> It was a room on the ground floor, up a dark and narrow entry, and about 12 ft. square [in Lancashire]. Here 43 boys and girls were assembled, of all ages from 5 to 14. Patches of paper were pasted over the broken panes of one small window, before which also sat the master intercepting the few rays of light which would otherwise have crept into the gloom. . . . [He had] laid aside his coat. In this undress he was the better able to wield three canes, two of which, like the weapons of an old soldier, hung conspicuously on the wall, while the third was on the table ready for service. When questioned as to the necessity of this triple instrumentality, he assured us that the children were "abrupt and rash."[20]

Meanwhile, thousands of children avoided broken heads. Reverend Watkins noted on a Liverpool street that 175 children went to school but 375 did not. In a detention house he found that a third of the little children had never heard of Christ, half were ignorant of the Queen's name, two-thirds couldn't read. Schools in Yorkshire were close to extinction for lack of funds—and the state's contribution would never save many. All inspectors noted the shortage of staff—and deep hostility to schooling. "Even now," the Rev. Mr. Watkins wrote six years after Arnold began inspecting, "it is no uncommon thing to hear it said that the modern elementary education tends to unfit the young for their work in life, to make them discontented . . . jealous . . . envious of those who were above them."[21] The Rev. Mr. Kennedy reported that the Factory Acts were unobserved, that education had no chance in his district against social class prejudice and vested interest. When a teacher encouraged drawing and pinned up pupils' pictures in one class, irate school managers burst in, abused the teacher for allowing workers' boys to indulge in drawing, and tore all the pictures down.

Replying to despondent reports, Kay fed the H.M.I.s with ideas. He held that "mechanical" training in the "3 Rs" could never amount to education whatever school managers said, for "wider views must be taken of what it is requisite to teach," and good teaching appeals to the whole child, to the "mind" and "heart."[22] He made his H.M.I.s into emissaries, propagandists. He set up inspectors' conferences at which his men criticized the Council Office and he encouraged initiative. His staff proposed new systems of ventilation and new kinds of industrial schools, drew distinctions between what was fitting to teach and what was not, even compared educational methods in France and Germany. By the time Kay retired, the inspectors were amateur sociologists, even if they failed to find "springs" and "principles" motivating the lower orders.

No less devoted to hard work, his successor Ralph Lingen was a circumspect bureaucrat with a brain like an adding machine. A dazzling career at Trinity College Oxford, a fellowship at Balliol, and three years of success with the law at Lincoln's Inn never taught Lingen tact; he alienated most of the H.M.I.s in 1849 and 1850. Yet he rightly sensed Parliament was restive over costs: his predecessor had cajoled money—but inspectors had wasted it with philosophical disquisitions. (One of Fletcher's reports had run to a volume of 211 pages, with five maps, and cost £100 to print.) Lingen foresaw that the H.M.I.s would have to be restrained if the hard-pressed office were to survive.

Thus, hired in 1851 in Lingen's tenure and appointed to inspect "Wesleyan" and other Dissenter-run "British schools," Arnold began when efficiency and economy were the office's watchwords—and if he waited to get a list of schools, he found himself drowned in forms and regulations. Lingen sorely advised him that if he capered on river banks or leapt over railings in any sense *now,* he would lose his job. Lingen had known him well at Balliol. At any rate, Arnold's annual reports of the fifties catch the gray, unadventurous temper of the office. Knowing little about schools, he wrote of what he saw and drew modest inferences.

A sporadic diarist, he had to submit a "weekly diary"; and, as a man impatient with factual details, he had to compose reports on a visited school under a battery of headings:

1. *Mechanical arrangements*
   Buildings, size and ventilation of class-rooms and number of children in each.
   Arrangement of Desks—whether on Mr. Bell's or on the Lancastrian plan.
2. *Means of Instruction*
   Details of Books and apparatus.
3. *Organization and Discipline*
   Classes—Whether each child is under one teacher all the time.
   Number of Monitors (and/or) pupil teachers
   Rewards and punishments. . . .
4. *Methods of Instruction*
5. *Attainments*
   In Reading, Writing, Arithmetic . . . etc.[23]

Implicitly optimistic since charity day schools sometimes lacked books and floors, this outline—a brief version of the one proposed in 1839 for Church of England schools—gave him one model for report writing. He escaped the dreariest hellholes. The Dissenter-run schools he saw in country towns were often good or "moderately good." In a memo of 1852 made at Loughborough Wesleyan School, Arnold reports for example on a fairly pleasant establishment and seven "Attainments" of the pupils:

NOV. 19

3 divisions [or class levels]

		R[eading]	Wr[iting]	Ar[ithmetic]	Gr[ammar]	Geo[graphy]	Hist[ory]		Dict[ion]
i	13	m	g	S			2	t	mod
div.	boys	o	o	e				h	one
		d	o	e	m	m	o	e	or
ii	16	m	d				r		two
div.	boys	o		r	o	o	3	r	excel-
		d	g	e				e	lent
iii	17	F	o	p	d	d	g	s	
div.	boys	a	o	o			o	t	
		i	d	r			o		
		r		t			d	b	

furniture dirty. books d[itto] & ragged but abundant   a
                              spelling bad   d
                    boys' school dirty.[24]

On the other hand Arnold was to see pupil-teachers pale with overwork, who taught until they became ill. He was to note in his reports "bad class," "bad classrooms," "bad approaches and ventilation," "great . . . numbers in teaching sections" and "[school] very short of teaching force." He was to see many children who never came to school—and who had drawn the attention of James Kay—"a multitude" of starving, half-naked urchins "without hope."[25] He was admired by teachers for sympathizing with their plight; he abominated the fact that illness or poor school conditions could affect a teacher's salary and prospects and, at the risk of his job, he apparently bent rules. "Morton has been at work," Arnold writes in a private diary, "for his sake gave 1 P.T. [that is, allowed him one pupil-teacher as an assistant] but this is the last whole [writing illegible] . . . with the bad. . . ."[26] "Morton" seems to have been an ailing teacher who, according to the rules, did not merit help Arnold accorded him. Or again in the London slums over the years Arnold praised a Rosella Pitman, whom an H.M.I. had found "wanting in animation." Arnold observed this woman at Bethnal Green's Abbey Street, amid ragged pupils and teaching on a grimy asphalt floor in the cold. "In this excellent school," he wrote with some truth,

> the diffusion of the instruction continues to merit no less praise than its solidity.

The school had got a new floor—and he further informed his superiors:

> March 15/66 Miss Pitman's school continues to merit the highest praise. Matthew Arnold.

> March 13/67 Miss Pitman's school is in the highest possible state of effectiveness. Matthew Arnold.

> March 9/71 This school ranks with the one or two very best girls' schools I have ever known, and I take leave of it with great regret.[27]

One looks at H.M.I. Fletcher's statement that Miss Pitman was an *unanimated* teacher. Perhaps she became livelier as she aged over the bitter years. By focusing on the merits of the *school,* rather than on the teacher, Arnold gives the impression he desires at Council Office and poor Miss Pitman is helped.

In Lingen's regime at Council Office the emphasis in inspecting shifted away from ambassadorial work to the strict, factual reporting of conditions and standards. Arnold misjudged the temper of the Council Office, of its Secretary, and of a cost-conscious deadlocked Parliament throughout the 1850s. He began as a naïve H.M.I. and became, in time, a mediocre one, if one considers his work quite apart from his foreign reports. He couched reasonable arguments in the emotive style. "No one feels," he wrote in his Report of 1854,

> more than I do how laborious is [the schoolteachers'] work, how trying at times to the health and spirits, how full of difficulty even for the best: how much fuller for those, whom I too often see attempting the work of a schoolmaster—men of weak health and purely studious habits, who betake themselves to this profession, as affording the means to continue their favourite pursuits: not knowing, alas, that for all but men of the most singular and exceptional vigour and energy, there are no pursuits more irreconcilable than those of the student and of the schoolmaster.[28]

That was James Kay's style; it cut little ice with Lingen (who perhaps wished Arnold would save the elegiac note for Scholar-Gipsies, and who definitely *did* try to cut off his salary before a foreign tour—an action which almost prevented the Inspector from going abroad). Clever inspectors, under Lingen, had less and less scope. Arnold was known to be too ebullient, too careless, too frank and sympathetic in classrooms. Later he had a reputation for being distractable. But he was a good emissary from the republic of letters. First he would write for a school appointment (one trustee replied that no "emissary of Lord John Russell" or "any other Turkish Bashaw" would get inside *his* school).[29]

Most teachers were as glad to see him perhaps as Reverend Dymond was at Edmonton one day. Surprised by his "loud voice" and a "moppy abundance" of hair parted in the middle, Dymond noted: "a good half hour behind the appointed time he burst into the school." Arnold apologized for his want of punctuality "by some joking reference." He gave an amusing lecture to Dymond, five minutes long, "on the functions of a 'foot-scraper,'" while pupils sat on their hands. Coaxed into a classroom, the inspector with a booming voice promptly "frightened a little girl into a crying fit."[30]

Arnold called the little girl to his knee: "His patience with the children," says Dymond, "was wonderful." Either then or at another time, he put his face next to a girl with a bandaged head and ascertained she had an earache: "Ah," boomed Arnold, "I know what that is! I used to have bad ears when I was a little boy. I know how they hurt me. Go home and take that to your mother"—slipping the girl a shilling—"and tell her to tie your head up in hot flannel, and don't come back to school until you are quite better."[31]

Quite evidently his questions for toddlers were delightfully simple, if he reserved hard meaningless queries for older boys. "Well, my little man," Arnold might begin, "and how do you spell dog?" "Please sir, d-o-g." "Capital, very good indeed. I couldn't do it better myself. And now let us go a little further, and see if we can spell cat." (Chorus excitedly,) "C-A-T." "Now, this is really excellent."[32]

Dymond however noticed that when he left the Edmonton four- and five-year-olds, he was "riled" by an older smart aleck—until that boy volunteered that Shakespeare's knowledge was not so much "learnt" as "picked up." "Now," Arnold stated, "I must give you credit for that."[33] (Literary answers charmed him: when in a recital a boy, keeping to an iambic beat, came down heavily on an unpronounced syllable in Byron, Arnold declared he had a good ear.) Walking to the railway station with him later, Dymond expanded upon the scenic beauties and said that Charles Lamb lay dead and buried near Edmonton's church. "A fine smile" rippled over Matthew Arnold's face as he replied: "Poor Lamb!"[34]

Understandably he hurried to get *out* of a school. Sneyd-Kynnersley, who envied him, heard from a "school manager" that H.M.I. Arnold "shakes hands with the managers and teachers; and talks very pleasantly for a few minutes; then he walks through the classes between the desks, looking over the children's shoulders at some exercises, and so makes his way to the door, and we see him no more." Probably there is even more malice in Sneyd-Kynnersley's remark that a colleague, glancing at the poet's marks for a girls' school, "noticed that every girl had got the highest mark possible, and he commented on this monotony of excellence. Arnold merely purred—'They are such charming girls.' "[35] Malicious or not, Sneyd-Kynnersley seems right about the poet's blandness and haste and occasional neglect of detail.

Between 1851 and 1862, Arnold never examined every child in a class, for he was supposed to pick a random number to quiz on subjects of instruction. His work was "as nothing" compared with later years, when the "Revised Code" made him account for each pupil. Periodically, his district would be reduced in size; and he was to be given an assistant. Yet he slaved for committees while hating committees and marked scripts often with bloodshot eyes. Having sampled pupil attainments in seven subjects, given good conduct certificates and taken leave of a school, he would write up a report; he would digest and assess the school reports later in one of his annual reports (of which he wrote nineteen in all); meanwhile he corresponded with qualified masters about apprenticed pupil-teachers, inspected these individually, and read their examinations. Since the pupil-teacher system lay at the heart of his fieldwork, how did that system work? Often modified over the years, its essentials were these: At a school approved by an H.M.I. a boy (or girl) of thirteen might become a pupil-teacher for five years, indenturing himself to a head teacher and earning the small sum of £10 to £20 per year while he taught, and then compete for a Queen's Scholarship and matriculation at a normal school. (If the child survived the normal school, he might become a certified teacher.) Reportedly "pale and thin," the pupil-teachers taught all day, took 1½ hours of instruction from the master after school, prepared classes, and often worked for their parents at night. Reverend Watkins reported that five "P.T.s" in his district died in a year.[36] But across the nation 3,580 pupil-teachers worked in 1849 and over 15,000 in 1859—and so the system (in an era of expendable children) was perhaps a success. If a head teacher pleased Her Majesty's Inspector, he earned one pupil-teacher for every twenty-five pupils he had. Thus teachers liked the "system."

But the system almost broke Arnold. He had to talk to every pupil-teacher in his district once a year, hear them recite in the winter and spring, and mark large numbers of their scripts in January—and inspect the normal schools at other times. Pupil-teachers hoping to obtain certificates for normal schools, as the official rules read, "will be examined by the Inspector:—

1. In the composition of an essay on some subject connected with the art of teaching.

2. In the rudiments of algebra, or the practice of land surveying or levelling.
3. In syntax, etymology and prosody.
4. In the use of the globe or in the geography of the British Empire. . . .
5. More completely in the Holy Scriptures, Liturgy and Catechism. . . .
6. In their ability . . . to conduct the instruction . . . in any subject selected by the Inspector.

"In the examination the Inspectors will observe the degree of attention paid by the Pupil Teachers to a perfect articulation in reading, and the right modulation of the voice in teaching a class. A knowledge of vocal music and of drawing (especially from models) though not absolutely required, because the exact means of teaching it may not exist in every school, will be much encouraged."[37] Girls offered needlework to show their expertise at examinations. Arnold refused to have anything to do with "vocal music" *or* needlework. He knew not a great deal about "the art of teaching" and less about algebra; but for pupil-teachers and other students he prepared such handy "rudiments" as these:

Multiply $x^2 - 2ax \div 3a^2$	Voltaire b. 1694 d. 1778. 84.
by $x^2 - 2ax + a^2$	Rousseau b. 1712 d. 1778. 66.
Ans. $x^4 - 4a^3x + 3a^4$	

$864239 \div 7$	325681	5 cwt. 2 qrs. 8 lbs.
Ans. $123462 + 5$	$- 248723$	at £3 . . 4 . . 6
	Ans. 76958	Ans. £17 . . 17 . . 6

How many pounds in 143 iron plates, each weighing 5 tons. Ans. 1601600 lbs.

With income tax at 7^d in the £. I am left with £254 after paying tax—what was my gross income? [problem noted in year 1866][38]

He was happier with "syntax, etymology and prosody," "the use of the globe or geography," and "Holy Scriptures."

"Up to my ears in Grammar papers worked by the schoolmasters & students at their Xmas examinations," he writes appropriately to his old tutor Mr. Hill.[39] "I am holding an examination of pupil teacher apprentices," he tells Wyndham Slade, "surrounded by an innumerable company of youths and maidens." Sometimes everything came at once: "When I have finished these papers," he tells his sister Jane, "I have a General Report and a Training School Report to get out of hand, the inspection of schools going on alongside this all the while."[40] Just before one lecture, *On Translating Homer,* he had 587 sets of papers to correct; he did the 445th a week before the lecture. He turned from one thing to the next like an automaton; some days he was magnificently Herculean, as when he examined orally 307 pupil-teachers in a single day. One year 25,000 children came under his inspection; 13,000 were specially examined for grants. Usually he inspected 18,000 or 19,000 children a year and seldom fewer than 500 a week (except during a six-week holiday and another four weeks which H.M.I.s mercifully had for paperwork). He examined 173 "elementary schools" and 117 "institutions," 368 pupil-teachers and 97 certified teachers, as well as 20,000 pupils in a typical year (1855) in the early phase of his inspectorate.

Thinking of a Goethean epigram, he tells his diary again and again: "*Heute, heute!* and "*Nur heute!*" Arnold was the spiritual fox of Goethe's brief "Sprichwortlich" or "Proverbial":

> *Nur heute, heute nur lass dich nicht fangen,*
> *So bist du hundertmal entgangen.*[41]
> (Just today, just today, don't let yourself get caught,
> Thus you've escaped a hundred times.)

Only let me *not* be caught by fatigue! Only let me escape despair! Only let me out-distance the demon of discouragement ... "just today!" As an H.M.I., he salved his guilty social conscience ten thousand times over, and from time to time scratched out realistic notes: "I am too utterly tired out to write." "I am worked to death."[42]

Agreeing with Goethe that life is a hell one must get through as best one can, he read every year for the remainder of his life an unusually beautiful lyric by Goethe.

> AUF DEM SEE
>
> *Und frische Nahrung, neues Blut*
> *Saug ich aus freier Welt;*
> *Wie ist Natur so hold und gut*
> *Die mich am Busen halt!*
> *Die Welle wieget unsern Kahn*
> *Im Rudertakt hinauf,*
> *Und Berge, wolkig himmelan*
> *Begegnen unserm Lauf.*
>
> *Aug, mein Aug, was sinkst du nieder?*
> *Goldne Träume, kommt ihr wieder?*
> *Weg, du Traum! so gold du bist;*
> *Hier auch Lieb und Leben ist. . . .*[43]

(ON THE LAKE

And from these open spaces I suck fresh nourishment and new blood; how sweet and kindly is Nature who holds me to her breast! Our boat rocks up and down on the water in time with the oars, and mountains rise cloudily skywards in our path.

Eyes, oh my eyes why are you drooping? Are you
returning, your golden dreams? Begone, dream, golden as
you are! There is love and life here too.)

Arnold became the elegiac figure of his own poetry: for in years
ahead he lost the ability to write verse—and for the sake of his success
as a free-spirited artist he had lived. Thus occasionally he clearly
"drooped" and saw himself in Goethe's line, *"Aug, mein Aug, was
sinkst du nieder?"* On the other hand, he gained much from the
"freier Welt" or the open spaces of life as a traveling inspector, and
even from what was almost a dance of death in the elementary school.
He gained authority as a social critic, since he came to know the
English middle class experimentally and dined with Dissenting school
managers and saw homes and shops of the middle class, day in and
out. He gained perspective on media of his day, newspapers and
sermons and tracts and political pamphlets and speeches, since he
saw the gap between real conditions in the country and the perennial
"claptrap" of her spokesmen. He saw bitter suffering, and was drawn
to his father's sense of the need to reform a smug, unequal society. His
aestheticism never diminished, but it became enriched and complicated by a sense of reality aesthetes seldom have. His formula, "Poetry
is . . . a criticism of life,"[44] is one bridge Arnold built between his
aesthetic sense and social experience (a bridge that involved him in
aesthetic-didactic difficulties).

His poetry describes the meaning of an age of unbelief to a modern
man; and as a continuation of his poetry, his prose as a whole searches
for a world view adequate for man and remains important a century
after his death. The prose has its authority because he became a
"Turkish Bashaw" of the Council Office. Even the office's need for
facts helped him: he learned to keep his eye on the object and began to
write more objectively before he made foreign tours for Her Majesty.
Certainly the years ahead tested his moral courage, which was the
greatest attribute Dr. Arnold's eldest son happened to have.

Looking in his diary—in January 1852—at names on his itinerary
such as *New Jerusalem Day School* and *Graham Street Protestant
Dissenters,* he perhaps thought of the fractured modern age and of his
almost fractured poetic career. "Au reste," he tells Clough, "a great
career is hardly possible any longer—can hardly now be purchased
even by the sacrifice of repose, dignity and inward clearness—so I call
no man unfortunate. I am more and more convinced that the world
tends to become more comfortable for the mass, and more uncomfortable for those of any natural gift or distinction—and," he comments
with fairness, "it is as well perhaps that it should be so—for hitherto
the gifted have astonished and delighted the world, but not trained or

inspired or in any real way changed it." In January he is "sometimes in bad spirits" "but generally in better than I used to be. . . . Goodnight and keep alive, my dear Clough."[45]

He inspected Jerusalem Day and Graham Street Protestant cheerily —saved from "purgatory" when his wife traveled with him—but when she went to her parents to await childbirth, he was isolated. The worst of inspecting was that it divided one from friends, wife, books. "We had a flying visit from Matt," reports Palgrave a little later from Kneller Hall, a training school where Temple was the head. "He finds one great nuisance in his Inspecting work, in that it cuts him off from congenial spirits."[46]

Though lonely, Arnold wrote verse. So far his best periods coincided with times when a sense of security mingled with an aching sense of loss. His security at Oxford and grief over his father had helped him to produce "Mycerinus," and early sonnets. Surrounded by friends in London but affected by Tom's and Willy's emigrating he had written "Fragment of an 'Antigone'" and "Forsaken Merman." Strains in a romance had helped him to write "New Sirens," *Switzerland,* and "A Modern Sappho"; his fear ("not based in reason") of losing Jane Arnold contributed to the inward intensity of *Empedocles on Etna* —and his severance from his friends in no way handicapped meditations during his own engagement and honeymoon such as "Buried Life" and "Stanzas from the Grande Chartreuse," in both of which he is deliberately in lonely retreat. He missed "congenial spirits" now such as Brodie, Blackett, and Slade of bachelor days of Berkeley Square and Mount Street as well as the essential Todo Walrond and Clough, with whom he discussed "congenial books." As "One of Her Majesty's Inspectors" he thus began his last, brief period of splendid work on poetry—and began it unpromisingly.

Fermenting with aesthetic theories, he jotted in a copy of Goethe and Schiller's letters a plan for a collection Fellowes might print in 1852:

> Empedocles.
> Tristram & Iseult.
> La Châtelaine architecte
> The Death of Sohrab
> Hylas
> ? the wandering Mesmerist
> Obermann Stanzas.
> world religion stanzas
> short poems.[47]

It is reasonable to suppose that, by January, he had "Empedocles" and "Tristram" and "Obermann" in polished form. He may have been too nervous with approaching fatherhood to write such long-meditated poems as "La Châtelaine architecte" and "Death of Sohrab" and "wandering Mesmerist"—which saw daylight in 1853 as "Church of Brou," "Sohrab and Rustum," and "The Scholar-Gipsy." He apparently was never satisfied with "Hylas"; in any case no trace of it survives.

His chief new poems of 1852 are "The Youth of Man" and "Morality." The first relates to "The Youth of Nature" (which he finished on January 4, 1852) as well as to the diary note, "Pindaric 'sink o youth in thy soul.'" Its Pindaric qualities are hardly more than triadic structure and a hectoring, elevated style:

> *We, O Nature, depart,*
> *Thou survivest us! this,*
> *This, I know, is the law.*
> *Yes! but more than this,*
> *Thou who seest us die*
> *Seest us change while we live;*
> *Seest our dreams, one by one,*
> *Seest our errors depart;*
> *Watchest us, Nature! throughout,*
> *Mild and inscrutably calm.*
>
> *Well for us that we change!*[48]

The speaker might be a penitent Roman centurion at the Stoical school of wisdom at Nicopolis. The verse has less imagery than many sermons, less charm than street songs. In fact, the setting is Richmond Hill, near Lord Lansdowne's pretty Cardigan House estate above the Thames, where a poet encounters an aged couple. He has known them since they were young. Once the pair had boasted "Man, man is the king of the world!" and denounced mystics who prattled of Nature's beauty, and now old and infirm they cannot comprehend Nature's secrets—its mysterious serenity, its divinity. Perhaps they had never read Spinoza. Finally in the manner of Goethe's "Das Göttliche" the poet turns to time-ridden children of a modern epoch:

> *While the heart still pours*
> *The mantling blood to thy cheek,*
> *Sink, O youth, in thy soul!*
> *Yearn to the greatness of Nature;*
> *Rally the good in the depths of thyself!*[49]

The poet's Spinozism has made nature at once material, impassive, and divine, and his weariness during a hard year of inspecting has perhaps made him accept Epictetus's counsel without that philosopher's gaiety. Youth in this poem is too arrogant to find inwardness for life—age, too feeble.

More subtle and ironic, "Morality" opens presciently with a lament for ebbing poetic inspiration:

> We cannot kindle when we will
> The fire which in the heart resides;
> The spirit bloweth and is still,
> In mystery our soul abides.
> > But tasks in hours of insight willed
> > Can be in hours of gloom fulfilled.[50]

Here one of Shelley's romantic verbs, *kindle*, is arresting. Nature, observing man's earnest strife and "tasked morality," cries to man with delicious pity and wonder from the viewpoint of her *Witch-of-Atlas*-like freedom and her *Cloud*-like creative power:

> 'There is no effort on my brow—
> I do not strive, I do not weep;
> I rush with the swift spheres and glow
> In joy, and when I will, I sleep.'

But Nature admits that she had observed something like man's frenetic "morality" when she "lay upon the breast of God."[51] Arnold implies that nature is more consoling and restorative than the grave, dusty deity of Victorians. He printed "Youth of Man" and "Morality" when he had inspected schools run by the Dissenting clergy for exactly one year, and when he had begun to feel he had no aptitude for his work "whatever."[52]

12

THE MYTH OF THE "SCHOLAR-GIPSY"
1852–1857

For God's sake don't mope.
      —*Arnold to Clough*

THE dark splendor and grave elegiac beauty in Arnold's verse are shadows of an affirmation of life—a complex affirmation having to do with his gusto, ebullience, and zest. He had large reserves of energy, a great sense of fun, a ready wit, natural optimist's nerve and pluck. Joking with teachers over his "disgust" with inspecting to ensure the teachers of his sympathy, he cut a splendid figure in classrooms and he began this year to enter more sympathetically into Fanny Lucy's views. He hardly complained about his work to friends: "I submit," he told Clough with mock humility, "and revolve with the solar system."[1] Great talents are not easily destroyed. An intelligent, sensible, strong young man is well-served by his egotism if he finds he has unusual talent. He may enter too lightly into the problems of his friends—without being so callous as he appears.

Arnold did worry about Clough, who had been fired from one job and was drawing only a pittance from a chair of English. That poet was luckless. When he tried for work with "Mr. Lingen" in the Education Office, Arnold gently advised him. (Lady Ashburton, a friend of Lord Lansdowne, was trying to help the handsome, black-eyed Clough too.) "I think an Inspectorship would be better suited to you," wrote Matthew, "than an Examinership." Perhaps he and Clough could inspect schools *together*. Little girls terrified by one tall gentleman in class would perhaps faint at the sight of two hulking poets. But an inspectorship wasn't the *only* chance for Clough in the Council Office if he would hurry to apply: "With Lady Ashburton's help and your own character you have an excellent prospect of getting *some* situation in the C.O. . . . But be bustling about it; we are growing old, and advancing towards the deviceless darkness."[2]

Clough seldom bustled. He vanished for days before sending a cryptic note from Shairp's whisky-stocked house at Rugby.

"I did not know what had become of you," Matthew replied after calling at his empty rooms. "I called at Doubting Castle." He proposes a weekend meeting at Derby where he means to cajole his friend, and after snubbing a bad Shakespeare text he shows his urgent concern. "Something wrong every page" in Edward Capell's edition of Shakespeare, he writes to Clough.

> "Their currents turn *away*" instead of *awry*—and heaps more [errors in the text of *Hamlet*]. But I stick to Homer.
>   Adieu and love me. . . . Kindest regards to Shairp. Flu sends her kind regards to you. I have a real craving to see you again. Tell me if you are likely to have anything to do. —How life rushes away, and youth. One has dawdled and scrupled and fiddle faddled—and it is all over.[3]

Failing to see him at Derby and more worried, he sent Clough a list of projects. Publishers are rich as kings! Clough could perhaps translate for one of them the Greek lyrics or turn Laertius's metaphysical gossip into flesh and blood—leaving out "trash"? Very timid and confused, the London publishers print *excerpts* from poems without understanding the meaning of whole forms, or reissue bad *Hamlets*. Even lower than Arnold's view of publishers was his opinion of book reviewers who review books without giving samples from the works under review! Now, as Clough is a clever man, he can live by his wits and find a publisher with money. He might write lives of the English poets from where Johnson ends and in a Johnsonian method perhaps, "biographical but above this, *critical*"? (Matthew anticipates *Essays in Criticism* with the last suggestion in April 1852.) His concern was generous, but though aiding Clough in the attempt he lately had fretted when that friend applied for a post in Australia; he knew he needed Clough nearby to remain a poet himself. Their talents and fates were linked since his friend's willingness to commit feelings to verse gave Matthew a similar boldness. In the coming months and after their last quarrel, he wrote of his deep respect for Arthur's glittering "literary ability, and wholesome abundance, so unlike the strangled poverty stricken driblets of some of us."[4] He seldom praised that friend so freely, during the give-and-take of real intimacy.

In the early summer, he had less cause to feel optimistic about friendship. Quite fed up with job seeking, Clough announced that he meant to emigrate to Boston—to set up as a tutor with Ralph Waldo Emerson's help! News of Clough's American emigration plans reached Arnold at about the time that his wife, on July 6, gave birth to a frail little boy. The child was christened "Thomas Arnold." That name was a "pill" to swallow, as Matthew told his mother, but he was glad enough to use his father's name.

Fanny Lucy worried him more than the child did. Her confinement had been difficult—and when she recovered, her features had lost an earlier freshness. So far he had treated her often as a good-natured, animated doll, even as she obligingly emphasized her own delicacy by deriding the male sex and eyeing him warily, noting his reddish face and consumption of wine, cold drinks, and "ice." Arnold's view of sexual love is enlightening in his poetry but it is enlightening most often, as in "The Buried Life" or *Switzerland,* from the male viewpoint. The male ethos of the Victorian age supported him in his condescending grateful manner of ravishing his wife whenever he wished. And their game—with Flu offended by male boorishness and Matthew striving to be gallant before enjoying his privileges—might, after all, have been designed by male gods, or by Centaurs in the "Reveller" as he played it. He need not confide in her; he had kept much of his life separate from her, even *stopped* being gallant when convenient: he had not considered her feelings at the Grande Chartreuse or in the Alps. Her suffering as a young mother did affect him, and led him to understand her better than he had so far.

With the birth of Tommy, Flu had the option of staying in London. Their child proved unhealthy. In the summer they looked at a pallid head in its ornate, large crib—and Matthew walked with the child in his arms. He had doubts about the "heart," as he wrote, "having constantly remarked its singular agitations. . . . But I should not be the least surprised if Brodie or whoever sees him pronounces it only to be an infantine irregularity."[5] A doctor however told the Arnolds that the child had a cardiac defect and "was not to cry," lest crying should strain its heart.

This gave Fanny Lucy every reason to throw herself on her parents, to plead for a house at Teddington or in London. She might be a loyal wife while staying with Tommy in perfectly quiet rooms. Yet she declined this option and elected to travel with a handicapped child. She was not swayed by Arnold's optimism at this point—she was too sensible—and there is no reason to believe that Arnold demanded she stay with him in rough lodgings during inspecting months, or told her this would be easy. (She soon found it was not easy.) She seems, rather, to have sensed Arnold's need for her, and to have decided that he was capable of looking after her welfare and that her companionship, in turn, would help him. Her courage and gallantry in months ahead surpassed his own—and changed him. Sharing new troubles, they came to a new intimacy; and as Arnold depended on her help and listened to her advice, he gave up some earlier notions. He ceased dividing women into Heroines and Things and abandoned a prejudice against women in classrooms. Having agreed with George Sand that women have "certain forces of weakness, docility, attractiveness, suavity," he later insisted that the *chief* force in women is intelligence. He was to praise American women for being informed and capable in conversation and then become concerned with inhibitions upon English women imposed by an oppressive social class structure. Arnold did not escape all the prejudices of his time; but he knew, and tried to show, that we *always are* limited by prejudices of our social class, creeds, nations, and brief span of time in history. He thought about the position of women in modern society, and that thinking evolved. He was one of the least dogmatic of writers: a central characteristic of Arnold was his mobility, his capacity to evolve and correct his mistakes. He abhorred the rule or dogma, the fixed and established idea, and his concepts of culture and criticism are essentially means, processes, and avenues for mental perspective and intellectual change.

Fanny Lucy not only helped him to find values in opera, painting, sculpture, and modern novels, but criticized his lectures and manners. She had neat habits, a trim wardrobe, a readiness to pick up her things and be on her way, which contrasted with Arnold's tardy arrivals and slow habits. Her letters suggest that she could be terse, sharp, and ironic. She scorned literary bores and publishers' parties, and preferred men of simple manners and frank speech. She must have ridiculed Arnold's affected wincing, grimacing, and smirking, because he became easier and more natural. As the daughter of a logical, decisive Judge, she was resolutely practical when she had to be. Wishing to live in London and believing that recognition of Matthew's abilities at the Council Office would do him good, she hoped for his advancement and urged him to seek the secretaryship at the office. He wavered over this—wavered too in applying for other posts. He was nearly as uncertain as his friend Arthur Clough, about whom Fanny Lucy seems to have felt kindly. (By 1852 Clough no longer regarded her as a rival.) But it was in the area of Arnold's relations with Clough or in his whole trammeled life as a poet that she felt herself a stranger. From this she was still excluded.

She never disregarded her husband's poetry and may have sensed the poignancy of his need for Clough, and even the loneliness, absurdity, and suffering in this odd situation of two men who played Hamlet and Horatio lightly with each other to show their independence from the times and to disguise their own seriousness. Arnold's work was mixed with abstractions, theories, and speculations which made him doubt himself or take offense at friends, and even more deeply and darkly entangled in family relationships which Fanny Lucy might fret over or respect but with which she couldn't interfere. Eager to support him with her presence, she traveled willingly between hotels and lodgings in factory cities, and yet did not enter into his intense, main effort in these years. That effort was to write poems of national significance and to find strong ideas to make his new poetry viable. Arnold lived out *this* phase of his life apart from her, and suffered alone in his coming breakup with Clough, as Clough suffered quite alone.

He did what he could to help Fanny Lucy; his diaries suggest that he rented rooms costlier than he could afford and traveled hard to return to her. Of his kindness, gentleness, and love she had no reason to complain—and their mutual trust is evident. He believed that after a few years he might afford a house; he had no early intimation of the bitter personal tragedies ahead for them both and he saw hundreds who lived more wretchedly than any inspector. Yet once after a misunderstanding with "other lodgers" who had a prior claim to their rooms Fanny Lucy was expelled from a lodging and roughly driven from "pillar to post" for a week with a choking, crying baby. After this Arnold adopted a new tactic and tried to get her to take holidays with her sisters or parents so she could feel that in principle she shared his travels. He looked for quiet, rentable houses when he could; yet she was often with him and so was the baby. Tommy resembled a "skinned ape" with "legs smaller than ever,"[6] as Matthew noted.

He tried to be stoical about his prospects. But he certainly had family worries and larger, social worries on his mind by the time *Empedocles on Etna, and Other Poems* appeared under his bare initial on October 27, 1852. Here were "Buried Life" and "Summer Night," his lapidary and finished "Memorial Verses," his European poems to baffle the critics such as "Tristram," and "Parting" in the manner of *passion réfléchissante*. In all these shimmering mirrors of himself, in thirty-five brilliant poems, in "Excuse," "Indifference," "Too Late," and the others, he found little to sustain him and nothing that might console Fanny Lucy—and he could feel the poems were "all wrong" in view of what he now saw. The landscapes in which he worked were full of smoke, blackened factory walls, tenements and warehouses, narrow alleys, basement dwellings, filth and sewage. Workers and the unemployed seemed thrown into monstrous slums and schools here seemed beyond anyone's care. The government did nothing for the slums and next to nothing for schools or teachers or pupils. He would leave his wife and handicapped son only to find dozens of ill or "cheerlessly isolated"[7] teachers, abject poverty in city classrooms, death and suffering in the streets. This bleakness seemed unending and everywhere the shortage of money and help was evident. He traveled too many hours, talked to too many school managers: his weariness never helped him to adjust to social misery. In the cities were "children eaten up with disease," as he wrote later with parental feeling, "half-sized, half-fed, half-clothed, neglected by their parents, without health, without home."⁸

"Woe was upon me," he wrote this year, "if I analysed not my situation." Not even Goethe's *Werther* with its introspective ending in suicide or Chateaubriand's *René* with its doomed analytical hero had dealt with the poet's "modern situation in its true *blankness* and *barrenness, and unpoetrylessness.*"⁹

This language in a letter to Clough at least made his situation bearable: he could feel that he too, like Goethe and Chateaubriand, struggled as an artist in a wasteland. Yet the "*blankness* and *barrenness*" did not go away since he *saw* and *heard* the dilemma of elementary schools and knew that help for children was inadequate. The spirit of James Kay was dead. "Voluntaryists" hating the state's intervention in schooling (and others fearful of it) ensured through the decade that no new education bill would pass in the Commons. As for leadership Frederick Temple summed that up not long after *Empedocles.* "I think," Temple declared after talking with Lord Granville, the Lord President of the Cabinet, "these fellows have got into a mess in regard to Education. . . . They had not, no not one of them, the slightest notion of what ought to be done."¹⁰ The lack of ideas in government leaders prepared the way for Arnold's final defeat as a poet.

As yet he had no psychological vision of himself besides that of the poet; he did not wish to *be* anything else, to *do* anything else; and his sense of vocation and memory of his father's work and death at Rugby told him that he must persist. Flu could not help with poetry—she was not involved in his past, his childhood, his memory of his father, or in lines of connection with "K" or his mother. But, surely, to know some of the modern "*blankness* and *barrenness*" might be helpful—and he turned to one Old Rugbeian who had helped him to *think* about his art. "Let us, as far as we can," he wrote when Clough was boarding the S.S. *Canada* at Liverpool docks, "continue to exchange our thoughts, as with all our differences we agree more with one another than with the rest of the world." Looking ahead to a transatlantic debate with Clough, he proposed a "bi-monthly mail."¹¹ Under much pressure Arnold felt that this might be his main chance to improve his poetics, or his grasp of the ideas of his art—ideas he was reluctant to share with others. Only Clough's hard opposition could help. He certainly thought about their "differences." What were the real issues between them? Clough was getting some of the new urban scenery into his poetry but Arnold still believed that the poet's *matter* was "*the hitherto experience of the world, and his own*" and distrusted his friend's "direct communication, insight, and report." Clough's poetic aims seemed too novelistic, time-limited, or circumscribed by the present. Unlike Clough, Arnold would *group objects,* subordinate his images and details for the sake of an organic work, allowing for a full result of beauty and pleasure.[12] Embracing the Coleridgean idea that a poem brings unity out of multeity, Matthew believed that a poet's symbols might connect the past and future; yet Clough preferred mere glimpses and character sketches, a kaleidoscope of images to cast light on the "damned times" of the present—and wrote of that "multitudinousness" with moral satire, refractory vision, and multiple perspectives. Seeking an inner perspective and an idea of the world, Arnold would treat the age in view of *all* the experience of man's spirit, ancient as well as modern, in unified poems of beauty.

To entertain Clough out on the Atlantic Ocean, he turned his ship-letter into an interesting manifesto. "Critics," he tells Clough on October 28, 1852,

> still think that the object of poetry is to produce exquisite bits and images—such as Shelley's *clouds shepherded by the slow unwilling wind* . . . whereas modern poetry can only subsist by its *contents*: by becoming a complete magister vitae [guide or teacher of life] as the poetry of the ancients did: by including, as theirs did, religion with poetry, instead of . . . leaving religious wants to be supplied by the Christian religion.[13]

Like a skater veering from right foot to left, Arnold develops his poetics along an axis—and here he leans on his moral rather than his aesthetic foot. He doesn't wish poetry to replace religion—but sees that religion's best insights *are* in poetry. That a work should include "religion with poetry" anticipates his liturgical anthology of Western verse in "The Study of Poetry"[14] and such a work as *Literature and Dogma.* His idea turns far backwards: his "ancients" or Greeks had used the mythopoeic method: their strong myths included "religion with poetry" and gave to their epics and tragedies just that inwardness and universality he admired. After his friend sailed, Matthew with new incentive opened a delicate path through memory to the religious and mythical time of his own childhood. Up at Lincoln in November, he sat every evening for a week in the nave or transept of the cathedral and then traveled down the Trent; he "looked affectionately in the bright morning" at his mother's village of Fledborough: "My recollections of it are the only approach I have to the memory of a golden age."[15]

In "The Church of Brou," he assesses a divine myth of his childhood. Taking his data from a French essay of Quinet he locates the church in hills instead of on the plain of La Bresse, but plausibly tells about Philibert II, the young Duke of Savoy, who dies in a boar hunt, and then of his Duchess who watches the sculpting of their tomb effigies before she dies. When the royal pair are buried, a narrator speaks as if they *existed* in stone atop their tombs—

> *Where thou, young Prince! shalt never more arise*
> *From the fringed mattress where thy Duchess lies.*[16]

After a few more lines, the awakening of Duke and Duchess in the lonely church seems plausible. The beautiful statues eerily open stone eyelids—and Arnold offers the most moving couplets he ever wrote:

> *Let it be on autumn nights, when rain*
> *Doth rustlingly above your heads complain*
> *On the smooth leaden roof, and on the walls*
> *Shedding her pensive light at intervals*
> *The moon through the clere-story windows shines,*
> *And the wind washes through the mountain-pines.*
> *Then, gazing up 'mid the dim pillars high,*
> *The foliaged marble forest where ye lie,*
> *Hush, ye will say, it is eternity! . . .*
> *And, in the sweeping of the wind, your ear*
> *The passage of the Angels' wings will hear,*
> *And on the lichen-crusted leads above*
> *The rustle of the eternal rain of love.*[17]

"Brou" exposes the divine myth of Heaven he learned as a child—its pressure and beauty arising from his nostalgia for a lost faith.

More complex myths appear in "The Scholar-Gipsy," which creates a "map myth" looking back on Berkshire walks with Clough, and then vents Arnold's furious despair over the social *"barrenness."* Janus-faced, pointing to his lyric past and critical future, the poem is really an elegy on elegies—asking if any individual life is meaningful enough to merit an elegy in the *alto stile* of the Greeks and Milton. Central to it is a story in Joseph Glanvill's *The Vanity of Dogmatizing or Confidence in Opinions* (1661), a copy of which Arnold had owned in his last year at Balliol. Explaining the deceptiveness of the senses and the folly of solipsism (as Epictetus does too), Glanvill praises the modest good sense of Descartes, and argues that science has limits and that we need "Hypotheses" or what he interestingly calls "convenient supposals for the use of life." This little book seems as wise today as it did to its first readers, and Glanvill tells good anecdotes. One had caught Arnold's eye: a "Lad in the *University of Oxford*," having joined gipsies because he is "tir'd of knocking at preferment's door," one day meets two scholars at an inn—as Matthew after a walk might have met Todo Walrond and Tom. He performs a trick to show that he doesn't run with low gipsies for nothing. After his Oxford friends chat in another room, he rejoins them and tells them what they had said. He had put into their heads what he *wanted* them to say; and when he fully learns the gipsies' "wayes of heightening the Imagination to that pitch, as to bind anothers,"[18] he will report to the world.

That story might have charmed the author of *Biographia Literaria;* it enchanted the Clougho-Matthean set and made Arnold pore over *Vanity of Dogmatizing*—the title of which might stand for his own main approach to religion as well as culture. Indeed Glanvill's book is just vivid, rich, and suggestive enough to have delighted him. "The knowledge I teach," Glanvill wrote in *Vanity* when attacking "sciolists" and the absurdity of dogmatists in religion, "is ignorance."[19] As Glanvill appreciates the limits of human intellect and the virtues of nondogmatic lore, so Arnold's Gipsy shuns academic Oxford and searches for a mysterious "spark"—perhaps the one mentioned in Emerson's "The Transcendentalist"—and very brilliantly embodies a modern expressivist view of man.

Arnold as a part-time student of Germanic culture knew of Goethe's and Herder's very influential "expressivist anthropology" of the 1770s. Herder, in *On the Origin of Language* (1772), had seen man's *Besonnenheit,* or reflective consciousness, as being realized only by man's words; for Herder, man is not an imitator, but, uniquely through language, a creator. Goethe stresses a purification (*Läuterung*) that words effect, and sees *the poet* as a deific agent of nature. From the time of Herder and Goethe on in the West, as a good Hegelian has said, "art begins to take on a function analogous to religion, and to some extent replacing it."[20]

Matthew's wish to be chic, clever, and European had led him to read Goethe, but that sage's fears at length became his own. Goethe believed that new cities, communications media, and democracy all endanger the artist's self-possession: "*Daily criticism in fifty different places,*" Goethe had told Eckermann, "*prevent the appearance of any sound production. He who does not keep aloof (or) isolate himself by main force, is lost.*" And Matthew had lamented "cities, newspapers" and used terms such as *Besonnenheit* (for deep self-possession) and *bedeutendes Individuum* (for important subjectivity) to suggest what he lacked.[21] His Gipsy is, then, first of all, an artist in quest of full possession of his own uniqueness.

Fleeing distractions, the Gipsy embodies more than a German myth. He wanders in lovely tracts of Berkshire scenery near an old university—partly medieval and unchanging—as if he were in search of truths obscured since the ending of medieval Europe. With transferred epithets as in "shy retreats," "retired ground," or "lone wheatfields," the narrator describes the land in a way that applies to a lone, sensitive, bohemian wanderer—whose peregrinations are silent, strange, inexplicable. The Gipsy's elusive comings and goings might be those of creative inspiration, or suggest even the reappearances of a deity.

But the power of the Scholar-Gipsy lies in his ambivalent meanings. He exists by eyewitness report, in stanzas full of Berkshire flowers that so delighted Jane. He is seen and not seen, real and unreal, long buried and yet freely alive. Gradually the lovely stanzas move to a climax:

> *Thee at the ferry, Oxford riders blithe,*
> *Returning home on summer nights, have met*
> *Crossing the stripling Thames at Bab-lock-hithe,*
> *Trailing in the cool stream thy fingers wet,*
> *As the punt's rope chops round;*
> *And leaning backwards in a pensive dream,*
> *And fostering in thy lap a heap of flowers . . .*
> *And then they land, and thou art seen no more!*
> · · · · · ·
>
> *The blackbird picking food,*
> *Sees thee, nor stops his meal, nor fears at all;*
> *So often has he known thee past him stray,*
> *Rapt, twirling in thy hand a withered spray,*
> *And waiting for the spark from heaven to fall.*[22]

The mysterious quest and lustrous images show how Theocritus and Keats, the *Bhagavad-Gita* and Emerson's vatic essays mingled in Arnold's mind. That the Gipsy is convincing points to an autobiographical source. He is, at least partly, an Arnold or an Obermann looking for the key to his being while knowing that fertilizing moments of insight follow upon a disregard of time. Again he is the *Prelude*'s hero, who defies clock and sun by skating in darkness on the star-reflecting ice of a lonely lake.

Having created a symbol of Western man as unified, "pure," and expressivist, Arnold turns to a critique of modern society in which he holds aloft the Gipsy:

> *Thou hadst one aim, one business, one desire;*
> · · · · · ·
>
> *Thou waitest for the spark from heaven! and we,*
> *Light half-believers in our casual creeds,*
> *Who never deeply felt, nor clearly willed,*
> *Whose insight never has borne fruit in deeds,*
> *Whose vague resolves never have been fulfilled;*

> *For whom each year we see*
> *Breeds new beginnings, disappointments new;*
> *Who hesitate and falter life away. . . .*
> *Ah! do not we, wanderer! await it too?*[23]

As an ideal against which our "sick fatigue" and "languid doubt" may be measured, the Gipsy is a useful myth; he reminds one of T. S. Eliot's early praise of James Joyce's *Ulysses:* "the myth," as Eliot said, "is simply a way of controlling, of ordering, of giving a shape and significance to the immense panorama of futility and anarchy which is contemporary history."[24] Arnold's Gipsy represents stability in a world of flux and change, creative inwardness in a world of lassitude, stagnation, frustration, and dividedness. With irony, the narrator berates Tennyson as "our wisest," in a stanza replete with allusions to *In Memoriam* and "The Palace of Art":

> *. . . and amongst us one,*
> *Who most has suffered, takes dejectedly*
> *His seat upon the intellectual throne;*
> *And all his store of sad experience he*
> *Lays bare of wretched days;*
> *Tells us his misery's birth and growth and signs,*
> *And how the dying spark of hope was fed,*
> *And how the breast was soothed, and how the head, . . .*
>
> *This for our wisest!*[25]

That pitying irony embarrassed Arnold. In America thirty years later, he claimed he had had Goethe "in mind when he wrote."[26] And so he had. It is the enfeebled intellectual strain he sees in *In Memoriam,* the wrong, fragmented quality of Tennyson's nostrums ("And how the breast was soothed, and how the head") that he sets against his memory of cool wisdom in *Dichtung und Wahrheit;* only Goethe had *not* been an imposter on Europe's "intellectual throne." This stanza precedes an attack on modern English writing in *On Translating Homer.*

His coda switches the poem's scene to an ancient Mediterranean of encroaching Greeks and Tyrian traders, for the details of which he drew on Grote's *History of Greece,* Herodotus, Isaiah, and his own father's writings. As "young light-hearted masters" the Greeks were famous for easy, slick commercial dealings; the Tyrian (like the Gipsy) fled from men who would blight his soul—and with indignation on the windswept North African coast unfurled his fluttering sails,

> *where down cloudy cliffs, through sheets of foam,*
> *Shy traffickers, the dark Iberians come;*
> *And on the beach undid his corded bales.*

The ending expands the poem's theme. Contrasting spirituality with restlessness, past with present, and East with West, Arnold condemns the practical legacy of the Greeks for its Apollonian, present ascendency in the Western mind. He also suggests a fine Dionysian inwardness,[27] which is perhaps "what we want."

Yet "The Scholar-Gipsy" was not after all what he wanted. "I am glad you like the Gipsy Scholar," he wrote to Clough harshly late in 1853, "but what does it *do* for you? Homer *animates*—Shakespeare *animates*. . . . The Gipsy Scholar at best awakens a pleasing melancholy. But this is not what we want." And he cites his own "Youth of Nature":

> *The complaining millions of men*
> *Darken in labour and pain—*

"what they want is something to *animate* and *ennoble* them—not merely to add zest to their melancholy or grace to their dreams."[28] What made him accept this didactic view of poetry—which was his sister Jane's view—and turn against his brilliant work?

Unluckily, a barrage of complaints from Clough in the United States had begun to reach him in January. That poet's loneliness in Boston had given him time to reflect on past slights and insults. Clough's letters are lost—but they apparently accused Arnold of pride, ambition, smugness, egotism, and coldness over five years. It is hard to reply to an angry friend who is half-right and knows he is. Arnold made the very great mistake of trying to account for his failures in friendship historically. He begins with a little special pleading, as an "exchange" on poetics is dropped. "I am past thirty, and three parts iced over," he tells Clough, "—and my pen, it seems to me is even stiffer and more cramped than my feeling."

"I do not know," he confesses later, "that the tone of your letters exactly facilitates correspondence."[29] Clough damnably seemed *satisfied* with nothing he might say. Matthew throws up smoke screens; he admits he has been "egoistic and anti-social," but tries to justify himself: "So entirely indeed am I convinced," he recalls of flaunting Clough two years earlier, "that being in love generally unfits a man for the society of his friends, that I remember often smiling to myself at my own selfishness." He forgets that he neglected Clough to dine with Melville Portal, and raises a thick screen over his past anger with friends who "ridiculed" him about Thun, Mary Claude, and his love vigil in the Swiss Alps, though he admits to "coldness and want of intellectual robustness" and "languor of spirit, and fickleness and insincerity."[30] In brief, he poses as the laughing *philosophe* he believed Clough saw in him; and then stops being a *philosophe*. One's sentences, Matthew flings out, "correspond to nothing in one's inmost heart and mind, and only represent themselves. It was your own fault partly for forcing me into it. I will not go on with it: only remember, *pray* remember that I am and always shall be, whatever I do or say, powerfully attracted towards you, and vitally connected with you . . . for ever linked with you by intellectual bonds—the strongest of all."[31]

That complex, inner fracture or fault in Arnold's will to continue as a poet was caused by his revolt against intuition and his belief in a more rational outlook; and Clough's explosions—which testified to that poet's need for him—helped the final change to occur. Without consciously renouncing poetry, Arnold wrote less and less verse after 1853. He was puzzled and depressed by the change that occurred in him; but, in the years 1853 to 1857, he did very consciously and deliberately turn against subjective feeling. He had jotted an ironic line from *Faust:*

Gefühl ist alles (Feeling is all).

Under that phrase, he had noted:

Die ewige solo (The eternal solo.)[32]

He clearly believed that *feeling* had hoodwinked Goethe's Faust; again, that it is perfect folly to imagine oneself as a René or Hamlet. If the age occasioned a "dialogue of the mind with itself," could one forget the lucid Greeks' sense of social community? His feelings had led him to behave in an "egoistic and anti-social" manner to which he confessed, and he could hardly deny that in a sense Spinoza and Locke, in a ghostly way, accused him.

Citing those authors, he had told Clough: "*My respect for reason as the rock of refuge to this poor exaggerated surexcited humanity increases and increases.*"[33] Spinoza had advised against confusing feeling and imagination with conduct. Locke's support of "reason," in turn, inspired Arnold's theory of maturing development—which had led him to tell Jane that "we *must*" all leave "the aimless and unsettled but also liberal and open state of our youth." Instead of apologizing to Jane, he had promised to reform his whole character. Having thrown the theory of development in her lap, he had taken a hard inspectorship which left him little time for the "aimless and unsettled" life a poet may require. Further, his maturing intellect really found less outlet in his poetry after *Empedocles;* and he had sensed that analysis, rather than intuition and feeling, was natural to him and demanded of a man.

"I catch myself desiring now at times political life, and this and that," he pleads to Clough in May, "and I say to myself—you do not desire these things because you are really adapted to them, and therefore the desire for them is merely contemptible—and it is so. I am nothing and very probably never shall be anything." After that humble admission, he declares he has "just got through a thing" which pleases him "better than anything."[34]

The "thing" was "Sohrab and Rustum"—or a lesson in objectivity for Arthur Clough. In Sainte-Beuve's essay about Mohl's French translation of a Persian work, "Le Livre des Rois, par Firdousi," Matthew had read a tragic tale about a father and son. That essay gave him, as he later told Sainte-Beuve, "*courage de commencer enfin mon poème*"—and his courage rose without more help from Firdousi.[35] He never read more than a few paragraphs in translation of the Persian myth about the Tartar Sohrab, killed in a duel by his own father Rustum the Persian. Certainly, works such as Burnes's *Travels* and John Malcolm's *History of Persia* supplied background for his poem.

As an "Episode" told in the Homeric vein, "Sohrab and Rustum" has tragic irony, epic similes, a recognition scene. Yet its style is plainer than Homer's, its epic similes have a soft Virgilian tenderness, and its "scenes" give a version of epic history while almost neglecting Persians and Tartars, a contemporary culture, nation-state, or national destiny. Sohrab yearns for *one man*—

> one alone—
> Rustum, my father; who I hoped should greet,
> Should one day greet, upon some well-fought field,
> His not unworthy, not inglorious son.

What delays a mutual recognition, between father and son, on a sandy dreamlike waste between two armies? Rustum believes his only child was a girl, though he calls his own son girlish. Sohrab can hardly credit his good luck in meeting a parent. As a mortal duel begins, the similes remind one of Goethe and Schiller's searching debate over Homer's "retarding manner"—and of Schiller's valid idea that Homer gives "the quiet existence and operation of things in accordance with their natures."[36] The similes have inevitability, but suggest just that uncertainty about "fate" which appears in Sohrab's vast wave—"a wave," as Miss Martineau cruelly wrote in the *Daily News*, such as was never "seen at Brighton":

> 'For we are all, like swimmers in the sea,
> Poised on the top of a huge wave of fate,
> Which hangs uncertain to which side to fall.
> And whether it will heave us up to land,
> Or whether it will roll us out to sea,
> Back out to sea, to the deep waves of death,
> We know not, and no search will make us know;
> Only the event will teach us in its hour.'[37]

Though subpoetic, the wave and other features in "Sohrab" are compelling; for all relate to a personal theme. Matthew is concerned with the dissimilarity between himself and his father, and also with the need to gain his father's sense of social purpose. "Sohrab," "Balder Dead," and the play *Merope* all reflect his painful lack of any social purpose, and inability to give himself to *any* man's cause. "I too," he admits to his brother Willy, who literally sacrificed his life to the schools of India,

> have felt the absurdity and disadvantage of our hereditary connection in the minds of all people with education, and am always tempted to say to people, "My good friends, this is a matter for which my father certainly had a specialté, but for which I have none whatever." You however will throw yourself into [educational and social work]. . . . I on the contrary half cannot half will not throw myself into it, and feel the weight of it doubly in consequence. I am inclined to think it would have been the same with any active line of life on which I found myself engaged—even with politics . . . since I cannot bring myself to do more than a halting sort of half-work in other people's way.[38]

Sohrab indeed fights to discover—and protect—a psychic self. Arnold in writing perhaps made no conscious autobiographical connection, but drew on a very rich experience of filial love mixed, as it was, with anxiety about his identity and aims. There are family echoes in the text: Sohrab is not merely a tawny, muscular bravo—but is, like the Strayed Reveller, "softly" nurtured and surprisingly thin, handsome, and boyish. Rustum is a father with a vast reputation, a "tower" quite as solid as Laleham Church's or Rugby's. Matthew's father had kissed him on the lips; mortally wounded, Sohrab crawls on the sand as if to repay kisses given:

> *Sohrab crawled to where he lay, and cast*
> *His arms about his neck, and kissed his lips,*
> *And with fond faltering fingers stroked his cheeks.*

Dying, Sohrab is as alert as Prince Hamlet to the need to remember the dead. "Mourn for me," he appeals to a blunt-minded father,

> *That so a passing horseman on the waste*
> *May see my tomb a great way off, and cry:*
> Sohrab, the mighty Rustum's son, lies there,
> Whom his great father did in ignorance kill![39]

"Sohrab" was meant very deeply to touch Mrs. Arnold and Jane Forster, with its pathos and air of renunciation. This summer Matthew thought of withdrawing *Empedocles on Etna* from circulation, and even of writing an objective preface. He would bring his poetic theories truly in line at last with his practice. "Nearly stupefied by 8 months inspecting," he visited Froude in Wales where he found the angry young atheist who wrote *Nemesis of Faith* wonderfully changed. "See Froude," he wrote happily to Clough. "He goes to church, has family prayers, says the *Nemesis* ought never to have been published etc. etc. . . . He conforms. . . . He is getting more and more literary . . . instead of beating the air," Matthew adds in prediction of his "ineffectual angel" image for Percy Bysshe Shelley.[40]

Froude advised against writing a preface, but epitomized the conservative, renunciatory outlook on life and art which Arnold now eagerly sought. Another stimulus for his very interesting Preface was a harsh notice in *The North American Review* (July 1853), entitled "Recent English Poetry" and written by Arthur Clough.

In this singular review, Clough exteriorizes his long private debate with Matthew on poetry. He ends their friendship; he very nearly cuts Arnold's poetry to ribbons—or, rather worse, he explains why modern poetry ever since about 1840 has become less vital than the modern novel: "There is no question," says Clough (who has been talking lately with Emerson and hearing about Henry Thoreau of Walden Pond),

> that people much prefer Vanity Fair and Bleak House. Why so? . . . Poetry should deal more . . . [with] the actual, palpable things with which our every-day life is concerned; introduce into business and weary task-work a character and a soul of purpose and reality; intimate to us relations which, in our unchosen, peremptorily-appointed posts, in our grievously narrow and limited spheres of action, we still, in and through all, retain to some central, celestial fact. . . . The novelist does try to build us a real house to be lived in; and this common builder, with no notion of the orders, is more to our purpose than the student of ancient art who proposes to lodge us under an Ionic portico. We are, unhappily, not gods, nor even marble statues.[41]

Clough not only attacked Matthew's 1849 and 1852 volumes as inferior in spirit to poems by Alexander Smith (a lace-pattern designer of Glasgow and "Spasmodic" poet) but also demanded a raison d'être for poetry in the modern world. After all, if Thackeray's *Vanity Fair* or Dickens's *Bleak House* depict our lives, feelings, and ourselves in a social context, why do we need lyrics? This challenge, by no means fully answered in the famous Preface of 1853, was to give focus to Arnold's thought in dreary years ahead and to be taken up in his finest essays. Moreover, Clough's detailed points were fair. Matthew made eleven changes in the text of "Tristram" based on Clough's comments, and thanked him: if his own people at Fox How felt the book review "obscure and peu favorable," he told Clough, he didn't think either of these things.[42]

Their intimacy did not survive such polite, gracious, one-sided understanding. Clough returned to take a desk job in the education office and marry, but resigned from his hard, exploratory debate with Matthew—with whom he remained coolly cordial. Their friendship became only less tepid, shortly before Clough died, when the two poets tried (and failed) to get Tom Arnold a Catholic inspectorship.

Having finished the Preface by October 1, Matthew sent it to Longmans for his *Poems* (1853), the first book to appear under his full name. Despite echoes of Wordsworth's second preface to *Lyrical Ballads,* his Preface is a bold, original act of criticism, at once delightfully readable and as reactionary as Boileau's *L'Art poétique* or Horace's *Ars Poetica*. Its reception did not lift his discouragement—as we shall see—but made him controversial. Reviewers found fault, but debated his Preface. *Fraser's,* the *Edinburgh,* the *Sun,* and mighty *Blackwood's* even defended it. Arnold's fame as a critic was prepared in the 1850s; that fame was to increase in England, sweep him into the limelight, and leap to North America so that by the time he left for an "invasion of the United States" in 1883 people six thousand miles away knew his name. Excitement over his critical writings was to draw attention to his poetry, so that Matthew Arnold would be hailed as the foremost living English man of letters and a classic before he died. It was not through poems that he conquered England but through controversial prose; Arnold gained fame because he was audacious, challenging, fresh, witty, on the move in his ideas and topics, in the thick of controversy, and undaunted in probing the weakness of an industrial society. He was not ephemeral or superficial; it is not difficult in a lifetime to write as much as he did, and his output was surpassed by other critics; but he was unique in his voice and presence, irony, range, urbanity, and sensitivity, as he brought into his essays a sense of the Western literary heritage. In his armory was a grand sense of fun and of the ridiculous—which he could apply mockingly to himself.

Arnold's Preface does nothing it sets out to do but establishes "criticism" as a dialogue with the future, as a matter of comparison and insight rather than hard definition. The critic's authority rests on his being on the way to a subject and never quite there, on his ability to set ideas, authors, or received viewpoints against each other to suggest the insight he wants.

He begins by saying why he will not reprint *Empedocles*—and highlights the work he would suppress. His greatest poem fails to inspirit and rejoice, for it involves a "modern" time, as he says with a fine phrasemaking talent,

> [when] the dialogue of the mind with itself has commenced; modern problems have presented themselves; we hear already the doubts, we witness the discouragement, of Hamlet and of Faust.[43]

He withdraws *Empedocles* because his intuition has placed him in a false position in which his intellect is prevented from analyzing, searching into, or saying more about modern society. (His suicide poem implied that nothing "is to be done" about England.) His notes and Preface argument show him as quite obsessed by society. *"When young,"* he told himself in a desk-note, *"we sometimes represent best: for curiosity is here most active, & reflection least active; therefore we represent appearances in a lively . . . manner; whereas later our occupation with our own thoughts & society powerfully distracts us."*[44] Occupation "with our own thoughts & society" is made worse by reviewers who goad us into thinking, as he quotes from the *Spectator* in the Preface, that the poet should draw "subjects from matters of present import"; or again as he cites from *North British Review,* that "a true allegory of the state of one's own mind in a representative history is perhaps the highest thing" a poet can write. "No," Matthew protests, "assuredly, it is not, it can never be so."[45]

To choose subjects only of "present import," or to write out one's autobiography in blood to comfort the public is to accept a narrow, ugly, utilitarian view of art. His aesthetic consciousness kept him from any such thing. He implores young poets (to whom his Preface is addressed) to imitate the Greeks; they knew that the date of an action is nothing and the wholeness of the action, everything. They mastered the grand style, "so simple and well subordinated." With a few allusions to "confusion of the present times" and the "bewildering" counsel given to young poets, he recommends the "exquisite sagacity of taste" of Greek tragedians. Matthew thus appears as an Aristotle who has heard the music of John Henry Newman's sermons. He classically opposes the tendency to take *the lyric* as a norm in poetic theory and vividly treats the Greeks in terms of plastic and graphic arts—and shows a debt to Lessing. But the Preface's two main weaknesses—its limited view of style and its vagueness as to how the objective poet may fathom the "inward man" of his hero—pave the way for his failures in "Balder Dead" and *Merope.*

Thus he claims with rather hollow truth,

> The outward man of Oedipus or of Macbeth, the houses in which they lived, the ceremonies of their courts, [a poet] cannot accurately figure to himself; but neither do they essentially concern him. His business is with their inward man.[46]

But if one avoids autobiographical insights, subjective intuition, "sentiment capriciously thrown in," and frets over "not a word wasted," how is one to *get at* one's Oedipus or Macbeth? Distrusting feeling, he placed himself, as an artist, in the hopeless unresolved position he described in a note: "If it is said," he jotted for his own eyes, "that the mature & thoughtful poet abandons the outward appearances of objects to seize their inward being: I reply that . . . the inward being of man, which is unseen, can never be absolutely rendered [*overwritten* "represented"]. . . . but the poet, endeavouring to put himself in the place of the person represented, tries his own soul in certain situations, and reports accordingly, a great opening being here left for the subjective and arbitrary."[47] His objective view of art kept him from seizing the "inward being" of any man, even from writing with full lyric freedom.

All the same, his *Poems* (1853) contains a rich Preface, a compelling "Sohrab," and a beautiful "Scholar-Gipsy" within green cloth boards. Some critics were moved by the poems. But Mrs. Mary Arnold's failure to applaud loudly had a painful, consequential effect on Matthew and angered even Harriet Martineau up in the Lake District.

Clearly Mrs. Arnold did not end her son's poetic career—but her impatient feeling that, at thirty, he should take up his father's social causes beset him. Arnold's strength as a poet depended in large measure on the approval of women in his family. But Mrs. Arnold would not admit to herself that poetry of any kind was the best work he could do—even though people told her otherwise. This case was plain. Matthew *truly needed help,* as Miss Martineau felt: "Speaking of Poems," that lady wrote to a friend, "I am throbbing all through with Matt. Arnold's. *Have* you read his Preface? & Rustum? To think that his father underrated, even insulted, his quality of mind,—setting his soft, pious younger brother over him,—(a mere girl in comparison) & here is Matt: absorbing all the Arnolds that ever were & ever will be! I don't see that his mother sees it a bit. How amazed she w^d be to know how his good, earnest, narrow father shrivels up before his torch! But I suppose it w^d kill her. '*Do* write to Matt' she says to me. But I dare not. It w^d be an impertinence."[48]

Rocks and stones of the Lake District seemed to Harriet Martineau to cry out that Matt Arnold had become something unusual. He had proved himself. Harriet took varying views of his poetry and expressed the worst in her reviews: but what support did Arnold ladies of Fox How give him? She felt that we seldom understand the people in our midst, who need our help most. To encourage *them* costs us very little, but we seldom imagine the need. Suppose in the case of "Matt" that one of the strongest elegiac talents in England's poetical tradition had shown itself and that this talent was faltering and in the process of being destroyed?

At all events no English friend—not even Harriet—came to the defense of his poetic life in the years between 1853 and 1857, when he lived like a man in a quagmire in a nightmare. He tried again to turn his "Mythologica" notes into a drama on Lucretius and produced nothing. He used William Forster's influence to get elected to the Athenaeum Club in London: "I hear that people are admitted," he wrote to Forster, "on the very smallest grounds—even for a single pamphlet, or essay."[49] He entered the club with its large drawing room and quiet literary and scientific membership in February 1856 yet he made small use of its library; he was out of touch with his imagination —and "so dead sick of criticism,"[50] as he soon told Fan. (Instead of replying to critics of his 1853 Preface, he had written a brief, tepid, apologetic piece for a reissue of his *Poems* in 1854.) He promised Lewis Carroll an essay on Charles Kingsley's novel *Hypatia* and could not write it; planned a vivid piece on "Oxford Life" and either burned the essay or wrote nothing. For a week or two, he thought of a grand escape—from England, his mother and sisters and past—and almost took a government post on Mauritius in the warm Indian Ocean. After Sir James Stephen happily talked him out of it, Matthew mused of sitting with Flu "all day on a coral rock, bathing my legs in the Southern Ocean."[51]

He lacked confident dedication, a valid cause, a genuine belief that society had a right to claim his energies. He wrote bad verse to find out why he couldn't write well, to discover some mole's avenue around psychological obstacles and release himself from deadlock and inch his way on. "Balder Dead" (1855) suggests that the condition for release may be a new adjustment to his father's active, social outlook—and yet, more deeply, a realization that he cannot *live* his father's life, that he would seek a dialogue with a paternal spirit while expecting nothing from it. Using the Scandinavian myth of Balder the Sun God in the Norse *Edda* of Snorri Sturluson which he knew from Paul Henri Mallet's *Northern Antiquities,* he wrote a good story in a stiff, brusque style with military metaphors. Hermod, a fair brother god, travels to Hela's dark realm to retrieve the dead Balder's valiant spirit. What arouses Arnold's interest in the Norse Hel is the plight of a dazzling, deific spirit locked into death, though all the brother gods would die to bring Balder back. Despite his obvious charisma and strength of character, Balder is singularly hard, belittling, ungrateful:

> *Hermod the nimble, gild me not my death!*
> *Better to live a serf, a captured man . . .*
> *Than be crowned here, and rule the dead.*[52]

Hermod returns empty-handed to the sunlit upper world through picturesque alpine scenery. In Hel, Balder at last describes a City of the Gods, in which "a small remnant" of workers will build a new society.[53] But this idea—which suggests Dr. Arnold's comments on Isaiah, as well as Coleridge's *clerisy* of disinterested leaders and guardians for society—is offered with a curious lack of enthusiasm, tentatively, or as a theory or viewpoint to be tested. Arnold was to return to "the remnant" in a late essay, "Numbers."

Merope, written in 1857, fails as a play. It was meant to show "the effectiveness of Greek poetical forms" and Attic beauty according to its loose preface. Arnold's play is too literal to match blood-drenched Attic tragedies; he might have learned about the metaphoric handling of the antique from Racine or Corneille, as critics suggest, but he rejected authors too involved with intuitive feeling: "Racine," he agreed with Joubert, "is the Virgil of the ignorant."[54] On the other hand its speeches are lovely and never more so than when Merope describes her memories of her son Aeyptus or imagines his life in lyric, timeless valleys of Arcadia. Arnold is really concerned to represent his own mother's early unobsessive feeling for his welfare, her tenderness and gentleness, her natural faith in him, and the perfect fairness of her implicit demands—as if psychologically *she* were not responsible for choking his talent or dismaying him. The play veers away from psychological issues into political reality. Certainly Polyphontes the tyrant comes quite to life, as a worried, busy, sympathetic man, to be hustled off stage so that Merope may think of her son. Dramatically the problem is whether the son, Aeyptus, will forget his lackadaisical upbringing in Arcadia, kill his mother's tyrannical lover, and sit on a throne. With the lover (Polyphontes) dead, he enjoys his mother's warm political approval. The theme reflects at all levels one problem: just how soon will an inspector of schools find his social cause, what is it, how can he possibly take it up as his own?

Arnold admitted *Merope* was anything but classical. When someone later told him it was "not a bit Greek," he replied with half-shut eyes, "No doubt you are right; but it is *very* beautiful." He forgave its critics: "The comparison of the rhythm of some of the choruses in *Merope,*" he admitted, "to the noise of a stick drawn along a railing was . . . one of the happiest things I ever read."[55]

In these years, he tried to be resigned to a degree. Fanny Lucy, ill and in serious difficulty with each childbirth, followed him from lodging to lodging. She hoped for peace, comfort, a roof over her head, a pretty carriage to travel in, and kept hoping as a later diary shows; she still feared for her ribbons and frocks; but her day-to-day endurance and resilience in dreadful rooms with sick and fragile children put Arnold to shame. He tried to be cheerful for *her* sake and treated her with loving respect which by now surpassed the respect he showed "K," with whom he was often abrupt. His children increased his deep, secretive adoration of his wife. Fanny Lucy bore him beautiful blond or brunette infants, who had horrid coughs and seemed almost too frail to live. The healthy exception appeared to be fat, blond Trevenen or "Budge," who was born in October 1853 and soon became Matthew's special darling. Richard Penrose Arnold (who ran up large debts as an Oxford student) was born in November 1855. Lucy Charlotte arrived on Christmas Day in 1858, and her sister "Nelly," in February 1861. Basil Francis was born in 1868, by which time Fanny Lucy had given birth to one child in a filthy lodging with a workhouse behind, "and a penitentiary in front."[56] Only one of the Arnolds' four little boys—Richard Penrose—was to survive even to the age of twenty.

Six years of marriage changed Fanny Lucy's life. Despite her husband's wishes she had spent few days with relatives, had hurried to rejoin him during inspecting months and spent time in forlorn rooms. Tumult, dirt, and roughness in industrial cities surpassed anything she had known, and bleakness in poor areas where they lived weighed on her. Her worries fixed on details; she had fretted over the wind on her veil, discomfort in Italian hotels, the horridness of the Catacombs or the inconvenience of a carriage bogged in snow—with Matthew, in coat and boots, helping other men to move it. Small worries were her salvation, since illness and death hung over her children and indeed if summer holidays refreshed her the winter and spring found her nursing sick infants. Had her husband not suppressed his frantic worry, let her sleep late in the morning, breakfasted with the children who were well, and returned from schools as quickly as he could to help her, her life would have been unbearable. Arnold had two or three children with him whenever he was home; he worked after she went to bed, rose while she slept, and gave her reason to feel she had his devoted, practical, strong support. His verse writing was poor enough; but he had become an excessively attentive husband and a generous, indulgent, doting father, whose main fault was that he could never say no to a child. Fanny Lucy's small body, slim but rounded and filled out by heavy winter skirts and shawls, flourished because he treated her as more important than himself. He took the luxury of one brief rest, at the day's end, and then was up with the children. Coming home, weary and discouraged, he would fall exhaustedly on a bed, and find a blond head on his pillow. "When I come in," Arnold wrote about that head, "—Budge, who never sits down at any other time, announces that he is very tired and must lie down with Papa on the bed, and there he reposes asking me from time to time if I love him, and assuring me 'ur do love Papa' . . . the fat old duck."

Arnold's father wept when admitting new boys at Rugby; Matthew, it seems, looked with foolish misty eyes at his boys. He hated restraint in the family and encouraged Budge to express love, amply expressed his own affection, and couldn't bear to leave the children because the warmth of their love was the best antidote for discouragement. Once he was kissed at the door by the thin, handsome Tommy who cried out comically, "God bless you, Matt." That boy imitated his fatalism. "Did I tell you," Matthew informs his mother, "of [Tommy's] describing to me Diddy's illness. . . . 'He is in the nursery—he's very ill—he's had a fit—he's dead—where shall we put him?'—all in the most perfectly unconcerned tone."[57]

"Dining-room before breakfast," he jots on an occasion which illustrates his forbearance with the children. Tommy is in one window, and Budge in the other, "watching a band play." " 'Papa dear, is it going?—it *is* going—' " cries one of the boys in shock, as the cymbals and hollow drums fade away up the street. Arnold gets up, goes to the window, shuts doors, soothes the boys, and imitates a whole musical band. Now Tommy is "playing the Marseillaise on a paper knife and Budge dragging the litter-basket round & round the room to the tune of *Cheer Boys Cheer*." He was lenient because he knew from physicians how uncertain his boys' lives were and found Tommy so "fragile that we cannot take too much care of him," as Matthew explains to his mother.[58] "The little darling says if he hears me say we will do so and so if we live—'Yes—Please God we all live.' " And now Budge "has taken to exclaiming on all occasions PLE GO WE ALL LIB."

When he thought of the thin chance of getting an Oxford poetry professorship, he remembered the Gipsy. Having maligned that lyric he approves his "Scholar-Gipsy" in a note about the Oxford Poetry Chair. He wrote no more "Gipsies" or even "Sohrabs" these days, and his failures set a pattern. Inspecting duties tired him. Though he worked hard for Fanny Lucy, he perhaps failed her. How was he improving her life? What hope could he offer her? Delighted or moved to tears by the sweetness of his children, he feared for the future when he heard doctor's reports.

He wrote poor verse, almost no prose. His schemes came to nothing. In a banal manner, he was *living* the themes about "repeated shocks" which wear us out, and about each year breeding "disappointments new" and showing us how we have lost ground. In 1857 he might have been awaiting the "spark from heaven"; he now saw very little of Clough, and even less of John Duke Coleridge—who despite normal loyalties had accused him of committing plagiarism in "Sohrab." (He had sent Coleridge a mollifying letter and printed a full explanatory note with "Sohrab" about his borrowings.) Time and the schools divided him from friends; but with his name in nomination for Oxford's chair, he asked Balliol men only to vote for him.

To be at Oxford again! Elected by the university's convocation of M.A. degree-holders (or by any who cared to vote), the Oxford Poetry Professor gave about four talks a year. Paying next to nothing, this chair would add to his practical burdens and never relieve him from one day of school inspecting. As an *elected* chair, it embodied the spirit of Oxford over the years—a cynic might say the spirit of mean politics, factionalism, pedantry, and religious warfare. Some holders of the Poetry Chair knew nothing of poetry, but a few poets had won election. The chair might even suggest Oxford's real interest in literature and faith in poetry. Electors had voted in 1757 for Thomas Warton, Dr. Johnson's warm friend, who held the chair for two five-year terms and lectured on Greek bucolic poets and undertook a history of English poetry. Arnold's godfather John Keble had held this professorship from 1831 to 1841, and dedicated his lectures from the chair to Wordsworth.

Arnold needed to hope; he really needed spirit and energy to do more for his wife and himself. To have the post would give one a platform, make one's essays marketable. Arnold saw much in the Poetry Chair—and in being in the land of the Gipsy even if this wouldn't relieve him from schools. If he won, he would have a new forum, new stimulus, a renewed sense of himself as a poet (and less guilt over having lost his art). He felt he had little chance; and many signs were against him. The Christ Church men were active for "their candidate, Bode," and vastly outnumbered Balliol men. "Their numbers will overpower me," he felt.[59] The post paid only about £100 and its lectures had been given in Latin. On May 5, 1857, he wrote, *"These lectures I hope to give in English."*

That afternoon, he and Fanny Lucy went to Charing Cross telegraph station; they meant to buy toys for Budge and Tommy, bright wagons "with horses of precisely the same colour." At four they had a telegram from Theodore Walrond, who was still up at Oxford. It read vaguely: "NOTHING CERTAIN IS KNOWN, BUT IT IS RUMOURED THAT YOU ARE AHEAD." The votes were then being counted, but they were coming in like leaves from the Cumnor Hills and surprising almost everyone; for it was a tired, demoralized School Inspector who heard, late that day, that he had won "an immense victory."[60]

after all why am I restless because I have no one to say with tearful eyes to — I am wretched — & to be answered by — mon pauvre enfant; allons — sortons — dinons — &c ... Could we imagine a character we could be it — but we can only hope it: this is a bastard imagination: yet do young Heloises thrive on it & its warmth, or on its absence & the lmeverhip of the constructive faculty?

Arnold's desk-note on love and imagination—written when he knew Mary Claude, the blue-eyed French Protestant. BELOW: Hôtel Bellevue at Thun where he waited for his blue-eyed lady. (*Beinecke Rare Book and Manuscript Library, Yale University*) (*Bottom photo Courtesy of the Hôtel Bellevue, Thun. H. Meier, Photo-Kino, Thun*)

ABOVE: Fan Arnold, Matthew's youngest sister, who remained at Fox How
with her mother. RIGHT: his sister
Mary or "Bacco," who married three
times and was amused by his antics
and confessions. (*Courtesy of Mrs.
M. C. Moorman*)

One of Arnold's well-treasured photographs of his mother. BELOW: Fan and the aging Mrs. Mary Arnold in a typically Victorian portrait pose. (*Courtesy of Mrs. M. C. Moorman*)

Matthew Arnold, as a married School
Inspector. (*The Mansell Collection*)

Mrs. Matthew Arnold, the former Frances Lucy
Wightman. (*Courtesy of Mrs. M. C. Moorman*)

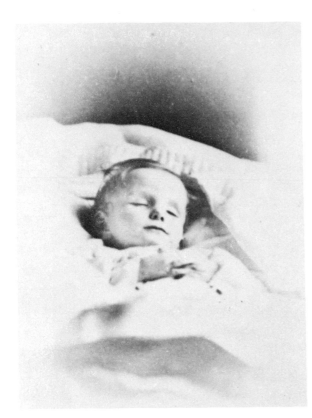

After sitting up half the night with him, Arnold to console Fanny Lucy had this photograph taken of their dead infant Basil, on January 4, 1868. BELOW: the Fox How drawing room in 1923 with Dr. Arnold's pictures and a likeness of Mrs. Mary Arnold on the walls. (*Courtesy of Mrs. M. C. Moorman*)

Matthew Arnold's daughters, Lucy and Nelly. (*Courtesy of Mrs. M. C. Moorman*)

Matthew Arnold, near the time of his first journey to the United States. (*BBC Hulton Picture Library*)

13

THE MAKING OF A POETRY PROFESSOR
1857–1862

> Buddha, of Magadha
> upadana—the cleaving to existing objects
> karma—action—the aggregate result of all
> previous acts, in former births, from the
> commencement of existence
> these cause new births . . .
>
> —*Arnold's Diary of 1860*

A RNOLD at thirty-four had won the elected Oxford Poetry Chair, founded in 1708. While still inspecting schools, he gave about three English lectures a year, over the next five years—and won reappointment at Oxford in 1862. Within a decade he became the leading critic of his age while practicing a *comparative* principle. Narrowness of mind, as he came to realize, is lethal in a scientific age. Criticism must be international, and may be of use against Philistine insularity. He was to teach that we must sympathize with remote cultures, and understand foreign ways of feeling to know ourselves. He would bring European sensibilities into *Essays in Criticism,* and ask in a report why England gives no training in "Hindustani" and "Malay" and "Chinese" and "Japanese."[1] He became England's first great comparative critic.

In May 1857, he felt relieved and happy. Even his father's old opponents voted for him: "Keble voted for me," he told his mother in triumph. "Archdeacon Denison voted for me . . . and Henley, of the high Tory party. It was an immense victory—some 200 more voted than ever before."[2]

Nowadays some 32,000 graduates are eligible to elect the Poetry Professor; few vote—and some ballots every five years are cast for film stars, chimpanzees, and even "the Vice-Chancellor." But bona fide poets such as W. H. Auden, Robert Graves, and Roy Fuller have all held the chair after Arnold, and when the novelist John Jones won the

Poetry Chair in 1978 (with 470 votes out of 1,498 cast) he wisely noted: "No one since Matthew Arnold has realised that the Chair of Poetry need not confine itself to English Poetry."[3]

Still, Matthew's lectures began badly, and became even worse. He reached Oxford after sitting up at dawn to write a talk—only to speak in a half-empty hall. Oxford threatened to fine him for giving too *few* talks, and many tutors noted his ignorance. He claimed that the Elizabethans were ornate, and cited Scott's *Kenilworth* as his proof; he even praised Periclean Athens as a time "of the most entire freedom,"[4] forgetting Greek slaves, the low status of Greek women, and the simple fact that in 440 B.C. only one in ten Athenians voted. But he carried ideas into a series of lectures entitled "On the Modern Element in Literature" (of which only the first talk and part of another survive), a series called "On Translating Homer," and yet a third series, "On the Study of Celtic Literature." In gaps in his schedule, he gave the pieces he revised for *Essays in Criticism,* and used his last Oxford lecture for the opening of *Culture and Anarchy.*

So far in life, he had looked for a positive, coherent ideal. In his "inaugural," he connects that search with his father. Speaking in the Sheldonian, Dr. Arnold in 1842 had cited "laws of history" when asking whether knowledge helps us to save a nation or whether we are, rather, "cursed with that bitter thing, a powerless knowledge, seeing an evil which we cannot escape." Dr. Arnold's last "great question" before he died involved the historical process. Can we influence our fate or do "laws of history" condemn the West to holocaust? We must not think, Dr. Arnold had said, "that in us or our actions is placed the turning power of the world,"[5] for we lack the intuition to control historical destiny—and cannot affect the nightmare of history.

Matthew's "On the Modern Element," this November, begins with his Empedoclean theme of a modern information explosion. Literature, he states, offers a mountaintop overview of an age's facts, and thus gives a large viewpoint on history. Like his father, he holds that history is cyclical, that Periclean Greece and Republican Rome teach us because those ages are "modern." But he adds that literature is an *illuminating force*, and recommends cultural comparativism—his central doctrine. "No single event," Matthew declares in a pompous style in November 1857,

> no single literature, is adequately comprehended except in its relation to other events, to other literatures. . . . 'We must compare.' . . . To know how others stand, that we may know how we ourselves stand; and to know how we ourselves stand, that we may correct our mistakes and achieve our deliverance—that is our problem.[6]

He illustrates very poorly from Greek and Roman poets. He cites Sophocles as a humanistic norm, but finds his *own* antisocial traits in Lucretius (whom he describes in terms borrowed from Coleridge's descriptions of Hamlet in *The Friend* and the second volume of *Literary Remains*); he even finds his own elegiac strain in Virgil, his own lack of "faith" in Horace. The Romans, he concludes, were not "adequate"[7] interpreters of their epochs.

Tutors who heard him were very unimpressed; they told students to avoid his talks. In some ways, Matthew *was* a dilettante straining to be professorial. He needed to discuss his critical details with friends, with whom he was out of touch. The only colleague he had befriended lately was a "mad" Inspector Laurie: "Be kind to him," he told Jane about this pop-eyed man. Poor Scottish Laurie had "nearly starved" before he became a School Inspector. "It is Dicky's birthday," Matthew explains to his sister again, "and we have to dine with us . . . our favourite Mr Laurie (mad, but excellent with children)."[8]

Tom Arnold, however, was back from Tasmania with a wife who was furious with him for becoming a Catholic. He was lonely enough to be a good audience. A remarkable letter sent to Tom this year is fascinating because it comes so early in Matthew's professorship, and displays his enthusiasm for ideas and real neglect of persons and nuances.

"How refreshing," he tells Tom excitedly in December 1857,

> it is to meet with any one who knows anything about any literary matter! . . . A great transformation in the intellectual nature of the English [is] inevitable. When this transformation comes the popularity of Wordsworth, Shelley, Coleridge, and others, remarkable men as they are, will not be the better for it. I am very much interested in what you say about Pope. I will read the "Essay on Criticism" again—certainly poetry was a power in England in his time—which it is not now. . . . You ask why is this. I think it is because Pope's poetry was *adequate,* (to use a term I am always using), to Pope's age—that is, it reflected completely the best general culture and intelligence of that age. . . . But it was a poor time. . . . Our *time* is a first class one—an infinitely fuller, richer age than Pope's; but our poetry is not *adequate* to it: it interests therefore only a small body of sectaries: hundreds of cultivated and intelligent men find nothing that speaks to themselves in it. . . . The eternal greatness of the literature of the Greece of Pericles is that it is the *adequate* expression of a first-class epoch. Shakespeare again, is the infinitely *more than adequate* expression of a *second class* epoch. It is the immense distinction of Voltaire and Goethe, with all their shortcomings, that they approach *near* to being adequate exponents of first-class epochs. . . . All this is the very matter debated in my inaugural lecture, & the debating of which will be continued in my two next.[9]

His mind typically seizes on a grand overall framework and a few, key phrases to come to terms with complex insights on art and history. But he hardly bothers to say why Shakespeare's epoch is "second class," or why reputations of "Shelley, Coleridge, and others" will plunge. "In literary matters," he assures Tom, "we may still have strong sympathy, —*Là, vous ne vous êtes pas cramponné à une légende morte.*—Admire my politeness in having recourse to French to say an uncivil thing. . . . always your most affectionate—M.A."[10] His uncivil French words attack Tom's Catholic faith—which had upset Tom's own sisters. Tom needed sympathy more than light mockery, and Matthew only derides him by saying that with literature he "won't be clinging to a dead legend." Lost in contemplating epochs of history and poetry (and failing to see very much in English romantic poetry), Matthew, at this point, was brash. Yet he was to become more aware of living qualities in religion and literature; he was to call Tom's Catholicism a promise of the religion of the future, and to become far better attuned to personalities, subtleties, and nuances of feeling as a critic.

Fanny Lucy helped him by declaring war on him. So far, he perhaps had heard from her very few, if any, negative comments on his poems; she probably withheld her fire after listening to his inflated inaugural speech. She did not withhold her fire forever. "Matt was always so earnest about the use of time, & the duty of *all* to be up & doing," recalled Fanny Lucy, who lay in bed mornings partly because she was efficient in the household. Matthew's "earnest" anxiety to succeed at Oxford was what hindered him now. He headed towards empty halls: "Hardly any undergraduates," he notes after talking in the Sheldonian again, "and the theatre was, to me, depressingly too big." One aspect of the empty bigness which, perhaps, should have cheered him more than it did, was that he could see his wife. She was one of his more discerning listeners—sitting in her assured, neat, compact delicacy of being whether or not she smiled behind a light veil. What seems to have been disconcerting was that she could think, criticize, and judge his texts and delivery. We know from remarks to his mother, and these are confirmed by Fanny Lucy's letters to Annie Fields and Sarah Orne Jewett, that Matthew's wife was very sensitive to lecturers and audiences. She seems to have told him that his earnest desire to dazzle the Oxford crowd kept him from being simple enough to move anyone. He was too obsessed, too ready to let a preparation swallow him; even after he relaxed, Fanny Lucy was ironic about his preparations: "Matt up to his eyes with his lecture," she records tersely, or "Matt up at 3 A.M. to finish his lecture which he did by 6." Did the man mean to kill himself? What *she* looked for in humanity was what she called "*understanding* sympathy," or sane feeling with comprehending intelligence; and this attitude she applied to audiences, since a "very good" audience in her view would be intelligently "attentive" and "most appreciate and sympathetic." If these qualities seemed missing in an audience, the intelligence of the lecturer was at fault.[11] There was good sense in her view: the cheerful wisdom of a father, who, irascible as he might be at trials, always loved Fielding's *Tom Jones,* had descended to a daughter who tried to make Arnold love Austen's *Emma* and *Persuasion.* She attacked Arnold for doing very little in his lectures to arouse "*understanding* sympathy."

Arnold told his mother that "Flu" disliked his second lecture, and he destroyed the text. Fanny Lucy did not learn to be quiet; she knew a good High Church sermon when she heard one. Were not his auditors men of intellect and of *some* feeling, too? Of what use is stiff, arrogant, bold, and sweeping brilliance if it never affects people? Arnold heard her, and only slowly took in the central theme of her crossfire: that he must relax, be himself, strive not to impress Oxford men, but rather to use a natural voice and manner. Of his third Oxford lecture, nothing at all survives. "How difficult it is to write prose," he had fretted, "and why? because of the *articulations of the discourse:* one leaps over these in Poetry—places one thought with another cheek by jowl without introducing them. . . ."[12]

He slid back into old obsessions. His wife's comments may have reminded him of his father's very natural, terse manner. Yet Dr. Arnold was exceptional. Matthew could not lightly shuffle off his career as a poet, or find a style that was not either his clever undergraduate manner or the bluff style of a "doctor." Vexed and irritable, he planned a piece on "Dante, the troubadours, and the early Drama" in relation to "the origin of what is called the 'romantic' sentiment about women, which the Germans quite falsely are fond of giving themselves the credit of originating."[13] That topic suggests his fear of sentimentalism—and just that self-mistrusting impulse which had led him, in the *first* lecture, to dismiss Roman poets of feeling as "not adequate." Deeply at war with old impulses, he was tense, nervous, self-absorbed, and far from his father's honest clarity.

His life was easier in 1858. He had paid off debts. Relieved to have a smaller school district, he rented a house at 2 Chester Square in London, where for the first time in seven years he fully unpacked. Fanny Lucy sighed with relief to be near the Wightmans at 38 Eaton Place, even if her husband now made a fool of himself at soirées. "Saw Matthew Arnold," writes the sculptor Thomas Woolner in March. "He was a regular swell, in brilliant kid gloves, glittering boots, and costume cut in most perfect fashion."[14] Chatting with the poet

Coventry Patmore, that night, the "high Oxford don"—as the sculptor facetiously called him—was aware that his father was again in the limelight.

Tom Hughes, the old Rugbeian, had in 1857 published *Tom Brown's Schooldays,* a sentimental novel of Dr. Arnold's Rugby. It was reviewed by James Fitzjames Stephen—a son of the Colonial Secretary (and uncle to Virginia Woolf). This Stephen was a handsome iconoclast with a fair beard—a busy, efficient man, who in a four-year period wrote 852 articles for *Pall Mall Gazette* while working full time at the law. Matthew saw in his review of *Tom Brown* a hint that Dr. Arnold had been a "narrow bustling fanatic," and after a delay wrote "Rugby Chapel," in reply to Stephen. "Blots existed in his character and administration," Matthew admitted about Dr. Arnold, "but [Stephen's] review does not hit them, and invents for him a physiognomy which no one who had ever seen him would recognize."[15]

In a poem of bolero-like rhythms, the Headmaster now appears as a guide who saves the whole "host of mankind" in a wasteland. Dr. Arnold is seen from a boy's viewpoint; and Willy or Widu's way of depicting Rugby athletes—"all eager, courageous, zealous"[16]—enters into Matthew's own style. What redeems the poem is its sketch of two kinds of work. Most workers are simply forgotten,

> *and no one asks*
> *Who or what they have been,*
> *More than he asks what waves,*
> *In the moonlit solitudes mild*
> *Of the midmost Ocean, have swelled,*
> *Foamed for a moment, and gone.*[17]

But some souls work in a manner linked with a school field, the few boys "late at their play," and the radiant Dr. Arnold. These workers have detachment, self-sufficiency, even a sense of play—qualities that may appear in a man's tone: "At your voice/Panic, despair, flee away."[18] Our social march to the City of God, or to a humane society, will be led, perhaps, by cheerful, objective thinkers and doers.

"Rugby Chapel," a check on Matthew's Hamletism and discouragement, links his familial tendencies with an element of play and drama in his outlook. He planned the poem while marching twice a week with militia; he joined Westminster Rifle Volunteers, during a crisis in British relations with Napoleon III.

He needed the therapy of parties and soldiering. He still felt the dull, heavy monotony of inspecting, and when depressed by work he found bitter crises at home. "We thought he would not live through the day," he writes of Tommy, late in 1858. That day, his son was treated with "hot pomentations to the chest"—and Matthew sat with the pale rasping boy "until the darling fell into a doze with his arm round my neck fondling my hair." Arnold had dismissed a strict nursemaid and hired a fat, Irish nurse, "Tuffy" or Mrs. Tuffin, who happily talks of "soldiers—her husband having been a dragoon."[19]

When out of the wintry blue, in January 1859, he read a note from Fitzjames Stephen about a mission abroad, he thought of taking his family to Paris. He enthused over this idea to Fanny Lucy. Under the Duke of Newcastle, a Royal Commission meant to report *"what Measures, if any, are required for the Extension of sound and cheap elementary Instruction to all Classes of the People."*[20] Clearly, the Newcastle Commission wanted to quiet Parliament's uproar over the *cost* of schools. In the education office, Lingen tried to bar as Commissioners all men who were not penny-pinching: "such men are deaf," he wrote, "to everything but the cry for higher grants."[21] Goldwin Smith, Edward Miall, and William Lake among others would look at home schools; Mark Pattison was going to Germany; and Matthew Arnold—who, it was felt, would give the Commission tone—was asked to see primary schools in France, the French cantons of Switzerland, and Holland.

He gladly agreed to go, and persuaded his wife to prepare for a journey. Abroad, he was to collect data for *England and the Italian Question, Popular Education of France, A French Eton*—and meet men such as Renan, Sainte-Beuve, Guizot, and Cousin, whose books he knew. Further, he was to be helped by polished insiders who knew French schools, Villemain and Alfred Magin, Duc de Broglie and Jean-Jacques Rapet. One evening at Sorèze he would even meet Lacordaire—and later find the key notion of a powerful state, and a transformed, awakened middle class.

"I like the errand," Matthew decided. "You know," he told Jane, "I have no special interest in the subject of public education, but a mission like this appeals. . . . I shall for five months get free from the routine work . . . of which I sometimes get very sick. . . . Then foreign life is still to me perfectly delightful, and *liberating*."[22] Liberated after giving his fifth Oxford lecture, he reached Hôtel Meurice, at Paris, on March 16. Three days later he was joined by his wife and Tuffy with the baby Lucy—and the babbling, excited Tommy, Budge, and Dicky.

A *"liberating"* life darkened. Tommy developed a fever. Their rooms overlooking Rue de Rivoli and the Tuileries became hot and clammy with a hospital air as a grave, fuddled doctor called. *"Pauvre chat,"* he would say, looking at Tommy. Bills horribly soared; money vanished. "I am being ruined," cried Arnold, "as our bill here averages about 500 Fr. (£20) a *week*, exclusive of all incidental expenses. . . . My total

receipts from the Commission amount to only £18 a week." He fell ill
with acute bronchitis ("which it takes a good deal to give me") and his
wife felt desperate in the prison-like rooms. "I have had little heart for
writing," he admits in a letter about Tommy's "congestion of the lungs"
which is "complicating his disease of the heart." The poor boy moaned
and tossed at night: "He, Flu, and I," writes Matthew grimly, sleep in
one French bed and it is "rather warm work."[23] He got two or three
hours' sleep only by slipping away in the dark. But when Tommy was
at lowest ebb, he slowly improved; one morning he was "certainly
better," and that cool evening, "wonderfully better." Relieved, Arnold
was now able to go about Paris to see Cousin and Guizot. Invited by the
British Ambassador, he met Ernest Renan and then Prosper Merimée;
and he found especially in M. Rapet, a school inspector and author of
educational works, a shrewd little guide to "French schools and the
practical working of their system."[24] He nearly forgot money problems:
one night he and Flu dined at the Trois Frères, and later saw at the
Variétés a flamboyant sexual skit on Michelet's *L'Amour.*

Then on April 12 he received an unexpected telegram about his
brother Willy: "DANGEREUSEMENT MALADE." Willy had lost his wife
Frances, and their children were then coming back from India. On his
own return voyage, Willy had been carried off a ship at Gibraltar. On
the thirteenth, M. Rapet happened to call at the hotel. As they were
leaving together, Matthew was handed a letter from his sister Susan
and later he recorded with shock: "Susy's letter—'Dear Willy died at
San Rogue'!"[25]

Thus it was—with news of his brother's death and with his son
barely well and hard work ahead—that he began the most stimulating
few months in all his years as an Inspector.

In a note to his mother about Willy, he admits he has undervalued
that brother, and failed in "tenderness."[26] Willy had written a novel,
Oakfield, about his Eastern experiences and after being invalided
home had returned to India to organize schools in the Punjab. Neither
his wife's death nor the Indian mutiny had prevented him from
working even as his health failed. His four orphans with their "frail
ethereal looks" were to be adopted by the William Forsters—and at the
early age of thirty-one, he lay dead at Gibraltar.

When Tommy improved, Fanny Lucy and Tuffy took the children
back to England. Matthew, alone with his memories and a feeling of
remorse over his coldness with Willy, entrained for Brittany and eight
days of school appointments. Everything reminded him of his family:
even the features of the Bretons were like his brother Tom's, and the
names of small towns might have been litanies on his own "Budge" or
Trevenen:

Trevignon
Tremorvezen
Trevannec
Treve

From Auray on May 6, he visited the prehistoric stones at Carnac, where he wrote with a certain numb stoicism his "Stanzas from Carnac." The poem has a bland, sunlit emptiness—

> *I climbed; beneath me, bright and wide,*
> *Lay the lone coast of Brittany.*
>
> *Bright in the sunset, weird and still, . . .*
> *Bearded with lichen, scrawled and grey,*
> *The giant stones of Carnac sleep,*
> *In the mild evening of the May. . . .*
>
> *From bush to bush the cuckoo flies,*
> *The orchis red gleams everywhere.*[27]

The one pitiless universal is death—*the orchis red gleams everywhere*. Willy lies at Gibraltar and no myth or idea either accounts for his loss, or consoles the heart: "No Druids bow"[28] in reverent ceremony at Carnac where sheep nibble among gaunt, gray stones. Yet after seeing Renan again and reading his *Essais de Morale et de Critique*, Matthew did use, in a later poem, Renan's myth about the voyager Saint Brandan of Galway. Sailing for a Land of Saints, Brandan found Judas in the polar sea. In Arnold's "Saint Brandan," it is Christ's betrayer —released once a year from a "pit of fire" for having aided a leper—who instructs an Irish saint:

> *'That germ of kindness, in the womb,*
> *Of mercy caught, did not expire;*
> *Outlives my guilt, outlives my doom,*
> *And friends me in the pit of fire.'*[29]

The "pit of fire" suggests a deep vein of guilt in Arnold's elder-brotherism or his rivalry with siblings, in his tendency to love and hate those who came between himself and his mother. He could not fathom himself, or explain *why* he had failed in "tenderness." Written in southern France this May his formal elegy on Willy, "A Southern Night," concerns his own perplexity. He repeats an Empedoclean idea: each man is astray and out of touch with the soul's depth. His own normally blind, jealous view of rivals, his need for fame, his rush to succeed have left him without self-knowledge. And in this, he is British:

> *In cities should we English lie,*
> *Where cries are rising ever new,*

> *And man's incessant stream goes by—*
> *We who pursue*
>
> *Our business with unslackening stride . . .*
>
> *And see all sights from pole to pole*
> *And glance, and nod, and bustle by,*
> *And never once possess our soul*
> *Before we die.*[30]

The English mind is hopelessly divided from its essence or soul. This is the nugget from lyric fire that he repeats in brief poems for the rest of his life. His awareness of his own lack of perfect self-understanding did not diminish; and that awareness becomes a talisman which he keeps by him.

He echoes the theme of self-ignorance, for example, in "Palladium," where man's soul resembles that cool image of Pallas which Trojans kept to guarantee their city's safety. We see the Palladium rarely, and like Hector fight blindly on life's plain:

> *We shall renew the battle in the plain*
> *To-morrow; red with blood will Xanthus be;*
> *Hector and Ajax will be there again,*
> *Helen will come upon the wall to see.*
>
> *Then we shall rust in shade, or shine in strife,*
> *And fluctuate 'twixt blind hopes and blind despairs,*
> *And fancy that we put forth all our life,*
> *And never know how with the soul it fares.*[31]

And never know how with the soul it fares. The theme recurs in "Growing Old," "Pis-Aller," "Rome-Sickness," in "Epilogue to Lessing's 'Laocoön,' " and even in that threnody on a canary with a name like Matthew's own, "Poor Matthias":

> *Birds, companions more unknown,*
> *Live beside us, but alone; . . .*
> *No, away with tales like these*
> *Stolen from Aristophanes! . . .*
> *What you feel, escapes our ken—*
> *Know we more our fellow men?*[32]

His poetry clearly dies with this theme—but the theme helps to vitalize his prose, and keeps him from resting with any one doctrine, any one world outlook, any one set, fixed answer to social problems.

The intense theme in "A Southern Night" is interestingly related to new attitudes to poetry, truth, and society forming in his mind this summer. If the truth of self can never be known, then *all* epistemologies are suspect and most questions demand a plurality of approaches. "To try and approach truth on one side after another," he argues a little later, and "not to persist in pressing forward, on any one side, with violence and self-will—it is only thus" that we see the Goddess of Truth in outline, "but only thus even in outline."[33] Genuine truths about life appear to lie in interanimating polar oppositions such as his "Hebraism and Hellenism" and even "Culture and Anarchy." If we fluctuate between "blind hopes and blind despairs," then literature has an enlightening value, since it *touches* the deepest level of human experience. In this way poetry finely interprets, makes life the whole subject of its interpreting, and is "a criticism of life." If we deny the value of poetry, we lose one of the most efficacious means of understanding human nature we have; yet poetry *as a way of knowing* does not rival anything else—but supplements what we learn, of life and man, from religion and the sciences.

He became less dogmatic and more open to plural values and observable facts, even this spring and summer. When on May 13 he forced the French inspectors to let him choose a school to see, he began like Tocqueville and Burke to look for the reason of things in society. The French bureaucracy had planned his tour and he had gone from school to school, thinking about Willy and finding relief in the gossip of soldiers and others who talked of war. (Waging her easy campaigns against Austria, France was embroiled in the Italian provinces in 1859.)

Now, in an inspectors' office in Bordeaux, he demanded a chance to *select* a French school. "A map of the department [of the Gironde] hung upon the wall, and they told me to choose where I would." Arnold chose the village of Blanquefort, for its association with "mediaeval wars" and campaigns of the Black Prince. Then he went out to a high, sunny region with large, silent fields of vineyards and strawberries and in a dusty village school entered a classroom under a drooping banner and observed the pupils:

> Many are absent . . . (just the old story in England), for field labour; but the field labour of Medoc, not of England—to clear the vineyards of snails and caterpillars, and to gather the strawberry harvest. . . . The highest class was reading a lesson on the ostrich, similar to the lessons on natural history in the third Irish reading-book. . . . Their writing was such as in an English school an inspector would describe as very fair.[34]

For the first time, he drew detailed contrasts between a French and an English school; he was becoming a comparative social critic. A few days later he seemed to cross the border of life itself: he was paid to visit state-run primary schools—not Catholic colleges—but from the Papal Nuncio, at Paris, he had asked for permission to see the man who revived the medieval Dominican order in France. Editor, preacher, and controversialist, Lacordaire had sacrificed his career to run a boys' small *collège* at Sorèze.

The book which reports Arnold's meeting, *A French Eton,* is perhaps the most forceful and cogent book on schools he ever wrote. He knew of odd coincidences involving Lacordaire, who had raised the number of enrolled boys at Sorèze up to 300 (as Dr. Arnold had at Rugby). Arnold notes that Lacordaire desired to "form Christians" and "placed character above everything else" and, unlike many teachers, believed so strongly in freedom he devolved authority upon boys. While asking for "firm order, solid government," he yet resorted so often to expulsion of unfit pupils as "to alarm people." After describing him, Matthew refers to "my father."[35]

His visit took him emotionally into his father's presence; Matthew was divided from his family, troubled by Tom's Catholicism, still agonized by Willy's loss. His yearning for the European past was greatest when he was alone on the Continent; it is his intense feeling for the past that enriches most of his comments on the present in *Culture and Anarchy* and helps him to know the meaning of cultural tradition. From Toulouse, one day, he arrived at an "old Visigoth place," on a bare, windswept hill. He waited for a small coach that took him across the bleak Montaigne Noire: "The air, even on the 18th of May in Languedoc, was sharp, the vast distance looked grey and chill, and the whole landscape was severe, lonely, and desolate." He noticed that Father Lacordaire's Sorèze lay "on the other side"[36] of dark mountains—and in the evening he came to a slanting, tree-lined lane.

Then he stopped at a Dominican abbey, founded eight centuries after Christ. The light had faded. "I waited," Matthew recalled, "in the monastic-looking court." At last he heard that a famous schoolmaster in France had consented to see him. He was shown, without lights, across an old, worn courtway, and in silence "up an old stone staircase, into a vast corridor; a door in this corridor was thrown open, and in a large bare room, with no carpet or furniture of any kind, except a small table, one or two chairs, a small bookcase, a crucifix, and some religious pictures on the walls, Lacordaire, in the dress of his order, white-robed, hooded, and sandalled, sat before me."

In the darkness he could not, at first, see either the objects in the room or the shadowy face of the hooded man, who asked about "Oxford."[37] A minute or two passed before "lights came." Arnold was very moved; and his emotion finds its way into *A French Eton,* which confuses Lacordaire with his recollection of Dr. Arnold. Both men gave their lives to small, special schools. Both had a largesse of social commitment, and wanted society to "*transform itself.*" Writing *Eton* after Lacordaire's death, Arnold identifies his own social mission at home: to guide the British middle classes to a much less insular, more seeking and open mental outlook. "Very likely," he argues, "France is to be pitied for having no Etons," but does England have schools for her middle classes so good "as the Toulouse Lyceum and the Sorèze College? That is the question."³⁸ His father, and more shadowily Lacordaire, stand behind his argument that by empowering a strong authority (the state) England may have such a fair, workable school system as France.

Lacordaire, that night, led him round the college. He saw the *Salle d'Illustres* with the bust of Henri de Larochejaquelein, in "his Vendean hat, and the heart and cross on his breast," who died at twenty-three in a rebellion against the government in 1793. Having seen the busts of the school martyrs, he followed Lacordaire to chapel. "Scarcely a Sunday passed," Matthew wrote of him, "without his preaching in chapel."³⁹

Parting with the schoolmaster after prayers, he went rather dejectedly to an inn, where he fell in with "old boys" of Sorèze. With elation, Matthew drank blackish wine. "Much *vin de Cahors* we drank, and great friends we became," he observed of the tipsy scholars—one of whom swore "(God forgive him!)" that he knew the poems of Arnold almost by heart.⁴⁰ Then at dawn he was in a slow, freezing coach and moving over blue and gray mists of the lovely Cevennes ranges, having seen for the last time the face of Lacordaire.

After that, his brief journeys in Holland and Switzerland had to be prosy and anticlimatic. The Dutch seemed on the whole sluggish (perhaps because they didn't wave French flags); but the Dutch word *Christelijke* (or humanely Christian) struck him as admirable in school law, purged as it was of "theological subtleties" that only divide a people.⁴¹ The very broad Dutch meaning of "Christian" influenced *Literature and Dogma*—where it consorts with Spinoza's ideas. With schools on holiday in Switzerland, he tried to find out if compulsory education was enforced in the cantons and worded his report so oddly that it was misconstrued, a little willfully, by his superiors.

In the Alps, he could hardly take his mind off France's war with Austria, or forget the gossip he had heard about Napoleon III from Guizot, and the British Ambassador Lord Cowley, at Paris. Even on trains, he had heard about the pure intentions of the French Emperor, and purer intentions of the army. If Austria occupied Italy, the aim of the French must be to thrash the Austrians for the sake of *liberté*. He began to believe in the goodness, if not the strength, of Napoleon III—who had pledged to free Italy of all Austrians, "from the Alps to the Adriatic."

"I shall put together a pamphlet," Arnold wrote home on June 25.

And a fortnight later, "How interesting are public affairs! I really think I shall finish and bring out my pamphlet. . . . I hope the Emperor does not mean to stop before the Austrians are out of Venice."[42]

Alas! even before *England and the Italian Question* appeared under Longmans imprint in London at the end of July 1859, he had noticed that Napoleon, at Villafranca, had ensured Austria would remain a power in Italy. Arnold weakly defends Napoleon in the pamphlet, but also argues reasonably that Englishmen have been unaware of civic progress in France for the past fifty years. His piece is a first draft for *Popular Education of France,* even if it portrays Napoleon III as an Englishman in epaulettes.

His foray into political writing is naïve—but he had found a talent for controversy in the act of defending France. He would need to master his silly, dangerous, romantic trust in the goodness of soldiers, a superficial residue of his trust in a militant father—from whom he dissociates himself at last in the autobiographical "Celtic" essays. But the *Italian Question* did him no harm with French friends when, in a high mood, he returned to Paris in August to work on his Newcastle notes. He stayed with Le Comte Adolphe de Circourt and his wife, who kept a literary salon and were to send Leo Tolstoi to see him in London. His cultivated hosts read Arnold's pamphlet aloud. Villemain, a former education minister, introduced the pamphleteer to a friend as one "who judges us perfectly."[43] In giving a French viewpoint on the war, the pamphlet helped foster an Anglo-French cultural dialogue—which Arnold's works in general abetted.

Moreover, his foray into politics delighted Sainte-Beuve, to whom he had sent a copy of his *Poems* with "Sohrab and Rustum" and a letter, in January 1854, naming him as Goethe's true successor. Even by then, Sainte-Beuve had led several lives—he had written poems and a novel, seduced Madame Victor Hugo and given up poetry, listened to George Sand and befriended Flaubert and a wide range of French geniuses. He had begun his fine "Lundi" or Monday biographical and critical essays for the Paris *Constitutionnel,* which Arnold gratefully read as reprinted in *Causeries du lundi* (1851–62) and *Nouveaux lundis* (1863–70). Embarrassed to be called by Arnold "the sole hope of those who love above all else the truth in the arts," he translated the Obermann "Stanzas" into French and called Matthew in print a Briton "whose talent combines simplicity with passion."[44]

With his bonhomie and Parisian finesse, his love of gossip and fondness for taking street girls back to grubby rooms in the rue de Montparnasse, Sainte-Beuve quite enjoyed British candor. Arnold delighted in his gossip and fund of stories about famous sexual affairs. One evening after dining together, Sainte-Beuve showed him the letters Musset and George Sand had sent him during their love affair, explaining gustily "all the evil they say about each other is true!" Matthew was much amused. "De Musset's letters were, I must say, those of a *gentleman*," he told Fanny Lucy.[45]

Sainte-Beuve in daily life was a truckling, rather absurd little gossip; but as a critic, as Matthew noticed, he wrote as "a man discharging with delight the very office for which he was born."[46] His *Causeries* suggested how one might set critical abstractions in warm, humane biographical contexts while using wit and irony to advantage. The Frenchman's crass idea of poetry and neglect of the ideas of romanticism, on the other hand, did Arnold little good. "He it was," wrote Sainte-Beuve very typically,

> one who knows what he was talking about [namely Goethe], who so justly said: "by classic I understand sound, and by romantic, sickly." . . . Classical literature never complains, never groans. . . . Romanticism, like Hamlet, has home-sickness, it seeks for what it has not, seeks it even beyond the clouds; it dreams, it sees in visions. In the nineteenth century it adores the Middle Ages. . . . Chrysostom's young friend Stagirius, or Augustine in his youth, were of this kind, Renés before their time. . . . Hamlet, Werther, Childe Harold, the true Renés, are sick men of the kind who sing and suffer, who enjoy their malady —romantics more or less in a dilettante way; they are sick for sickness' sake.[47]

That comment on Hamlet-worship seems clever and shallow; but Arnold forgave the Philistinism in Sainte-Beuve—who taught him a lightness of manner and easily earned a place in a pantheon of writers from whom he learned "habits, methods, ruling ideas." In 1872, Arnold named four in this pantheon as John Henry Newman, Goethe, Wordsworth, and Sainte-Beuve.[48] Another prime five were his father, Epictetus, Spinoza, Voltaire, Edmund Burke. But it must be said that Arnold was nobody's disciple, for he defined aspects of what he could believe in the light of his understanding of other writers too—from Sophocles, Plato, and the Hebrew prophets to Montaigne, Pascal, Montesquieu and Vauvenargues, and on into modern realms. Matthew's careful reading lists are culled not only from Hebrew, Greek and Latin, but from Italian, French, German, and English sources; he had read much, of late, in Buddhist and Hindu texts and manuals. He knew Moslem works. He still pored over *Revue des Deux Mondes* and *Revue germanique et français*, and extracted opinions from every Renan or Villemain he met. He had never given up the ranging intellectual habits of Oriel days—and his reading was to give immense authority to his force as a critic. Sainte-Beuve helped him to move freely among his bookish discoveries, and modified his Hamletism.

Before leaving Paris he attended an open session of the French

Academy; and then he was back in England with Fanny Lucy, the children, and too many notes on schools. He failed to begin a report. In December with not a word written, he dreamed yearningly of Paris and of Guizot and Cousin as if those spirits might help him to write. "I don't much think I shall go," Matthew sighed.[49] Then after a week in the British Museum, he cleared a table at Chester Square and wrote rapidly. His report appeared in March 1860 as "Strictly Confidential," and a year later as Volume IV of the Newcastle Reports and at his own risk with Longmans as *The Popular Education of France with Notices of Holland and Switzerland.*

Written with some of the wonder of *Gulliver's Travels,* the readable book is a model of lucidity. If you accept Arnold's facts, you accept his tight argument that Britain needs something like the French municipal organization and that whereas France has a school system, England has chaos. He admits that his search for facts met with rebuffs. When asked to say what the 1789 Revolution gave education, François Guizot had replied: "A deluge of words, nothing else."[50] But the facts he gathered give him insight for some unusual comparisons. In a passage overlooked by modern critics Arnold explains, for example, that book-loving Prussians are enfeebled by pedantry. It is *not* learning but "crude primitive vigour" that is the force of nations —and *not* their reading but their "*constitutional preference for the animal over the intellectual life*" that is the good strength of England and France.[51] Because he is assured of the primitive sensuous quality in the English (which may save them from tolerating too much state control) he can recommend to them later Swift's "sweetness and light." He has not seen America, but has met enough Americans to believe they suffer from crude vanity: Prussia and America help to define his England—which suffers from anarchy of individualism and laissez faire. He demands a balance of national attributes and, in this work, spells out the idea that we correct tragic or lethal errors by comparing our nation with foreign cultures.

In a preface later called "Democracy," he replies to Miss Martineau's remarks about his slighting of Protestant Dissent in the original report. Harriet had criticized his text, up at Ambleside, and stimulated social ideas. Arnold now surveys his England: Parliament is being transformed from an aristocratic to a democratic body and industrialism generates class-consciousness—so that workers desert the Anglican Church of the governing classes for Miss Martineau's Dissenting churches. Religion is political by 1860. But what is society? Borrowing from Renan, Tocqueville, and especially from Burke's *Reflections on the Revolution in France,* Arnold holds that society is a timeless partnership in all science, in all art and "virtue," and that the state—which is the people in a *"collective and corporate character"*[52] —is the prime unifying force in a modern nation.

He does not swallow Edmund Burke whole. That enemy of Tom Paine and of revolutions had upheld social classes, and an idea of economic inequality. Arnold satirizes the class system in *Culture and Anarchy* and in his essay on "Equality" argues for propertied equality. He rejected "class" as a positive factor, though he referred to classes, and especially to a "middle class" of bankers, barristers, architects, engineers, and other entrepreneurs and professional people as those newly in power. It was this bourgeois class for whom he wrote; this class, which might lead England to a new life of culture. The lower class should be our first object of interest, he admitted to Richard Cobden, in 1864,

> but one must look, as Burke says, for a *power* or *purchase* to help one in dealing with such matters [as aiding the poor], and I find it nowhere but in an improved middle class.[53]

"Democracy" contains a nostalgic lament for the decline of an aristocratic power; but having lamented the Lord Lansdownes of his day, Arnold pleads for "collective action."[54] As a funeral oration on an aristocratic laissez faire ethos, the essay neatly introduces *Popular Education of France*—itself a plea for communal action in England.

Selling about 300 copies, the book failed to meet its own costs: Longmans sent him a bill for £80.16.4—and he *paid out* more than the total sum he had earned in thirteen years as an author.

He might perhaps have despaired. At Oxford, his lectures had gone so very badly that he was shifted to the humble, mote-filled "Taylor Institution"; but there on November 30, 1860, he took up the topic of translating Homer. At his second Homer talk there were fewer empty seats, and at his third, he was surprisingly cheered. *On Translating Homer: Three Lectures* duly appeared early in 1861. In these pieces he ridiculed a feebly correct version of the *Iliad* by his old *bête noire*, Francis Newman, then Professor of Latin at University College. When Newman wrote a 104-page pamphlet on *Homeric Translation in Theory and Practice: A Reply to Matthew Arnold, Esq.*, Arnold responded with "Last Words" on Homer in November 1861. Written when he was grieving over Clough's death, "Last Words" was his best lecture to date.

The Homer talks released his critical talent with the rush of a spring flood—and like most floods they lack moderation. They prove that it may be wise to press conclusions to near absurdities, to indulge one's whims as well as one's insights to find one's style and method. They are grand pieces of theatre, shrewdly, hilariously witty. Oxford loves erudition when it is mixed with the blood of pedants and Arnold was a verbal prizefighter. He quoted a hideous example of Francis Newman's translation of Homer's *Iliad,*

> *Chestnut, why bodest death to me? from thee this was not needed,*
> *Myself right, surely know also, that 't is my doom to perish,*

and took up the corpse of Newman to batter it rhythmically: "To bad practice he has prefixed the bad theory which made the practice bad: he has given us a false theory in his preface, and has exemplified the bad effects of that false theory in his translation. It is because his starting-point is so bad that he runs so badly. . . ."[55]

He was surprised, and slightly hurt, that Francis Newman took this amiss in the *Reply;* but Arnold never attacked an enemy who was incapable of hitting back. Newman's defense of his Homer translation was long, angry, and diffuse; and this offered Arnold a grand opportunity to discuss, in *On Translating Homer: Last Words,* the nature of criticism itself.

In "Last Words," Arnold is at once controlled, entertaining, and profound. He himself shows the temperament of the ideal critic—not so sharp with fools as to avoid urbanity, not so clever as to make art simple. He remembers Wordsworth's "disinterested imagination," and Glanvill's idea of the totally free, intuitive sensibility. He regrets his earlier "vivacities of expression" which troubled Francis Newman. "Well," adds Matthew,

> the demon that pushes us all to our ruin is even now prompting me to follow Mr. Newman. . . . And he ends by saying that my ignorance is great. Alas! that is very true. . . . [I wish] my ignorance were even greater. [In criticism] there is needed a poise so perfect that the least overweight in any direction tends to destroy the balance. . . . Erudition may destroy it. To press to the sense of the thing itself with which one is here dealing, not to go off on some collateral issue about the thing, is the hardest matter in the world. The "thing itself" with which one is here dealing,—the critical perception of poetic truth,—is of all things the most volatile, elusive, and evanescent; by even pressing too impetuously after it, one runs the risk of losing it. The critic of poetry should have the finest tact, the nicest moderation, the most free, flexible, and elastic spirit imaginable; he should be . . . the *undulating and diverse* being. . . . The less he can deal with his object simply and freely, the more things he has to take into account in dealing with it,—the more, in short, he has to encumber himself,—so much the greater force of spirit he needs to retain his elasticity.[56]

His picture was subtle and true. In proposing what the critical sensibility might be, he began to fashion the voices of later critics of literature and society such as Eliot and Richards, Leavis, Tillotson and Wilson Knight, Trilling and Tate and Blackmur and Ransom, or the more recent voices (to cite very different examples) of Northrop Frye in *Anatomy of Criticism,* Iris Murdoch in *The Sovereignty of Good,* or Raymond Williams in *Culture and Society* and his later books. Inevitably some of those most influenced by his methods will misconstrue his ideas; if Arnold in spirit is the father of modern critics, he has at times been treated with willful blindness by his children. The errant children, in turn, might note what can really be held against him thus far—his misjudgments of Virgil and Lucretius in "The Modern Element," and of Tennyson and Shakespeare in "Homer." His practical criticism was uncertain in 1861, but our debt to his thought about what criticism *is* begins with his "Last Words," written in the autumn after he had heard of Arthur Clough's death.

Despite rhetorical blunders, Homer in translation was for him an ideal topic—ancient and modern, surrounded by the pedantry from which he neatly rescued it. He fixes Homer in a glittering four-pointed star (Homer is *rapid, plain, simple,* and *noble*) and raises the star aloft to move under it almost too easily. As his topic is style, he attacks Shakespeare for including in each tragedy some of the worst style of all ("the affected style").[57] As his territory is translation of the *relation* between literary languages, he criticizes recent English literature for provincialism. Viewed as a living intellectual instrument, the literature of England ranks after "the literature of France and Germany," he contends. In Europe like a rising tide the modern effort has been "a *critical* effort"—the endeavor to see the world in the light of those revolutionary changes that ended medievalism and to hold and view in the disciplines of philosophy, history, theology, art, and science, "the object as in itself it really is."[58] Arnold seeks that clear, detached, easy and free view of reality that he finds in the best thought of Europe.

As for Francis Newman, whose treatise on *The Soul* epitomized the glibness of modern clergymen, he had done with him. Clough praised that man—though he never printed the review in which he hailed Francis Newman at the expense of Dr. Arnold.

Of Arthur Clough's ailments, of his nervous depression and scarletina and fits of neuralgia, Matthew had heard a little. He knew of his sick leave from the Council Office—but nothing of strange anxieties and compulsions besetting that friend. Clough had become bald and portly, with a massive white face. At forty-two in 1861, he had impressed a stranger as a neatly dressed and soft-spoken "man of business, a poet-banker or publisher," badly misplaced "behind a desk." Gentle "as a woman can be" with his sensitive mouth and dreamy eye, Clough seemed lost in an "arcanum of thought," or some curious "life beyond the actual life, into which he withdrew, and out of which he came to speak." He recovered his creativity at the last, for he was writing his *Mari-Magno* poems when he wandered about France by himself in the summer of 1861. In failing health, he thought of Italy. Having met his wife at Paris, he traveled "up the Rhône valley and over the Simplon." At Bologna, he had an attack of neuralgia. He and his wife pressed on to Florence by October 10. A few days later, he suffered a stroke: what was called his "low malarial fever" was succeeded quickly by symptoms of paralysis, first in the eye and one leg and then in the lungs. Arthur died at Florence on November 13 and was buried under cypresses in the Protestant Cemetery.[59]

Matthew could say little of him this year. In "Thyrsis: A Monody," printed five years later in *Macmillan's Magazine*, he at first sees Clough in terms of mutability and loss. He revisits the Hinkseys:

> *In the two Hinkseys nothing keeps the same;*
> *The village street its haunted mansion lacks,*
> *And from the sign is gone Sibylla's name.*[60]

Sybella Curr of the Cross Keys Inn had died by 1866. Yet the poet in "Thyrsis" stations himself one evening in the hills above an unchanging city:

> *Lovely all times she lies, lovely to-night!*

Behind him is the elm tree he and Clough had prized. It is a sign of the Scholar-Gipsy's imagined life and a symbol of symbols, suggesting all insights and artistic images he and Clough had ever sought. He accuses Clough now of having left Oxford too soon, of abandoning a quest, of taking up social causes too early. But, even if his *own* earlier transfer to Lansdowne House had been to an Oxford-of-the-Mind, his failures seem more grievous to himself. He has had a facile regard for truth; he has misjudged intellectual and artistic difficulties, and he has felt that he could elude time—or preserve youthful hope and fire.

If time conquered his friend, it conquers Corydon or Arnold, too. "Round me too the night," he writes,

> *In ever-nearing circle weaves her shade.*
> *I see her veil draw soft across the day,*
> *I feel her slowly chilling breath invade*
> *The cheek grown thin, the brown hair sprent with grey;*
> *I feel her finger light*
> *Laid pausefully upon life's headlong train.*[61]

If Clough is lost to him, the sensibility of that "subtle soul" is a reminder of delicate, balanced, plural truths he must seek while he lives. It is important that he completed "Thyrsis" when writing of "disinterestedness"[62] in a work dedicated to Oxford; and again that the unrushed, reflective view he needs is evident in a "Creweian Oration" which he had given at Oxford. The oration deeply illuminates "Thyrsis." Nobody listened perhaps to Latin Creweian talks, though people pretended to. "Arnold was the orator," recalls Ellis Yarnall of one of them. "He appeared in a reading-desk or pulpit projecting from a side gallery." If "nobody seemed to listen," his manner gave one the feeling "that he did not in the least expect attention would be paid to him."[63] "*Academici*," Matthew said, as if to scholars past and future, "*Pergite igitur. . . . Quid censetis, qui ante ad agendum quam ad cognoscendum plerumque accedunt. . . .* Academicians, continue as you have always done. What do you think of those who turn to action before learning, whom labour itself exhausts in the city, in the field, and daily business before they can conjecture anything about leisure? What fine and great cultivators of learning do you think they will be? . . . For my part I promise you this and will ever fulfill it: that I shall neglect nothing by which your studies and the glory of Oxford's founders may seem in any way to be aided; and to this end I shall devote my whole life."[64] His doctrine of reflective leisure points to readings in Eastern as well as Western mysticism, and to a new feeling for academic Oxford. "Thyrsis" shows that leisure of mind is the true condition of a meaningful quest for light. Clough, the Gipsy, Oxford, and the Tree all finally blend in his elegy as enduring quest symbols. Through the town's harsh, heart-wearying rear, it is Clough's mild voice that he hopes to hear:

> Let in thy voice a whisper often come
> To chase fatigue and fear:
> Why faintest thou? I wandered till I died.[65]

But in 1861 he could express very little of his anguished feeling for Clough. He did no more than allude to that poet's courage and integrity, and to his poem *The Bothie,* in the final Homer talk. The loss was like a symbol of the ending of his *own* life as a poet—and everything he once lived for. He felt an anxious grief deeply enough: he sensed that he had given up lyric poetry to gain applause as a critic, whereas his great friend never compromised, never once joined in a vile "saturnalia" of struggle for literary success. Taking his wife to her sister's home in Copford, Essex, late this year, he felt the full weight of the loss of Arthur Hugh Clough. Poetry once linked them; old intellectual bonds, Rugby and Oxford, critical ideas and easy bachelor-hood cemented their friendship. But now that had ended and everything was over. At Copford he walked through rainswept woods, and felt that he might lie down perhaps forever. "It is a place," Arnold wrote, "where I could be well content, if I was the rector of it, to think that I should end my days and lay my bones."[66]

14

CRITICAL ACTS: "ESSAYS IN CRITICISM"
1862–1867

> Whoever sets himself to see things as they are will find himself one of a very small circle; but it is only by this small circle resolutely doing its own work that adequate ideas will ever get current at all.
>
> The critic must keep out of the region of immediate practice in the political, social, humanitarian sphere, if he wants to make a beginning for that more free speculative treatment of things, which may perhaps one day make its benefits felt.
>
> *—Arnold on the nature of criticism*

E VEN before he was grieved by the news of Clough, Arnold read notices of *On Translating Homer*. The reviewers carped at his personality. *The Economist* called him supercilious and the *Athenaeum*, "authoritarian." A few other journals found him brutal, conceited, and defamatory—and only mildy cogent. The *Saturday Review* flared up at his "contemptuous and insulting" language with a decent (but oddly verbose) London University professor of the classics, poor F. W. Newman, and at his most "outrageous conceit" verging on "personal abuse, and sometimes on low buffoonery" in the Oxford chair!

"The whole of the Lectures are one constant I—I—I," fumed the *Saturday*.[1] Arnold at forty was free from self-conceit. He had a strong ego, much pride of which he was aware, and a desire to take chances with his critical personality to gain in *effect*. Amused by the attacks, he told one reviewer that most people noticed nothing "except that I abused F. W. Newman, and liked English hexameters." But when Jane called his manner "dogmatic," he tried to assess what he had done.

At Oxford, he had pleaded for a full attention to European ideas and a more open critical sensibility. He had discovered his accent as a writer: he could put *himself* into essays. He was using wit and irony to show how a critic might be concerned but detached, committed but flexible, intellectually serious but also lambent and enjoyable. Like Alexander Pope, he too was at war against dullness—and would deserve Leavis's praise for being "one of the most lively and profitable of the accepted critics."[2] He was getting pace and movement into his critical prose. Saturating himself in a topic, he could produce a rapid first draft and fill in insertions later: "It is odd how much easier I find it to write a thing for insertion in a particular place when what is before and after it stands finished," he noticed, "than to write it when I come to it in its regular course." His style appealed to the auditor's ear and reader's eye. Journals that wouldn't print "speeches" would print his lectures unchanged, or *as is.* "That," he told his new friend Mark Pattison, who became Rector of Lincoln College, Oxford, "is because of the rhythm."[3] His prose had such intimacy it gave the effect of his being in the room with the reader; but faults in *Translating Homer* he soon perceived: he had been too cavalier and vague. His worst fault involved the fact that his *illustrations* only poorly bore out his *ideas.*

Still, he was a celebrity. Some thirty reviews of the Homer pieces were advertising his name. Even the liberal leader, Gladstone, himself a Homer scholar, sent him a compliment. Arnold was glad to be *"getting at"* the public, even if he was haunted by the notion that "negligence, self-mismanagement, and want of patience"[4] could destroy his power.

He felt a new sense of urgency after Clough's death, as he told his sister Fan. "I have a conviction," Matthew worried, "that there is a real, an almost imminent danger of England losing immeasurably in all ways, declining . . . for want of what I must still call ideas, for want of perceiving how the world is going and must go, and preparing herself accordingly. This conviction haunts me, and at times even overwhelms me with depression."[5] He anxiously focused on one idea: that England's real enemy was her mental insularity. If the middle class could not take in foreign ideas, if they failed to see that "Europe tends constantly to become more and more one community" so that we are by rights "Europeans instead of merely Englishmen, Frenchmen, Germans, Italians," then in her isolation England would go down. "If we are doomed to perish," Arnold believed, it will be from "want of patience with ideas, our inability to see the way the world is going." While France taught her people Persian and Hindustani and Chinese and Japanese, Arnold's countrymen lived as if Moslem, Hindu, and Buddhist cultures never existed. England lacked a single school for the study of Eastern cultures, or languages, yet had large Eastern interests. Arnold foresaw an England with "all her colonies" gone, and looked beyond that to a nation *lacking a daily infusion of foreign ideas in her press** and culturally moribund.[6]

He took pains with his character since he meant to *exhibit* the sensibility of a man open to fresh modes of thought. Trying to master his ego, he held close to family traditions and asked his mother to change her legal will, so that he might later buy Dr. Arnold's Fox How. He pleaded for pictures: "I think I told you I had grandfather Arnold's portrait," Matthew told her. "I want you to bring me grandpapa Penrose and Sir Charles Penrose—I will frame them and hang them up." Seeing a photo of himself, Matthew called it "a perfect beast."[7]

Though genial with other writers, he never wrote an essay on a major living English author. He viewed contemporaries much as he had Clough—as foils or mirrors which told him about himself or the narrow-minded modern age: Carlyle was a "genius—part fanatic —and part tom-fool."[8] Ruskin seemed to lack "coherence" and John Stuart Mill, for all his suggestive good sense, displayed that rather Cloughian fault of being blind to the value of religious traditions. Arnold was too excited by his contemporaries to judge them fairly; and his emotional involvement in *In Memoriam* was so great that he was most foolish about Tennyson. That poem, with its rich ideas and subtle psychological structure, concerns the poet's grief for his university friend Arthur Henry Hallam; its quiet diction and brilliant cadences had been in Arnold's mind ever since 1850:

> *Come; let us go: your cheeks are pale;*
> *But half my life I leave behind. . . .*
>
> *Dear friend, far off, my lost desire, . . .*
> *Sweet human hand and lips and eye,*
> *Dear heavenly friend that canst not die,*
> *Mine, mine for ever, ever mine . . .*
>
> *I hear it now, and o'er and o'er,*
> *Eternal greetings to the dead;*
> *And 'Ave, Ave, Ave,' said,*
> *'Adieu, adieu' for evermore.*

That beauty moved him too much; and the truest, best compliment he ever paid Tennyson was to misquote him in the *Homer* talks. (Tennyson was sensible of the compliment: to misquote is to imply that one reads a poet often enough to know him nearly by heart.) Tennyson's work he supposed was formless and insular: *In Memoriam*

---

*Arnold believed England nearly had sealed herself off from foreign viewpoints since 1815. A major index, and cause, of any modern nation's decline will be the tendency of her newspapers to neglect foreign ideas, beliefs, and viewpoints; her writers will cease experimenting with ideas and with language. Arnold comments on the "provincialism" of the press in major essays such as "Function of Criticism," "Academies," "My Countrymen," *Culture and Anarchy,* and *Friendship's Garland.*

was only one of his "holdings forth in verse" without "beginning middle or end," wrote Matthew,[9] with an uneasy memory of how closely *In Memoriam* was connected with his tumult over Jane.

Still, among the poets, Matthew did befriend Robert Browning by 1862. Here was a cosmopolitan genius, ten years older than himself and steeped in European life. A gray-bearded, olive-skinned man of about fifty with Italian gestures and a loud, affectionate manner, Browning came to dine at the Arnolds' usually with visiting Parisians such as Fanny du Quaire or the critic Joseph Milsand, and knew stories that could make Fanny Lucy's eyes pop. In candlelight and over the port, his high-pitched voice lowered and Browning became a good listener, too. In a shadowy room, he seemed to command shadows or to know about old ghosts and strange old customs. A "quite remarkably agreeable converser," Matthew wrote of him, and a "man of genius with a reach of mind compared to which Tennyson's reach of mind is petty." This genius read Rabbi Benjamin of Tudela; he understood Jewish culture, Italian writers, and indeed had lived at Paris, Florence, Rome. Still, his poems were too full of the anarchy of sensations to please Arnold, who found them not "pellucidly and absolutely clear," and saw in their style a dark emotionalism he feared in himself.[10]

Some of Fanny Lucy's happiest hours were spent in candlelight, among good friends. She now disliked large parties, but she was apparently fond of small dinners—and even of waiting for Mr. Browning to speak quietly over the port. These dinners were small respites during Matthew's hectic inspection months; on four days a week he left Chester Square for his schools at about nine, and came back at seven. Meanwhile, she was left with the children. Tommy was her chief worry—and almost constant companion—since this thin asthmatic boy with his weak heart avoided healthier children. Tommy, who was clever, played on her sympathies; hence she was seldom able to go out alone to her loved museums and galleries, or to the evening concerts and little parties that pleased her. We know that she took the children to relatives or friends in London, for a day, but even so they were seldom out of sight. She hoped to keep them alive—and looked forward to summer holidays which were usually spent at Fox How. At times her husband's optimism astonished her. He was less naïve about health than about people, but he had quite failed to see for example how F. W. Newman would be *bound* to feel attacked and insulted by the Homer talks! (She enlightened Matthew on that.) On the other hand, her days and nights with Tommy were extremely difficult and she relied on Matthew's hope and gaiety, even on his optimism. Her comments in diaries are never bitter or despairing, and her irony is restrained. She knew that *he* needed respite from his chores: she wanted him to stay with fishing or hunting friends when he could, or to go to the theater; and she raised no objection apparently even to his meetings with a clever, pretty Lady de Rothschild.

Sharing confidences with Flu, Arnold believed he had her complete trust and depended on her great help. He was these days not a very ebullient husband in the evenings; he worked nights with school papers and found it hard to sleep. Tommy wanted company: "Flu is with him almost constantly, and sleeps with him, while I sleep with Budge," Matthew notes wearily. "I think [Tommy] prefers this and finds it less exciting than my being constantly awake . . . from my quite natural difficulty of sleeping, when I am with him."[11] He did not always get through a night well with Budge. He had felt very raw and weary when a smooth-nosed Russian Count arrived from the De Circourts, to ask about science teaching, in 1861. Arnold exchanged a few words in French with the Count, who perhaps mentioned his experience of firing at British troops in the Crimea. Later he was to find in this Russian's *Anna Karenina* a subtle "piece of life,"[12] as he wrote in his admiring essay, "Count Leo Tolstoi."

He managed his time shrewdly. Needing as ever to appear superior to "Didu" or Edward, who was now a hard-working School Inspector and whose wife Caroline Orlebar had died and left poor Edward with a son, Matthew sent his mother terrible bulletins about his *own* hard days:

> Up at six, writing and working till breakfast at 8½. In the Saffron Walden School at ¼ to 10, and from then till half past 12; [and then I] drove to Great Bardfield, through the heart of Essex, 12 miles in the rain; reached the school at 2, there till ¼ past five—then [after dining with a Quaker farmer] at ½ past 6 the carriage at the door again; and at 8 I was put down in Saffron Walden again, where the Scholars of a night school kept me till nearly 10.[13]

This was truthful propaganda, a hectic day summarized for his family's wonder. His schedule varied. Putting off bores by claiming that he inspected all day, he kept whole afternoons free for essay writing at the Athenaeum Club or the British Museum's North Library, one of the few libraries not lit by gas (which made his eyes run).

His friendship for Louisa, Lady de Rothschild, who was as petite as Fanny Lucy, began as a convenience. He took Dicky to the "fairy land" of her Aston Clinton in Buckinghamshire, and stayed overnight there or at her glittering Mentmore estate, when looking at nearby schools. Born in 1821 as Louisa Montefiore, she had as a girl of nineteen married plump Anthony de Rothschild, a grandson of the Frankfurt banker who put five sons in five nations to protect the House of Rothschild. Louisa's girlhood in Italy had made her cautious about herself: "I must never," she told a diary, "permit myself to have any affections unfounded on esteem, and must never, either from self-interest or caprice or thoughtlessness demonstrate [more] than I feel."[14] She entered this under a bold headline "AFFECTIONS."

One day, when Sir Anthony had asked their daughter what she wanted for her birthday, the girl had replied, "An infant's school." To Connie de Rothschild's delight, a real school had sprouted on the family estate; it was inspected in 1858 by a "tall pleasant faced man" with "amiable looks," the child decided.[15] Louisa herself admired the handsome school inspector, and tried to get Matthew to call back.

Matthew sent her debonair notes, and she replied with gifts for his family, a pocketbook in ivory for Lucy, bonbons for the boys, pheasants for Christmas. "So you did actually get to Skye," Matthew writes to Lady de Rothschild. "I am glad I did not know your whereabouts, or I should never have kept my resolution of coming straight back [home]." Fanny Lucy, he adds, is having a "tedious recovery."[16] He implies that if his wife's condition is tedious, Louisa's attraction for him is nearly irresistible. "Why do not *you* come over and hear me lecture at Oxford," he asks. "I only hope he did not think," Matthew assures Louisa when asking her to thank Sir Anthony for partridges, "I was like Oliver Twist asking for more."[17]

He asked for no "more" from this petite lady in her forties than a special, affectionate friendship. But he felt compelled to see her, and after a while took pains to arrange their meetings: "[Let] me come to dine with you in London . . . you and your daughter Constance," he offers, "and then we might go together to see *Hamlet,* which I much want to see."[18]

At Louisa's parties he saw bankers, musicians, politicians. At Aston Clinton in 1864, he met her friend "Dizzy," who looked blackly at the hors d'oeuvres until he recalled who Arnold was. "I had a great respect for the name you bore," Disraeli volunteered, speaking slowly across the candlelight like a witch in *Macbeth.* "Now you are well known, you have made a reputation. But you will go further yet, you have a great future before you, and you deserve it." Matthew bowed, and then discussed Cicero, Bolingbroke, and Burke with the Tory, then four years from his first premiership. "It is only from politicians who have themselves felt the spell of literature that one gets these charming speeches," Matthew noted afterwards. After Disraeli had made the Queen the Empress of India, Matthew met him for the last time. A feeble old man then hung on his arm at Lady Airlie's and rasped, "I want to talk about *you.*" Having praised him as a living classic, Disraeli became intimate:

"You have heard me called a flatterer."

Arnold could not deny it.

"Yes, and it is true," Disraeli whispered. "Everyone likes flattery —and when you come to Royalty you should lay it on with a trowel."[19] Matthew preferred his smooth, comical urbanity to William Gladstone's puritanism and liberal nostrums. If Disraeli denied Judaism, he had written *Alroy* and *Tancred*. Louisa's intelligent, orthodox faith was of course more important to Matthew; she read the New Testament as well as the Old, and knew Emanuel Deutsch, whose article on "The Talmud" in the *Quarterly Review* she might have written herself. In fact Matthew's light flirtation with her was more than a matter of *beau monde;* opening his eyes to the complexity of Jewish culture, Louisa talked with him of her supreme poet, Heine, while others waltzed at her parties.[20] In appealing to his whole sensibility, she helped him to recover his trust in feeling: Matthew found himself writing to her about Sainte-Beuve's *Chateaubriand et son groupe,* the Liège lectures about the author of *René*,[21] and then jotting in his notebook:

CHATEAUBRIAND ON THE TRUE PATHETIC
CHATEAUBRIAND ON DESIRE

In a curious sense, Lady de Rothschild's temperament was elegiac. Cultivated, learned, realistic, she had a sense of impermanence and change, of the suffering of her race, of the pathos of the historic past. Her depth of view touched Arnold: "I have a great *penchant*," he told her intimately, "for the Celtic races, with their melancholy and unprogressiveness."[22] She helped him to think more deeply about religion, and even encouraged him to profit from his brusque defeat at the hands of Robert Lowe, in an education battle. Arnold had underestimated his foremost enemy. In 1859 Robert Lowe had become his highest superior at the education office, Vice-President of the Committee of Council until 1864 (when he resigned for tampering with Inspectors' reports). An acid-tongued albino with white hair, a red face, and weak eyes, he canceled the Inspectors' meetings and denounced the whole staff of "H.M.I.s" in the Commons. As Lord Lansdowne's protégé, he was a very able M.P. for Calne and a Whig. It is said that, in his attacks on electoral reform in the 1860s, he gave the best case against democracy the House of Commons heard in the nineteenth century: "His hair," wrote an observer, "shone and glistened. . . . His complexion had deepened into something like bishop's purple. There he stood, that usually cold, undemonstrative, intellectual, white-headed, red-faced, venerable arch-conspirator; shouting himself hoarse."[23]

With Lingen's help, Lowe had proposed a cost-saving plan for granting moneys to schools, based on "payment by results." If the plan wasn't cheap, he said of the Revised Code, it would be efficient, and if not efficient cheap—but in fact it struck hard at Inspectors. Instead of looking into the whole civilized condition of a school, they were now asked to quiz every child in a class. Grants to schools would *depend* on children's being able to answer questions in the "3 Rs"; a small sum would be deducted from a grant for each pupil missing or who couldn't answer a question.

Few schools could afford to lose grant money. Pupils ill with diptheria, scarlet fever, or other diseases would have to be taken from sickbeds to class when the H.M.I. appeared. "Paroxysms of whooping cough," "pustules of small pox," infants "wrapped up and held in their mothers' arms or seated on a stool by the fire because they are too ill to take their proper places"[24] were among sights Matthew was indeed to see in class. Slum schools or those with backward or handicapped pupils, who faltered over the "3 Rs" and couldn't answer Inspectors' questions, would get poorer. A few rich, privileged schools would profit.

Lowe's Code was opposed by thousands of teachers and by every H.M.I. to a man. James Kay wrote an unreadable, technical pamphlet, supposedly beating out "the brains of the Code";[25] but Arnold hung fire. Then as Parliament was debating Lowe's plan, he sent in February 1862 the angriest piece he ever wrote, an essay called "The Twice-Revised Code," to *Fraser's Magazine.* "My hand is so tired I can hardly write," Matthew noted after correcting proofs. Though his superiors "strictly" forbade him to write on the Code,[26] Arnold's essay attacks Lowe as a demagogic bureaucrat animated by "a spirit of hostility to the system which he administers," and Ralph Lingen as a flunky lacking "love for the very course" the Department was "created to follow." What is at stake is *humanity* in education: Arnold had argued in one of his inspired annual reports that pupils misapprehend English writing because we overstress facts; our education forgets young minds. Now, Lowe would make schools even more mechanical and turn H.M.I.s into useless clerks, as if, Arnold writes, "there might not be in a school most grave matters needing inspection," or as if generals were asked to look only at the infantry's ammunition boxes. "The organization of the army is faulty:—inspect the cartouch-boxes! The camp is ill-drained, the men are ill-hutted, there is danger of fever and sickness. Never mind; inspect the cartouch-boxes!" But the whole army "is going to a disaster!" Arnold exclaims bitterly. "That is not your business; inspect, inspect the cartouch-boxes!"[27]

He thus struck at mechanization in crippling, modern schemes of education and at plans that overlook the whole child. At the practical level of politics, he *applied* here a developing theory of culture. In writing the *Fraser's* piece, he hardly risked his job; his employers would not have dared to fire him—but he risked making his working days unpleasant for the rest of his life. "I don't think, however, they can eject me," he told his wife about Lingen and Lowe, "though they can, and perhaps will, make my place uncomfortable." Fanny Lucy was far from certain he would keep a roof over her head: "If thrown on the world I daresay we should be on our legs again," Matthew told her.

He kept his job, and further attacked the Code in reports and two more essays. James Kay sent a copy of Arnold's "Twice-Revised Code" to every member of the House of Commons, and out at Aston Clinton, Lady de Rothschild made Disraeli read it. Soon Arnold was to be given an assistant named Thomas Healing, who made his inspecting easier. But the fact is that Lowe humbled Arnold.[28] Adding a few provisos and amendments, a cost-conscious Parliament approved Lowe's Revised Code in 1862.

"How short could Mill write Job?" Matthew once wrote with spite.[29] In his view, Mill lacked the religious sensitivity to "write" the Book of Job, in any number of words. Significantly after his defeat by Lowe he thought of "translating the Book of Job" afresh, and then in November, or nine months after attacking the Code, he wrote the piece that became "Maurice de Guérin" for *Essays in Criticism*.

No longer was there any large gap between what he felt as an Inspector and what he wrote in essays. The hard literalness of intellectuals, he felt, was paralleled by the mechanical spirit of entrepreneurs and intolerance in the schools. In an industrial nation, as Arnold reasoned, we tend to stress what is practical and to neglect what is not of immediate *use*. In a Protestant country, we call Catholics fanatics and Jews unenlightened. Of what use is a strange religion? Preferring our settled ways, we seldom look beyond our own culture; and he jotted a classroom song—

> *Of all the tongues from east to west,*
> *I love my native tongue the best.*

The utilitarian spirit does not train the moral sense; hence for our advantage we shall find excuses for killing blacks in Africa, natives in India, or aborigines in the Antipodes; and again Arnold records in his diary:

History
The aborigines (of New Zealand) are a degraded and ferocious cast of people but owing to the introduction of firearms and spirits they are gradually decreasing.

(3rd yr. girl)[30]

Essays in Criticism was to declare unyielding war against the utilitarian, insular spirit.

In "Maurice de Guérin," he opposes that spirit in a delicate study of a young French poet who died at twenty-eight before achieving practical success. Indeed, he writes the finest brief portrait in English of the artistic temperament. Against the background of Guérin's idyll at La Chênaie in Brittany with the overpowering Abbé Lamennais, his nature descriptions and "Centaure," his sense of being between "two worlds" and struggle in Paris, the essayist shows him as a man who helps us to define ourselves. For the first time, Arnold relates a major thesis to a fitting illustration: if poetry interprets by its natural magic or moral profundity, Guérin, like John Keats, had natural magic. His life and writings show him as a free Strayed Reveller: "He goes into religion and out of religion, into society and out of society, not from the motives which impel men in general, but to feel what it is all like."[31] Yet even when he renounced the religious life, Guérin remained a sensitive Catholic.

This piece is meant to show that, if we are not Catholic, we are incomplete as citizens in a Western nation until we understand a Catholic sensibility at its finest. Arnold's four Spinoza essays and his "Heinrich Heine" are, again, proof enough that we are incomplete, mechanical, unless we know minds that have been enriched by Hebraic culture. These essays have other interests, too. Arnold replies to recent public furor over John William Colenso, or the Bishop of Natal, who returned "trembling" to England to print in 1862 a book on the Pentateuch after intelligent Zulus had shown him mathematical and other factual errors in the Bible. In Arnold's view, the Bishop confused mythical truths in the Bible with statistics—just as Lowe confused children with numbers, exams, money.

In fact, Colenso is only his starting point. Satisfied with his piece on Guérin, Arnold intended to publish an essay a month from late 1862 to June 1863. To counter the utilitarian spirit, he would explore the difficult topic of religious faith and take advantage of new journals. Older journals such as the *Quarterly* and *Edinburgh* "amuse a public whose intellectual and spiritual growth has long since stopped," he told one editor.[32] But Froude, now, was renovating *Fraser's*. *Macmillan's Magazine* was launched in 1859, two months before George Smith's *Cornhill Magazine,* which was to print "My Countrymen" and the installments of *Culture and Anarchy*. Again in Smith's new *Pall Mall Gazette,* Arnold was to print "Theodore Parker," and the Arminius letters which became *Friendship's Garland*. For the *London Magazine* in December 1862, he now reviewed a translation of Spinoza's *Theologico-Politicus*. Then in the January, February, and

December 1863 issues of *Macmillan's Magazine,* he printed his very important "Bishop and the Philosopher," "Dr. Stanley's Lectures on the Jewish Church," and "A Word More about Spinoza"—which he was to expand as "Spinoza and the Bible."

As a minor theme, he explores rather fastidiously the privileged role of a philosophical elite. After a loud outcry in the liberal press, Arnold modified his views of the elite for *Culture and Anarchy.* But more deeply, these pieces seek to show that the Dutch philosopher, Baruch Spinoza, offers the only sound modern basis for interpreting biblical truth. "If the English clergy must err, let them learn from this outcast of Israel to err nobly," writes Arnold.[33] Though not infallible, this "outcast" may help us.

Arnold now states his *credo* after his talks with Lady de Rothschild and defeat in a public debate: if Lowe has won the day in England, what can be mustered against the utilitarian spirit? First, we must see the Deity as Spinoza did. Spinoza's God directs nature according to universal law—but *not* "as the particular laws of human nature" require. Hence the world does not exist "for the sake of man," and, says Arnold, man's happiness lies in active Stoicism and in seeking to discover what is valid for his nature.[34] It is of course misleading to approach Arnold as Lionel Trilling did in 1939, ignorant of much of his reading, of his manuscript notes, and of his unpublished letters, and then to find in him unintended contradictions. Trilling's factual errors are less important than his remorseless politicizing of Arnold's thought, and his failure to see that Arnold came to Spinoza after very carefully reading Berkeley and Epictetus. In Berkeley's *Siris,* he had seen that outward nature—trees, hills, lakes, the geography of England—has a dual aspect: nature may inspire man, but may also "ensnare" the feelings and mislead. "Quiet Work," in which the stars inspire, and "In Harmony with Nature," in which nature is "cruel" and "fickle," must be taken together: both are Berkeleyan. The paradoxical Berkeleyan dual view of nature had seemed less oppressive to Arnold, later, when he studied Epictetus, who cautioned him against drawing easy analogies from nature: a man is not a horse, tree, flower, or sunset: *"Turn your thoughts upon yourselves, find out what kind of preconceived ideas you have,"* said Epictetus. *"What element of superiority, then, do you possess? The animal in you? No. . . . Your reason is the element of superiority which you possess: adorn and beautify that."*[35] Arnold came to Spinoza's books with Epictetus's view that man belongs to nature yet is separate by his "reason," and that "reason" may criticize our "preconceived ideas" and yet attach us to God. He then considered Spinoza's propositions closely. "When Spinoza," he observed at his desk, arguing against the doctrine of final causes says—God did not make the world for Man's sake, because if he did [God worked for an end, and whoever works for an end, necessarily reaches for something he lacks*] . . . he argues like a schoolman and not like himself.

But only rarely did Spinoza argue like a "schoolman."[36] His argument that the Deity is utterly vast and coextensive with the universe, impassive, yet concerned *for* all things and hence capable of being worshipped, impressed Arnold. Spinoza approached the Bible as a *metaphorical* text and in effect gave a sanction for criticizing it as one would any other literary text. Further, Spinoza suggested that romantic nature philosophies must be false—and Arnold in due course was to condemn even Wordsworth's "philosophy" as illusion.[37]

Romantic poets, as Arnold believed, usually had implied that man has a unique status and that the whole spiritual life *in* nature depends on the poet's active imagination. In "Yes! in the sea of life," he had given nature a Spinozan inner life of its own:

> *The islands* feel *the enclasping flow,*
> *And then their endless bounds* they know.[38]

He had found it convenient to speak of "islands" and to use "feel" and "know," as equivalents for what matter endures. But there is nothing sentimental in Arnold's poetic image. Similarly in "Dover Beach," the sea with its separate, enduring, inner existence sounds its own note, which Sophocles once interpreted as we do now. In our own time of advanced nuclear physics, Arnold's lyrics show a convincing respect for the complex independence of matter. His painstaking study of Spinoza influenced his lyric metaphors, increased his respect for nature, and saved his belief in a Deity.

Now, at forty in 1863, he takes Spinoza's subtle rationality-with-faith as a measure or test of the critical attitude he wants to show in *Essays in Criticism*.

The very impressive features of these essays—six of which began as lectures and all nine of which appeared in periodicals—are their sympathy, confidence, and intuitive judgments of European Catholic and Jewish writers. As Oxford lectures, they were well-received. (He made a solemn audience "laugh aloud with two pages of Heine's wit," though it was only after a later, Celtic lecture that an old Oxford Principal muttered aloud: "The Angel ended.") Arnold was now, in his cautious way, deeply intrigued by a woman who strongly sympathized with Hebraic culture. As the feeling in his poetry would not really exist but for Mary Claude, Jane Arnold, and Fanny Lucy, so the feeling

---

*God "worked *propter finem*, and *qui propter finem agit aliquio necessario appetit quo caret*." The desk-note incorporates Spinoza's Latin.

which humanizes the *Essays,* as well as *Culture and Anarchy* and *Literature and Dogma,* is partly inspired by Lady de Rothschild. Impressionable and sensitive, he needed strong female images as a means of organizing his emotions. His creative and intellectual life coalesced around "memory pictures"; he had needed to *see* and *hear* George Sand and Rachel and had arranged his scenic rendezvous with Mary Claude; and so, too, in the 1860s until the end of his life he quietly arranged meetings with Louisa in settings of importance to him. His loyalty to Fanny Lucy, respect for marriage, and fear of losing his power through "self-mismanagement" kept him from making outright love to Louisa. Moreover he understood himself: the image, the symbol of the woman and not the possession of her was what meant so much to the creative Arnold. And, for him, religion was as necessary as love. His Spinoza essays worked out a rationale for his faith, even if he had not reconciled his understanding of the Spinozan Deity with his own practice of a ritualistic, High Church Anglicanism.

A year before his book was published in 1865 by Alexander Macmillan, he had thought about its title: "I must not call the volume 'Orpheus,'" he told Macmillan. "I had thought of 'Essays of Criticism' in the old sense of the word *Essay—attempt—specimen.* . . . What do you think of 'Essays *in* Criticism'?"[39] His urbane, contrasting method was what he chiefly wanted to stress in these nine "specimens" or essays:

The Function of Criticism at the Present Time
The Literary Influence of Academies
Maurice de Guérin
Eugénie de Guérin
Heinrich Heine
Pagan and Mediaeval Religious Sentiment
Joubert
Spinoza
Marcus Aurelius

In "Heinrich Heine," in which the ideas are as important as the method, Arnold is at his best. He uses the career of an exiled German Jewish poet to explain a dissolvent attitude to tradition, and evokes the quality of his author: Heine's free play of mind led him to reject every "stock" notion. This poet epitomized the wit and ardor of France and the culture, sentiment, and thought of Germany as he battled against *Philistinism*—or against those who invoke outworn beliefs against reason, and who fail to value ideas "irrespective of the practical convenience of those ideas." Less perfectly than Goethe, he embodied "the modern spirit"[40]—a spirit which Arnold explains in one of his finest tributes to *Dichtung und Wahrheit* and the *Gespräche mit Goethe*:

> Goethe's profound, imperturbable naturalism is absolutely fatal to all routine thinking; he puts the standard, once for all, inside every man instead of outside him; when he is told, such a thing must be so, it has been held so for a thousand years, he answers with Olympian politeness, "But *is* it so? is it so to *me*?"[41]

Yet, Arnold paradoxically adds, it is self-defeating to prefer darkness of our own to "light" that exists in sources foreign or strange to us. This is the subtle theme of *Essays in Criticism*—a work of gradual assessment and great critical insight, which finds its unity in interpreting the lasting meaning of the French Revolution. For Arnold no idea relating to morality, art, religion, politics, or any other aspect of life is to be credited unless it passes the test, "*Is* it so? is it so to *me*?" But before we discard what we do not happen to like, we must identify *our own* narrowness or Philistinism, our hostility to light.

Where shall we find light? In "A French Coleridge," the subtle, brilliantly comparative and illustrative piece that was retitled "Joubert," he discusses a gentle, Jesuit-trained Neoplatonist who opposed the political spirit of 1789. Living his invalid's life at Paris and Villeneuve-sur-Yonne, the Catholic Joubert inscribed maxims of this kind:

> The idea of God is a light.
> Political systems have need of elasticity. They lose it when everything is regulated by laws fixed and inflexible.
> Acquaintance with other intellects is the charm of criticism; the maintenance of rules is only its machinery and its least utility.
> For children in literature, nothing but what is simple.[42]

Does Protestant England, in which children write of "degraded and ferocious aborigines," have light? Joubert's mild light came from his Church. Even so, he may have misinterpreted the wisdom of his teachers, for as a layman he was too ascetic, "too ethereal," lacking in sensuous delight.[43] To define the exact quality of Joubert's work, Arnold sets up a series of delicate comparisons between Joubert and Coleridge, Byron and Chateaubriand; and it is important that after his biographical background he gives, through quotation, a sense of the range of Joubert's tone, voice, attitudes, and insights. Perhaps in no earlier essay in English have so many critical techniques been used together. Arnold defines a French sensibility, and shows its importance. He implies that Joubert's discrimination and subtlety, mild amenity, and the sensitivity of his Catholicism are all missing in England.

Arnold loved no writers more than the Stoics. He took up the vivid, easy Seneca now and then, turned to Marcus Aurelius for consolation, and to Epictetus for nerve and strength to continue as an Inspector and writer. In "Marcus Aurelius" (1863), he mounts a fine strategic attack against Mill's claim that Christian morality is "negative"[44] and then considers Stoic morality. A new outlook for man would, in his view, take into account the Greek Stoic tradition which comes to perfection in Epictetus's *Discourses,* a work which influenced *Meditations* of Marcus Aurelius. But, says Arnold, the moral injunction is inferior to the religious precept; thus the Roman Emperor Aurelius is only a sentinel for the modern spirit, a reminder of the *religious ingredient* lacking in our philosophies: "We see him wise, just, self-governed, tender, thankful, blameless; yet, with all this, agitated, stretching out his arms for something beyond."[45] More broadly, in "Pagan and Mediaeval Religious Sentiment" (1864), with the wit, irony, and facetiousness which mark his greatest criticism—and humanize it—he looks for a synthesizing approach to human nature. He doffs his hat to the Catholic Church, an institution for which every imaginative person has a "weakness" and whose wonders are seen in the Catholic Encyclopaedia at the British Museum, "its right mounting up into heaven among the white folios of the *Acta Sanctorum,* its left plunging down into hell among the yellow octaves of the *Law Digest.*"[46] The comic tone creates just that atmosphere of sane, easy urbanity in which he can comment on religion freshly, without arousing the reader's defenses or prejudgments. If pagan religious sentiment, in Theocritus's idylls, is cold and cheerless, as he shows, medieval Catholic sentiment in the Canticles of St. Francis is warmly restorative. Yet pagan poetry from Pindar to Sophocles is so "well balanced" as to satisfy our intellect and religious sense alike, since it appeals to "imaginative reason."

That phrase, which had been used by John Davison and J. H. Newman, is reminiscent of similar bipolar terms used around midcentury by those seeking a synthetic philosophy of mind. Arnold offers it as an algebraic "x," a sign or symbol of the new integrated view of life he seeks.[47] *Culture and Anarchy* was to elaborate on "imaginative reason."

All of his major essays are comparative. In "The Literary Influence of Academies" (1864), he describes a fine "sensitiveness of intelligence" fostered by the French Academy ever since 1629; and he relates that quality to popular culture. Writing in the heyday of the popular press and often going out to buy Fanny Lucy her copy of *Once a Week* (a Victorian forbear of England's modern *Woman* or *Woman's Own*), Arnold sets us "flexibility of intelligence" as a value by which we might measure British popular prose.[48] Here, as in "Eugénie de

Guérin," he attends to *values* in popular culture quite as perspicuously as two Arnoldian men of our own time, Richard Hoggart and Stuart Hall, have done at England's Centre for Contemporary Cultural Studies, at Birmingham. The critic's scope for Arnold is the *entire quality of a nation's life;* hence criticism is to attend to what is said in—or written for—the streets. Matthew himself had shocked friends with splendid variations on the pungent street-word *shits* (*shit, shite, Shite's Oracle*) and the anatomical word *ass,* (*hass, obverse*). He was beginning to see that language of streets and of the daily press may determine a nation's life. The truly vulgar, brassy newspaper style of "Corinthian prose" for example has mere "glitter without warmth, rapidity without ease, effectiveness without charm,"[49] and in a newspaper's style we may see clues to the character of a society. In "The Function of Criticism," he submits this example of a press item:

> A shocking child murder has just been committed at Nottingham. A girl named Wragg left the workhouse there on Saturday morning with her young illegitimate child. The child was soon afterwards found dead on Mapperly Hills, having been strangled. Wragg is in custody.[50]

Arnold was writing in October 1864, or just a month after Elizabeth Wragg killed her baby on September 10. (Before the court sentenced her in 1865 to twenty years in prison, Elizabeth offered this in her defense: "I should never have done it if I had had a home for [the child].")[51]

He comments on the "Wragg" news item during a time of social and political reform, a few years before the Reform Act of 1867 and the Elementary Education Act of 1870. His remarks counter the superficial, reformist zeal of his time, with courage.

Wragg has a "hideous name," he claims. "What a touch of grossness in our race . . . is shown by the natural growth amongst us of such hideous names,—Higginbottom, Stiggins, Bugg!" He alludes ironically to politicians who have boasted, "the old Anglo-Saxon race are the best breed in the whole world" and "I pray that our unrivalled happiness may last":

> And "our unrivalled happiness" . . . the workhouse, the dismal Mapperly Hills,—how dismal those who have seen them will remember,—the gloom, the smoke, the cold, the strangled illegitimate child! "I ask you whether, the world over or in past history, there is anything like it?" Perhaps not, one is inclined to answer: but at any rate, in that case, the world is not very much to be pitied. And the final touch—short, bleak, and inhuman: *Wragg is in custody.* The sex lost in the confusion of our unrivalled happiness; or (shall I say?) the superfluous Christian name lopped off by the straightforward vigour of our old Anglo-Saxon breed![52]

For Arnold Britain's *mental insularity* is revealed in the "Wragg" item.

He had in his diary evidence that pupils wrote in praise of the killing of blacks; under Lowe's Revised Code pupils might be credited for such compositions. He had seen, in London inspections, many Elizabeth Wraggs "without home, without hope." He knew the workhouses. He had begged for money for working-class schools; he had attacked even Lingen for a plan that was prejudiced against impoverished children, and that would further harden middle-class attitudes—and he had failed to influence the public. Arnold believed, now, that enemies would never yield to a frontal attack. Facing sharp, biting ridicule for his comments on Wragg, he used this case to make his great point about criticism. "Mr. Roebuck," Arnold says of the M.P. who spoke of our unrivaled happiness, "will have a poor opinion of an adversary who replies to his defiant songs of triumph only by murmuring under his breath, *Wragg is in custody;* but in no other way will these songs of triumph be induced gradually to moderate themselves."[53] The critic, in short, influences society by practicing the method of "disinterestedness":

> And how is criticism to show disinterestedness? By keeping aloof from what is called 'the practical view of things'; by resolutely following the law of its own nature, which is to be a free play of the mind on all subjects which it touches. By steadily refusing to lend itself to any of those ulterior, political, practical considerations about ideas, which plenty of people will be sure to attach to them, which perhaps ought often to be attached to them, which in this country at any rate are certain to be attached to them quite sufficiently, but which criticism has really nothing to do with. Its business is . . . simply to know the best that is known and thought in the world, and by in its turn making this known, to create a current of true and fresh ideas.[54]

The ultimate end of the critic is to *change the sensibility of a modern nation.* In "Eugénie de Guérin," he offers a case study of two modern sensibilities. He contrasts the charming sister of Maurice de Guérin with her practice of confession, her saints' lives, her apparently enriching Catholicism—as against the blank, mean, lightless "brick-and-mortar" Margate Protestantism of the third-rate popular poet Emma Tatham. Eugénie is not used by Arnold to illustrate the superiority of French to British faiths, but to show that in Eugénie's "distinction" of mind is some of "the best" that we may emulate. Varieties of "the best that is known and thought" he has tried to illustrate in his essays on modern French Catholics, a pagan emperor, German poets, a Dutch philosopher, Hebraic values, and an Academy of Letters.

In his Preface he declares war on "Philistines," invokes Oxford, and conjures up a future—monolithic in its stupefying grandeur—in which with "the whole earth filled and ennobled every morning by the magnificent roaring of the young lions of the *Daily Telegraph,* we shall all yawn in one another's faces with the dismallest, the most unimpeachable gravity."[55] Irony and wit are to be among his weapons. But "a brother and sister" at Fox How to whom he read the Preface, as he told Lady de Rothschild, "received it in such solemn silence that I began to tremble."[56] Some reviewers understood his wit, but the *Guardian* echoed Fox How complaints: "What is the unsatisfactory element in Mr. Arnold as a writer? Why, with his great gifts, is he of little or no weight as a teacher?" it complained. "Misplaced jokes are dangerous things," it felt, "and rash personalities are out of place, whether we are joking or in earnest."[57]

Nevertheless, with *Essays in Criticism* he was conquering England. Some reviewers found it more than the sum of its parts, his methods provocative and vital. From this time on, his name appeared in newspapers read by bankers, architects, barristers, M.P.s, deans, and businessmen over morning coffee. His name was placarded at W. H. Smith's railway bookstalls; he was debated by students, teachers, and the clergy, damned in journals, mocked behind his back in polite society, killed by logical philosophers, resurrected again in a leading article. His view that literature *matters* became part of the national faith; and his message that literature gives us a critical habit of mind—which saves us from living like rats in a cage, mice in a tunnel—became a more uncertain part of that faith. The middle class could help England most by broadening its habits, reading foreign books, and bringing to bear foreign ideas on its industrial life and culture. That class's insularity became Arnold's target. Yet he was not doctrinaire; he implied that the critic is fair, just, and useful when tentative, that the judgment which forms itself along with fresh knowledge is valuable, and that the critic must dwell "much on foreign thought." By communicating knowledge "not as an abstract lawgiver" but as a "companion and clue," any critic does the most good.[58]

He was changing the English quality of life and "flexibility of intelligence" was now to be reckoned with. Students at Oxford, Cambridge, London, and the Scottish universities were reading him. His *Essays* made him the leading critic of his age and set the characteristic viewpoint—and many of the terms—for criticism in the next century. Arnold's Christian humanism seemed nourished by diverse religious traditions and by a knowledge of works of art and intellect past and present. He demanded only a belief that art is *not* moralistic, but moral in concerning men and women in society even when it thrusts beyond morality into the playful, demonic, or antisocial.

This spring, he eluded some of the minor hubbub over the *Essays*. In parliament M. E. Grant-Duff, who admired *A French Eton*, had urged the Liberals to set up a Schools Enquiry Commission under Lord Taunton—with William Forster, Frederick Temple, and Edward Baines among others—to look into secondary education. The Commission was hardly "open-minded"[59] to a national system of secondary schools, as Arnold noticed. Lord Taunton was dull and cool; Baines as a "voluntaryist" was an archenemy of state aid; even Temple, hostile to state support since becoming Rugby's new Headmaster, tried to keep Arnold off the board. Lingen tried to sabotage Arnold's salary and then sent him a captious letter. Still, his appointment to the Commission was approved.

His mission in France, Germany, Italy, and Switzerland for the Taunton Commission gave him ammunition for a book on European higher education. His children were not happy to have him leave, and neither was Fanny Lucy. He wanted to bundle them all to the Continent; Flu clearly was less happy about that and funds were short. But she agreed to meet him, with the children and a governess, for a holiday in the Black Forest after he had "done" France and Italy. He was to cram all the school-seeing possible into the very fewest days, swelter in the Italian heat, and then presumably recover in Germany. At first all went well. Leaving his family in April 1865, he spent four busy weeks looking at the Paris *lycées* and then crossed the Alps. "We began to go through the Apennines," Arnold wrote back. "I could just see what a beautiful place Bologna was on the lower slopes . . . and the descent was before us. Everything was changed; it was the real Italy; the weather had cleared, it was all sunshine and white clouds. . . . It was for this country I was predestined."

Despite that good beginning, he found schools shut and officials hard to see in Italy. Affected by the heat, he lived for days on a diet of bread, black coffee, and "ices."[60] One morning at the Bay of Spezzia he hired a boat, and half a mile from land stripped off his clothes. Believing that Shelley had drowned in this "soft blue Spezzian Bay," he plunged into the water, and his blackish hair swirled round his face. Matthew hardly wanted to surface. Red from the sun, a forty-two-year-old Inspector found the sea so welcoming "it was difficult ever to bring one's head up out of it." Finally, back in the boat, this heavy, red walrus of an Englishman was touched by delicate beauty in the scene: going back to land, he watched ascending outlines of hills and cypresses "rising up like spines" among lovely towers, and then the majesty of ferns, waving everywhere.[61]

After imitating the Forsaken Merman in green depths, he became oddly disoriented. He jotted confused nonsense about schools—and listened in naïve wonder to Carlo Matteucci, an electrophysicist who served as a harassed Minister of Public Instruction to Victor Emmanuel II. With more credulity, he heard some poppycock from George P. Marsh, American Minister to the Kingdom of Italy, and walked with him in the sun at Turin. Marsh envied young men in the American legation who spoke Italian fluently. "There is great truth," writes Arnold (who spoke French and Italian, and struggled with German and Dutch), "in Mr. Marsh's remark that the speaking several languages tends to make the thought thin and shallow."[62]

In acute misery from the heat, he survived four hours of classes at Milan, on June 24, and the next day set out for Germany. The Alps refreshed him. Then at Berlin, the air was crisp. His metabolism troubled him not at all in this lively, bracing city. He walked into a class in Friedrich-Wilhelms Gymnasium just as Dr. Ferdinand Ranke (a brother of Germany's famous historian) began a lesson on Sophocles' *Philoctetes;* and he saw other schools and universities when they were preeminent in Europe. The former Prussian Minister Wilhelm von Humboldt, a friend of Goethe and Schiller and veritable founder in 1810 of the University of Berlin, had lifted Prussia to cultural glory. Here, at Berlin, teachers distrusted examinations; they believed in "total cultivation" of pupils, and in Humboldt's thesis that schools exist "to raise the culture of the nation ever higher and higher."[63]

Less than eighty years later, a Berlin Reichskanzler appointed an Education Minister from the Nazi party. Fearing the political dependency of schools even in France, Arnold in 1865 found a snake in Germany's paradise. The Prussian system was entirely dependent on the whims and control of a single Minister, Dr. von Mühler, who refused, at first, to appoint a school director because "his politics . . . were unacceptable." Arnold interviewed that school director and began to "dislike"[64] the language of Von Mühler. "They all told me," Arnold writes uneasily in his German report, "that the State administration of the schools was in practice fair and right; that public opinion would not suffer it to be governed by political regards."[65]

His aim in "Germany" in his *Schools and Universities* is to show how England, lacking even school boards, may learn from Prussia's organized, strong state system. Thus it is noteworthy that he observes a flaw. Before his eyes the German ideal of culture, having passed from the Weimar circle to Von Humboldt who embodied it in a humane school system, was being mocked by a practice (invidious in Germany even late in the twentieth century) of refusing to confirm school directors because of their "politics." Arnold benefited from what humane, shrewd teachers told him at Berlin—but after taking "pains" to inquire, he felt that freedom in most German schools was marginally less imperiled than in French schools.

In July he vacationed with his family at Kiefernadel Bad, in the Black Forest. For once, the boys were well. Budge and Dick, now eleven and nine, became sailors on a clear and shallow stream at the bottom of their Gernsbach hotel garden. "Dick has his trousers rolled up to his hips and his feet bare" and "Budge has an old pair of waterproof leggings," Matthew noted. Taking his girls Lucy and Nelly, now six and four, by either hand, he looked in forests for wildflowers. He even noticed that Tommy, fragile as ever at thirteen, was keeping a diary. Tommy rose to eloquence:

> A thunderstorm came on. I never saw anything to equal it. The sky was so black that I thought there would either be an earthquake or that night was coming before its time.

With the children, "it is almost impossible to be depressed," Matthew felt. They "have so good an effect on my spirits."[66]

In September he went on across the German states to Schulpforta and then to Dresden, Prague, Vienna. At a meeting with Lingen in Vienna, he pleaded for a month to see Württemberg and other places he had missed. Having learned that his commission couldn't be extended, he came home by November 1 with an "ocean" of documents to fill his study. Slowly, amid much other work, he turned that ocean into the report which appeared in March 1868 as *Schools and Universities on the Continent*.

That book might be a giant x-ray of his mind. With the Alps as a boundary, everything Arnold says about northern nations is rational and cogent; but nearly everything on Italy is bizarre, emotive, and suggestive of a dreamworld. What is so interesting is that in "Italy" he denies the evidence of his senses and appears, as he wrote of the Celts, *"to react against the despotism of fact."*[67]

In "Italy," he imagines Ugo Foscolo of *Letters of Ortis* teaching with men who never taught with Foscolo. Having *seen* vivid paintings in the Uffizi Gallery, Arnold calls the Italian Renaissance a "literary" movement. Next follows a history of Italy more bizarre than anything suggested by Carlo Matteucci's *Raccolta di Scritti* or *Istruzione pubblica*—although it may reflect what he had heard from Matteucci and Marsh. After the Renaissance the Church, Arnold explains, became an "anti-intellectual influence" so "fatal" as to take the "soul" out of Italian schools. "Natural sciences alone" thrived. Then came the arrival of French troops. Since the Church had fought against "the liberal culture of the human spirit," French bayonets did good by bringing to Italy the spirit of 1789. Indeed, says Arnold,

> the great merit of the French Revolution, the great service it rendered to Europe, was *to get rid of the Middle Age*: very few Englishmen yet perceive even that.[68]

Pressed for time in England, he thus boils up several chapters out of notes composed in Italy when he was drenched in sweat and living on black coffee. He then offers firsthand evidence about Church schools —and *all* of it tenderly supports the Church! Classes under ecclesiastical management were among the "best" he saw; priests who suppressed culture were teaching pagan *"Virgil"* (underlined by Arnold) better than anyone else; "nowhere on the Continent" did he see better accommodation than in one Church school, "nowhere in Italy"[69] did he hear Greek so well taught as at another. One rubs one's eyes. Were all of the priests and nuns *perfect* teachers? His bizarre report on "Italy" seems written by two men, the first hostile to the "Middle Age," the other anxiously yearning for it.

A year before going to Italy, he had walked in Wales with the easy, reflective Tom Arnold. "All interests are here," Matthew wrote happily of Wales, "—Celts, Romans, Saxons, Druidism, Middle Age. . . ."[70] His paradoxical longing for faith and the "Middle Age," and rational dislike of that yearning, are explored in the engaging lectures he printed in 1866 and collected a year later as *On the Study of Celtic Literature*. For pages in this delightful work, with its racial theories occasionally mocked by its author, there is nothing very logical. We might be reading a psychoanalytic transcript by a relaxed Matthew, dreamily telling us what he *sees* when we say to him words such as "German," "Celt," or "Englishman." "The German," writes Matthew easily,

> has the larger volume of intestines (and who that has ever seen a German at a table-d'hote will not readily believe this?), the Frenchman has the more developed organs of respiration. That is just the expansive, eager Celtic nature; the head in the air, snuffing and snorting [and] sentimental,—*always ready to react against the despotism of fact. . . .* Balance, measure, and patience are just what the Celt has never had. . . . No doubt the sensibility of the Celtic nature, its nervous exultation, have something feminine in them, and the Celt is thus peculiarly disposed to feel the spell of the feminine idiosyncrasy. . . . [All of this] points to a certain mixture and strife of elements in the Englishman; to the clashing of a Celtic quickness of perception with a Germanic instinct for going steadily. . . . No people, therefore, are so shy, so self-conscious, so embarrassed as the English, because two natures are mixed in them, and natures which pull them such different ways.[71]

Having parted company, as he says, with "brother Saxons," Arnold uses the terms "Celtic" and "German" and "Saxon" to define aspects of himself. He *denies* none of himself; even his laughter is racially respectable since it belongs to the impressionable Celt who is "sociable, hospitable, eloquent, admired, figuring away brilliantly," in love with "bright colours" and easily audacious. He not only pictures and organizes his emotive temperament, but objectifies his tensions by finding in Englishmen a "clashing" of traits.[72]

He thus explores his mind before writing two textured, brilliant masterpieces—two books which T. S. Eliot believed could be read any number of times; and we see in the Celtic book one reason why *Culture and Anarchy* and *Friendship's Garland* are always fresh, never to be put aside. Since he identifies with classes and races his social comments have the added intensity of autobiography. His best essays are emotionally as taut as scenes in Shakespeare; the emotive attitude to the idea, in Arnold, enriches the idea, so that we feel he is driving at the heart of human life.

For *Celtic Literature* he drew on talks with his philological friend, Max Müller, and on works by Renan, Eugene O'Curry, Lord Strangford, and others, to make a case for Irish and Welsh poetry. His book caused Oxford to set up a chair of Celtic studies. Veering into politics, he begs for sympathy for the Welsh and Irish and very deliciously cites some "asperities" from the press. " 'The Welsh language is the curse of Wales,' " he quotes from an anti-Celtic tirade in which the London *Times* pontificated:

> Not only the energy and power, but the intelligence and music of Europe come mainly from Teutonic sources, and this glorification of everything Celtic, if it were not pedantry, would be sheer ignorance. The sooner all Welsh specialties disappear from the face of the earth the better.

"I have made a study of the Corinthian or leading article style," Arnold comments blandly. This newspaper style is "no more to be quarreled with than the law of gravitation. So, for my part, when I read these asperities in *The Times* . . . what I said to myself, as I put the newspaper down, was this: '*Behold England's difficulty in governing Ireland!*' "[73]

He remembered a genial employer who wanted cuts in relief, while predicting "1,000,000 of deaths" in Ireland; he could recall, too, Arthur Stanley's sentimental Oxford liberalism. Stanley loved the Irish and termed them "Barbarian." Arnold adopted that easy political liberalism, too, by writing idly of "independent Ireland" while implying the Irish are "Children," and adding that "the Irish article is not to my taste." Phrases such as "even the Irish" came to him easily. One reason for Arnold's lack of faith in Gladstone's Irish policies, later, was his *own* experience with a facile liberalism.

The Time's generous wish to improve the world, by making "all Welsh specialties disappear from the face of the earth," reminded him of British history. For England and Ireland this was a tale of bloody suppression, commercial jealousy, neglect, indifference, and anti-Catholic prejudice. British policy during the Elizabethan wars had been to deprive the recalcitrant Irish of their means of livelihood. Controlling Irish legislation, England destroyed Ireland's manufacturing industries in the south and west by commercial restraints, inhibited cattle-raising, and forbade the people to export wool. The Irish were taught to break laws to survive; an illicit traffic in wool between Ireland and France kept many people alive. Land became the main property, potatoes the main Irish crop. When potato harvests failed, Irish peasants even in the eighteenth century starved. Only Irish Protestant freeholders voted until 1793 and indeed eight years later the Act of Union between Britain and Ireland (effective on January 1, 1801) wiped out the Irish Parliament and imposed on a mainly Catholic people a Protestant hegemony. Between 1830 and 1870 every attempt to solve the "Irish Question" was defeated in Parliament by a coalition of great English landlords and Ireland's "Protestant garrison," ascendant since 1801. M.P.s proposed land settlement bills, agricultural education, new housing ideas, state-owned railways, laws protecting the peasant from landlords. The wreckage of these ideas bred cynicism in England about Ireland; and if Gladstone was the first statesman "in whose thought the Irish problem was central,"[74] Parliament would continue, into the next century, to do too little thinking about Ireland—to inquire, to listen, and to propose too little. Even in the 1970s there was no permanent Parliamentary fact-finding and negotiating committee in violent Ulster.

In Arnold's time the Irish economy was *always* fearful. Low wages, recurring famines, absentee landlords demanding exorbitant rent for mere cabins, the brutal and large-scale eviction of tenants—which could incite homeless parents to crush a child's head, or stifle a baby in crib or hamper, to get Burial Allowance money—all led to deeper hatred of the British and then to guns and dynamite in the Fenian campaign for independence. As brutality was repaid by mindless violence, one might see the ending of cohesiveness in that same British Empire which made *The Times* so proud: "we have a great empire," Arnold warned his countrymen; "so had Nebuchadnezzar."[75]

He identified the obtuse manner of thinking which politics engenders, and criticized in the light of Ireland our fine beliefs in liberty, political parties, and democracy. Arnold asks us to consider the limits and disadvantages of even our best ideas. Democracy encourages us to imagine opponents: "to *go contrary*"[76] is our habit in democratic politics and to hate the nation that lacks political liberty is our rule. But what if the *terms* for solving an "Irish Question" are not of opposition, but of active intelligence and understanding, historical perspective and sympathy? Calling himself "a Liberal tempered by renouncement,"[77] he edited Burke's *intelligent* Irish speeches, and refrained from party loyalties himself but supported M.P.s who lacked blind partisan feeling. "Gladstone is simply using Ireland for his party purposes, and the danger is that Balfour may do the same," he wrote later, but "there is really a large number of men on the Conservative side determined not to throw in their lot with the Irish landlords and anxious to do what is right."[78]

Arguing in *Celtic Literature* that British greatness springs from a mixture of Celtic, Teutonic, and Norman bloods, he would ask the Irish to be forgiving. He felt that it might be too late for forgivingness. "In order to attach Ireland to us," he wrote in *Irish Essays,* the "English people have not only to *do* something different . . . they have to *be* something different."[79] He brooded over Land Tenure, Rent Law, Ulster, and a witch's tangle of factors behind unrest. In "A Word More about America," in February 1885, he proposed dividing Ireland into three or four provincial areas, each with its own assembly, based on the system of the United States. Then in "Up to Easter" (May 1887), written eleven months before he died, he suggested two provinces based on religion. His "overwhelming anxiety over Ireland"[80] led him, in short, to propose for the "Irish Question" a tireless search for new light and solutions. In the deepest sense, he viewed Ireland as a part of himself.

With "My Countrymen" in 1866 he dropped literary criticism for ten years, and with new and at times desperate worry over the violence in the United Kingdom, he turned to social comment. He began his "Baron Arminius" letters for *Friendship's Garland* and gave his last Oxford speech, on "Culture and Its Enemies," before a slim green volume of *New Poems* appeared in July 1867.

Now that his lyric talent was virtually dead, critics enjoyed and even praised *New Poems.* Matthew's friends, too, were helpful. Browning had urged him to reprint *Empedocles* and prompted him to collect his new sonnets such as "East London" and "West London"—which allude to urban squalor in reply to Wordsworth's London sonnets. The volume is heavy with sonnets, and rather prosily impassioned. In "Anti-Desperation" and "Austerity of Poetry," as in the more lyrical

"Monica's Last Prayer" and paradoxical "Immortality," he alludes to the inward force a social critic will need. In "Last Word," Matthew treats his own social zeal more ironically:

> *Vain thy onset! all stands fast.*
> *Thou thyself must break at last.*
>
> *Let the long contention cease!*
> *Geese are swans, and swans are geese.*
> *Let them have it as they will!*
> *Thou art tired; best be still.*
>
> . . . . . .
>
> *Let the victors, when they come,*
> *When the forts of folly fall,*
> *Find thy body by the wall.*[81]

To offset the gloom of *Empedocles,* he imagines a sumptuous dawn breaking over the Swiss Valais in "Obermann Once More" and hears Senancour speaking of a "joy whose grounds are true." When Sainte-Beuve told him that he had portrayed an "Obermann transfigured,"[82] he replied that he had *meant* Senancour to sound like an arid ghost of 1789. Poetry, for Arnold, was not a good vehicle for optimism. His best pieces in *New Poems* are his darker "Heine's Grave" and "Lessing's 'Laocoön.' " The first concerns the "love" for mankind that Heine truly lacked; and the second, the complex "movement" of life which is ideally poetry's subject—and in which culture is to operate.

Very limited and ungodlike in strength, after all, Matthew of late had tried to find a new job. In Germany, he had told the surprised and admiring teachers, "*Ich hatte nicht die Absicht die Schulcarriere zu machen*" (I never meant to take to school-inspection work).[83] In England, he tried and failed to become a Charity Commissioner and then an Endowed Schools Commissioner. When he applied to be Librarian of the House of Commons, Gladstone flatly turned him down and invited him to breakfast. Yet he did not try very hard to obtain these jobs; he of course meant to convert or enlighten the middle classes, come what might. "I shall do what I can," he had written to Jane, "with the risk always before me, if I cannot charm the wild beast of Philistinism while I am trying to convert him, of being torn in pieces . . . and even if I succeed," he added very lightly, "of dying in a ditch or a workhouse at the end of it all."[84]

15

THE IDEAS OF
"CULTURE AND ANARCHY"
1866–1872

Something bookish, pedantic, and futile has got itself
more or less connected with the word culture. . . . A man
without books or reading [has culture, if he] gets nevertheless a fresh and free play of the best thoughts upon
his stock notions and habits.

—*Culture and Anarchy*, 1869

Budge!
showers in day—hard rain at night.
Budge's funeral!
rain
heavy rain
—*Diary*

WHY did Matthew Arnold turn so urgently in 1866 to pure social
criticism? He stated his aim as a social critic when he said he
meant to exhort a nation "to healing measures and an attractive form
of civilisation." Broadly his view of society was uncomplicated: the
British aristocracy seemed moribund, and the working class lacked
political power. Hence he would exhort the middle classes—mainly
the busy Dissenters of the day (members of sects other than the
Anglican one). These people had "a defective type of religion, a narrow
range of intellect and knowledge, a stunted sense of beauty."[1] They
were politically ascendant but almost oblivious to their failings.

One only had to look at Prussia and France, Arnold believed, to see
how nations with strong, well-organized school systems and govern-
ments were getting far ahead of England. Prussia lately had detached
the duchies of Schleswig and Holstein from Denmark. Now in a
position to fulfill the dream of Frederick the Great, Bismarck was
ready to unite the German states—and thus England might soon
contend with an immensely potent new Germany. France seemed
almost equally strong, with her good schools, fine capillary network of

communes and cantons, and effective idea that the state exists to *help* all the people.

England, in contrast, seemed disorganized, chaotic, and vulnerable to panic. An outbreak of cattle disease or the fall of a commercial house sent tremors everywhere. Only one-sixth of the male population could vote (as late as 1866) and most of the working class was unrepresented in Parliament, which now debated laws against the working-class trade unions. At giant meetings of the Reform League, speakers angrily demanded the franchise. Ireland, too, was seething. Resorting to murder and mayhem, the Irish Fenian nationalists were taking their guns and explosives into English streets. Late in 1867 they blew up a barrel of gunpowder at Clerkenwell, killing twelve people and injuring a hundred. "I was dining at the Garrick Club," wrote Arnold, "when one of the guests came in saying that his hansom had nearly been knocked down by a string of cabs with policemen filling them inside and out, hurrying to Clerkenwell prison, which had been blown up by the Fenians."[2] What Arnold called "anarchy"—or the Do Nothing, Think Nothing, laissez faire attitude to politics and economics, religion and morals—could be discerned throughout the nation.

For sixteen years, he had been an empirical observer of the English people in scores of communities and had talked with farmers and engineers, clergymen and businessmen, working-class trainees and children, day in and out. He had looked into European societies, in two five-month tours abroad, and had come back from Prussia and France with very exact findings. In his official reports and books he had tried to assimilate his data. Now, in the light of his comparative experience, he could see how England's crises pitted one social class against another and kept people from getting any detached, free perspective. The Governor Eyre case, perhaps, was symptomatic.

Brutality in Jamaica, lately, had divided even English intellectuals at home. Governor Edward John Eyre, after a riot in Jamaica in October 1865, had hanged a civic leader and innocent black citizen named George Gordon, and then had brought terror more largely to the sugar colony. In a month his troops burned a thousand homes, flogged 600 men and women, and hanged or shot 586 black Jamaican citizens. Letters from the British officers in Jamaica were soon quoted in the British press. For example Colonel Elkington, then Deputy Adjutant-General at Jamaica, wrote to a fellow officer and was quoted in the *Saturday Review* in April 1866: "*Hole is doing splendid service with his men about Manchioneal, and shooting every black man who cannot give an account of himself. Nelson, at Port Antonio, is hanging like fun by court-martial. I hope you will not send us any prisoners; civil law can do nothing. . . . Do punish the blackguards well.*"[3]

There was indignant fury in England. Led by John Stuart Mill, a committee was formed to indict Governor Eyre for murder—and a Royal Commission looked into the case. (Eyre was quickly removed from office.) But since black men had massacred white settlers at Haiti, both *The Times* and *Punch* spoke up for Eyre and the principle of blunt authority. Carlyle's "Eyre Defense Committee" drew support not only from aristocrats, such as Lord Elcho, but from Ruskin, Tennyson, and even Dickens. Perhaps the English schoolchild who wrote about "ferocious aborigines"—and whose words Arnold quoted in his diary—had sounded *one* of the age's keynotes. In India, Jamaica, and Tasmania, white settlers and troops used vicious force to control natives partly because Victorians felt no compunction about exploiting and ruining cultures unlike their own (and in fact genocide on the island of Tasmania was to be totally effective—not one Tasmanian aborigine was left alive, later in the next century).

Refusing to take part in the bitter Governor Eyre controversy, Arnold only alluded to "Jamaica" in a letter to the *Pall Mall Gazette* in March 1866: "In hearts we are (except when we find ourselves in India or Jamaica) very well off; but in heads there is always room for improvement."[4] Nevertheless, he used the Jamaican occasion to strike to the heart of a conventional belief in political liberty. The murdered black Jamaicans had not been especially "free"; and perhaps, by equating freedom with "political liberty," Englishmen blind themselves to humane lessons they might learn from nations less democratic than their own. His argument focuses on France. "So the *Morning Star* and I are to go on crying 'We are free! We are free!' " writes Arnold, attacking his countrymen for failing to compare themselves with the French (who may be instructive even though they lack liberty under Napoleon III). Arnold believed that the Englishman's penchant for boasting about political freedom, or of the right of "Doing as One Likes," does itself contribute to the lethally insular state of mind. He reasonably explains his interest in France: "What makes me look at France and the French with such inexhaustible curiosity and indulgence is this,—their faults are not ours, so we are not likely to catch them; their merits are not ours, so we are not likely to become idle and self-sufficient from studying them."[5]

His attitude to the "Eyre" case was at least "healing" and mild; but the very near view of political events filled him with worries and emotional conflicts. For example, he was hardly detached and calm when London's commissioner of police prohibited a large meeting in Hyde Park which the Reform League had set for July 23, 1866. The League's leaders, Edmond Beales and Sheffield Dickson, on that day tried to take their demonstration past the park to Trafalgar Square. At

Bayswater Road and Park Lane, the crowds became violent and smashed down a thousand yards of Hyde Park railings. That evening, rioters surged into Chester Square and stoned the windows of Sir Richard Mayne, the police commissioner, as Matthew and Fanny Lucy watched from their balcony. Matthew, later on, went to sit in the visitors' gallery at the House of Commons "to hear what was said about the rioting." He came away utterly furious over the weakness of the police and the "talking and shilly-shallying and crying" of the Home Secretary, yet paradoxically relieved not to live in a police state and glad the police were *not* stronger: "I do not think it, in itself, a bad thing that the principle of authority should be so weak here,"[6] Matthew told his mother.

He was too emotional to see politics in the near view steadily; and in these years he was irritated by the political successes of his brother-in-law William Forster, who had become an M.P. for Bradford and a leader of advanced Liberals. Coming down with Jane from their Yorkshire house, "Wharfeside," to 80 Eccleston Square in London, and seeing a good deal of the Arnolds, Forster soon proved his competence as a political strategist. As a Privy Councillor and Vice-President of the Education Council (and Matthew Arnold's official superior) he was to introduce in the Commons in February 1870 his splendid, if flawed, Elementary Education Bill. Astutely, Forster guided it to success. If it failed to settle the problem of religious training in state-sponsored schools, Forster's act set up a workable system of school boards and became the basis for England's later national system of education.

"A man has no business to deal with matters of public concern without having seriously studied them," Matthew writes to his mother indignantly in 1867; and then with much venom and jealousy: "Soon men like William Forster, who entirely give up real study and think they are or can keep qualified for public affairs by . . . going into Bradford, reading the newspapers, going to the House, going to the Cosmopolitan [Club], will be left behind. I can see signs."[7] Matthew was not jealous by nature; but he still found it hard to endure a brotherly rival, and particularly one who seemed likely to achieve practical success in the field of education beyond anything he himself had accomplished. He *liked* the tall, simple, hoarse Forster, and even meant to love him for "K's" sake. In his published work, Matthew tried to purge himself of bitterness and self-pity, even as Forster, in the 1860s, went on from one parliamentary success to the next.

To soften the caustic effect of his essay "My Countrymen," he had sent in July 1866 to the *Pall Mall Gazette* a letter quoting a funny Baron Arminius von Thunder-ten-Tronckh, a blue-eyed, pipe-smoking

Prussian who visits his friend "poor Matthew Arnold" of Grub Street. The Baron is descended from Voltaire's *Candide.* He puffs blue smoke, drinks Matthew's ale, enjoys finding "poor Mr. Matthew Arnold" pilloried in the press as a "high priest of the kid-gloves persuasion," and writes to the *Gazette* himself.[8] The real author of these various dramatic letters (collected later as *Friendship's Garland*) is so charming, funny, and self-effacing that he seems almost invulnerable to criticism. Arnold here typically laughs at his own doctrine of the grand style; "Arminius (his real name is Hermann, but I call him Arminius because it is more in the grand style)"; and, indeed, he urbanely makes fun of himself at every turn:

> There was that broken-down acquaintance of my early youth, Mr. Matthew Arnold . . . snivelling and crying in a corner. [But] Mr. Matthew Arnold counts for nothing.[9]

Zealous about what he calls "Geist" or Intelligence, Baron Arminius brightly comments on the stupidity of English Liberal nostrums such as a deceased wife's sister bill which would enable a man to marry his dead wife's sister—an epitome of Liberal reforms. Winningly, he puts forth Arnoldian views on foreign policy, on education, or on newspapers such as the *Daily Telegraph,* which has the largest circulation in the world and a fusty patriotic style. Matthew has to correct Arminius's view that the *Telegraph* is "incorrigibly lewd":

> Though I do certainly think its prose a little full-bodied, yet I cannot bear to hear Arminius apply such a term to it as "incorrigibly lewd;" and I always remonstrate with him. "No, Arminius," I always say, "I hope not *incorrigibly.*"[10]

So urbane that he knows the best people, Matthew introduces the Baron to Viscount Lumpington—a mindless Etonian who represents the landed interests—and then to a fatuous Rev. Esau Hittall, a Tory who stands for the Church. Matthew's third friend is Bottles, Esq., a millionaire bottles manufacturer who rides the Reigate train while dreaming of marrying his dead wife's sister. Bottles has read nothing of importance, and thought nothing of importance, ever since leaving Lycurgus House, Peckham, where his teacher was Archimedes Silverpump, Ph.D.—the Ph.D. being then uncommon in England and suggestive of pedantry. Sure enough, he is exuberantly proud of his education. Speaking like Dickens's Mr. Jingle in *Pickwick,* Bottles boasts of his schooling: "Original man, Silverpump!" he tells the poor Matthew, "fine mind! fine system! none of your antiquated rubbish —all practical work—latest discoveries in science—mind constantly kept excited—lots of interesting experiments—lights of all colours —fizz! fizz! bang! bang! That's what I call forming a man!"[11]

Few passages in Arnold's comic prose are more interesting. *None of your antiquated rubbish—all practical work* are phrases that might apply to the schooling of William Forster, who was educated at Fishponds House, Bristol, and at Mr. Binns's School, Tottenham, before he went to work twelve hours a day in a woollen mill. *Lights of all colours—fizz! fizz! bang! bang!* reminds one of Mrs. Mary Arnold's love of excitement and of the sputtering, winking lights of panoramas and dioramas she adored; and the *whole* portrait of Bottles seems to attack Mrs. Arnold's, Jane's, and Forster's simple faith in "Reform." That word is at the core of Matthew's entire experience of his family, and in the 1860s it is on everyone's lips in England. Bottles "has always gone straight as an arrow about Reform." "Table," as Arnold cries, "the whole Liberal creed, and in not a single point of it will you find Bottles tripping!" The same could be said of William Forster, Liberal M.P. for Yorkshire. In a later dramatic letter, Arnold specifies one enemy of fresh ideas in England as "the earnest liberalism and nonconformity of Lancashire and Yorkshire."[12]

And yet far from deliberately holding Forster up to ridicule, he purged much of his bitterness in the Baron Arminius letters, and strongly clarified his own ideas. By April and May 1867 when he began preparing the Oxford lecture that became "Sweetness and Light" for *Culture and Anarchy,* he had defined two types of man.

Comically and exaggeratedly, the first type of man is represented by Mr. Bottles; the second type, by Baron Arminius. In life the first type of man is William Forster, the person with a practical view who puts his trust in political nostrums and embodies the self-reliance of the English. The second type puts his trust in "culture," because he knows that he does not *know enough*. In Arnold's life, the man of culture is represented by such a figure as Crabb Robinson, whom he happened to meet at the Athenaeum Club on a January night of this year.

He had found this meeting unusually moving. At ninety-one, Henry Crabb Robinson, the Arnold family's vocal friend, had made his way over to the club from 30 Russell Square. Robinson, in himself, was a record of European cultural history ever since his birth in 1775. Having heard John Wesley preach, he had later met Goethe and Schiller and then William Blake, and actually befriended not only Charles Lamb, but S. T. Coleridge and Robert Southey. Loyal to Wordsworth, Crabb Robinson was with that poet in Switzerland, and again with him in Italy. He had found young Matthew Arnold rather trying but had seen that Matthew the dandy was very bright and promising. Lately, he had seen the fuss over *Essays in Criticism* in the reviews. After an exchange of compliments, on this January evening, Matthew offered to send him a copy of those *Essays*.

"No, no, I'll buy them. Don't throw them away upon an old fellow like me," replied the friend of Goethe and Wordsworth. "I shall be dead in a fortnight."[13]

If Matthew wished to get home to Fanny Lucy's dinner, he had to wait. Robinson smiled up from an armchair and began to recite the epigrams of Goethe, filling the yellow air of the Athenaeum Club on a winter night with German verses. Arnold knew these verses by heart:

> *Musst immer tun wie neugeboren* (You must always behave like one new born.)
> *Was ist ein Philister?* . . . (What is a Philistine? A hollow gut, stuffed with fears and hopes. Merciful God!)
> *Ich traumt und liebte* . . . (I was dreaming and loving clear as day; I realized that I was alive.)[14]

A day or two later, Crabb Robinson received a copy of Matthew Arnold's *Essays*. He read the first piece in the book. Then in a firm hand he wrote the final entry in his famous old battered red-leather diary:

> Thursday 31st JANUARY During the last two days I have read the first *critical* essay—On the qualifs of the prent age of Critcism . . . Mat Arnold . . . thinks of Germany As he ought And of Goethe with high admiration—On this point I can possibly give him assistance which he will gladly (but I feel incapable to go on)

> *In pencil in another hand:*

> H C R died
> 5 February 1867[15]

When he heard that Crabb Robinson had died, Arnold wrote a moving paragraph in which he told his mother, he "most called up the thought of old days, and passed away people."[16] In the "old days" at Fox How when Dr. Arnold and Wordsworth were alive, Robinson had spoken of Goethe, Schiller, Mme de Staël and many others. Some of these associations were in Arnold's mind when on June 7, a few months after seeing Robinson, he finished "Culture and Its Enemies," and drove up with his wife and boys to give it as a lecture at Oxford. The university was then in trouble. In the exciting political air with talk of "reform" everywhere, Oxford seemed to many observers a place of the past, losing its prestige and effect. Rousing with the spirit of Robinson's "passed away people," Arnold certainly aimed to tell a badly divided audience of old Newman Ritualists, Broad Church dons, young university men and students that *their* Oxford still had a crucial role to play. What he offered was his most searching, dramatic piece of social criticism.

First, he quotes in his lecture some of his recent, outspoken critics and opponents. In response to a notion of culture aired in his *Essays,* he says, the *Daily Telegraph* has called him an "elegant Jeremiah." John Bright, the reforming M.P. and tribune of the people, who was so quick to support Mill in the "Governor Eyre Case," thinks the idea of "culture" is effete. Frederic Harrison, a bright young Comtian critic, calls culture "the silliest cant of the day."[17]

Instead of refuting these men, Arnold admits, in this final talk at Oxford, that he himself is a political Liberal tempered by "experience" and "renouncement." He simply intends to explore culture's usefulness. What then is culture? He cites Montesquieu, Bishop Wilson, and Epictetus to show that it may be intellectual curiosity, a passionate desire to help society, or a temper of mind. Viewed too narrowly, culture becomes a shibboleth or a nostrum, a divider of the social classes and a thing only for the educated. In a later piece for *Culture and Anarchy,* he defines culture, almost dutifully, as

> a pursuit of our total perfection by means of getting to know, on all matters which most concern us, the best that has been thought and said in the world; and through this knowledge, turning a stream of fresh and free thought upon our stock notions and habits.[18]

But he is less specific at the outset since he wants to suggest an *inward operation,* or an attitude of mind which alone guarantees intellectual and creative freedom in an urban society.

If we are to be free to develop in mind and spirit, we must know our enemies. Arnold's analysis of the "enemies" of culture is so profound that it applies to societies more than a century later. First, he says, "the mechanical and material civilisation we esteem" imperils *inwardness* of the spirit. Without inward life, no man or woman is imaginatively free. Second, our competition separates us from our fellows. Without sympathetically helping others in their development, we are "stunted and enfeebled." Third, "our intense energetic absorption in the particular pursuit we are following" forestalls the development of our own nature. Thus, what culture demands for each individual is an *harmonious* expansion of powers; unless we have inward lives, assist our fellows, and refuse to be limited by specialization in work we cannot fulfill ourselves. But what are to be the sources of that "stream of fresh and free thought" thrown "upon our stock notions and habits"?[19]

Contrary to what is sometimes said of him, Arnold condemns any pure trust in the higher culture. He draws a distinction between bookishness, which he sees as inadequate and provincial, and the natural and unfussy love of books, which he sees as an attitude ensuring for us an inexhaustible source of liberation and refreshment. He stresses the tyranny of the political man with one set of books on the shelf, of "men with a system, of disciples, of a school." At Oxford he had read one writer to be free of another; and now he recalls being under the spell of Benjamin Franklin until he found "a stretch of humanity" beyond Franklin's good sense and then of being caught by Jeremy Bentham's seemingly cogent books until he was "delivered from the bondage of Bentham."[20] Culture, then, is a psychological attitude which implies a refusal to be locked in, finally enrolled, or seduced by any idea except the idea of mental freedom. From *Empedocles* and on to *Culture and Anarchy*, he attacked knowingness, the fetish of stuffing oneself with either facts or elegant culture. "Something bookish, pedantic, and futile," he admits, "has got itself more or less connected with the word culture." A calm, reasonable attitude to reading immensely helps us; but in *Culture and Anarchy* he most interestingly qualifies even his belief in reading. Any man or woman's life seems to depend each day "for its solidity and value" on whether the person reads during that day, and, far more still, on what is read during it. But this is a matter for each "private conscience and experience," for if a person

> without books or reading, or reading nothing but his letters and the newspapers, gets nevertheless a fresh and free play of the best thoughts upon his stock notions and habits, he has . . . that for which we prize and recommend culture. . . . This inward operation is the very life and essence of culture, as we conceive it.[21]

That is a key statement in *Culture and Anarchy* of 1869; when they neglect it, modern critics garble the book's meaning. Arnold's "culture" depends not on libraries but rather on an attitude of mind which is not content with "stock notions and habits."

He chiefly opposes a belief in nostrums, in "machinery," in shibboleths or gimmicks such as the belief that Liberal reforms will alone improve life. Opposing these, he recommends John Henry Newman's pursuit of beauty and intelligence, and speaks of these as "sweetness and light."[22] That Swiftian catch-phrase popularized Arnold's ideas, but drew ridicule, too. He concludes "Culture and Its Enemies" with allusions to Herder and Lessing, humanists who tried to make the best thought of their time prevail. Arnold knew of Herder's and Goethe's idea of man's free inward potential, or *Humanität*, and of their concept of *Bildung*, the process of learning, seeing anew, changing, and developing. Arnold's view of "culture" is derived from Herder, though he enriches the term and emphasizes the *inward freedom* that is the prime condition of mental and spiritual development.

Urbane and mild, his prose style illustrates the attitude of culture as his arguments do. His natural grace in this lecture, his use of what John Holloway calls "value frames" to persuade,[23] his intimacy with the reader and the "portrait" he sketches of himself all raise his work to the level of literature.

As never before, he had "got at" the shallow patriotism and mindless trust in action in his nation. When his lecture appeared in the July *Cornhill,* there was an uproar that lasted for the rest of the year. His "culture" is founded, *The Morning Star* believed, "on the most absurd and obvious misconception." Some, not all, reviewers saw him as a personification of everything dull, absurd, and patrician at Oxford. *The Daily Telegraph* imagined his foppish limbs clothed in a "flowered dressing-gown."[24] "Cultivated hysterics," decided the *London Review.* Arnold is only a sneering mouse in Oxford robes: "Mr. Arnold does not shriek, he only squeaks. . . . We do not forget that he has sneered at our Protestantism, sneered at science, and when he could find nothing else, sneered at English surnames."[25] *The Spectator* accused him of slighting the Christian faith, of proposing in "culture" something that "really has no direct moral authority." Edward Miall for the Noncon-formists, and Henry Sidgwick writing at Cambridge, tended to agree that "culture" left little room for religion.

Shrugging his shoulders, Arnold bided his time. He laughed until he cried over Frederic Harrison's funny, absurd, "Culture: A Dialogue," which made him yearn to respond.[26] However, he only launched late in 1867 and in 1868 his five essays on "Anarchy and Authority" (which became in *Culture and Anarchy* his Chapters 2 through 6). Written thus over the fourteen-month period from June 1867 to August 1868, *Culture and Anarchy* became an intimate dialogue with his critics—a feature which makes it puzzling to read unless one bears in mind that its later chapters reply to what the critics had said of earlier ones. Starting with Chapter 2, Arnold proposes the term "anarchy" for the laissez faire or Do Nothing view in modern society. Disraeli's Reform Bill of 1867, which added a million mainly of the working class to the electorate, is not mistaken, but even this is for Arnold a nostrum, a substitute for England's lack of a strong and humane governing state. The violence of Irish "Fenian" terrorists concerns him. Irishmen turn to violence, partly because *we* use no ideas, no imagination to solve Ireland's troubles. "We are not in danger from Fenianism" or terrorists, says Arnold; we are endangered by a selfish spirit of anarchy which says, "Every man for himself."[27]

"Our social machine is a little out of order," he comments. "There are a good many people in our paradisiacal centres of industrialism and individualism taking the bread out of one another's mouths."[28] His economic criticism of society is here couched in the terms of culture, as critics have noted, but he uses explicit economic terms later in "The Future of Liberalism." Significantly, too, when writing of industrial economics at such *"hell-holes"* as Bolton and St. Helens, where capitalists profit to the neglect of the jobless, Arnold agrees that one may "discover, like those unionist workmen whose words Mr. John Morley quotes, that 'free political institutions do not guarantee the well-being of the toiling class.' "[29] In Arnold's belief that culture "seeks to do away with classes," and that free institutions alone do not guarantee the workers' well-being, he resembles young university radicals of the day such as John Morley, Frederic Harrison, or even James Bryce, who deplored the "alarming increase in the political and still more the social power of wealth."[30] Yet Arnold's outlook is quite as aesthetic as it is economic: he would look to the whole, harmonious development of man's nature. Let us, he asks, arrange our societies so they foster *that*.

In his third piece, in 1868, he calls aristocrats, middle class, and working class England's "Barbarians, Philistines, Populace." These witty poetic fictions describe only a *tendency* or an "average self" in each class, and suggest that the pleasure-loving Barbarian, the dull Philistine, and the violent Populace exist within each citizen. The witty terms also suggest the limits of politics: the parties appeal only to an "average self" in each social class. A democracy cannot dispense with politics; but neither can it do without culture, which is concerned in the "best self" of each citizen. Arnold neglects the social culture of the working class, but he rightly shows how we belong to his "Populace" every time "we snatch up a vehement opinion in ignorance and passion," or "long to crush an adversary by sheer violence," or "adore mere power or success."[31] He assumes we have a "best self" in this: each person, normally, is able to employ his mind and personality to discover what his intellectual or creative goals should be, and is able to make some advance towards them.

As early as "Butler's Sermons," he mocked simplistic, fixed terms in psychology:

> *Affections, Instincts, Principles, and Powers,*
> *Impulse and Reason, Freedom and Control—*
> *So men, unravelling God's harmonious whole,*
> *Rend in a thousand shreds this life of ours.*[32]

In the piece that became "Hebraism and Hellenism," he uses his terms almost in the structuralist manner of Claude Lévi-Strauss. We do not "treat *terms* as independent entities," says that French anthropologist, but take instead as the "basis of analysis the *relations between terms.*"[33] In Arnold's prose, a verbal term throws out its magnetic field and is modified by the field of an opposing word. "Hebraism" for Arnold is the urge to develop moral awareness and "strictness of conscience"; "Hellenism" is the urge to see things as they are, to take delight in clearness, beauty, intellect, and "spontaneity of consciousness."[34] As with the land and sea in "Forsaken Merman," the interactions between these opposites are suggestive.

Forces of Hebraism and Hellenism alternate throughout Western history and in each psyche. Neither force is adequate alone; and the human spirit is "wider" than either of them. Arnold offers the striking example of man's idea of immortality, which seems grander and truer than any single expression of it. St. Paul the "Hebraist" is confused and inconclusive, Plato the "Hellenist" is oversubtle and sterile, in writing about immortality. The implication is that human expression is never equal to the grandeur, depth, and strength of man's spirit.

Man's spirit nevertheless is capable of immense evil (as Hebraism recognizes). It is valid, says Arnold, to view Western man as a "chained captive, labouring with groanings that cannot be uttered," so ridden with sin and inclined to violence that Socrates seems almost a ludicrous optimist.[35] Socrates is terribly at ease in Zion, or complacent about evil. But has not England in the 1860s *too much* concerned herself with moral sin, and *too little* concerned herself with intelligence? Arnold argues that his nation needs more Hellenism, but adds that there is no one doctrine or code that can save a society; again he returns to the plurality and freedom of culture. Letting a "play of thought live and flow round all our activity," we rid ourselves of fanaticism, stock notions, and merely optimistic or fashionably pessimistic views of man. In "Our Liberal Practitioners," which reads like a manifesto for the election of 1868, he holds that the Liberals despite their reforming plans neglect "the sunken populace of our great cities." Why is it that reformers neglect what *would* be socially useful?

> Mr. Sidgwick says that social usefulness really means "losing oneself in a mass of disagreeable, hard, mechanical details," and though all the believers in action are fond of asserting the same thing, yet . . . to lose ourselves is not what we want, but to find ourselves.[36]

Usefulness begins with the Socratic "Know thyself." Lacking self-knowledge, we only misjudge or overlook society's deepest needs. We foment what is ugly, inhumane, and stupid. "Mr. Disraeli educates, Mr. Bright educates," but "we," says Arnold of himself, "pretend to educate no one, for we are still engaged in trying to clear and educate ourselves."[37]

Gathering up his *Cornhill* pieces, he published them on Monday,

January 25, 1869, as *Culture and Anarchy: An Essay in Political and Social Criticism*. The book made slow headway in its time—but its focus on the relation between economic enterprise and Protestant dissent, its study of the emotional liabilities of Puritanism and its toughminded idea of "culture," and above all its view of the forces that inhibit our inward freedom have influenced writers as different as Max Weber, Eliot, Tawney, I. A. Richards, and Raymond Williams. Creative discussions of the individual in society, today, show the book's direct or indirect influence.

What did catch on in his time were phrases such as "Sweetness and Light," since the newspapers picked them up. When he was given the degree of D.C.L. at Oxford in 1870, he was told by the Chancellor that he should have been called *"Vir dulcissime et lucidissime."*[38] "I think *Barbarian* will stick," he wrote earlier to his mother. "A very charming Barbarianess, Lady Portsmouth, expresses a great desire to make my acquaintance." Yet the reviews, in general, were grudging. Glancing at a memo on wooden, smelly latrines or "earth closets" sent by Fanny Lucy's cousin to the India Board, he believed he could smell plenty of dung and piss in reviews: "You will have seen," he wrote to Grant Duff, "all the earth closets lately emptied on my head for my Culture and Anarchy Essays."[39]

His wife, meanwhile, tried to see that he did not become ill with overwork. In these years he seemed at work night and day in London; but he and Fanny Lucy were managing longer holidays in the Lake District, and she encouraged her husband to accept country-house invitations when he could. She was amused when, in September 1866, Matthew had spent a few days with the Grant Duffs in Scotland and made what the papers called his "first salmon capture." First the Banffshire paper reported *that* as a great event; then the *Morning Star* picked it up in London, and Matthew was famous even as a fisherman! He came back from Perth, humbly enough, on a slow train that reached London at night; the train was an hour delayed, yet she and the boys had sat up for him.

He had become, as she knew, a cultural force in the nation's life. He hardly needed to catch a salmon in an ink-black river, under a rainswept Scottish sky, to make the papers take notice. Matthew's name was often before her eyes; and as an intelligent woman Fanny Lucy noticed that he was felt—he was a real presence—in popular criticism, in reviews, in the leading articles, even when he wasn't mentioned. Writers who did not boisterously take sides, or thump for a cause, but who let intelligence play over a topic, revealed his mark and style. He might criticize the insular overly patriotic Young Lions of *The Daily Telegraph;* but even *Daily Telegraph* writers showed their respect when meeting him at parties. Arnold told her of the occasion when one of the aging Young Lions, George Sala, leaned across a dinner table to explain a pet theory about Virgil—that Virgil was a simple, hearty, muddy-booted farmer, as the *Georgics* might prove. Matthew had listened with an infinitely patient smile!

The literary life, in Fanny Lucy's opinion, was an absurdly bizarre carnival in which few of the performers appeared to have the sanity or decency of her husband. Matthew, she believed, had overstepped himself once or twice in gratuitous criticisms of persons; but he had been attacked so often himself that by now she was impressed by his good-natured restraint and resort to mainly inoffensive wit. What she found objectionable was the simple, heavy, boring, pontificating strain of those she called the "Literati." These people were large, bewhiskered men who came late to dinner, sat late, talked about themselves, and left her with new feelings about the nature of men as "pigs." How her Jane Austen would have dealt with them. How her own father had detested them! Arnold, in the light of them, was an angel of delicacy and grace. Not that the poor man enjoyed himself as much as he should; she still saw his life as an Inspector as the central drain on his energies—and worried every time she told her diary, "Matt came home with a bad cold" or "Matt's cold very troublesome." Wanly, she put up with his garrulous friends such as Walter Bagehot and Leslie Stephen, and despite many misgivings she tolerated publishers' dinners in 1867—though she was glad to get him away from them. "Large party of Literati," she writes with an eloquent *but,* "but pleasant."[40]

She notes on April 18 that "Mr. Huxley" came to dine at Chester Square. Here was a champion of science, whose strident demand for more science in the schools was opposed by Matthew, who wanted a balance between science and literature in classrooms. She was surprised that the two men struck it off well, and that Matthew went later to Thomas Huxley's Geological Society dinners. Huxley helped her husband to define his views. Both men were propagandists, selfless in wanting to aid society, and rather overworked and put upon. Matthew later told this unique friend, "My life is very hellish" and signed a note to him, "Ever yours, in spite of old age, poverty, low spirits, and solitude."[41]

There was much about Matthew which Fanny Lucy felt the world would "never guess," much that wouldn't occur to a reader of "My Countrymen" in which he had complained of England's "narrow, unintelligent, repulsive" religion[42]—when he had in mind chiefly the evangelical low Anglicans and Dissenters. Matthew after all was an Anglican Ritualist. He faced to the east when the Anglican creed was read (even when the clergy failed to do so). And who would think that despite his insults to the Church, he took Holy Communion? "Matt & I went to early Communion," Fanny Lucy observes one Sunday; she often records the name of their High Church Oxford friend, Melville Portal, whom Matthew had sought out in 1851 just before their marriage: "Matt lunched with the Portals" or "Mr. Portal and Mr. Herbert called."[43] She never had reason to doubt that Matthew's outlook was profoundly religious or any regret that *she* had led him to a source of his strength. His own father, she knew, had opposed the Anglican Ritualists. By fastening himself to the strength and greatness of the Church of England, Matthew, as she perhaps rightly felt, gained freedom, ease, and confidence as a critic. She was eager to take her children to church.

With a new sewing machine given her by Matthew, she worked during March on "flaired petticoats" for her "chicks." Nelly and Lucy would be lovely in them; they were adorable girls even if their dresses and petticoats were much too time-consuming. She was not very attentive when her nearly one-year-old Basil, the baby, was restless after a vaccination. While Matthew was up at a girls' school at Hoddesdon, she took Basil over to the Forsters to see Fan and Mrs. Arnold, who had come down from Fox How. Matthew's youngest sister, Fan, was quite "charmed with Basil."[44]

A ferociously hot summer and the infant's teething, however, left Basil weepy. Matthew carried him about, a blond pretty boy in a red flannel dressing gown, every morning in October and November to see downstairs "pictures." Yet on December 18, Dr. Hutton shook his head. Basil seemed feeble. Worried, Matthew next night fell down a flight of unlit steps at Cannon Street Station and broke several teeth; coming to rest with his face on a stone step in the dark, his mouth full of blood, he mused about his ruined "beauty." Fanny Lucy sympathized, but now she wrote in her diary:

BAD NIGHT

On December 23 Dr. Hutton saw Basil and "tried calomel, injections, mustard plasters, leeches—but had little hope for our darling."[45] On January 3, Matthew sat up with exam scripts and went over to the crib after every second paper. At two in the morning he leaned over the crib, "and," as he wrote, "put my finger into the poor little twitching hand." This magic very nearly worked, for the baby next began to drink from a spoon until his teeth shut convulsively. Just after noon, Basil died.

A few days later at Laleham, Matthew and Flu walked after a clergyman's assistant who carried the small white coffin on his shoulder: "Flu stood with me in the sleet by the grave and saw our darling laid in it." Arnold was deeply affected by the loss; but to cheer up his wife, he went out the next week to Howell and James's shop and bought her a handsome sealskin coat.

He had taken a rather foolish view of his boys, while writing beautifully of them. At Dover beyond "the piles on which the railway runs" near Shakespeare's Cliff, for instance, he had watched Dick and Budge at play. "And you should have seen that lovely little figure of Dick's laid down flat," he wrote, "on the bright shingle with his sweet face upwards and his golden hair all floating about him waiting for the wave to come up and wash over him." Fearful about the boys' health, he admired their beauty, overindulged them, and then wanted them to be manly. Budge's leaving home for six hours was a trial for Matthew, not Budge; but when the boy came home he "wept copiously," Matthew admitted, "when I told him I almost cried at leaving him."[46] Budge learned the power of tears as did Tommy. Matthew simply had to kneel at a bookcase to be overwhelmed with tears, squeals, and kisses.

All fathers like to see their children at somebody else's party, or at the theater; but Matthew's passion for shows and masquerades was absurd. He bought the boys masquerade clothes, and forced them to go to children's dances as if he wanted to fix them in a new world. When Tommy refused to go to a ball, Matthew dressed him in spangles and velvet. That night as a waltz began, Tommy "brightened up." He "tried to waltz," stretching up his spangly, starry arms to the hostess, as she turned him round on the shining floor. The boy became so tired he had to be carried home, but Matthew enjoyed the evening immensely because Budge "danced every dance."[47] The very sight of his boys in "black velveteen," or in "new black velvet with a large gold stud," moved him; and when Mrs. Baldock, a perfect stranger at Beaumont Gardens, admired Dicky Arnold in church Matthew gushingly paid a call upon that lady. (The name "Bald[r]ock," like "Balder Dead," "Harrow," and "Pains Hill," had one of those double meanings which he was well aware of, as when he joked about staying at "West Humble" and said that *that* name deeply suited him.) When Mrs. Baldock invited the boys to a *"bal costumé,"* he surely could have kissed her. Dicky "the duck will be in his blue satin and point lace," the father enthused. "Budge will be in powder as a fashionable highwayman," and "dear little Tom *will* be a Matador," though Matthew smiled at the idea of Tommy the Matador fighting a bull or even a frog. Outside the party season, he took his children even to the most wearisome children's pantomimes, where he composed poetry in his head. "A fearful performance," he writes, "but I did two stanzas of a poem, and so suffered less."[48]

His passion for dress and theaters did his boys no harm; but his folly over schools could be damaging. Here, the case of Budge became alarming. That boy did so poorly at Miss Leech's day school that the Arnolds resolved to send him to Laleham, where Matthew once had suffered. The school was run, now, by a hearty Matt Buckland, who one day held Budge's hand—as Matthew gripped the other—while the three figures walked by the Thames. The sight of Chertsey ferry and the barge path and the willows reassured the father; but after he left his son, Matthew began to "think of him all day long."[49] The boy was too fat and he hated fishing. Impulsively, Matthew went to the school to see how he was doing.

Far in the distance, he spied a red face. Budge ran up pell-mell with other boys, getting redder until he was alone with his father; and then, with great effect, he burst into tears. Hugging him, Matthew inquired as to why he was the lowest boy in the whole school "but one"? Budge only replied by asking him to repeat "Nelly," "Lucy," and "Dicky," and welcomed each name "with a new outburst of grief."

Matthew then rose to go. Having called his father "darling," Budge gave his apostolic blessing and called out as Matthew walked away, "God bless you! God bless you!"[50]

Surely, Laleham would *never* do for Budge! The Arnolds next thought of Rugby. Temple the headmaster was willing to please, since he was ashamed to have opposed Arnold on the Taunton Commission board. Matthew admired Temple and Flu hoped for the best. Thus in January 1867 an "enormously fat" Budge, now thirteen and with a small notion of Latin, was driven up to one of the nation's most demanding schools. For a few months, he was almost happy. "Budge looks well," Matthew observed in the spring, "but he brings a terrible character for idleness. I shall take him away if he brings another such [report] at the end of next half."[51] At the end of the next half year, Budge was doing very poorly.

Matthew was baffled. Rugby School was costly and Budge disliked books. What "suited me from the first times when I began to read at all," Matthew later told Bulwer-Lytton, were books with a "*European* tone of reflection and sentiment,"[52] such as Bulwer's books; but his own son Budge couldn't feel this sentiment. Matthew actually thought of sending him "to a school at St. Germain, near Paris," and then had another idea. He had succeeded in tutoring the boys *himself* in the summer, or with the help of a home tutor; or again when taking them out to look for wildflowers and getting them to find the right picture in

Anne Pratt's *Wildflowers*. When he gave them a simple book they were delighted. Lucy got Andersen's *Tales* when she didn't cry at the dentist, and adored it. Tommy and Dicky were pleased (and a little staggered) when Matthew took them to hear his "Culture and Its Enemies," a special privilege since he forbade his own mother from ever hearing him lecture.

He concluded from all this that his boys *might* learn, if they lived with him and went to a public school. Having thought of Harrow, he made inquiries. The old buildings of Harrow School perched on a hill from which one could see on a clear day the tower of Westminster and the mild line of the Thames in front of London. Masters in gowns and boys in straw hats, with much depth of brim, walked over the hill into Harrow Village, where one Polly Arnold who had sold Lord Byron his Latin "cribs" still ran a stationery shop. This was, of course, Lord Byron's old school. Sleepy for nearly 300 years, it had been revived by Charles Vaughan of Rugby and now it was entering a brisk, alert phase under Henry Montagu Butler, who at thirty-five admired the late Dr. Arnold. Nearly strapped for funds, Matthew found that if his boys lived as "home boarders" he could educate three of them at Harrow for a mere £123, which was "nearly £50 less," he told his mother, "than it costs to educate one."[53]

Looking for a home, he found one almost on top of the hill in "Byron House"—a large red-brick pile with more than an acre of garden and apricot, peach, and pear trees. For five years from 1868 to 1873, this was to be his home. At Byron House he grew cauliflowers, Brussels sprouts, and artichokes and even kept pigs and a milk cow. The whole area passed his "wildflower test" for it was near open country. He noted that George Hughes, who had kept order with his fists at Rugby, once lived in Byron House; but many tenants had lived here since 1691. One dark oddity about the house was that nobody ever lived in it for long.

Matthew now asked Lady de Rothschild to inquire of Lady Charles Russell if *her* invalid child, a boy named George, was happy at Harrow. Hearing a good answer, the Arnolds sold their lease at Chester Square and packed up their things. On March 28, 1868, they moved into Byron House with three boys, two girls, one kitten, and three surprised canaries.

He felt that he had quit London just in time not to be overwhelmed as a social celebrity; but at Harrow, a small community of sports, religion, and Latin, he was welcomed as if he were Lord Byron. Young George Russell called and found the tall, smiling Arnold "blithe and friendly" and quite fond of "a fine vintage."[54] Arnold soon watched cricket matches and played lawn tennis with Harrow boys; he sensed the almost Rugbeian atmosphere of the school, and this made him eager for his sons. "Farrar," he writes, "asks to take the three boys in his pupil-room without fee." F. W. Farrar, Dicky's tutor and later Dean of Canterbury, was a gifted teacher. Even so, the most interesting person at Harrow for Matthew was the school organist, Farmer, who "has been out in the streets with the Chartists throwing stones at the military."[55] Farmer was not so tame as the average teacher.

Budge and Tommy enjoyed being home boarders. While mocking the stuffiness of what he called the "catch-scholarship" of the school in those days, Matthew was pleased. "Budge loses ground by his bad arithmetic," he noticed, but does "well in his Latin and Greek." Tommy set a song to music, then sang it in a clear voice bravely at a school concert. The singing whetted a father's appetite for more progress. Glad that his boys were achieving, Matthew encouraged them in outdoor sports and perhaps became a little careless of Tommy's health. That summer up at Fox How, Tommy fell from a pony.

"The fall from his pony," Matthew remarked, "seemed nothing."[56] Perhaps the summer should have gone on forever, with Matthew bathing every day in the shallow Rotha with his laughing boys; but he now returned to Harrow without Tommy. When Fanny Lucy at last arrived with him, Tommy stayed in bed. An attack of rheumatism brought a doctor, then an alarmed Headmaster and Lady Charles Russell, to Byron House. One Monday, when Matthew entered the sickroom, he heard the boy's breath growing "shorter." Tommy whispered, "Don't let Mamma come in," and a little while later he was dead.

Arnold was deeply stunned with shock and grief, and he was agonized for his wife, since Tommy had been "the occupation of her life." Next day he was reading Marcus Aurelius. Later Flu ensconced herself in his dressing room and read "a little book of devotion" Lady Charles Russell had given her; and then he struggled to answer condolences: "People say—do not answer—but it seems to me an affectation not to answer," he wrote in his grief, "and one forces oneself . . . until one is almost stupefied, and words lose all their sense and truth."[57]

The loss left him feeling less worldly, but more realistic. He gave up a hopeless project, that of writing on the early Greek poets so as to make them as popular in England as the Bible. After starting his *Culture and Anarchy* Preface on November 22, a day before Tommy died, he couldn't for weeks go on with its "persiflage." (Even so, "persiflage" gets into the finished piece, as when he roundly berates "the university of Mr. Ezra Cornell"[58] in New York State for training chiefly miners, engineers, and architects.) But he soon felt that Tommy's loss was an epiphany for himself, an "awakening" or a "new beginning," and in fact he was beginning the boldest work of his life in bringing the methods of literary criticism to bear on the Bible. Yet he struggled to keep up his spirits in his routine work and noted caustically Robert Lowe's blatant hypocrisy in "expressing himself shocked to see me still an inspector."[59] When Arnold's collected *Poems* came out in June 1869 he told his mother to read Alfred Austin's savage, deflating essays on Browning and Tennyson, but then calmly defended his own achievements. "My poems represent," he insisted, "the main movement of mind of the last quarter of a century." Perhaps he has less sentiment than Tennyson, less "vigour and abundance"[60] than Browning, but he believes his own work involves modern ideas, and hence in future will be read widely. Coming after Tommy's death, this resurgence of his ego was healthy.

And now he watched "the misty line of the Thames," where poor Tommy lay. Before going to his schools, he helped Flu up onto a wagonette laden with plants, wreaths, and crosses for the two Laleham graves.

However, Flu was too busy to be obsessed with loss. She had the grand duty, now, of caring for Prince Thomas of Savoy who had been sent to Harrow by his uncle—the King of Italy. On behalf of his mother the Duchess of Genoa, Matthew had pressed Harrow School to admit him. The new Thomas was an angular, soft-spoken boy, who greatly liked Budge. Though pestered by visits from his Italian advisers, he made himself quite at home in Byron House and Matthew took him to see the gimcrack estate of Bulwer-Lytton's Knebworth —and was very amused by Bulwer's gushing reception of the Prince. Though Bulwer didn't imagine it, a "theatrical" mind such as *his* might have accused Arnold of starting the whole Franco-Prussian War, by advising this "august pupil."[61] To everyone's amazement the Spanish Cortes, late in 1869, offered the crown of Spain to Prince Thomas, whereupon Montagu Butler and Arnold told him to stick to his algebra and avoid Machiavellian kingmakers. The boy heard mixed advice from his Italian advisers, some of whom were very upset; and, for the only time in history, a Harrow schoolboy refused to become King of Spain! The Cortes next offered the crown to a German princeling, an act which helped to galvanize France into a war with Prussia.

In July 1870 the Arnolds received a legacy of £2000—not, it seems, as a bequest of Sir William, who died in 1863, or of Lady Wightman, who lived until April 1871—but probably from Mrs. Mary Arnold's commercial Penrose relatives. Trying to save the capital sum for his wife, Matthew invested some of it abroad to quicken his "interest in modern history."[62] He bought Turkish, Spanish, and Italian stocks as well as Pennsylvania and New York Central bonds and shares. The proceeds, however, tended to be eaten up by his expenses. He was now sending Lucy and Nelly to classes run by a "Mrs. Goose." His pay rose slightly when he became Senior Inspector in 1870, and his morale rose when he was given, early the next year, a "perfect" inspection district in Westminster and the rural area around Harrow.

He was wryly amused when the Italian King made him a *Commendatore* for taking care of the Prince, who had become a true old Harrovian. Matthew felt Harrovian, too, when he approved the song, "Forty Years On," which the organist Farmer had asked him to see. Chanted like thunder in Arnold's day, this school song is chanted by aging Old Harrovians today:

> *O the great days, in the distance enchanted,*
> *Days of fresh air, in the rain and the sun,*
> *How we rejoiced as we struggled and panted,*
> *Hardly believable, forty years on!*[63]

He walked alone in his garden, where his cow "lowed" to see him. At times, he wanted to be under the ground, with Tommy and Basil. Now and then he skated on a nearby pond in the darkness. He approved Harrow School, now, only because Budge had done well. Having threatened to send him away to Westphalia, Arnold had seen him rise from fortieth to fourteenth in his class! "No, no, Budge mustn't go to Westphalia."[64] Prince Thomas had pleaded and Budge had wept; but by threatening to send him to a Prussian school, Matthew felt, he had made Budge into a scholar. Unfortunately, he left Budge behind one summer at Fox How to study when he took Dicky and Flu to Switzerland to climb the "Gemmi." But if *that* made Budge downcast, how good it was to see him doing nicely!

Pleasing his father, the fattish Budge at eighteen took part in school running events on the sports fields at Harrow. Puffy and short, he came home one day looking "much knocked up running a mile very fast."[65] He had had trouble getting his breath. A few days later, he was in bed with a "bilious cold." Matthew that night went into his room three times. Once he found him "lightheaded wandering about the room." Budge looked at him wonderingly, recognized him, and said "Ah, papa!" and then the boy seemed to fall into a heavy doze, from which in fact he never awoke. He died on February 16, 1872, with the physicians of Harrow at his bedside.

After this loss, people tried to comfort mainly the father. Harriet Martineau was too grieved to write, but knew that the event came to the Arnolds without "warning." Nelly tried to console people inside Byron House,

> Oh! Budge come back, come back,
> And cheer a lonly home.
> . . . and when I am alone,
> I think and think of thee
> How that we n'er shall meet again
> Axcept in heaven above
> Where God has taken you to rest.[66]

But Arnold wrote no elegy. He was simply "terribly cut up." When he went off to a school to examine pupil-teachers, "Mr. Forster found him there with his poor eyes full of tears, yet keeping order and doing his duty till he was relieved."[67] He had come to Harrow mainly for Budge; he had woken in the night thinking of that boy, when "Toss" the cat roused herself on the covers to stare at him. His Harrow experiment had never worked and he had failed as a father.

He had begun to keep very regularly a "rain" diary, and he resorted to that this week:

> Budge!
> showers in day—hard rain at night.
> Budge's funeral!

This became almost a poem:

> heavy rain
> heavy rain
> heavy rain.
> . . . . . .
> hard rain
> rain
> rain in morning
> rain in morning
> rain in evening.
> rain
> rain in evening
> rain all day
> rain at night
> rain.[68]

For Matthew this rain suggested the rivers of Isaiah and the poetry of the Bible, grace in the spirit, and that which literally nourishes all of life. He was not cast down for very long. He could not for months easily write Budge's name, and when he *had* to do so, he stopped in "stupefaction"[69] to think the boy was not alive. Yet he felt he could still do something useful with his life. Arnold meant to affect the public in his writings about religion; and what he wrote was exciting and advanced and cogent. Outside the grieved and slowly recovering world of Byron House, he had become a scandalous figure.

16

MR. LUKE'S VIVACITY
1870–1878

One can endure anything, except a series of wonderful
days.
—Goethe

Jesus was far over the heads of all of his reporters.
—God and the Bible

All the seriousness, clear-mindedness, and settled purpose is hitherto on the side of the Reds.
—Arnold on the "Red" Paris Commune in 1871

A T the age of fifty, Arnold lifted a monocle to his eye with an elegant
twist of his hand or else let the glass dance on a black ribbon. He
was a ruddy-faced, rather gushing man in company and too loud-
voiced to be the author of "Scholar-Gipsy," Henry James felt. Looking
at him closely, one saw narrow lines in his face. He had lost weight
lately—but his blue eyes and a thickish mop of blackish-brown hair
were youthful. One day in town he met Henry Coleridge—who arose
like a fat, gray ghost from the Oriel College years: "I thought he would
never let my hand go," recalled Arnold. "At last he said—'Matt!! I
expected to see a white-headed old man.'" "All my white hairs," he
replied to Henry, "are internal."[1]

Though grieving for his three sons, he tried not to dwell on the past
and took great consolation in his three living children. As Matthew
turned fifty, his son Dick was a handsome blond boy of seventeen,
Lucy was fourteen with long hair and pretty features, and Nelly was a
boyish eleven. With a glance at his children no doubt, he jotted
Goethe's sane advice in a diary:

One must continually change, renew oneself, become young, in order
not to stultify.[2]

Matthew played lawn tennis with Dick and the girls, and played
croquet on a smooth straight lawn with Fanny Lucy. He walked with

his children up at Fox How, in the beautiful mountainous valley of the Rotha, over the Christmas holidays; and now and then he left to go shooting with Victor Marshall over at Coniston. Then thirty, Victor was a plump grandson of Lord Monteagle. "My dear Victor," Matthew informs him, "I shall start at ½ past eight on New Year's morning [from Fox How]. . . . I never remember the shooting party starting earlier. Will this do?"

Odd things happened at Victor's shooting parties even before the whisky vanished, and once Matthew came home in the wrong trousers. "Victor," he pleads later in despair, "why did you add insult to injury by taking my clothes?" If *Victor* didn't steal Arnold's trousers, *who did*? The Hellenic spirit of the region? Or perhaps Hartley Coleridge's ghost? "I have ascertained that it was not the man with the divine voice, Farquhar," writes Arnold, as he recalls the shooting party, "—I do not think it could have been Jim, because the trousers I have got are too short for him, . . . too roomy round the waist; it must, therefore have been you," he tells Victor, who loved to talk in a "Jolly Students" vocabulary. "You have no doubt, unlike me, many changes of raiment. When I was a jolly student, I had."[3]

As for the shooting, Arnold was hardly better at fifty than at sixteen. "How I miss!" he laments, "but what a pleasant three days I had at Coniston!"[4]

Refreshed by these sprees he was writing notoriously on theology. In 1870 he drove reviewers into a frenzy with *St. Paul and Protestantism*, then stirred up more terrible hornets' nests with *Literature and Dogma*, and finally in 1875 provoked the clergy to fury with *God and the Bible*—a book which applies the word "clap-trap" six times to the Bishop of Winchester. Arnold was perfectly right in believing that *God and the Bible* contains some of his best expository prose—but the wit and descriptive clarity of his religious books almost conceal their real modesty and deeper design. Starting with three *Cornhill* pieces of 1869 and 1870 which he collected as his *St. Paul*, he tried to establish the truth of Christianity empirically or on the ground of human experience. He anticipated the later theology of Tillich and Bultmann —and illuminated many of the processes of literary criticism.

Why does he offer his biblical criticism "neither as something quite new nor as something quite true"? St. Paul's thought, he believes, will "grow more," and cannot stand in future "as we now exhibit it," for it will "gain some aspects" which Arnold fails to show in it and "drop some" which he gives it.[5] This doctrine of a work's *developing meaning* lies at the heart of Arnold's approach to all literature: if St. Paul's epistles, or Keats's odes, change in meaning as society evolves, then these works grow beyond the range of their older critics and need new interpreters. Hence criticism must always be tentative, exploratory, and undogmatic.

He evokes Goethe's *Zeitgeist* or Time-Spirit, that ever-changing mental outlook of a people, to show why the Bible calls for more intelligence in an age of science. St. Paul, misconstrued by puritans, neither focused on divine miracles nor denied the goodness of "being in love."

Arnold's treatment of "being in love" is fascinating. Delays—or failures—in sexual fulfillment in life, often caused by the close intimacy of the family and by brother-sister relationships, led Victorians to write as insightfully on the state of "being in love" as, today, we write on the quality of the orgasm. Emily Dickinson, Elizabeth Browning, and Matthew Arnold wrote well of the psychology of love. Arnold had shown in his Mary Claude *passion-réfléchissante* lyrics the relation between failed love, isolation, and insights into the psyche; and in "Dover Beach" and "The Buried Life," how being in love is, itself, a means of spiritual survival and of self-discovery. "Being in love," he writes in *St. Paul,* "makes animation and buoyancy where before there was flatness and dullness," gives "light, and movement where before there was stagnation and gloom." He only needed to see Louisa, Lady de Rothschild now and then to feel this:

> A powerful attachment will give a man spirits and confidence which he could by no means call up or command of himself; and [it is true] that in this mood he can do wonders which would not be possible to him without it.[6]

The sensible person, Senancour says, is in love with love. Arnold agrees with Senancour, but for this reason he frankly associates "conduct" with sexual moderation. The casual affair, he argues in *Literature and Dogma,* "has an attraction for all of us." England develops the sexual person under "doubts," grossly. But France develops the sexual person "confidently and harmoniously," and not "with madness, into a monstrosity, as the Italy of the Renaissance did" and hence she attracts us with casual sex. Paris "has much reasonableness" in all her "arrangements; a sort of of balance . . . as goes with the ideal of *l'homme sensual moyen.* . . . All of us feel, at some time or other in our lives, a hankering after the French ideal, a disposition to try it."[7]

He is influenced by social concern and sexual passion. Sex outside marriage was attractive to *him.* He called pupil-teachers by their first names and tried to help them, and when they became young teachers they adored him. He chatted with the pretty young teachers before spending his lonely nights in hotels, and after his sons died his nights away from home did not become less lonely. Moreover, one "Barbari-aness" after another was inviting him, without his wife, to dine in a milieu in which casual sex was so commonplace as to bore gossipers. His old fear that indulging in casual love affairs can rob one of spiritual innocence and mental freedom kept him, no doubt, sexually loyal to his wife. What he intuited strongly, he related often enough to a theory of the Celts. "The pure Celt, the Irish, is chaste," Arnold writes in French to the worldly French Protestant clergyman, Ernest Fontanès, after comparing Irish and French writers in 1873.

> The latinized Celt, the French, is something quite else. Proudhon said, according to Sainte-Beuve, that "France was turning completely to-wards fornication"—and that's just your trouble. Now in this way, Ireland offers to other countries an example truly admirable, her own faults lying elsewhere.[8]

The Irish are "chaste" in their literature, but he has no illusion that they are inherently virtuous. What he struggles with is the paradox that while "being in love" invigorates one's whole mind (as he says in *St. Paul*), rids one of "gloom," is of spiritual value, and is wrongly discounted by Puritans who detest beauty and by bishops who can't think, yet inward or mental freedom and spontaneity of feeling depend, perhaps, upon constancy in love and sexual fidelity.

"Righteousness" has implied fidelity for St. Paul, who confirms Cicero's good sense. "Hold off from sensuality," Arnold quotes Cicero, "for, if you have given yourself up to it, you will find yourself unable to think of anything else."[9] Cicero—like St. Paul and even like Senan-cour—had urged *reasons* for any course of conduct. Arnold would oppose *all* forms of restraint not observably warranted in the eyes of rational men and women; in love we are not to betray others, not to be obsessed by the sexual chase, nor to lose innocence to the point of "being unable to think of anything else."

In *St. Paul* he takes a new, exploratory view of the etymology of Bible terms, and of the need for "unity" among the Christian sects. (Christian "unity is not very important," he admits in his Preface.) What he strongly opposes are two "spurious and degenerate" forms of Hellenism and Hebraism in daily life: Hellenism may become "Millism," or that stupid revolt against all religion, which is epito-mized too often by J. S. Mill. Modern Hebraism degenerate is only "Mialism,"or that spirit of watchful jealousy among the Christian sects, which is typified by Edward Miall. (It was Miall who edited the middle-class *Nonconformist,* and whose brash, fractious, unreligious motto "The Dissidence of Dissent and the Protestantism of the Protestant religion"[10] Arnold had mocked as the "Puritan ideal" in *Culture and Anarchy.*)

Having indulged in name-calling to draw attention to Mill's and Miall's errors, he was pleased by the storm in the reviews over *St. Paul.* The book even had a few defenders, in 1870.

Meanwhile, he was moving to a stronger defense of both literature and the Bible. He needed a clearer faith; his Anglican worship was still deeply at odds with his abstract Spinozism. His own "Hellenism" could not be so surely opposed to "Hebraism," or seen as unreligious. Ernst Curtius's *History of Greece* (which Arnold began to review in 1868) was now showing that Hellenic culture had depended on the Apolline priesthood of Delphi and on Greek religious festivals. In two memorial pieces, on "Obermann" and on "Sainte-Beuve" for the new intellectual journal, *Academy,* Arnold had touched on the need for a vital, credible faith and on the possibility of a new disinterested criticism—which might extend to the whole Bible. Senancour once complained that religion in the West had not "done" enough.[11] But in England, even though people chattered about God and had church quarrels and church entertainments, the public was beginning to reject the Bible.

Why was the Bible likely to be unread, in a future England? Arnold believed nobody was likely to read it less intelligently or readily because of the "higher criticism" of European scholars. Stemming from the work of J. G. Eichhorn and other eighteenth-century German scholars, who had advanced biblical studies in one wave with historiography, philology, and anthropology, the new Bible criticism was hardly flawless. In *God and the Bible* Arnold attacks F. C. Baur (1792–1860)—who at Tübingen argued against the authenticity of the Fourth Gospel—and he also attacks Heinrich von Ewald (1803–75), who at Göttingen opposed Baun. Yet Arnold's point is only that the German biblical scholars lack critical tact and literary experience; he welcomes their intelligence, untiring search for historical fact, and in general their enlightened attitude to the New Testament. That attitude is seen in D. F. Strauss's *Leben Jesu,* which Arnold read in the French translation by Dollfus and Nefftzer. "We have to realize," Strauss had argued, that the narrators of ancient Israel

> testify sometimes, not to outward facts, but to ideas . . . [and] constructions which even eye-witnesses had unconsciously put upon the facts, imagination concerning them, reflections upon them, reflections such as were natural to them and at the time of the author's level of culture. . . . [A New Testament narrative] is a plastic, naive, and, at the same time, often most profound expression of truth, within the area of religious feeling and poetic insight. It results in a narrative, legendary, mythical in nature, illustrative often of spiritual truth in a manner more perfect than any hard, prosaic statement could achieve.[12]

In England the clergy neglected this sensitive approach to the Bible's poetic truth. Popular preachers, in effect, reduced that truth to mere "fairy-tale." A "very powerful preacher," Arnold admitted after listening to Flu's friend Reverend Wilkinson at St. Peter's in Eaton Square. "He was so evidently sincere, more than sincere, burnt up with sorrow . . . and half the church was in tears."[13] *But of what good is emotion without light?* Wilkinson's ideas were fixed—at a time when all of Huxley's science was remaking itself. People's experience, Arnold notes, "widens, and they get a clearer view of what a fact is and what proof is, they are more aware when they talk nonsense and more shy of talking it." English theology lacks intellectual seriousness. Physicists and biologists have lately "corrected their old data from top to bottom; half of these data they have clean abandoned, and the other half they have transformed. But theologians have not yet done so."[14]

Moreover, as he noticed, dogmatic believers now clashed with skeptics. A day or two after receiving his D.C.L. degree in June 1870, Arnold was alarmed when Oxford's Chancellor, Lord Salisbury, announced this at Keble College:

> There shall be no more within these walls the idea of severing religion and dogma than there is the idea of severing daylight from the sun.[15]

Dogmatists like Salisbury, who lacked Newman's open intelligence, were loud and ferocious. Lately the High Church Anglicans, at Oxford, had denied the liberal Mark Pattison his appointment as curator of the Bodleian Library, and deprived Benjamin Jowett of his salary as a professor of Greek. They had "tremendously beaten" Max Müller for the Boden chair of Sanskrit, because Müller held "Germanic" ideas about the Bible. And if these were Oxford's tempests, the whole nation was embroiled in a larger tempest over whether religious education in tax-supported schools was to be secular or not. Even local elections to the London School Board were bitter in 1870. Elected to the Marylebone Division of the Board, Thomas Huxley, of all people, defied his secular colleagues by asking "to make the Bible a part of every day's study in the schools."[16]

Huxley, who admired *St. Paul,* very warmly encouraged Arnold. But there were too few Huxleys. Dogmatists like Salisbury only ensured the Bible would be dropped in disgust sooner or later by *all* the schools—and hence the public would lose just that source of religious and poetic insight which might correct its deadly literal-mindedness. Arnold foresaw all of Europe locked in sterile conflicts—religious, secular, and patriotic. One of the smallest of these battles began in 1870 after Arthur Stanley (as the new Dean of Westminster) invited a committee of New Testament revisers to take Holy Communion in the

Abbey. Because he had invited a Unitarian to the ceremony, there were demands for Stanley's excommunication! As the cries over *that* reached fever pitch Samuel Wilberforce, the Bishop of Winchester, lashed out at poor Stanley for denying "the Godhead of our Lord Jesus Christ"![17]

Arnold's anger over these absurdities took the form of savage ridicule. "And to the eloquent and impetuous Chancellor of Oxford," he writes of Lord Salisbury in *Literature and Dogma,*

> who cannot away with a hazy amiability in religious matters, and brandishes before us his dogma, not vague, he says, but *precise*: —"Precise enough," we answer, "precisely wrong!"[18]

As for Bishop Wilberforce,

> he freely permitted himself the use of clap-trap . . . and he was signally addicted to clap-trap. . . . Those who use clap-trap as the late Bishop of Winchester used it . . . only prove their valuelessness.[19]

Even the demands for Stanley's excommunication faded, as the Franco-Prussian War unfolded in 1870. In cavalry charges of French and Prussians, in men beheaded and horses disemboweled by nitroglycerin shells, in the loss of 25,000 soldiers in a day, Arnold's countrymen took interest. By the spring of 1871 the French seemed defeated, for Napoleon III had surrendered and von Moltke's heavy siege guns were in the Paris suburbs. German infantry were in the Champs-Elysées.

At that point, oddly enough, a red flag appeared in the *arrondissements*. On March 22, a red flag had flown at Lyon, and on March 23 at Marseilles. The presence of a "socialistic and red" workers' commune in Paris now scandalized most of Europe.

Frustrated by the myopia of bishops, Arnold was fairly elated by the red flag—and "not so angry" over socialism. He believed the French upper classes were "corrupted"[20] and that workers for the second time in his life, if they lacked "moral" force, were acting decisively. "What news from France!" he exclaims with relief. "What is certain is that all the seriousness, clear-mindedness, and settled purpose is hitherto on the side of the Reds."[21] In May, as the Communards fought to the last in the XI and XII *arrondissements*, Matthew Arnold noted for the twentieth century

> that fixed resolve of the working class to count for something and *live,* which is destined to make itself so much felt in the coming time, and to disturb so much which dreamed it would last for ever.[22]

He felt about Communards or "Reds" much as he did about science. Since England has a "blundering and miserable constitution of society," its lower classes must surely change a social order which only gives them poorer schools, feebler health, worse houses, and fewer opportunities than their employers. Workers are "destined" to disturb so much that dreamed it would last forever. But similarly, science will radically change the whole social fabric.

What Arnold feared was this: profound changes in the social order as they *continue in future*—and involve revolutions more radical than the founding of "socialistic and red republics" and more sweeping than anything dreamed yet by biologists and physicists—will separate people from the past collective wisdom of the race. Life is sterile and barren if we lose the past, no matter how fair our new society may look. At fifty, Arnold is neither revolutionary nor conservative and no more opposed to science than to social evolution. He is correctly seen as a "humanist" (if we do not ascribe to him the antireligious bias of an Auguste Comte, or of the early Walter Pater). The ultimate effect of the Commune on his outlook was to make him more urgently a propagandist for literature itself: for literature embraces the past, gives to its readers some lucidity and compassion, some largeness of heart and mind. But then, what headway do its advocates ever make? "For anyone who believes in the civilising power of letters and often talks of this belief," he writes in his *Bible Reading for Schools,* in 1871, in which he offers a version of *Isaiah,* 40–64, for schoolchildren,

> —to think that he has for more than twenty years got his living by inspecting schools for the people, has gone in and out among them, has seen that the power of letters never reaches them at all and that the whole study of letters is thereby discredited and its power called in question, and yet has attempted nothing to remedy this state of things, cannot but be vexing and disquieting. He may truly say, like the Israel of the prophet: "We have not wrought any deliverance in the earth!"[23]

He was so depressed when he went to Birmingham in October, to give a lecture in the Masonic Hall on Moslem religious drama, that he consoled himself by walking out the Hagley Road, past Newman's Oratory, until he could see Bromsgrove's Lickey Hills, "fading in the evening." Then he went back to the Masonic Hall—and miraculously found that 900 people had come to hear him and that 200 had to be turned away! His Birmingham talk was a vital turning point. He printed this lecture as "A Persian Passion Play" in his third edition of *Essays in Criticism;* and despite his pessimism in *A Bible Reading* he felt in 1872 that he could, as a critic, get people to look anew at the Eastern, "Oriental" Bible. One of Arnold's central insights was that society in the West *lacks* feeling and intuition of the East. He had symbolized that idea in "The Scholar-Gipsy," and graphically spelled it out in a sonnet of 1867, "East and West." His sonnet uses the legend of the two Anglesey saints, Seiriol and Kybi, who represent the East and the West as they walk towards "two springs" each day. Seiriol's face is in sunlight, Kybi's in shadow:

> Seiriol the Bright, Kybi the dark! *men said.*
> *The seër from the East was then in light,*
> *The seër from the West was then in shade.*
>
> *Ah! now 'tis changed. In conquering sunshine bright*
> *The man of the bold West now comes arrayed;*
> *He of the mystic East is touched with night.*[24]

The "mystic East" has a source of power in Moslem culture, which he considers in his Birmingham lecture—even as he exalts that "Oriental" work, the Bible.

And Birmingham made up for a bad setback. After printing two pieces for his planned *Literature and Dogma* in the *Cornhill* in July and October 1871, he was politely told by Leslie Stephen—that journal's new editor—that *Cornhill* would accept no more of his new book. Having relied on the magazine's deadlines, Arnold now boldly changed the book's scope. Instead of writing a polite treatise on literature in connection with "dogma," "physics," and "natural science," as he had planned, he produced a critique of the Bible in a vigorous popular style.

Published in February 1873, *Literature and Dogma* made him notorious but not rich, though in small editions it eventually sold as many as 100,000 copies. Today one is impressed by the book's moderation. Arnold cautiously accepts Spinoza's idea that biblical miracles must be discounted, again that an anthropomorphic Deity does not exist and that scripture is *not* a trapeze for metaphysicians or theologians. He discusses the nature of biblical language, and the reliability of Jesus' reporters. The Bible's Hebrew is the language of those who were helped *and* limited by the poetry of Israel—language "thrown out" to express difficult religious experience. Much of that language, he contends, is best described by the German word *Aberglaube,* or extra-belief, since it concerns matters which nobody "can prove impossible to turn out true, but which no one also can prove certain to turn out true."[25]

"The Son of Man coming in the clouds" is thus *Aberglaube,* Arnold maintains, and so too are the other Messianic prophecies and all biblical miracles. Some of his rejections seem premature, but qualified. When Mill asserted that there was a law of nature against miracles, Arnold later replied: "No such law of nature as Mr. Mill describes has been or can be established against the Christian miracles."

And I may be wrong, Arnold admits in effect. "We may be wrong in *our conjectures.*"²⁶ Much that we say may be "dropped" by future biblical critics; but in a materializing society overly impressed by science, we only discredit religion by pinning faith on the miraculous. We credit the unlikely and so make Christianity *seem* "a cheat and an imposture." Asking his readers to accept only what can be demonstrated, he describes religion as *"morality touched with emotion"* and offers clear examples:

> "By the dispensation of Providence to mankind," says Quintilian, "goodness gives men most satisfaction." That is morality. "The path of the just is as the shining light which shineth more and more unto the perfect day." That is morality touched with emotion, or religion. . . . "We all want to live honestly, but cannot," says the Greek maxim-maker. That is morality. "O wretched man that I am, who shall deliver me from the body of this death!" says St. Paul. That is religion. . . . "Live as you were meant to live!" is morality. "Lay hold on eternal life!" is religion.²⁷

Despite what both F. H. Bradley and T. S. Eliot claimed about him, Arnold never attempted a fixed definition of religion. He came to the Bible not as a professional theologian but as an experienced critic. He meant to illustrate what can be shown, what is patently true, what at once may *convince* us that the Bible holds psychological truth. And the whole critical delicacy of his argument is underestimated when T. S. Eliot, for example, calls him at best, "in some respects the most satisfactory man of letters of his age," or when F. R. Leavis writes that Matthew Arnold "is not disposed of as a literary critic by pointing out that he was not a theologian or philosopher."²⁸ Why is it that since Eliot and Leavis's time, we have seen that Arnold's criticism refreshes and renews biblical texts, and that *Literature and Dogma* is one of the most suggestive of his books? Why, among theologians ninety and a hundred years after he died, is a substantial interest in his theological writing growing?

A work such as Frank Kermode's *Genesis of Secrecy* (The C. E. Norton Harvard lectures printed in 1979), easily the best critical work in English of its year, borrows Arnold's insight that classic and sacred texts depend on interpretation for their vitality. The Bible is dead unless we interpret it. To interpret it well, Arnold holds, we must see that it is a metaphoric work. Religion, then, in a sense may be metaphorical. There is a distinction, for example, between the truth of Jesus' ideas and the metaphoric mode of his parables, but in the parable is the key or seed of its interpretation, or as we would say, its demythologizing or deconstruction. The metaphoric parable ensures the survival of Jesus' truth throughout time; but the deconstructing critic is needed to expose its insight for *this* time.

Two things follow for Arnold. As the Bible is a metaphoric work, unusual *literary* tact and experience are required to interpret it. But, secondly, the process of interpreting is a continuum in time involving theological critics past, present, and future. Hence the critic may begin with a criticism and an assessment of the critical act. (There is much that we might call "metacritical," or *about* criticism and interpretation, in both *Literature and Dogma* and *God and the Bible*.) The critic need not presume to evaluate Christian institutions, but will ask how the Catholic Church and how Protestantism have furthered our understanding of Jesus' metaphoric language. It is the Catholic Church's achievement to have laid hold of Jesus' "secret" of self-renouncement, for example, Arnold writes, and an achievement of Protestantism to have illuminated Jesus' "method" or that important "labour of inwardness and sincerity in the conscience of each individual."[29] Among Jesus' best interpreters have been four—all Catholics or Anglo-Catholics. Arnold mentions Thomas Wilson (1663–1775), Anglican Bishop of Sodor and Man, whose services in the Isle of Man were attended even by Catholics and whose *Sacra Privata* was later edited by Newman—there we find insights into Jesus. Or, Arnold asks, let the critic turn to the German mystic Johann Tauler, or to the founder of the Visitandine order of nuns, St. Francis of Sales, or to the author of *The Imitation of Christ*.

Criticism, enriched and prepared by such prior commentary, the best that we have, will at least be respected in the future. It will not be dogmatic or definitive, but will be *something like* useful biblical commentary to come. "We present our conceptions, neither as something quite new nor as something quite true," as he had said in 1870. In fact, he does connect with a later time: his insights foreshadow those of theologians such as Rudolph Bultmann, Paul Tillich, H. Richard Niebuhr, and even Dietrich Bonhoeffer and Martin Buber. Bultmann's demythologizing of creedal language and his effort to "remythologize" biblical miracles are reminiscent of Arnold's reinterpreting the Bible as poetry. Tillich's existential view that religion speaks for the human experience of estrangement from a potential inner freedom, and his view that language cannot incarnate the divine but that it serves to get at unspeakable but final truths about experience, both connect with Arnold. So, too, does Niebuhr's discussion of revelatory knowledge that comes from imagination united with reason.[30] Arnold's argument that "Jesus was far over the heads" of his "reporters" is not fanciful, but seems confirmed by detailed studies of the evangelical reporters, as in M. D. Goulder's *Midrash and Lection in Matthew* (1974) and John Drury's *Tradition and Design in Luke's Gospel* (1976). Arnold emphasizes "the difference between the logos of Jesus and the deliberate inventions of the

Evangelist—and, a finer distinction, between the tenor of Jesus and the metaphoric language of his parables," writes Leslie Brisman of Yale; he "sees the concept of rebirth through Christ" as

> the spiritual capacity for self-transcendence. Every individual recapitulates the archetypal distinction between a first and second dispensation, a literal and a figurative birth. The first birth makes us creatures, the second (because it is the birth of the imaginative faculty) creators. This distinction is also manifested in the historical development of a religion and civilization at large. It is Arnold's special message for his time that the more scientific our perspective about our creaturely origins, the stronger our faith in creative rebirth ought to be.[31]

Distinctively modern, too, are his empirical terms and, perhaps, his view of the Church. God may be described as "The Eternal, not ourselves, that makes for righteousness," Arnold writes, because in *that* sense many men and women experience the deific force and truth. But *what right* have we, he asks, to call God, anthropomorphically, a "person who thinks and loves"? "It is because we cannot," he states, "trace God in history that we stay the craving of our minds with a fancy-account of him." The mystery of God demands our modesty —more especially in an age of science and literalism. Partly to escape the linguistic limits of the age, Arnold goes to church. He believes that long-used rites and liturgical traditions help him to worship at once deeply and moderately; and to be an Anglican is to maintain "connexion with the past."[32]

Arnold carefully had studied Hebrew to get at the meaning of words for his edition of *Isaiah,* for the "paramount aim" of getting Isaiah "enjoyed" and widely read. To reach the widest audience for *Literature and Dogma,* he often uses colloquial prose, as when he says that "the Bible hardly meddles with" art or science. This later caused critics such as Bradley, Eliot, and Trilling to attack his book for amateurish, inexact language. But, as Arnold told his sister Fan, "ponderous works produce no effect; the religious world which complains of me would not read me if I treated my subject as they say it ought to be treated." In fact, he is informal but exact. His view of the Bible's language has survived many attacks. Lionel Trilling, for example, felt that by calling biblical language "poetry" he had reduced the Bible to mere pseudo-statements, which are subjective, emotive, and untrue. But Arnold had insisted on the "natural truth of Christianity" and had held that the Bible's mythopoetry covers "more of what we seek to express than the language of literal fact and science." As a conveyor of religious experience, the terms and definitions of modern science would be shallow, simplistic, and untruthful. The New Testament authors were conscious of "immense truths which engaged their affection and awe" and concerning which *"adequate statement is impossible."*[33] Hence their experience, as given in the Bible, is in truthful myths.

Since Arnold's time, Wittgenstein and others have shown that religious language has its own meaning and logic. Certainly Arnold's views are foreshadowed by Strauss, by Renan. But his criticism refreshes today as theirs does not; and it is Arnold, as one modern High Anglican, A. O. J. Cockshut, has fairly said, who undertakes the task of transforming the modern "religious consciousness"[34] by interpreting Christ's message as one which applies to our real experience in this world. This attempt was the ultimate test of his idea of criticism. By advancing from literary and social comment into theology in *Literature and Dogma,* he was offering a nearly comprehensive vision of modern society and showing that his critical methods could be useful in the most difficult field of all. Arnold's *God and the Bible* began as a series of essays in 1874 and 1875 in reply to "objections to *Literature and Dogma,*" and includes his response to the purely negative or hostile biblical criticism he finds in W. R. Cassels's *Supernatural Religion.* Arnold importantly asks that we be willing to change our set, pat views of a developing Bible: "Englishmen enjoy pounding away at details," he writes. What they dislike "is having to face the new ideas which await them when the detail-hunt is done with." Though he calls anything he dislikes a "theory" and anything he likes an "idea," he offers an informed reading and defense of the Fourth Gospel.[35] We know more about that gospel than any of his contemporaries did—and still *God and the Bible* has not been superseded. Nor is it likely to be. We have no better demonstration of his true greatness as a critic, or of that combination of delightful readability, intelligence, delicacy, tact, and insight which writing about the Bible should have.

In 1873, he was weary and much in the limelight. Avoiding the reviewers' tumult over *Literature and Dogma* just three days after that book was published, he took his family abroad. At Cannes, Fanny Lucy, he, and the two girls thawed out in March—and in a Monte Carlo gambling casino Arnold grandly proved his superb "conduct" at red, black, and green tables. He won at roulette before he lost his stake. "Conduct and character, my dear Smith," he reports to his London publisher, "*will* tell, and a habit, instead of skipping about and abandoning your colour when you have lost upon it, of simply raising your stake until your colour wins." Later, he took Fanny Lucy to a gambling casino with no money in his pockets ("except one 5 franc piece for *her*"[36]) and noted how pleased she was.

She was more pleased to be in Italy. He was trying to distract Fanny Lucy from her grief for her lost sons, and hence—after Dicky joined them from Harrow—Arnold took her to galleries and churches where "one sees far too much." Meekly, he tried to admire frescoes. The Church of Minerva in Rome was refreshing because it had Michelangelo's strong "Christ"—one of the few images of Jesus he really liked. Later: "I saw as much of the statues as the children would let me see," and "then I was dragged off to see [a] famous bronze wolf."[37] For Arnold the fine arts were a duty, a ritual, even a necessity, but seldom a pleasure—and yet he felt more like himself at a wine party, in Rome, given by the American sculptor W. W. Story and his wife. There he met Henry James. Astonished by Arnold's coarse red face in those tapestried Roman rooms, James found him "decidedly a disappointment, in a superficial sense." Matthew talked as idly and loudly as if he were an American—a fault or a virtue shared by his own daughters. James later found young Lucy, at a soirée, "as pretty as an American girl and chattering as freely."[38]

"I am ruined," Arnold cried out at last. When his family later finished shopping in Paris, he felt his ruin complete. "The Continent has become too expensive for little people," he wrote in despair, feeling that he had been gouged by hotels. By the time he landed in England on May 17, *Literature and Dogma* had gone into a third edition—but the book was not going to make much money, and he had heard of damning comments by reviewers. At Dover, he picked up a journal announcing that "the Rev. Something is going to lecture in St. George's Hall against Literature and Dogma. Shall we go and hear the blasphemer?" he wrote to George Smith the publisher.[39]

To save money, and also to free themselves from associations at Harrow, the Arnolds moved into a "nutshell" of a house in Surrey soon after their return. Not too far from a northern railway to London, Pains Hill at Cobham was to be Arnold's home from 1873 to the end of his life. The cottage fronted open fields not far from heather and pine groves in the "valley of the Mole," near the muddy River Mole. If he had to leave home at 8 A.M. to get to London schools, Matthew on weekends could now put on his boots, slosh about in the fields, and then watch a long green view from his study. Almost book-free, the study room was immaculate. As a visitor, Tom Arnold's bright daughter Mary Ward was much struck by its neatness: "No litter in the room, every drawer and shelf scrupulously tidy," she noted, and "his table at the window from which he could see the garden." Yet dreadful cats and spoiled dachshunds ruined this harmony. The Arnolds had turned with increasing wonder and affection to pets: Huxley had gone to Harrow to put a splint on a cat's leg. Mary Ward came to Cobham "eager to talk to 'Uncle Matt' about a book or an article" and the talk would dissolve with "Uncle Matt" red-faced and breathless, chasing some dog "through field after field," where it harried sheep or cows, "with the dear poet, hoarse with shouting, at his heels."

"Aunt Fanny Lucy," as Mary felt, was a "dear gracious little lady" who indulged the dogs, too. The horrid drawbacks to Cobham "were the 'dear, dear boys'—i.e. the dachshunds, Max and Geist, who, however adorable in themselves, had no taste for visitors. . . . The dogs were always *in the party,* talked to, caressed, or scolded like spoilt children."[40] Matthew's sense that he had demanded too much of Tommy and Budge, and an inner isolation increased by his fame in the late 1870s, made him dote on his responsive dogs. They were less to him than his real children, and so he could be ironic and bring all his feelings into play with them. The floppy, brown-and-black "Geist" was named after Arminius's spirit of intelligence in *Friendship's Garland*; when that brown sausage died in 1880, Arnold wrote "Geist's Grave"—a seriocomic elegy in which dog and poet almost blend:

> *That liquid, melancholy eye,*
> *From whose pathetic, soul-fed springs*
> *Seemed surging the Virgilian cry,*
> *The sense of tears in mortal things—*
>
> . . . . . .
>
> *Then some, who through this garden pass,*
> *When we too, like thyself, are clay,*
> *Shall see thy grave upon the grass,*
> *And stop before the stone, and say:*
>
> People who lived here long ago
> Did by this stone, it seems, intend
> To name for future times to know
> The dachs-hound, Geist, their little friend.[41]

Only three of his "pet" poems survive. Toss the cat (named after Atossa, daughter of Cyrus the Great) and Rover the dog are both included in "Poor Matthias," Arnold's requiem for a canary, and also in "Kaiser Dead," on a dachshund.

By renting a house in London for a few months each year starting in January, the Arnolds kept up some urban social life. In the winter they saw the Rev. Hugh Haweis, the five-foot-high author of *Music and Morals*—who later took a mistress and sired an illegitimate child. Arnold wrote one night in an autograph book for the sprightly clergyman's legitimate child, Hugolin Olive:

> *Little baby Haweis*
> *Playing with your corals;*
> *Papa will teach you music,*
> *But who will teach you morals?*[42]

His mother, the most youthful Christian spirit he ever knew, would have enjoyed these verses. Ill, shriveled, and feeble on her eighty-second birthday, Mrs. Mary Arnold talked, in her quiet and sweet voice, with the enthusiasm of a girl. But she died a month later, on September 30, 1873, leaving Arnold with the feeling that part of himself had died. Nothing consoled him in his grief. In all his work, Arnold in effect explained himself to his parents. With his mother, he had tested the clarity and persuasive effects of beautiful language; he had tried to win her approval, awe, and delight, tried to win her sympathy by getting her to experience his feelings. Nearly every aspect of his thought he had reported to her; every poem from his pen he had written for her to admire—even though he addressed some of those poems to Jane (his father's representative). Some poems he had felt too trivial for her to notice; but he had always hoped to write the perfectly beautiful work for her. He had sent her every one of his prose compositions, and lately had received her sympathetic letter about *Literature and Dogma* and felt acutely her "power of appreciating what might not be in her line." Her literal belief in a personal God had seemed to him, finally, no barrier dividing him from her. She was the perfect Christian of light. He could recall her delight in what she called "the history of Rugby Chapel," when the school's chapel was being renovated; her habit of calling Rugby servants her friends; her love for France, Switzerland, and "dear old Father Thames"; her girlish ecstasy in Dublin's Phoenix Park and when watching the "Salmon Leap in the Liffey," during the briefest of family visits to Ireland in August 1836; and above all, her sane, healthy, intimate, prismatic attitude to time and death. For if no woman loved the excitement of life more, his mother knew death as a true friend and inspiration: he could recall and read in the household journal of her belief in death as the event "which gives *reality* to what in life is often so Phantom like." Death makes us sane. She memorialized in her diaries and talk, the better to understand the astonishing beauty of this earth.

Arnold, as a writer, always faced his parents: psychologically, they were the dynamic force in his creative life. He reached through his family to others, and his mother especially helped him to define himself. His opposed, interacting elements were also hers. It was his mother who could admire "spontaneity" and "conscience," who resembled the free Merman and the pious Margaret in "The Forsaken Merman," and who could respond to violent revolution with as much interest as to the morally conservative idea of a strong state.

It was not in letters of condolence to sisters that he mourned her. He wrote to *them* of her charity, intelligence, sympathy, or fine spirit. But when he was alone he surely recalled how much she had evoked from him; and that, perhaps, she had withheld approval of his lyrics, especially after the *Reveller,* to get him to discover other talents and make himself fully effective. He wrote to her habitually in a spirit of confessional defense, as if recommending himself, because he feared her probing intuition. In middle age he became franker, as when he told her how much more inquisitive Flu was than he—or of how he would wait for Flu's "impulsion" before he could get up steam "to go anywhere, except on business errands" on their European journeys.[43] His mother was hardly surprised by his franker admissions. Fondly, she had studied him all her life.

That subtle, psychological dualism in his thinking which made him look for the healthy interaction between amoral and moral forces, between sex and love, beauty and piety, or Hellenism and Hebraism became polarized after she died. Thus he was not at his best in *Last Essays on Church and Religion,* comprising four of his essays of 1876. In that book, "Bishop Butler and the Zeit-Geist" acknowledges Arnold's debt to Butler's sound religious intellect; and "A Psychological Parallel," on the seventeenth-century Cambridge Platonists, offers a rearguard defense of *Literature and Dogma* by showing that the psychological truth of Christianity was grasped by one Cambridge Fellow, John Smith (1618–1652), even during a time of credulity about witchcraft. But *Last Essays* also contains ossified remarks on "the fact of the two selves" which contend in man. Arnold's first self is that of "impulse," which leads to "death and misery"; the second is "reason," which leads to "happiness."[44] But his more valid, earlier view of human possibilities is that spontaneous "impulse" and moral "reason" must both be respected for happiness and creative activity.

To regain his balance after his mother died, he turned away from religion and back to literature, while fretting over moral questions. His later horror over "Lubricity" or the Goddess of Sexual Pleasure, "Aselgeia," suggests that he feared his impulses more than he did while his mother lived; furthermore his political views became narrower, less patient and even less charitable. Yet as a literary critic he continued to think and to mature; and he was not to become self-satisfied or complacent. At fifty-two, he wrote these candid verses about himself for young George Cullum of Trinity College:

> *Our aspiration quits us, not our need.*
> *The unrest of youth departs—We cease to strive,*
> *We do not cease to doubt; we cease to search,*
> *But we've not found; we cease to build ourselves,*
> *But we've not ceased still to be incomplete.*
>
> Matthew Arnold.—
> *August 6th 1875*[45]

His "unrest" continued, and his "search" for a better understanding of himself and of human life remained.

His lines on aspiration are too honest for self-parody. Over a famous parody of himself in William Mallock's satire of current ideas in the *New Republic* (1877), he was amused but not enchanted. "I think Fan and Edward would like to look at the *New Republic*," Matthew told Flu. "But I myself and my conversation are not well hit off." Arnold was seldom so grave as Mallock's funny "Mr. Luke," who appears in a fashionable country house with "Mr. Storks" (Huxley), "Mr. Herbert" (Ruskin), "Mr. Rose" (Pater), and "Dr. Jenkinson" (Jowett) in the company:

> "Culture," said Mr. Luke, ". . . sets aside the larger part of the New Testament as grotesque, barbarous, and immoral; but what remains, purged of its apparent meaning, it discerns as a treasure beyond all price. And in Christianity—such Christianity, I mean, as true taste can accept—culture sees the guide to real significance of life, and the explanation," Mr. Luke added with a sigh, "of that melancholy which in our day is attendant upon all clear sight."[46]

Taking that satire in good spirit, he appeared very debonair and carefree at parties in London. Among "rolls of brocade" and "quite superbly dressed women" at a Rothschild party, he took Nelly once to sit near Thomas Carlyle. He wanted his daughters to be at ease in society and Carlyle, for once, fully cooperated. "We sat with Carlyle more than an hour; he was very easy to get on with, and very kind to Nelly; he shook hands with her several times, and said she was just entering life, and he wished her 'a clear and prosperous course.' " Yet Arnold felt that the old man's opinions were still "very mad."[47]

About their son Dicky, Matthew and Flu were infinitely anxious. This handsome, thin-featured, blue-eyed, pert, and merry boy with his "yellow mop" of hair had been terribly pampered. A tutor at St. Leonard's had got him through the entrance exam at Balliol College, then under the mastership of the demanding Benjamin Jowett.

Arnold was not an obtuse father: but he was almost paralyzed by love. Nelly and Lucy once compared him with Emma's doddery, doting father Mr. Woodhouse in Jane Austen's *Emma*. He worshiped Dicky and accepted the boy's wishes as law: Dicky's demand for money soon sent the Arnolds more than £1000 into debt. When Dicky injured himself in rugby football, Matthew spent days at Oxford uselessly nursing him. And it was "natural," as Matthew wrote after the boy had begun at Balliol, that "we hear a great deal of football, the river, and breakfast parties, and hardly a word about reading."[48]

At Jowett's Balliol, one read day and night. Nonreaders died slow deaths—and often involved their parents in unmentionable agony before the last ax fell.

Dick was in deep trouble by 1875; and even then Matthew could not bear to be sharp. As the boy failed to turn in papers and alienated his tutors, Matthew did, however, lash out at Oxford's History Honours course in which Dick was enrolled. "Nothing but read, read, read, endless histories in English, many of them by quite secondrate men," Arnold fumes. In Dick's course there is nothing even to exercise the mind, such as "learning a new language, or mathematics, or one of the natural sciences."[49]

Huxley sent him a letter about "Old Darwin," who declared that *his* mind was amply satisfied "by the domestic affections and by natural sciences." Far from quarreling with Darwin, Arnold felt that natural sciences amply trained young minds at a university. Mathematics and sciences at Oxford were sound. What were feeble—and became much feebler, he believed in his later years—were Oxford's *humanities* offerings. If Oxford only added to its History some books "in other languages," such as "Thucydides, Tacitus, and either Montesquieu's *Esprit des Lois,* or Guizot's *Civilisation in France,*" the classes "would be incalculably improved, and would be a real training." He had no objection to studying foreign works in translation. "The one matter which gave the mind something to school it, the Roman Law, which used to go along with the History, they have now taken away."

"The fact is," Arnold continued, "it is at Oxford as it is in our schools. The regulation of studies is all important, and there is no one to regulate them, and people think that anyone can regulate them. We shall never do any good till we get [people to regulate curricula at a university] who have the highest mental training themselves."[50] Clearly, the minds of young people at university are among a nation's delicate assets; these minds can be stultified with verbiage by second-rate authors, or by works from only one "language" or one national culture, or by merely fashionable and popular reading lists. Those who set courses at a university must be highly experienced, he believed, and must never pander to the students' wishes.

When visiting his son at Oxford he stayed with Humphry Ward —the Brasenose College tutor who had married Tom's daughter Mary. Aesthetic and up-to-date, the Wards lived among blue pots and William Morris designs in a house just opposite Walter Pater, who also lived among blue pots and Morris wallpapers, with his sisters, and had caused a sensation in 1873 with his *Renaissance.* Pater's aestheticism is indebted to Arnold but as a rule aesthetic Oxford was drearier and more puritanical than Newman's earlier, religious Oxford. Dinner parties in the 1870s were simple and short; ladies in smocked "Liberty" dresses with "Watteau pleats" scorned the new low dresses of London—which Mary Ward thought ugly and "fast." That earnestness amused Matthew. When Mary gravely sighed over Sarah Bernhardt in Racine's *Phèdre*, "Uncle Matt" quite angered her by laughing and patting her hand as he said: "But, my dear child—you see, you never saw Rachel!"[51]

Not all the Humphry Wards' friends were stuffy. They knew Mark Pattison, the Rector of Lincoln, and later met Rhoda Broughton—who quarreled with Pattison when he took George Bradley's niece, Meta, as his mistress.[52] Arnold knew the novelist Rhoda Broughton and persuaded her to settle at Oxford in 1878.* And, if the Wards were rather more earnest than their friends, Humphry *did* take a kindly, sympathetic interest in Arnold's son Dick—and that interest was now exploited. With Ward's help the boy might get through Balliol. "My dear Ward," a father writes sweetly from Cobham, "I consider you Dick's best and most valuable friend. . . . I got a very kind letter from Jowett," admits Matthew, "saying that he would do anything for Dick's good, but that, if he might venture to say so, I was not strict enough with the boy." Indubitably, Dicky is "a great baby" and may have said a few "cheeky" things to the Balliol tutors—but surely Humphry can help him to pass his Oxford Moderations exam, which Dicky has terribly failed? "Take Dick under your guidance," Matthew pleads. On holidays the boy with his "blond mop" of hair and engaging manners lamentably does "not much, and is much interrupted by invitations; I can do little or no work with him," Matthew sighs, "as I am in full career of inspection."[53]

Quite soon, Balliol tutors told Dick that he was too far behind to get anything from college lectures. Then he met a fate worse than his father's second-class Oxford degree. Matthew was devastated: "I had hoped Dick might scramble into a fourth [class degree]," he wrote to Humphry Ward in a pathetic letter, "but his course has been so fruitful in anxiety and disappointment . . . that I was foolish, perhaps, to expect anything pleasant, even relatively pleasant. For the fourth class would not have qualified him for the [Education] Council Office—the best opening I could see for him." The very lowest clerkship in the education office was, for Dick, "absolutely out of the question."[54] A

---

*Arnold flirted facetiously with the intense, witty Rhoda Broughton (1840–1920), who wrote romantic tales and then comic satiric novels such as *Second Thoughts* (1880) or *Belinda* (1883)—in which Arnold's friend Pattison is caricatured as Professor Forth. "I am *wanted* tomorrow night to meet Rhoda Broughton," Arnold told the publisher George Smith. "Suppose R.B. and I were to collaborate on a novel?"

Fourth Class would have been nearly disastrous, but Dick did not rise to that. He left Oxford with an enormous gambling debt—and no degree at all.

Matthew blamed neither himself nor his son. He yearned now to keep the boy alive, well, nearby—and yet when Dick spoke "eagerly" of being a banker in Australia, Matthew and Flu, despite their anguish over losing him, helped him to go.

Dick's career did not make Arnold wiser as a parent or a man; but it confirmed him in believing that inner freedom is after all better than success. If Dick wished to go to Australia, he must go. In his son's shoes, Matthew would have worked abroad as a "farm-hand," as he told Ward, "in Canada or New Zealand."[55] And consistently, though Arnold at fifty-five dined among leading *literati* and political figures of the day, and had his ideas discussed by them, and saw in the journals that he was a formative influence on his nation, he was detached from his success. He was ironic and aloof at dinner parties. He declined "honours." He refused to stand for a virtually certain seat in Parliament, refused to head public committees, refused to be "honorary" rector at St. Andrews University—because he felt that post might clash with his liberty as a "subordinate" School Inspector, a job which "has always left me perfect freedom in my literary productions." A certain weary exasperation with his fame, and petulance over the thickheadedness of insular clergymen, contributed to his vowing to write no more popular books on religion. He had decided by 1877 to return to the best guarantor of human freedom he knew, or "literature proper." He was only returning, he told the public in *Last Essays*, "to devote to literature, more strictly so-called, what remains to me of life and strength and leisure."[56]

He would not compromise a boy's freedom by insisting on a "factory inspectorship" in England. Dick was bent on becoming very rich as a clerk in the Union Bank of Melbourne. Matthew wondered if Dick had the discipline to hold any job; but Dick "says that he shall first repay me all I have had to spend on him, and then shall enable me to retire! His passage is taken and he sails."[57]

After Dick left Gravesend on a November day, the parents went on to Plymouth to see his boat for the last time. Arnold indulged his sentimental feelings on this occasion; he found relief in Fanny Lucy's outright weeping over Dick's departure. They took a tugboat out to the waiting, enormous vessel. "Dick stood with many others at the ship's side; he had taken off his cap, and the dear fellow's 'yellow mop' was all visible." As the ship left Plymouth for the sea, Arnold watched his wife; she "behaved admirably, quite admirably; made no scene at all, had no burst of weeping, did not even cry much at all, though from time to time tears ran down her dear cheeks." Evening came over Plymouth Harbour and a "new moon was visible." Self-consciously he tried to comfort Flu. Then he tried to believe that Dick would reach Australia and return some day to his parents—who could think of nothing else. He felt, as an anxious father, that happiness and well-being utterly had left him: "I shall go on as usual, but I shall never have a happy day until I see him again."[58]

17

INVASIONS OF THE
UNITED STATES
1878–1886

MATTHEW ARNOLD ARRIVES

THE APOSTLE OF SWEETNESS AND LIGHT
SOJOURNING HERE AWHILE

ENGLAND'S INCOMPARABLE EGOTIST GIVES
A FEW OF HIS IMPRESSIONS ABOUT CHICAGO
—*Headlines in North America, 1883 and 1884*

I would not go to see the pig-sticking at the stock yards.
Certainly not! Why should I wish to see pig-sticking?
—*Arnold in the United States*

H IS blond son Dick's headstrong departure from England in
1878—like his brother Tom's and Clough's earlier sailings
—deeply affected Matthew Arnold. When news came that Dick's ship
was at Cape Verde Islands, he wrote "S.S. 'Lusitania'."

This interesting sonnet, the last from his pen, contrasts the fabled
drowning of the hero, Ulysses, with the safe, global voyage of the
happy Dick: "Of my child I thought," writes Matthew as an anxious
parent of fifty-six,

> *In his long black ship speeding night and day*
> *O'er those same seas; dark Teneriffe rose, fraught*
>
> *With omen; 'Oh! were that Mount passed', I say.*
> *Then the door opens and this card is brought:*
> *'Reached Cape Verde Islands, "Lusitania".'*[1]

Arnold's own last decade was to have its splendid voyages—but why
does he fear the "omen" of Mt. Tenerife in the Canaries? Once a wind
from the Mount overwhelmed Ulysses' ship. The hero watched dark
"sea-waters" overhead, and sank in black depths under the seafloor to
Inferno, where he sings forever of death. Ulysses knows the pain of
inwardness, of creativity; he is a lost poet; but blond Dick is spared

that anguish as he travels over surface waters to sunny Melbourne.

When Arthur Stanley died in 1881, Arnold turned him into a more complex symbol. This Old Rugbeian was feebler than "the narrowest Evangelical" and lacked "deep religious power of any kind";[2] but, then, the strength of Arthur Stanley lay in his candid innocence: perhaps he remained a "child of light" all his life. Arnold's "Westminster Abbey" links him with the Thames, with the lovely legend of St. Peter's consecrating the old Abbey, and with a Goddess Demeter who cared for the infant Demophoön and who knows the future for all poets. Stanley's life, from his childhood to his futile years as Dean of Westminster, suggests a poet's life:

> *Warm in her breast, by day,*
> *He slumbered, and ambrosia balmed the child;*
> *But all night long amid the flames he lay, . . .*
>
> . . . . . .
>
> *'Had human cry not marred the work divine,*
> *Immortal had I made this boy of mine; . . .'*
>
> . . . . . .
>
> *Why should he pray to range*
> *Down the long age of truth that ripens slow;*
> *And break his heart with all the baffling change,*
> *And all the tedious tossing to and fro?*[3]

Society's human "cry" destroys *any* lyric talent; the world nearly engorges the poet, then breaks his heart with a ceaseless flux of events, with distracting, modern changes. As Arnold's last two substantial poems, "Lusitania" and "Westminster" interestingly return to his early symbols for lyric creativity—to depths of water, children, and beings who transcend time—and both lyrics seem addressed to his sisters.

Those sisters admired him as England's foremost man of letters, yet revered him especially for *Culture and Anarchy* and his work as a social critic. Though meaning to return to "literature," Arnold to placate his sisters and his conscience—and to earn money—now wrote a few tracts such as "Ecce, Convertimur ad Gentes" (Lo, We Turn to the Gentiles), which he delivered at Ipswitch Working Men's College in 1879. He asks, here, that workers support the idea of state middle-class schools so the working class will have "a more civilised middle class to rise into, if they *do* rise." He no sooner gave that tactless parody of *Culture and Anarchy* than he turned to his sisters: he had said nothing at Ipswitch, as he told Jane, "which you will dislike." Then he smiled at Fan: "I am very glad you liked my Ipswitch discourse, and praise you give it as being well adapted to its audience pleases me particularly."[4] He hardly bothered to solicit their approval for his late literary pieces.

His social aim became less certain—and except for the remarks on unemployment in "Future of Liberalism," his late social essays are less cogent than speeches by Bright or Gladstone. But, by shifting from society to poetry, he gives his last *literary* essays new depth and reality. Each of his late volumes contains some fine things. In February 1879, his *Mixed Essays* appeared with these pieces:[5]

Democracy (1861)
—reprinted from *Popular Education of France*

Equality (1878)
—on the need for social equality in a democracy

Irish Catholicism and British Liberalism (1878)
—on Anglo-Irish misunderstanding

"Porro Unum Est Necessarium" (1878)
—"But One Thing Is Needful," on a state system for secondary schools

A Guide to English Literature (1877)
—on Stopford Brooke's survey of literature

Falkland (1877)
—a brilliant essay on the seventeenth-century statesman, Lucius Cary Viscount Falkland, and the tragic principle in history

A French Critic on Milton (1877)
—on comparative criticism and the Geneva critic Edmond Scherer

A French Critic on Goethe (1878)
—on Edmond Scherer and against "systems" in criticism

George Sand (1877)
—on memories of Nohant and George Sand's qualities as a writer

After visiting Dublin to see "K" and her husband Forster, who was then under severe pressure as Chief Secretary for Ireland, he published in February 1882 *Irish Essays and Others,* a miscellany on politics, the schools, social questions, and poetry:

The Incompatibles (1881)
—Arnold's most interesting "healing" essay on Anglo-Irish relations

An Unregarded Irish Grievance (1881)
—on state support for Irish grammar schools

A Speech at Eton (1879)
—on Greek values, to the Eton Literary Society

The French Play in London (1879)
—on Sarah Bernhardt's French repertoire and the need for a British state theater

"Ecce, Convertimur ad Gentes"
(1879)
—his Ipswitch address on
secondary schools

The Future of Liberalism (1880)
—on politics and unemployment

Copyright (1880)
—on human rights and
Anglo-American copyright law

Prefaces to Poems (1853, 1854)
—reprinted from earlier
volumes of *Poems*

In June 1885, he next published the book he most wanted to be remembered by, a green octavo *Discourses in America* with three lectures on society, education, and literature from his American tour of 1883–84:

Numbers; or The Majority and the Remnant (1884)
    —written for his American lecture tour and delivered eighteen times in the U.S. and Canada
Literature and Science (1882)
    —written for his Rede lecture at Cambridge of June 14, 1882, in reply to Huxley's attack on literature in liberal education (at the opening of Sir Josiah Mason's new Science College in Birmingham on October 1, 1880), and given 29 times in North America
Emerson (1884)
    —written in the United States and given as a lecture eighteen times, first at Boston on December 1, 1883

With its format and title planned not long before he died, his *Essays in Criticism: Second Series* appeared with a notice by John Duke Lord Coleridge in November 1888. All these pieces were meant for fairly wide audiences:

The Study of Poetry (1880)
—written to introduce Humphry Ward's anthology of *English Poets*

Milton (1888)
—a memorial speech at Westminster

Thomas Gray (1880)
—written for Ward's selection of Gray's poems

John Keats (1880)
—written for Ward's selection of Keats

Byron (1881)
—written to introduce a *Byron* selection for Alexander Macmillan

Shelley (1888)
—an essay on Edward Dowden's *Shelley* (1886) about Shelley's life; it was meant to be followed by one on Shelley's poetry, which Arnold did not live to write

Count Leo Tolstoi (1887)
—mainly on *Anna Karenina*

Wordsworth (1879)
—written to introduce the
Wordsworth volume in
Macmillan's "Golden Treasury"
(and remaining in print for a
hundred years in that series)

Amiel (1887)
—written soon after Mary
Ward's translation in 1885 of
Amiel's mystical *Journal intime*

Among the essays he never collected are a *locus classicus* for his views on American intellect and literature, "Theodore Parker" (1867); his fine essay on a sensitive Savoyard friend of the Geneva writers, "Joseph de Maistre on Russia" (1879); his best piece on Sainte-Beuve titled simply that (1886); and critiques of the United States such as "A Word" and "A Word More about America" (written just before and after his American tour), "General Grant" (1887), and the last essay he published, "Civilisation in the United States" (1888).*

He fully *meant* to write poetry again. He hoped that he might, somewhere, find a locale for poetry writing; but his sisters, interestingly, seem later to have tried to suppress evidence about his plans. When Professor J. J. Sylvester of Woolwich accepted a mathematics chair at Baltimore, in the "brain drain" of 1876, Arnold for example thought of the States. "Matthew Arnold spoke to me about the University," Sylvester wrote to President Gilman, of Johns Hopkins. "He would prefer a congenial appointment as a professor. . . . He even went so far as to say that I might acquaint you that he could be approached."[6] But he gave up dreaming of English Chairs in Maryland; he couldn't after all, emigrate with "relatives" or his four sisters to Johns Hopkins. ("This would have been a very great catch indeed,"[7]

---

*Other pieces Arnold wrote in his last, prolific decade fall into three main groups. (1) The best are critical or biographical: "On Poetry" (1879); "A Genevese Judge" on Eugène Colladon (1881); "An Eton Boy" on Arthur Mynors (1882); "A French Worthy" on Rapet the school inspector (1882); "A Liverpool Address" on science, nervous excitement in culture, and "negative lucidity" or seeing the faults in received ideas (1882); his Wordsworth Society address (1883); "A Comment on Christmas" on a secular meaning in the Resurrection (1885); and "A 'Friend of God' " on Johann Tauler (1887). He also wrote prefaces to editions of Johnson (1878); Burke (1881), Isaiah (1883), and Mary Claude (1887). (2) His last school writings include his official general reports; his last *Special Report* on German, Swiss, and French primary schools (1886); his oral statements to the Cross Commission (1886); and some unofficial writings: "Common Schools Abroad" (1886), "Schools in the Reign of Queen Victoria" with curt comments on William Forster (1887), and his Westminster Farewell speech (November 12, 1886). (3) His uncollected political essays include "Nadir of Liberalism" (1886), "Zenith of Conservatism" (1887), "Up to Easter" (1887), "From Easter to August" (1887), and "Disestablishment in Wales" (1888). Finally his letters to *The Times* concern schools and politics: "The Irish University Question" (July 31, 1879), "The Cost of Elementary Schools" (October 20, 1879), "The Political Crisis" (May 22, 1886), and "After the Elections" (August 6, 1886).

wrote Sylvester to the Johns Hopkins president, in one of the finest understatements of the time.) He next meant to go to Florence with Flu to write verses; and then in 1885, tried to regain Oxford's Poetry Chair—and only changed his mind because he had implied, earlier, he would back Palgrave *if* Palgrave still wanted the chair and thought he could get it. "I must now write to him," Arnold wrote at sixty-two to Humphry. If Francis Palgrave thinks he has "a fair chance of success if I abstain, I cannot stand."[8] Since Palgrave wanted Oxford's Poetry Chair, in 1885, Arnold abstained from the election. (He might have retired quietly to Oxford, for lectures and poetry writing, and would have been eligible for two terms until 1895.)

His dream to recover his lyric talent remained a dream—but he longed to give up school inspecting. He had too many projects he would *like* to try and too little energy left for pupil-teacher papers. In April 1882, when his son had decided to return to England, he faced the idea of *never* having funds to retire. His accounts were bleak:

overdrawn Jan^y £12 . . 16 . .
overdrawn Feb. £33 . . 14 . . 10
overdrawn March £130 . . 7 . . 9
overdrawn April £142 . . 9 . . 7[9]

He seldom pleased a bank manager, and really went through life borrowing, lending, gambling, and giving away what little he had with an imperial largesse—but his real endurance was failing in 1882. He pushed himself on days full of reports, exams, letters, articles and the reading in Spenser, Mme De Sévigné, or Montalembert that kept his mind alive:

Tuesday	in Jonah nur heute!
	in Anthology
	in Sévigné—Fauriel
	letters of day
	begin writing article
	in Spenser
Thursday	finish Ewald
	in Spenser
	P[upil] T[eacher] papers
	letters of day
	in Montalembert
	in Feydeau
	in Renan
	in Fauriel
	Whiskey—Mrs Shand
Friday	in Gk. Test[ament] nur heute, heute!
	20 papers
	200 of [illegible]

Friday	in Gray
(cont.)	in Neander
	in Molière
	letters of day
	P[upil] T[eacher] notices
	in Lob Nor[10]

"Twofold are the gates of sleep," he scribbles wearily, "one of which bears hours."[11]

To get money to retire, he edited six of Johnson's *Lives* and then a selection of Burke's speeches as Irish conditions worsened. With accounts nagging him, he brought out *Prose Passages* from his works, then helped Nelly to choose 365 mottoes for a *Matthew Arnold Birthday Book.* "The fashion of compiling 'Birthday books,'" winced the *Daily News,* "flourishes, though, as with our coal supplies [it is] predestined to exhaustion." Nelly's book showed a puffy Matthew with an overfed dog: "Love me," sighed the *Guardian,* "love my dog."[12]

His late literary essays more boldly *oppose* their time. Young critics of the 1870s and 1880s such as Edward Dowden, Edmund Gosse, F. W. H. Myers, and George Saintsbury had been taught sophistication by Arnold himself; Arthur Symons now appeared regularly in the *Fortnightly* and *Cornhill;* and Leslie Stephen between 1874 and 1879 published three series of *Hours in a Library,* just as John Morley's *Critical Miscellanies* and Swinburne's *Essays and Studies* appeared. These critics dismayed Arnold paradoxically, because, as he felt, their "methods" in aesthetic or scientific criticism excluded many readers while oversimplifying literature.

In a review of the popular poems of Charles P. O'Conor, called "A Deptford Poet," Matthew really had "returned" to criticism in 1875. He began this piece by saying that "the right function of poetry is to animate, to console, to rejoice, to *strengthen*"—a Schiller-like thesis that he was to develop.[13] He next quoted 122 lines of O'Conor to get him to show his own range, power, and faults, and would use the same technique in "A Septuagenarian Poet" on Rossetti's friend William Bell Scott. No book, Arnold felt, is reviewed unless its texture is displayed by the reviewer, who must know *why* he should quote: the good critic displays, compares, and gets out of the way while yet offering a mind "qualified in a certain manner."[14]

His own mind respects texts, and values a world literature. A "provincial infatuation," he says, mingles even in British verdicts on Shakespeare. Our nations for intellectual and spiritual purposes are "one great confederation," hence English poetry is only one contributory stream to the world-river of poetry. This thesis is developed in

"Wordsworth," and also in "The Study of Poetry," which Arnold wrote as the introductory essay to a four-volume anthology of English poets from Chaucer to Rossetti, under Humphry Ward's general editorship. Ward had over thirty people writing essays on individual poets for this large anthology, and Arnold offered "Thomas Gray" and "John Keats" for it. He plays out in these pieces a little drama, in which he attacks, for, example, in "Gray," the lavish praise of Collins over Gray in Swinburne's piece on "Collins" for the same anthology.[15] Arnold appeals for critical moderation in his own pieces, but rises to perfection because he has opponents to refute.

He wrote "Byron" and "Wordsworth" to introduce selections of those poets for Macmillan, but "The Study of Poetry" is the locus for most of his central ideas in this period. That essay displays his best methods, even his own sensitive, tactile consciousness. He had a habit of touching people, of throwing his arms around surprised Americans later in the United States, for example. He now looks back from a more sophisticated England of the 1880s to a cruder, less inhibited nation of the 1840s when his critical ideas were forming. The older nation of railway barons and Irish navvies, of extreme filial affection and solicitude, of brothers who kissed sisters on the lips and of male friends who walked hand in hand at school, was itself part of him. His fondness for the palpable appears even in "touchstone" passages he offers in "Study of Poetry." (His father in a review once condemned moral abstractions in poetry, while recommending touchstones to critics.) Matthew offers eleven brief passages from Homer, Dante, Milton, and Shakespeare—such as this one from *Henry IV*, Part II:

> *Wilt thou upon the high and giddy mast*
> *Seal up the ship-boy's eyes, and rock his brains*
> *In cradle of the rude imperious surge. . . .* [16]

Since it reveals poetry's highest power, that passage educates the critic. Arnold does not object to the technical study of literature—but holds that we cannot fully *define* poetic excellence, and insists that we respect the extremely elusive nature of art. In this he foreshadows Roland Barthes's later view of the literary work as almost infinitely complex, onion-like,

> a construction of layers (or levels or systems) whose body contains, finally no heart, no kernel, no secret, no irreducible principle, nothing except the infinity of its own envelopes.[17]

If literature is so elusive, it is hard to sum up, grasp, get one's critical hands on. Yet, in its complexity, it offers life's best interpretations; and in this way it is religious. If "religion to-day" is external and we attach religious emotion only to exploded dogmas, rather than to Christian and Hebraic ideas, then religion as currently conceived is of less use than literature. Arnold seems to lose his faith neither in imagination nor in religion; he believes that if a poet's imagination is hampered by an age of half-hearted beliefs, then critics must help in bringing about a new intellectual and spiritual ethos. Meanwhile poetry *does* strenghen us with its insights: and the importance of "touchstones" is that they put art into our minds—and inform and structure the modern consciousness.

Arguing for literature's necessity, he turns his best essays into impassioned models of critical acts. He is tough-minded, unapologetic, at home in "Byron." "Amidst snow and ice, I have done that volcano, Byron," he told an editor, "and have sent him off."[18] But "John Keats" reminds him of nagging quarrels with Clough and with himself; he temperamentally upbraids sensual Keats, then ranks him high. In "Wordsworth," he sets a poet in his European context—in which Wordsworth belongs to a wide tradition involving "Lessing, Schiller, Uhland," as well as "Filicaia, Alfieri, Manzoni, and Leopardi" and "Racine, Boileau, Voltaire, Andre Chenier, Béranger, Lamartine, Musset" and "M. Victor Hugo"—and yet must be ranked above them all. "The greatness of a poet," he writes as he bridges a gap between his own ethics and aesthetics, "lies in a powerful and beautiful application of ideas to life."[19] He tries to show that Wordsworth *has* that greatness—and indeed his "Wordsworth" essay assisted that poet's reputation, even if he cites as Wordsworth's best lyrics "The Fountain," "Michael," and "The Highland Reaper" (getting the title straight later as "The Solitary Reaper") and in his anthology, following the essay, fails to print "The Thorn," "Peter Bell," and "The Idiot Boy." (A lyric anthology omitting them, one feels, is hardly fair to Wordsworth.) If Arnold pulls the Rydal poet's teeth, he does offer an easily readable Wordsworth, even as he recalls, perhaps, Macmillan's advice about the British public: " '*Bottles' touched with emotion* is the sort of audience you seek to reach—and create," that publisher had reminded him before he set to work on "Wordsworth."[20]

Two key pieces—"A French Critic on Milton" and "A French Critic on Goethe" show his comparative approach at its best: both involve Edmond Scherer, the silver-haired Geneva critic and deputy whom he had met in 1859 and ranked with Sainte-Beuve. The first essay (with Dr. Johnson's help) attacks Milton for contempt of women and discusses the sins of modern criticism and book reviewing: fashionable rhetoric, conventional views, and failure of flexibility. (It might be a reviewer's Bible.) In the second "French Critic" he takes his happiest fling at systematizers and narrow historical critics—at all who forget that criticism involves the whole sensibility.

"Many and diverse" are the "judgments" we make about authors, writes Arnold delightfully, in a profound comment on the element of commitment that lies at the root of "disinterestedness" and as if by way of warning to a future generation of critics who bring an arid positivism into their work. Let Dullness paste *this* into its hat:

> There is the judgment of enthusiasm and admiration . . . the judgment of gratitude and sympathy . . . the judgment of ignorance, the judgment of incompatibility, the judgment of envy and jealousy. Finally, there is the systematic judgment, and this judgment is the most worthless of all. The sharp scrutiny of envy and jealousy may bring real faults to light. The judgments of incompatibility and ignorance are instructive, whether they reveal necessary clefts of separation between the experiences of different sorts of people, or reveal simply the narrowness and bounding view of those who judge. But the systematic judgment is altogether unprofitable. Its author has not really his eye upon the professed object . . . of his criticism at all, but upon something else which he wants to prove. . . . He never fairly looks at it, he is looking at something else. [21]

His late essays that matter the most are the two "French Critics," "Thomas Gray," "Byron," "John Keats," "George Sand," "Wordsworth," "Emerson," "The Study of Poetry," and "Literature and Science"; these with the earlier *Essays in Criticism,* the Preface of 1853, and the Homer lectures amount to his chief legacy as a critic of literature.

His effort in writing pieces of the late 1870s such as "Wordsworth" was made no easier by the toil of school inspecting, and indeed in 1880 he had the first sign that his health might give away. He was ill at ease and short of breath. Fanny Lucy urged him in September to join the Sandfords and Mundellas without herself in one of the coldest parts of eastern Switzerland. He never had more congenial supervisors in the education office: Sandford, an old Balliol friend, was its Secretary, and the liberal A. J. Mundella had Lowe's old commanding position as Vice-President of the Council—and thus was Sandford's and Arnold's chief. Mundella was more than a boss: he was a political mentor, a confidant, a bureaucrat who urged Arnold to write more poetry—and who loved his poetry. He had a pretty, flirtatious daughter who would be coming along, too, to the icy, blue-and-white Ober Engadine in the eastern Alps.

Matthew, settling into a hotel at Pontresina that September, was so overcome by the beauty of scenery that he yearned to tell Fanny Lucy about it: he missed her acutely. At first he had little time for the genial Mundella or even narrow-waisted Miss Mundella. He fell in love with the Morteratsch glacier, and even with its name. A mass of blue and greenish ice below the Bernina, it seemed beautiful, cold, and severe as anything in the Bernese Oberland. The freezing air did him good, and his health improved, although the air and scenery were so stimulating that he could not sleep very deeply and rose early. He looked out on white magnificence: "In every direction from Pontresina," he wrote to Flu, "you are led up to beauty unutterable." He took walks high above the Morteratsch in snow fields and watched "the great glacier below running up the great snow-vested sweep of the Bernina and his fellows, all their upper parts sparkling in sunshine, but the deep black shadows steadily creeping up them." He was fascinated by the black shadows and very pleased to be, like Thoreau, an inspector of snowstorms. Hunting for gentians and Alpine asters one day, he was surprised to meet a man carrying a measuring can: "I asked him what he was doing up there."

"Ich messe die Bewegung des Gletschers" (I am measuring the movement of the glaciers), replied his friend.

"Sind Sie Militar?" (Are you in the army?) he asked.

"Nein, Gelehrte," replied the man, shaking his head and explaining that he was employed by a scientific group.

"I thought these glacier measurers were very appropriate inmates of the solitude," Arnold wrote with great satisfaction to Flu. But he enjoyed best his total isolation, when beauty appeared in every haunting alpine line and shadow: "I wandered on by a path along the mountain side to a hut from which the ascent of the Bernina and the great peaks near him begins. I have seldom enjoyed anything more," Matthew reports. "I did not see a soul. The moon rose, the black shadows gradually stole up the sparkling snow-sides of the mountains, and I could hardly tear myself away." How important was this natural symbolism of beauty and death to him? He was not a morbid man nor a romantic like Rousseau, but the beauty of nature in its extreme severity reconciled him cheerfully to the fact of death, to the likelihood that "black shadows" might overtake him soon, and told him that something beautiful that he had seen in this world would remain. To love the Morteratsch glacier was to escape, for a few days, from mortality. He went back to his friends the Mundellas and Sandfords in high and ebullient spirits, joined them in walks, and laughed when a "gigantic St. Bernard" leaped up between himself and Miss Mundella at one luncheon. The dog put an end to a relationship that was, after all, becoming flirtatious. Seated on an empty chair between Miss Mundella and himself, this wet, huge, delightful St. Bernard "entirely refused bread, and would eat nothing but beefsteak." A day or two later, a happier and healthier Arnold went through Vicosoprano on the way back to England: "I am glad to be drawing nearer to you, for I miss you constantly," he wrote with a good conscience to Fanny Lucy, "but if you were with me I should be in despair at turning my back upon Italy."[22]

Still, when back in England he yearned not so much for glaciers, as for a new perspective on *human* society. As the months passed his routine work seemed to eat into his morale and he thought more often of a grand "invasion" of the United States. In 1882 he felt perfectly healthy and yet indescribably and wearily hemmed in, eager to escape with Fanny Lucy. He was captious and displeased with the old sources of his inspiration and more than ever bored and restless. Not even a meeting with Newman two years earlier in the Duchess of Norfolk's reception line, or the few play reviews he wrote for *Pall Mall Gazette* as "An Old Playgoer," really refreshed him. He barely approves H. A. Jones's funny *The Silver King* or Henry Irving and Ellen Terry's acting in *Much Ado;* and in fact, his later review of Wilson Barrett in *Hamlet* shows him captious about play and actor. "All Hamlets whom I have seen," he writes, "dissatisfy us in something."

But he strikes a happier note in 1882 in "A Word about America," in which he sees promise in the United States, despite its Philistines, and alludes to "Jumbo"—an African elephant, in Regent's Park, purchased that January to the despair of the British public by an American circus man. Jumbo *was* going to the U.S.A. as Barnum's circus elephant: would Arnold, people wondered, go over too?

His son's return from Australia decided him: Dick needed funds even *after* he became a Manchester factory inspector and married his Melbourne sweetheart, Ella Ford. The quickest way Arnold might recoup money he had already lost on Dick was to speak in the States. At Mrs. Henry Yates Thompson's party in London, in June 1883, he now met a cheerful, square-faced American of forty-eight known as the Star-spangled Scotchman—Andrew Carnegie. Rising from a Dunfermline cottage to become Pittsburgh's iron king, Carnegie was not yet what J. P. Morgan called him—the richest man in the world—but he was agreeable and obliging, eager to listen and perhaps to confide: he was under the thumb of his old Scottish mother and engaged to a woman in her twenties, Miss Whitfield, who was three inches taller than himself. He thirsted for European culture, while saying things such as "By golly boys, there's a great treat in store for us here,"[23] and he adopted Arnold as the most charming of men.

Arnold so far, had taken his notions of America mainly from Tocqueville, Ampère, Renan, and Guizot, elegant watchers of that democratic experiment. He knew few Americans of the "Mr. Bottles" type, such as Carnegie, although he did know men who understood New England culture—such as the Rev. Moncure Conway; Charles Eliot Norton, the Harvard professor of fine arts; or James Russell Lowell, poet, author of *Biglow Papers,* and minister to the Court of St. James's. Carnegie almost symbolized an unrefined, middle-class America—which might listen to critics.

The Star-spangled Scotchman in 1883 invited Matthew, Flu, and Lucy to stay at his hotel in New York. Matthew made travel plans, and near sailing time irritated the New York press. He had accepted from that "Pericles" Gladstone a small Civil List Pension though, in fact, wary of taking "£250 a year more" from a nation paying his normal salary "of nearly £1000."[24] John Morley, the M.P., advised him to take the pension; and the *New York Times* advertised this in September:

HAPPY MATTHEW ARNOLD
WHO TAKES A PENSION FROM A FUND FOR THE POOR[25]

On the eve of sailing, Arnold worsened matters by naïvely telling a reporter he *hoped to profit* in the United States from lectures. This item was promptly telegraphed to New York.

Whatever Americans liked, he would give them "Literature and Science," his Cambridge piece on the need for a balance between literature and science; and also "Numbers," in which he argues for a dedicated "remnant" of new leaders, and against the tyranny of numbers in a democracy. That piece was finished at the last moment. For a third lecture, on "Emerson," he took along the Emerson-Carlyle letters and a pile of other books to read at sea. "I wish my invasion of America were over," he cried out at last. "I don't like going, I don't like lecturing, I don't like living in public."[26] But Lucy was cramming gifts as if she were going to be married into Stateroom 92 of the Cunard steamship *Servia.* Flu tucked at her bonnet and waved good-bye to Nelly; horns sounded in the damp air and a large ship moved out of Liverpool.

Arnold faced a murderous ordeal—with seventy speaking engagements ahead. At the other shore were entrepreneurs who acted as his agents, the Savoy opera's Richard D'Oyly Carte and James B. Pond, the promoter; as well as a vast lovely America, waiting to be seen and to see him.

The United States in a "Gilded Age" eighteen years after its Civil War was worth seeing. It had welcomed people from every nation as its citizens, flung railways 3,000 miles out to California and turned

Northern Pacific and Sante Fe into household names. Here were fifty million vigorous people producing more than five billion dollars' worth of manufactured products a year. They were advanced: typewriters were in use by 1883. With her vast panorama of rich green farmlands, thickly wooded hills, enormous grazing lands enclosed with barbed wire and dotted with cheap metal windmills, her one thousand steel plants, her refineries massed around Pittsburgh and Cleveland, her mines and pipelines, her trains carrying manufactured goods from the Mississippi Valley and huge crops of the Middle West, America was leading the capitalist world.

How long would she stay on top of the wave? Arnold was to tally up real strengths of the United States: her wonderful Constitution, laws, and federal system, the vigorous forward-looking and hopeful attitudes of her people, her natural resources, and her machine production and factory system. Her weakness lay at the heart of her success: the speed of change had made the quality of life in the United States very poor, as he considered, and it is not pleasant to live in a sterile, bright, shiny, metallic culture which cuts itself off from roots in Europe and in ancient Greece and Israel. We need long traditions, a sense of our connection with the human past, to be truly humane, tender, sympathetic, and interesting to one another. A society lacking in that cohesiveness given by traditions, and in which the quality of life is poor, can become brittle and finally a prey to its enemies. America of President Jackson's day had been a country of farmers and artisans and small-scale businessmen dependent on wagons, river steamers, and canal boats—but since the Civil War she had become an industrial giant with the three key industries of steel, meat packing, and oil at the heart of her wealth, and dependent on large-scale enterprise, vicious greed, and masses of the proletariat teeming in her cities. American men were typically loud, boastful, crude, literal, and optimistic; they loved fistfights, chewing tobacco, brass spittoons, bourbon whisky. Except when they became wealthy, and sent their girls to college or married them well, they exploited their women and kept them hard at work in factories or the home. Again, Americans thrived on shoddy advertising and sales campaigns, on buncombe and ballyhoo and bizarre political oratory—though as a rule their industrialists dominated politics and had reduced Lincoln's humane Republican party to one with few ideas, but two main policies: free land and high tariffs. Ruthless aggression in America had not been mellowed by a developing culture or softened by much social legislation.

Not more than 17 percent of the people were illiterate, however, by 1883. A flood of immigrants had put pressure on American schools and a fine federal system responded: the Supreme Court upheld

Kalamazoo's right to have a free school and many states had compulsory education laws. Americans were *demanding* to be educated—and the free library, free public school, and Chautauqua movement bringing lectures to adults (and finally six United States Presidents to talk by the shores of Lake Chautauqua in New York) were typical of the day. Americans worshiped technology and science. Their clergymen, with amazing ease, reconciled Darwin's evolutionary theory with theism; even Princeton's president declared that God works through natural selection. As a mechanical sign of the times, Mark Twain wrote on a $125 typewriter and felt that it "piles an awful stack of words on one page."[27]

Yet wealth and technology left the nation oddly anxious, rootless, and uneasy. New England writers such as Emerson and Lowell tried to connect with Europe's cultural traditions while Mark Twain and Whitman—though Whitman took a keen interest in Europe and in his English friends—looked for a unique American national identity. Wealth and progress offered feeble, fragile values, no real substitutes for aristocracy, ritual, and the national churches which tended to stabilize European life. America had a brief, rich history—some of Arnold's Virginia hosts still signed "C.S.A." after their names—but by 1883, Yankee and Confederate nostalgia seemed not enough for life.

Often insecure with new wealth, Americans craved approval and love; they boasted and wanted you to marvel. They sought "culture" as a badge or as proof of success, leisure, and good manners while wanting you to admire their hard work. What, after all, did Arnold mean to them? His books were quite unknown to most, and generally disliked by the Yankee literary establishment (except perhaps by Henry James and Charles Norton). The *New York Times* only imagined that his essays were better known in America than in England—and, by October, London's *Times* believed that myth. The American press was now inventing a coolly outrageous critic, who seemed to be arriving from Britain to make money and scoff. As Arnold, the sillier he seemed, would draw crowds, D'Oyly Carte the promoter hoped he would give many press interviews.

After a somewhat rough crossing, the *Servia* docked at Staten Island for a quarantine check. Matthew was up for landfall: "Not a single Mohican running about!" he remarked with cheer.[28] Just before 9 A.M. on October 22, 1883, he set foot in the United States.

Pushing through crowds, Carnegie and his secretary saved the Arnolds from newsmen, and drove them to Hotel Windsor on Fifth Avenue at 46th Street, where the party settled into rooms. Matthew then went for a drive in Central Park with old Mrs. Carnegie, who pointed out Scottish "nooks and glens." Newsmen, surrounding the hotel entrance, did not find much gossip value in his climbing out of Carnegie's carriage. Arnold seemed a friendly, long-legged, rather unkempt and massive fellow—but no more poetic than the manager of a grocery. Later this day, he actually faced a nimble New York *World* reporter: "Very sorry indeed to have kept you waiting," Matthew began among the Windsor's potted flowers. "Let us take a seat in this sunny, beautiful corner where we can talk."

He was to be subjected to scrutiny in America beyond anything he ever met with in England. The reporter noted his low shoes, "dark blue socks," whiskers with a touch of gray, and pleasant florid face with light blue eyes. Did he have a good crossing?

"No voyage is pleasant to me," Matthew returned with a smile: he was not a "good sailor."

"Shall you stay long in America?"

"Let me see," he paused, thinking of the calendar and certainly of his crammed schedule, "this is the 22nd—about four months."

Did he have specific, personal plans?

"None at all. I am entirely in the hands of Mr. D'Oyly Carte. Probably I shall not see all of America that I could wish. It will be impossible for me to go far West, but I hope to see many of your bright towns."

What would he lecture about?

"I shall talk on politico-social lines. . . . I thought I would wait until I came here before I wrote anything about Emerson," and he "lingered" oddly on that name. "I wanted to see [the] old Concord battle-field and the other places of which he wrote."

Any other subjects in mind?

"No," replied Matthew cheerfully; he didn't mean to ram himself stiffly "down people's throats at meetings, dinners, and the like. In fact I hate speaking."[29]

But soon after this interview he was rammed down glittering throats at Carnegie's parties, and closely watched by hordes of writers and socialites, including the naturalist John Burroughs, who thought him oddly sailor-like and rough:

> [Arnold's voice is] more husky, more like a sailor's, I thought. . . . When he talks to you he throws his head back . . . and looks out from under his heavy eyelids, and sights you down his big nose—draws off, as it were, and gives you his chin. It is a critical attitude, and not sympathetic. Yet he does not impress one as cold and haughty.[30]

He dismayed some Americans: "A great disappointment," noted H. C. Bunner, editor of *Puck*, after being pawed by him. "The mighty Arnold" has a plebeian look and possibly wears Lincoln's old trousers:

"He is naturally *common,* yes common. He looks and talks like an intelligent and educated brick-layer—spokesman of a strikers' delegation. [He] desires to make himself agreeable, and treats everyone with indiscriminate and rather undignified friendliness. The queerest man in the world as a critic of manners and customs."[31]

At a large reception on October 27, Hotel Windsor's parlor was aglow with floral wreaths spelling out, queerly, the names of Arnold's own books (*"Church and Religion"* or *"Essays and Criticisms"*)—and General and Mrs. Grant, Theodore Dwight, George W. Cable, and other notabilities shook his hand. Carnegie's elderly mother played hostess, with her Scottish brogue, after seeing to the floral designs. Then three days later, at Chickering Hall, Arnold gave his first lecture on "Numbers"—to a crowd of 2,000 people, a larger audience than he had ever faced. He looked "like an *édition de luxe,*" as the *Times* man gloated; Arnold calmly began the talk by comparing Plato on Athens "with Isaiah's account of the Kingdom of Judah. During this part of his lecture he was interrupted with cries of 'Louder!' 'Can't hear you.' " Plato and Isaiah, he said, saw that an unsound state could not possibly stand. "Mr. Arnold, we cannot hear you," called a voice from the dark. Only the first few rows in the house heard anything; a few people stood up to leave. Ulysses S. Grant got to his feet: "Well, wife," he supposedly said out loud, "we have paid to see the British lion; but we cannot hear him roar, so we had better go home." Enough people actually survived to give a fine ovation, "though many remarked, while they were leaving the hall, that they had heard not half of it." The *Sun's* reporter felt that people left in "good humor, each man imagining himself to be one of the remnant."[32]

But, even allowing for the *Times* man's prejudices, Arnold's voice was dreadful. The *New York Tribune,* whose friendly George Smalley was trying to keep the *texts* of Arnold's lectures out of the press so the lectures would seem fresh, admitted that his voice couldn't carry. There was now a council of war in Carnegie's rooms in the course of which Arnold was advised to stop his lecture tour—and was perhaps comforted by Mrs. Carnegie's advice when he asked *her* about his "first lecture in America." What had she thought of it?

That lady told him slowly: "Too meenisteerial, Mr. Arnold, too meenisteerial."

Later he enjoyed repeating the remark: "She hit the nail on the head,"[33] Arnold claimed.

He was quite sanguine about his voice: if he *had to shout* at Americans, he would shout! In fact he despaired only after Harvard students invited him up for a poetry recital on November 12. While reading "Thyrsis," two pet-animal poems, Obermann "Stanzas,"

"Philomela," and a few lines from "The Future," at Sanders Theatre in Cambridge, he watched young men leave at the back. "Almost impossible to hear," one of them later felt. Behind brocaded curtains at President Eliot's neat colonial house at Harvard, a lecturer might get a good drink after a disaster. Arnold appeared at Eliot's door sunk in misery and was perhaps given whiskys to cheer him up and to make his flushed face redder. During that long evening, Matthew was so depressed over being inaudible that he "sat on the sofa at [President] Eliot's house with his head in his hands, rubbing his hands back over his hair, and obviously feeling so badly that Eliot sent away those faculty members whom he had invited to meet Arnold."[34] He was then put in touch with a Professor Churchill, an elocution specialist at Andover, who gave him two lessons in speaking and after that he was pretty well heard.

"I have liked best a visit to Dartmouth," Matthew wrote back to "K." Dartmouth men knew about "papa,"[35] and enjoyed "Literature and Science"; and it was in part by speaking to college people that Arnold influenced the nation. His message to *them* was that literature offsets materialism in a democracy, and that the intelligent young must be willing to set their own desires second to the task of leading and improving the new democratic society. From New England in the 1880s to S. N. Whitney's idealistic Deep Springs, in California, and Hutchins's University of Chicago a half century later, and on to modern Oberlin and Swarthmore and Reed and Antioch—and other colleges and universities in the United States—one "voice" encouraging intelligent idealism and service has been Arnold's. Idealism has fashions, yet it has not died out; it causes some of the young to work more generously in industry and the professions with an eye to bettering the republic.[36]

"What I like," Arnold in the autumn wrote to his sisters, "is the way in which people far lower down than with us, live with something of the life and enjoyments of the cultivated classes." Indeed: "buoyancy, enjoyment, freedom from constraint" are American assets. Yet "the love of quiet and dislike of a crowd is gone," and there isn't "much real depth"[37] about uproar in the United States. Money still creates class. Only wealthy Americans escape the uproar. Attracted to wealth and class, Arnold had just visited on the Hudson some wealthy people at Steen Valetje, north of Hyde Park. The host's niece had given birth on January 30, 1882, to a boy named Franklin Delano Roosevelt. "A Delano married to an Astor," Matthew lightly tells "K"; "but he grumbled, ungrateful man, because every one took a right of way through his grounds."[38]

The public—or D'Oyly Carte—took hard "right of way" with Arnold's time and energy. His schedule took him to New England's cities and college towns in November and December; for the Christmas season he would go to Philadelphia, Washington, Richmond, and Baltimore and in January swing out as far as Madison, Chicago, and St. Louis, and then return through Toronto, Ottawa, Montreal, and Quebec and finally sail from New York on March 8. Though fatigued, he tried to be genial with authors. He became very fond of Whittier and of Dr. O. W. Holmes, and liked William Dean Howells better than his novels: he invited Howells to "a small hovel I have in Surrey, where I have never yet succeeded in decoying Henry James."³⁹

Under pressure of time he had written "Emerson" by mid-November; he sent the rough copy to a Boston printer, who demanded a fair copy; then C. E. Norton assured him that Harvard Press could read *anything,* and took the manuscript there. (Some of Harvard's inevitable misreadings were kept by Arnold even in the final version.) He corrected proofs hastily on a train and delivered "Emerson" at Boston and at Cambridge, and then felt relieved when the Wellesley students "telegraphed to beg" for his Emerson at *their* college."⁴⁰ In the lecture he struggles with his mixed feelings about Carlyle but names Emerson as the writer of the "most important work" done in English prose in the nineteenth century.⁴¹ He denies Emerson, even so, a first-rate talent; but he meant to keep standards very high, to flatter in no way, to overcome personal feelings in an effort to be just. Having learned "that the young ladies are charming," he was pleased by the Wellesley College women, who welcomed him (according to the college's alumnae records) "with great pleasure and thorough appreciation."⁴² In fact Wellesley on December 6, Smith College at Northampton on December 11, and Vassar College at Poughkeepsie in New York on January 7, 1884—all gratified and impressed him. "I have never met such takingness," Arnold said later of American women. "The ladies are much more engaging than English ladies—are better informed and more capable in conversation."⁴³ This was perhaps unfair; his sisters and daughters were frank and outspoken—and in chatting with articulate American college girls, he perhaps felt very nearly at home in Fox How or in Cobham. Few Englishwomen whom he knew were so unrestrained as his own relatives. Having once called young women "things," he had learned by the time of his "George Sand" and "Critic on Milton" to sympathize with female viewpoints. What Arnold disliked was timidity or reticence in man *or* woman—but he had yet to meet Mrs. Erminnie Smith, who scheduled him to speak to her tuneful Jersey City Aestheticians and who (as we shall see) made timidity seem a virtue.

As convivial as he was, he longed to be by himself. In New Jersey, when his hosts failed to meet him, he was glad to hitch a ride in "an empty hay-waggon." He rode along like a pig going to market, three miles, until he was let off at Princeton, where he wearily gave "Literature and Science" on November 20. He had to repeat the same talk next day at New Haven, Connecticut; then at Newport, Rhode Island, on the twenty-third; at Newton, Worcester, and Salem a few days later; yet again, up a steep hill with a good view of an old American city, in Sayles Memorial Hall, Brown University, Providence, on December 3; at the Music Hall in Taunton, Massachusetts, on December 5; and at Amherst College on December 7. He switched to "Emerson" at Phillips Academy, on December 13—by which time his patience with American faculty members and food was wearing thin. He either had a nightmarish breakfast at Andover or horrendously dreamed it: a "breakfast at eight with a party of professors and their wives—coffee, fruit, fish-balls, potatoes, hashed veal, and mince-pies, with rolls and butter."⁴⁴

The liveliest evening, so far, had been at Hartford, Connecticut, where he ran into Howells at a reception. "Who—who in the world is that?" asked Matthew, gazing at a flamboyant man with a swirl of bright, red hair, streaked with gray. Laughing, showing his teeth, gesturing, talking to several ladies at once, this was the wildest madman he had seen! "Oh," said Howells, "that is Mark Twain." After talking with him, Arnold went to dine at Twain's with Edwin P. Parker among others. He was charmed. Twain "kept a perpetual gale of laughter going, with a string of comment and anecdote." When he left Twain's that night Arnold repeated funny things Twain had said, and then asked Parker: "And is he never serious?" Edwin Parker replied solemnly: "Mr. Arnold, he is the most serious man in the world."⁴⁵ Though he liked Samuel Clemens and later read his works, Arnold could not forgive "Mark Twain" for trying to create an American sensibility too divorced from Western cultural roots. No doubt, what is new in the American national experience and what that experience owes to the Western heritage create tensions in American national life; Arnold respected what was new, and felt it was "ceasing" to be true that "American literature has no original individuality of its own"—but he was hostile to pure democratic apologists. "Whitman," he had written, is "a genuine American voice, not an echo" of Europe. But then, he felt, it isn't enough to be an "American" voice in cultural isolation: "for a real spiritual lead it is necessary to be a European voice." The essence of Arnold's ideas about writers and intellectuals in the United States was just what he had said, in 1867, in his essay, "Theodore Parker":

When American intellect has not only broken, as it is breaking, the leading strings of England, but has also learnt to assimilate independently the intellect of France and Germany and the ancient world as well as of England, then, and not till then, may the spiritual construction of an American be a "many-gated temple."[46]

America would be strongest when assimilating a complex heritage dating back to Greece and Israel, and weak when trying to exclude Europe or the Near East.

He felt more at home in the "English" American South, which, indeed, he had hoped might win the Civil War so as to humble Yankee pride. On December 17 he lectured in Washington, where he was introduced by W. E. Chandler, the Secretary of the Navy. He dined with Henry Adams, whose political novel *Democracy* he knew; then with the historian George Bancroft, where he met "half a dozen politicians"[47] and liked Senator R. L. Gibson of Louisiana the best. Against the advice of agents who said there was no money or culture in Virginia, he spoke at Richmond's Mozart Hall, and stayed with Gen. Joseph Anderson, C.S.A., the "Carnegie of the South," who during the war had owned the Tredegar Iron Works or "the mainstay of the Confederacy in the manner of munitions." For Arnold, Virginia was the most beautiful state—and here perhaps he felt in harmony as critic, elegist, and school inspector. Mrs. Anderson, a pretty woman, took him in her carriage to see Richmond with the gleaming James River bending through it, then to the Confederate cemetery with a "great pyramid over the common soldiers"[48] in the darkening evening.

To her dismay, Arnold asked to see an all-black school, where he was astonished by "the line of demarcation between the white and the negro in the south still." He made a speech to a class of black children—who sang for him "Dare to Be a Daniel." "I could have passed hours there," he felt.[49]

But he hurried on. A day after his sixty-first birthday, he took Flu and Lucy to the White House to call on President Chester Arthur—a good-looking, spotless man. "The house," Arnold felt, "is far handsomer than I expected." The President "told Lucy that if we would stay on in Washington he would 'make himself personally responsible' for her enjoying her winter there more even than in New York."[50] But Lucy, who had just turned twenty-five, dreamed of New York. She was a talkative, animated, rosily pretty girl, with large naïve eyes, and so compassionate that she appealed to shy and reserved men. At a Carnegie party, she had met a stiff, taciturn young lawyer named Frederick Whitridge—who in due course, after another party or two, seemed to be gentle, kindly, abashed, and single-mindedly in love with her. She had come to America to see Niagara Falls and a Negro baby (as she said) but had found her "Fred." Fred was soon to prove his terrier-like devotion, and much audacity in courtship.

At Philadelphia Arnold met Wayne MacVeagh—the pleasantest of all Americans, as he believed. (With that unique Scottish-American version of "Mr. Bottles," Andrew Carnegie, and a Confederate soldier and schoolmaster of Petersburg named William Gordon McCabe, Wayne MacVeagh was one of the three Americans whom Arnold found the most sympathetic.)* After a Yale degree and much drudgery in the law, MacVeagh had become minister to Turkey and Attorney General; he was now fighting Philadelphia's corrupt, tough Cameron Republican machine. He was too indecisive and had too many scruples to succeed, for long, in the rough arena of politics. But he had courage enough for five politicians, and his Yale idealism was typically American. If MacVeagh was all combat and svelte charm, Mrs. Erminnie Adelle Platt Smith was the soul of the new American middle class.

On a memorable day, in late December 1883, Arnold looked out over a sea of hats, at last, belonging to members of the Jersey City Aesthetic Society. Their President, Mrs. Smith, was an honorable white member of the Tuscarora Indian Tribe. He had survived a luncheon with her. And now, even before she introduced him as the age's leading aesthetician, there was trouble: peculiarly he had a view of only *half* of her church. Rustling the papers of "Emerson," he looked towards Erminnie Smith in despair. Erminnie led him to a "music stand," and repositioned him. But instead of sitting down, she "extended to the Society the holiday greeting," as a reporter noticed, "and quoted some appropriate lines from Mrs. Robert Browning and Margaret Fuller" (two authors whom Matthew rather disliked) "which drew from Mr. Arnold a smile, and a look of appreciation."[51] Certainly he might now begin his talk? As he looked up, a quartet known as the Meigs Sisters stood up and sang "God Save the King." Feeling that he was pretty well introduced, Arnold looked apprehensively round the church. Mr. Courtland Palmer rose with a "few remarks laudatory" of the Aesthetic Society of Jersey City. Arnold listened. Was he being *deliberately* tortured? Did they want him to speak or not? Who were these people? Would an ecclesiastical sign be given to tell when he might open his mouth? Miss Henrietta Markstein now stood up, walked to a piano, and played a "solo, 'Old Black Joe,' with variations." After applause for

---

*William Gordon McCabe (1841–1920) in the year of General Lee's surrender took off his Confederate uniform and founded McCabe's University School, at Petersburg, where he was headmaster until 1901, and then moved to Richmond. Isaac Wayne MacVeagh (1833–1917) after his diplomatic career in Turkey lived usually in Washington or Philadelphia.

Miss Markstein died down, Arnold opened his mouth. He began reciting "Emerson," as a reporter felt, in a wavering, indistinct voice as if "reading prayers," and finally, just as his British voice ended, Mrs. Clementine Lassar Studwell stood up and sang "The Star Spangled Banner." Arnold had trouble even in sitting down. After the national anthem, there was a new outburst of Aesthetic Society energy. An Aesthetician complimented him, whereupon Mrs. Studwell stood up again to sing "Within a Mile of Edinburgh Town." Arnold's eyes studied exit doors. He might break his way out rudely, get through a cluster of ladies at the side exit if something distracted them, or, of course, he could run to the door while smiling normally. He settled on a smile and a brisk walk. Just as all four Meigs sisters stood up to sing "Little Jack Horner," as the reporter noticed, "Mr. Arnold took his leave."[52]

Quite understandably after this as 1884 began, he thought with anxiety and passion of going home. Instead he went on to Swarthmore, Vassar, Utica, and Wells. At Colgate College in Hamilton, New York, there were the first outbreaks of revolution in an Arnold student audience—" 'Oh, I'm mashed.' 'Say, Mr., please wake me when he is through.' 'Whew, he is English, though.' . . . 'He is a dude.' "[53] Vassar girls greeted him with enormous respect, but in upstate New York his morale wavered; once he rushed past his hosts to see a river in the freezing night, and felt near the breaking point for lack of solitude. He also felt that the beauty of America was compromised by a people who forgot the eighteenth-century idea that the *look* of things—cities, landscapes—affects daily work and leisure, the whole quality of life. "On my journey to Buffalo," wrote Arnold, "I saw a sledge standing still on the snowy, frozen lake, with the horses half turned round, which struck me as the only picturesque thing I have seen in America."[54] Later he had to push himself. "Sometimes in the dead unhappy night, I pour a little Scotch whisky which yet remains to me into a glass of milk," he writes from Bloomington in Illinois on January 31, "and things wear a milder aspect. . . . The sleeping cars, of which they talk so much, are all babies . . . and as they know I am fond of children they always put a fretful baby near me." He kept incipient paranoia under control, however, by laughing at himself and the press: "I am getting through, however, and the newspapers treat me wonderfully well on the whole; though sometimes, out west here, they are in this style (fact)

WE HAVE SEEN HIM ARRIVE!

'He has harsh features, supercilious manners, parts his hair down the middle, wears a single eyeglass and ill-fitting clothes.' "[55]

He enjoyed lively audiences at teetotaling Oberlin College (where he asked for whisky) and at Cleveland where Col. John Hay "who was Lincoln's private secretary" had secretly bought up all the unsold tickets to Arnold's lecture and given them to Western Reserve students.[56]

An indifferent Detroit crowd was nearly forgotten, next day, at the spreading new University of Michigan, at Ann Arbor, where "1,300 in the hall" applauded "Literature and Science." "I like to see those young men sit there and take such an interest in what I said," Arnold told a *Chicago Tribune* man next day; "I think a great deal of my own university at home, and that sight last night did me good."[57]

The *Tribune* man, boarding his train on the way west, gives us a glimpse of the Arnold party dressed for Chicago's winter:

> Mrs. Arnold is a very pleasant, matronly-looking lady, with iron-gray hair, and Miss Arnold is a bright, pretty, rosy-looking English girl, apparently enjoying the best of health. Mrs. Arnold was quietly dressed in black, and she wore over her travelling dress a plain gray knit jacket.

Arnold wore a black necktie "loosely tied in a sailor-knot around a pointed stand-up collar," and as if he were a romantic poet dressed for the Arctic, "upon his feet were slippers, upon his head was a small silk cap, and around his neck was thrown a black and white worsted scarf."[58]

Chicago was his last stiff ordeal. Chicagoans suspected "the rubber-framed eye-glass pendant from his neck," and were not kind to a poet lecturing them on the terrifying dangers of democratic majorities. Arnold took in "a whiff of the Chicago River," wrote Eugene Field in the *Daily News*; "then he returned to his hotel and wrote a pale-green poem that will have to be disinfected and deodorized before it is printed."[59] But he was housed grandly, by General McClurg the bookseller, and fed by the Chicago Literary Club where, after having just dined, he "had to go through the whole course from oysters to ice, with plenty of champagne."[60] Four hundred people heard "Numbers" at the Central Music Hall on Tuesday, January 22, 1884, and about 700 heard "Emerson" on the Thursday. A hoax essay by "Mr. Arnold" on Chicago's cultural faults was printed later in New York, and believed quite genuine by the *Chicago Tribune*. To set the record straight on that, Arnold discussed the city: Chicago was too "new" and "beastly prosperous," he told a reporter. Carnegie had urged him to see the stockyards, but "I would not go to see the pig-sticking at the stock-yards. Certainly not! Why should I wish to see pig-sticking? Still, as I have said, nowhere did I meet more charming people than in Chicago. I liked Milwaukee and St. Louis better as cities, but I prefer Philadelphia to any American city."[61]

Philadelphia's Chestnut Street reminded him of Bond Street—and he had ached for London. Yet his statement about the "charm" of Chicagoans was meant. Sensitive observers such as T. S. Eliot and Nelson Algren praise the bracing effect of that city—where enthusiasm for culture is traditionally strong; that spirit was in the city perhaps in 1884. Even so he had shivered and fretted: Chicago's temperature plunged to nine above zero with winds knifing in from the northeast across Lake Michigan.

At Madison on January 25, he delivered "Literature and Science" to University of Wisconsin undergraduates and others; here he met Mary Claude's immigrant brother Louis—who mentioned Ambleside days of the 1830s, and begged him to write a preface for Mary Claude's *Twilight Thoughts*. He feared that this task would be troublesome; days of "Marguerite" and of the Clougho-Matthean set were somewhat embarrassing, now, to a famous, critical, middle-aged family man. Yet Arnold was proud enough of "Yes! in the sea of life," which Mary Claude helped to inspire. When the journal *Light* praised that lyric as a work beyond fault, in 1878, Matthew had sent the review to his sister, Susy, to whom he had first recited the poem and who was always moved by it.[62] He told Louis Claude he would try to write a preface to *Twilight Thoughts*. After Madison, he spoke at Galesburg, and then in a blur of days, at St. Louis, Indianapolis, Cincinnati, again at Cleveland, and Buffalo, before he entered Canada. In Toronto he met Goldwin Smith, his prosperous Oxford friend, and gave "Numbers" on February 12 to a full audience of women at Shaftsbury Hall who "occasionally took notes on paper, using their muffs as writing desks."[63] He drew another good Toronto audience next day with "Numbers." The aristocratic English society flocked to him, and on February 16 the audience at Ottawa's Grand Opera House looked regal. But it is important that he preferred French Catholic Society at Quebec, where he gave "Literature and Science" on February 18; and at Montreal, where he repeated that lecture and gave "Numbers." Quebec's people "gave me an excellent reception, and were pleased at my talking French to them," he wrote; "Quebec is the most interesting thing by much that I have seen on this Continent."[64] That beautiful old city with its mingling of traditions in the New World setting of Canada gave him, at last, a sense of what he hoped for in the States: a culture becoming "new" by absorbing the humane customs and best ideas of Europe. With a sigh, he headed south—to finish a love-hate tour in New York. On February 21, he gave "Numbers" at Portland, Maine, and two days later "Emerson" at Albany, for the last "dismal" performance. An Albany paper found him "more like a prosperous rope manufacturer"[65] than an author.

Relieved to be in New York, he spoke at the new Authors' Club down on Fifteenth Street on February 28. "Gentlemen, I owe everything to the literary class," Matthew told an audience of young, fledgling authors. If the public never comprehends what he is after, he said, the literary class *does*. Literary people find "in me," Arnold declared, "that which pleased Gil Blas in the road to Merida when he cried, '*Le coeur au métier*.' Put your heart into your business. . . . Gentlemen," he concluded, "suffer me to leave you with these words, *Le coeur au métier*."[66] Criticism demands not only the mind, but all of the heart.

Young listeners, that day, such as R. W. Gilder and Hamilton Mabie praised his unique, insightful, intelligent criticism; they kept his torch burning well into the next century. He had won the United States by appealing to the young; and though he left with a sense of failure, the fact is that no other English critic has so influenced the nation.

His essays seemed to oppose literal, simplistic ways of thinking and feeling just as the brash frontier culture of America was ending. As muckraking reformers and antitrust laws began to unsettle the old era of ruthless, uninhibited capitalism, Arnold offered the nation an example of the critical habit. He asked for an awareness of foreign ideas and for flexible, delicate, and subtle comparative techniques in social, religious, and literary criticism. He called for disinterestedness *and* for a committed personal response: he taught American critics to bring new light and a free play of mind to their subjects, to avoid pedantic or provincial verdicts, to love their nation for its spiritual and intellectual achievement, and to compare its culture in the light of real and often better achievements in Europe, in Russia, and the Eastern countries.

He vastly encouraged literary study in America. He became the "unacknowledged legislator of twentieth-century criticism"[67] because his sensitive, probing methods did justice to the uniqueness of literature as an invaluable synthesis of form, feeling, and idea. Literature is not intellectual; it is not a substitute for philosophy or religion, according to Arnold; it is something which appeals to the whole sensibility and is aesthetic, entertaining, and delightful. Because it engages the whole sensibility, it is uniquely valuable in training the mind to use and assimilate other forms of knowledge: thus it is the only "answer" to the modern information explosion, and necessary in the early training of every scientist, architect, engineer, or other specialist. Educators believed him: more and more often in American primary schools, secondary schools, and in the first two years in liberal arts courses at universities, literature became the core subject in new curricula.

Arnold confirmed the rightness of America's democratic experiment. He was, and remains, one of the few modern thinkers to propose a comprehensive attitude to life: he suggested in *A French Eton,* in *Essays in Criticism,* in "Democracy," and in *Culture and Anarchy* that the role of the intellectual is to make the best thought prevail in a nation—and that masses of people can understand and value what helps them. "This is the *social idea,*" he told Americans in effect in the first chapter of *Culture and Anarchy;*

> and the men of culture are the true apostles of equality. The great men of culture are those who have had a passion for diffusing, for making prevail, for carrying from one end of society to the other, the best knowledge, the best ideas of their time; who have laboured to divest knowledge of all that was harsh, uncouth, difficult, abstract, profession-al, exclusive; to humanise it, to make it efficient outside the clique of the cultivated and learned, yet still remaining the *best* knowledge and thought of the time, and a true source, therefore, of sweetness and light. Such [men] were Lessing and Herder in Germany. . . . And why? Because they *humanised* knowledge; because they broadened the basis of life and intelligence.

He had seen in Germany that political institutions, or even the educational framework of a state, can subvert humanists; he had not forgotten the Prussian Minister Von Mühler, who fired academic staff for political reasons and held schools in a demogogic grip. Democra-cies are brittle, as Arnold believed, and a nation's institutions are no more than "machinery" which can break down and fail a whole people. An often hideous United States with a poor quality of life, crude and blunt manners, insensitive personal relationships, enor-mous city slums, inequalities in wealth, racial segregation with "the line of demarcation between the white and the negro in the south still," and an exploited and underpaid work force, had no reason to be smug or to neglect lessons it could learn from Europe. He meant to strike hard at a few, key, omnipresent glaring faults in the Yankee-and-Southern paradise, and hoped that American critics in future wouldn't forget that their nation's whole quality of life was their subject.

But at last, his seventy speaking engagements were over.

Having spoken to 40,000 people—from Madison and Toronto in the west to Maine and Virginia in the east—he arrived back at Cobham in March 1884. He had netted over £1000 from his tour and felt that at least some of his hosts had been fair to him: Emerson's own daughter, Ellen, at Concord, after all had approved "Emerson." When he gave that same lecture at the Royal Institute, *Vanity Fair* in London damned it as "a tissue of captious contempt rather than analytic criticism." Over in America, Boston papers had been furious, but Americans warmed up after *Discourses in America* appeared. "We have had time to ponder his remarks," wrote a repentant reviewer in the States. "The truth of his utterances . . . is now more generally acknowledged."[68]

He had loyal friends among the Americans—and unfortunately, perhaps, a suitor for Lucy's hand, since the once shy, abashed Frederick Whitridge, the lawyer, came over from his New York firm to woo her. Whitridge was now polite, agile, and intent. He was more outspoken too. Arnold had called one of Lucy's former suitors "The Wolf"—but he hardly had time to find a nickname for "Fred." The Arnolds' frank, pretty, rosy daughter married her American to the delight of Cobham village, just before her twenty-sixth birthday. The newlyweds, Fred and Lucy Whitridge, sailed back to New York around January 1, 1885.

Matthew was happy for Lucy's sake and made her feel she had done just the right thing. But the wedding happened suddenly. He had become an international parent with a daughter wed to a New York lawyer, and a son to a Melbourne girl, Ella. Lucy's marriage, perhaps, put Dick's Ella into a rather better light—at least Ella was not taking *Dick* overseas! "I like Ella more and more, I am glad to say," Matthew admitted just before Lucy sailed.[69] He missed Lucy constantly and painfully; when her letters arrived, Flu had to recite them. "I always cry when they are read to me," wrote Arnold, "but it is a happy cry."[70] On *family* questions he was often the doting, ineffectual Mr. Woodhouse in Austen's *Emma* his ladies said he was.

About North America, he meant to be strictly truthful. "I am writing," he writes to Lucy in January 1885, when she is back in New York, "a long promised thing . . . —'A Word more about America'; I often think of you, as I write it; and that it would be unpleasant for you if it gave offense over there; but I do not think it will. Mamma, however, is in a thousand agonies."[71]

His "agonies" were perhaps worse than Flu's, in February, when "A Word More about America" was printed in Knowles's *Nineteenth Century*. Arnold's essay praises the Americans for their federal system, which fits like a "wonderful suit," and for their admirable "straightness," yet implies that the nation isn't fit to live in. Its "human problem"[72] is unsolved; its brash society lacks depth, beauty, good manners, human interest. *Because* America has vast latent strength, its quality of life ought to be measured with Europe's. Yet an English person of taste "would rather live in France, Spain, Holland, Belgium, Germany, Italy, Switzerland, than in the United States, in spite of our community of race and speech with them!"[73] Americans do not need to improve their framework, legal system, or wonderful Constitution —but need to enrich *themselves!*

That perhaps was well said; but this essay, with other complicating factors, shortened his life. Fearing that he had offended the New York Whitridges, he heard, in the spring, that Lucy might not visit Cobham in 1885. He was very badly upset; and ten days after that news he could hardly breathe.

His odd, sharp chest pains on May 8 were so severe that Flu worriedly took him to see Sir Andrew Clark. Arnold was then sixty-two, overweight, hard-pressed by schools, feeling perhaps the strain of his recent tour. He heard he had "indigestion," and would have to drink and eat less. "My liquors," he wrote in May, are "confined to one small half-glass of brandy." And yet: "I cannot get rid of the ache across my chest . . . ; imagine my having to stop half a dozen times in going up to Pains Hill! What a mortifying change," Matthew informs Lucy. "So one draws to one's end."[74]

Lucy came to England very quickly. In August, Matthew knew that he had angina; but the pain relented enough to let him play lawn tennis. He drank "cool champagne" and took his illness as philosophically as Epictetus might have wished. "At the end of April I positively resign," he wrote about inspecting early in 1886, "and shall regain my liberty—but how late in life, alas, how far, far too late!"[75] Yet he eagerly had accepted a last mission to report on German, French, and Swiss primary schools—and stayed busily out of the country from November 1885 to late in March 1886, except for a return at Christmas. When the journey was over, he reached the climax of his schools career by giving 1,227 oral replies to a famous "Cross Commission."

Sir Richard Assheton Cross headed a Royal Commission, created in 1886, to look into workings of primary schools ever since Forster's 1870 Education Act. Arnold as a "Chief Inspector"—an honorific title—spoke to the board on April 6 and 7, at Old Palace Yard in London, rather grandly attacking the Revised Code again, and showing what he had learned from France and Germany and perhaps from seeing public schools in Boston with T. W. Higginson. His testimony is long and technical, but he makes two very clear, prophetic points. He believes the minds of the young are wretchedly thwarted by examinations; and that we err in making a "distinction" between clever and average children—who ought to be trained *together*.

When the Bishop of London asked about examinations in primary schools abroad, Arnold stressed those two points:

ARNOLD: Yes, abroad they do not consider, I think, the enabling a child to do a number of sums right at the examination to be the object in view.

Q. Do you think there is any difference between doing a sum in an examination and doing it on the counter of a shop?

ARNOLD: I think there is a difference between preparing [children] to do rightly the sort of sums that are set in an examination and preparing them to use their heads. . . .

Q. (*Mr. Alderson*) Is it not rather at present the case that the examination dictates the instruction?

ARNOLD: Yes.

Q. Do you think [examinations are] good for ascertaining the attainments of the clever children, as distinct from the medium children?

ARNOLD: No, but I do not like to see a distinction between the two. I do not think them good means for operating on either sort of children.

Q. Probably they are best for operating on the average child?

ARNOLD: I should be inclined to say that I see faults in them for all sorts of children.

In one reply, he complains of his own rushed, exam-heavy schooldays: "they would hurry me on as a boy too fast when I was learning arithmetic, for which I had no particular taste. I was taught by a very able man, but I was hurried on much too quickly. I never learned arithmetic until I taught it myself later in life when I had to inspect schools."[76]

In April, just as he gave that sensible and considered testimony, Fanny Lucy left for the United States to care for Lucy, who was ill with a pregnancy. "We are too old for these separations," Matthew wrote to his wife.[77] After completing his last foreign schools report he left for the States himself, on May 22 aboard the Cunarder *Umbria*. In North America on this visit, he said nothing at all that might embarrass Fred or Lucy. He gave a lecture, "Common Schools Abroad" at the University of Pennsylvania, and once at Buffalo. Later he played with Lucy's newborn girl, "Midget," who was lively in the summer. "She snatched a five dollar note out of my hand," Arnold writes from the Whitridges' summer home at Stockbridge, Massachusetts. "A true little Yankee." He could not get his fill of being a new grandfather: "She has clutched my eyeglass and played with it."[78] Once he visited the plump, rich Coddington girls up in the scenic Adirondacks; Fannie Coddington was soon to marry Robert Browning's only son, Pen.

In August, he sweltered in 90 degree heat at Stockbridge and tired of botanizing and walking. Before leaving Lucy he had an accident. It was "nothing," he explained.[79] He had been in swimming, when a wave carried him "against a taut rope under water," and the shock led to nights of frightening angina. But he felt better when, at last, he boarded ship for England in September. His visit had passed so quietly—almost eerily—that few Americans understood he was in the States. Out at sea he thought chiefly of the married daughter he had left behind: "My darling child," Arnold began in a letter written on the *Aurania*. "This day week I have left you—my darling, precious child! How I love you, how I think of you!"[80]

18

AT THE FORT:
"DEBEMUR MORTI NOS NOSTRAQUE"
1886–1888

I quite agree with you that we ought to work as long as
the day lasts.
> —*Benjamin Jowett to Matthew Arnold, 1887*

Spare me the whispering, crowded room, . . .
Nor bring, to see me cease to live,
Some doctor full of phrase and fame, . . .

Bring none of these; but let me be,
While all around in silence lies,
Moved to the window near, and see . . .
The wide aërial landscape spread.
> —*"A Wish"*

Be sure to send a lazy man for the Angel of Death.
> —*Proverb*

O N the eve of leaving for the States, Matthew happily had retired
from school inspecting. Delighted to be home on Sunday,
September 12, 1886, he was jobless and free. As for his thirty-five
years as "H.M.I.," he felt as if he had "lived through the French
Revolution: *J'ai vécu!* "[1] After visiting Dick and Ella or the "Dicks" in
Manchester, and then his sisters Fan and Jane, he spent a few weeks
clearing out papers at the education office and settling accounts.

His fortune had changed as a result of his lecture tour in the United
States; he had come back with a "Draft on Morgan" for £1198. Despite
a large advance to Dick Arnold and then monthly payments to him of
£8 (which he often sent to Ella, since Dick gambled), he ended the
year 1886, about £251 to the good. Arnold had two-thirds of his salary
as a retirement pension; that plus his Civil List Pension, small
legacies, and payments from publishers brought his income in 1887 to
£1655.17.8.[2]

He felt financially secure. The fuss this autumn over his retirement was a nuisance; but, on November 12, he faced a testimonial at St. Peter's School (Lower Belgrave Street), where Westminster elementary teachers gave him a silver claret jug and a salver. "Very beautiful," he felt; "I was afraid of a tea service." George Bradley, Dean of Westminster, was on hand to recall their fifty years of friendship. After the schoolteachers cheered him, Arnold spoke about his own years as Inspector: "Ladies and gentlemen, I thank you," he boomed loudly in a small school hall.

> I will begin where my obligations are least. To Government I owe nothing. (Cheers and laughter.) But then I have always remembered that under our Parliamentary system the Government takes little interest in such work, whatever it is, as I have been able to do in the public service.[3]

What he felt very strongly was that his superiors in "government" had belittled him. Balliol men such as Ralph Lingen, Francis Sandford, and Patrick Cumin had been promoted over his head; the education office never willingly had given him a post of influence. "The recognition and opportunity which would have been useful," Matthew later wrote to A. J. Mundella this autumn, "they never gave me."[4] Government officials tried to keep him off foreign commissions; they quarreled over his salary, nearly sabotaged his application for leave of absence even in 1883.[5] Lingen, Lowe, and some of their successors turned a stone-deaf ear to his remarks on the Revised Code. That mechanical Code was still in force; secondary education was a shambles—and lacked state support of the kind given to lycées in France, and high schools elsewhere. England even lacked a Minister of Education. The nation was depressingly class-ridden; and educators were likely to perpetuate social-class distinctions into the future by dividing "clever" from "average" children and having one quality of schools for the wealthy, another kind for the poor.

Clearly, William Forster's Elementary Education Act had not greatly changed attitudes to schooling in England. Sadly, Forster had died in April 1886. When Humphry Ward asked Arnold for a piece on "Schools in the Reign of Queen Victoria," for a survey he was preparing, Arnold in 1887 offered two-edged comments on Forster —which only partly reflect jealousy. Arnold perhaps shocked Jane Forster, but he is strictly truthful:

> Mr. Forster [did] what was possible to be done [in Parliament in 1870]. For the extension of our popular instruction, he was able to do much more than Sir James Shuttleworth. He made [our elementary schools] for the first time national. . . . But Mr. Forster was not, like Sir James Shuttleworth, a born educator, an earnest student of methods and problems of education [with a] mind trained and interested to weigh all

questions of teaching. . . . The false direction given by the Revised Code to teaching, Mr. Forster did not correct; "payment by results" he left as he found it. I doubt whether he even took its faults and fallacies into his mind at all.[6]

"Schools in the Reign of Queen Victoria" gives the impression that Jane's husband was a man with few ideas, an opportunist who had seen that the nation might be grateful to a Liberal who could straighten out the worst mess in the lower schools, in 1870.

Refusing to let Forster's ghost rest in peace, Matthew implicitly attacks him, again, in no less than two letters to *The Times* and five late essays on Ireland. (Forster had been advanced by Gladstone, and Arnold identified him somewhat unfairly with Gladstone's Irish views.) These pieces begin with fury over Gladstone's Home Rule policy, which, in Arnold's opinion, would destroy the Kingdom by setting up a parliament in Dublin. That would encourage Ireland to separate from England—and play into the hands of Nationalists and papers such as William O'Brien's *United Ireland*. After Gladstone's Home Rule bill was defeated, and Lord Salisbury's Conservatives took office, Arnold next demanded greater British firmness with the restive Irish public. In "The Zenith of Conservatism," for example, he asks that freedom of speech, freedom of assembly, and freedom of the press be reduced in Ireland. Weak in detail, forgetting his own principles, recommending the suppression of liberty on the one hand and the sensible idea of better local government for Ireland on the other, he is not at his best in these essays. What does appear, to Arnold's credit, is his humane anxiety for a political solution to the Irish question; and again, at least, an openness, or willingness to alter his stance.

His feeling that the British must be *tougher* in Ireland makes him almost too partial to Lincoln's "perservering" Civil War hero in the essay "General Grant," and too impatient to write very sympathetically in "Shelley," in "Amiel," or even in "A 'Friend of God' " (on the German mystic, Tauler). Having complained that Parliament seems "to flounder and to beat the air,"[7] Arnold is delighted to end his Shelley essay, after attacking first Shelley's mistreatment of Harriet and then Edward Dowden's scandalous *Life of Shelley*, with these words echoing what he had said in "Byron": "The man Shelley, in very truth, is not entirely sane, and Shelley's poetry is not entirely sane either. . . . In poetry, no less than in life, he is 'a beautiful and *ineffectual* angel, beating in the void his luminous wings in vain.' "[8] Again, he neglects Shelley's *ideas*; that poet figured too strongly in his own dreamy, emotive early life. In October 1886, writing his Preface for Mary Claude's *Twilight Thoughts*, he found Mary's stories taking him uneasily back to "the Westmoreland of Wordsworth and Hartley

Coleridge." He rejects Mary's love for German sentimentalists and her "English sadness," yet hails her radical "Chartist" strain—which reminds him of Wordsworth.[9] Living a retired life at Ambleside, Mary Claude perhaps smiled over the Preface. Few people saw her in these years. Her niece, May Cannon, glimpsed her only once—when Arnold's "Marguerite" appeared at the door "in a red dressing gown."[10]

Arnold wrote well, when he truly balanced thought and emotion. He always tried to find ways to integrate his intellect and his spontaneous feelings; at his best, he combines the impulse and check-upon-the-impulse in his work, or, in effect, presses brake and accelerator simultaneously. His ideas of "criticism" and "culture" are not answers to his problems; but they offer *ways* of looking, attitudes of use, to us, in any intellectual search. He had rejected the romantic tendency to find encompassing truths or raise fixed ideals; his own poetry, like Browning's, is modern in seeking inside the self and down to the mind's ocean-floor for traces of meaning, unities, and values. What he most appreciated, in the months before he died, was the psychological depth of Russian novelists. Drawn more and more to novel reading, he recited fiction aloud to Flu and Nelly. He "greatly" liked Turgenev, and preferred English and American novelists to the new, "hard" French school of Flaubert. Of the Russians, Tolstoi at first appealed to him for finding communal or "socialist" ideas in the Bible: "Tolstoi," Arnold notes in 1887, "says" that the Bible's "true, socialistic teaching has been overlooked, and attention has been fixed on metaphysical dogmas . . . which are . . . says Tolstoi, secondary."[11] Matthew spent more time preparing "Count Leo Tolstoi" than any other essay in 1887, and sent it off gladly to the *Fortnightly* on November 15. He treats Tolstoi's pacifism, internationalism, and dislike of oath taking with much good nature—but cordially praises *Anna Karenina* beyond anything else, and advises Tolstoi to return to novel writing.

A letter from Churton Collins, late the previous year, reminded him of the new, eager pressure to set up a chair of "English literature" at Oxford. Arnold replied to Collins that he would be glad to see "great works of English literature taken in conjunction with those of Greek and Latin." His comparative emphasis remained strong to the end: at the root of his thought is the idea that nothing "English," either in history or culture, is understood unless we cross national borders to draw comparisons. Criticism, study, education are useless within narrow, national horizons. "But," he admits to Collins, some university men can't see beyond their noses. "I have no confidence," Arnold repeats, "in those who at the Universities regulate studies, degrees, and honours. To regulate these matters great experience of the world, steadiness, simplicity, breadth of view" are needed.[12] Far from being a mere apologist for the arts, he would give due place in schools to science: we must "give ourselves as much training" in science as we can, Arnold held. His quarrel with Huxley had been smaller than critics and biographers later noticed: Arnold wanted *both* science and the arts studied widely; there is "really no question between Professor Huxley and me as to whether knowing the great results of the modern scientific study of nature is not required as a part of our culture."[13] At university level, where science is enough for any mind, he would admit students without qualification in Greek.

In 1887 his social life was vigorous. He had rented for £31.10 a month through White and Berry, the estate agents, a house at 3 Wilton Street in London from January to April 1887. He and Flu went to Lady Dorothy Neville's parties, saw Browning, hoped to meet the "Roosevelts," and later looked forward to seeing the Franklin Delanos. Once in Browning's company at Lady Dorothy's, Arnold sat back and listened, with amusement, to a Mrs. Potter recite his friend's "How They Brought the Good News from Ghent to Aix." This recital drove Robert Browning "mad," Mary Ward reports. Mrs. Potter "galloped like a horse" and "rode like a jockey, and shrieked like a good 'un!"[14] Matthew on occasion twitted Browning over poetry; and once on the steps of the Athenaeum Club, when feeling ill, took leave of Browning for what may have been the last time by exacting a promise. If only that prolific friend would not write an elegy on him! "Now, one promise, Browning," Matthew told him airily, "please, not more than ten lines."[15]

Underneath his own gaiety was a sadness that even John Coleridge now sensed. When that friend asked him to name the most characteristic lines in Horace, Matthew, it seems in the privacy of Coleridge's elegant London study-room, replied quickly:

> *Linquenda tellus, et domus, et placens*
> *Uxor; neque harum, quae colis, arborum,*
> *Te, praeter invisas cupressos,*
> *Ulla brevum dominum sequetur.**[16]

Still, after helping to eat at Cobham a gigantic Christmas turkey sent by Andrew Carnegie, Arnold faced the year of 1888 with plans. As an Inspector, he had traveled steadily. In retirement, his conscience nagged him; he was restless; hence he accepted a few lecture ordeals for the new year. "I am just off for the North to make a horrid

---

*"Earth, home, and winsome wife, thy fate will have thee leave, and not one tree of all, save cypress that we hate, O transient lord, shall follow thee."

discourse about America," he notes on January 27. "I have then to prepare a horrid discourse about Milton, and a horrid article about Welsh disestablishment—all before the middle of February."[17] The first "horrid" piece, which he delivered at Hull, Bradford, and Bristol as "Life in America," was to be printed in April 1888 as "Civilisation in the United States." This had been a "very ticklish subject"[18] as he told Lady de Rothschild, whom he saw for the last time in March; for, without shocking Americans, he meant to show *why* they hadn't yet solved their "human problem." His essay denounces England's own class system, then shows that Americans, though less inhibited by class, utterly neglect beauty in their towns and cities, tolerate worthless newspapers, and fail through their own boastfulness to see and correct "shortcomings." Again he refers to the United States, and its faults, in "Milton." On February 18 he gave that piece at St. Margaret's Church, near Westminster Abbey, on the occasion of G. W. Childs's gift of a stained glass window to celebrate Milton and his second wife or "late espoused saint." Childs, the donor, was an American; thus Arnold's speech rather gingerly attacks the United States for discouraging the Miltonic ideal of "high and rare excellence."[19]

His British audiences at Hull, Bradford, and Bristol, and the few Americans present at St. Margaret's Church, did not object to these remarks. But as his daughter Lucy's journey from New York, in 1888, drew nearer, Arnold began to worry. What would American newsmen say of "Civilisation in the United States" when they saw it in print—glaring and staring at them in April's *Nineteenth Century*? Arnold had tried, in the essay, to approve what he could: he praised "American women" because they seemed outspoken, natural, and at ease, in contrast with the "English" middle-class woman who is tied in knots because she always worries what an "upper class, as it is called" is thinking about her.[20] (He could not forget Wellesley, Smith, and Vassar, or the intelligent women he met in Chicago, for that matter.) For all his qualifications, he indicted American society, more severely now, for lacking in interest, beauty, depth, and the self-critical attitude. His "American daughter" Lucy might find life miserable if New York's press screamed abuse at him, and kept it up. She was pregnant again; she was leaving Fred behind and risking her health this year to cross the Atlantic. One cannot underestimate the force of Arnold's anxiety for his children—and he thought the worst of the press.

Yet he expressed no regret for any of his criticism of America; and "Civilisation" rounded off his career. He had thought about the United States most of his life, had traveled over and drawn comparisons, talked to its people, seen their cities, read their books. Arnold's best insights were retrospective; and since 1884 he had had time to reflect on the States in the light of thirty-five years of firsthand inspections of a hundred towns and cities up and down England. To have kept silent about America or *not* to have written "Civilisation" would have been unthinkable. The contrast between British and American societies lies at the heart of his thought after 1884; it can be felt in his Irish essays, which reflect his belief that the United Kingdom cannot match the sane, efficient, democratic federal system of the United States. Like Stephen Spender later,[21] Arnold believed Americans were in many ways "adolescent," but also that in some ways they could rise above Europe: their state-system, Constitution, energy, and respect for freedom seemed unique.

All that he failed to see was that, by April, his life was in danger. Anxiety over American papers *could* compound itself with excitement over Lucy's arrival to send his heart racing. His face had become dark red; he was beefy and girthy, now that he weighed in the region of 17 stone (almost 240 pounds). His face had been thin enough, in 1870, to cause Charles Dickens to ask an illustrator to portray Edwin Drood as "Mr. Matthew Arnold."[22] (One picture of the villain of Dickens's novel *Edwin Drood* shows Arnold's thin, ominous face.) But nobody could have used him to illustrate a villain now. Whether or not he usually followed Sir Andrew Clark's diet, Arnold drank rather too much. Possibly Sir Andrew was giving him nitroglycerin, which had been introduced in London in 1875 for the heart; but Arnold does not say so, and in any case it would not have sent his weight soaring.

George Smalley read "Civilisation in the United States" on March 31, and opened up with cannon fire. As London correspondent of the *New York Tribune,* he cabled to his paper a violent attack on his old British friend. Arnold's essay is an "elaborate lampoon on America," Smalley begins. "It is the most acrimonious of all recent attacks on America," a "skilful scandal," bitterly deplorable, and "almost an international calamity."[23] On April 1, 1888, the *Tribune,* sensing a wonderful windfall, gave Smalley's piece a column and a half on page one.

Editors at the *New York Times* must have been puzzled by this, since it was usually left to *them* to put Matthew Arnold in his place! Here was the *Tribune* firing at him! Not to be outdone, they came into action by April 9, at which time Arnold's whole hateful essay was being printed by American newspapers. Arnold is infected by snobbishness, declared the *Times,* and "lives in a social atmosphere thick with antiquated nonsense"; this makes him pitiable.[24] The *Tribune* fired again, and by now many sharpshooters were in the fray. Satires on Arnold, mock interviews, poems defending American place names by attacking English names made the New York press lively. Arnold as an English critic had dared to mock "the Briggsvilles, Higginsvilles, Jacksonvilles, rife from Maine to Florida"![25] He was supposed to be chanting, for example, in snobbish Britain:

> *At Scrooby and at Gonerby,*
> *At Wigton and at Smeeth,*
> *At Bottesford and Rumcorn*
> *I need not grit my teeth.*[26]

A copy of Smalley's *Tribune* dispatch, with a letter, reached Cobham by April 13. On that day, Arnold wrote a mollifying reply to Smalley, and a more worried note to George Russell—one of the last letters Arnold ever wrote: Smalley has written a letter full of shriekings and cursings about my innocent article; the Americans will get their notion of it from that, and I shall never be able to enter America again."[27] He had two days in which to imagine how Smalley's "shriekings and cursings" would upset his pregnant daughter, Lucy.

He put aside his projects. He meant to write on Shelley's poetry and a piece on Alexandre Vinet; also he had found "G. Sand's correspondence" so very lively he planned an "article on 'the old age of George Sand.'" Like Benjamin Jowett, he believed that old age is for work: "I quite agree with you," Jowett had told him in 1887, "we ought to work as long as the day lasts."[28] Matthew hoped to see Jowett at the Palmerston Club, on June 2. As for his health, he was not troubled by it. The greatest felicity is to have a sudden death, he had jotted from Sainte-Beuve; again he had looked at Senancour's *Obermann* and told Fanny Lucy: "When I am dying, *'qu'on place ma chaise sur l'herbe courte'*—may they put my chair on the short grass—says Obermann, and I quite share his feeling."[29] He hoped to die with his eyes on nature, and not near "some doctor,"

On April 14, he and Flu left Cobham for the home of Matthew's sister Susanna, who lived at Dingle Bank at the edge of Liverpool.

The Dingle, south of Liverpool's southernmost boundary in 1888, was a place of odd contrasts. When the Croppers, a Quaker family who made money in paper manufacturing, settled there early in the century it was a delicious suburban nook with sculpted flower beds, pretty paths, and a few well-kept lawns and villas. By the time Matthew's sister Susy married John Wakefield Cropper, in 1858, it was already changing. For one thing Liverpool's port facilities were always too small—even if they happened to be the largest on earth. "From Rimrose Brook to Dingle Point," J. A. Picton says with pride in *Memorials of Liverpool*,[30] "hydraulic works" of "magnitude and grandeur of construction" line the River Mersey's shore. And that was in 1875; thirteen years later the Mersey Dock Board actually had purchased much of the Cropper estate.

When Arnold took an evening walk with John Cropper on April 14 and again the next day, when he walked to catch a tramcar which would take him to Lucy at Liverpool's Landing Stage, his eyes gazed at a decaying landscape. There was a "faint" dilapidated air in this green region, so close to wharfs, docks, steam cranes, and smokestacks of a city. Yet he was delighted to be near Liverpool; he was always overjoyed to see his family, and he must have kissed Susy very warmly.

He had twenty-four hours before Lucy was due.

Lucy Whitridge with her daughter "Midget," in fact, were nearing Ireland, on the *Aurania* from New York. On Saturday evening, after a chatty supper with the Croppers, Matthew suggested an evening walk with Susy's husband. Outside the house, he noticed an iron railing about 2 feet 9 inches high, dividing the lawn from a ragged meadow running to the high bluff above the Mersey shore. Years before as a schoolboy, he had cleared a Rugby obstacle known as "Cole's Gate"—it was over five feet high—and later on, as an Oriel student, he had risked his neck (and a £5 bet) to jump Wadham College's high spiked railings, which stood at 5 feet 3 inches, between Wadham's grass and paved street of Oxford. Perhaps as he laughed and tried to jump a low fence this evening, he recalled that Wadham leap as vividly as a friend did. Back in the 1840s, Matthew had made a fantastic jump which might have suggested much to him: instead of leaping *from the city street* onto soft green college lawn, as others did, he went through Wadham's gate and placed his "back against the college wall." He intended to leap from greenery into the hard city—just as in life he had come from pastoral, quiet Westmorland into a hard inspectorship.

"There is nothing in the jump," Matthew announced at Balliol College. "I will undertake to clear the Wadham railing myself this very afternoon, and to forfeit five pounds if I fail."

No sooner said than done. Ten or twelve [young men] . . . made their way quietly along Broad-street, and turned to the left, when the end of Holywell-road was reached. A few steps brought them face with Wadham, where the iron spikes lifted their heads aloft to an alarming height. Without losing a moment Mr. Arnold . . . entered the iron gate, and placing his back against the college wall [began to run]. . . . Although his style of jumping was far from graceful, as his legs seemed to be jointed at the knees like those of a German doll, and flew outwards spread-eagle fashion at right angles to the thighs from which they depended, Mr. Arnold cleared the spikes by a couple of inches, amidst the subdued applause of the spectators, who hurried away from the spot, fearful of being interviewed by the Proctor and questioned by him as to their ideas of the proper method of spending Sunday afternoon.[31]

He became instantly famous that day—but with what a *thwack!* he must have landed!

On this quiet evening, a man of about 268 pounds who had been ill with angina pectoris ran at the 2-foot 9-inch railing, and abruptly stopped. He turned round with a smile, came back, and then to his great delight made the jump. But from then on, that night and the next morning, images of Lucy's arrival and of Smalley's "shriekings" about the American essay perhaps often made his heart race. On Sunday after a Presbyterian church service at Sefton Park, and luncheon, Flu and Matthew at last began their 800-yard walk to a tramcar stop. The air was then warm, windless, and mild. A complete change, according to the newspapers, had just taken place in the weather over England so that barometers were quickly rising in the north and falling in the south. Nearly all of England was covered with rainclouds, except for the "extreme Western coasts"[32] —and Liverpool oddly was in sunlight.

Fanny Lucy walked by Arnold's side for a few hundred yards. The lane inclined to a small degree uphill; and now all around him was greenery but in the distance lay the great city. "Twice in that short journey" to the tramcar "it was noticed that he paused a little to take breath. This was not unusual with him and at the end of the lane Mrs. Arnold, seeing the tramcar ready to start, hurried forward to detain it."[33] Arnold may have quickened his pace or run a few steps; but as he was about to enter the horse-drawn car, he fell forward into the dusty street. His wife knelt at his side, and cried for brandy.

He was carried unconscious to the nearby house of Dr. Little, who was roused by a "violent ringing" of his front doorbell. In his study-room Dr. Little discerned that Arnold was still alive. Ventricular fibrillation probably had begun: the heart, in cases of fatal coronary thrombosis, may beat idly and wildly and unrhythmically until it stops. Having sent for an ambulance, Dr. Little tried to pour brandy down the throat of the slowly breathing Arnold. After "three or four minutes,"[34] and shortly before 3 P.M. on Sunday, April 15, 1888, Matthew Arnold died. He had lived sixty-five years and three months.

Fanny Lucy could not go to the landing stage to meet Lucy that day; she was an admirable woman but in fact she had to be carried back to the Croppers' house at Dingle Bank. "I," Dick Arnold wrote, "with my wife & my sister [Lucy] were on board the Aurania and were just getting out of the cab at the hotel in Liverpool when my uncle [John Cropper] met us with the sad and dreadful news."[35]

On Monday morning, the only paper to print that news was the

Liverpool Daily Post. But evening papers were alerted; and next morning great journals ran obituaries. "The esteemed poet and critic," wrote the *Daily Telegraph,* "died by as swift and painless . . . [a] death as mortal man can well hope to undergo." As for his rewards, Arnold "will 'go not crownless to PERSEPHONE'" in the shades of Hell.[36] Americans were cabled the news; and they responded: "Mr. Arnold always seemed to us," wrote New York's *Herald,* "somewhat over-strained." "Regret will not be selfish," judged the solemn *New York Times;* "Mr. Arnold's latest writings [show] he had reached the limit of his productivity." But other United States papers were rather kinder: "Arnold is dead," wrote *The Springfield Republican,* and "the intelligence falls with a sensible shock."[37] The American press was surprised, later, by the fact that he had left an estate valued at only £1040 (or about $5000).

Arnold's sisters wanted his body dispatched to Laleham almost at once; but his wife's wishes, in what seems to have been a mild dispute, now prevailed. Arnold's body went to Cobham for a day or two, before the Laleham service.

On Thursday, April 19, an impressive special train left London's Waterloo Station for Laleham, at a quarter to eleven. Aboard were four Members of Parliament with Lord Coleridge and Robert Browning, Jowett and Henry James, George Smalley of the *New York Tribune* and many clergymen as well as ladies who held wreaths of primroses. Arnold's body, meanwhile, was conveyed through the narrow lanes from Cobham Village. People lined the route as the horse-drawn hearse went from sun into rain. As Inspector, Arnold had known all kinds of weather during thirty-five years of travel from school to school—and indeed before he died his face was coarsened, his teeth were cracked and chipped, and his smile had become crooked. George Bradley was now at Laleham gate; the coffin was borne into the church just before Bradley recited "I am the Resurrection and the Life," and as it went through the low portal all the "tasteful wreaths" piled on the oak box were swept off its lid. Rain was falling, obediently, when the service ended at the graveside. Dean Bradley's voice was "broken with emotion" when he said the words, "ashes to ashes, dust to dust." Then Arnold was laid in a vault near the remains of his three boys.

Words from a poet, that April, perhaps helped Fanny Lucy. "After all," Browning told Mrs. Arnold, "you will just hear a word, true as Truth's self, that tells you I shall hold in veneration—to my own dying day—the memory of one of the noblest and best men I ever knew and ever loved."[38]

Fanny Lucy was also moved by the sight of enormous wreaths from schoolteachers, who could hardly afford the tributes they sent to Laleham. She tried to comfort the tall, pale, and silent Jane Forster. Letters between Matthew and "K" in recent years had become oddly impersonal, if not less affectionate, with passing comments on politics but no very intimate confidences. Timid and resigned, "K" interested herself in her grown and active Arnold-Forster children, and lived quietly until 1899.

Tom Arnold was doubly shattered because on April 7 at Oxford, a few days before Matthew died, he had lost his wife Julia. He returned to Ireland, where Julia, who never became reconciled to his Catholic faith, had refused to live. Tom was now Professor of English at University College, Dublin, where for the past few years he had been intimate with the holder of the Greek chair—Father Gerard Hopkins. Two years after Matthew died, Tom began one of the happiest periods in his life. He married Josephine Benison, a middle-aged Roman Catholic from Slieve Russell, county Cavan; he also began to write the vivid memoir, *Passages in a Wandering Life*—easily his best book —and to his delight and surprise noticed that two of his little grandchildren, Julian and Aldous Huxley, were affectionate even though they were precocious and spoiled by their mother (Tom's daughter Julia, who had married Thomas Huxley's son Leonard). A fragile and handsome gentleman in his seventy-seventh year, Tom fell ill and died on November 12, 1900. He was buried at Glasnevin.

Fanny Lucy kept busy trying to help her children Lucy, Nelly, and Dick and their families while concealing her grief—but admitting to her distant friend, C. E. Norton in Massachusetts, her "sense of loneliness" and "the weight of sorrow which presses on me so heavily."[39] Lucy and Nelly saw her as an unselfish, tiny and pretty lady with a swirl of gray hair and a heavy shawl. This year Lucy gave birth to a baby, John, who died on July 4, but she later gave birth to a vigorous son, Arnold Whitridge, who became a French scholar at Yale University and a friend to critics. Nelly became engaged in 1888 to Armine Wodehouse, a younger son of Lord Kimberley of the India office.

That engagement pleased Fanny Lucy, without easing her grief. She wrote at Cobham to her friends the C. E. Nortons, on December 29, "This season used to be specially joyous, as Christmas Eve was my beloved Matt's birthday, and Christmas Day is Lucy's. It *is* heartbreaking to think of all that has been, & can never be again. I am sure the sense of loss increases if possible, more & more as time goes on—& the sorrow seems as if it were greater than could be borne." Later she arranged to meet Mrs. Arthur Clough in London to talk about "Thyrsis." Her comfort was to keep every item in Matthew's room at Cobham "just as he had left it" and "waiting"—his "coat hanging behind the door, his slippers beside his chair, the last letters he had received, and all the small and simple equipment of his writing-table ready to hand."[40]

Matthew had been lucky in his marriage, lucky with his teachers and friends—who included Temple and Tait who became Archbishops of Canterbury, as well as Wordsworth, Clough, and Browning. His son Dick perhaps inherited that luck, along with a real quality of sympathy which became clear in his forties when he and Ella lived at Eastbourne Lodge, in Worcester. His "blond mop" of hair was then much darker and thinner; he was "given to whimsical and witty remarks" and very loyal to Ella and his family. He shared a passion for family, which had been one secret of Matthew Arnold's success—and of Matthew's effort to fulfill himself partly in the light of what Mrs. Arnold, "K", and his other sisters suggested might be true about his nature. Dick, in Worcester, now befriended "Ted" Elgar, a lean, nervous, emotional man with an army captain's mustache and a habit of fluttering his eyes. As a composer, he was almost unknown. Dick and Ella, as amateur musicians, went over to Elgar's house in the woods below Malvern to help him read through his music "as it came in proof."[41] Soon after this friendship began, Elgar had the idea of sketching "portraits" of friends in musical variations. "There are wonders in true affection," wrote Sir Thomas Browne in *Religio Medici,* a copy of which lay on Edward Elgar's shelf; "it is a body of *Enigmas,* mysteries, and riddles. . . . I love my friend before myself, and yet methinks I do not love him enough."[42] Dick Arnold, as "R.P.A.," became the subject of the fifth of Edward Elgar's *Enigma* Variations. For as long as Western culture lasts, Matthew Arnold's son will have his living portrait in Elgar's lovely music.

Arnold never believed that his own work would be popular—but he is the Victorian who matters the most. His poetry seems to give us to ourselves, even as it portrays a modern mind, sensitive to the historic past and to its own past; and he is with Milton one of the two best elegiac poets of England. His essays have set a precedent for a flexible, informed, readable criticism—which seeks far and wide, which looks always for what really sustains the human spirit, and which is surely more realistic and sound in its "social idea" or its intelligent concern for society than are the fashions of many shallow optimists and shallow pessimists of any age. "We have not won our political battles,"[43] he wrote very fairly of Oxford and of himself in *Culture and*

Anarchy; "we have not carried our main points, we have not stopped our adversaries' advance, we have not marched victoriously with the modern world; but . . . we have prepared currents of feeling which sap our adversaries' position when it seems gained, we have kept up our own communications with the future."

REFERENCES

Some names, such as "Thomas" and "William," appear in more than one generation of Arnolds. Section One is a brief list of names and nicknames of the Arnolds in three generations, together with dates and remarks. Section Two is a list of Cue Titles used in the notes; and Section Three contains notes to the chapters.

SECTION ONE   THE NAMES OF THE ARNOLDS, IN THREE GENERATIONS

William Arnold (b. 1745; d. 1801), H.M. Inspector of Customs at the Isle of Wight	in 1779 married	Martha Delafield (b. 1750; d. 1829) of Aylesbury

The children of William and Martha Arnold were:

1. William   Married in London and emigrated to Tobago in the West Indies where he died in 1806.

2. Martha   Married, in 1803, John Ward, successor to her father as customs officer at Cowes; grandmother of Sir Adolphus Ward, Vice-Chancellor of Manchester University.

3. Lydia   Married, in 1814, the seventh Earl of Cavan—whose country seat overlooking Southampton Water was "Eaglehurst."

4. Susanna   Lived as an invalid with her mother and her Aunt Delafield, at Laleham, from 1819 until she died in 1832. A godmother to the poet Matthew Arnold.

5. Frances   Married in 1816 Rev. John Buckland, and helped him to run the school he began in 1819 at Laleham with her brother Thomas; she died at age 73 in 1863.

6. Matthew   Army chaplain under Wellington and later Classical Professor at the Royal Military College at Marlow. Drowned 1820.

7. Thomas   Born June 13, 1795; died June 12, 1842; the most famous of English headmasters, and father of Matthew Arnold the poet and critic. Schoolmaster at Laleham in 1819. Married in 1820. Elected Headmaster of Rugby School in December 1827, moved to Rugby in August and took his D.D. degree in December

426

1828. Regius Professor of Modern History at Oxford in 1841–42. In religion, Dr. Arnold advocated a latitudinarian or "broad" church (to include all Christians); he brought critical intelligence to the schoolroom with comparative approaches to history and literature, and turned Rugby into a democratic hierarchy, in which the eldest boys (Sixth Formers) had power and responsibilities almost equal to the teachers'. He wrote a drinking song, a number of poems, and published pamphlets, journalism, sermons, a *History of Rome,* and a translation of Thucydides. His book reviews rebuke poems of moral abstractions and recommend "touchstones."

Thomas Arnold, on August 11, 1820, married the daughter of a Nottinghamshire clergyman. She was Mary Penrose (born in Cornwall, August 21, 1791; died at Ambleside, September 30, 1873), an amateur poet of religious as well as light comic family verse, avid diarist and letter writer. Their children were:

1. Jane Martha (b. August 1, 1821; d. October 21, 1899). Family nickname: "K." Married William Edward Forster (1818–1886) on August 15, 1850. Adopted the four children of her brother, William Delafield Arnold, after he died in 1859. Jane or "K" was Matthew's confidante throughout his life, his most valued critic, and the sister he most heeded.

2. *Matthew Arnold, the poet and critic (b. December 24, 1822; d. April 15, 1888). Family nicknames: "Crab," "Crabby," "The Emperor." Private secretary to the Marquess of Lansdowne, 1847–1851. Married Frances Lucy Wightman on June 10, 1851; they had six children. His career for thirty-five years as one of Her Majesty's Inspectors of Schools for working-class and lower-middle-class children, aged from 4 to 13, began in 1851.*

3. Thomas Arnold, teacher and literary historian (b. November 30, 1823; d. November 12, 1900). Family nickname: "Prawn." Sailed for New Zealand in November 1847. At Hobart in 1850, he married Julia Sorell, who bore him eight children. Became a Roman Catholic in 1856, lapsed in 1866, and later returned to the Catholic faith. After working at Birmingham Oratory School under J. H. Newman, he became Professor of English at University College, Dublin, where he knew Gerard Manley Hopkins. Married again in 1890. "Tom" was Matthew Arnold's best-liked brother and "Popish Duck."

4. Mary (b. March 29, 1825; d. 1888). Chief family nickname: "Bacco." The frankest, most outspoken of the four Arnold sisters, she studied Christian Socialism in London. Married three times: (1) in April 1847 to William Aldred Twining, who died in 1848; (2) to Rev. J. S. Hiley of Leicester, in 1856, with whom she had two sons, Lewis and Arnold; and (3) to Rev. Robert Hayes.

5. Edward Penrose Arnold, Fellow of All Souls College, Oxford, and H.M. Inspector of Schools (b. October 28, 1826; d. April 6, 1878). Family nickname: "Didu," "Pig," "Swiney," "Ducktail." Married Caroline Orlebar and had one child, Edward, who founded the London Publishing house of Edward Arnold, Ltd.

6. William Delafield Arnold (b. April 7, 1828; d. at Gibraltar, April 9, 1859). Family nickname: "Widu." Sailed for India in 1848, married Frances Anne Hodgson there in April 1850. Wrote a novel, *Oakfield,* and became Director of Public Instruction in the Punjab; his wife died in the Punjab, March 1858. Their four children, Edward Penrose, Florence, Hugh Oakeley, and Frances Egerton, were adopted in 1859 by Matthew's sister Jane and her husband and later took the name Arnold-Forster.

7. Susanna Elizabeth Lydia (b. August 25, 1830; d. June 6, 1911). Family nicknames: "Babbat Apbook," "Susy," "Master," "Maestro." Married in 1858 John Wakefield Cropper (1830–1892) of Liverpool.

8. Frances Bunsen Trevenen Whately (b. October 10, 1833; d. September 9, 1923). Among her nicknames: "Bonze," "Fan," "Fankiss," "Junx," "Congus," "Skatrell." Living at Fox How, she survived many Arnold and Arnold-Forster men who were killed in the Zulu war and the First World War, and befriended Theodore Roosevelt and Woodrow Wilson. Known as "Aunt Fan" to generations of relatives. Her drawing room in 1923 looked much as it did in 1842.

9. Walter Thomas Arnold (b. August 19, 1835; d. September 27, 1893). Family nicknames: "Quid," "Corus." Began as a boy sailor at age 12, later gave up the merchant navy, married, and settled at Greenhithe, Kent.

Another child, Frances Trevenen, was born May 13, 1832, and died in infancy.

The six children of Matthew Arnold and Frances Lucy Wightman were:

1. Thomas (b. July 6, 1852; died at sixteen on November 23, 1868). Nicknames: "Tommy," "Little Tom," "Tiddy Tom."

2. Trevenen William (b. October 15, 1853; died at eighteen on February 16, 1872). Nickname: "Budge." Arnold's favorite son, Budge was a fat, sensitive boy who hated fishing, called his father "Darling," wept over the names of his family when at school, and had original and odd opinions.

3. Richard Penrose (b. November 14, 1855; d. 1908). Family names: "Dick," "Dicky." The only one of Arnold's sons who reached adulthood, he ran into debt and other difficulties as a student at Oxford, went to Australia as a bank clerk, met Ella Ford of Melbourne, and later married her in England. H.M. Inspector of Factories, 1882. He lived at Shrubbery Avenue, Worcester, and befriended the composer Elgar.

4. Lucy Charlotte (b. December 25, 1858; d. 1934). Married Frederick W. Whitridge of New York. They had four children: Eleanor or "Midget"; John, who died in infancy; Joan, who married Henry Forsyth; and Arnold Whitridge, who married Janetta Alexander and became Professor of French at Yale and the author of scholarly works on Matthew Arnold and a biography of Dr. Arnold.

5. Eleanor Mary Caroline (b. February 11, 1861; d. 1936). "Nelly"; nickname in infancy: "Gorilla." Edited a small selection of her father's notebooks in 1902. Married (1) in 1889 the Hon. Armine Wodehouse, with whom she had a son, Roger; (2) in 1909, William Mansfield, Baron Sandhurst.

6. Basil Francis (b. August 19, 1866; d. January 4, 1868).

The children of Matthew Arnold's brother Thomas Arnold (1823–1900) and Julia Sorell were:

1. Mary Augusta (1851–1920), who married Thomas Humphry Ward (1846–1926) and wrote *Robert Elsmere* and twenty-four other novels as Mrs. Humphry Ward; 2. William Thomas; 3. Theodore; 4. Lucy; 5. Arthur; 6. Julia, who married Leonard Huxley (1860–1933) and became the mother of Julian Huxley the naturalist, and Aldous Huxley the novelist; 7. Ethel; 8. Francis.

SECTION TWO   CUE TITLES

"M.A." is Matthew Arnold the poet and critic (1822–1888); "T.A." is his father, Dr. Thomas Arnold (1795–1842), Headmaster of Rugby.

Alexander Turnbull MS.	Thomas Arnold Papers (MS 321: folder 4) at Alexander Turnbull Library, Wellington, N.Z.
Balliol MS.	Letters, diaries, or other manuscripts in the Balliol College Library at Oxford.
Bodleian MS.	Letters in the Bodleian Library at Oxford.
Brotherton MS.	Documents in the Brotherton Collection at the Brotherton Library, University of Leeds.
Humanities Res. Center, Texas	Letters in the Humanitarian Research Center, the University of Texas at Austin.
Letters, ed. Bertram	*New Zeland Letters of Thomas Arnold the Younger, with further letters from Van Diemen's Land, and Letters of Arthur Hugh Clough, 1847–1851*, ed. James Bertram (London and Wellington: Oxford University Press, 1966).
Letters, ed. Whitridge	*Unpublished Letters of Matthew Arnold*, ed. Arnold Whitridge (New Haven, Conn.: Yale University Press, 1923).
Letters of M.A.	*Letters of Matthew Arnold, 1848–1888*, ed. George W. E. Russell (New York and London: Macmillan and Co., 1895), 2 vols.
M.A. Diaries	*Matthew Arnold's Diaries, the Unpublished Items: A Transcription and Commentary*, ed. William Bell Guthrie, diss. University of Virginia, 1957, 4 vols.
M.A. to A.H.C.	*The Letters of Matthew Arnold to Arthur Hugh Clough*, ed. Howard Foster Lowry (London: Oxford University Press, 1932).
Mulhauser	*The Correspondence of Arthur Hugh Clough*, ed. Frederick L. Mulhauser (London: Oxford University Press, 1957), 2 vols.
Note-Books	*The Note-Books of Matthew Arnold*, ed. Howard Foster Lowry, Karl Young, and Waldo Hilary Dunn (London: Oxford University Press, 1952).

Poems, ed. Allott	*The Poems of Matthew Arnold,* ed. Kenneth Allott (London: Longmans, Green and Co., Ltd., 1965).
Stanley, *Life*	Arthur Penrhyn Stanley, *The Life and Correspondence of Thomas Arnold, D.D.* (London: Ward, Lock and Co., 1890).
Super	*The Complete Prose Works of Matthew Arnold,* ed. R. H. Super (Ann Arbor: University of Michigan Press, 1960–77), 11 vols.
Univ. of Virginia MS.	A. K. Davis–Matthew Arnold Collection (4885), Manuscripts Department, University of Virginia Library.
Wordsworth MS.	Letters in the Wordsworth Library, Grasmere.
Yale MS. (Tinker 21)	Notes in pencil and ink in the hand of Matthew Arnold, on thirty-seven sheets bound in blue levant morocco, and designated Item 21 in the Tinker Collection of the Beinecke Rare Book and Manuscript Library at Yale University.
Yale University MS.	Letters in the Beinecke Rare Book and Manuscript Library, Yale University.

SECTION THREE   NOTES

Chapter 1. Childhood, 1822–1836, pp. 3–26.

Epigraph: Balliol MS., in pencil, October 15, 1830.

1. Brotherton MS., 1836 Notebook of Mrs. Mary Arnold. Matthew was lazy, careless, truant, vain, unreliable, and too sociable, according to his mother; he had outgrown the more deplorable fault, *obstinacy,* by the age of 13; for disfiguring Tom's face, see William T. Arnold, "Thomas Arnold the Younger," *Century Magazine,* LXVI (1903), 118.

2. "The First Sight of Italy," lines 45–47, 29–30, composed in March 1836.

3. Brotherton MS., Mrs. Mary Arnold to Lydia Penrose, September 17, 1838.

4. Brotherton MS., 1836 Notebook of Mrs. Mary Arnold.

5. Brotherton MSS., extract from a letter by Trevenen Penrose, October 18, 1821; Mrs. Mary Arnold's Journals, I, October 1, 1823.

6. Brotherton MS., extract from a letter by "Grandpapa" [Rev. John Penrose], Fledborough, December 31, 1822.

7. Brotherton MS., Mrs. Mary Arnold's Journals, I, March 22, 1824.

8. Ibid.

9. Brotherton MS., Notebook of Laura Ward, "Rugby April 1836."

10. Brotherton MS., Mrs. Mary Arnold's Journals, I, July 1827.

11. *Autobiography of Mrs. Fletcher, of Edinburgh, with Selections from her Letters and Other Family Memorials,* ed. by the Survivor of her Family [Lady Richardson] (Carlisle, 1874), pp. 160–61.

12. Diary of Aubrey de Vere, March 5, 1845, quoted by Wilfred Ward, *Aubrey de Vere: A Memoir* (London, 1904), p. 68.

13. Brotherton MS., Mrs. Mary Arnold's Journals, I, February 1831.

14. Ibid., I, February 25, 1822.

15. Ibid., I, September 1823.

16. Brotherton MS., T.A. to his wife, January 10, 1825.

17. Brotherton MSS., Frances and Susanna Arnold, his sisters, to "Tom" [c. 1800]; T.A. to his Aunt Delafield.

18. "Ode on the 20th of November, 1812, Sung at the Common Room Anniversary Meeting by G. Cornish, Esq., Written by T. Arnold, Esq.," *The Pelican Record* of Corpus Christi College, Oxford, II (March 1895), 181–82, lines 12–16.

19. Stanley, *Life,* p. 33 (November 20, 1819).

20. Brotherton MS., Mrs. Mary Arnold's Journals, I, January 8, 1822, and February 24, 1822.

21. Stanley, *Life,* p. 51 (to Tucker, March 2 [1828]).

22. Ibid., p. 223 (June 11, 1834).

23. Ibid., pp. 138 (to Mrs. Evelyn, February 22, 1829), 99 (to Sir T. Pasley [n.d.]).

24. See Norman Wymer, *Dr Arnold of Rugby* (London, 1953), p. 73; and Brotherton MS., T.A. to Cornish, April 4, 1823.

25. Wordsworth MS., T.A. to Mrs. Frances Buckland, July 21, 1824; Brotherton MS., Mrs. Mary Arnold's Journals, I, July 27, 1824.

26. Brotherton MS., Mrs. Mary Arnold's Journals, I, August 9, 1824.

27. *Letters of M.A.,* I, 27 (November 25, 1852).

28. Lines 10–11, 14–16, 25–27, 140–143.

29. Brotherton MS., to George Cornish, September 23, 1824.

30. Brotherton MS., 1836 Notebook of Mrs. Mary Arnold, entry in M.A.'s hand.

31. M.A. wore iron leg-braces regularly from September 1824 to June 1826 and off and on in the months before his fourth birthday, as his mother (against medical advice) "gradually discontinued" them. In the next few years, he walked abnormally; physical clumsiness, noted by Mrs. Arnold in the 1830s, partly accounts for burning his hand at Winchester; yet M.A. seems to have regulated his clumsiness to appeal to his mother. Shuttlecock, hoop-rolling, and a long walk from Wythburn to Keswick indicate that by the age of 10½ he was active when he wanted to be. The most complete record of the "leg-irons" is in Mrs. Mary Arnold's Journals, I; but see also her Diaries, T.A.'s letter of September 23, 1824, and *Arnold Newsletter* I (Autumn 1973), 11–12.

The biographer has discussed Mrs. Arnold's comments on Matthew's "bent" legs with Dr. W. H. P. Cant, Professor Peter Eckstein, and Keith Norcross, F.R.C.S., of Birmingham. Another specialist, P. L. Frank of Manchester, sent in a summary of knock-knee and bowleg in 1,200 children (1973) to Mr. Norcross. Probably M.A. suffered from rickets caused by a mild Vitamin D deficiency and not from osteomyelitis (which would have been recognized in London in 1824) or another disease. In dairy land with insufficient irradiation from the sun, the products the child consumes may be deficient. Leg-braces in the 19th century were so heavy that bowleg and knock-knee in children could be iatrogenic; one of Matthew's legs bowed *after* he began to wear the apparatus. The "irons" delayed his cure.

32. Stanley, *Life,* p. 460.

33. William T. Arnold, "Thomas Arnold the Younger," *Century Magazine,* LXVI (1903), 123.

34. Brotherton MS., Mrs. Mary Arnold's Journals, I, April 1829.

35. Ibid., I, April 1829, and September 1830 [written in April 1832]. This well-praised walk from Chertsey by M.A.'s brother, Tom, was on August 31, 1824; and his father outwalked a pupil, Hoskyns, on October 3, 1825. Mrs. Arnold's praise of physical action, and her complaints about M.A.'s lassitude and clumsiness, continued after the family moved to Rugby in August 1828.

36. (London, 1900), p. 9.

37. Brotherton MS., Mrs. Mary Arnold's Journals, I, August 1828.

38. Ibid.

39. Brotherton MS., 1836 Notebook of Mrs. Mary Arnold.

40. Ibid.

41. Brotherton MS., Mrs. Mary Arnold's Journals, I, June 1826 [written on or just after March 16, 1828].

42. Ibid., I, February 1828.

43. Ibid., I, December 1827; T.A.'s poem is dated April 30, 1827.

44. Stanley, *Life,* p. 54 (to Hull, July 29, 1828).

45. Brotherton MS., T.A. to Mrs. Frances Buckland, January 3, 1832.

46. Brotherton MS., 1836 Notebook of Mrs. Mary Arnold.

47. Brotherton MS., May 17, 1830; and Yale University MS., Diary of Mrs. Mary Arnold [n.d.].

48. Brotherton MS., Mrs. Mary Arnold's Journals, I, July 1828.

49. Ibid., I, August 1828.

50. Stanley, *Life,* pp. 197 (to the Archbishop of Dublin, February 1, 1833); 136 (to F. C. Blackstone, September 28, 1828).

51. Brotherton MS., T.A. to his Aunt Delafield, May 15, 1811.

52. See Norman Wymer, *Dr. Arnold of Rugby* (London, 1953), p. 138.

53. W. P. Fishback, *Recollections of Lord Coleridge* (Indianapolis and Kansas City, 1895), p. 123.

54. Brotherton MS., Mrs. Mary Arnold's Journals, I, December 1828.

55. Balliol MS., October 15, 1830.

56. Balliol MS., February 11, 1863.

57. Balliol MS., January 2 [1848].

58. Brotherton MS., October 18, 1831.

59. Balliol MS., February 29, 1832.

60. Brotherton MS., March 21, 1832.

61. Douglas Bush, *Matthew Arnold: A Survey of His Poetry and Prose* (London, 1971), p. 3.

62. Brotherton MS., to Mrs. Frances Buckland, January 3, 1832.

63. Brotherton MS., March 21, 1832.

64. Stanley, *Life,* p. 197 (February 1833).

65. Ibid., p. 389.

66. W. P. Fishback, *Recollections of Lord Coleridge* (Indianapolis and Kansas City, 1895), p. 73.

67. December 15, 1833.

68. Brotherton MS., T.A. to M.A., March 21, 1832.

69. Wellesley College Library MS., February 18, 1861.

70. *Passages in a Wandering Life* (London, 1900), pp. 8–9.

71. Brotherton MS., Mrs. Mary Arnold's Journals, I, July 1831.

72. *Passages in a Wandering Life* (London, 1900), p. 45.

73. Stanley, *Life,* p. 177 (to Cornish, "RYDAL!!! December 23, 1831").

74. Brotherton MS., Mrs. Mary Arnold's Journals, I, August 1833.

75. *Letters of M.A.,* I, 74 (to Jane, August 6, 1858).

76. "Resignation," lines 44–47, 61, 64–67, 69–71, 82, 84–85.

77. Quoted by H. D. Rawnsley, *Literary Associations of the English Lakes* (Glasgow, 1906), II, p. 117; Canon Rawnsley felt that Miss Brontë's imagination had carried her too far: Fox How could not have been "half buried in flowers and creepers" when she saw it in August 1850: " 'flowers and creepers' note, for the dark Scotch firs and the delicate birches . . . planted by Dr. Arnold." But Mrs. Arnold had planted climbing roses along the walls, as Anne Clough noted.

78. *Passages in a Wandering Life* (London, 1900), pp. 12, 38.

79. Brotherton MS., Journals of Mrs. Mary Arnold, I, 1831: Mrs. Arnold wrote her poem soon after July 26, 1832, the date of T.A.'s eight stanzas headed "Brathay Hall." See also "How still this upland vale!" in *Poems,* ed. Allott, pp. 610–11.

80. Kenneth Allott, "A Birthday Exercise by Matthew Arnold," *Notes and Queries,* CCIII (1958), 225.

81. 1836 transcript, lines 14–16, 22–24, 27–31.

82. Brotherton MS., to Willy and Susy [Arnold], July 10, 1836.

83. Ibid.

84. "Lines written on the Seashore at Eaglehurst," lines 1–2, 11–12. See *Poems,* ed. Allott, p. 565.

85. *M.A. to A.H.C.,* p. 111 (September 23 [1849]).

86. Brotherton MS., Mrs. Mary Arnold's Journals, II, February 1837.

Chapter 2. To Winchester and Then to Dr. Arnold's School, 1836–1841, pp. 27–47.

Epigraph: From the *Fox How Magazine* MS., July 1, 1839, by M.A.'s sisters Fan and Susanna, then aged 5 and 8. The Arnold children produced a single copy of the "magazine" twice a year from 1838 to 1841; some of M.A.'s contributions (usually signed "C.C.C.") appear in *Poems,* ed. Allott, pp. 568–75.

1. *Letters of M.A.,* II, 267–68 (November 15, 1883).

2. Stanley, *Life,* pp. 128, 160.

3. Laura Ward recorded while visiting Rugby, "On being asked if he was fond of statuary [Dr. Arnold] said I cannot say I am. . . . I can understand it very well with regard to the figure of a horse or a Dog but not of a Man [since statues reveal no] Mental Expression whatever" (Brotherton MS. notebook, 1836). He took his children to see "the colossal statues of Melpomene and Jupiter" in the Louvre (M.A.'s Travel Journal of 1837) and knew that he was not the best judge of art.

4. See *Memorials of William Charles Lake,* ed. Katharine Lake (London, 1901).

5. Balliol MS., M.A. to his mother, June 14, 1862.

6. "Lines Written on First Leaving Home for a Public School," 12–13, 37, 28, 32, 34–35.

7. T.A. explained several of the Anglican Articles and warned M.A. against studying them on November 4, 1836; Mrs. Arnold transcribed T.A.'s letter in her Diary (Yale). See also "Matthew Arnold," By One Who Knew Him Well [Tom Arnold], *Manchester Guardian,* May 18, 1888. M.A. entered the *Quinta Classis Senior Pars* or Senior Fifth at Winchester at age 13, on August 31, 1836. Set books for M.A. would have included Homer's *Iliad* and *Odyssey,* Sophocles' *Electra,* Virgil's *Georgics,* and Horace's *Satires;* see Warren D. Anderson, *Matthew Arnold and the Classical Tradition* (Ann Arbor, Mich., 1965), p. 5. I am grateful to the Winchester Archivist for data.

8. Brotherton MS., Mrs. Mary Arnold's Journals, II, September 1836.

9. Tom Arnold, quoted by Katharine Chorley, *Arthur Hugh Clough: The Uncommitted Mind* (Oxford, 1962), p. 17.

10. *Rugby Magazine,* January 1836.

11. Mulhauser, I, 45 (Clough to Simpkinson [May 5, 1836]).

12. Ibid., I, 57 (January 1, 1837); and Brotherton MS., Mrs. Mary Arnold's Journals, II, January 1837.

13. Mrs. Humphry Ward, *A Writer's Recollections* (London, 1918), p. 52.

14. "The Bishop and the Philosopher," Super, III, 42.

15. See Three Beetleites, *Winchester College Notions* (Winchester, 1901); and Thomas Arnold, *Passages in a Wandering Life* (London, 1900), p. 14.

16. Brotherton MS., T.A. to his son Tom, with postscript by Mrs. Arnold dated April 9 [1837]. If M.A. tried to give the whole speech from Byron's *Marino Faliero,* starting "I speak to Time and Eternity" (V, iii, 26–104), the Warden and masters may have cut him short—for they limited a boy to 14 or 18 lines at Easter and Commoner speakings.

17. Brotherton MS., Mrs. Mary Arnold's Journals, II, April 1837; the entry was composed in July 1839 from diary notes.

18. Brotherton MSS., Mrs. Mary Arnold to her sisters, May 29, 1840, and March 19, 1840.

19. Brotherton MS., Mrs. Mary Arnold's Journals, I, February 1830; the entry was composed on February 14, 1832.

20. See Brotherton MSS., Mrs. Mary Arnold's Journals, II, August 1837; and T.A., "Excursion to France, August, 1837."

21. Brotherton MS., 1838 Notebook of T.A.

22. Balliol MS., M.A.'s 1837 Travel Journal ("M. Arnold. Bought at Dover July 11th 1837, and respectfully inscribed, to D.D.D.F.P. wch is being interpreted *E. P. Arnold*"); entries for August 11, 12, and 21. M.A., at fourteen, bought his first "Eye-Glass at Harris the Optician's in G^t Russell Street" while his father went for passports on Poland Street in London.

23. Balliol MS., February 18, 1863.

24. Balliol MS., M.A.'s 1837 Travel Journal, August 16. The Arnolds saw Chartres on the 15th (Festival of the Assumption) and stayed on the square, at the Hôtel du Grand Monarque, which still stands.

25. Ibid., August 17. They had two nights in Paris, at the Hôtel de Bristol, before going back by way of Amiens and Beauvais to the Channel.

26. August 21, 1837.

27. Norman Wymer, *Dr. Arnold of Rugby* (London, 1953), p. 178; Mulhauser, I, 63 (Clough to Simpkinson [September 2, 1837]).

28. *M.A. to A.H.C.*, p. 110 (September 23 [1849]).

29. Brotherton MS. notebook.

30. Margaret Woods, "Matthew Arnold," *Essays and Studies by Members of the English Association*, XV (1929), 9; and Wordsworth MS., T.A. to Susanna Arnold, January 12, 1832.

31. Balliol MS. notebook, "Rugby School. Fifth Form. 1837." M.A.'s 31-line Latin *vulgus* or assigned composition on "Juvat Ire Jugis" is dated October 21, 1837.

32. Ibid. Prizewinning Latin prose assignments by William Henry Townsend ("First Prize") and by M.A. ("Second Prize") in this notebook respond to the topic, "Forsan et haec olim meminisse juvabit," from Virgil's *Aeneid*, I, 203 (Perhaps one day it will be pleasant to remember even these things). M.A.'s essay, quoting from Juvenal, Pope, Byron, Southey, and Keble, is dated December 8, 1837.

33. Brotherton MSS., Mrs. Mary Arnold's Journals, II, June 1838; and notebook of T.A., "June 15th Friday [1838]."

34. Thomas Arnold, *Passages in a Wandering Life* (London, 1900), p. 39.

35. George Foster Braithwaite, *The Salmonidae of Westmorland, Angling Reminiscences, and Leaves from an Angler's Note-Book* (London and Kendall, 1884); Philip Guedalla, *Mary Arnold* (London, 1928), p. 24; and "Stanzas from the Grande Chartreuse," lines 191–92.

36. Brotherton MS., Jane Arnold, to her aunts at Coleby, posted September 2, 1838.

37. Ibid., postscript in Mrs. Arnold's hand; also Brotherton MSS., Jane to her aunts, April 8, 1840, and Mrs. Arnold to her sisters, November 30, 1838.

38. Brotherton MSS., Mrs. Arnold to her sisters, November 30, 1838, and December 19, 1839.

39. Brotherton MS., Mrs. Arnold to her sisters, December 24, 1838.

40. "The Roman or the Graecian Page," lines 51–53. In an 1853 notebook of M.A.'s

juvenile verses, a transcript of the poem is followed by: *"Age 15 years & 7 months.* July 10th 1838. *Matt Arnold."*

41. "Land of the East! Around thy shores are flung," lines 13–14, 27–28.

42. Diary of Henry Crabb Robinson (Dr. Williams's Library transcript), December 27, 1835; and T.A.'s "So eighteen hundred years have fled away," lines 31–32, 64, dated November 15, 1829, in Mrs. Mary Arnold's Journals, I.

43. Composed December 30, 1838.

44. *Fox How Magazine* MS.

45. Brotherton MS. notebook, December 21, 1838.

46. *Letters of Mary Wordsworth 1800–1855,* ed. Mary E. Burton (Oxford, 1958), p. 214.

47. "The Youth of Nature," lines 99–102.

48. Alexander Turnbull Library MS. (Moorman transcript), Mrs. Arnold to her son Tom, January 27, 1848; Brotherton MS., Mrs. Arnold's Journals, II, June 1839.

49. Frederick Sessions, *Literary Celebrities of the Lake District* (London, 1905), p. 213; Thomas Arnold, *Passages* (London, 1900), p. 47.

50. See "Maurice de Guérin" and "Byron."

51. *The Times,* November 2, 1891; Brotherton MS., Mrs. Arnold, "Saturday morning" [December 1839].

52. Thomas Hughes, *Memoir of a Brother* (London, 1873), p. 33.

53. Ibid.

54. Brotherton MSS., T.A.'s Rugby notebooks of 1838–40. M.A. was examined by his father in Plutarch, Price in Plato's *Crito,* Buckoll in "Hebrew," e.g.—and seemed to his parents to look better *on paper* than he was, for they measured a banal Sixth in 1839 and 1840 against a dazzling, earlier Sixth Form of Stanley, Lake, Vaughan, Greenhill, and other bright, hard-working boys. M.A.'s 13 "LATE"s (almost breaking a tardiness record) in autumn 1840 were symptomatic of his cavalier, lazy attitude. A Sixth-Form chart for a first half-year shows M.A. with a bad 10 in Greek Verse (Lushington 24, Walrond major 21, Hughes 20). His marks in German (200 out of 300), French (140 out of 200), and Latin Prose (120 as against Doxat's 140) were not exceptional; but that in Latin Verse (125) was second highest in the form. Latin Verse saved him. One "total" for M.A. of 476 (Doxat 530, Lushington 505, Bradley 403, Hughes 395) kept him just inside the upper quarter of his class. He is listed as "Arnold" in years when he was the only Arnold in the Sixth.

55. Brotherton MSS., Mrs. Arnold, April 30, 1840, and May 29, 1840; Mary Fletcher, quoted by E. K. Chambers, *Matthew Arnold* (New York, 1947), p. 5.

56. *Letters of M.A.,* II, 28 (to his mother, December 13, 1869).

57. "The Church of England," Super, VIII, 65.

58. An Old Boy [Thomas Hughes], *Tom Brown's Schooldays* (London, 1862), p. 105—first published on April 24, 1857. Hughes's Crab resembles "Crab Arnold" in belonging to School House, playing a little football, and being cool, self-possessed, untroubled. Hughes was in M.A.'s form and heard "Crab" in use at Fox How; but it may be that only T.A. and George Cotton are positively identifiable in this classic novel of Rugby School in the 1830s, "though various suggestions have been made." See E. C. Mack and W. H. G. Armytage, *Thomas Hughes* (London, 1952), p. 94. If applicable, Thomas Hughes's portrait of Crab Jones carries an exuberant Christian Socialist's rebuke of M.A., who preferred Thomas's brother George.

59. W. H. D. Rouse, *A History of Rugby School* (London, 1898), p. 265. M.A. was low down in the school cricket team, but played "Bat Fives" well and liked it; see *Manchester Guardian,* May 18, 1888.

60. Quoted in N. Wymer, *Dr. Arnold* (London, 1953), p. 186.

61. See Brotherton MSS., Mrs. Arnold, "Wednesday night"; December 8, 1839; and May 15, 1840. Queen Adelaide visited the school on October 15, 1839.

62. Brotherton MSS., March 15 and March 29, 1840.

63. March 5, 1840.

64. F. A. Mignet, *History of the French Revolution* (London, 1846), p. 387.

65. Ibid., pp. 313, 408.

66. *M.A. to A.H.C.,* pp. 142–43 (September 6 [1853]).

67. See Brotherton MSS., Mrs. Arnold, April 8, 1840, and "Wednesday night" [April 1840].

68. Balliol MS., December 20, 1864.

69. Margaret Woods, "Matthew Arnold," *Essays and Studies by Members of the English Association,* XV (1929), 9; E. C. Mack and W. H. G. Armytage, *Thomas Hughes* (London, 1952), chap. 2.

70. Brotherton MS., Mrs. Arnold to her sisters, January 25, 1840.

71. Lines 24, 47–48, 53–54.

72. Lines 169–72.

73. Lines 200, 213, 215.

74. See *Poems,* ed. Allott, p. 3.

75. Brotherton MS., posted May 15, 1840.

76. Brotherton MS., June 16, 1840. For Mrs. Arnold, prizes were a mark of seriousness and promise; for M.A., a means of getting prestige and money. A Rugby Exhibition, or a Balliol Scholarship, paid one for being at university; and the latter carried much prestige. (Schools sent candidates to Oxford to compete in examinations there for the Balliol.) Keeping his eye on prizes, M.A. won something each year at Rugby School. In 1838 he won the Fifth-Form Prize for Latin Verse (on "Dissipatae religiosorum societates, direptae domus") and Second Prize for Latin Prose. On May 25, 1839, T.A. noted: "Eng. Verse decided.—Lushington.—Prizes, Walrond, Hughes, & Matt." (Brotherton notebook). In 1840, he won the Sixth's Prize for English Verse (for "Alaric"), the English Essay Prize (for "Europe in the Sixteenth and Seventeenth Centuries compared"), and a token prize for fourth place in the Exhibitions; see R. H. Super, in *Notes and Queries,* CC (1955), 357. Typical subjects for Exhibition examinations were Aristophanes' *Birds,* Aristotle's *Politics,* Cicero's *De Oratore,* and "Europe from 1640 to 1715" (T.A. notebook for 1839). In 1841, M.A. was elected an Exhibitioner and shared prizes for Latin Prose and Latin Verse. Franklin Lushington (and others) won the Greek prizes.

77. Brotherton MS., December 8, 1839.

78. Brotherton MS., August 30 [1840].

79. Jane Arnold to her brother Tom, November 23, 1849, quoting an earlier letter from M.A.

80. Quoted in *Memorials of William Charles Lake,* ed. Katharine Lake (London, 1901), p. 161 (August 17, 1840).

81. Bodleian MS. Eng. lett. c.189 fol. 212, to Burbridge, November 22 [1840].

82. December 5, 1840. See J. P. Curgenven, "Matthew Arnold in Two Scholarship Examinations," *Review of English Studies*, XXII (1946), 54–55.

83. Quoted by N. Wymer, *Dr. Arnold* (London, 1953), p. 186.

84. Leon Gottfried, *Matthew Arnold and the Romantics* (London, 1963), p. 210.

85. Brotherton MS., T.A. to his sister Frances, Bayonne, July 12, 1841.

86. Brotherton MS., T.A. "Tours, July 5th [1841]."

87. *Manchester Guardian,* May 18, 1888. Success in the Exhibition would depend on more than one translation—see note 76, above, for typical essay and translation topics. Six Exhibitioners were elected at Rugby in 1841; M.A. came in second, and was awarded £60 per annum for Oxford. For emoluments of the Balliol Scholarship (reckoned at about £30 by Archdeacon Palmer), see E. Abbott and L. Campbell, *The Life of Benjamin Jowett* (London, 1897), I, 103.

Chapter 3. Gardens of Oxford, 1841–1842, pp. 48–63.

Epigraph: Preface to *Essays in Criticism,* 1865 (Super, III, 290).

1. H. W. Carless Davis, *A History of Balliol College,* revised by R. H. C. Davis and Richard Hunt (Oxford, 1963), p. 33.

2. E. Abbott and L. Campbell, *Benjamin Jowett* (London, 1897), I, 39.

3. R. E. Prothero and G. G. Bradley, *Arthur Penrhyn Stanley* (London, 1894), I, 297; K. Chorley, *Arthur Hugh Clough* (Oxford, 1962), p. 86.

4. Prothero and Bradley, I, 342.

5. Abbott and Campbell, I, 63n; and *Memoirs of Archbishop Temple,* by Seven Friends, ed. E. G. Sandford (London, 1906), II, 412.

6. *Manchester Guardian,* May 18, 1888.

7. *The George Eliot Letters,* ed. Gordon S. Haight (London, 1956), VIII, 20; and Mulhauser, I, 114 (November 10, 1841).

8. Thomas Arnold, *Passages in a Wandering Life* (London, 1900), p. 55.

9. Brotherton MS., Rugby, November 5, 1841.

10. Edward Walford, in *M.A. to A.H.C.,* pp. 23–24.

11. Prothero and Bradley, *Stanley* (London, 1894), I, 359.

12. Balliol College MS., Master's Examination Register or "Master's Book." For each of the three Oxford terms—Michaelmas, Lent (later Hilary), and Easter and Act (later Trinity)—the Master commented on each student under "Morals" and noted texts assigned. Some tutors may have assigned additional texts; see Warren Anderson on the "Undergraduate Syllabus" in *Arnoldian,* VI (Winter 1979), 2–6.

13. "Master's Book"; Abbott and Campbell, *Jowett,* I, 59; E. H. Coleridge, *Coleridge,* I, 101; and *M.A. to A.H.C.,* p. 142.

14. Fox How, "Saturday morning" [August 1842].

15. Kathleen Tillotson, " 'Yes: in the Sea of Life,' " *Review of English Studies,* N.S. III (1952), 351.

16. R. T. Davidson and W. Benham, *Life of Archibald Campbell Tait* (London, 1891), I, 72.

17. "Bishop Butler and the Zeit-Geist" and "A Guide to English Literature," Super, VIII, 12 and 237.

18. *Review of English Studies,* N.S. III (1952), 350–51.

19. *Manchester Guardian,* May 18, 1888.

20. Jane wrote for the family:

> *Eau de Mille Fleurs, Eau de Cologne and twenty eaux beside*
> *Rowland's Odonto, scented soaps, jostle his books aside.*

21. For the ubiquity of A. Rowland & Sons' notices see John W. Dodds, *The Age of Paradox* (London, 1953), p. 16.

22. Balliol MS., "Sunday" [c. June 1844].

23. J. P. Curgenven, "Matthew Arnold in Two Scholarship Examinations," *Review of English Studies,* XXII (1946), 55–56. M.A. sat for the Hertford Latin Scholarship on March 7, 1842.

24. Brotherton MS., T.A. to Frances Buckland, December 7, 1841.

25. Prothero and Bradley, *Stanley* (London, 1894), I, 308.

26. Thomas Arnold, *Introductory Lectures on Modern History* (Oxford, 1842); Prothero and Bradley, I, 308; and M.A. quoted by Super, V, 436 (November 18, 1865).

27. "The Incursion: A Dramatic Fragment," lines 10–11, 34–35, 40–43, 19, 23.

28. See *Poems,* ed. Allott, p. 573n.

29. Lines 148–50, 162. For T.A.'s health, see Brotherton MS., Mrs. Arnold, March 15, 1840.

30. T.A. recorded for February 2, 1842: "Breakfasted with Crab.—Beautiful walk with Lake, Didu, Widu, & K. to Shotover & Home by Bullington.—Dined in Hall at Oriel, & met Newman" (Brotherton MS.); for Newman's account, see Meriol Trevor, *Newman: The Pillar and the Cloud* (London, 1962), pp. 263–65.

31. E. H. Coleridge, *John Duke Lord Coleridge* (London, 1904), I, 91.

32. Ibid., I, 81.

33. Ibid., I, 155. The friend was C. E. Prichard.

34. *Memoirs of Archbishop Temple,* ed. E. G. Sandford (London, 1906), II, 457.

35. M.A. began to shock his family with slang at age eight; see the *Times,* April 17, 1888. The Yale holograph shows wavy lines and six exclamations dancing around "Shite's." See *M.A. to A.H.C.,* pp. 60, 56, 81, 86, and 115.

36. David J. DeLaura, "Matthew Arnold and John Henry Newman: The 'Oxford Sentiment' and the Religion of the Future," *Texas Studies in Literature and Language,* VI Supp. (1965), 690–92. M.A.'s words are in "Emerson," written October–November 1883 (Super, X, 165).

37. Rev. T. Mozley, *Reminiscences, Chiefly of Oriel College and the Oxford Movement* (London, 1882), II, 48; and Rev. W. Tuckwell, *Reminiscences of Oxford* (London, 1900), p. 184.

38. Quoted by Lady Chorley, *Clough* (Oxford, 1962), pp. 44–45.

39. Balliol MS., "Balliol, Sunday" [c. June 1844].

40. Lines 36–40. Newman did not speak in an Anglican church after September 1843.

41. See "Literary Influence of Academies," Super, III, 244, 250; and *Letters,* ed. Whitridge, pp. 65–66 (M.A. to Newman, May 28, 1872).

42. Stanley, *Life*, p. 462.

43. Balliol MS., June 14, 1862.

44. Quoted by Charles R. Moyer, "Matthew Arnold and His Father," diss. University of Kansas, 1958, p. 18.

45. *Times*, December 1, 1884.

46. Prothero and Bradley, *Stanley* (London, 1894), I, 312.

47. *Memorials of William Charles Lake*, ed. K. Lake (London, 1901), pp. 163–64.

48. Ibid., p. 164.

49. Fox How, "Saturday morning" [August 1842].

Chapter 4. Very Select Company, 1843–1845, pp. 64–80.

Epigraph: "Thyrsis," line 104.

1. *Letters*, ed. Bertram, p. 155; *Letters of M.A.*, II, 31; and Lady Chorley, *Clough* (Oxford, 1962), p. 123.

2. Mulhauser, I, 94; and Bodleian MS. Eng. lett. d. 177 fol. 11, September 14, 1851.

3. C. and F. Brookfield, *Mrs. Brookfield and Her Circle* (London, 1906), p. 294; F. J. Woodward, *The Doctor's Disciples* (Oxford, 1954), p. 137; *M.A. to A.H.C.*, p. 130 (February 12, 1853); and Bodleian MS. Eng. Lett. e. 77 fol. 1, Dec. 30, 1851.

4. Chauncy Hare Townshend, *Mesmerism Proved True, and the Quarterly Reviewer Reviewed* (London, 1854), pp. 62–63.

5. Yale MS. (Tinker 21).

6. Bodleian MS. Eng. lett. e. 77 fols. 17–18, Clough to Miss Smith; and *M.A. to A.H.C.*, p. 173 (December 5, 1851).

7. Bodleian MS. Eng. poet. d. 120 fol. 26 (1847 notebook).

8. *Dipsychus*, IX, 107–110.

9. *Amours de Voyage*, Canto II, 83–85, 252–56, 262–65, 272–75.

10. Lady Chorley, *Clough* (Oxford, 1962), p. 234; *M.A. to A.H.C.*, p. 130 (February 12, 1853).

11. M.A. to his brother Tom, May 15, 1857, quoted by Mrs. H. Ward, *Recollections* (London, 1918), p. 54.

12. Margaret Woods, "Matthew Arnold," *Essays and Studies by Members of the English Association*, XV (1929), 18–19; Lady Chorley, *Clough* (Oxford, 1962), p. 141.

13. Mrs. Ward, *Recollections* (London, 1918), p. 54. Properly the farm is "Chilswell"; but it is "Childsworth" in the Ordnance map of 1830 and for Arnold.

14. Lady Chorley, *Clough* (Oxford, 1962), pp. 141–42; "The Scholar-Gipsy," lines 16–18, 22–28, 30.

15. *Publii Virgilii Maronis Opera: Notis ex Editione Heyniana Excerptis* (London, 1839). The copy inscribed "M. Arnold Ball: Coll: 1843" has notes in M.A.'s hand chiefly in Book IV of the *Georgics* (courtesy of the Rev. John Leonard Miller of New York); this copy was probably given to M.A. by his family's friend, Christian Bunsen, who had known the philologist and editor of Virgil, Heyne, in Göttingen. See the interesting essay by Robert O. Preyer, "The Dream of Spiritualized Learning and Its Early Enthusiasts: German, British and American," in *Geschichte*

und Gesellschaft in der amerikanischen Literatur, heraus. von K. Schubert und U. Müller-Richter (Heidelberg, 1974), p. 67.

16. Virgil, *Aeneid,* II, 61; Bodleian MS. Eng. lett. c. 190 fol. 137 [August 1847]; and "In Utrumque Paratus," lines 15–21. M.A.'s poem contrasts Plotinian and evolutionary views of the origins of human consciousness.

17. Lines 143–45.

18. March 11, 1843, quoted by E. H. Coleridge, *Lord Coleridge* (London, 1904), I, 125.

19. In The Decade, M.A. was accused of flippancy, and of failing to appear when he was supposed to defend the poetry of Wordsworth against the idea that "Alfred Tennyson is the greatest poet of the age." Clough spoke gravely, at one meeting, on the concept of the "gentleman" from its medieval origins. Other members included Stanley, Shairp, Riddell, Blackett, Conington, and J. D. Coleridge, who helped to get M.A. into the club: "Matt, you must make a speech." "Why, I never did such a thing in my life." See *Memoirs of Temple,* ed. E. G. Sandford (London, 1906), II, 453; and A. Dwight Culler, *Imaginative Reason* (New Haven and London, 1967), pp. 85–86.

20. *Memoirs of Temple,* ed. Sandford, I, 81.

21. Brotherton MSS., Notebook of Laura Ward, and Mrs. Arnold, December 5, 1839.

22. Kathleen Tillotson, "Matthew Arnold and Carlyle," *Proceedings of the British Academy,* XLII (1956), 139; Prothero and Bradley, *Stanley* (London, 1894), I, 45.

23. E. H. Coleridge, *Lord Coleridge* (London, 1904), I, 124.

24. "Cromwell," lines 79, 81–82, 89–92.

25. Lines 219, 221–24; K. Tillotson, "Matthew Arnold and Carlyle," *Proceedings,* XLII (1956), 140.

26. Brotherton MS. notebook, June 13, 1842; and Mrs. Arnold to Gell, quoted by F. Woodward, *Disciples* (Oxford, 1954), p. 182.

27. See F. Woodward, *Disciples* (Oxford, 1954), p. 185 (May 9, 1847); and Brotherton MS. notebook, September 1867.

28. E. H. Coleridge, *Lord Coleridge* (London, 1904), I, 129 (Hawker to J. D. Coleridge, July 3, 1843).

29. Ibid., I, 129n.

30. Ibid., I, 145–46 (July 29 [1844]).

31. Mulhauser, I, 141 (Clough to Gell, November 24, 1844); I, 249 (Clough to Hawkins, March 3 [1849]).

32. *Letters,* ed. Bertram, pp. 210, 209, 211.

33. Balliol MS., "Balliol, Sunday."

34. Stanley, *Life,* p. 273.

35. David Gordon Osborne, Jr., *Matthew Arnold, 1843–1849: A Study of the Yale Manuscript,* diss. University of Rochester (1963), pp. 68–69; and *Poems,* ed. Allott, p. 45.

36. *M.A. to A.H.C.,* p. 131 (February 12–13, 1853).

37. Ibid., p. 110 (September 23 [1849]).

38. R. H. Super, "Emerson and Arnold's Poetry," *Philological Quarterly,* XXXIII (1954), 396–403.

39. Mulhauser, I, 129 (July 13 [1844]).

40. Ibid., I, 131 [July 21, 1844]; I, 135 (July 31, 1844).

41. George Butler, "Reminiscences of the Lakes in 1844," *Longman's Magazine,* XII (1888), 623–25.

42. E. H. Coleridge, *Lord Coleridge* (London, 1904), I, 146; and David J. DeLaura, "A Background for Arnold's 'Shakespeare,'" in *Nineteenth-Century Literary Perspectives: Essays in Honor of Lionel Stevenson,* ed. C. de L. Ryals (Durham, N.C., 1973), pp. 129–48.

43. See Mulhauser, I, 137–38, 146; and Abbott and Campbell, *Jowett* (London, 1897), I, 80n. Some constraint in Oxford's intellectual atmosphere between *Tract 90* (1841) and Ward's degradation (1844) helped to ensure M.A.'s poor result in finals or "Schools"; and no doubt the Schools were dull, as examinations go: "Clough failed [i.e. achieved only a Second Class in May 1841] because he looked for more meaning in the questions than they were intended to have," wrote Temple at the time. Clough, perhaps, knew too much; M.A., who devoted three weeks to three years' reading assignments, knew too little. His downfall was swift. He began paperwork on November 13, orals on November 18; his Second Class result was announced on November 29, 1844.

44. Balliol MS., to Trevenen Penrose, April 8 [1845]. M.A. in February 1845 replaced Algernon Grenfell, who died March 6; Richard Congreve replaced M.A. in April on Rugby's staff.

45. *M.A. to A.H.C.,* p. 113.

46. See Kathleen Tillotson, "Rugby 1850: Arnold, Clough, Walrond, and *In Memoriam,*" *Review of British Studies,* IV, 122–125.

47. Margaret Woods in *Essays and Studies by Members of the English Association,* XV (1929), 8.

48. M.A.'s reading list for the Oriel examination included Kant's *Critique of Pure Reason,* two books of Mill's *Logic* (which Clough liked) Plato's *Republic* and *Phaedrus,* Augustine's *In Johannis Evangelium Tractatus,* Descartes's *Méthode,* and Berkeley's *Siris* and *Dialogues.* "It will be no loss to your mind," William Lake told an Oriel candidate. "Scholarship and some Metaphysics, versus knowledge" and the electors "are influenced more than they acknowledge to themselves by other things than the examination." M.A.'s election owed to his "power of writing" and to his being the son of J. H. Newman's antagonist, especially since the Oriel Provost was trying to rid the air of Newmanism in 1845. See *Temple,* ed. E. G. Sandford (London, 1906), I, 88; *Lake,* ed. K. Lake (London, 1901), pp. 187–88; and K. Allott, "Reading-Lists in Three Early Diaries," *Victorian Studies,* II (1959), 258.

Chapter 5. An Oriel Fellow "in the Depths of the Sea," 1845–1847, pp. 81–113.

Epigraphs: Yale MS. (Tinker 21).

1. Balliol MS., to Trevenen Penrose, April 8 [1845].

2. Wordsworth MS., extract from Mrs. Mary Arnold to Miss Trevenen, April 2, 1845.

3. Yale University MS., Diary of 1846.

4. See Austin Duncan-Jones, *Butler's Moral Philosophy* (Portway, Bath, 1969).

5. Rev. W. Tuckwell, *Reminiscences of Oxford* (London, 1900), p. 193; and G. C. Richards, "Oriel College and the Oxford Movement," *Nineteenth Century,* CXIII (1933), 728.

6. C. Kegan Paul, *Memories* (London, 1899), p. 144.

7. Quoted by G. C. Richards, "Oriel College," *Nineteenth Century,* CXIII (1933), 727, 729.

8. W. Tuckwell, *Reminiscences* (London, 1900), p. 190; Mulhauser, I, 117 (to Gell, April 17 [1842]).

9. *M.A. to A.H.C.,* p. 59.

10. Yale MS. (Tinker 21). Most of M.A.'s notes, on 37 sheets now at Yale, were jotted between 1843 and 1856; many relate to his poems and reading lists of the late 1840s. For help in interpreting the notes, I am indebted to Professor S. O. A. Ullmann and to his "Editing Yale's Tinker 21," *Arnoldian,* III (1975), 6–9, as well as to K. Allott, "Three Early Diaries," *Victorian Studies,* II (1959), 254–66, and D. G. Osborne, Jr., *Matthew Arnold, 1843–1849: A Study of the Yale Manuscript,* diss. University of Rochester (1963).

11. Diary of 1846.

12. Yale MS. (Tinker 21).

13. Ibid.

14. "Stanzas from the Grande Chartreuse," lines 67, 69–70, 73–75, 77–78.

15. Yale MS. (Tinker 21).

16. Quoted by Walter Benjamin, *Illuminations,* ed. Hannah Arendt (London, 1973), p. 179.

17. Preface to *Essays in Criticism* (1865); Super, III, 290.

18. Brotherton MS., T.A. to M.A., October 18, 1831.

19. E. H. Coleridge, *Lord Coleridge* (London, 1904), I, 124 (Fox How, March 2, 1843).

20. Ibid.

21. Yale MS. (Tinker 21).

22. *M.A. to A.H.C.,* p. 110 (September 23 [1849]).

23. Tom Arnold, in *Manchester Guardian,* May 18, 1888; see *Poems,* ed. Allott, p. 22.

24. Lines 2–3, 17–18.

25. Yale MS. (Tinker 21).

26. "To a Gipsy Child by the Sea-shore: Douglas, Isle of Man," lines 29–32, 37–38, 39, 53–56.

27. "Matthew Arnold's Summer Holiday," *English,* VI (1946), 77–81.

28. "The Forsaken Merman," lines 30–32, 35–36, 38–45.

29. Ibid., lines 50–53, 106–107, 77–79, 83–86.

30. See page 88.

31. "The Forsaken Merman," lines 114–123, 139–143.

32. Balliol MS., February 11, 1863.

33. Balliol MSS., October 15, 1830 and February 29, 1832; Brotherton MSS., October 18, 1831; January 3 and March 21, 1832; September 17, 1838.

34. See page 8.

35. F. Schiller, *Works* London, 1879), VI, 273–74.

36. R. T. Clark, *Herder* (Berkeley and Los Angeles, 1955), p. 399. M.A., at the end of his 1845 diary, cited Herder's *Metakritik zur Kritik der reinen Vernunft* (1799), which

expresses hostility to Kant at once: "One does not 'criticize' a faculty of the human mind; instead one defines, delimits it, shows its use and misuse" (see J. G. Herder, *Sammtliche Werke,* ed. B. Suphan et al. [Berlin, 1877–1913], XXI, 2).

37. See Ralph Cudworth, D.D., *The True Intellectual System of the Universe,* ed. Thomas Birch (London, 1820), I, 55; and Edward Stillingfleet, D.D., *Origines Sacrae* (Oxford, 1836), II, 465.

38. Plutarch, "On Isis and Osiris."

39. *M.A. to A.H.C.,* p. 59 [1845 or 1846].

40. "Matthew Arnold," *Manchester Guardian,* May 18, 1888.

41. J. P. Eckermann, *Conversations with Goethe,* trans. John Oxenford (London, 1930), p. 103.

42. *M.A. to A.H.C.,* p. 59 [1845 or 1846].

43. Lines 51–55.

44. Lines 22–24, 37–40.

45. See René Wellek, *Immanuel Kant in England* (Princeton, 1931), pp. 154–56.

46. J. P. Eckermann, *Conversations with Goethe,* trans. Oxenford (London, 1930), p. 205; and see E. D. Hirsch, Jr., *Wordsworth and Schelling: A Typological Study of Romanticism* (New Haven, 1960), p. 131.

47. E. Abbott and L. Campbell, *Jowett* (London, 1897), I, 90.

48. "La Philosophie Allemande: des derniers travaux sur Kant, Fichte, Schelling et Hegel," *Revue des Deux Mondes* (1846), I, 311–12.

49. Yale MS. (Tinker 21).

50. Ibid.

51. Reading lists in M.A.'s Diaries of 1845 and 1847 (Yale); and see R. T. Clark, *Herder* (Berkeley and Los Angeles, 1955), p. 330.

52. F. W. J. Schelling, "Concerning the Relation of the Plastic Arts to Nature," trans. M. Bullock, in Herbert Read, *The True Voice of Feeling* (London, 1953), p. 341.

53. *M.A. to A.H.C.,* pp. 59, 143.

54. Schelling, "Concerning the Relation of the Plastic Arts," trans. M. Bullock, in Read, *The True Voice* (London, 1953), pp. 341, 345–47.

55. "To George Cruikshank, Esq. on seeing for the first time his picture of 'The Bottle,' in the country."

56. Balliol MS., 1837 Travel Journal.

57. *M.A. to A.H.C.,* p. 99 [February 1849].

58. J. C. L. Simonde de Sismondi, *Études sur les Constitutions des Peuples Libres* (Paris, 1836), pp. 1, 135.

59. See "In Utrumque Paratus," lines 8, 11–14; and G. Robert Stange, *Matthew Arnold: The Poet as Humanist* (Princeton, 1967), pp. 118–26.

60. See Victor Cousin, *Cours de l'histoire de la philosophie, histoire de la philosophie du xviiie siècle* (Paris, 1829), II, 230–35; M.A. in 1846 knew one or both of the attacks upon Cousin by the Abbe V. Gioberti (*La Panthéisme de M. Cousin* [1842] and *Considérations* [1844]). One cannot be sure that he finished reading W. von Humboldt's "Über die unter dem Namen Bhagavad-Gita bekannte Episode des Mahá-Bhárata." It occurs three times in his Oriel reading lists.

61. Yale MS. (Tinker 21).

62. *M.A. to A.H.C.,* pp. 71 and 69 [March 1848].

63. Yale MS. (Tinker 21).

64. Ibid.

65. Ibid.

66. Ibid.

67. See Clough's " 'Blank Misgivings . . .,' " V, 1–4, 13–16; VI, 1–3; VII, 7.

68. See Stanley, *Life,* p. 239 (to Stanley, March 4, 1835), and pp. 97, 387.

69. MS. Diaries of Anne Jemima Clough, June 1845.

70. Ibid., April 1849.

71. Ibid., n.d.

72. Balliol MS. [c. 1850].

73. Balliol MS., "London, Friday" [c. January 1851].

74. Quoted by Mary Arnold-Forster, *The Right Honourable Hugh Oakeley Arnold-Forster, A Memoir* (London, 1910), p. 140.

75. Curtis Cate, *George Sand* (Boston, 1975), chap. 17; A. Maurois, *Lélia* (London, 1953), p. 171; *Letters of M.A.,* I, 123 (August 21, 1859).

76. Mulhauser, I, 159 (October 27 [1845]).

77. George Sand, *Jacques,* nouvelle édition (Paris, 1900), partie xxix, p. 142.

78. *Lélia,* nouvelle édition (Paris, 1900), partie xviii, p. 67.

79. "George Sand" (1877); Super, VIII, 220.

80. *Lélia,* nouvelle édition (Paris, 1900), partie lxvii, p. 161.

81. "George Sand," Super, VIII, 221.

82. *Lélia,* nouvelle édition (Paris, 1900), partie xxv, p. 108.

83. Ibid., partie xiv, p. 56.

84. "George Sand," Super, VIII, 217.

85. Ibid.; and Diary of 1846.

86. "In Utrumque Paratus," lines 16, 18–19.

87. "George Sand," Super, VIII, 217.

88. Diary of 1846.

89. "George Sand," Super, VIII, 217–18.

90. *Letters of M.A.,* II, 151 [June 11, 1876].

91. See Chapter 1.

92. *Letters,* ed. Whitridge, p. 18 [c. July 1849].

93. Yale MS. (Tinker 21).

94. Bodleian MS. Eng. lett. c. 190 fol. 52, J. C. Shairp [September 1846]. M.A. was at Rugby from September 3 to October 17, 1846.

95. "The French Play in London" (1879), Super, IX, 65.

96. Quoted by John W. Dodds, *The Age of Paradox* (London, 1953), p. 47.

97. *M.A. to A.H.C.,* p. 81 [May 24, 1848].

98. See "A Courteous Explanation" (1866), Super, V, 34.

99. John W. Dodds, *The Age of Paradox* (London, 1953), p. 48. In Paris, M.A. saw Rachel in Racine's *Phédre* and *Andromaque* and in Corneille's *Horace, Cinna, Le Cid,* and *Don Sanche D'Aragon,* as well as in *Marie Stuart,* Lebrun's version of Schiller (Diaries of 1846 and 1847).

100. See *Poems,* ed. Allott, p. 485.

101. Jean-Marie Carre, *Michelet et Son Temps* (Paris, 1926), pp. 180–81.

102. Eckermann, *Conversations,* trans. J. Oxenford (London, 1930), p. 201. For Goethe's influence, see James Simpson, *M.A. and Goethe* (London, 1979).

103. Bodleian MSS. Eng. lett. c. 190 fols. 80, 78, Clough to Shairp [February 22, 1847] and to Anne Clough [February 15, 1847].

104. Mulhauser, I, 181 (April 18 [1847]).

105. Brotherton MS., October 17, 1847.

106. Clough's report of "Sunday, May 3rd 1846" about "Matt's inspectorship" is not misdated (Bodleian MS. c. 190 fol. 22), but it is overlooked by Mulhauser.

107. M.A. vacillated over the secretaryship; but he had spoken with his future employer as early as February 27, 1847. He served as Lord Lansdowne's private secretary from April 2, 1847, to April 15, 1851 (Diaries).

108. Mulhauser, I, 181 ("Oriel, Sunday 18th" [April 1847]).

Chapter 6. Discoveries in London, 1847–1848, pp. 114–143.

Epigraph: *Poems,* ed. Allott, p. 579.

1. Yale MS. (Tinker 21).

2. *M.A. to A.H.C.,* p. 128 (February 12, 1853); Yale MS. (Tinker 21).

3. The *Lucretius* fragment dates from either c. 1846–49 or c. 1855–56; *Poems,* ed. Allott, pp. 587–88.

4. *M.A. to A.H.C.,* pp. 65 [December 1847], 97 [c. 1848–49].

5. For a typical concert at Lansdowne House see Charles Lacaita, *An Italian Englishman: Sir James Lacaita, K.C.M.G. 1813–1895* (London, 1933), p. 87.

6. See "Index of Ministers" in Chris Cook and Brenan Keith, *British Historical Facts, 1830–1900* (London, 1975), and N. G. Annan, "The Intellectual Aristocracy," in *Studies in Social History,* ed. J. H. Plumb (London, 1955), pp. 243–87.

7. Mulhauser, I, 306 (February 12 [1852]).

8. Charles Lacaita, *Sir James Lacaita* (London, 1933), p. 84.

9. Ibid., p. 130; *M.A. to A.H.C.,* p. 60 [late 1847].

10. Evelyn Abbott and Lewis Campbell, *Life and Letters of Benjamin Jowett* (London, 1897), I, 158.

11. John Prest, *Lord John Russell* (London, 1972), p. 225. Lord Lansdowne was not inhumane and his views on state-sponsored education were ahead of his time; he had, however, a weak grasp of economic theory, as Miss Martineau rightly said, and much influence on the Prime Minister (who distributed extracts from Adam Smith to Irish delegations). Lansdowne's holdings amounted to the second-largest landed property in Ireland; and his advice on Ireland counted. He believed (as did other conservative Whigs) that the government's famine-relief funds would dry up the flow of help to Ireland from the charities. The facts remain that Lansdowne

predicted, early in 1847, one million deaths in Ireland and kept arguing for cuts in famine relief.

12. M.A. had seen Lord Lansdowne on February 27, 1847; Jowett, who had heard accounts of the starvation at Skibbereen, on March 10 repeated Lansdowne's prediction of "1,000,000" deaths to Ralph Lingen (who was joining the education office), and added that he had heard it from Arnold and that a small fraction of the gross national income might save the Irish. Jowett, Blackett, and Temple were among Balliol friends of M.A. who were appalled by the Whigs' Irish policy. See E. Abbott and L. Campbell, *Jowett* (London, 1897), I, 158. Irish deaths from famine and related causes in the period July 1846 to July 1848 (including 14 months when M.A. worked for Lansdowne) totaled between nine and ten hundred thousand.

13. "Horatian Echo (To an Ambitious Friend)," lines 10–21.

14. *M.A. to A.H.C.*, p. 78 [April 1848].

15. Ibid., p. 68 [March 1, 1848].

16. "The Buried Life," lines 57–60.

17. "Matthew Arnold," By One Who Knew Him Well [Tom Arnold], *Manchester Guardian*, May 18, 1888.

18. *M.A. to A.H.C.*, p. 60 [late 1847].

19. See Charles Lacaita, *James Lacaita* (London, 1933), p. 102; and "Lansdowne House" in Victorian editions of Baedeker's *London*.

20. Quoted by Mrs. Humphry Ward, *A Writer's Recollections* (London, 1918), pp. 48–49 (February 8, 1848).

21. Thomas Arnold, *History of Rome* (London, 1838), I, 6. M.A.'s copy is in the biographer's possession.

22. MS., Baron Bunsen to Mrs. Mary Arnold, April 28, 1847.

23. *Manchester Guardian*, May 18, 1888.

24. *Letters*, ed. Bertram, p. 2; *M.A. to A.H.C.*, p. 81.

25. *Letters*, ed. Bertram, p. 1 (April 16 [1847]).

26. *Manchester Guardian*, May 18, 1888.

27. *Letters*, ed. Bertram, p. 9 (October 9, 1847).

28. William T. Arnold, "Thomas Arnold the Younger," *The Century Magazine*, LXVI (1903), 120; and Bodleian MS. Eng. lett. c. 190 fol. 153.

29. Balliol MSS., August 19, 1852, and May 10, 1851.

30. Quoted by Mrs. Humphry Ward, *Recollections* (London, 1918), p. 66.

31. Dr. Williams's Library MS., Diary of Henry Crabb Robinson, June 19, 1847.

32. *M.A. to A.H.C.*, p. 36 [shortly after December 6, 1847].

33. Ibid.

34. Balliol MS., January 2, [1848].

35. See the notes to Chapter 7.

36. Balliol MS., M.A. to his sister Jane, with a draft of "Written in Kensington Gardens."

37. "Fragment of an 'Antigone,'" lines 17–23.

38. Lines 3, 28–32.

39. Lines 97–98, 103.

40. *Poems,* ed. Allott, pp. 578–79.

41. Ibid., p. 579.

42. Yale MS. (Tinker 21).

43. Bodleian MS. Eng. lett. c. 190 fol. 34, Shairp to Clough [August 1846].

44. Quoted by Frances Woodward, *Disciples* (Oxford, 1954), p. 200 (December 19, 1852).

45. New York University Library MS., January 24, 1885.

46. William E. Buckler, *Matthew Arnold's Books: Toward a Publishing Diary* (Geneva and Paris, 1958), p. 97 [c. September 1, 1875].

47. *M.A. to A.H.C.,* p. 105 [March 1849]; and "The New Sirens," lines 33–34, 81–85.

48. *M.A. to A.H.C.,* pp. 105–106.

49. "The New Sirens," lines 93–104.

50. Lines 105–109, 112–14, 119–30.

51. *M.A. to A.H.C.,* p. 106.

52. Yale MS. (Tinker 21).

53. "To the Reverend Memory of Thomas Arnold, D.D.," in *Ambarvalia: Poems by Thomas Burbidge and Arthur H. Clough.*

54. *M.A. to A.H.C.,* p. 61 [early December 1847].

55. Ibid., p. 63 [shortly after December 6, 1847].

56. Ibid., p. 99 [early February 1849].

57. Ibid., p. 101 [c. March 1, 1849].

58. See *Victorian Poetry,* I (1963), 117–18.

59. Epictetus, *Discourses as Reported by Arrian, the Manual, and Fragments,* trans. W. A. Oldfather (Cambridge, Mass., and London, 1967), I, 213–45.

60. *M.A. to A.H.C.,* pp. 64 [c. December 1847], 66 [c. February 24, 1848].

61. *Letters,* ed. Bertram, p. 75 (January 31 [1848]).

62. *M.A. to A.H.C.,* p. 66 [c. February 24, 1848].

63. Ibid., p. 69 [March 1, 1848].

64. Mulhauser, I, 215 (July 16 [1848]); and *M.A. to A.H.C.,* p. 68 [March 1, 1848].

65. Balliol MS., March 10, 1848.

66. *M.A. to A.H.C.,* p. 69 [March 1, 1848].

67. Balliol MS. [May 1848].

68. *M.A. to A.H.C.,* p. 79 [April 10, 1848].

69. *Letters,* ed. Bertram, p. 33 (March 20, 1848).

70. Balliol MS., March 10, 1848.

71. *Letters,* ed. Bertram, p. 78 (February 26, 1848); and *Amours de Voyage,* Canto II, lines 16, 18–20.

72. *Letters of M.A.,* I, 8 [April 12, 1848]; *M.A. to A.H.C.,* p. 66 [c. February 24, 1848].

73. Circulated at Oxford on July 4, 1848.

74. "Louis Philippe," *The Examiner,* March 4, 1848, pp. 145–46.

75. *M.A. to A.H.C.*, p. 75 [March 8, 1848].

76. See "Goethe's Works" in Carlyle's *Critical and Miscellaneous Essays*.

77. *Poetical Works of Matthew Arnold*, ed. C. B. Tinker and H. F. Lowry (Oxford, 1950), p. 1.

78. Balliol MS. [May 1848].

79. "The Buried Life," lines 45–48, 55–56.

80. "On the Study of Celtic Literature," *The Cornhill Magazine*, XIII (April 1866), 483; Super, III, 335.

81. Super, III, 297, 299–300.

82. Balliol MS., March 1, 1848.

83. *M.A. to A.H.C.*, pp. 116–17 (October 23, 1850); he may have read Jacobi's and Goethe's exchange of letters at any time between 1848 and 1850.

84. "The Buried Life," lines 65–66, 67–76.

85. Kenneth Allott, "Matthew Arnold's 'Stagirius' and Saint-Marc Girardin," *Review of English Studies*, N.S. IX (1958), 289.

86. See R. H. Super, "Arnold and Literary Criticism," in *Matthew Arnold*, ed. K. Allott (London, 1975), pp. 162–63.

87. "On the Study of Celtic Literature," Super, III, 381.

88. Balliol MS., M.A. to his sister Jane [July 31, 1848].

89. *M.A. to A.H.C.*, p. 47.

90. Ibid., p. 132.

91. Ibid., p. 89 (August 12, 1848).

92. Quoted in "Fox How after Dr. Arnold's Death" (in the possession of Arnold family descendants).

93. *M.A. to A.H.C.*, p. 92 (September 29, 1848).

Chapter 7. The Intensity of Love, 1848–1849, pp. 144–167.

Epigraph: "Parting," lines 59–62, 71–74.

1. Thomas Arnold, *History of Rome* (London, 1843), III, 88–89.

2. Balliol MS., July 2, 1859; and *M.A. to A.H.C.*, p. 92 (September 29, 1848).

3. *M.A. to A.H.C.*, p. 91; and *Letters*, ed. Whitridge, p. 13.

4. January 29, 1848, p. 10.

5. *Murray's Handbook for Travellers in Switzerland*, ed. J. Simmons (Leicester, 1970), p. 107.

6. *M.A. to A.H.C.*, pp. 91–92.

7. Ibid., p. 92.

8. Alexander Turnbull MS., Mrs. Mary Arnold, April 3, 1848.

9. *M.A. to A.H.C.*, pp. 92–93.

10. Ibid., p. 110 (September 23 [1849]).

11. Ibid., pp. 111, 109.

12. "Self-Dependence," lines 1–8. See Stanley, *Life*, p. 54 (to Hull, July 29, 1828). The first two lines of M.A.'s poem are virtually translations from Senancour's *Obermann;* at least one line in "Parting" is a translation from Goethe; and several lines in "Church of Brou" translate from Edgar Quinet's French. Unlike Eliot in *The Waste Land*, M.A. seldom acknowledged his borrowings, which reveals lack of confidence in himself as a poet. Unacknowledged borrowing, though never extensive, became a settled habit and continued in his prose writings; *Celtic Literature* lightly commits plagiarism-by-translation from Renan, for example.

13. Senancour, *Obermann*, Édition Critique (Paris, 1931), Lettre IV, p. 23.

14. Lines 89–96.

15. Senancour, *Obermann* (Paris, 1931), Dernière Lettre, p. 246.

16. *M.A. to A.H.C.*, pp. 109–110; and "Stanzas in Memory of the Author of 'Obermann,' " lines 137–38, 161–68, 175–76, 181–84.

17. *M.A. to A.H.C.*, pp. 109–110.

18. Ibid., pp. 110, 111.

19. *Matthew Arnold, Poète: Essai de Biographie Psychologique* (Paris, 1947), p. 76.

20. *M.A. to A.H.C.*, p. 93 (September 29, 1848)

21. "Stanzas in Memory of the Author of 'Obermann,' " lines 5–12, 33–36, 129–32.

22. *M.A. to A.H.C.*, p. 91.

23. The "long letter" of November 25 by Mrs. Twining (Mary or Bacco) about "Matt's romantic passion for . . . Mary Claude" left Gravesend on the Sydney mail ship *Midlothian* on December 1, 1848; the letter is missing, but Tom Arnold's reply to it (Nelson, June 14, 1849) was saved by his daughter Ethel. Its text, published in 1966, in *Letters*, ed. Bertram, offered a starting point for seven years' research by this biographer and others working in England, the U.S., and on the Continent, into the Claudes who were baptized (as Mary Claude was) at Friedrichstadt's French Reformed Church. Tom had sailed for New Zealand in November 1847; by mid-1848, his sisters began to send him timely accounts of family news, writing to catch mail ships which left England on the first of each month.

24. *Letters*, ed. Bertram, p. 120. That M.A. was ridiculed is clear from Tom's letter, M.A.'s letter of November 1848, his "To my Friends, who ridiculed," and later letters of Clough. Mary Claude lived a mile from Fox How; see line 74 in "A Farewell" for "neighbouring," though this is not an unmistakable allusion.

25. *M.A. to A.H.C.*, pp. 94, 113; Mulhauser, I, 270.

26. *M.A. to A.H.C.*, pp. 94–95 [November 1848].

27. Ibid., pp. 129, 95, 96–97. See also Yale MS. (Tinker 21), and *Letters*, ed. Whitridge, p. 13 [early 1849].

28. Humanities Res. Center, Texas MS., Mrs. Louise Claude to H. Coleridge [c. 1842].

29. Lines 37–38, 1–2, 9–10; Arnold published the poem as "A Memory Picture" in 1869; this is its title in *Poems*, ed. Allott.

30. Lines 21–22, 25–30.

31. Mary Claude was M.A.'s model for "Marguerite." Descriptions of her physical beauty, blue eyes, paled features, and tensions between mockery and gravity, and of her intimacy and "moonlight" walks with the Clougho-Matthean set, appear in the MS. diary of Anne Jemima Clough and in MS. letters between the Claudes (formerly

of the Friedrichstadt French community in Berlin) and Hartley Coleridge. In 1848 "Matt's romantic passion for . . . Mary Claude" was known to all of his family.

By 1840, French Protestant exiles named Claude, Reclam, Papin, and Chambeau were intermarried with representatives in the Swiss cantons, Magdeburg, Berlin, and Liverpool. Mary's father Louis Claude (a *"Marchand à Liverpool"* who was in fact a commission merchant) had married in 1818 the daughter of a Chambeau in the French Reformed Church, Friedrichstadt. Mary Claude was baptized in that church, after her birth in the Berlin French-speaking community, on March 21, 1820. She was taken to England as a child. Louis Claude died at Liverpool in 1828. His will shows that James Brancker, who summered at Clappersgate near Ambleside, was one of his legal executors. From 1829 to 1839, Mrs. Claude and her five children summered at Rothay Bank, near the Branckers and the site of Fox How; M.A. befriended Mary's only brother, Louis Claude. Mrs. Claude by 1843 had bought the thick-walled Broadlands, not far from Rothay Bank. At a party in Liverpool in April 1845 Anne Clough met Mary Claude, and later when staying at Broadlands drew her into the Clougho-Matthean set for pony rides, waterfall-scrambles, boat rides, "moonlight" walks, literary conversation, and teas at Fox How. Surviving reports about Mary Claude emphasize her unusual beauty. She was a close friend to (and godmother to the child of) her own aunt, the former Jeanne S. E. C. Reclam, who was a descendant of the Reclams of Geneva and who (like Mary herself) was baptized in Friedrichstadt's French Reformed Church. Some Reclams remained in the Swiss cantons. Mary imitated Foscolo's sentimental *Letters of Ortis* and other sentimentalists, notably Richter, in poems and stories about daisies, anemones, and the moon—all, for her, symbols of modern spiritual isolation. See: "A Note on Matthew Arnold in Love" (*Victorian Newsletter,* No. 39 [Spring, 1971], 11–15); "Fox How and the Continent: Matthew Arnold's Path to the European Sentimental School," and "Matthew Arnold, Mary Claude, and 'Switzerland,'" (*Victorian Poetry,* XVI [1978], 58–69 and 369–75); also Super, XI, 419; MS. Journals of Anne Jemima Clough; and the Coleridge-Claude letters at the Humanities Research Center, Univ. of Texas at Austin. James Bertram and Eugene August suggest that Clough may have twitted Arnold with "Mary" and "Claude" in *Amours de Voyage.*

32. "To my Friends, who ridiculed a tender Leave-taking," lines 33–38.

33. Humanities Res. Center, Texas MSS., Mrs. Claude to H. Coleridge, "Sunday 18th April" [1841], and H. Coleridge to his mother; also see Super, XI, 120.

34. "Tender Leave-taking," lines 42–46.

35. Lines 7–8. See *Hamlet,* I, v, 51.

36. "Tender Leave-Taking," lines 49–58.

37. MS., M.A. to Lucy Whitridge, October 29, 1886; quoted by permission of Arnold Whitridge.

38. See note 31 above.

39. Humanities Res. Center, Texas MS., February 25 [c. 1845].

40. Humanities Res. Center, Texas MS., Mrs. Claude, September 9, 1840.

41. See Balliol MS., October 21, 1886; *Letters of M.A.,* II, 266 (November 8, 1883); and Super XI, 120 and 418.

42. Humanities Res. Center, Texas MS., H. Coleridge collection.

43. Ibid.

44. Ibid.

45. Super, XI, 120.

46. Humanities Res. Center, Texas MS., Mary Claude to H. Coleridge.

47. MS. Diary of Anne Jemima Clough, 1847.

48. M.S.C. [Mary Sophia Claude], *Consideration* (London, 1847), pp. 2–3.

49. MS. Diary of Anne Jemima Clough, 1847.

50. "The Sea," lines 6–8, in Mary Claude's *Little Poems* (London, 1847). Her prose work, "The Moon," appeared in her *Twilight Thoughts* (1848), for which M.A. in October 1886 wrote a preface, at the urging of her brother Louis, for a Boston edition of Mary Claude's fables.

51. Super, XI, 120.

52. *Letters of M.A.*, I, 11.

53. See "Heinrich Heine" (Super, III, 108), written at first as a lecture in 1863.

54. Charlotte M. Yonge, *History of Christian Names* (London, 1878), I, 267.

55. "To Meta," lines 12–14, 19–20.

56. Diary of 1851, January 1, 4, and 5, Allott transcript.

57. "To Meta," lines 21–24.

58. Lines 25–26, 28, 33–40.

59. See De Senancour, *Obermann* (Paris, 1931), Lettres LXIII and XLVI.

60. Ibid., Lettre XXXVIII.

61. Mme. de Staël, *De la littérature considérée dans ses rapports avec les institutions sociales* (Paris, 1800), I, 311–13.

62. Chauteaubriand, *René,* Édition critique publiée par Armand Weil (Paris, 1935), p. 31.

63. De Senancour, *Obermann* (Paris, 1931), Lettre XLI.

64. See Ronald E. Becht, "M.A.'s 'Switzerland': The Drama of Choice," *Victorian Poetry*, XIII (1975), 35–45.

65. Lines 1–8.

66. Lines 9–16.

67. *M.A. to A.H.C.*, pp. 76 [March 1848] and 111 (September 23 [1849]).

68. "Parting," lines 1–4, 9–16.

69. Lines 17–22.

70. Lines 41–42.

71. Super, XI, 120.

72. "Parting," lines 59–64, 71–84.

73. See Kathleen Tillotson, " 'Yes: in the Sea of Life,' " *Review of English Studies,* III (1952), 352–53, as well as the critique in this article.

74. E. R. Vincent, *Ugo Foscolo: An Italian in Regency England* (Cambridge, 1953), p. 16.

75. "To Marguerite, in returning a volume of the Letters of Ortis."

76. *M.A. to A.H.C.*, p. 92. See W. A. Madden, *M.A.: A Study of the Aesthetic Temperament in Victorian England* (Bloomington and London, 1967), pp. 84–86.

77. *Letters of M.A.,* I, 17 (January 25, 1851).

78. "Parting," lines 37–40.

79. "A Dream," lines 23, 27.

80. Quoted by F. B. Malder, "M.A. and the Circle of Recurrence," *Victorian Poetry,* XIV (1976), 305n.

81. "The Terrace at Berne," line 52.

82. "A Farewell," lines 53–56, 73–76. Carlyle had praised Jean Paul Richter's *Traumdichtungen.* See J. W. Smeed, *Jean Paul's Dreams* (London, 1966), especially pp. 18–31.

Chapter 8. "The Strayed Reveller" 1848–1850, pp. 168–194.

Epigraph: *M.A. to A.H.C.,* p. 99.

1. Jane Arnold to her brother Tom, October 27 [1850], quoted in "Fox How after Dr. Arnold's Death." (The "tale" may have been Mrs. Gaskell's *Moorland Cottage,* as Elsie Duncan-Jones suggests.)

2. *M.A. to A.H.C.,* p. 98.

3. Ellis Yarnall, *Wordsworth and the Coleridges, with Other Memories Literary and Political* (New York and London, 1899), p. 158. As late as 1849, the letters "A" and "P" distinguished Arnoldians from Puseyites at Rugby.

4. Balliol MS., April 14, 1853. Fellowes was "willing to do" anything proposed to him, though M.A. "felt the objection of his obscurity and inactivity." It is doubtful that Fellowes or M.A. withdrew *Strayed Reveller* soon after it was published, despite M.A.'s vague statement in 1876 that the book was withdrawn; see R. L. Brooks, "The *Strayed Reveller* Myth," *The Library,* 5th series, 18 (1963), 57–60.

5. "The Hayswater Boat," lines 1–4, 6–8.

6. "A Question: To Fausta," lines 1–14.

7. "Resignation," line 152.

8. "Mycerinus," lines 8–12.

9. Ibid., lines 112–115, 121.

10. Balliol MS., "Notes on Athenaeus X and XIII," [c. 1856–57].

11. "Mycerinus," lines 125–27.

12. Super, III, 12.

13. See G. Robert Stange, *Matthew Arnold: The Poet as Humanist* (Princeton, 1967), pp. 23n. and 16–29.

14. "The Strayed Reveller," lines 15–22.

15. Ibid., lines 75–81, 94–95, 97.

16. Brotherton MS., Mrs. Mary Arnold's Journals, I, January 8, 1822. In T.A.'s hand.

17. Ibid.

18. Ibid., I, March 1, 1822. Signed "M[ary]A[rnold]".

19. Ibid., I and II. These are excerpts from verses composed by T.A. between 1822 and December 30, 1838.

20. "The Strayed Reveller," lines 131–32, 135–150.

21. Ibid., lines 208–211.

22. Ibid., lines 223–25, 227–34.

23. "The Strayed Reveller," lines 287–89.

24. The comparativist critic gains insight into one national literature or epoch by contrasting it with another; the method was used in T.A.'s classes at Rugby, and M.A. found it exemplified in critics such as Mme de Staël, Sismondi, and A. W. Schlegel. Because of its international aspects, the romantic movement encouraged comparativism. M.A. freed himself from the excessive influence of English romantic poets by balancing them against French and German romantic writers in the 1840s. His comparativism kept him from wholly rejecting Byron, Keats, and Shelley, and helped him to make use of their images, symbols, and styles, while remaining critical of those poets. As a critic, M.A. later exemplified the strength and soundness of comparativism; see, for the background of this method, D. L. Fanger, "Romanticism and Comparative Literature," *Comparative Literature,* XIX (1962), 153–66; and René Wellek, *Concepts of Criticism* (New Haven and London, 1963), especially pp. 160–98.

25. See *Poems,* ed. Allott, p. 75n.

26. "The Sick King in Bokhara," lines 177–80.

27. Ibid., line 221. See A. Dwight Culler, *Imaginative Reason* (New Haven and London, 1966), pp. 105–111.

28. *Matthew Arnold* (New York, 1955), p. 93. Elsewhere (pp. 82–89) Lionel Trilling in this often brilliant book (first published in 1939) does find philosophical confusion in M.A.'s work where there is none; in "Resignation," and in other poems of 1849 and 1852, M.A., for example, accepts the Idealist thesis that nature is to be seen *both* as a snare and a guide. (He had studied Berkeley's *Siris* carefully in 1845, and its deliberately ambivalent view of nature is not uncommon in post-Berkeleyan thought.) M.A. maintained that his poems were "Fragments," not equivalent to a philosophical system, but representing "the main movement of mind" over a quarter of a century (1842 to 1867); Trilling undervalues and misconstrues Arnold's poems as well as his religious ideas, but assesses the humanist insights in his essays with sympathy and discernment.

29. "Resignation," lines 5, 22, 24–25.

30. Ibid., lines 144–45.

31. Ibid., lines 199–200, 203–204, 206–213.

32. Jane Arnold's words were written a year after she had seen "Resignation," or in 1850, but M.A. had heard her Rugbeian argument often in the 1840s and possibly, as he implies, as early as 1843. "Fox How after Dr. Arnold's Death" (in the possession of Arnold descendants) records a portion of Jane's letter.

33. "Resignation," lines 220–22.

34. Charles Wilkins, trans. and ed., *The Bhagavat-Geeta, or Dialogues of Kreeshna and Arjoon* (London, 1785), p. 133.

35. "Resignation," lines 247–52.

36. See "Amiel," Super, XI, 272–78.

37. "Resignation," lines 269–70.

38. Ibid., lines 276–78; and see Manfred Dietrich, "Arnold's *Empedocles on Etna* and the 1853 Preface," *Victorian Poetry,* XIV (1976), 311–24, especially p. 317.

39. *Letters,* ed. Whitridge, p. 15.

40. Ibid.

41. Mulhauser, I, 247 [February 28, 1849] and 251 [March 6, 1849].

42. Clough printed only part of the poem, and without the "Resignation: to Faustus" title; see his lines beginning "O Land of Empire, art and love!"

43. *Letters,* ed. Whitridge, pp. 18–19 ("London, Saturday" [1849]).

44. *The Guardian,* IV (March 28, 1849), 208–209; *The Spectator,* XXII (March 10, 1849), 231; *Fraser's Magazine,* XXIX (May 1849), 575–80.

45. *Blackwood's Magazine,* LXVI (September 1849), 340–46.

46. XXXII (September 1849), 283–84; XXII (March 10, 1849), 231; and March 17, 1849, p. 188.

47. *Germ,* No. 2 (February 1850); *Letters of M.A.,* I, 26 (to Slade, October 22, 1852).

48. William T. Arnold, "Thomas Arnold the Younger," *Century Magazine,* LXVI (1903), 125; *Letters,* ed. Whitridge, p. 14 [c. May 1849].

49. *Letters,* ed. Whitridge, p. 22 [c. December 1853].

50. Ibid., p. 20 (October 31, 1853); and *Letters of M.A.,* I, 117 (August 13, 1859).

51. "Thyrsis," lines 167–70, 191–93; *Letters,* ed. Whitridge, p. 21.

52. Yale MS. (Tinker 21).

53. Quoted by Mrs. Humphry Ward, *A Writer's Recollections* (London, 1918), p. 43.

54. C. B. Tinker and H. F. Lowry, *The Poetry of Matthew Arnold: A Commentary* (New York, 1940), p. 290.

55. Ibid., p. 291.

56. Brotherton MS., Mrs. Mary Arnold's Journals, I, February 1832.

57. Diary of 1851, "March 28, Friday."

58. See, e.g., *Athenaeum,* August 12, 1848, p. 808.

59. C. B. Tinker and H. F. Lowry, *Commentary* (New York, 1940), pp. 291–92.

60. *Letters,* ed. Whitridge, p. 14.

61. Mulhauser, I, 270 (July 24 [1849]).

62. *M.A. to A.H.C.,* pp. 107–109.

63. "Consolation," lines 1–8, 41, 45, 48–50.

64. *Letters of M.A.,* I, 11 [1849 rather than 1848].

65. Quoted by Mrs. Humphry Ward, *A Writer's Recollections* (London, 1918), p. 52.

66. Super, III, 253.

67. J. D. Coleridge to his father, "Epiphany, 1864," quoted in E. H. Coleridge, *John Duke Lord Coleridge* (London, 1904).

68. "Sir William Wightman," *Dictionary of National Biography.*

69. *Letters,* ed. Bertram, p. 203.

70. Myron F. Brightfield, *John Wilson Croker* (London, 1940), p. 347.

71. Ibid., pp. 352–53; John Murray to Croker in 1853.

72. [George W. E. Russell], "Comments by the Way," *The Pilot,* July 6, 1901, pp. 13–14.

73. Ibid., p. 14; and Patrick J. McCarthy, "Mrs. Matthew Arnold: Some Considerations and Some Letters," *Harvard Library Bulletin,* XVII (1969), 386.

74. See page 4.

75. "Absence," lines 1–8, 17–20.

76. Quoted by C. B. Tinker and H. F. Lowry, *A Commentary* (New York, 1940), p. 169.

77. Ibid., pp. 169–70.

78. Mulhauser, I, 286 (July 23 [1850]).

79. "Youth's Agitations," line 1.

80. "Human Life," lines 16, 21, 27.

81. *M.A. to A. H.C.,* p. 114.

82. M.A.'s three known sources for *Tristram and Iseult* were La Villemarqué's "Les poèmes gallois et les romans de la Table-Ronde" and "Visite au Tombeau de Merlin" in *Revue de Paris* (3rd ser. xxiv [1841], 266–82; 2nd ser. xli [1837], 45–62) and Malory's *Le Morte Darthur* of 1485; he probably did not consult John Dunlop's *History of Fiction* (3d ed., 1845), until Froude suggested it to him in 1853—a year after M.A. printed his poem. M.A. then composed a note for the poem from Dunlop's sentences.

83. R. E. C. Houghton in *Times Literary Supplement,* May 19, 1932 (M.A. to Hill, November 5, 1852).

84. *Hamlet,* V, ii, 244–48.

85. *Tristram and Iseult,* I, 234, 238–42.

86. Ibid., I, 283–87.

87. Ibid., II, 1–8, 25–32.

88. Ibid., II, 193.

89. Ibid., III, 218–22. His "Marguerite" in *Switzerland* is a stereotyped female (as is Goethe's Lotte in *Werther*) who evokes a male's impassioned comments on love, friendship, isolation, the will, the self, or spiritual rebirth; but the widowed second Iseult in *Tristram* is recognizably a woman with an interior life of her own. See Barbara Fass Leavy's interesting "Iseult of Brittany: A New Interpretation," in *Victorian Poetry,* XVIII (1980), 1–22.

Chapter 9. *"Empedocles on Etna,"* 1850–1851, pp. 195–215.

Epigraph: *Poems,* ed. Allott, pp. 132.

1. See *Selected Prose Works of Arthur Hugh Clough,* ed. Buckner B. Trawick (University, Alabama, 1964), p. 20; and "Stanzas in Memory of the Author of 'Obermann,'" line 54.

2. Mary Moorman, *William Wordsworth, A Biography: The Later Years 1803–1850* (Oxford, 1965), p. 497 ("Evening Voluntaries").

3. Ibid., p. 604.

4. Ibid., p. 564.

5. See "Wordsworth," Super, IX, 51; and Tom Arnold, quoted in Moorman, *Wordsworth* (Oxford, 1965), p. 577. Mrs. Arnold's letter of January 27, 1848, reports one very recent talk between M.A. and Wordsworth, at Fox How, on S. T. Coleridge and "Italian poetry" (Alexander Turnbull MS.).

6. *M.A. to A.H.C.*, p. 99 [c. February 1849].

7. See the 1845 edition of Wordsworth's poems.

8. "A Speech at the Unveiling of a Mosaic," in *Essays, Letters, and Reviews by Matthew Arnold,* ed. Fraser Neiman (Cambridge, Mass., 1960), p. 256 (November 29, 1884).

9. *The Correspondence of Henry Crabb Robinson with the Wordsworth Circle,* ed. E. J. Morley (Oxford, 1927), II, 743.

10. Ibid., II, 769.

11. "On the Study of Celtic Literature," Super, III, 372.

12. "Memorial Verses: April 1850," lines 8–9.

13. Ibid., lines 23, 27–28.

14. Ibid., lines 62–63, 66–67.

15. Ibid., lines 42–44, 47–57.

16. "The Youth of Nature," lines 1–3, 8–9, 15–21. The poem was possibly begun in June 1850, laid aside, and finished in January 1852.

17. Ibid., lines 26, 28.

18. Ibid., lines 31–35.

19. *M.A. to A.H.C.*, p. 115.

20. Balliol MS., "London Tuesday" [1850].

21. Ibid.

22. Ibid.

23. Ibid.

24. *M.A. to A.H.C.*, p. 115. Clough, in two letters of 1847 printed in *The Spectator* (November 6 and 20), challenged F. Newman's idea in *The Soul* that "moral teaching is intellectually mephitic"; but in 1850—when suffering from nervous depression—Clough, in a review, hailed *The Soul* and savaged Dr. Arnold as one of the men who "know not what they do." The review was not printed until 1869; but M.A. either saw or heard something of this attack on his father; he focused his anger not on Clough but on Francis Newman, who remained his *bête noire.*

25. *Manchester Guardian,* May 18, 1888.

26. Super, X, 191–92.

27. "On Translating Homer: Last Words," Super, I, 174.

28. See *Poems,* ed. Allott, p. 149; the essential contrast is between Act I scene ii, and Act II.

29. *Empedocles on Etna,* I, i, 19–20.

30. Ibid., I, i, 149–53.

31. Ibid., I, ii, 87–90.

32. Ibid., I, ii, 122–25, 144–46, 257–60.

33. Ibid., I, ii, 319–31, 347–50.

34. Ibid., I, ii, 332–36.

35. "On the Modern Element in Literature," Super, I, 20–21.

36. *Empedocles on Etna,* II, 242–46.

37. Ibid., II, 329–30.

38. Ibid., II, 90–94.

39. Ibid., II, 190.

40. *Letters of M.A.,* I, 72–73 (August 6, 1858).

41. *M.A. to A.H.C.,* p. 130 (February 12–13, 1853).

42. Ibid., pp. 136 (May 1, 1853) and 126 (December 14, 1852).

43. Ibid., pp. 87 (July 20 [1848]) and 116 (October 23, 1850).

44. *Empedocles on Etna,* II, 345–90.

45. MS. Diary of Anne Jemima Clough, 1847.

46. *Empedocles on Etna,* II, 421–22.

47. Ibid., II, 457–68.

48. *M.A. to A.H.C.,* p. 99 [c. February 1849].

49. *Romantic Image* (London, 1971), p. 31.

50. "The River," lines 1–8, 14–16, 18, 27–28, 33–40.

51. See "Matthew Arnold," by One Who Knew Him Well [Tom Arnold], *Manchester Guardian,* May 18, 1888.

52. Ibid.

53. *A Writer's Recollections* (London, 1918), p. 35.

54. A transcript of the letter by Mary Twining, née Arnold, is given in "Fox How after Dr. Arnold's Death" (typescript in possession of an Arnold descendant).

55. Yale MS. (Tinker 21), and "Longing," lines 1–2, 5–16.

56. *Letters of M.A.,* I, 26 (October 22, 1852).

Chapter 10. "Fancy 'the Emperor' Married!" 1850–1851, pp. 216–246.

Epigraph: Seneca, *Ad Lucilium Epistulae Morales,* trans. R. M. Gummere (London and New York, 1925), pp. 222–23.

1. *M.A. to A.H.C.,* p. 116 (October 23, 1850). See the *vermischte Epigramme* of Goethe.

2. March 10, 1851.

3. *M.A. to A.H.C.,* p. 118.

4. *Letters of M.A.,* I, 15 (December 21, 1850).

5. "Rime of the Ancient Mariner," lines 178–80.

6. *Letters of M.A.,* I, 32.

7. Matthew Arnold, *Reports on Elementary Schools,* ed. F. Sandford (London, 1889), p. 2: General Report for the Year 1852.

8. Balliol MS., "Sunday."

9. Kathleen Tillotson, " 'Haworth Churchyard': The Making of Arnold's Elegy," *Brontë Society Transactions,* XV (1967), 112.

10. *Letters of M.A.,* I, 15–16 (December 21, 1850). The observing friend was Hippolyte Taine, who was six years younger than M.A. (see Taine to Mme Taine in *Life and Letters,* III, 57–58).

11. Kathleen Tillotson, *Brontë Society Transactions*, XV (1967), 114.

12. "Haworth Churchyard: April, 1855," lines 92–95, 99–100.

13. Balliol MS., April 14, 1853.

14. Balliol MS., January 25, 1851.

15. Diary of 1851.

16. Balliol MSS., "Friday" [c. February 28 or March 7, 1851] and May 10, 1851.

17. Diary of 1851; and Balliol MS., May 10, 1851.

18. Balliol MS., to his mother, May 30 [c. 1858].

19. See S. Coulling, *M.A. and His Critics* (Athens, Ohio, 1974), p. 325n.; and Balliol MS., December 18, 1861.

20. Mrs. Humphry Ward, *A Writer's Recollections* (London, 1918), p. 65; and *Letters,* ed. Bertram, p. 205.

21. Diary of 1851.

22. Ibid.

23. Yale MS. (Tinker 21).

24. Diary of 1851.

25. Quoted in Diary of 1851.

26. Arnold took the Marx quotation from John Macdonell's "Karl Marx and German Socialism" in the *Fortnightly Review* for March 1, 1875 (*Note-Books of M.A.*). Marx's and Arnold's views sometimes coincide. Though he held that conscious efforts cannot alter the social organism, Marx in *Theses on Feuerbach* praises "sinnlich menschliches Tätigkeit" (human sense activity), his idea being that we know the world through activity and that activity *implies* changing. Similarly, Arnold held that we cannot alter the *Zeitgeist,* but that we must yet work for a future, more equitable society. Arnold's acquaintance with Marxist thought was not extensive even in the 1870s.

27. Mulhauser, I, 290 (May 16 [1851]).

28. Diary of 1851.

29. Yale MS. (Tinker 21). The "pride is madness" notes were jotted between 1847 and 1851. Arnold may have seen the *Spectator* review (of April 18, 1846) which declares the plays of George Stephens to be products of Bedlam. "Tale of the Modern Time" by Aubrey de Vere, about a paranoid hero, was said in the *Quarterly Review* (1843) to represent "the introverted eye of the modern mind." "G. Planche & Barbier" refers to Planche's review of Barbier in *Revue des Deux Mondes* (July 1, 1837) in which the section of Auguste Barbier's *Lazare* entitled "Bedlam" is specially praised. Arnold owned the three-volume edition of Goethe's letters to Frau von Stein edited by Schöll (1848–51); the quotation "Gott hat . . ." is from a letter to that lady in which Goethe refers to his "mixed-up-necesses" ("Verworrenheiten"). Spinoza's *Ethics,* which Arnold finished reading in 1851, virtually summarizes Arnold's interest in the relation between madness, pride, modernity, and the creative imagination: "Pride . . . is a kind of madness, wherein a man dreams with his eyes open, thinking that he can do all things which he achieves only in imagination" (pt. III, prop. 26n).

30. Yale MS. (Tinker 21).

31. "A Summer Night," lines 1–5.

32. Diary of 1851.

33. "A Summer Night," lines 26–29, 31–33.

34. Ibid., lines 34–46.

35. Ibid., lines 68–69, 74–75.

36. Ibid., lines 76–77.

37. Edward Bouverie Pusey, "Lectures on Types and Prophecies of the Old Testament," MS., Pusey House, Oxford; Jerome Bump, "Hopkins' Imagery and Medievalist Poetics," *Victorian Poetry,* VX (1977), 99–119.

38. *Isaiah,* 43:2, 20.

39. "The Buried Life," lines 47, 49, 51, 73.

40. See Clough's "Recent English Poetry," *North American Review,* LXXVII (1853), 1–30.

41. Yale MS. (Tinker 21).

42. Ibid.

43. Ibid.

44. "The Buried Life," lines 1–8.

45. Ibid., lines 12–15, 21–23.

46. Ibid., lines 67–70.

47. Ibid., lines 77–84.

48. Ibid., lines 86–88, 95–98. See Robert Langbaum, *The Mysteries of Identity; A Theme in Modern Literature* (New York, 1977), chap. 3; and Alice N. Stitelmann, "Lyrical Process in Three Poems by M.A.," *Victorian Poetry,* XV (1977), 133–46.

49. Diary of 1851.

50. *Letters,* ed. Bertram, p. 203 (June 14 [1851]).

51. R. E. Prothero and G. G. Bradley, *Life and Correspondence of Arthur Penrhyn Stanley* (London, 1894), I, 428.

52. See "Dover Beach," lines 15–16.

53. Ellen S. Gahtan, " 'Nor help for pain': M.A. and Sophocles' *Philoctetes,*" *Victorian Newsletter* (Fall 1975), 22.

54. "Dover Beach," lines 1–6.

55. Ibid., lines 9–12.

56. Ibid., lines 15–18, 21–37.

57. In a university sermon of January 6, 1839, printed in Newman's *University Sermons* in 1843.

58. *Letters of M.A.,* I, 398 (November 9, 1866).

59. Ibid., I, 157 (May 14, 1861).

60. Diary of 1851; *Letters of M.A.,* I, 159.

61. *Letters of M.A.,* I, 403 [January 5, 1867].

62. Ibid.

63. Ibid., I, 216 (March 13, 1863).

64. Ibid., I, 327 (June 22, 1865).

65. *Letters of M.A.*, II, 349 (November 27, 1885); and see "Study of Celtic Literature," Super, III, 355.

66. Yale MSS., Mrs. Matthew Arnold: to Galton, August 15, 1888; to Mrs. Clough, December 16, 1893.

67. Paris, Hôtel Windsor, September 2, 1851.

68. Diary of 1851, September 1 and 2.

69. Paris, Hôtel Windsor, September 2, 1851.

70. Diary of 1851.

71. Milan, "Sunday" [September 14, 1851].

72. "Stanzas from the Grande Chartreuse," lines 7, 9–12.

73. "De Arte Poetica," line 63 ("We are doomed to death—we and all things ours").

74. "Sunday" [September 14, 1851].

75. "Stanzas from the Grande Chartreuse," lines 45–46.

76. "Sunday" [September 14, 1851].

77. "Stanzas from the Grande Chartreuse," lines 39–42, 65–66.

78. Ibid., lines 93–94, 110–12.

79. Ibid., lines 85–86.

80. Ibid., lines 115–116.

81. Ibid., lines 133–150.

82. Ibid., lines 157–62.

83. Ibid., line 69.

84. Ibid., lines 179–80.

85. Ibid., lines 205–207, 209–10.

86. Yale MS. (Tinker 21).

87. Epictetus, *The Discourses*, trans. W. A. Oldfather (Cambridge, Mass. and London, 1925), I, 245 (bk. II, ch. v).

88. "A Liverpool Address," Super, X, 86.

89. Yale MS., March 20, 1855.

90. "Sunday" [September 14, 1851].

91. Ibid.

92. Venice, September 19, 1851.

93. Lucerne, October 1, 1851.

94. Seneca, *Epistolae Morales*, XXXI; and see *Letters*, ed. Whitridge, p. 31.

95. *Letters of M.A.*, I, 20 (October 15, 1851).

Chapter 11. Lord Russell's "Bashaws," 1851 and 1839–1852, pp. 247–266.

Epigraphs: *Note-Books of M.A.*, p. 60; *Correspondence of Carlyle and Emerson* (1883), I, 207.

1. See John Snell, quoted by Mary Sturt, *The Education of the People* (London, 1967),

p. 201; Rev. John Dymond, "Matthew Arnold: Some Personal Recollections," *Wesleyan Methodist Magazine,* III (1888), 521; and Super, II, 103.

2. "Ordnance Maps," Super, II, 253 (composed in 1862).

3. *Letters of M.A.,* I, 21 (December 2, 1851).

4. Bodleian MS., December 29, 1851. M.A. at this date had a list only of those schools having pupil-teachers or certified masters, in his "most laborious and embarrassing" school district.

5. Bodleian MS. Autograph e. 10 fols. 9–10, December 29–30, 1851.

6. Frank Smith, *The Life and Work of Sir James Kay-Shuttleworth* (London, 1923), p. 215 (November 1848).

7. Ibid., p. 216 (Sunday, December 10, 1848).

8. Quoted by P. J. McCarthy, *M.A. and the Three Classes* (New York and London, 1964), p. 116.

9. Donald K. Jones, *The Making of the Education System 1851–81* (London, 1977), p. 10.

10. The statistics are not to be trusted as if they were modern sociological findings, but they are more nearly accurate than Lord Kerry's tables of 1833; see Francis Adams, *History of the Elementary School Contest in England,* ed. Asa Briggs (Brighton, 1972), pp. 94–95.

11. Mary Sturt, *The Education of the People: A History of Primary Education in England and Wales in the Nineteenth Century* (London, 1967), pp. 40, 58. M.A. heard of a master who pulled off a boy's ear; the H.M.I.s learned of schools that had ceased to exist because of the violence of a master.

12. "Schools in the Reign of Queen Victoria," Super, XI, 211. Lord Lansdowne perhaps "exercised a restraining hand" on Kay's "wording" only after Kay had sent to new H.M.I.s 174 questions on schools (printed in the Committee's *Minutes,* 1839–40, pp. 22–45). Lord Lansdowne advised Kay to adopt a "plain and dry" manner; see Frank Smith, *Kay-Shuttleworth* (London, 1923), pp. 96–97.

13. Mary Sturt, *Education of the People* (London, 1967), pp. 88, 91.

14. Cited by John Leese, *The History and Character of Educational Inspection in England,* diss. University of London (1934).

15. Donald K. Jones, *The Making of the Education System 1851–81* (London, 1977), p. 9.

16. *Minutes and Reports of the Committee of Council on Education,* 1846.

17. Richard Johnson, "Educational Policy and Social Control in Early Victorian England," *Past and Present,* XLIX (1970), 104 (*Minutes* of 1845).

18. *Minutes and Reports of the Committee of Council on Education,* 1845.

19. John Leese, *History and Character of Educational Inspection,* diss. University of London (1934), p. 64.

20. Mary Sturt, *The Education of the People* (London, 1967), pp. 39–40 (*Minutes* of 1840–41).

21. *Minutes and Reports of the Committee of Council on Education,* 1857.

22. Mary Sturt, *Education of the People* (London, 1967), pp. 172–73.

23. John Leese, *History and Character of Educational Inspection,* diss. University of London (1934), p. 32 (*Minutes* of 1839).

24. Diary of 1852; see *M.A. Diaries,* II, 27–28.

25. *M.A. Diaries;* and *Culture and Anarchy,* Super, V, 217.

26. Notes of May 15, 1855, on Great Queen Street School (Diary of 1855).

27. "Schoolmistresses Certificate," entries by M.A. from 1854 to 1871; the teacher was also helped by H.M.I. Alderson.

28. *Reports on Elementary Schools,* ed. F. Sandford (London, 1889), p. 40. M.A. used the emotive style ("no one feels," "alas," "it is even affecting") while pleading for more exactness in reporting in 1854; he had dropped this style by 1861.

29. "Schools in the Reign of Queen Victoria," Super, XI, 222.

30. Rev. John Dymond, "Matthew Arnold: Some Personal Recollections," *Wesleyan Methodist Magazine,* III (1888), 521–22.

31. Ibid., p. 522.

32. G. W. E. Russell, *Matthew Arnold* (London, 1924), p. 98.

33. John Dymond, "Matthew Arnold," *Wesleyan Methodist Magazine,* III (1888), 522.

34. Ibid., p. 523.

35. Fred G. Walcott, "Matthew Arnold, Her Majesty's Inspector of Schools," *Michigan Alumnus Quarterly Review,* LX (1954), 247.

36. Mary Sturt, *Education of the People* (London, 1967), p. 193.

37. Ibid., pp. 181–82.

38. Diaries of 1857, 1862, 1866, 1870, 1871.

39. To Hill, January 7, 1858; courtesy of the Syndics of Fitzwilliam Museum.

40. *Letters of M.A.,* I, 46 (November 6, 1854); 89 (January 21 [1859]).

41. See Goethe, *Werke, Gedenkenausgabe,* ed. E. Beutler (Zurich, 1950), I, 420. To judge from his diaries, starting in 1851 when he quoted it and in various years after 1851 when he quotes a phrase of it (*"Heute!" "Nur heute!"*), this couplet occurred to Arnold more often than any other epigram in any language.

42. *Letters of M.A.,* I, 32 (March 10, 1853); I, 37 (November 26, 1853).

43. "Auf dem See," lines 1–12 (it has twenty lines).

44. See M.A.'s versions of this formula in "Joubert," "Wordsworth," "The Study of Poetry," and especially "Byron," where he recognizes the trouble it gives him as a didactic definition of (aesthetic) poetry or literature.

45. *M.A. to A.H.C.,* pp. 122–23 (erroneously printed "June" for "Jan 7th 1852").

46. Mulhauser, II, 363; M.A. saw Palgrave just before Christmas 1852.

47. C. B. Tinker and H. F. Lowry, *The Poetry of M.A.: A Commentary* (New York, 1940), pp. 16–17.

48. "The Youth of Man," lines 1–11.

49. Ibid., lines 27, 114–18.

50. "Morality," lines 1–6.

51. Ibid., Lines 25–28, 36.

52. See *Letters,* ed. Whitridge, p. 31.

Chapter 12. The Myth of the "Scholar-Gipsy," 1852–1857, pp. 267–290.

Epigraph: *M.A. to A.H.C.,* p. 84 [summer 1848].

1. *M.A. to A.H.C.,* p. 120 [April 9, 1852].

2. Ibid., p. 118 [late 1851 or early 1852].

3. Ibid., pp. 119–20 [April 9, 1852].

4. Ibid., pp. 121 (April 22, 1852); p. 138 [July 27, 1853].

5. Balliol MSS., August 19, 1852, and November 25, 1852.

6. Balliol Mss., "Tuesday night"; "Monday"; and November 25, 1852.

7. *Reports on Elementary Schools,* ed. F. Sandford (London, 1889), p. 42.

8. See *Culture and Anarchy; Super,* III, 217.

9. *M.A. to A.H.C.,* p. 126 (December 14, 1852).

10. Mulhauser, II, 373 (Temple to Clough, February 3, 1853); M.A. saw Temple often enough to have heard this view; it was not uncommon during the parliamentary deadlock over education in the 1850s.

11. *M.A. to A.H.C.,* p. 124 (October 28, 1852).

12. Ibid., pp. 65, 99. See Dorothy Deering, "The Antithetical Poetics of Arnold and Clough," *Victorian Poetry,* XVI (1978), 16–31.

13. *M.A. to A.H.C.,* p. 124 (October 28, 1852).

14. "Arnold and Literary Criticism," *Matthew Arnold,* ed. K. Allott (London, 1975), pp. 124–26.

15. *Letters of M.A.,* I, 27 (November 25, 1852).

16. "The Church of Brou," III, 7–8.

17. Ibid., III, 32–40, 43–46; M.A. translates from several phrases of Quinet, his main literary source; see Edgar Quinet, "Des Arts de la Renaissance et de l'Église de Brou," in *Oeuvres Complètes* (Paris, 1857), VI.

18. Joseph Glanvill, *The Vanity of Dogmatizing* (London, 1661), pp. 196–98.

19. Glanvill's preface; and Ruth apRoberts, "The Theme of Vocation," *Victorian Poetry,* XVI (1978), 43–57.

20. Charles Taylor, *Hegel* (Cambridge, 1975), pp. 15–29.

21. Goethe to Eckermann, January 2, 1824; for M.A. on *Besonnenheit* and *bedeutendes Individuum,* see *M.A. to A.H.C.,* p. 110, and Mrs. H. Ward, *A Writer's Recollections* (London, 1918), p. 53.

22. "The Scholar-Gipsy," lines 72–78, 81, 116–20.

23. Ibid., lines 152, 171–78, 180.

24. T. S. Eliot, in *The Dial,* LXXV (1923), 198–201.

25. "The Scholar-Gipsy," lines 182–89, 191.

26. *The Worcester Spy* (Worcester, Mass.), November 29, 1883.

27. See "Scholar-Gipsy," lines 231–50. This view brings to bear ideas about the expressivist anthropology in my essay, "The Theory of Biography" (in *Novel: A Forum on Fiction,* XIII, 1979); I also have drawn on my talk with J. P. Curgenven and on his essays on "The Scholar-Gipsy" and "Thyrsis" in *Litera,* (II–VI, 1955–59); G. Wilson Knight's "Interpretation" (*Review of English Studies,* VI, 1955); and R. B. Wilkenfeld's suggestive remark that the poem is an "elegy for elegies," in his essay "The Argument of 'The Scholar-Gipsy' " (*Victorian Poetry,* VII, 1969).

28. *M.A. to A.H.C.*, p. 146 (November 30 [1853]).

29. Ibid., pp. 128 (February 12, 1853); 134 (May 1, 1853).

30. Ibid., pp. 128–29 (February 12, 1853).

31. Ibid., p. 130 ("Sunday" [February 13] 1853).

32. Yale MS. (Tinker 21).

33. He had been reading John Locke's *Essay on Human Understanding* (1690) and, in the Latin, Spinoza's *Ethica* or *Ethics* (1677), in October 1850 (*M.A. to A.H.C.*, pp. 116–17).

34. *M.A. to A.H.C.*, p. 135 (May 1, 1853).

35. M.A. to Sainte-Beuve, January 6, 1854.

36. "Sohrab and Rustum: An Episode," lines 49–52. See the exchange of letters, of April 1797, in *Briefwechsel zwischen Schiller und Goethe* (Stuttgart und Tübingen, 1828), II. M.A. jotted the title "Death of Sohrab" in his copy of this book.

37. See *Daily News* (London), December 26, 1853; and "Sohrab and Rustum," lines 390–97.

38. *Letters,* ed. Whitridge, pp. 31–32 (March 31, 1856).

39. "Sohrab and Rustum," lines 318, 337, 694–96, 790–93; both Culler (*Imaginative Reason,* New Haven, 1966, pp. 205–14) and Madden (*Arnold,* London, 1967, pp. 27–33), comment on autobiographical elements.

40. *M.A. to A.H.C.*, p. 140 (August 25 [1853]); see "Shelley," Super, XI, 327.

41. See *North American Review,* LXXVII (July, 1853), 1–30. Clough's name-calling (M.A. is an effete Westerner lost in "rehabilitated Hindoo-Greek theosophy") was not in itself offensive (M.A. had called him a "poor subjective," and worse); but his exteriorizing of a private debate to strike at M.A.'s poems signaled a wish to end the intimacy of that debate, and this damaged their friendship.

42. *M.A. to A.H.C.*, p. 140 (August 25 [1853]).

43. Preface to *Poems* (1853). See also Robert Langbaum, in *Modern Philology,* LX (1963), 300; and S. M. B. Coulling, in *Victorian Studies,* VII (1964), 233–63.

44. Yale MS. (Tinker 21).

45. Perface to *Poems* (1853).

46. Ibid.

47. Yale MS. (Tinker 21).

48. To Mr. Chapman, February 11, 1854.

49. Trinity College, Camb. MS., Dec. 19, 1855; courtesy of the Master and Fellows.

50. *Letters of M.A.,* I, 68 (February 3, 1858).

51. *Letters,* ed. Whitridge, p. 33 (March 31, 1856).

52. "Balder Dead, 2. Journey to the Dead," lines 264–65, 267.

53. See part 3, "Funeral."

54. "Joubert," Super, III, 204.

55. Eleanor Alexander, *Primate Alexander, Archbishop of Armagh: A Memoir* (London, 1913), p. 133; and Francis Otter (collection of A. K. Davis, Jr.).

56. Super, XI, 377.

57. Balliol MSS.: December 6, 1856; December 12, 1854; January 16 [1857].

58. Balliol MSS.: June 3, 1855; July 25, 1857; November 2 [1856].

59. Boston Public Library MS. (to George Sumner, April 11, 1857).

60. Mrs. Humphry Ward, *A Writer's Recollections* (London, 1918), pp. 55–56.

Chapter 13. The Making of a Poetry Professor, 1857–1862, pp. 291–311.

Epigraph: M.A.'s notes on R. S. Hardy's *Manual of Buddhism,* 1860 (Yale Diary).

1. *Schools and Universities on the Continent,* Super, IV, 137.

2. Mrs. H. Ward, *A Writer's Recollections* (London, 1918), p. 56. M.A.'s godfather John Keble held the Oxford Poetry Chair from 1831 to 1841 and printed his poetry lectures, in 1841, as *De Poetica Vi Medica.* (Among those who congratulated M.A. was Mrs. William Wordsworth.)

3. *Sunday Times,* November 5, 1978. For John Jones, in 1978, the poetry chair carried an annual salary of £1,079 and the duty of giving one lecture each term at Oxford for five years plus an annual Creweian Oration in Latin; in M.A.'s time the salary was £100, and the Creweian Oration was given in alternate years. M.A. rightly construed "poetry" to mean all literature.

4. "On the Modern Element in Literature," Super, I, 23.

5. P. A. Dale, *The Victorian Critic and the Idea of History* (Cambridge, Mass., and London, 1977), pp. 91–97.

6. "On the Modern Element in Literature," Super, I, 20–21.

7. Ibid., I, 34–36.

8. Balliol MS., November 14, 1863. M.A. refers to the "mad" British Schools Society Inspector, J. S. Laurie, as the Arnold children's special friend.

9. R. L. Lowe, "Two Arnold Letters," *Modern Philology,* LII (1955), 262–63, to Tom, December 28, 1857.

10. Ibid., pp. 263–64.

11. Fanny Lucy's Diary, June 6 and 7, 1867 (on the composing of "Culture and Its Enemies"). That she criticized his early Oxford lectures is clear from M.A.'s statement that she felt one of them to be, at least, "better" than his "last." That she commented on style, tone, manner, and detail may be inferred; she had listened for years to good High Church sermons in a Knightsbridge parish. It is incorrect to suppose that she was distressed by her husband's doctrines; she preferred his more nearly atheistical poems to his prose, and felt that he was a "good Christian" no matter what he *said.* See also P. J. McCarthy, "Mrs. M. Arnold," Harvard Library Bulletin, XVII (1969), 394, 390.

12. *M.A. to A.H.C.,* p. 144 (October 10 [1853]).

13. Super, I, 18 and 225. His second lecture was given on May 8, and his third on May 29, 1858; the fourth, on December 4, concerned feudal society and the scholastic philosophy; the fifth, given on March 12, 1859, was planned to include his " 'romantic' sentiment about women" and became a piece "on the Troubadours." The texts of these lectures are missing. All were a part of his "On the Modern Element in Literature" series; that title was attached to the inaugural when he printed it with complaints about his own style (that of the "doctor" and not the "explorer") and his "insufficient" knowledge, in *Macmillan's Magazine* in February 1869.

14. Amy Woolner, *Thomas Woolner, R.A., Sculptor and Poet* (New York, 1917), p. 145, Woolner to Mrs. Tennyson, March 11 [1858].

15. Balliol MS., January 18, 1858. M.A. met Fitzjames Stephen in May 1858.

16. M.A.'s brother Willy had used the triple-adjectival manner in writing of a Rugby "Big-side" football match; see *The Book of Rugby School,* with a preface by E. M. Goulburn (Rugby, 1856), p. 159.

17. "Rugby Chapel," lines 67–72.

18. Ibid., lines 7, 196–97.

19. Balliol MSS., January 19 and December 1, 1858.

20. Super, II, 327–28.

21. Quoted by Donald K. Jones, *The Making of the Education System, 1851–81* (London, 1977), p. 40.

22. *Letters of M.A.,* I, 90–91 (February 16, 1859).

23. Balliol and Whitridge MSS., March and April, 1859.

24. *Popular Education of France;* Super, II, 31. Alfred Magin (or Magin-Marrens), who became French Inspector-General of primary instruction, answered M.A.'s general questions; Jean-Jacques Rapet, the primary inspector, helped M.A. with details and later praised *Popular Education* for its value and "exactitude."

25. Diary of 1859.

26. *Letters of M.A.,* I, 92 (April 14, 1859).

27. "Stanzas from Carnac," lines 3–5, 10–12, 17–18.

28. Ibid., line 15.

29. "Saint Brandan," lines 61–64.

30. "A Southern Night," lines 61–65, 69–72.

31. "Palladium," lines 13–20.

32. "Poor Matthias," lines 95–96, 153–54, 161–62.

33. Preface to *Essays in Criticism;* Super, III, 286.

34. *Popular Education of France;* Super, II, 123, 125.

35. *A French Eton,* Super, II, 273–75, 291.

36. Ibid., II, 272.

37. Ibid., II, 273, 275.

38. Ibid., II, 279–80.

39. Ibid., II, 277.

40. Ibid., II, 278.

41. *Popular Education of France,* Super, II, 195. M.A. pays tribute to Dutch school reformers such as J. H. van der Palm and Adriaan van den Ende (who influenced Kay-Shuttleworth); Holland had led Europe in setting up a primary school system in 1806. Sectarian conflict had retarded English schooling; hence M.A. was impressed that Dutch Protestants, Catholics, and Jews alike could agree with a law stating that the young were to be trained in *"Christelijke en maatschappelijke deugden"* (Christian and social virtues). He had made an attempt to study Dutch.

42. *Letters of M.A.,* I, 111 (June 25, 1859); 113 (July 9, 1859).

43. *Matthew Arnold's England and the Italian Question,* ed. M. M. Bevington

(Durham, N.C., 1953) p. xxv. He first met Villemain in March 1859 (Diary).

44. See Arnold Whitridge on M.A. and Sainte-Beuve in *PMLA*, LIII (1938), 303–13; and R. H. Super's "Documents" on the friendship in *Modern Philology*, LX (1960), 206–10.

45. *Letters of M.A.*, I, 123 (August 21, 1859).

46. "A French Critic on Milton," Super, VIII, 175.

47. "Of a Literary Tradition," delivered at the École Normale, April 12, 1858.

48. *Letters*, ed. Whitridge, pp. 65–66; to J. H. Newman, May 28, 1872.

49. *Letters of M.A.*, I, 128 (December 19, 1859).

50. *Popular Education of France*, Super, II, 51.

51. See the key discussion of Prussia and America in Chapter XIV; Super, II, 158–62.

52. "Democracy;" Super, II, 26. Burke's ideas are central to M.A.'s notion of the State; and Burke's essay on the sublime influenced him (see J. T. Boulton's edition). But we must bear in mind M.A.'s eclecticism. Tocqueville's methods of argument are reflected in "Democracy," and not only Montesquieu, Dr. Arnold, Guizot, Renan, and Michelet, but what M.A. *had seen* in France helped him to form his doctrine that the state must be made to embody the nation's collective "best self" and give a humane character to society. The State *may become tyrannical* (as M.A. observes in close remarks on France and on Prussia); but England in his time has no cause to fear that danger. See R. C. Tobias in *M.A. and Edmund Burke* (University Microfilm, Ann Arbor, Mich., 1958).

53. W. H. G. Armytage, "M.A. and Richard Cobden," *RES*, XXV (1949), 251–52.

54. "Democracy"; Super, II, 28.

55. "On Translating Homer"; Super, I, 134, 139.

56. "Last Words"; Super, I, 170–74.

57. "On Translating Homer"; Super, I, 145.

58. Ibid., I, 140.

59. Lady Chorley, *Clough* (Oxford, 1962), pp. 324–26.

60. "Thyrsis: A Monody," lines 2–4.

61. Ibid., lines 21, 131–37.

62. See "The Function of Criticism at the Present Time."

63. Ellis Yarnall, *Wordsworth and the Coleridges, with Other Memories Literary and Political* (New York, 1899), p. 237.

64. The Creweian Oration of 1858, in *Essays, Letters, and Reviews*, ed. Fraser Neiman (Cambridge, Mass., 1960), p. 29.

65. "Thyrsis," lines 235–37.

66. *Letters of M.A.*, I, 178 (November 20, 1861).

Chapter 14. Critical Acts: "Essays in Criticism," 1862–1867, pp. 312–337.

Epigraphs: Both are taken from "The Function of Criticism at the Present Time."

1. *The Economist*, XIX (February 1861), 206; *The Athenaeum*, March 30, 1861; *The Saturday Review*, July 27, 1861.

2. G. W. E. Russell, *Matthew Arnold* (London, 1924), p. 37; and *Letters*, ed. Whitridge, p. 50 (February 8, 1861). F. R. Leavis was not able to "revaluate" Arnold as a critic of religion, but in other respects his "Revaluations (XI): Arnold as Critic" (in *Scrutiny*, VII, 1938, 319–32) is one of the two best apologies for Arnold's criticism that were written in the first half of the twentieth century. The other is of course Trilling's book.

3. *Letters of M.A.*, I, 402 ["January 11" for January 5, 1867]; and Bodleian MS., January 20, 1876.

4. See Sidney Coulling, *Matthew Arnold and His Critics* (Athens, Ohio, 1974), pp. 18–19; and Balliol MS., to Jane Forster [c. December 1864].

5. *Letters of M.A.*, I, 359 [c. November 1865].

6. "On the Study of Celtic Literature" and *Schools and Universities on the Continent* in Super, III, 376, 382, and IV, 137.

7. Balliol MSS., November 19, 1860, and December 11, 1861.

8. R. L. Lowe, "Two Arnold Letters," *Modern Philology*, LII (1955), 264.

9. Tennyson's *In Memoriam*, LVII, 5–6 and 13–16, CXXIX, 1 and 6–8; and Yale Univ. MS., to Mr. Graves, July 21, 1860. Also see Edward Alexander, *M.A. and John Stuart Mill* (London, 1965) and *M.A., John Ruskin, and the Modern Temper* (Columbus, 1973).'

10. Browning dined with M.A. at Chester Square in November 1862 and occasionally thereafter, meeting him also at dinner parties, the Athenaeum Club, and Oxford receptions. Browning's direct influence on his work except for "A Modern Sappho" (which imitates Browning's style) is slight, but the indirect influence is major, and is one of tendency and emphasis as in Arnold's essay, "Heinrich Heine," where several ideas coincide with Browning's. The deep link between Browning and Arnold is their common intellectual debt to Carlyle and transcendentalism, which influences their reception of European culture and their mutual dislike of, for example, Tennyson's ready, easy patriotism. See Balliol MS., November 13, 1862; and *From a Victorian Post-Bag*, ed. C. L. Davies (London, 1926), pp. 75–76.

11. Balliol MS., December 11, 1861.

12. Super, XI, 285.

13. Balliol MS., May 7, 1863.

14. Lucy Cohen, *Lady de Rothschild and her Daughters, 1821–1931* (London, 1935), p. 9.

15. Ibid., pp. 103–104.

16. September 24, 1866.

17. May 24 and September 24, 1866.

18. *Letters of M.A.*, II, 137 (November 6, 1874).

19. Ibid., I, 257–59 (January 28, 1864), II (February 21, 1881); and George W. E. Russell, *Portraits of the Seventies* (London, 1916), p. 45.

20. These comments owe much to Ruth apRoberts; M.A. read Emanuel Deutsch's "The Talmud" in 1867 in *The Quarterly Review*, CXXIII, 417–64.

21. M.A. read Sainte-Beuve's *Chauteaubriand et son groupe littéraire*, which prints a translation of M.A.'s "Obermann" Stanzas, late in 1861; "I got it because Sainte-Beuve wrote me word that he had quoted a poem of mine," he wrote to Lady de Rothschild on December 28, "but got quite fascinated as I went on. . . . [It

concerns] Chauteaubriand, Mme de Staël, and their contemporaries, the most interesting company possible. The book has made a scandal in Paris because of the havoc it makes with Chauteaubriand's reputation for good Catholicism—but it is well worth reading apart from the interest of this scandal, and I recommend you, who are one of the few people who still read anything, by all means to get it." The difference between M.A.'s smart polemic style from 1857 to 1861 and the intuitive, warm, flexible, and richer style of "Guérin," "Heine," "Joubert," "Aurelius," and other essays of November 1862 through 1864 is partly explained by Sainte-Beuve's book, which deepened M.A.'s sympathies and restored much his respect for the French "sentimental school." "Living" with this book for at least two months, he copied about 36 extracts. It is noticeable that France figures more prominently than Germany in *Essays in Criticism*. After 1862, M.A.'s German readings kept up in *Revue germanique,* Lessing, Jean Paul, and others; Goethe, Herder, and Von Humboldt were very important to him; but he became suspicious of modern German thought, partly because Heine had exposed a narrow nationalist yearning at the basis of the German "sentimental school," which once had helped to inspire M.A.'s poetry. See his attack on that group in "Heinrich Heine."

22. *Letters of M.A.,* I, 279 (September 25, 1864).

23. George W. E. Russell, *Portraits of the Seventies* (London, 1916), p. 76.

24. Stokes's report on midlands schools quoted in *Education of the People* (London, 1967), p. 279; see also S. J. Curtis, *History of Education in Great Britain* (London, 1967), p. 267.

25. Balliol MS., November 6, 1861.

26. *Letters of M.A.,* I, 183 (February 19, 1862); and E. M. Sneyd-Kynnersley, quoted by Fred G. Walcott, "M.A., Her Majesty's Inspector of Schools," *Michigan Alumnus Quarterly Review,* LX (1954), 254.

27. "The Twice-Revised Code," Super, II, 212–43. See also M.A.'s Annual Report of 1852.

28. *Letters of M.A.,* I, 194–95 (March 28, 1862); and see David Hopkinson, "Matthew Arnold's School Inspections," *History Today,* XXIX (1979), 29–37 and 98–105, esp. 101. Thomas Healing joined him on his rounds, and carried out routine work for M.A., who, in the 1860s began to inspect schools of all denominations.

29. *M.A. to A.H.C.,* p. 75 [March 8, 1848].

30. Balliol MS., July 20, 1862; and Diary of 1863.

31. "Maurice de Guérin," Super, III, 31.

32. Albert Peel, *Letters to a Victorian Editor* (London, 1929), p. 170: to Henry Allon, November 10, 1865.

33. "The Bishop and the Philosopher," Super, III, 55.

34. "Spinoza and the Bible," Super, III, 176–77.

35. Epictetus, *Discourses,* bk. III, chaps. i and xxii.

36. Yale MS. (Tinker 21).

37. Super, IX, 48.

38. Lines 5–6; see Elisabeth G. Gitter, "Undermined Metaphors in Arnold's Poetry," *Victorian Poetry,* XVI (1978), 275–79.

39. See William E. Buckler, *M.A.'s Books* (Geneva and Paris, 1958), p. 67; and Super, III, 493. Charles Williams, Principal of Jesus College (Oxford's Welsh foundation),

said aloud after M.A.'s fourth "Celtic Literature" talk on May 26, 1866, "The Angel ended." Arnold's "wooden" Oxford audiences had been a factor leading him to more wit; the "Angel" remark was a tribute to his defense of Welsh culture.

40. "Heinrich Heine," Super, III, 107–32.

41. Ibid., III, 110.

42. G. T. Fairclough, *A Fugitive and Gracious Light: The Relation of Joseph Joubert to M.A.'s Thought* (Lincoln, 1961), Appendix.

43. "Joseph Joubert," Super, III, 196.

44. Ibid., III, 189.

45. "Marcus Aurelius," Super, III, 157.

46. "Pagan and Mediaeval Religious Sentiment," Super, III, 213–14.

47. Ibid., III, 231. John Davison (The Oriel Noetic) had defined poetry as "impassioned imaginative reason" in 1811; M.A. could have found Davison's phrase in the 1852 edition of the volume Newman later entitled *Idea of a University*.

48. "The Literary Influence of Academies," Super, III, 237; it must combine, of course, with an "openness of mind."

49. Ibid., III, 255.

50. "The Function of Criticism at the Present Time," III, 273; the essay was delivered as an Oxford lecture on October 29, 1864, and first printed in *National Review* for November (with the second word in its title, "Functions").

51. Super, III, 379n. Four months after M.A.'s essay was printed, Elizabeth Wragg was sentenced to "twenty years penal servitude" on March 13, 1865. Her sentence was later remitted.

52. Ibid., III, 273–74.

53. Ibid., III, 274.

54. Ibid., III, 270.

55. "Eugénie de Guérin" and Preface, Super, III, 97, 287.

56. *Letters of M.A.*, I, 288 (February 11 [1865]).

57. *Guardian* (London), May 17, 1865, p. 502.

58. Super, III, 283. Much of the best twentieth-century literary criticism in English is in debt to M.A.'s *Essays in Criticism*. Among valuable approaches to the *Essays* and to M.A.'s methods, see especially the edition by Sister T. M. Hoctor and the essays by Noel Annan and Geoffrey Tillotson, as well as F. R. Leavis's "Arnold as Critic" in *Scrutiny*, VII (1938), 319–32, and Robert A. Donovan's "The Method of Arnold's *Essays in Criticism*," *PMLA*, LXXI (1956), 922–31.

59. December 1, 1864.

60. *Letters of M.A.*, I, 310–11 (May 23, 1865); I, 322 (June 5, 1865).

61. Balliol MS., June 21, 1865.

62. Super, IV, 299.

63. Ibid., IV, 214, 209.

64. Ibid., IV, 228–29.

65. Ibid., IV, 229.

66. Balliol MSS: September 17, 1865, and Diary of Tommy Arnold (M.A.'s son), July 21, 1865. Also *Letters of M.A.*, I, 344.

67. "On the Study of Celtic Literature," Super, III, 344.

68. "Italy," in *Schools and Universities on the Continent*, chap. IX.

69. Ibid., chap. XIII.

70. *Letters of M.A.*, I, 276–77.

71. "On the Study of Celtic Literature," Super, III, 343–44, 347, 359–60; see F. E. Faverty's *M.A., Ethnologist* (Evanston, 1951).

72. Ibid., III, 343, 359.

73. Ibid., III, 391–92. M.A. combines statements from September 8 and 14, 1866, issues of the *Times*, which was attacking the Eisteddfod or Bardic Congress of Wales, in which poems and speeches are recited in Welsh. He had attended one of these with his boys.

74. William Robbins, in *University of Toronto Quarterly*, XVII (1947), 54.

75. "Wordsworth," Super, IX, 38.

76. *Letters of M.A.*, II, 163 [December 1877].

77. Quoted by William Robbins, p. 55.

78. Harvard College Library MS., to Edwin Godkin, October 3, 1887.

79. See *Irish Essays*, pp. vi–ix.

80. Thomas S. Snyder, "M.A. and the Irish Question," *The Arnoldian*, IV (Winter 1977), 19.

81. "The Last Word," lines 3–8, 14–16.

82. *Poems*, ed. Allott, pp. 529 and 527n.

83. Super, IV, 348n.

84. *Letters of M.A.*, I, 240 (November 14, 1863).

Chapter 15. The Ideas of "Culture and Anarchy," 1866–1872, pp. 338–359.

Epigraphs: Preface of 1869; Diary of 1872.

1. "The Incompatibles" (1881), Super, IX, 276, 285.

2. *Letters of M.A.*, I, 437–38 (December 14, 1867).

3. *Saturday Review*, April 7, 1866, p. 397; see also George H. Ford, "The Governor Eyre Case in England," *University of Toronto Quarterly*, XVII (1948), 227–28.

4. "A Courteous Explanation," Super, V, 35.

5. Ibid., V, 33–34.

6. *Letters of M.A.*, I, 390 (July 27, 1866).

7. One must bear in mind that Mrs. Mary Arnold, Fan, and Jane or "K" all praised Forster's political successes. In writing to his mother, M.A. sometimes implied that Forster was a dullard; in writing to Jane, that he lacked "thought" but had "soul" (Balliol MS., c. December 1864). Yet he was on close, cordial terms with Forster, one of the best-informed M.P.s of the 1860s, chatted with him at times until 3 A.M., and learned from him. It *may* be valid, but in the deepest sense it may be meaningless, to accuse M.A. of hypocrisy. A complaint such as "men like William Forster, who entirely give up real study" (December 5, 1867), which M.A. sent to his mother, has meaning only in the sense that it controls jealousy, helps to purge M.A.'s sense of being outrivaled by the man who married his darling "K," and

further helps him to take a vivacious (not bitter) attitude towards English politics in the 1860s.

8. *Friendship's Garland,* Super, V, 57.

9. Ibid., V, 48, 314–15.

10. Ibid., V, 67.

11. Ibid., V, 71.

12. Ibid., V, 69, 318. The Arminius letters were stopped in 1867, and resumed again in 1869. They end with a satirical account of the Baron's death in the Franco-Prussian War in November 1870, written in the *Daily Telegraph* style of G. A. Sala; all of them appeared in *Pall Mall Gazette* and were republished as *Friendship's Garland* on February 24, 1871.

13. *Letters of M.A.,* I, 408 [c. February 10, 1867].

14. See Goethe's mixed epigrams, including "Lebensregel."

15. Dr. Williams's Library MS.

16. *Letters of M.A.,* I, 408.

17. *Culture and Anarchy,* Super, V, 87–88.

18. Ibid., V, 233.

19. Ibid., V, 94–95, 233.

20. Ibid., V, 111.

21. Ibid., V, 529.

22. Ibid., V, 99, 106–107.

23. John Holloway, *The Victorian Sage: Studies in Argument* (Hamden, Conn., 1962); and Ruth apRoberts in *Arnold and God* (typescript).

24. *Daily Telegraph,* July 2, 1867; *Morning Star,* June 28, 1867.

25. "Mr. Matthew Arnold Again," *London Review,* XV (July 13, 1867), 39–40.

26. *Spectator,* July 6, 1867; Sidgwick's and Harrison's notices are given in an edition of *C. and A.,* in 1971, ed. Ian Gregor.

27. *Culture and Anarchy,* Super, V, 121, 95.

28. Ibid., V, 122.

29. It is no longer possible to hold that Arnold shirked a criticism of industrialism economics. In "The Future of Liberalism" (1880), he deals with brutal social results in manufacturing areas when "demand ceases or slackens" and employers dismiss workers during "depression of trade" and "over-production" (Super, IX, 136–60). His criticism of the "paradisiacal centres of industrialism" in "Doing as One Likes" arises from his finding *anarchy* in the laissez faire attitude to economics.

30. See Christopher Kent, *Brains and Numbers: Elitism, Comtism, and Democracy in Mid-Victorian England* (Toronto, 1978).

31. *Culture and Anarchy,* Super, V, 144.

32. "Written in Butler's Sermons," lines 1–4.

33. *Structural Anthropology,* trans. C. Jacobson and B. G. Schoepf (London, 1969), p. 33.

34. *Culture and Anarchy,* Super, V, 165.

35. Ibid., V, 169.

36. Ibid., V, 218, 227.

37. Ibid., V, 229. Especially helpful on aspects of *Culture and Anarchy* are Patrick J. McCarthy's *M.A. and the Three Classes* (New York and London, 1964) and his essay in *University of Toronto Quarterly*, XL (1971), 119–35; F. G. Walcott's *Origins of "Culture and Anarchy"* (London, 1970); David Perkins's "Arnold and the Function of Literature" in *ELH,* XVIII (1951), 287–309; Sidney Coulling's *M.A. and his Critics* (Athens, Ohio, 1974); and the studies by Raymond Williams and John Holloway.

38. *Letters of M.A.,* II, 41 (June 25, 1870).

39. March 10, 1869.

40. Yale Univ. MSS., March 14 and 19 and April 6, 1867.

41. W. H. G. Armytage, "M.A. and T. H. Huxley: Some New Letters 1870–80," *Review of English Studies,* IV (1953), 350, 353.

42. Super, V, 19.

43. Yale Univ. MSS., April 7, 14, and 21, 1867.

44. Ibid., March 26, 1867.

45. Ibid., December 1867 entries.

46. January 1868; August 1859; October 1861.

47. January 16, 1861.

48. *Letters of M.A.,* I, 405 (January 12, 1867); and December 30, 1865.

49. February 11, 1863.

50. February 18, 1863.

51. *Letters of M.A.,* I, 417 (April 25, 1867).

52. Earl Lytton, *Life of Edward Bulwer* (London, 1913), II, 451–52.

53. Balliol MS., April 9, 1868. Enrolled at Harrow School on April 30, 1868, Arnold's son Tommy at fifteen went into the "4th Form, 3rd Remove"; and Budge, at fourteen, into a higher class known as "Shell, 3rd Remove." Dicky, at twelve, was tutored for a year until he entered on April 14, 1869 (in "Shell, 4th Remove") and thus had the easiest introduction to Harrow School; he got into the Football XI in 1873.

54. See George Russell's recollections in his *Matthew Arnold* (London, 1924).

55. Balliol MS., April 9, 1868.

56. *Letters of M.A.,* I, 461 (October 24, 1868).

57. November 28 and 30, and December 8, 1868.

58. Preface of 1869, Super, V, 244.

59. Balliol MS., November 6, 1869.

60. *Letters of M.A.,* II, 10 (June 5, 1869).

61. *The Harrow Life of Henry Montagu Butler, D.D., Headmaster of Harrow School (1860–1885),* ed. Edward Graham (London, 1920), p. 189.

62. *M.A. Diaries,* I, 281; he received the legacy of £2000 in July 1870.

63. Text from P. H. M. Bryant's *Harrow* (p. 118), courtesy of J. S. Golland.

64. December 17, 1869.

65. *Letters of M.A.,* II, 92 (February 18, 1872).

66. Balliol MS., "To my darling brother," February 23, 1872.

67. E. H. Coleridge, *John Duke Lord Coleridge* (London, 1904), II, 207.

68. *M.A. Diaries*, III, 808, 812, 813 (February, October, and December 1872).

69. Quoted by G. W. E. Russell, *Matthew Arnold* (London, 1924), pp. 188–89.

Chapter 16. Mr. Luke's Vivacity, 1870–1878, pp. 360–381.

Epigraphs: Goethe's epigrams; Super, VII, 241; *Letters of M.A.*, II, 62.

1. *Letters of M.A.*, II, 104 [c. December 23, 1872].

2. Transcribed in German five times in M.A.'s diaries from Goethe's *Unterhaltungen mit Müller* (Stuttgart, 1870, p. 140); "Mann muss sich immerfort verändern, erneuen, verjüngen, um nicht zu verstocken."

3. Univ. of Virginia MSS., [c. December 18, 1871] and January 7 [1872].

4. Univ. of Virginia MS., January 23, 1872.

5. *St. Paul and Protestantism*, Super, VI, 111–12.

6. Ibid., VI, 38–39.

7. *Literature and Dogma*, Super, VI, 390–91.

8. *Letters of M.A.*, II, 121 (August 15, 1873)—in French.

9. *Literature and Dogma;* Super, VI, 177.

10. *St. Paul and Protestantism;* and *Culture and Anarchy*, chap. 1.

11. "Obermann," Super, VI, 299.

12. M.A. relied, when he could, on French guides to modern German biblical scholarship; his main guide to Pauline doctrine was Édouard Reuss's *Histoire de la théologie chrétienne au siècle apostolique* (2d ed.; 1860), which he read in 1869. He knew George Eliot's translation of Strauss's 1835 *Leben Jesu*, as well as the authorized French one by Charles Dollfus and F. Nefftzer; from the French philosopher Dollfus's 1864 essay on Strauss, M.A. transcribed more than 3000 words.

13. *Letters of M.A.*, II, 102–103.

14. Preface to *God and the Bible*.

15. *Guardian*, June 29, 1870.

16. See William Blackburn, "The Background of Arnold's *Literature and Dogma*," *Modern Philology*, LXII (1945), 130–39.

17. Ibid., p. 135.

18. Super, VI, 280.

19. Introduction, *God and the Bible*.

20. *Letters of M.A.*, II, 46 (October 9, 1870).

21. Ibid., II, 62 (March 28, 1871).

22. Ibid., II, 66 (May 31, 1871). The last Communard rifles in Paris were silenced at about 2 P.M. on May 28, 1871.

23. Super, VII, 505.

24. "East and West," lines 9–14.

25. *Literature and Dogma,* chap. 2.

26. *God and the Bible,* chaps. 1 and 6.

27. *Literature and Dogma,* chap. 1.

28. See T. S. Eliot's *The Use of Poetry and the Use of Criticism* (1933), and F. R. Leavis in *Scrutiny,* VII (1938).

29. *Literature and Dogma,* chap. 9.

30. I am closely indebted here to Jerold Savory's comparisons in *The Arnoldian,* V, No. 2 (1978), 16–22.

31. "The Romantic Faith and the Primitive Logia," *The Arnoldian,* V, No. 2 (1978), 7–8.

32. *God and the Bible,* chap. 1; Preface of 1873 to *Literature and Dogma;* and *Letters of M.A.,* II, 151 [June 11, 1876].

33. See James C. Livingston, "M.A. and His Critics on the Truth of Christianity," *Journal of the American Acad. of Religion,* XLI (1973), 386–401.

34. *The Unbelievers: English Agnostic Thought, 1840–1890* (London, 1964), p. 72. Other studies of M.A.'s religious thought include William Robbins's *Ethical Idealism of M.A.* and Vincent Buckley's *Poetry and Morality.* No other aspect of Arnold studies late in the twentieth century was livelier, more intelligent, or more in motion, and one should see especially the works by D. J. DeLaura and by James C. Livingston, Ruth apRoberts's *Arnold and God* (which I read in typescript draft), and the MLA papers by Brisman, Savory, and apRoberts printed in the Winter 1978 *Arnoldian.* Frank Kermode's metacriticism and work on St. Mark seem to me much in Arnold's line.

35. *God and the Bible,* chaps. 4–6.

36. Yale Univ. MSS., March 2 and March 15, 1873.

37. *Letters of M.A.,* II, 114 (April 17, 1873).

38. Leon Edel, *Life of Henry James* (New York, 1977), I, 369, 538.

39. Yale Univ. MS., May 13, 1873; Super, VI, 453.

40. Mrs. Humphry Ward, *Recollections* (London, 1918), pp. 52–53; and *The Times,* December 23, 1922.

41. "Geist's Grave," lines 13–16, 73–80.

42. Sir Algernon West, *Contemporary Portraits* (London, 1920), p. 62, and K. Allott and A. W. Shipps in *Notes and Queries,* 1974 and 1978.

43. Brotherton MS., Mrs. Mary Arnold's Journals, II, March and September 1834, April 1835, August 1836; M.A. to his mother, April 12, 1865 (courtesy of Arnold Whitridge); and *Letters of M.A.,* II, 124 (October 11, 1873). His letters to his mother lack the confessional ease of those to Jane, but cover a wider range of topics. His first "Irish journey" occurred in 1836: with his family, M.A. had sailed on the night steampacket *Lady Lonsdale* on August 15, reached Douglas in the Isle of Man at daybreak, and Dublin twelve hours later. He stayed with the Whatelys at Redesdale, drove through Phoenix Park, went to the zoo, watched the Irish jig danced at a birthday party, and sailed for England on the 25th. Amusing as this was for a boy of thirteen, his first sight of Ireland was surely overshadowed by the idea that he would leave his parents, and begin as a Winchester schoolboy, just five days after returning home.

44. See William Robbins, *The Ethical Idealism of M.A.* (London, 1959), pp. 53–54.

45. Trinity College, Cambridge MS., courtesy of the Master and Fellows.

46. W. H. Mallock, *The New Republic: or, Culture, Faith, and Philosophy in an English Country House* (London, 1878), p. 31. Mallock wrote the funniest of contemporary British comments on Arnold, and began warming up to the subject as an Oxford student, in his *Every Man His Own Poet; Or, The Inspired Singer's Recipe Book* (1872), which tells how to write an Arnold poem: "Take one handful of involuntary unbelief, which has been previously flavoured with self-satisfied despair. . . . grate in finely . . . half-a-dozen allusions to the nineteenth century, one to Goethe, one to Mont Blanc. . . . This class of poem is concluded usually with some question, about which we have to observe only that it shall be impossible to answer."

47. *Letters of M.A.*, II, 160–61 (May 6, 1877).

48. Ibid., II, 137 (November 6, 1874).

49. Ibid., II, 142 [December 1875].

50. Ibid., II, 142–43.

51. Mrs. Humphry Ward, *A Writer's Recollections* (London, 1918), pp. 157–58.

52. Tamie Watters, "An Oxford Provocation & Caricature: Rhoda Broughton and Mark Pattison," *Encounter*, April 1971, pp. 34–42.

53. May 29 and July 12, 1875.

54. July 12, 1878.

55. October 6, 1877.

56. Preface to *Last Essays on Church and Religion* (1877), Super, VIII, 148. The uneven quality of the volume points to M.A.'s weariness in 1876. The Preface is a good brief statement of his religious position, and "Bishop Butler and the Zeit-Geist" and "A Psychological Parallel" are fairly strong essays; but "The Church of England" and "A Last Word on the Burials Bill" are weak.

57. October 22, 1878.

58. November 1878.

Chapter 17. Invasions of the United States, 1878–1886, pp. 382–411.

Epigraphs: New York *World*, October 23, 1883; Chicago *Daily Inter-Ocean* and *Chicago Tribune*, January 20 and April 7, 1884.

1. Lines 9–14.

2. Other letters and diaries show that M.A. considered Arthur Stanley, as a clergyman, trivial, misplaced, and ineffectual; Tom Arnold and Mary Ward describe the childlike appearance of this slight, silvery man of china blue eyes. Since his manner and outlook hardly changed, M.A. describes him as a "child of light" in "Westminster Abbey," where the elegist identifies with the elegized. See M.A.'s letter of April 5, 1869.

3. Lines 87–89, 104–5, 147–50.

4. *Letters of M.A.*, II, 175, 180, 177.

5. Arnold's late essays are illuminated by John P. Farrell's "Homeward Bound" in *Victorian Studies*, XVII (1973), 187–206, and his study of the essay on Falkland, in "M.A.'s Tragic Vision," *PMLA*, LXXXV (1970), 107–17; as well as by Fraser Neiman, "The Zeitgeist of M.A." in *PMLA*, LXXII (1957), 977–96.

6. Fabian Franklin, *The Life of Daniel Coit Gilman* (New York, 1910), pp. 374–75.

7. Ibid.

8. October 24, 1885.

9. M.A.'s "Smith's" Diary of 1882. (He kept both a "T. J. & J. Smith's Pocket Diary and Almanack" and a "Pawsey's London Diary and Almanack" in the years 1880–83)

10. "Smith's" Diary of 1882, April, August.

11. Ibid., end pages.

12. Clippings of 1883, from Nelly Arnold's scrapbook.

13. "A Deptford Poet," Super, VIII, 1.

14. "A French Critic on Milton," Super, VIII, 175.

15. See Edward A. Watson, "M.A.'s 'The Study of Poetry' in the Context of T. H. Ward's *The English Poets," The Arnoldian*, VII, No. 1 (1979), 2–7.

16. *2 Henry IV*, III, i, 18–20; the preferred reading is "Seel up," from the Elizabethan hawking term for "sew together." Another M.A. touchstone, from Dante's *Paradiso*, III, should be emended to: "e la sua volontate è nostra pace" (Temple Classics Ed.).

17. See Jonathan Culler, *Structuralist Poetics* (London, 1975), p. 259.

18. To George Grove, editor of *Macmillan's Magazine,* "Jan. 24th."

19. "Wordsworth," Super, IX, 36–55.

20. William E. Buckler, *M.A.'s Books: Toward a Publishing Diary* (Geneva and Paris, 1958), p. 133.

21. "A French Critic on Goethe," Super, VIII, 254.

22. *Letters of M.A.,* III, 198–212 (September 1880).

23. Between 1882 and 1884, M.A. wrote as "An Old Playgoer" for the *Pall Mall Gazette* five reviews, which treat comedies by H. A. Jones, Grove and Merivale, H. Aidë, and B. C. Stephenson, and then performances of Shakespeare's *Much Ado about Nothing* and *Hamlet.* He found a dramatic, amusing appeal in Andrew Carnegie's own personality at this time and later "performed" for that friend, as when M.A. impressed him with a speech at Keble's grave; see B. J. Hendrick, *Life of Andrew Carnegie* (New York, 1932), chap. 13; John G. Cawelti, *Apostles of the Self-made Man* (Chicago, 1965); as well as Carnegie's *Autobiography* and *Triumphant Democracy.*

24. *Letters of M.A.,* II, 251 (August 10, 1883).

25. September 16, 1883, p. 2, col. 5.

26. October 9, 1883. The *Servia* sailed from Liverpool to New York on October 13.

27. See Jay Martin, *Harvests of Change: American Literature 1865–1914* (Englewood Cliffs, N.J., 1967), p. 10.

28. *Letters of M.A.,* II, 258 [October 1853].

29. New York *World,* October 23, 1883; the interview text is longer.

30. C. H. Leonard, *Arnold in America,* diss. Yale University (1932), p. 80.

31. Ibid., pp. 81–82.

32. *New York Times,* October 31, 1883; *New York Sun,* October 31, 1883; and J. B. Pond as quoted by Leonard, *Arnold in America,* p. 37.

33. B. J. Hendrick, *Carnegie* (New York, 1932), I, 246.

34. Leonard, *Arnold in America,* pp. 106–107.

35. *Letters of M.A.,* II, 267–68; he spoke at Dartmouth on November 9, 1883.

36. Arnold, Emerson, and Thoreau are among the 19th-century sources of American social idealism—or the idea that it is *worth* devoting one's career and major efforts to improving a nation's quality of life. This idea flourished among the well-educated young, before and after Nixon, Watergate, and Vietnam. It was especially strong in the 20th century at small, high-quality American colleges such as Reed, Swarthmore, Antioch, Oberlin, or Deep Springs in California where the director in the 1940s (S. N. Whitney the economist) went so far as to recite "Rugby Chapel" to the students. See Sharon Johnson, "A School for a Select Few," *New York Times,* November 11, 1979, for Deep Springs.

37. *Letters of M.A.,* II, 262–63, 267.

38. Ibid., II, 268. The Arnolds stayed with Franklin Delano and the former Laura Astor at Steen Valetje, Barrytown, on November 3 and 4, 1883. (The host's niece was Sara Delano, who had married James Roosevelt and given birth to FDR, twenty miles south at Hyde Park.) M.A. met the Delanos and New York Astors at Carnegie's suggestion.

39. Houghton Library, Harvard Univ. Library MS., December 3 [1883].

40. See Super, X, 505.

41. "Emerson," Super, X, 182. Though he met and disliked Hawthorne, and disapproved of his Puritan topics, M.A. grants that Hawthorne (unlike Emerson) has a literary talent "of the first order" (X, 175).

42. Leonard, *Arnold in America,* p. 152.

43. *Pall Mall Gazette,* July 17, 1884.

44. *Letters of M.A.,* II, 282 (December 14, 1883); and Leonard, *Arnold in America,* p. 123.

45. W. D. Howells, *My Mark Twain* (New York, 1910), pp. 28–29; A. B. Paine, *Mark Twain* (New York, 1912), II, 758–59.

46. "Theodore Parker," Super, V, 81.

47. See "A Word More about America."

48. A. K. Davis, Jr., "Matthew Arnold Comes to Virginia" (typescript).

49. *Letters of M.A.,* II, 286 (December 19, 1883).

50. Ibid., II, 290 (December 27, 1883).

51. *The Jersey City Journal,* December 31, 1883.

52. Ibid.

53. Quoted from *The Madisonensis,* January 19, 1884, by Leonard, *Arnold in America,* p. 198.

54. *Letters of M.A.,* II, 293 (January 18, 1884).

55. Yale Univ. MS., January 31, 1884.

56. George Monteiro, "M.A. and John Hay: Three Unpublished Letters," *Notes and Queries,* CCVIII (1963), 461–63.

57. *Chicago Tribune,* January 20, 1884.

58. Ibid.

59. John P. Long, "M.A. Visits Chicago," *University of Toronto Quarterly,* XXIV (1954), 38.

60. Ibid., p. 37.

61. *Pall Mall Gazette,* July 17, 1884.

62. *Light: A Journal of Criticism and Belles Lettres,* no. 22 (August 31, 1878), 650, and *Letters of M.A.,* II, 172 (October 26, 1878).

63. Leonard, *Arnold in America,* p. 233.

64. *Letters of M.A.,* II, 309 (April 2, 1884); II, 308 (February 28, 1884).

65. As reported by Joshua Crane.

66. *New York Tribune,* February 29, 1884.

67. Stephen Spender, *The Struggle of the Modern* (Berkeley, 1963), p. 246.

68. See the *Vanity Fair* report in *New York Times,* March 30, 1884; and *Literary World,* October 3, 1885. For his reception by American critics, see D. J. DeLaura, "M.A. and the American 'Literary Class,'" *Bulletin of the New York Public Library,* LXX (1966), 229–50; and John Henry Raleigh, *M.A. and American Culture* (Berkeley and Los Angeles, 1961).

69. Balliol MS., December 25, 1884.

70. *Letters of M.A.,* II, 320 (February 24, 1885).

71. January 12, 1885.

72. *Nineteenth Century,* XVII (February, 1885), 219–36.

73. Ibid.

74. *Letters of M.A.,* II, 324 [May 10, 1885]; II, 326 [May 25, 1885].

75. August 26, 1885, and January 19 [1886].

76. See *First Report of the Royal Commission appointed to inquire into the working of the Elementary Education Acts, England and Wales* (London, 1886), qu. 5843–44, 6020, 6023–24, 5838.

77. *Letters of M.A.,* II, 383 (April 24, 1886), repeating his wife's words.

78. Ibid., II, 400 (August 10); M.A. had become a grandfather on April 17, 1886, when Lucy's first child Eleanor or "Midget" was born.

79. Ibid., II, 404 (August 30, 1886).

80. Begun aboard ship, September 5, 1886. The dates of Arnold's two stays in North America were: (1) October 22, 1883, to March 8, 1884; and (2) May 30 to September 4, 1886.

Chapter 18. At the Fort: "Debemur Morti Nos Nostraque," 1886–1888, pp. 412–425.

See Horace, *Ars Poetica,* 1. 63: "We and all things ours are doomed to die"; Balliol MS., Jowett, September 23, 1887; and "A Wish," 11. 13, 17–18, 29–31, 34.

1. September 19, 1886 (in *Pall Mall Budget,* April 19, 1888).

2. But M.A. was just solvent, not rich; in 1887 he spent £1685, or £29.2.4 more than he earned. Even his 1886 surplus of £251 meant that he would have to publish new work to stay solvent.

3. *The Times* and *Pall Mall Gazette,* November 13, 1886.

4. See W. F. Connell, *Educational Thought . . . of M.A.* (London, 1950), p. 285.

5. The Council had not notably advanced M.A. in the permanent bureaucracy, after he attacked Lingen and Lowe in print; he became a Senior (1870), then a Chief

Inspector (1884), but by 1886 the last rank also was given to D. J. Stewart, T. W. Sharpe, and Canon W. P. Warburton. Arnold's chief value, in education, was as a good propagandist for state primary and secondary systems—designed to reduce social-class distinctions and the examination-ridden bias of schools. (Critics and biographers who have not studied Minutes and Reports of the Committee of Council err in giving him credit for the new ideas of other H.M.I.s and in calling him the founder of Britain's elementary schools, thus confusing him with James Kay-Shuttleworth.)

6. "Schools in the Reign of Queen Victoria," Super, XI, 233.

7. "The Zenith of Conservatism," Super, XI, 124. M.A.'s visit to Dublin (September 21 to October 1, 1881) when Forster was Chief Secretary for Ireland had made him more restive over Irish riots and newspapers, and more inclined to firmness. For Arnold and Ireland, see P. J. McCarthy, *M.A. and the Three Classes* (1964), chap. 6, as well as William Robbins, "M.A. and Ireland," *University of Toronto Quarterly*, XVII (1947), 52–67, and Thomas S. Snyder in *The Arnoldian*, III and VI.

8. "Shelley," Super, XI, 327.

9. Mary S. Claude, *Twilight Thoughts. Stories for Children and Child-Lovers*, ed. Mary L. Avery, with Preface by Matthew Arnold (Boston, 1887)—the only one of her books to give the author's full name. M.A. had promised Louis Claude at Madison, Wis., on January 25, 1884, to write the brief preface—which "gives me more trouble than you would imagine," he wrote to Jane Forster in October 1886.

10. May Wedderburn Cannan, *Grey Ghosts and Voices* (London, 1976), p. 27.

11. To E. Fontanès [c. September 1887], in G. W. E. Russell, *Arnold* (London, 1924), pp. 26–61. Arnold's late novel reading took him mainly to Fielding, Sterne, Goldsmith, Jane Austen, Stevenson, George Eliot; Cooper, Hawthorne, Howells, and James; and to Stendhal, Balzac, Flaubert, and Zola, as well as to Tolstoi and Turgenev. Scott and Trollope had seemed congenial; he used Dickens's *David Copperfield* to make social points in "The Incompatibles," and imitated *Pickwick's* Mr. Jingle in *Friendship's Garland*. He looked for ideas, a world view of interest in novels, and put Hardy on his list before he died. If any Arnold could write a novel, he told Henry James apropos Mary Ward's *Robert Elsmere*, "I would have done it long ago."

12. *Letters from M.A. to J. C. Collins* (London, 1910), October 24 and December 29, 1886.

13. "Literature and Science"; and see David A. Roos, "M.A. and T. H. Huxley: Two Speeches at the Royal Academy 1881 and 1883," *Modern Philology*, LXXIV (1977), 316–24.

14. Quoted by W. S. Peterson, in a letter to the author.

15. Max Müller, *Auld Lang Syne* (New York, 1898), p. 143.

16. W. P. Fishback, *Recollections of Lord Coleridge* (Indianapolis and Kansas City, 1895), pp. 127–29. His Laleham and Balliol friend, lavish of praise in late years, had become Lord Coleridge in 1874 and Lord Chief Justice of England in 1880.

17. G. C. Brodrick, *Memories and Impressions, 1831–1900* (London, 1900), p. 263. M.A. took no fees for lecturing in England.

18. *Letters of M.A.*, II, 433 (January 4, 1888).

19. "Milton," Super, XI, 328.

20. "Civilisation in the United States," Super, XI, 356.

21. See Stephen Spender's *Love-Hate Relations: A Study of Anglo-American Sensibilities* (London, 1974).

22. James S. Bain, *A Bookseller Looks Back: The Story of the Bains* (London, 1940), p. 99.

23. *New York Tribune,* April 1, 1888.

24. *New York Times,* April 9, 1888.

25. "Civilisation in the United States," Super, XI, 359.

26. *New York Times,* April 11, 1888.

27. *Manchester Guardian,* December 22, 1906.

28. Balliol MS., September 23, 1887.

29. *Letters of M.A.,* II, 161–62 (May 7, 1877), *translation added.*

30. (London, 1875), II, 606–07.

31. *Daily Telegraph,* April 17, 1888. Cole's Gate at Rugby was about 5 ft 4 in high; *Pall Mall Gazette* gives the height of the iron rail near the Croppers' Dingle Bank as around 2 ft 9 in (April 19). Jumping had been practiced as a fine art at Dr. Arnold's Rugby.

32. *Times,* April 16, 1888.

33. *Pall Mall Gazette,* April 19, 1888.

34. "The Late Mr. Matthew Arnold. Further Details," *Liverpool Echo,* April 16, 1888, p. 4; the *Echo* received a detailed report with statements by Dr. Little, after either typesetting or planning to typeset *Liverpool Daily Post's* morning account of M.A.'s death, which is run on *Echo*'s p. 3. (Hence its p. 4 conflicts with p. 3.) The new report shows that M.A. did not die in the street: "Dr. Little . . . found that though unconscious he was still alive, and that he really lived for about three or four minutes." *Echo*'s p. 4 is confirmed by an Arnold family typescript: "they carried him to a doctor's house, and before an ambulance could be brought to take him home he was dead." The *Pall Mall Gazette* account of April 19, with fresh information, coincides with these details. R. H. Ronson's account of the death, in *TLS,* October 10, 1968, is mainly correct; but W. S. Peterson in the issue of August 28, 1969, emends it with Fan Arnold's statement that "they were on their way to meet Lucy" when Arnold fell at the "Tram." The myth, fostered by W. Y. Sellar's wife, that M.A. died just after leaping a fence, is contradicted by circumstantial accounts in MS. letters and in the press in April 1888.

35. Pierpont Morgan Library MS., April 21, 1888.

36. *Daily Telegraph,* April 17, 1888.

37. *New York Times, New York Herald,* and *Springfield Republican:* issues of April 17, 1888.

38. Balliol MS., April 17, 1888. Browning also played a role in getting money for Mrs. Arnold. Arnold's estate of £1040 was less than any one year's income in recent years, and pension payments stopped when he died. To help his widow, a Memorial Committee in 1889 raised £6,840; a motion to use £600 for a bust of M.A. in Westminster Abbey and to invest the remainder for Mrs. Arnold "was seconded by Mr. Robert Browning and passed" (*The Critic,* June 9, 1888, and May 11, 1889). Browning had helped to raise the money.

39. July 7, 1888; see P. J. McCarthy, "Mrs. Matthew Arnold: Some Considerations and Some Letters," *Harvard Library Bulletin,* XVII (1969), 396.

40. December 29, 1888; see P. J. McCarthy, p. 398, and Mrs. Humphry Ward, *A Writer's Recollections* (London, 1918), p. 242. Because "Matt did not keep a journal" she could not say when "a memorial poem such as Thyrsis" was written, as Mrs. Arnold wrote to Mrs. Clough on December 16, 1893. But "I should much like to come & see you when I am in London. All being well, I hope to be there with my daughter Nelly Wodehouse sometime after Christmas. Always, Very sincerely yrs. Frances L. Arnold."

41. Percy M. Young, *Elgar O.M.: A Study of a Musician* (London, 1955), p. 84.

42. Diana M. McVeagh, *Edward Elgar* (London, 1955), p. 26.

43. *Culture and Anarchy* (1869), chap. 1.

INDEX

Some of Matthew Arnold's more important ideas are indexed under his name. Titles are included under author.

486

Matthew Arnold (*cont.*)

PROSE:

"Amiel," *178, 386, 414; A Bible Reading for Schools,* 367, 371; "The Bishop and the Philosopher," 322; "Bishop Butler and the Zeit-Geist," 376; "Civilisation in the United States," 386, *417–418;* "Common Schools Abroad," 411; "Count Leo Tolstoi," 316, 385, *415;* Creweian Orations, Oxford, 310–11; *Culture and Anarchy,* 75, 223–24, 254–*326 passim,* 334, 343–50, 356, 363, 383, 408, 424–25; "Culture and Its Enemies," 336, 344–47, 355; "Democracy," *306–307, 384, 408;* "A Deptford Poet," *388; Discourses in America,* 385, 408; *see also essay titles;* "Dr. Stanley's Lectures on the Jewish Church," 322; " 'Ecce, Convertimur ad Gentes,' " 383, 385; "Emerson," 385, 391–408 *passim; England and the Italian Question,* 297, 303–304; "Equality," 307, 384; *Essays in Criticism* (1865), 210, 268, 291–92, 320–30, 344, 367, 391, 408, 469–70 n.21; *Second Series* (1888), 385–86, 388–90, 414–15; "Eugénie de Guérin," 327–28; "Falkland," 384; "A French Critic on Goethe" and "A French Critic on Milton," 384, *390–91,* 400; *A French Eton,* 297, 302–303, 330, 408; "The French Play in London," "A 'Friend of God,' " 386n., 414; *Friendship's Garland,* 314, 321, 334, 336, *341–43, 374;* "The *Function of Criticism at the Present Time," 314n.,* 324, *327–29;* "The Future of Liberalism," 348, 384–85; "General Grant," 386, 414; "George Sand," 105–106, 384, 391, 400; *God and the Bible,* 93, 361, 364, 370–72; "Hamlet Once More," (review of W. Barrett's staging of *Hamlet,* 1884, with essay remarks on the play), 202, 393; "Heinrich Heine," 321, 324–*25, 469 n.21;* "The *Incompatibles,"* 384; "Irish Catholicism and British Liberalism," *384; Irish Essays,* 336, 384; "John Keats," 385, 389–91; "Joseph de Maistre on Russia," 386; "Joubert," 324–25; "Journale Gastronomique," 33–34; *Last Essays on Church and Religion,* 376, 380; "The Literary Influence of Academies," *314n., 326–27; Literature and Dogma,* 273, 303, 324, 361–62, *368–73, 375–76;* "Literature and Science," 385 *and 416;* 391, 394, 399, 401, 405–406; "A Liverpool Address," 386n.; "Marcus Aurelius," 326; "Maurice de Guérin," *320–21, 324;* "Milton," 385, *417; Mixed Essays, 384;* "Numbers," 287, 385, 398, 405–406; *"Obermann," 364;* "An Old Playgoer . . ." (*reviews and review-essays*), 393, 478 n.23; "On the Modern Element in Literature," 205, 292–93, 309, 466 n.13; *On Translating Homer,* 261, 292, *307–309,* 311–13, 391; *Last Words,* 308–309; "Ordnance Maps," 248; "Pagan and Mediaeval Religious Sentiment," *326; Passages from the Prose Writings of M.A.,* 388; "A Persian Passion Play," 367; *The Popular Education of France,"* 297, 304, *306–307;* " 'Porro Unum Est Necessarium,' " 384; Prefaces: to *Merope,* 287; to *Poems* (1853), 75. 86–87,

209, *281–86,* 385, 391; to *Poems* (1854), 385; "A Psychological Parallel," 376; *St. Paul and Protestantism,* 361–65; "Sainte-Beuve" (1869), 364; (1886), 386; "Schools" (in the Reign of Queen Victoria), 413–14; "Schools and Universities on the Continent," 330–33; "A Septuagenarian Poet," 388; "Shelley," 385, 414; "Spinoza and the Bible," 322–23; *The Study of Celtic Literature,* 138–39, 292, 304, *333–36;* "The Study of Poetry," 273, 385, 389–91; "Theodore Parker," 321, 386, 401–402; "Thomas Gray," 385, 389, 391; "Tractatus Theologico-Politicus" (review), 321; "The Twice-Revised Code," 319–20; "Up to Easter," 336; Whitechapel address (1884), 62; "A Word about America," 386, 393; "A Word More about America," 336, 386, 409–410; "Wordsworth," 386, 388–91; "The Zenith of Conservatism," 414; *minor prose works of 1876–88: see* 386n. and 477 n.56

Arnold, Polly, stationer, 355

Arnold, Richard Penrose (M.A.'s son), 288, 316–83 *passim,* 412, 421, 423–24

Arnold, Susanna (M.A.'s aunt), 13

Arnold, Thomas (M.A.'s father): at Laleham, 8–13; at Rugby, 16–46, 133; at Oxford, 9, 51, 55–57, 66, 82; death, 61–63, 87; influence of his ideas and character on M.A., 5–296 *passim,* 302–304, 389

Arnold, Thomas (M.A.'s brother), 4–123 and 149–275 *passim,* 298, 302, 333, 374, 423; religious odyssey, 72–73, 293–94

Arnold, Thomas (M.A.'s son Tommy), 231, 268–98 *passim, 315–16, 332,* 374

Arnold, Trevenen William (M.A.'s son Budge), 288–332 *passim,* 353–59, 374

Arnold, Walter Thomas (M.A.'s brother), 4, 56, 101, 112, 122

Arnold, William, customs inspector, 8

Arnold, William Delafield (M.A.'s brother), 4, 40, 56, 71–296 *passim,* 298–302

Arrian, 133

Arthur, Chester Alan, 402

Aselgeia, 376

Ashburton, Lady Harriet, 116, 267

Astor, Laura, 399

Athenaeum Club, 286, 316, 343–44, 416

Auden, W. H., 291

August, Eugene, 451n.

Augustine, St., 442

Austen, Jane, 60, 232, 295, 481; M.A. as Mr. Woodhouse, 377, 409

Aytoun, W.E., 180

Bagehot, Walter, 64, 351

Baines, Edward, 253, 411

Baldock, Mrs., 353

Balfour, Arthur James, 336

Balzac, Honoré de, 105

Bancroft, George, 402

Barbier, Henri Auguste, 225, 227

Barnum, P. T., 393

Barrett, Wilson, 393

Barthes, Roland, 389

Baudelaire, C. P., 150

Baur, F. C., 364

Beales, Edmund, 340
Becht, R. E., 452n.
Benison, Josephine, 423
Benjamin of Tudela, 315
Bentham, Jeremy, 346
Béranger, Pierre-Jean de, 111, 131, 142, 146
Berkeley, George, 94, 207, 322, 442
Bernese Oberland, 106, 143, 238, 392
Bernhardt, Sarah, 379, 384
Bertram, James, 429, 451nn.
Bevington, M. M., 467n.
Bewick, Thomas, 17
Bhagavad Gita, 99–100, 178, 276
Bible, 5, 7, 17, 32, 221, 227, 277, 287, 320–23, 356–57, 359, 361–72
Bion, 52
Birmingham, 34, 251, 327, 367; as "manufacturing town," 248–49; Mason College, 385
Bismarck, Otto von, 338
Blackburn, W., 475
Blackett, John, 119, 264
Blackmur, R. P., 308
Blake, William, 39, 343
Blanc, Louis, 137
Boag, Mrs., 119
Boileau-Despréaux, N., 283
Bolingbroke, Henry, Viscount, 317
Bologna, 330
Bonhoeffer, Dietrich, 370
Bonnerot, Louis, 149
Borrow, George, 89
Boulton, J. T., 468n.
Bowe, William (Billy Boo), 36
Bradley, George Granville, 40, 45, 55, 79–80, 379, 413, 422
Braithwaite, George Foster, 36
Brancker, James, 35–36, 155
Briggs, Asa, 462n.
Bright, John, 345, 349, 384
Brightfield, M. F., 455n.
Brisman, Leslie, 371
British and Foreign School Society, 253–54, 256
British Museum, 236, 306, 326; M.A. works in North Library, 316
Brittany, 298–99
Brodie, Sir Benjamin Collins, (the 2nd), 119, 179, 264, 269
Broglie, A.-C., duc de, 297
Brontë, Charlotte, 6, 24, 190, 219–20
Brontë, Emily, 220
Brookfield, Mrs., 64
Brookfield, the Rev., H.M.I., 254
Brooks, R. L., 453n.
Broughton, Rhoda, 379
Brown University, 401
Browne, Sir Thomas, 424
Browning, E.B., 362, 403
Browning, Robert, 115, 138, 203, 336, 357, 411, 415–16, 422; nature of friendship with M.A., 315 and 469 n.10
Bruno, St., 238
Bryce, James, 348
Buber, Martin, 370
Buccleuch, Duke of, 112

Buckland family, 5, 12, 14, 19–21, 31, 19–21, 124, 354
Buckler, W. E., 448n., 470n., 478n.
Buckley, Vincent, 476
Bucknill, physician, 62
Buddhism, 72, 305, 313
Bultmann, Rudolph, 361, 370
Bump, Jerome, 460n.
Bunner, H.C., 397
Bunsen, C. C. J. von, 32, 76, 94–95, 120
Bunyan, John, 18, 55
Burbidge, Thomas, 123, 130–31
Burke, Edmund, 17, 117, 301, 305–307, 317, 336, 338, 468n.
Burnes, Alexander, 280
Burns, Robert, 185
Burroughs, John, 397
Bush, Douglas, 433n.
Butler, George, 76
Butler, Gray, 79
Butler, Henry Montagu, 355–57
Butler, Joseph, 52, 54, 75, 82
Byron, George, Lord, 25, 31, 35, 44, 89, 130, 185, 188, 197, 240–41, 325, 389–90; recited in schools, 259; at Harrow, 355; Byron House, 355–59

Cable, George W., 398
Cambridge University, 47, 116, 329, 347, 385; Cambridge Platonists, 376
Canada, 380, 385, 406
Cannon, May W., 415
Capell, Edward, 268
Carlyle, Thomas, 68–164 *passim*, 204, 209–10, 314, 340, 377, 400
Carnegie, Andrew, 393–94, 396–98, 403, 405, 416
Carpus, physician, 12
Carroll, Lewis, 286
Carte, R. D'Oyly, 394–96, 399
Cassels, W. R., 372
Cate, C., 445n.
Cato Minor, 31, 190
Centre for Contemporary Cultural Studies, 327
Chandler, W. E., 402
Charles I (of England), 69; Charles X (of France), 17, 135
Chartists, 135, 356
Chasles, Philarète, 111
Chateaubriand, F. R. de, 152, 198, 318, 325; on anarchy, 223; *René*, 140, 160, 207, 272, 279
Chaucer, Geoffrey, 389
Chéri, Rose, 109
Chicago, 399, 405–406
Childs, G. W., 417
Chinese, 291, 313
Chopin, F., 108
Chorley, K., 434n., 439–40nn.
Christie, J. F., 83
Church of England, 41, 254–56, 306, 328, 344, 352, 364–65, 370–72, 477 n.56
Church, R. W., 83–84
Churchill, Winston, 83
Cicero, 52, 317, 363
Circourt, Adolphe de, 304, 316
Clark, Sir Andrew, 140, 418

Field, Eugene, 405
Fielding, Henry, 186, 295, 481 n.11
Fields, Annie, 294
Firdousi, 280
Fishback, W. P., 21
Fitzgerald, Penelope, 89
Flaubert, Gustave, 304, 415
Fletcher, Joseph, H.M.I., 254, 256, 258
Florence, for poetry-writing, 387
Fontanès, Ernest, 363
Ford, G. H., 472n.
Forster, Jane Martha, *née* Arnold (M.A.'s
   sister), 4–424 *passim;* criticisms of M.A.,
   176–79, 181; engagement, 187–88, 200–201;
   marriage, 205, 213–15
Forster, William Edward, 104, 187–88,
   200–201, 213–14, 216, 219–20, 286, 298,
   330, 341–43, 359, 384, 410, 413–14
Foscolo, Ugo, 111, 152, 157–58, 163–64, 332
Fourierism, 134
Fox Ghyll, 22
Fox How, 23–25, 36–40, 61–63, 76, 127, 151,
   213–14, 221, 249, 282, 285, 314, 329, 361;
   Fox How Magazine, 37–38, 46, 56, 89
Fox, W. J., 218
France, 7, 42–43; M.A. visits, 33–34, 47,
   106–11, 237–40, 297–306, 330; French:
   influences on M.A.'s work, 98–367 *passim,*
   393, 469 n.21; Revolution (1789), 27, 42,
   140, 158, 325; Revolution (1830), 17–18;
   Revolution (1848), 134–37, 140; schools,
   218, 255, 297–98, 301–303, 332, 410; war of
   1870–71 and Commune, 366–67
Francis, St., 326
Friedrich, Caspar David, 150
Froude, J. A., 60, 179, 181, 281–82
Frye, Northrop, 309
Fuller, Margaret, 403
Fuller, Roy, 291

Gahtan, E. S., 460n.
Gainsborough, Thomas, 119
Gaskell, Elizabeth C., 168
Geist, dachshund, 374
Gell, J. P., 83
Genoa, Duchess of, 357
Germ (Pre-Raphaelite journal), 180
Germany, German language, 7, 17, 142, 306,
   333–34, 338; M.A. visits German provinces,
   151 and 214 (Rhineland), 331–32, 337, 410;
   German: education, 218, 255, 331–32, 410;
   influences on M.A.'s ideas and work,
   93–100, 111, 130, 137, 141, 151, 158–280
   passim, 295, 305, 324–25, 346, 364–65, 409
   n.21
Gibbon, Edward, 10, 44
Gibson, R. L., 402
Gilder, R. W., 407
Gilman, D. C., 386
Girardin, Saint-Marc, 140, 165
Gitter, E. G., 470n.
Gladstone, W. E., 18, 313, 318, 335–37, 394,
   414
Glanvill, Joseph, 274–75, 308
Glasgow, 53, 282
Goethe, J. W. von, 39, 43, 68, 76, 84–86,
   94–98, 100, 104, 111–216 *passim,* 224–25,

262–65, 272–305 *passim,* 324–25, 331, 344,
   346, 360, 362
Goldsmith, Oliver, 481
Golland, J. S., 474n.
Gordon, George, 339
Gosse, Sir Edmund, 44, 388
Gottfried, L., 438n.
Goulder, M. D., 370
Grande Chartreuse, Isère, 238–43
Grant, U. S., 41, 398, 414
Grant-Duff, Sir M.E., 330, 350
Granville, G. L.-G., 2nd Earl, 272
Graves, Robert, 291
Gray, the Rev. Dom Andrew, 238
Gray, Thomas, 389
Greece; Greek, 17, 21, 40–41, 52, 55, 95, 170,
   182–83, 273, 284, 292–93, 356, 364, 415–16;
   see also Homer, Sophocles, *etc.*
Greenhill, Laura, *née* Ward, 5, 42, 55
Gregg, William Rathbone, 142
Gregor, Ian, 473n.
Grenfell, 79, 442
Grey, C. Grey, 2nd Earl, 17
Grey, H. Grey, 3rd Earl, 120
Grote, George, 277
Grove, William, 286
Guercino, 119
Guérin, Eugénie de, 328
Guérin, Maurice de, 171, 321, 328
Guizot, François P. G., 42, 134, 297–98, 303,
   378, 393
Guthrie, W. B., 429n.

Hadrian, 119
Haiti, 340
Hall, Stuart, 327
Hamilton, Captain, 23
Hannibal, 144, 243
Hardy, Thomas, 190, 481 n.11
Hare, Julius, 76, 95
Harrison, Frederic, 345, 347–48
Harrow, 116, 355–59, 373
Harvard University, 398–99; proofs of
   "Emerson" essay, 400
Haweis, Hugh, 374
Hawker, J. Manley, 29, 68, 71, 86
Hawkins, Edward, 57, 72, 82–83
Hawthorne, Nathaniel, 479, 481 nn.
Hay, John, 405
Haydon, Benjamin, 39, 164
Hayes, Mary, *née* Arnold (M.A.'s sister 'Bacco'),
   4, 22, 56, 102, 123, 151, 201, 214
Healing, Thomas, 320, 470 n.28
Hebrew, 368, 371–72
Hebson, one-handed angler, 36
Hegel, G. W. F., 95–96
Heine, Heinrich, 158, 318, 337, 470
Helvellyn, 32, 40, 76–77
Henley, Joseph Warner, 291
Henry VIII, 238
Heraclitus, 127
Herder, J. G. von, 93, 96–97, 275, 346
Herodotus, 17, 21, 52, 87, 170, 277
Higginson, T. W., 410
"higher criticism," 364–65, 372
Hill, Herbert, 21, 25, 29, 40, 191, 261
Hindustani, 291, 313

Mack, E. C., 436–37 nn.
Macmillan, Alexander, 324, 385–86, 389–90;
  Macmillan's Magazine, 310, 321
MacVeagh, I. W., 403
Madden, W. A., 452, 465 nn.
Maffei, F. S., 140
Magin-Marrens, Alfred, 297
Malay, 291
Malcolm, Sir John, 280
Malder, F. B., 453n.
Mallet, Paul Henri, 286
Mallock, W. H., 377, 477
Malory, Sir Thomas, 191
Manchester, 244, 252, 393
Mann, Horace, 215, 218
Marcus Aurelius, 119, 326, 356
Markham, Mrs., 17
Markstein, Henrietta, 403–404
Mariott, Charles, 83
Marsh, G. P., 331–32
Marshall, Victor, 361
Martineau, Harriet, 75, 219–20, 280, 285, 306,
  358, 446 n.11
Marvell, Andrew, 70
Marx, Karl, 224, 459 n.26
Mason, Sir Josiah, 385
Matteucci, Carlo, 331–32
Maurice, F. D., 76, 201
Mauritius, 286
Maurois, A., 445n.
Max, dachshund, 374
Mayne, Sir Richard, 341
Mazzini, Giuseppe, 184
Meagher, Thomas F., 118
Meig Sisters, 403–404
Melbourne, 380, 383, 393, 409
Melville, Herman, 140
Mérimée, Prosper, 298
Mesmerism, 64–65
Meyerbeer, Giacomo, 226
Miall, Edward, 253, 297, 347, 363–64;
  "Mialism," 363
Michelangelo, 373
Michelet, Jules, 111, 242, 298
Michigan, University of, 405
Mignet, F. A., 42
Mill, John Stuart, 314, 320, 326, 330, 345,
  363–64, 368; "Millism," 363
Miller, John L., 440, n.15
Milnes, R. M. (1st baron Houghton), 136
Milsand, Joseph, 315
Milton, John, 56, 69, 77, 106, 108, 115, 172,
  223, 389–90, 417, 424
Moberly, George, 26, 28–31
Mohl, Jules, 280
Molesworth, Sir William, 224
Molière, 100
Moltke, H. Graf von, 366
Montaigne, M. E. de, 183, 305
Montalembert, C. F. R. de, 387
Monteagle, Thomas Spring-Rice, 1st Baron,
  224, 361
Monte Carlo, 372
Monteiro, G., 479n.
Montesquieu, Charles, baron de, 98, 305, 345,
  378
Montreal, 406

Moore, Thomas, 117
Moorman, Mary, 456 nn.
More, Sir Thomas, 96
Morell, J. D., H. M. I., 217, 244, 249
Morfill, Professor, 83
Morley, John, 348, 388, 394
Morris, William, 378
Moschus, 52
Moseley, the Rev. H., H.M.I., 254
Moslem culture, 305, 313, 367–68
Moyer, C. P., 440n.
Mozley, Thomas, 60
Mühler, Heinrich von, 331, 408
Mulhauser, F. L., 429n.
Müller, F. Max, 334, 365
Mundella, A. J., 391–92, 413
Murdoch, Iris, 309
Murray, John, the 3rd, 143, 145
Musset, Alfred de, 104, 114, 305
Myers, F. W. H., 388
Mynors, Arthur, 386n.

Napoleon I, 41, 106, 185
Napoleon III, 296, 303–304, 340, 366
Nathalie, Mademoiselle, 109
National Society for the Education of the Poor,
  253–54
Nazi party and education, 331
Nebuchadenezzar, 335
Nefftzer, F., 364
Neiman, F., 457–77 nn.
Neville, Lady Dorothy, 416
Newcastle Commission, 297–306
Newcastle, Henry, 5th Duke of, 297
Newdigate Poetry Prize, 59, 71
Newman, Francis W., 201, 307–309, 312, 315
Newman, John Henry, 48–51, 53, 56–61, 68,
  78, 82–85, 208, 224, 226–27, 235, 284, 305,
  326, 346, 367, 370, 393
New York Times, 394, 396, 398, 418, 422
New York Tribune, 398, 418–19, 422
New Zealand, 120–21, 123, 151, 380
Niebuhr, Barthold Georg, 43, 240
Niebuhr, H. Richard, 370
Nonconformists, 60, 253–56, 263, 266, 306,
  347, 351–52, 363, 366
Norton, C. E., 394, 396, 400, 423
Novalis, 134, 157–58, 198, 240

Oberlin College, 54, 399, 405
O'Brien, Smith, 118
O'Brien, William, 414n.
O'Conor, C. P., 388
O'Curry, Eugene, 334
Oldfather, W. A., 133n.
Once a Week, 326
Osborne, D. G., Jr., 441–43 nn.
Ottawa, 406
Ovid, 20
Oxford, 16, 56–61, 66–69, 78, 82–83, 274–76,
  286, 329, 344, 350, 365, 377–80, 424;
  colleges: All Souls, 64, 122; Balliol, 47–71,
  78–79, 87, 93, 95, 122, 186, 256, 274, 290,
  413, 420; Brasenose, 378; Christ Church,
  116, 122, 290; Corpus Christi, 9; Keble, 365;
  Oriel, 9, 39, 57, 79–113, 442; Trinity, 256;
  University, 64, 95; Wadham, 420; *the*

Turgenev, I. S., 415
Turner, J. M. W., 236
Twain, Mark, 396, 401–402
Twining, William Aldred, 123

Ullmann, S. O. A., 443 n.10
U.S.A. and Americans, 27, 30, 69, 71, 75, 168, 283, 306, 331, 385, 409; American: education, 218, 395–96, 405, 410; influence of Arnold, 407–408; lecture-tours of Arnold, 393–408, 411; literature and intellect, 400–402; newspapers, 394, 396, 417–19, weaknesses and social strengths, 135, 152, 306, 395–96, 399, 404, 409, 417–18; women, 395, 400, 403, 417

van den Ende, A., 467 n.41
van der Palm, J. H., 467 n.41
Vandyke, Sir Anthony, 33
Vassar College, 400, 404, 417
Vaughan, Charles John, 28, 35, 355
Vauvenargues, L. de, 305
Velázquez, D. R. deS. y, 119
Vere, Aubrey de, 6, 225
Vico, G. B., 43, 240
Victor Emmanuel II, 331, 357
Victoria, Queen, 41, 110, 253, 317
Vienna, 332
Villemain, A.-F., 297, 304
Villemarqué, T. de la, 191
Vincent, E. R., 452n.
Vinet, Alexandre, 419
Virgil, 20, 31, 52, 58, 67, 280, 287, 293, 309
Voltaire, 121, 140, 242, 293, 305, 34
Voluntaryism, 253, 272, 330

Wagner, Richard, 191, 236
Walcott, F. G., 463–74 nn.
Wales, Welsh, 333–35
Walrond, Theodore, 64–231 passim, 264, 275, 290; Walrond brothers, 40
Ward, Mrs. Humphry (Mary), 213, 373–74, 378–79, 386, 416
Ward, T. Humphry, 378–79, 385, 387, 389
Ward, William G., 49–50, 53–54, 71–72, 83, 103
Warton, Thomas, 290
Watkins, the Rev., H.M.I., 255, 260
Watson, E. A., 478n.
Watters, Tamie, 477n.
Weber, Max, 350
Wellek, René, 454n.
Wellesley College, 400, 417
Wellington, A. W. 1st duke of, 41, 47, 75

Wesley, John, 343; Wesleyan schools, 254, 256
Westminster Abbey, 365–66, 417
Westminster Rifle Volunteers, 296
Whately, Richard, 9, 82; Whately family, 13, 120
White, Blanco, 82
Whitman, Walt, 396, 401
Whitney, S. N., 399
Whitridge, Arnold, 423
Whitridge, Eleanor (Midget), 411
Whitridge, Frederick W., 402–403, 409, 411, 417
Whitridge, Lucy Charlotte, née Arnold, 288, 297, 317, 332, 352–423 passim
Whittier, J. G., 400
Wightman, Sir William, 186–87, 190, 212–13, 221–24, 230, 237, 270, 351, 357; Lady Wightman, 231, 244, 357
Wilberforce, Samuel, bishop of Winchester, 366
Wilkenfeld, R. B., 464n.
Wilkins, Sir Charles, 99
Williams, R., 309, 350
Wilson, Thomas, 345, 370
Winchester College, 8–31 passim, 247
Winckelmann, J. J., 97
Winn, Joe, 36, 242
Wisconsin, University of, 406
Wittgenstein, Ludwig, 372
Woodward, F. J., 440–448 nn.
Woolner, Thomas, 295
Wordsworth, Dora: see Quillinan, Dora
Wordsworth, Dorothy, 38, 195, 209
Wordsworth, Mary, 38–39, 195, 466 n.2
Wordsworth, William, 10, 22, 24–415 passim; impresses young Arnold, 26, 38–39; talks at Fox How, "disinterested imagination," and Arnold's verses, 195–99; Jane's opinion of him, 177; Arnold's essay, 389–91
Wragg, Elizabeth, 327–28
Wycliffe, John, 49–50

Xenophanes, 183
Xenophon, 21

Yale University, 371, 403, 423
Yarnall, Ellis, 311
Yeats, W. B., 206
Yonge, Charlotte, 158
Yorkshire, 255, 341, 343
Young, P. M., 483n.

Zeno of Elea, 183